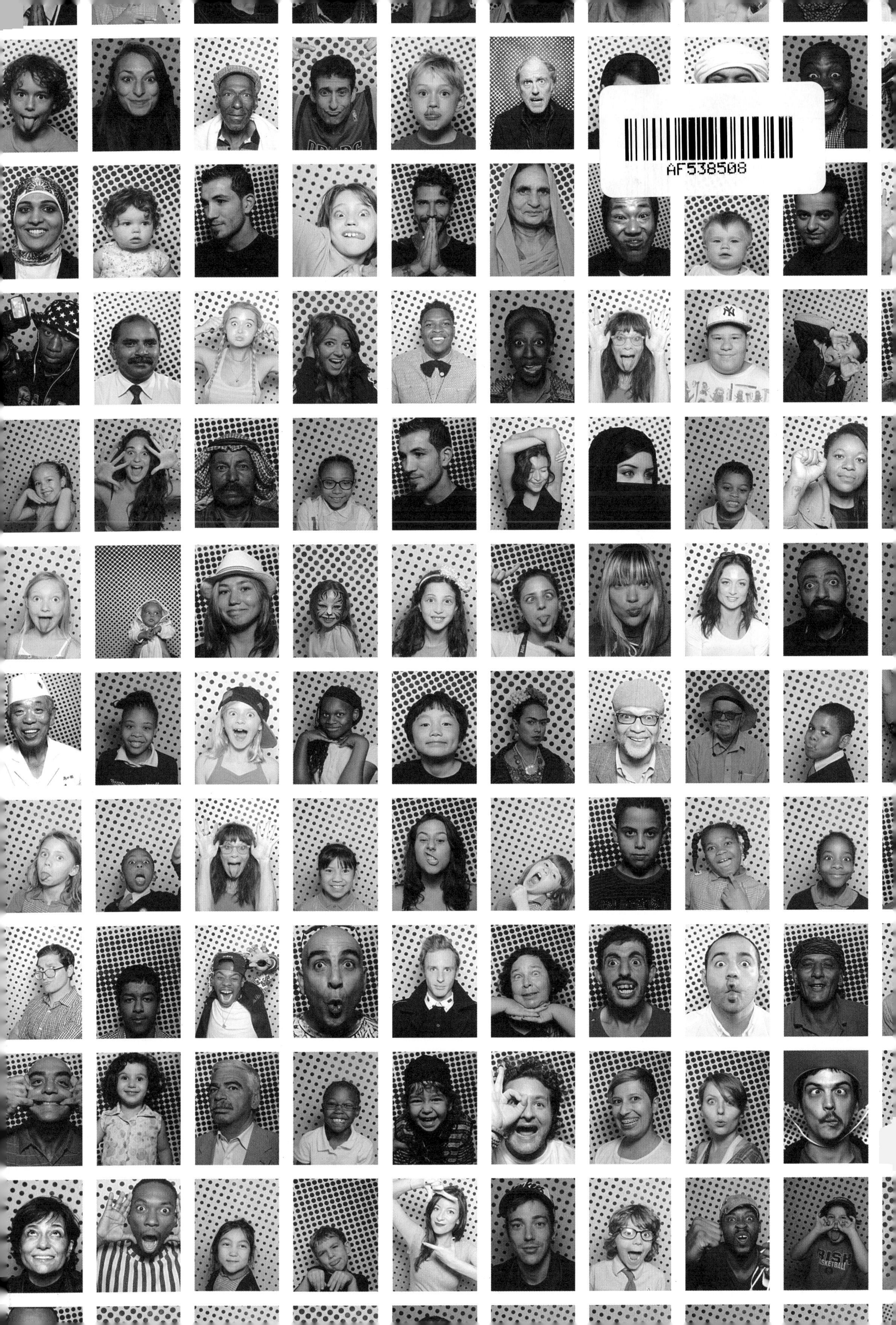

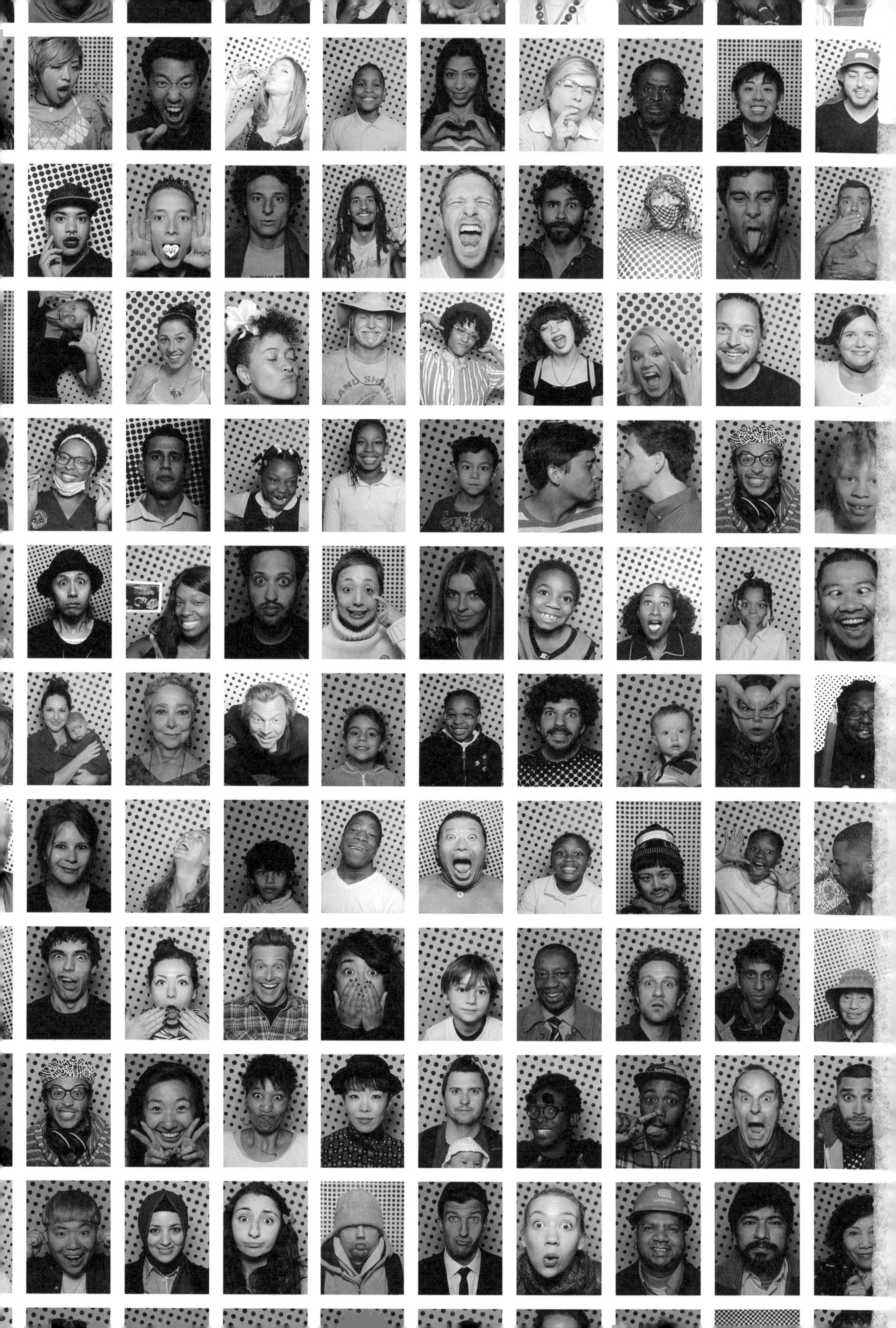
Inside
OUT

JR

INSIDE

OUT

JR

INSIDE OUT

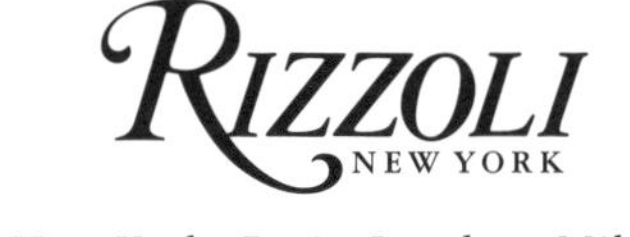
New York · Paris · London · Milan

The Inside Out Project is financed only by its participants and not by any brand, company, or NGO. Since March 2011, we have been able to finance it by voluntary donations. More than 300,000 posters have been sent so far to more than 140 countries. The project will continue as long as donations by contributing participants will allow to cover the costs of the ones who can't pay for their posters.

The project is free and open to everyone, at www.insideoutproject.net

EDITORIAL AND CONTENT COORDINATION BY INSIDE OUT PROJECT TEAM
Lola Iteanu, Luana Saltiel, Marc Azoulay, Manon Delaselle, Ohana Nkulufa, Viviane Cohen;
and all previous team members that helped organize and sort through our archive.

ART DIRECTION AND DESIGN BY NR2154
Jacob Wildschiødtz, Elina Asanti, Betina Bethlem

First published in the United States of America in 2017 by
Rizzoli International Publications, Inc.
300 Park Avenue South
New York, NY 10010
www.rizzoliusa.com

2017 2018 2019 2020 2021 / 10 9 8 7 6 5 4 3 2

Printed in China

ISBN-13: 978-0-8478-5864-4
Library of Congress Control Number: 2017936073

TABLE OF CONTENTS

Introduction

7 JR

9 Chris Anderson

11 Pharrell Williams

13 Marc Azoulay

14 **Actions**

249 **Inside Out Project Team**

253 **Credits**

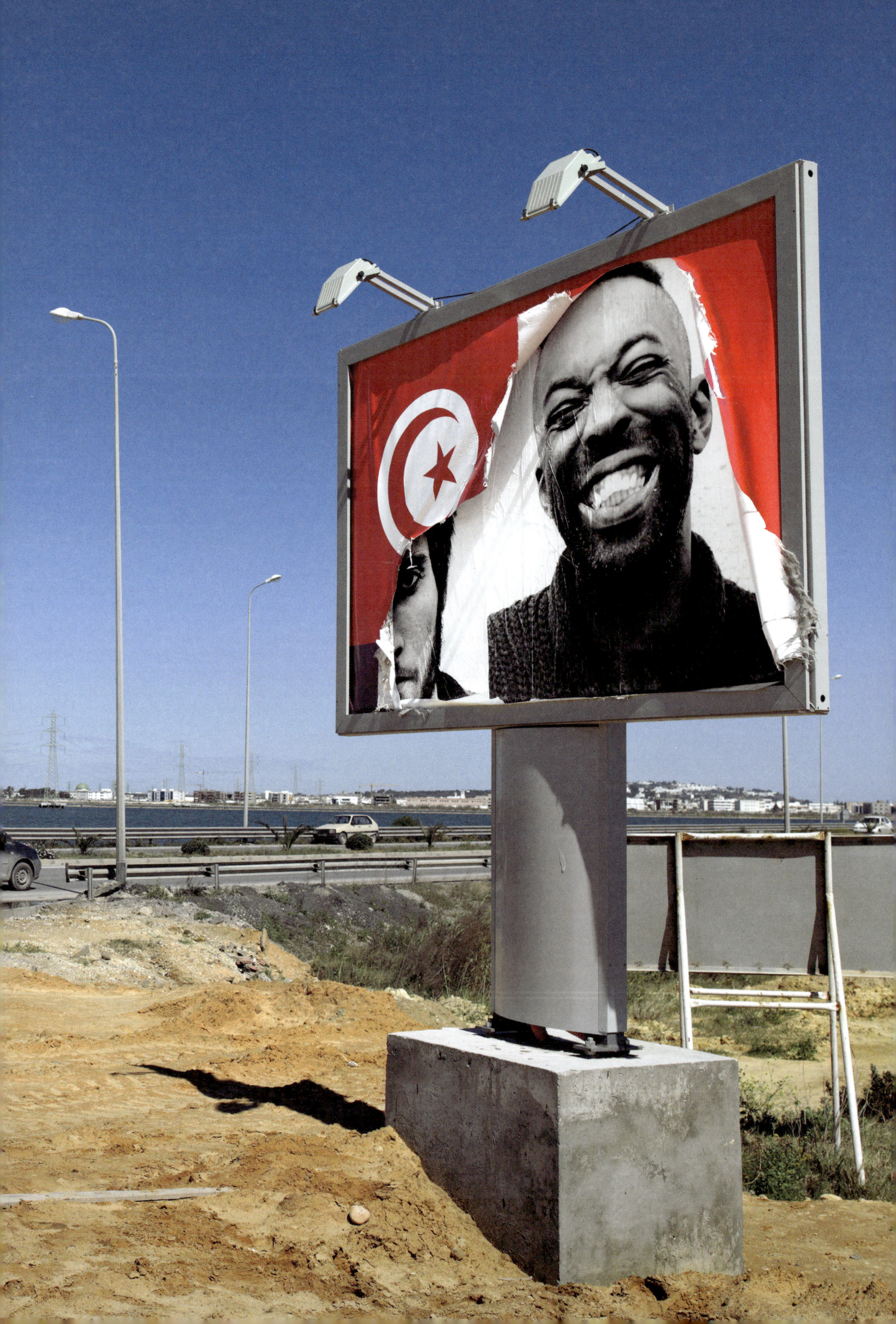

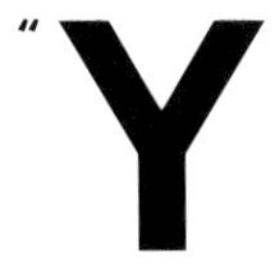

our JR—did he invent black-and-white or the portrait?"

This was what the lawyer of a large company that was preparing an advertising campaign had asked our group. A campaign that I obviously refused to endorse. He was pitching a "Clients Are Heroes" campaign that roughly copyied my project "Women Are Heroes."

Three days later, he changed his campaign.

He wanted us to convince him that I had invented something. Or perhaps he felt that it would not be appropriate to plagiarize such a project. Maybe he understood that doing so would suggest that I supported his products when that was not my role. Maybe he finally accepted the idea that art and advertising can share the public space, but that if brands copy art they no longer allow the artist to exist.

A few days later my lawyer called me. "I saw your speech at TED. You were ready to blow up this company that had copied your work, even kidnap the boss! But now you offer to the whole world to do the same thing that you're doing. It's interesting."

Indeed, it is interesting. Creating an artistic space, a way of working that is yours, means that your work is recognized, and after succeeding in creating that identification, you explain to the world how to incorporate the concept. You even help them to do so. In fact, you free yourself from what you created . . .

I believe in a tradition in which artists share their approach with other artists who will customize it, contextualizing it to make it theirs. They will then create their own projects that will retain the vague footprint of my presence, just as my work has been influenced by what I saw on the walls.

A few days after I was awarded the TED Prize, I witnessed the first Inside Out group action. I arrived in Tunis and went from theory to practice. A team of Tunisian photographers who called themselves the Artocrats had already done a lot by gathering portraits from across the country. Posters were printed in Paris and, as we were in a hurry, I gave them the paper rolls and taught them how to paste. From the first contact, I felt we knew each other well. That may be because for weeks they had been selecting strangers on the streets, they had listened to them to understand, and, after that, they took their picture. It's an experience that marks us all.

With paper and glue, they hit the cities. Here, more than anywhere else, they had to interact with people each of whom all had plenty to say. They also sometimes had to cope with their posters being torn down, and also to defend their project with courage. And if at first we took it for a demonstration of hostility, we soon felt that it was the expression of a new freedom, the right to say "no." I watched this spectacle with amazement and admiration.

This first group action was a beautiful experience, and I learned to leave the process completely in the hands of thousands of people all over the world. Six years later, I am still amazed everyday by the creative power of participants, and by giving away my process, I feel that I made it grow stronger, and actually enabled more ideas to be expressed everywhere . . .

JR

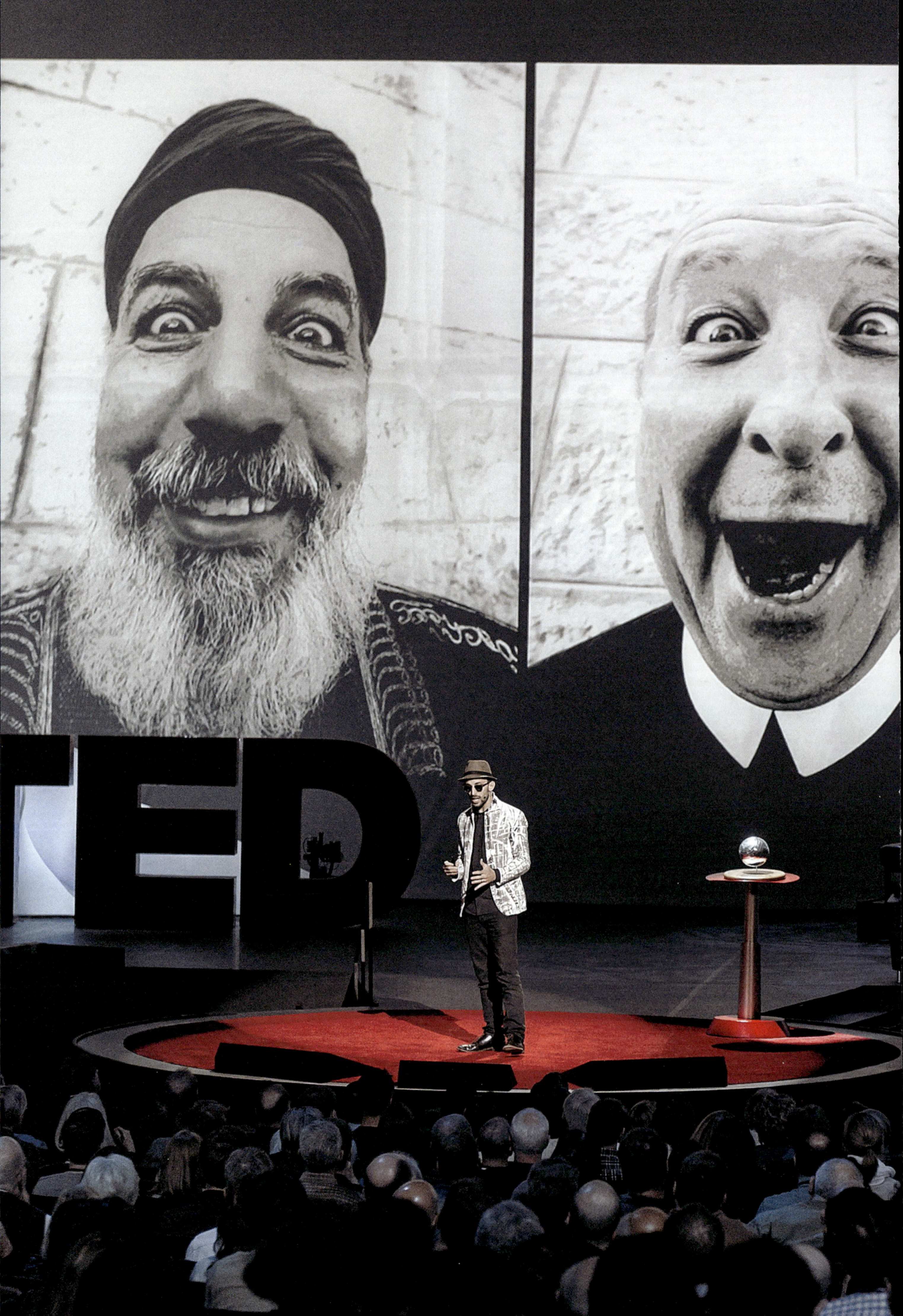
TED

I spend, as you might imagine, a lot of time listening to people who are sure they've got the next "big idea." Whether it is a way to reverse climate change or eradicate poverty or put a colony on Mars, I'm all ears. I love my job, because it puts me in touch with some of the world's most passionate people working on some of the world's most wicked problems.

There is no problem more pressing than humanity's continued struggle to honor one another's inherent and inalienable dignity. When we don't see one another, we are in danger of harming one another. And in these increasingly interconnected times, turning people into "the other" can have fast-acting consequences.

And that's why the book you're holding matters so much. JR is an iconoclastic, unapologetic visionary who has essentially offered up an elegant hack for dehumanization. The Inside Out Project is the world's largest participatory art project. It invites people to stand up for what they care about, to document and archive their communities for the whole world to see.

Since its creation in 2011, as part of his TED Prize wish, more than three hundred thousand actions have taken place in 139 countries, from Haiti to Nepal, Paris to Palestine. These actions have focused on everything from empowerment of women to the conservation of Indigenous land and rituals, from the battle against poverty to religious reconciliation—always with a commitment to making the invisible, visible, and the voiceless heard.

To experience the Inside Out Project is to be collectively transformed. The images are iconic and the process of capturing them filled with vulnerability and surprise. The experience of pasting is so visceral—hundreds of thousands of people have bonded elbow deep in wallpaper glue, holding ladders steady for one another, pulling the image of a grandmother or a teacher or a shop clerk taut while a neighbor smoothes the edges. And the witnessing—that moment when passersby crane their necks, kids drag their friends over to see, traffic stops. Whole communities feel legitimized by the beauty at such scale. It is playful and also undeniably profound.

Known for his large-scale street pastings in Kibera, Rio, Paris, and beyond, JR's work embodies the spirit of TED's community: untamable innovation and wild moral imagination. And there's no end in sight. All these years after JR received the TED Prize, his wish continues to take on a life of its own. That elegant hack, that open source artistry, could not be more needed now. I can't wait to see what people paste next.

CHRIS ANDERSON

Curator, TED Conference

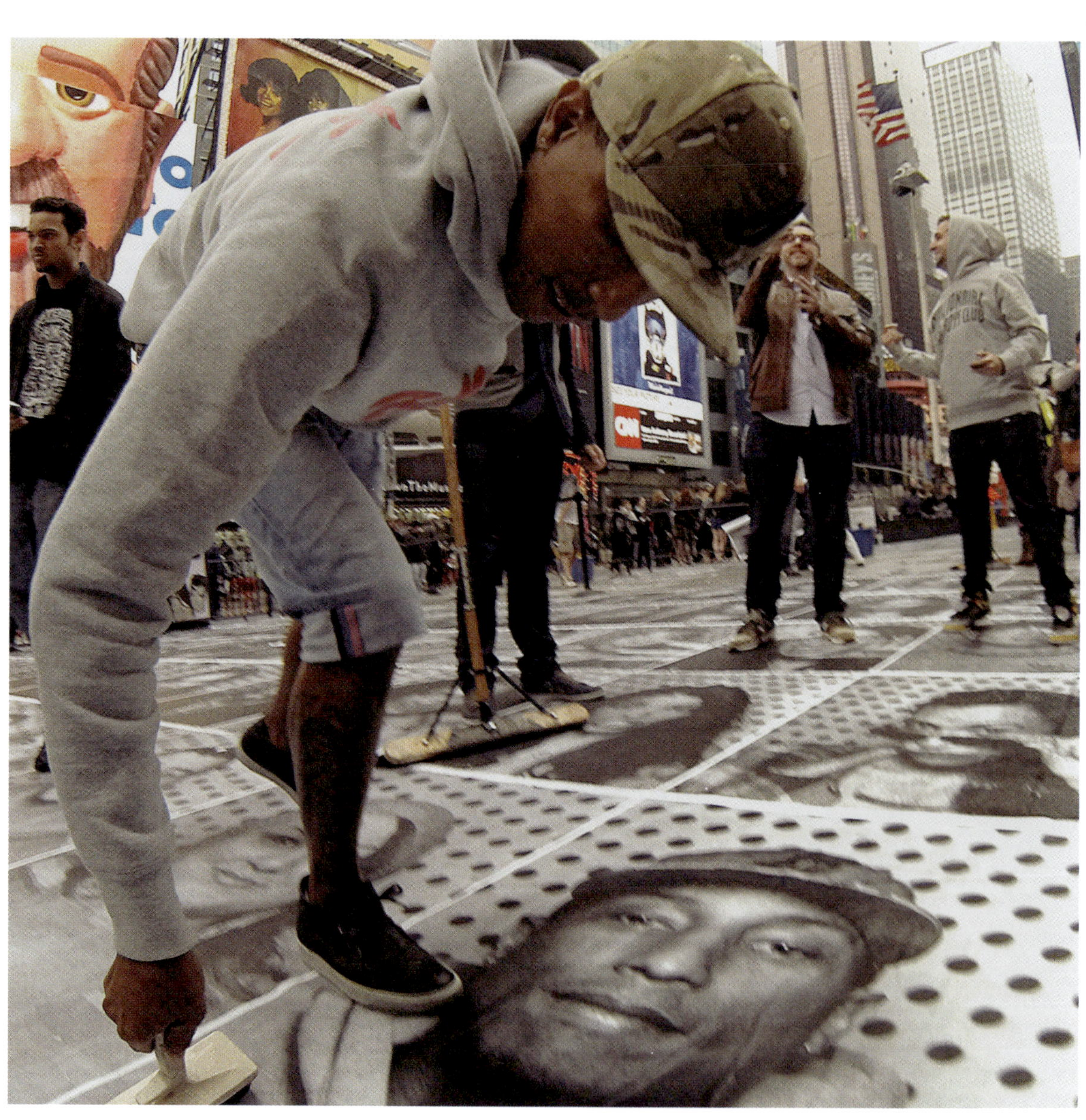
CNN

I remember the first time I heard about the Inside Out Project. JR had this thing he was very excited about, that really lit him up. He told me to come to Time Square to participate in an Inside Out photo booth action. They had outfitted a vehicle the size of an ice-cream truck, but when you looked inside, instead of seeing ice-cream machines and racks of candy bars, there was a printing machine; the set-up was like some fantasy chocolate factory. People were lined up to take their pictures and plaster them on the pedestrian areas of Times Square. When you stood back and saw all these portraits together, you understood the true beauty of this project: to show the connective tissues between people and their lines of communication. It allows us to utilize each of our differences as a kind of passport, to meet and understand different cultures. It allows us to understand that, ultimately, we are one, and those differences are what make us beautiful.

A picture speaks a thousand words, and by initiating the Inside Out Project, JR gave the means to everyone around the world to use the powerful tool of imagery as a vehicle for personal expression. Unlike his other projects, this is a process solely based on trust, human nature, and democracy. The people have absolute control over their image and once they receive their posters, they can put them wherever they please. Often, people immediately paste their posters right next to each other, because it seems that they recognize that just as bees work together when they are building a beehive, these people and their posters are stronger together. Inside Out says so much about our society. It harnesses the natural ebb and flow of humanity and how it endures. It is also a healing process. People seek answers to their questions, print by print and through human collaboration. When you see all the prints gathered together, like in Times Square, it heals a neighborhood, it heals a community. By looking at each other and making that initial new connection—not the visual, judgmental, esthetic connection but that blind connection, where literally what is connecting us is our willingness to allow our spirits to connect—I feel a spiritual connection is conveyed through these photos, this project, and these installations. We literally stop looking at what's on the outside and see deeper, inside out.

PHARRELL WILLIAMS

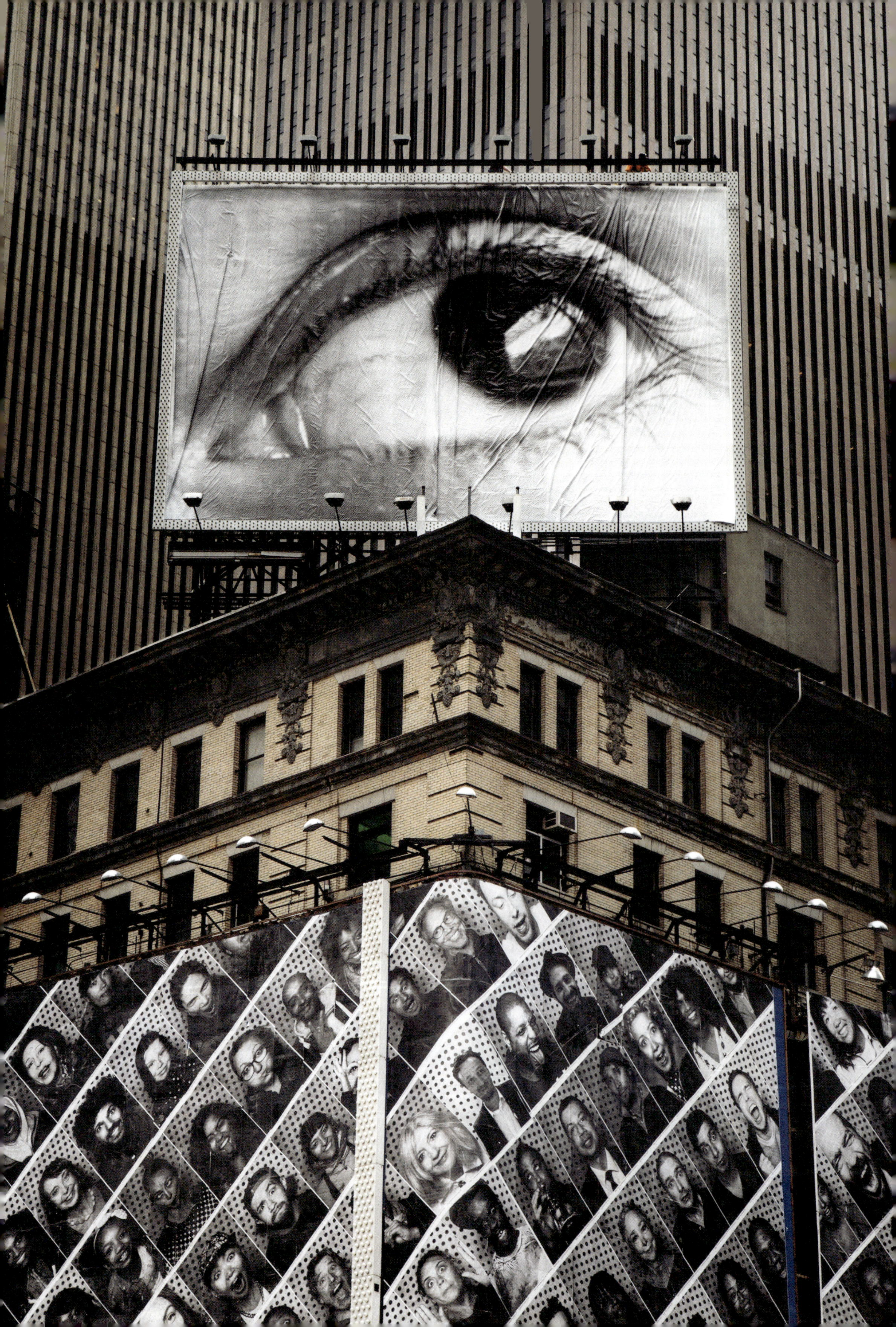

I remember the day when JR called me in 2011 to let me know that he was awarded the TED Prize and was asked to make a "wish to change the world." His idea was pretty simple: every day, people could contact him from anywhere across the globe asking him to bring art to their streets and to make their issues visible. JR couldn't be everywhere, so he decided to create a platform where anyone could order oversized posters for free in order to make a statement in their community.

JR offered me the opportunity to help him set up the project and to open a studio in New York City. The next day I became part of this incredible adventure.

Over the years, the Inside Out Project evolved into many different forms. We started by sending single portraits, but we found that most people wouldn't paste them, they would rather keep them for themselves and hang them in their homes. We decided to establish a minimum number of five portraits, and later increased the minimum to fifty. This developed the concept of "group actions" which created links within communities all over the world around a basic idea: to put faces in the streets in a huge format in order to pass on a message in a very visual and different way. It takes a vast amount of energy to organize a group action: to gather people around a statement, to take their portraits, to receive the posters, to request authorization (or to choose not to), to paste the images in the streets or on a building, to get help from volunteers or participants to put up the posters, and to communicate around the project.

And it worked, poster after poster. Thousands of people in more than 140 countries have accepted the challenge and participated. They were provided with a way to express themselves through portraits, through images.

Another more instant way of participating, the Inside Out photobooth, has been wildly popular. People have waited up to eight hours to get their portrait printed, and to feel as if they are a part of something bigger than they are. It is beautiful to observe that when already provided with a surface to paste—a wall, the floor—they wanted to be part of it. They wanted to add their face to the artwork, instead of bringing back home a huge portrait of themselves. Connections and conversations sprouted within the waiting lines, and we found that the impact of seeing oneself in a large format is very powerful. It provokes a smile automatically.

Times Square was somehow the epitome of this. In a place where every available space is already covered with eye-catching, colorful billboards and screens displaying retouched images trying to sell products, the Inside Out photobooth truck printed more than six thousand black-and-white faces of "everyday" people. They were then pasted onto the floor and onto a gigantic billboard, as if to watch the thousands of daily passersby.

Like JR's other projects, Inside Out is a project of its time. In an era of omnipresent social media and self-portrait sharing, we have to remember that in 2011, the term "selfie" had hardly been coined—and smartphones were not yet widespread. Portraits being shared more publicly were just starting to become ubiquitous. Instagram launched around that time, and "visual literacy" was nowhere near as prevalent it is today. Regardless of this recent prevalence, all those massive black-and-white faces, with nothing to sell or advertise for, create drama and intrigue.

Participation has also been a key element of the project. Anyone, anywhere, can participate for free if they have the courage to display their face in public to make a statement. The process is somehow very democratic. At a time when many live almost exclusively online, disconnected in the permanently connected world, Inside Out requires its participants to actually put themselves out there in a vulnerable way and to join the physical world—a real community.

Over the years at the studio we have been amazed by the creativity of people using their portraits to demonstrate their passions—pasting them underwater, on trees, and in impossible locations. Provide people with a very basic frame and set of rules—one poster size, one person in the poster, looking straight at the camera—and you get thousands of elaborate variations. It is also fascinating to observe that an image can have a very different meaning, depending on where it is placed: a fun selfie in one country; a powerful political tool in another. Teachers have even used Inside Out as an educative tool—approximately 20% of actions have been done in schools. We are impressed daily by the hundreds of images we continue to receive. The beauty of an ongoing project is that there is no real goal to achieve. Inside Out is a living platform that empowers its participants and evolves with them. As with every participatory project, nothing would have been possible without the hard work of hundreds of volunteers and team members, thousands of group action leaders and generous donors—people helping other people to create art, connections, meaningful exchanges, and smiles.

When we started, we prepared ourselves for group actions that wouldn't be acceptable for us. How would we respond to someone who wanted to make an action to ban immigrants, or to someone who would want to build walls here and there, or to a person who would promote racist ideas? We discussed it for hours, but it never happened. I still wonder why.

MARC AZOULAY

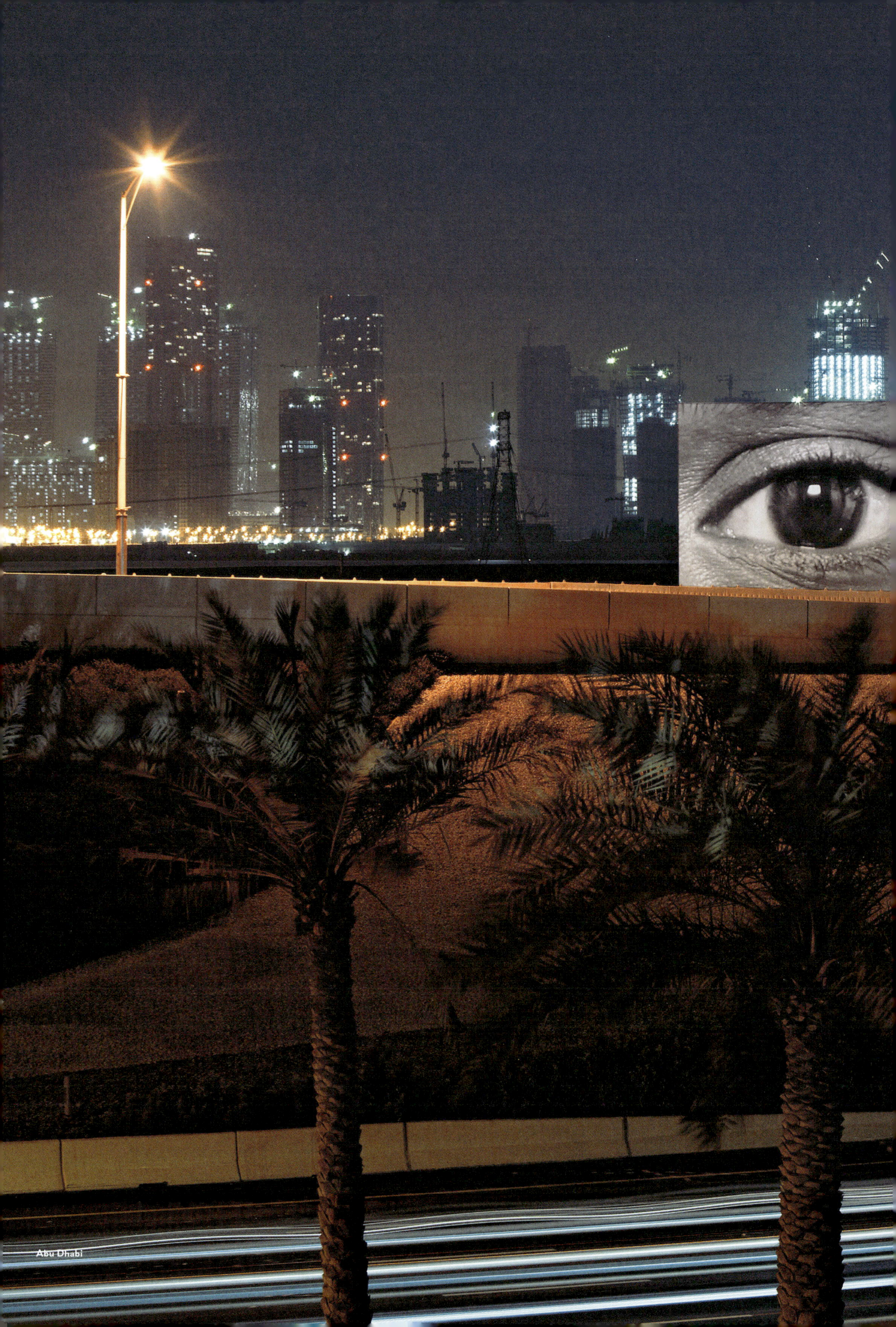

Abu Dhabi

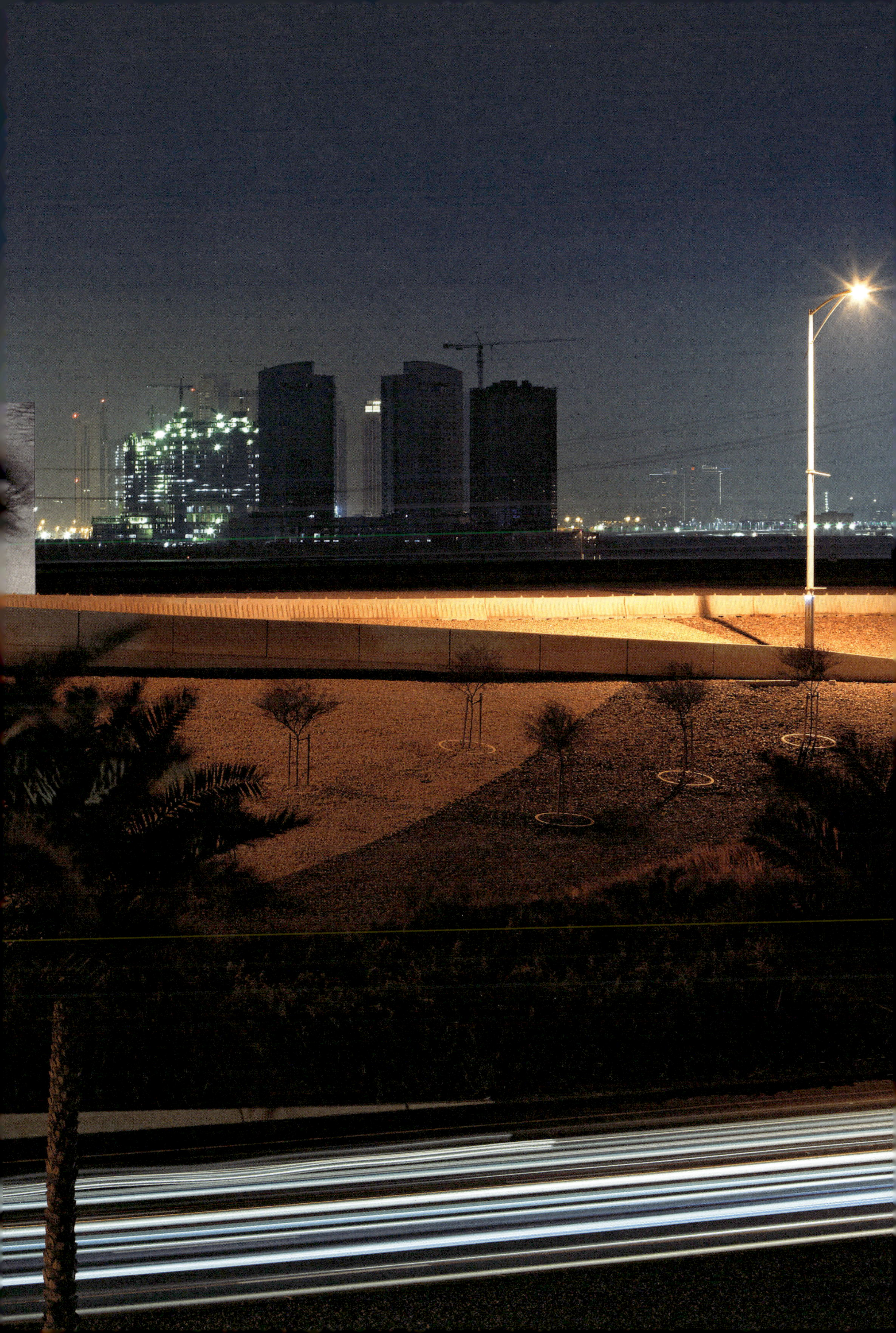

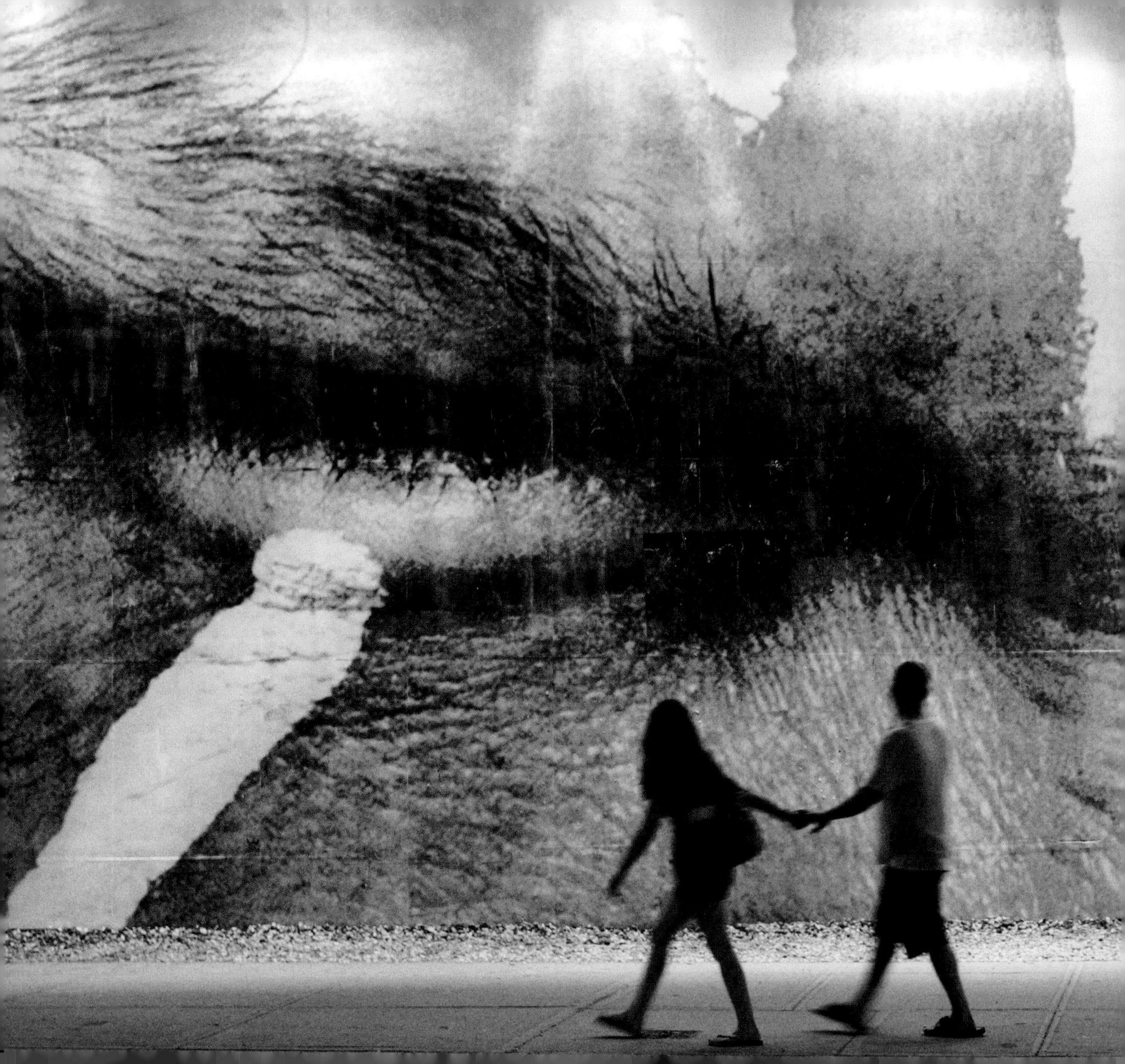

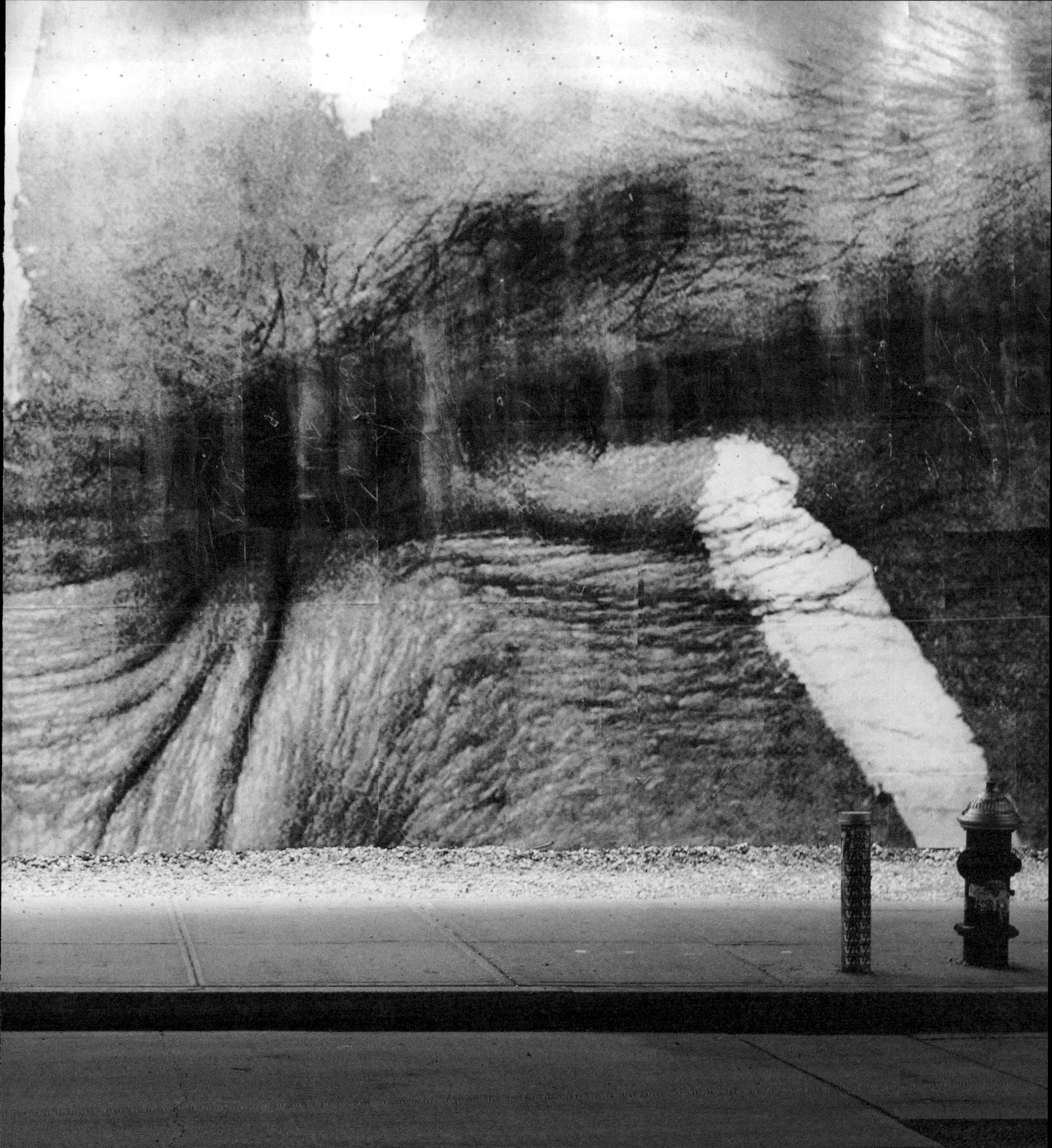

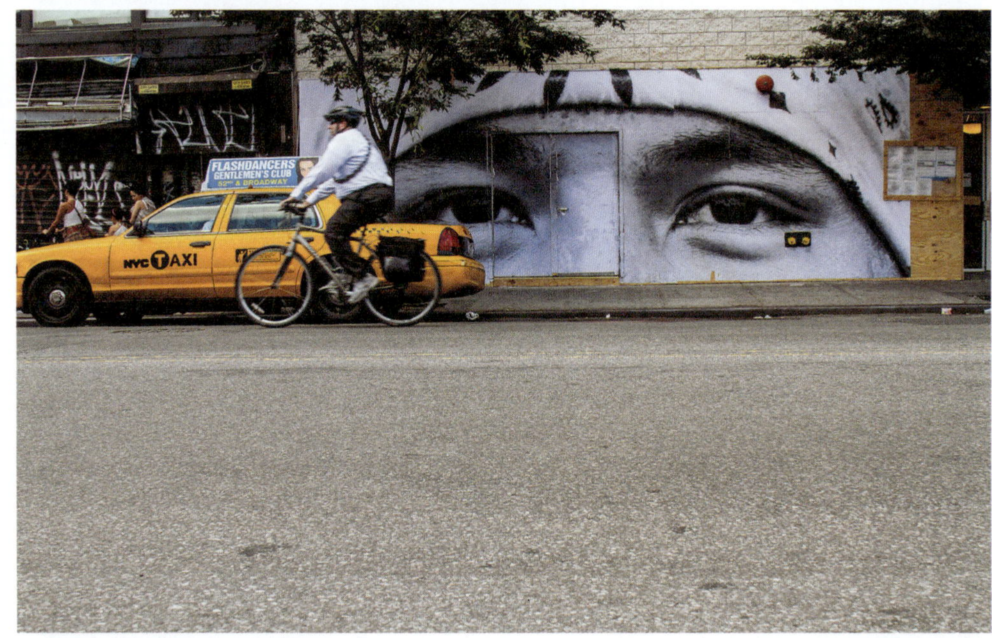

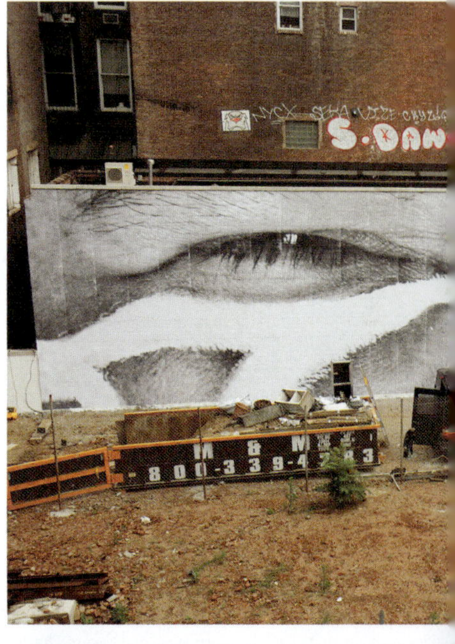

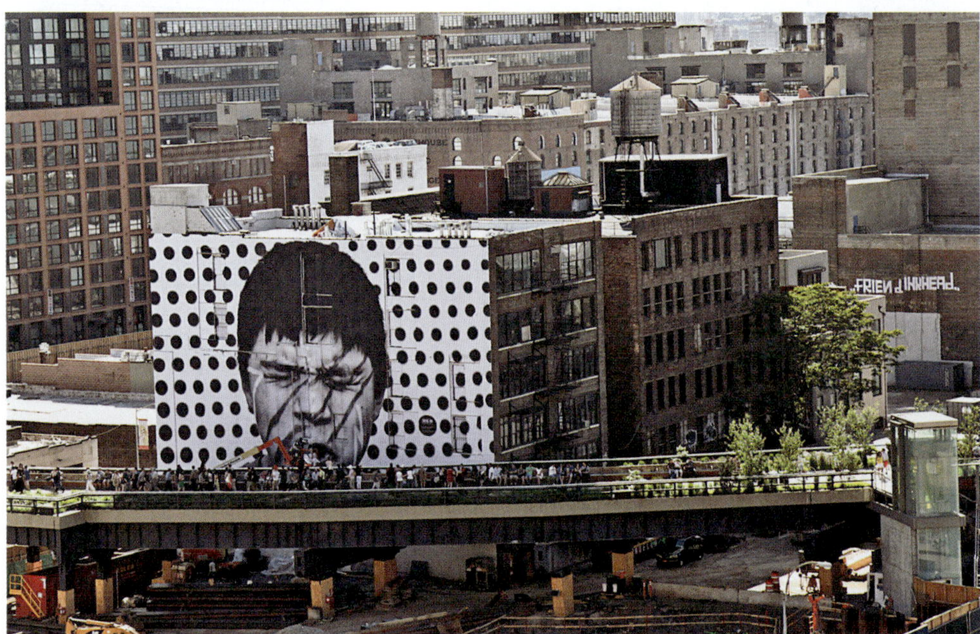

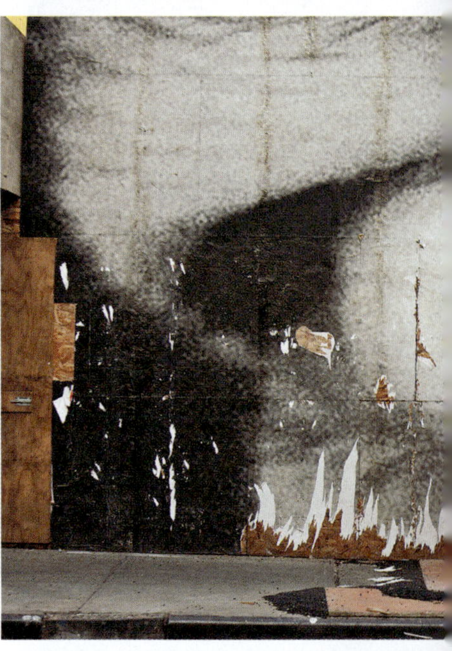

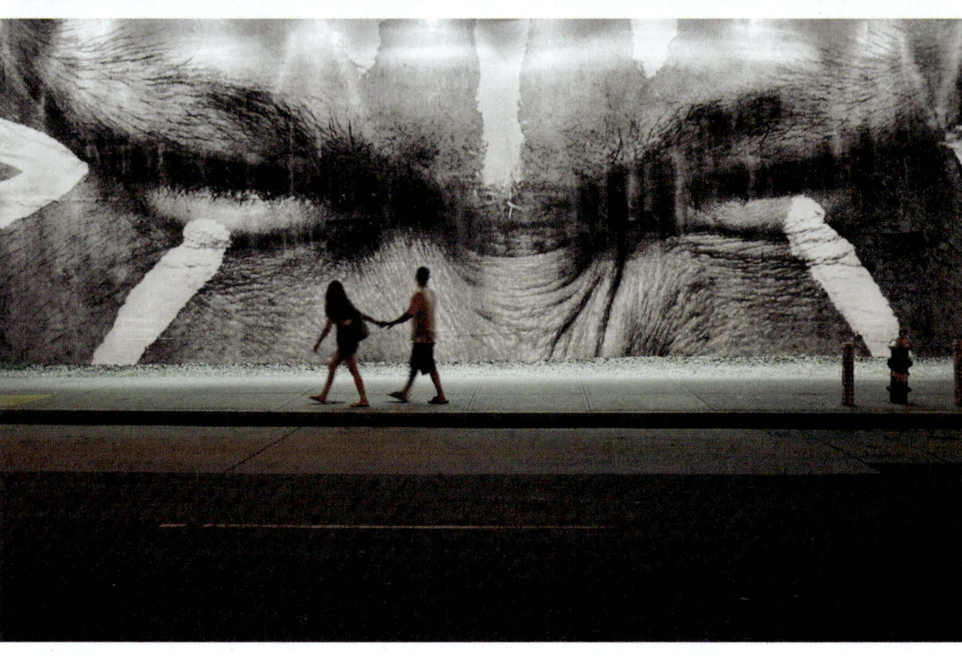

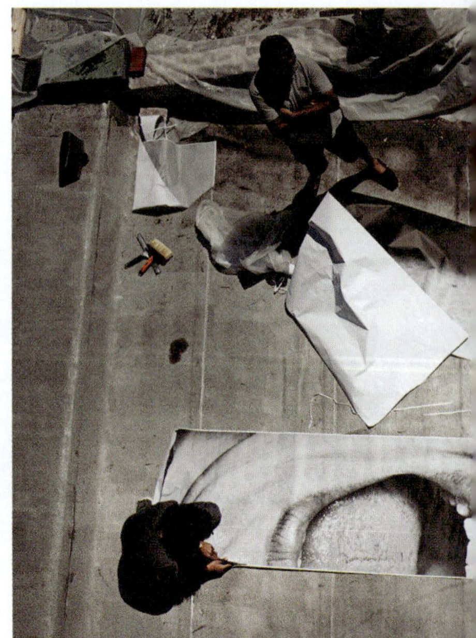

Standing Rock, NY

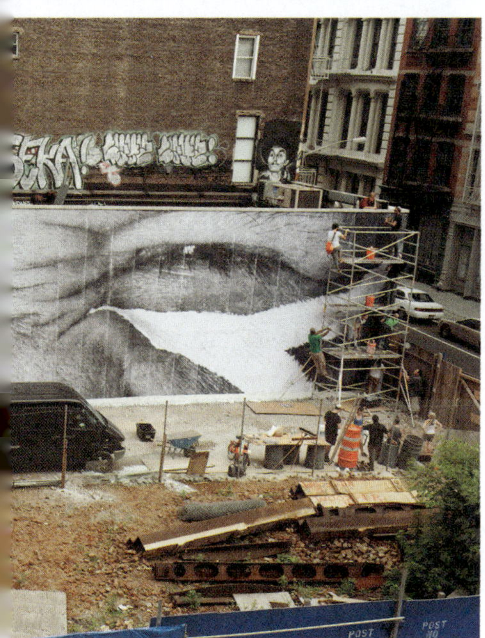
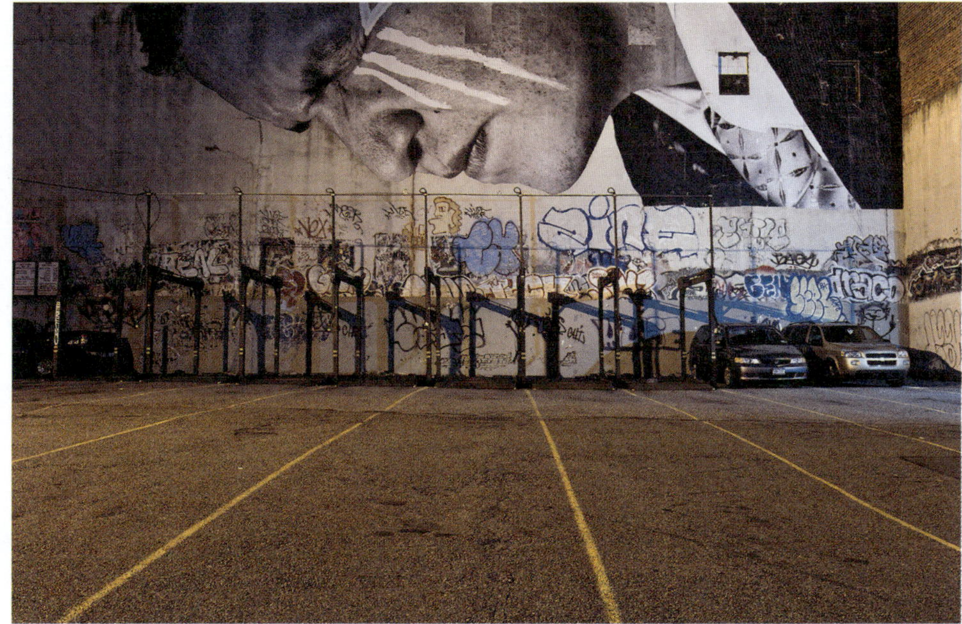
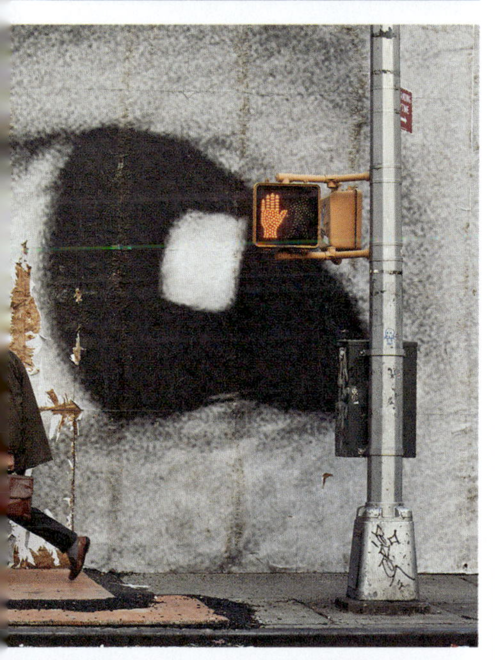
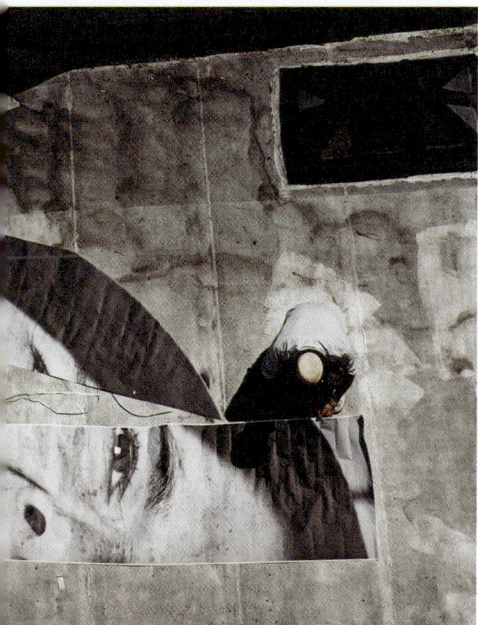

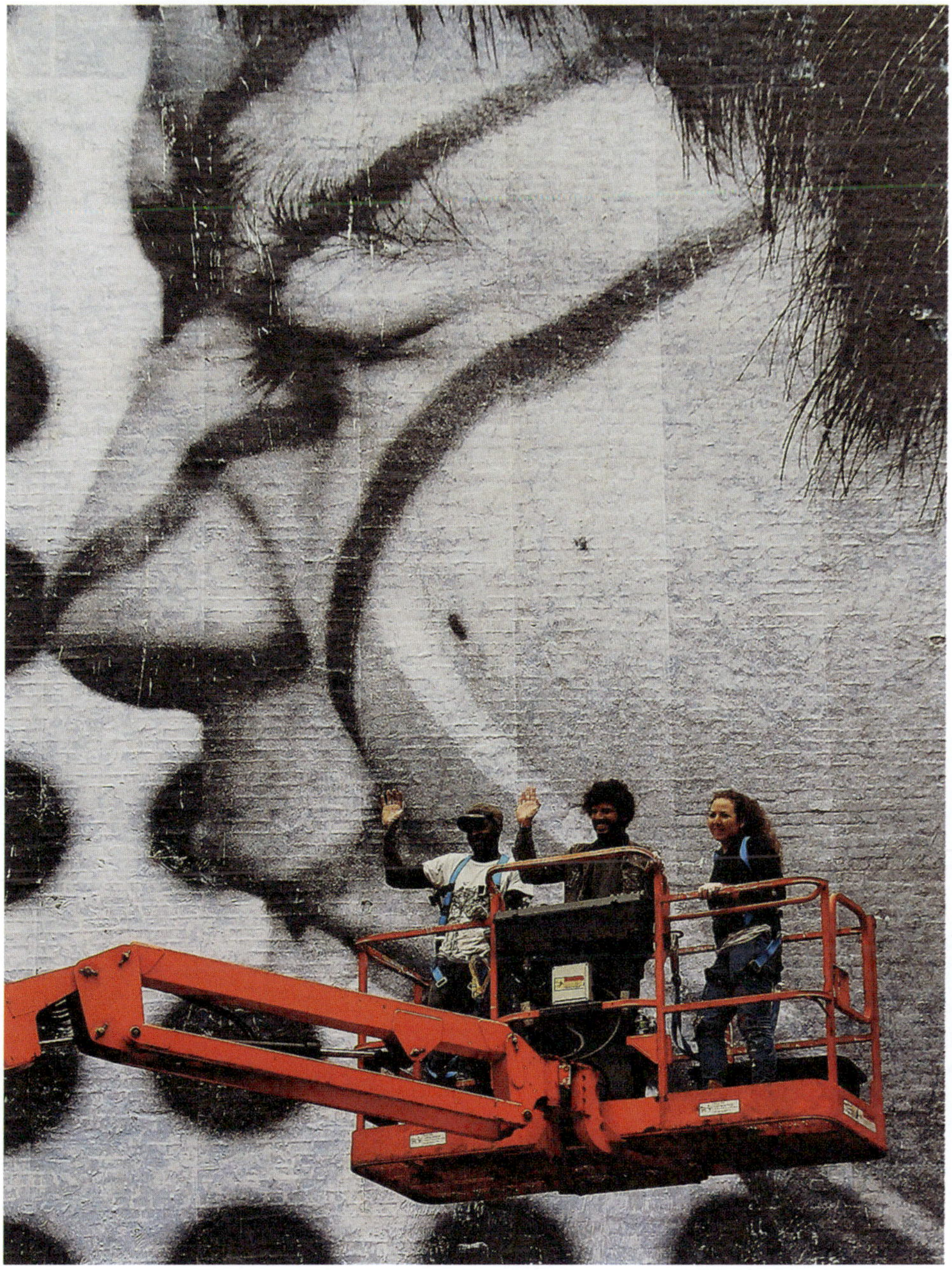

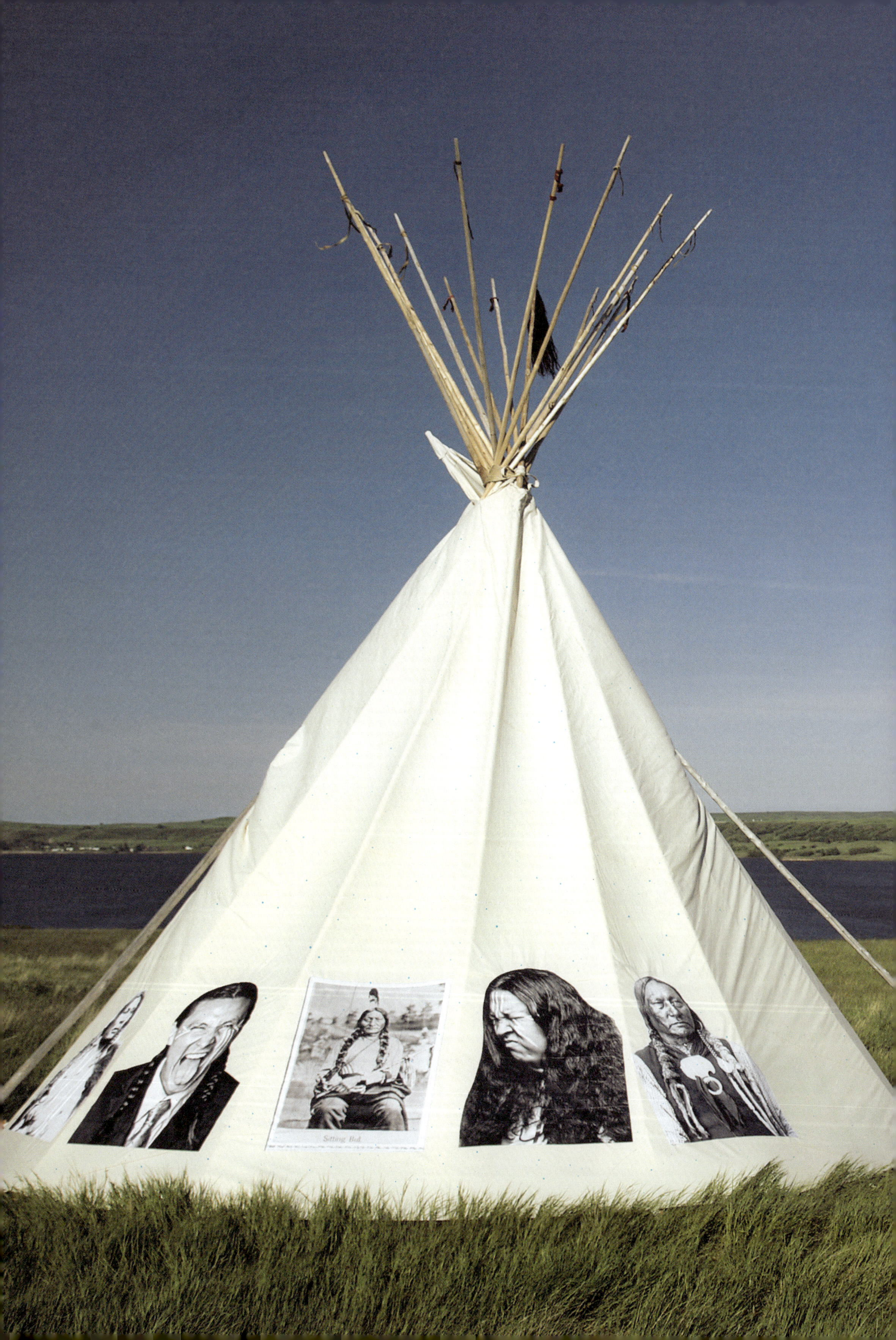

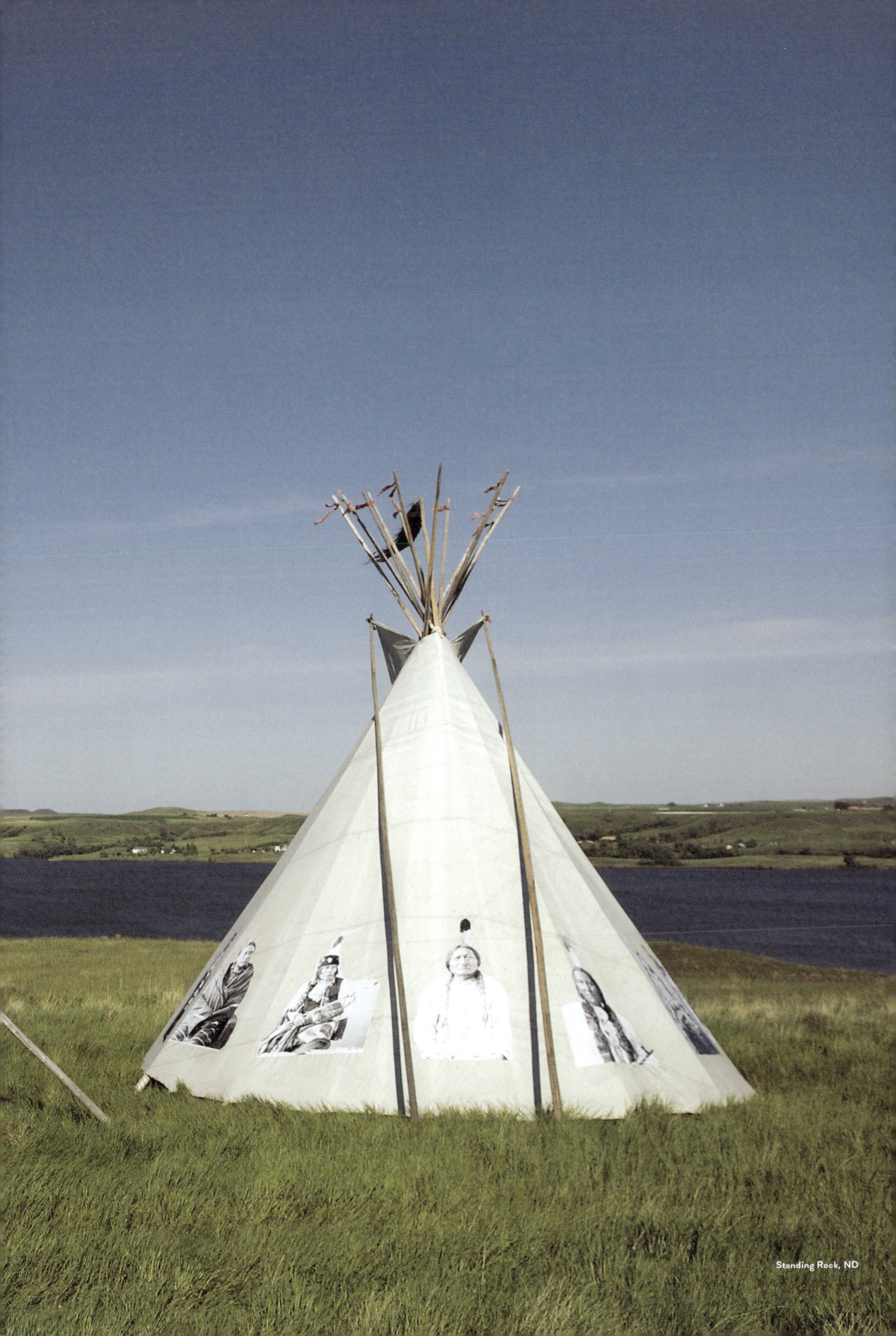

Standing Rock, ND

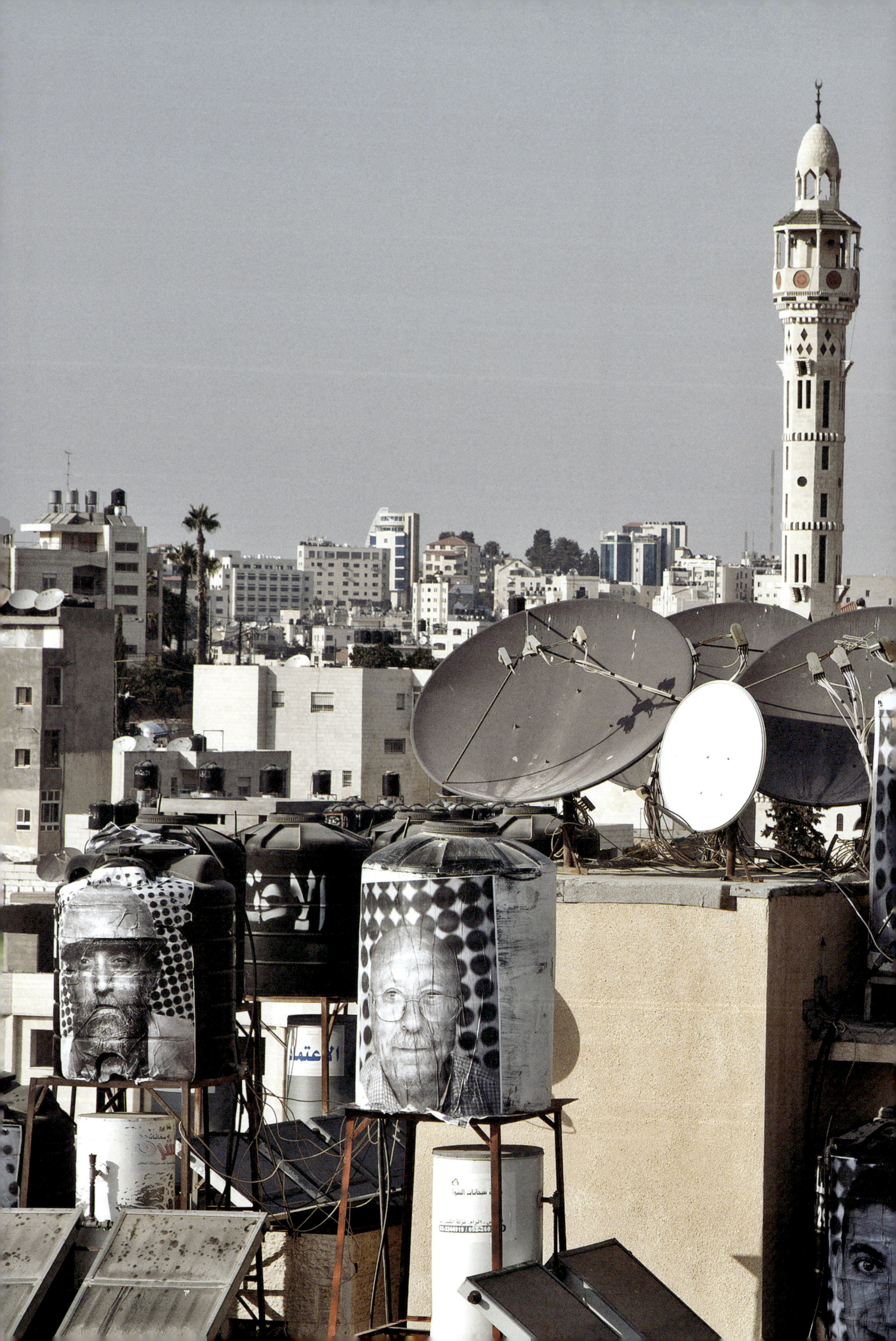

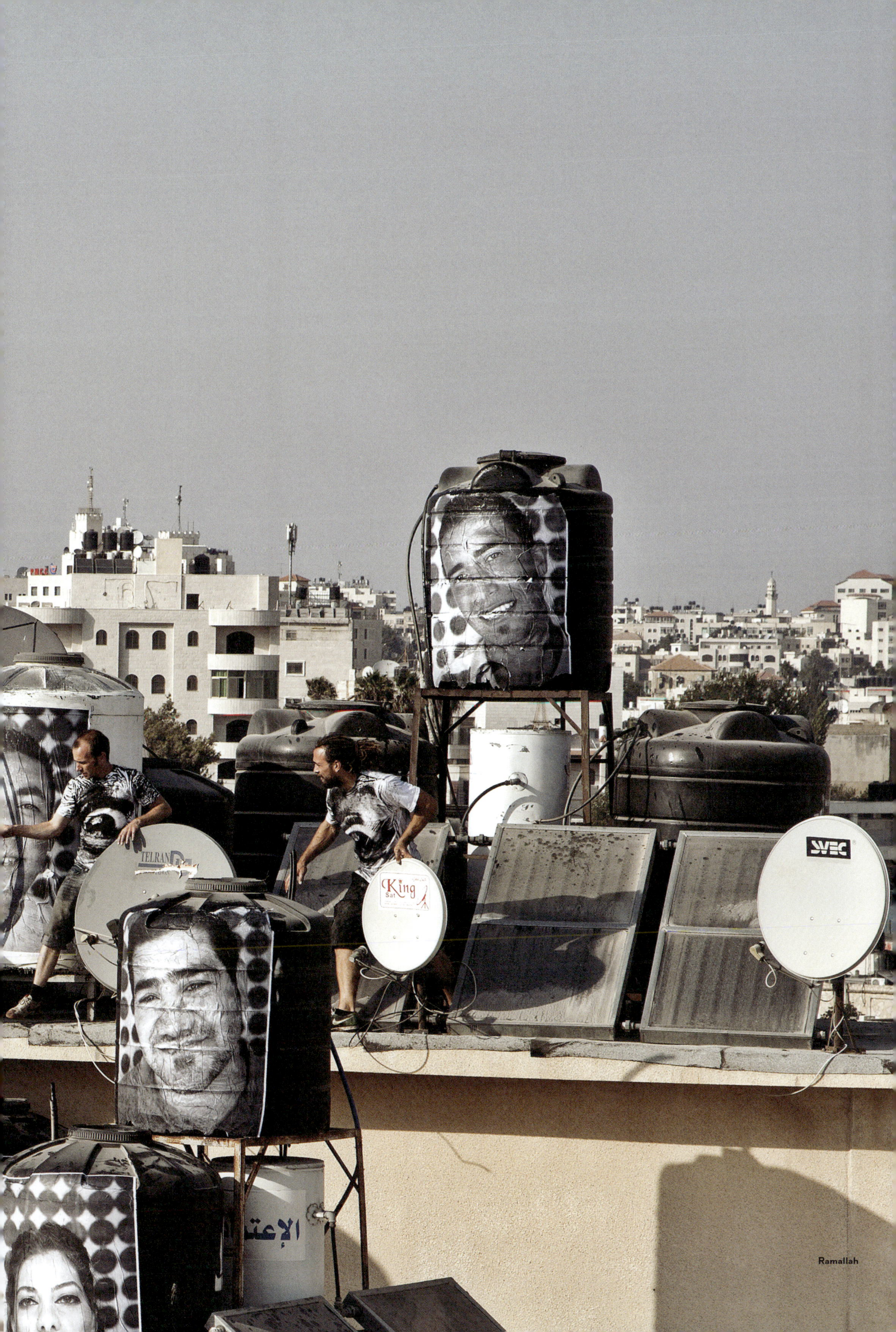

Ramallah

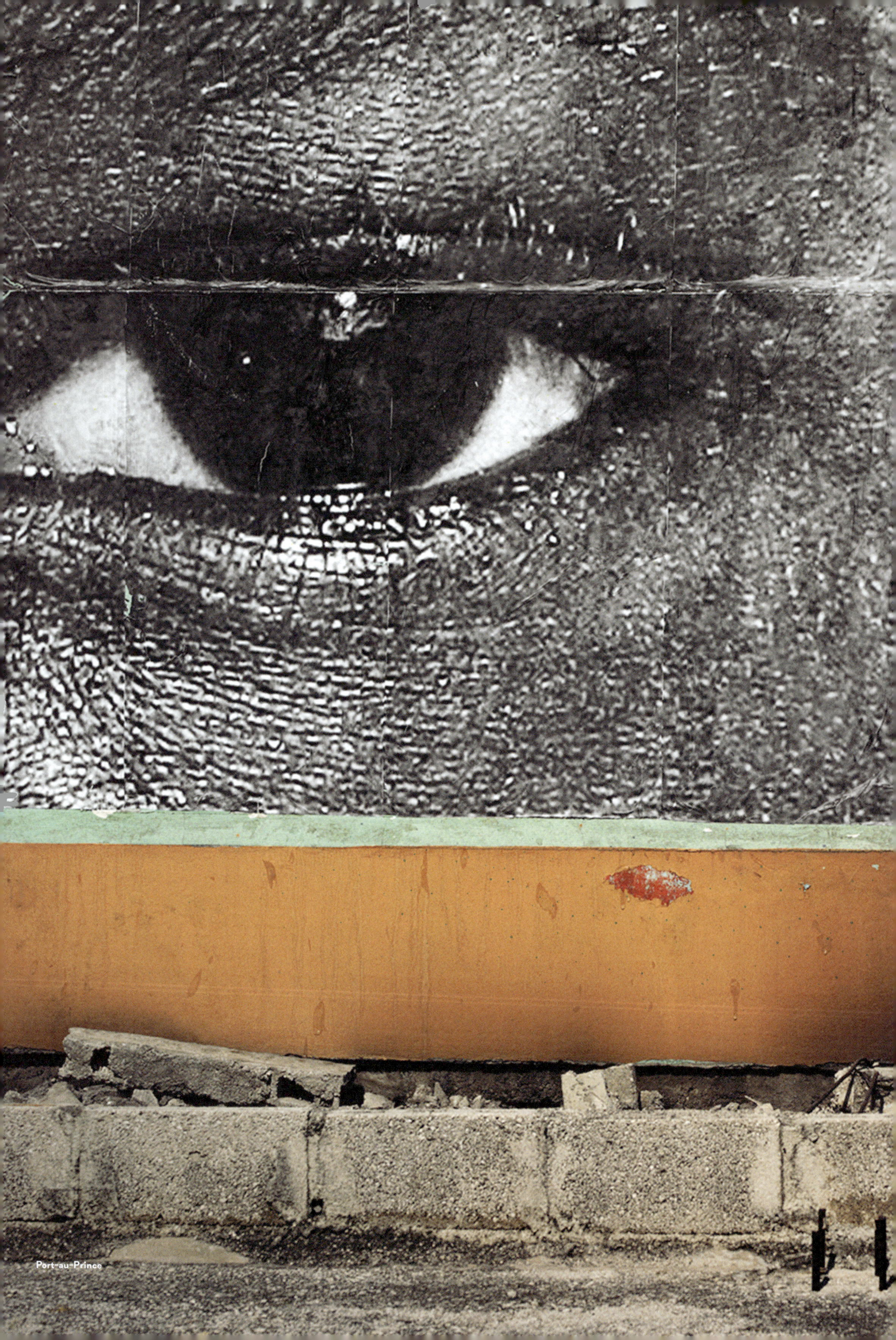

Port-au-Prince

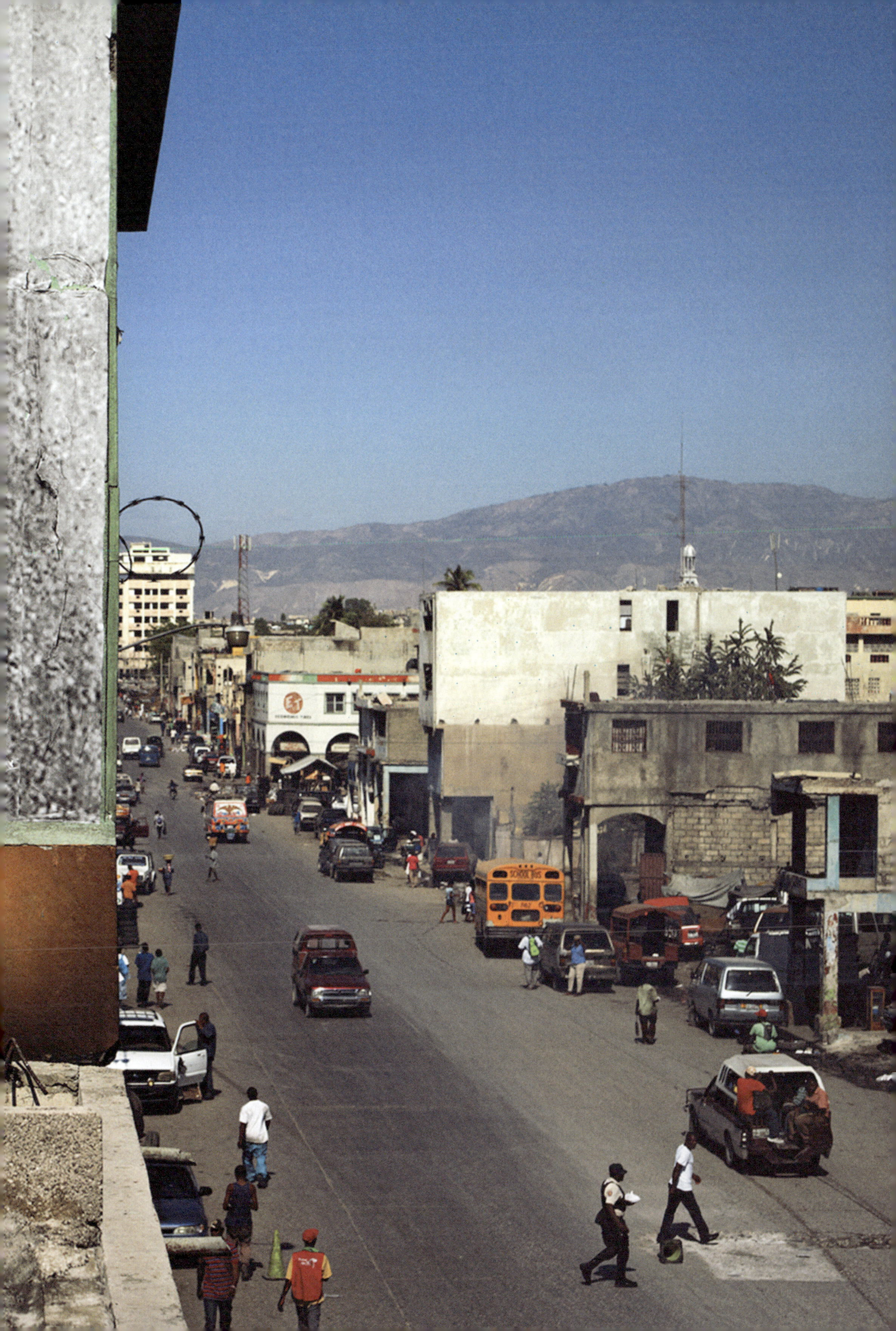

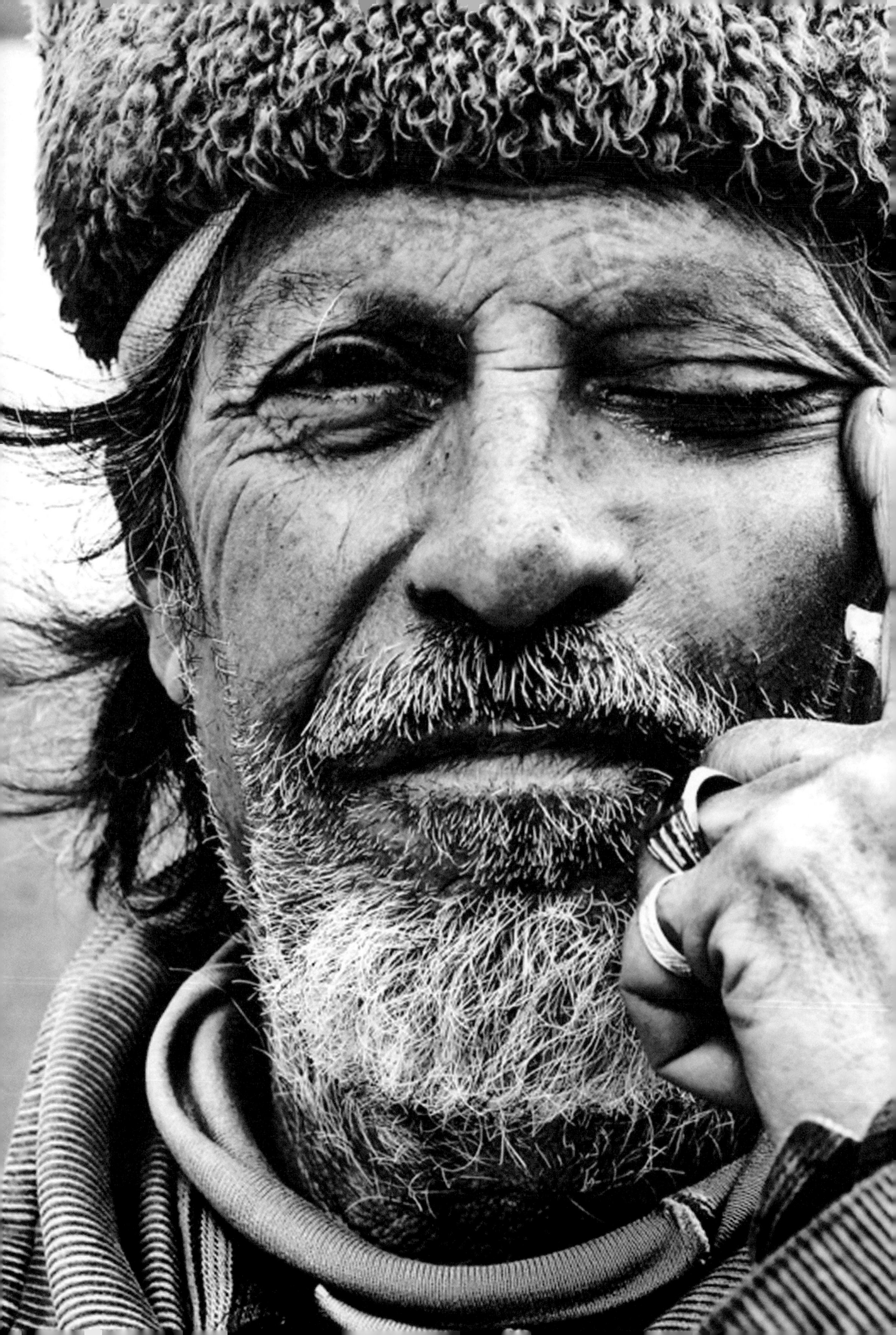

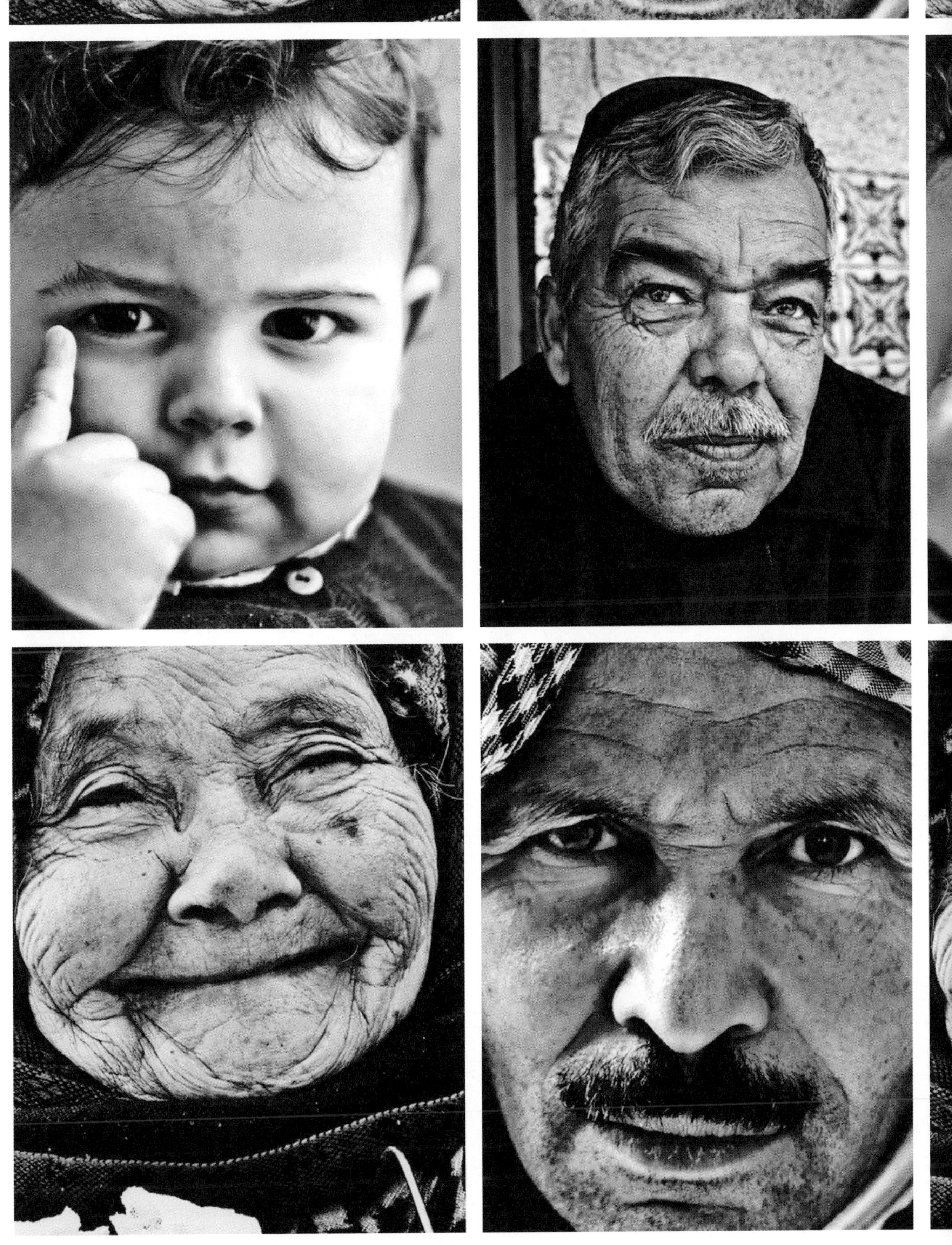

“These people represent the different faces of Tunisian society, people who agree to live with mutual respect for others.”

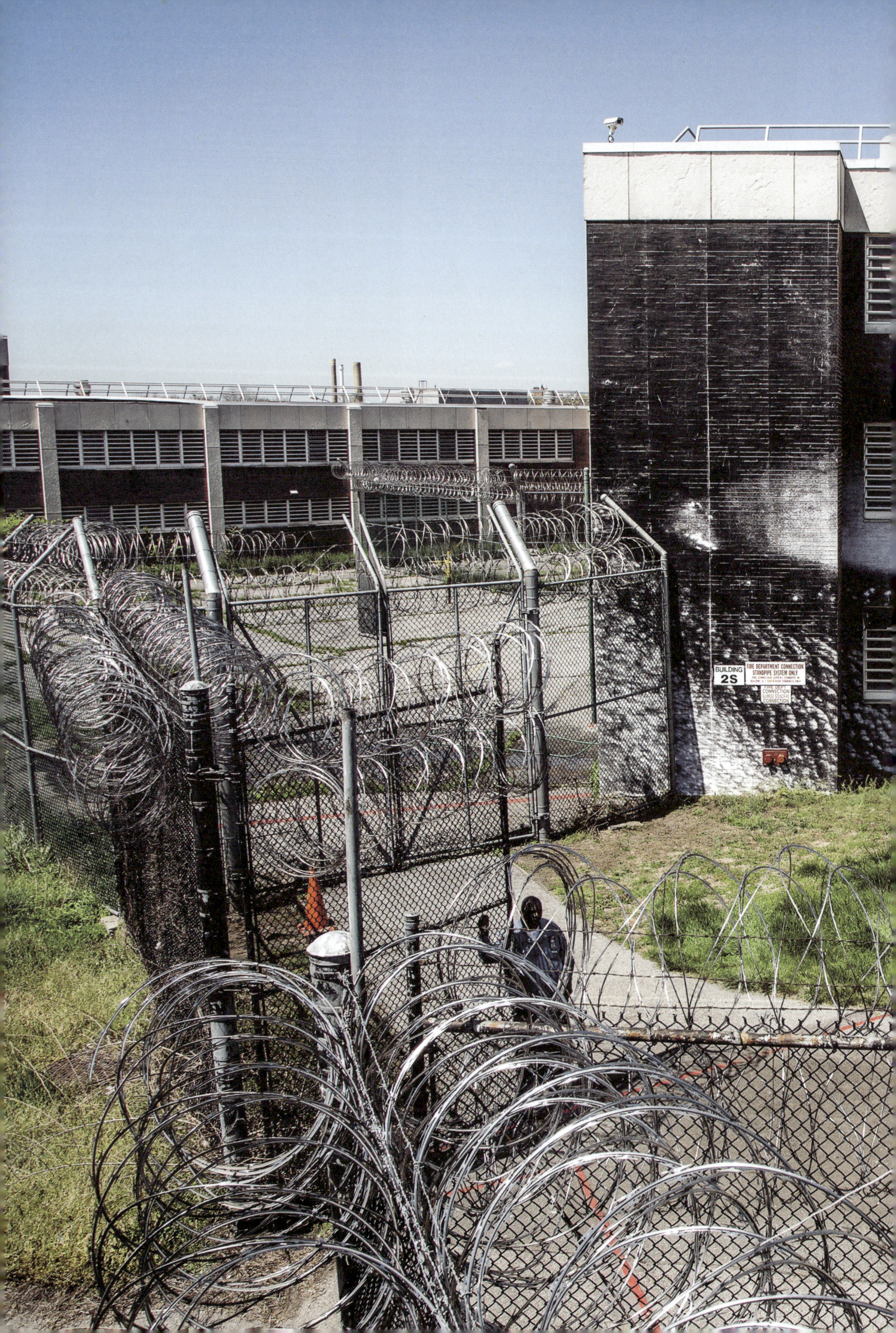
BUILDING
2S
FIRE DEPARTMENT CONNECTION
STANDPIPE SYSTEM ONLY
CONNECTION
CONNECTION

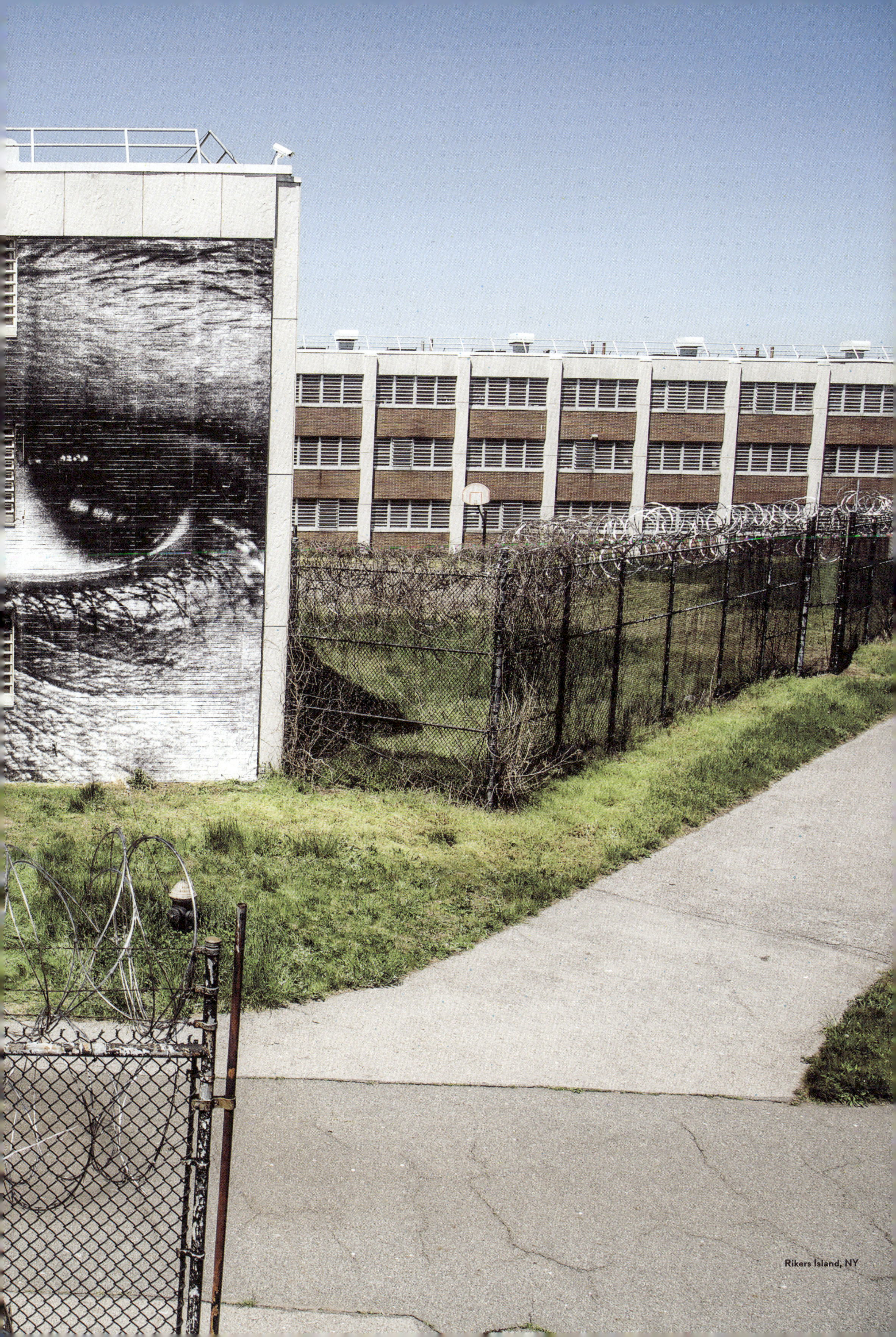

Rikers Island, NY

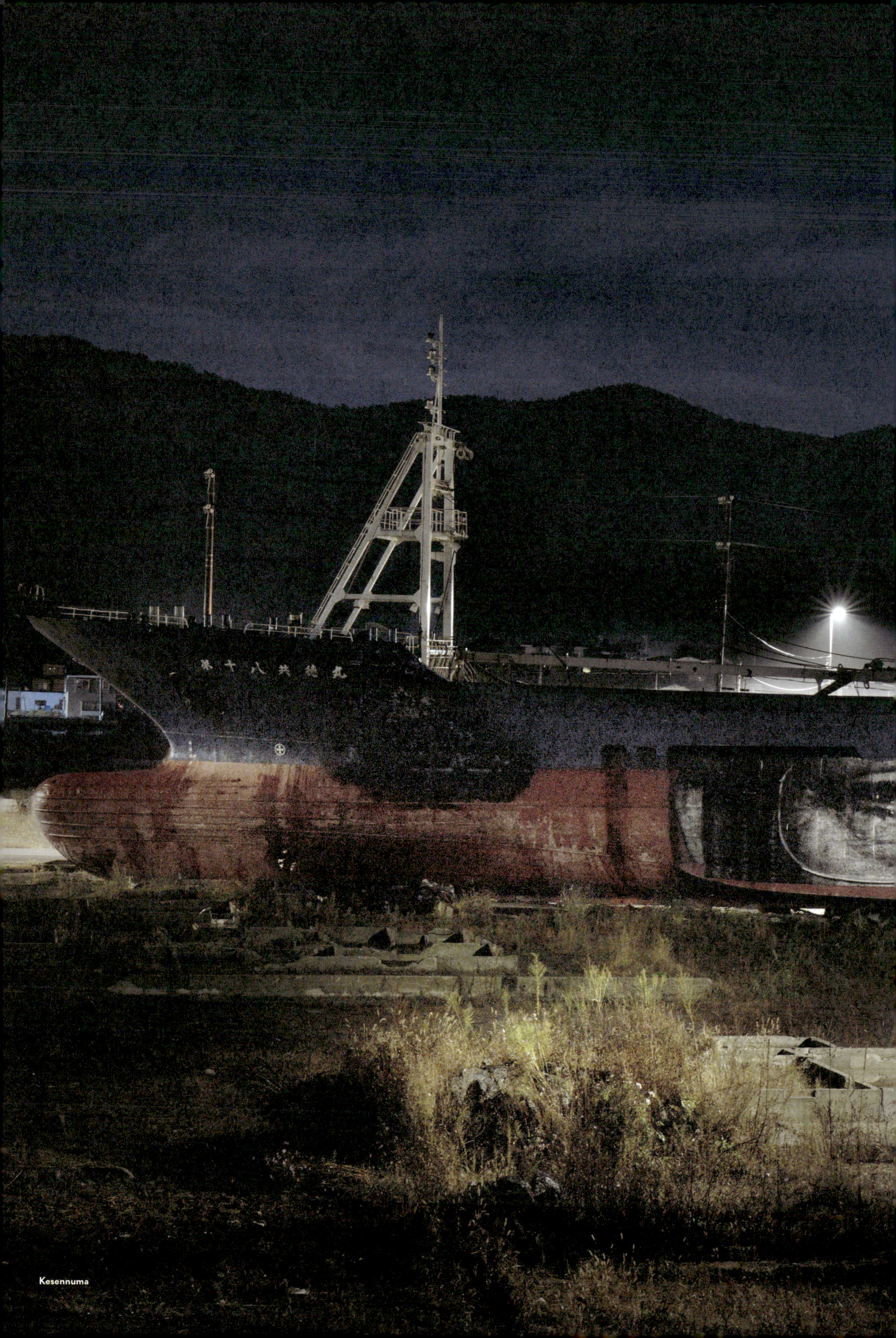

Kesennuma

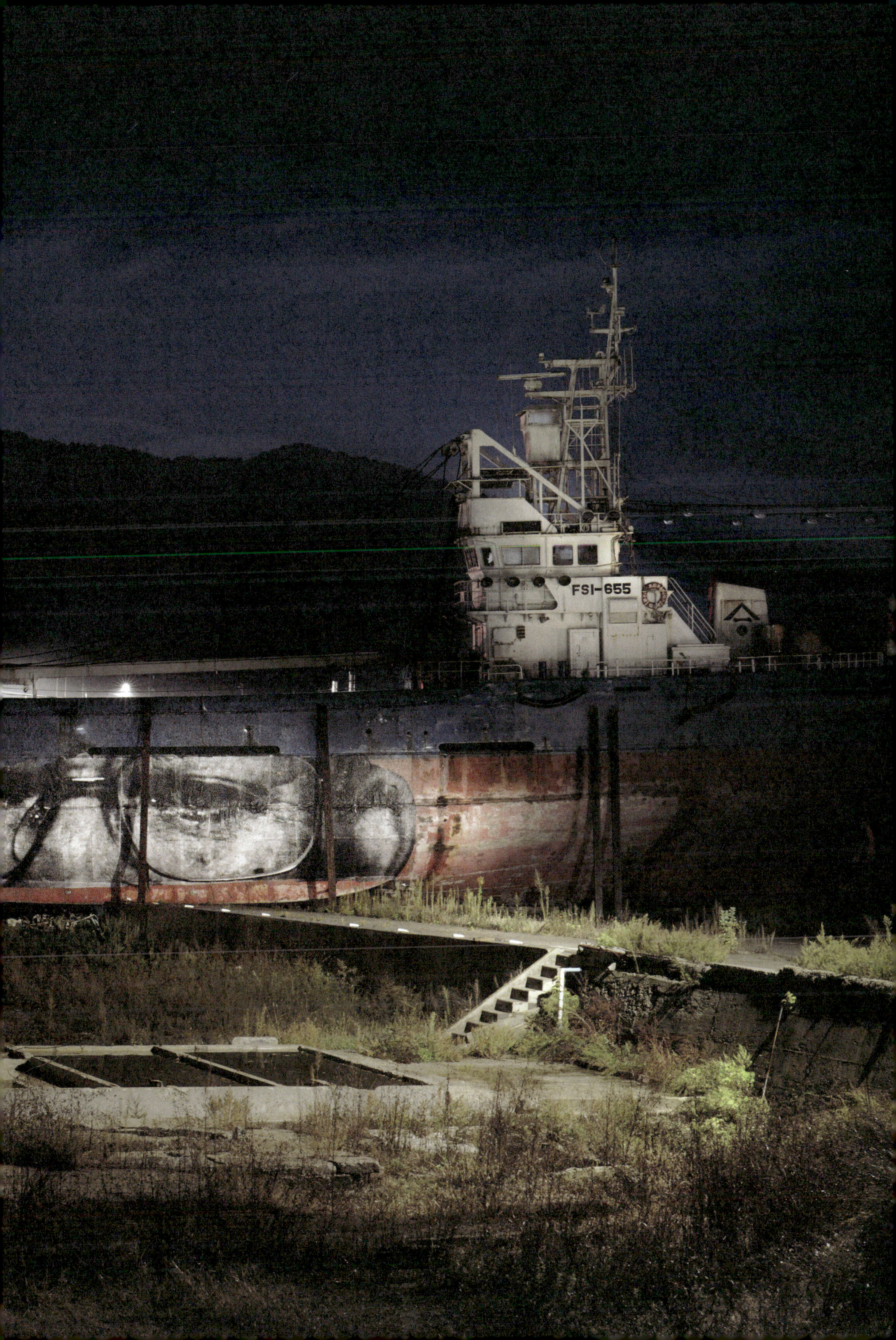
FSI-655

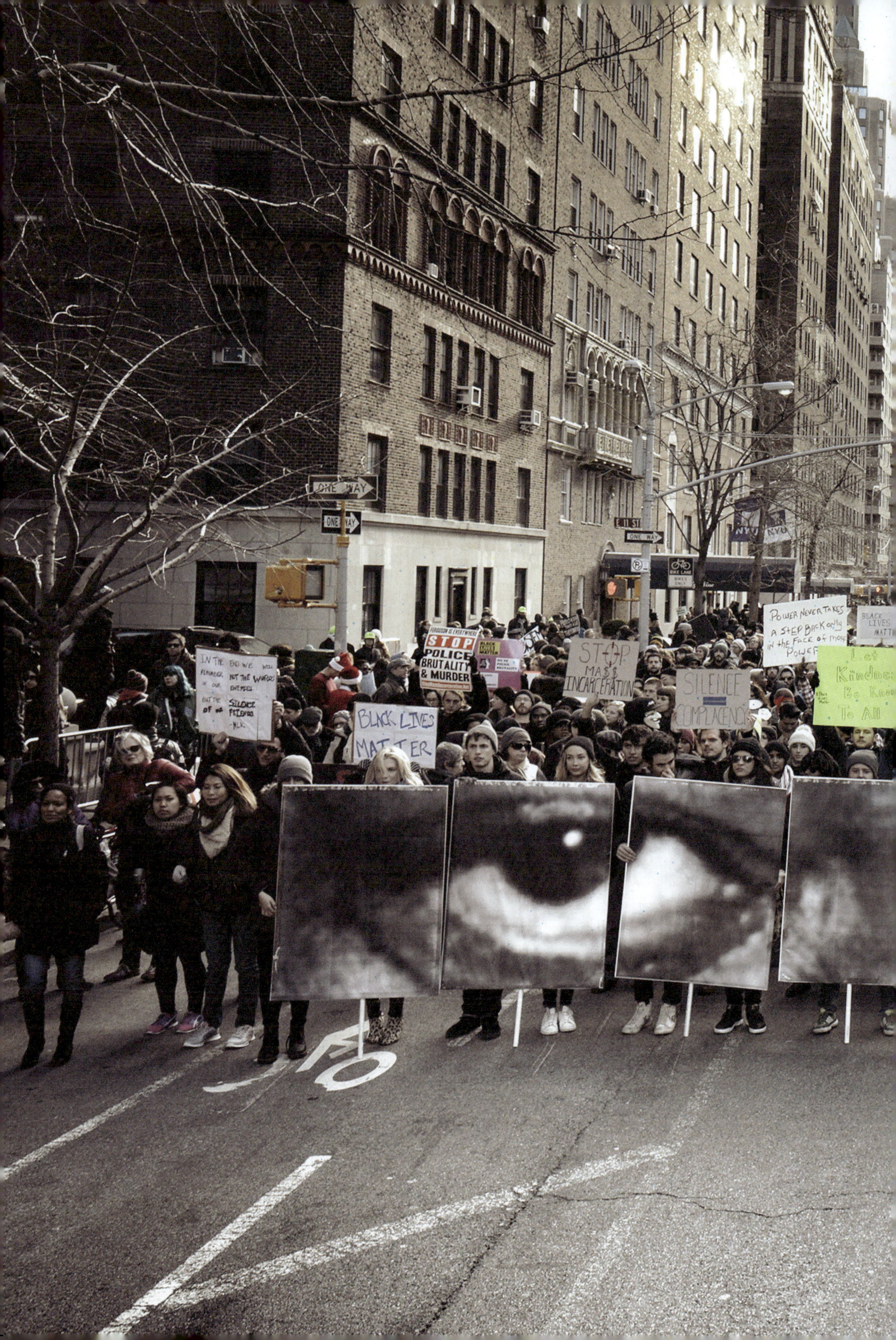
ONE WAY
ONE WAY
ONE WAY
BIKE LANE BIKES ONLY
FERGUSON IS EVERYWHERE
STOP POLICE BRUTALITY & MURDER
STOP MASS INCARCERATION
SILENCE = COMPLACENCY
BLACK LIVES MATTER
POWER NEVER TAKES A STEP BACK only in the FACE of more POWER
Let Kindness Be Known To All

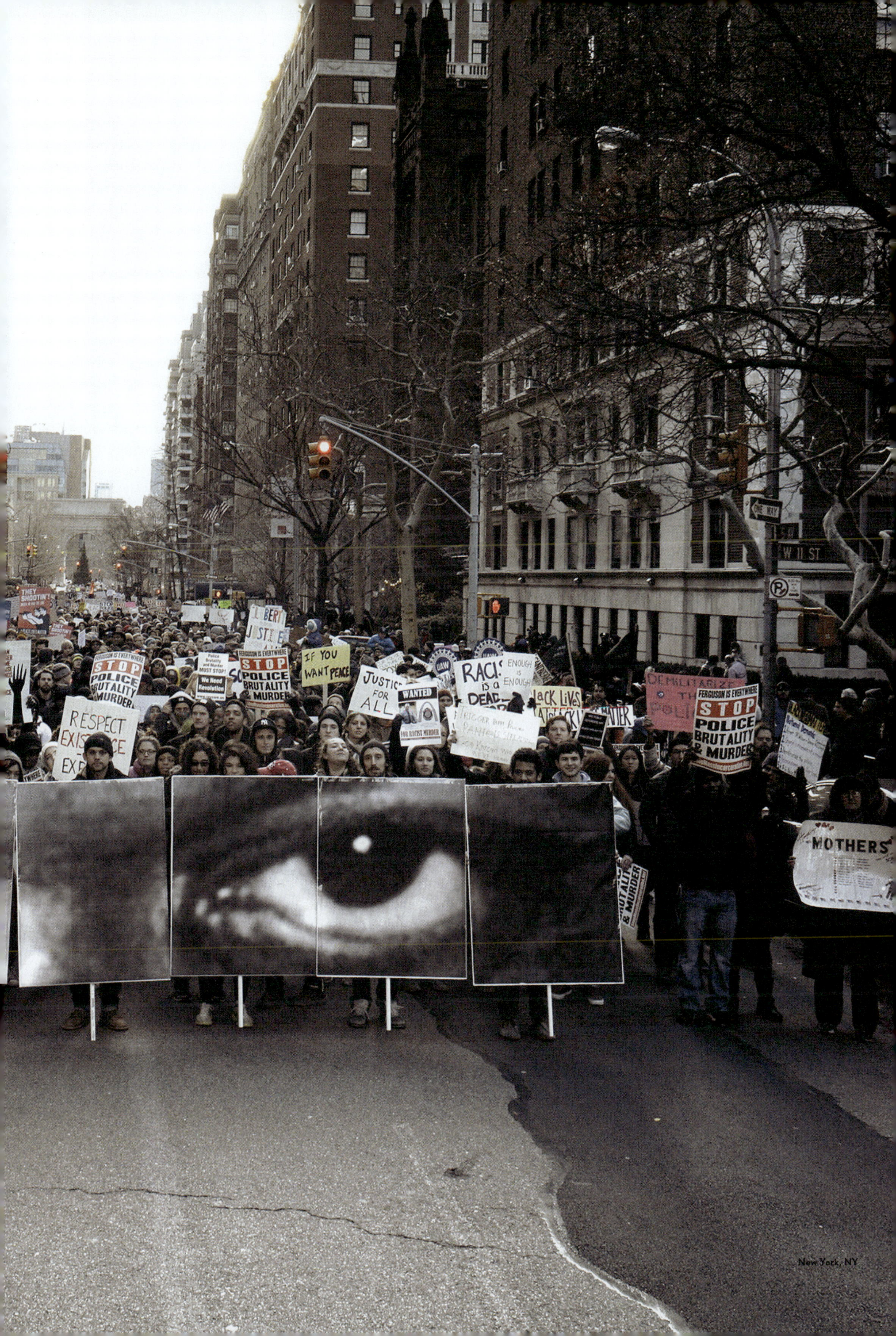
ONE WAY
W 11 ST
FERGUSON IS EVERYWHERE
STOP
POLICE
BRUTALITY
MURDER
IF YOU WANT PEACE
JUSTICE FOR ALL
WANTED
ENOUGH IS ENOUGH
RESPECT
MOTHERS

New York, NY

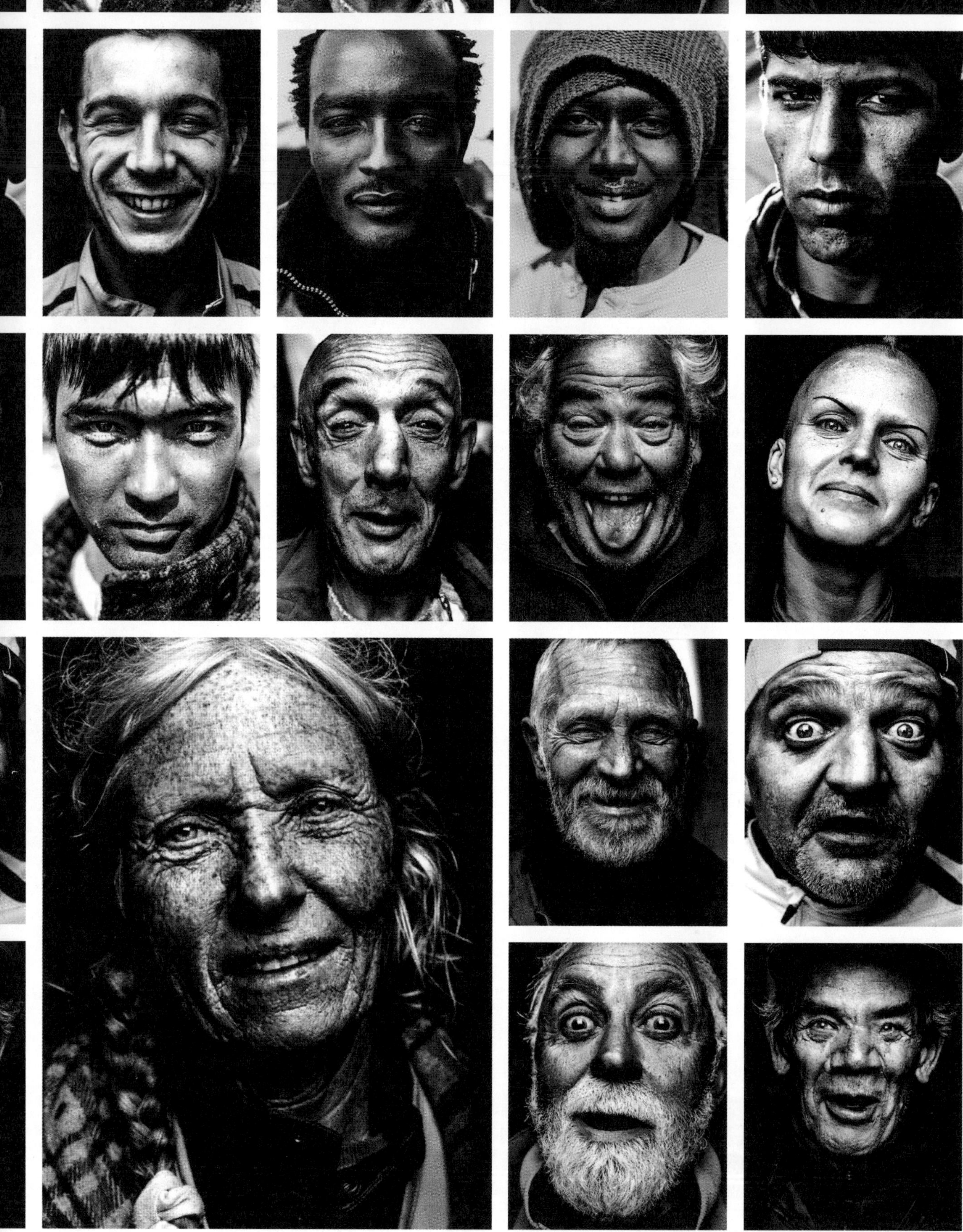

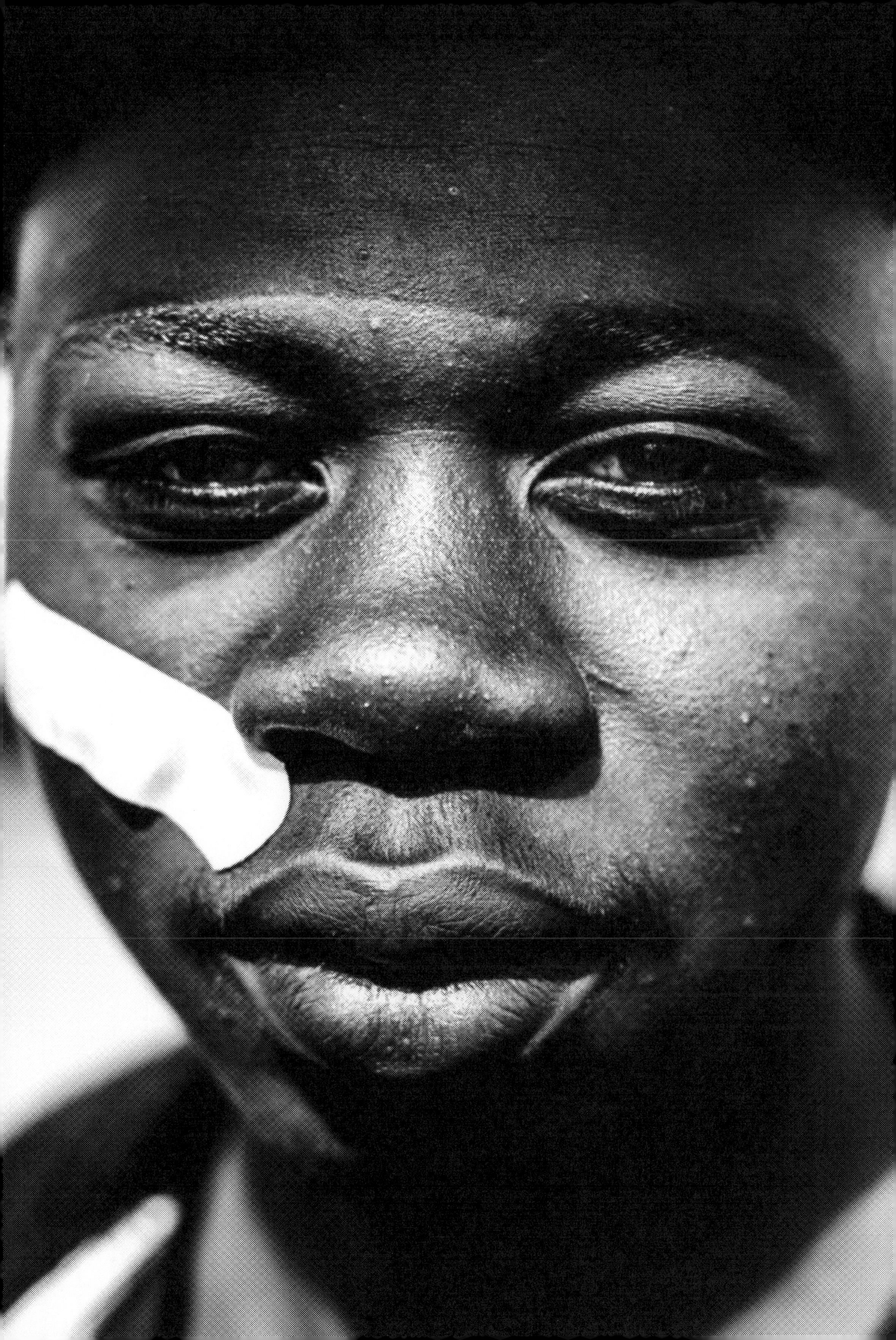

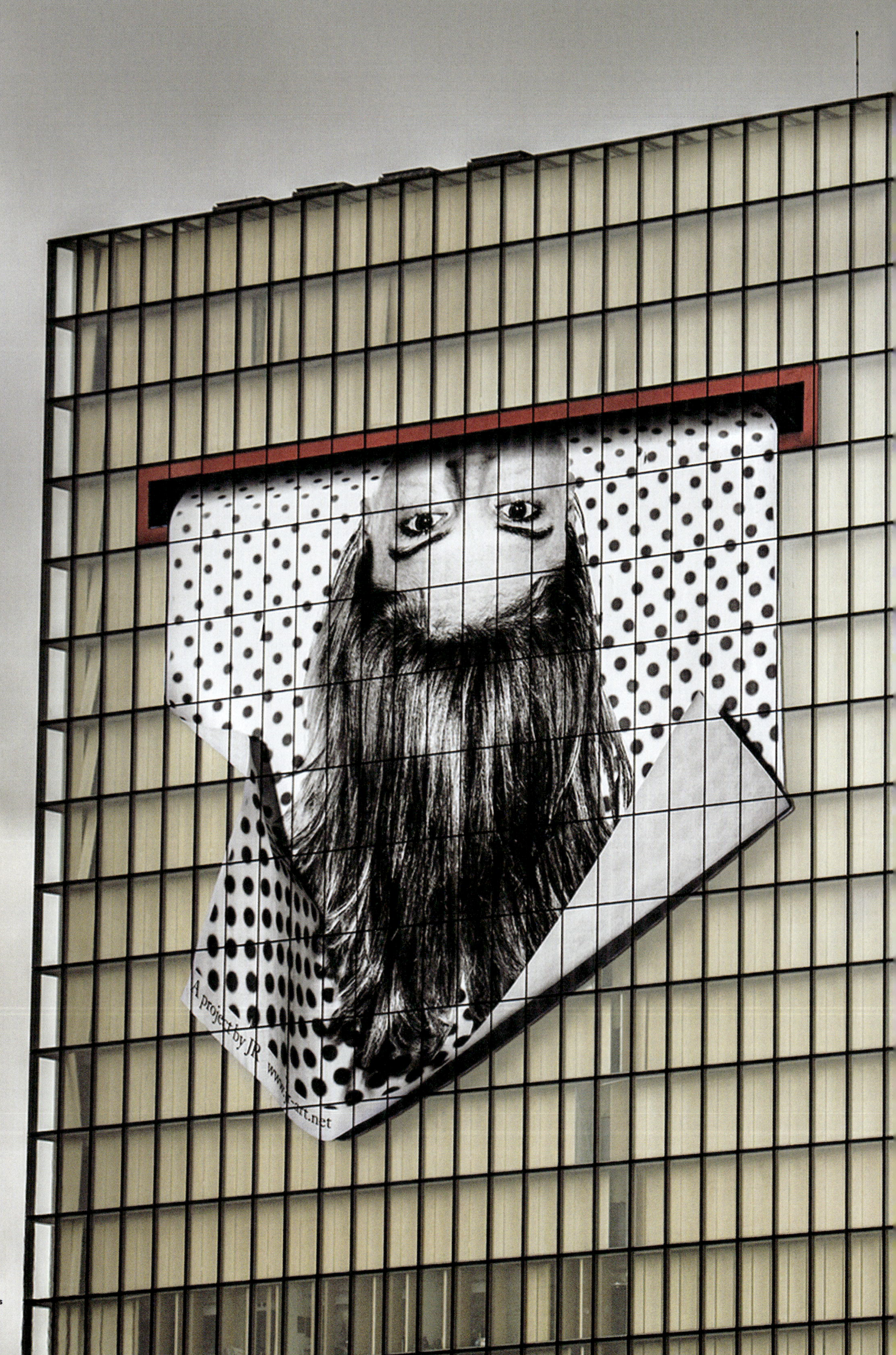

Paris

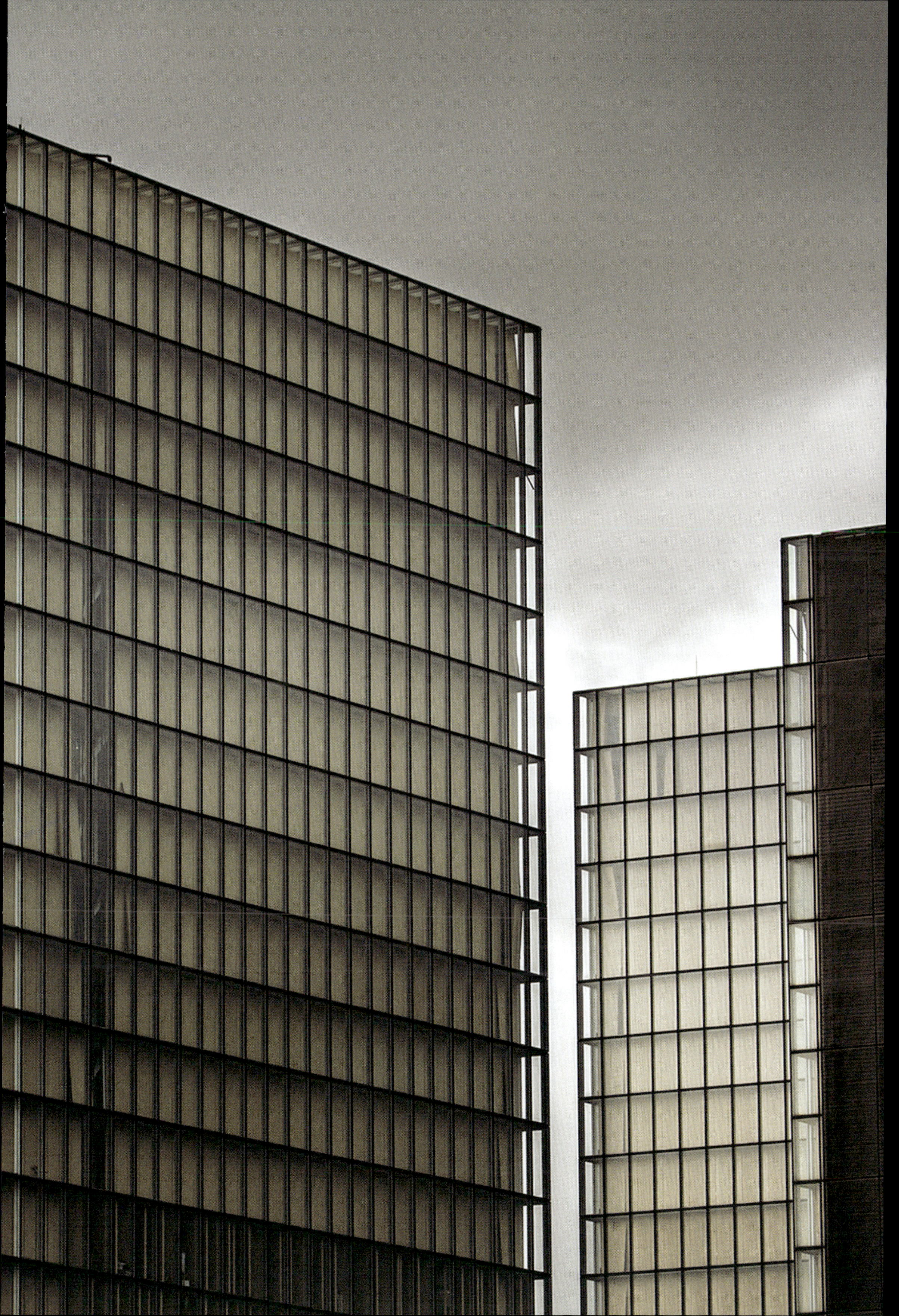

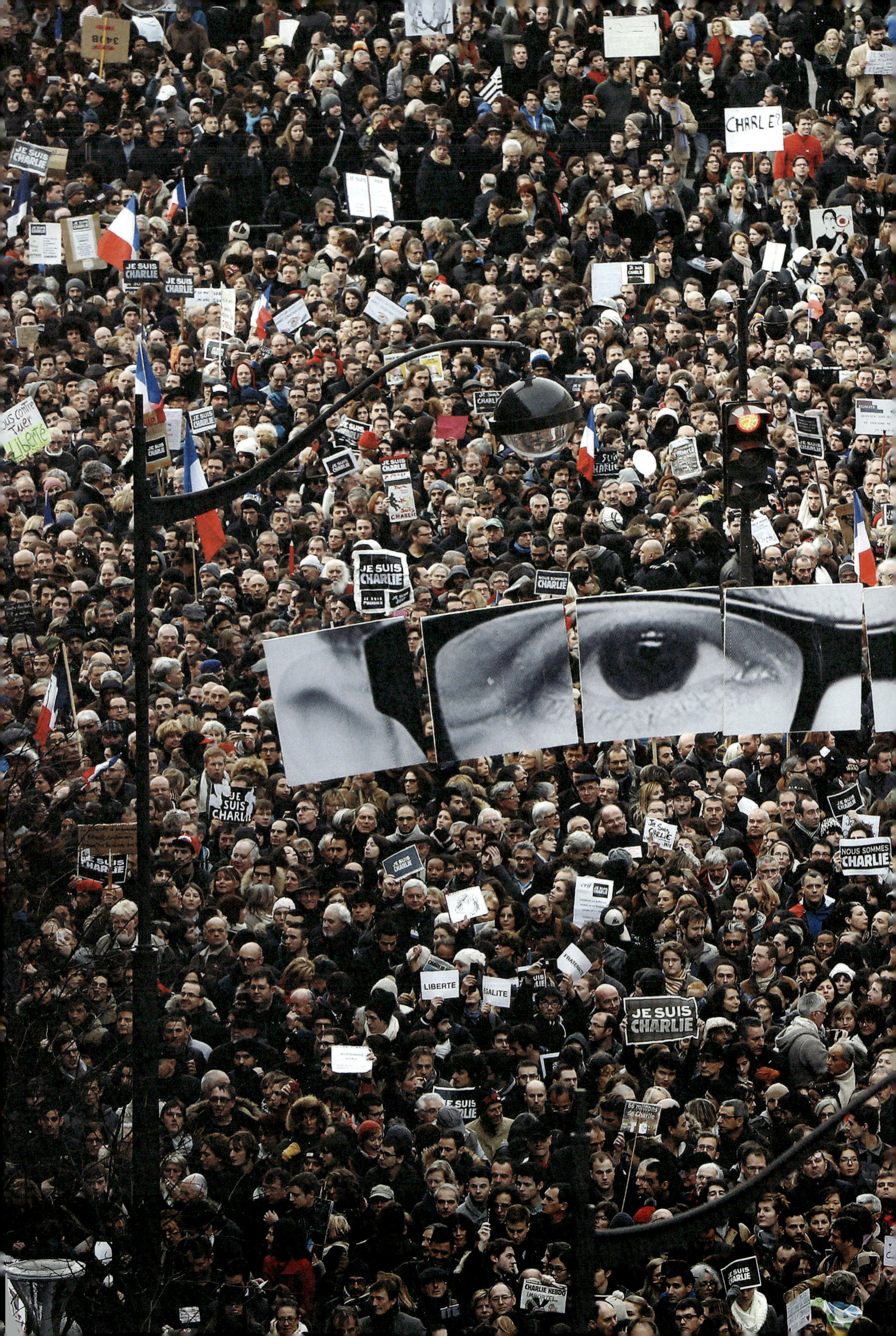
JE SUIS CHARLIE
NOUS SOMMES CHARLIE
LIBERTE
JE SUIS CHARLIE

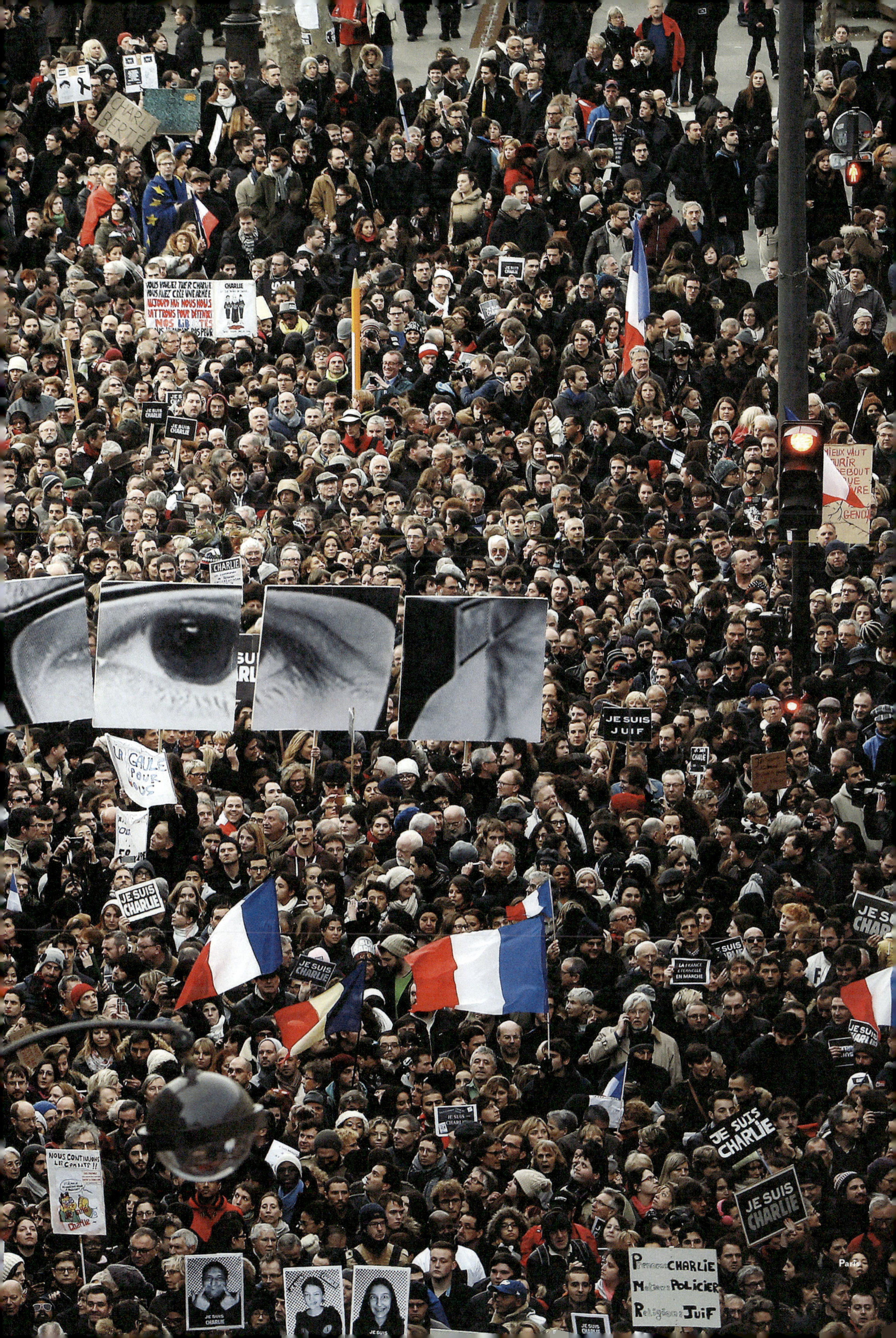
JE SUIS JUIF
JE SUIS CHARLIE
JE SUIS CHARLIE
JE SUIS CHARLIE
CHARLIE
POLICIER
JUIF

Paris

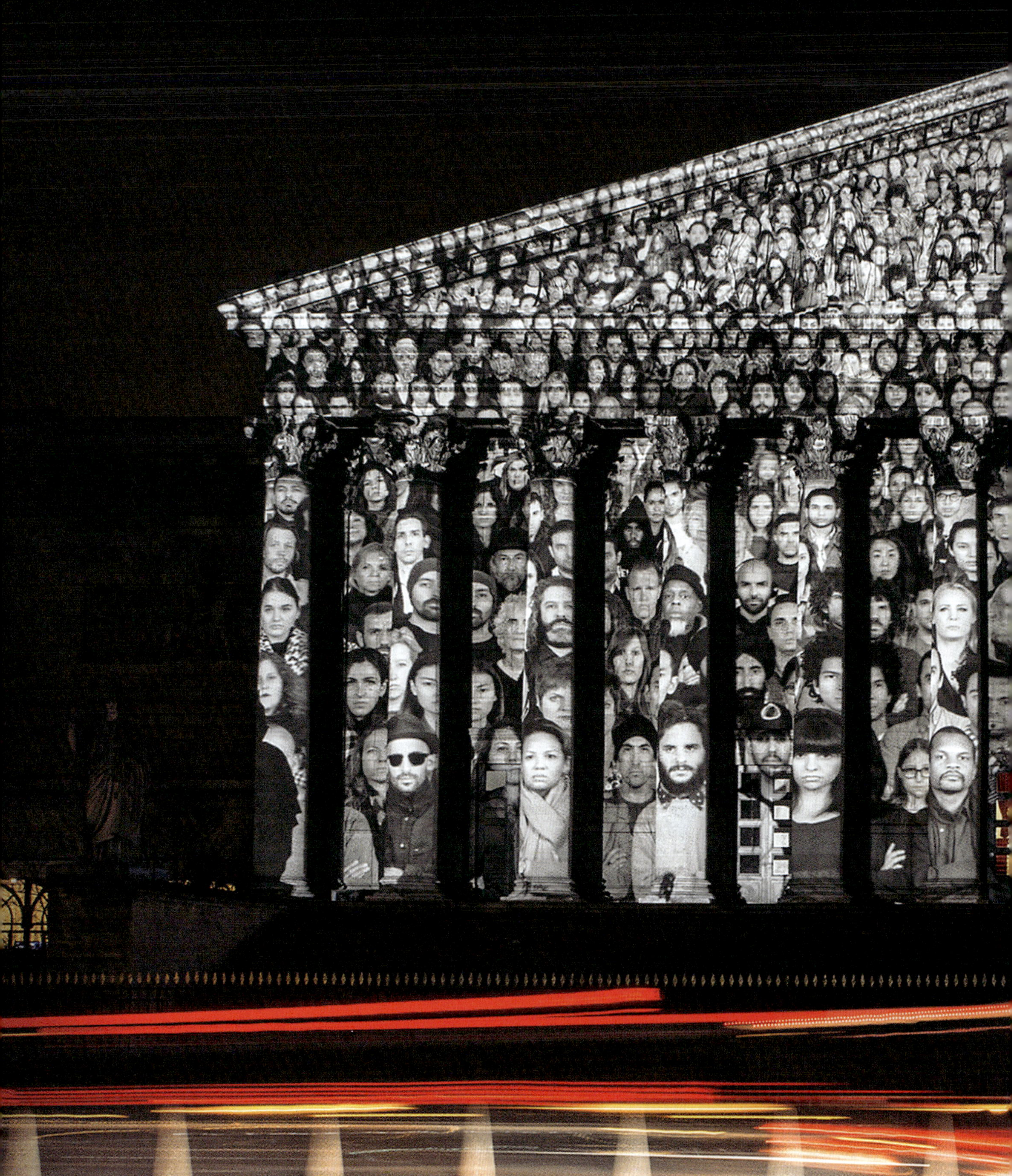

Paris

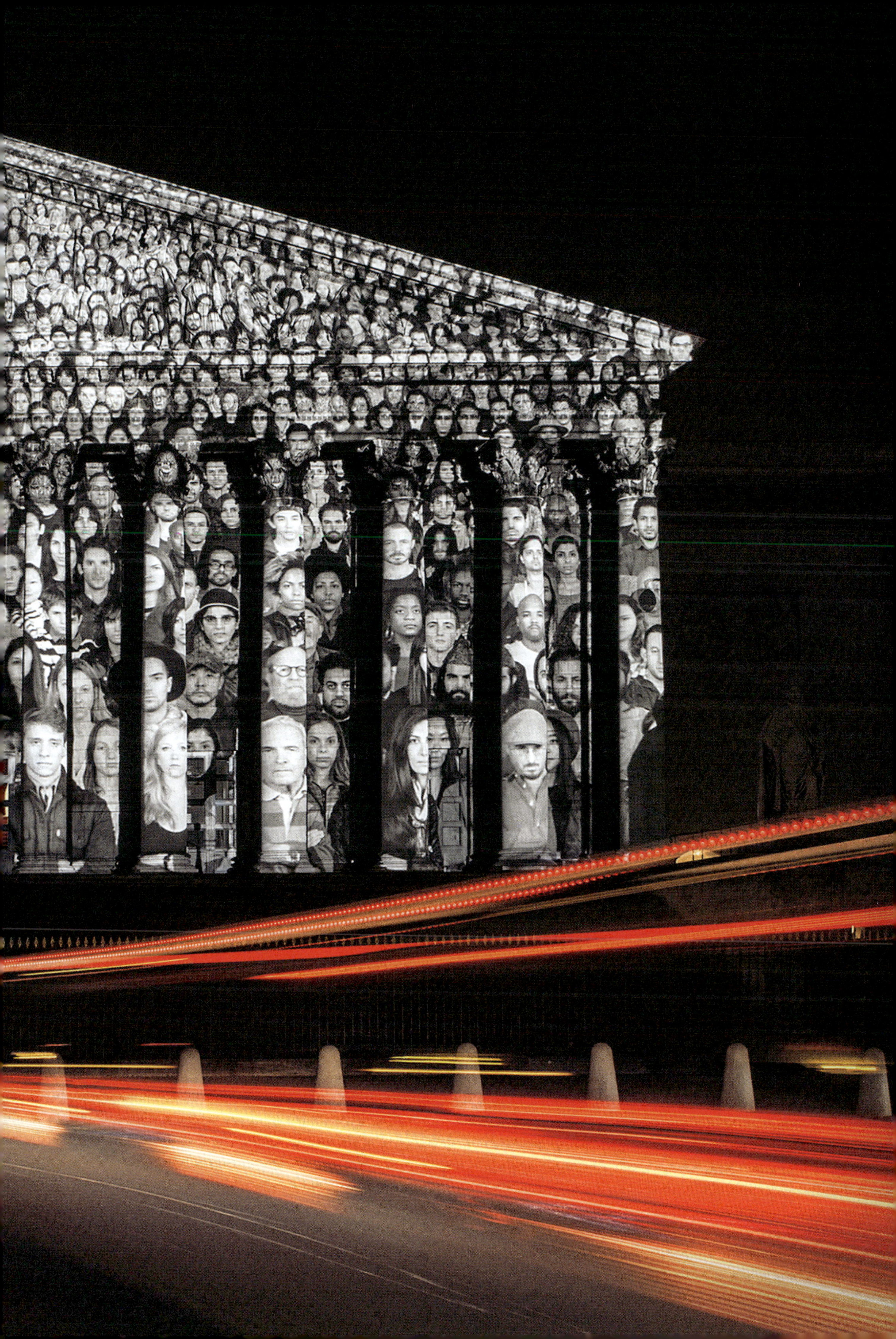

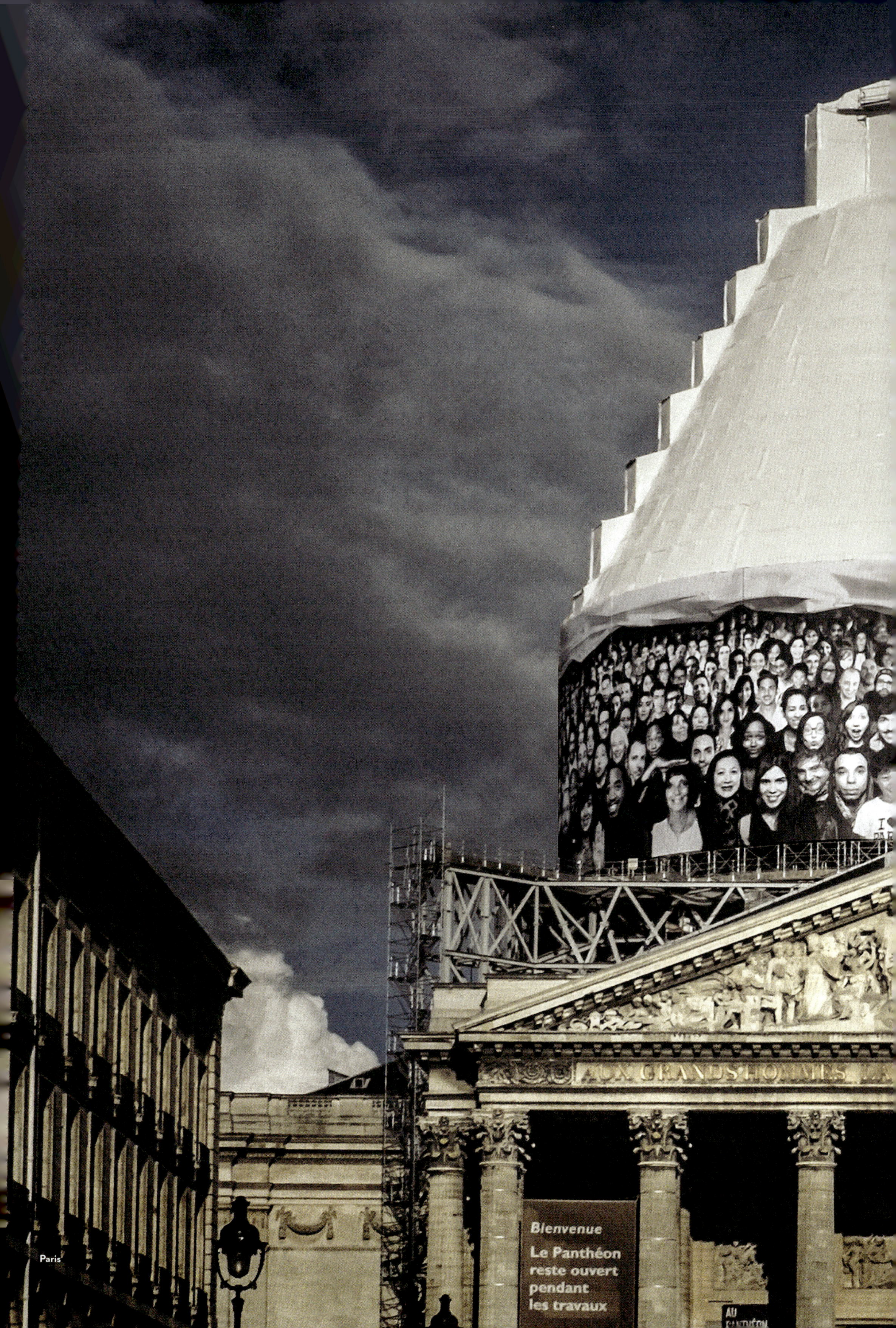
AUX GRANDS HOMMES
Bienvenue
Le Panthéon
reste ouvert
pendant
les travaux

Paris

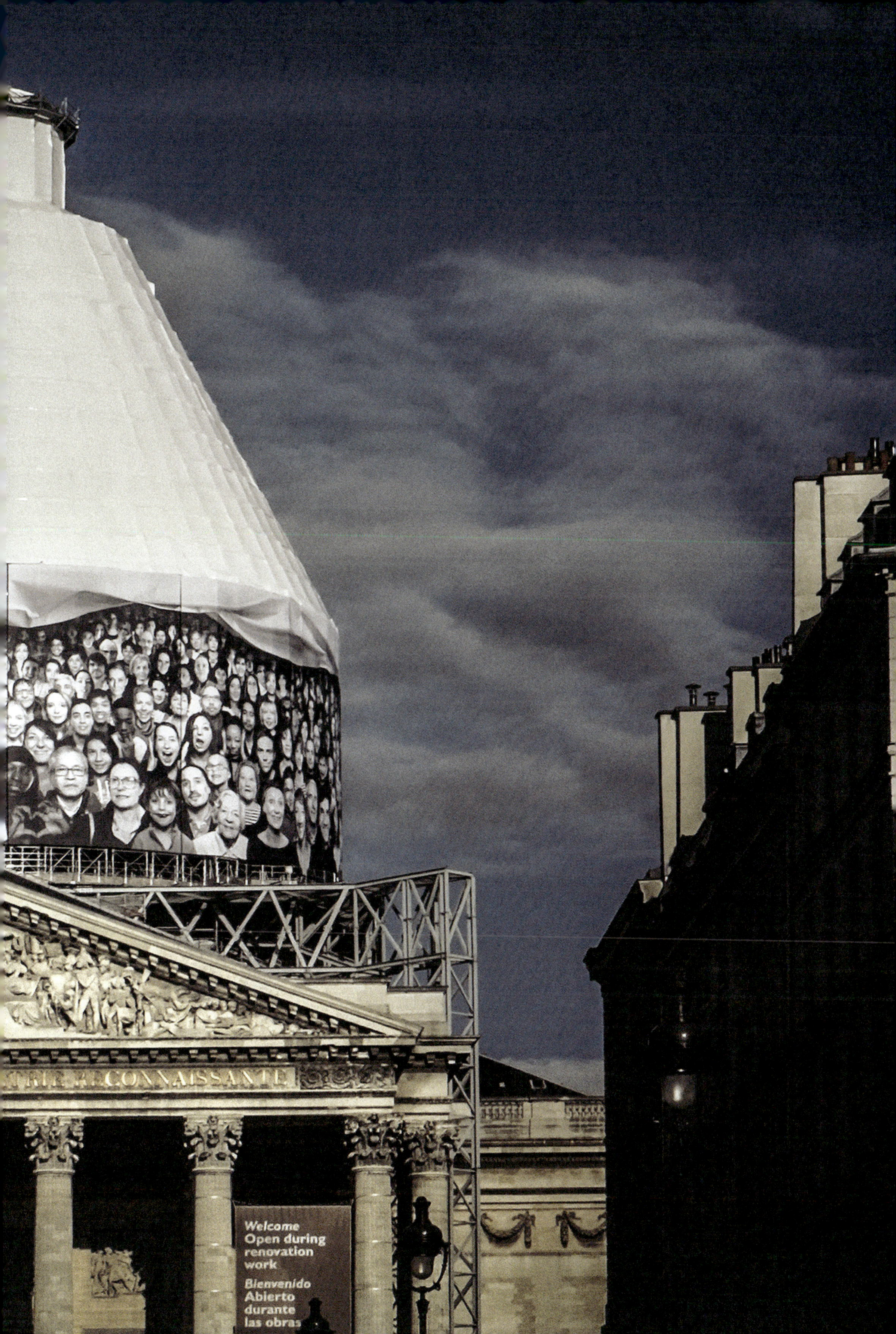
Welcome
Open during
renovation
work
Bienvenido
Abierto
durante
las obras

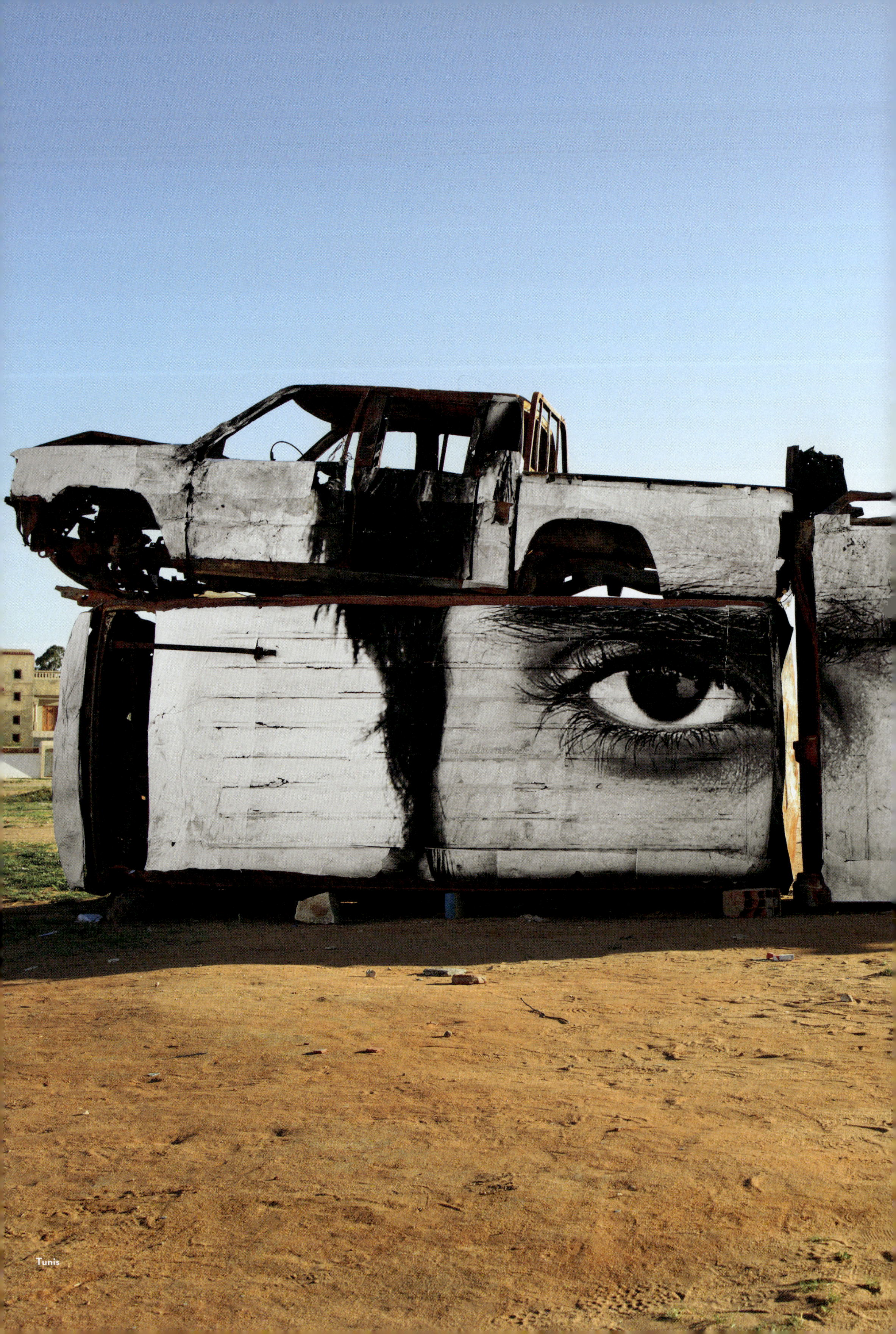

Tunis

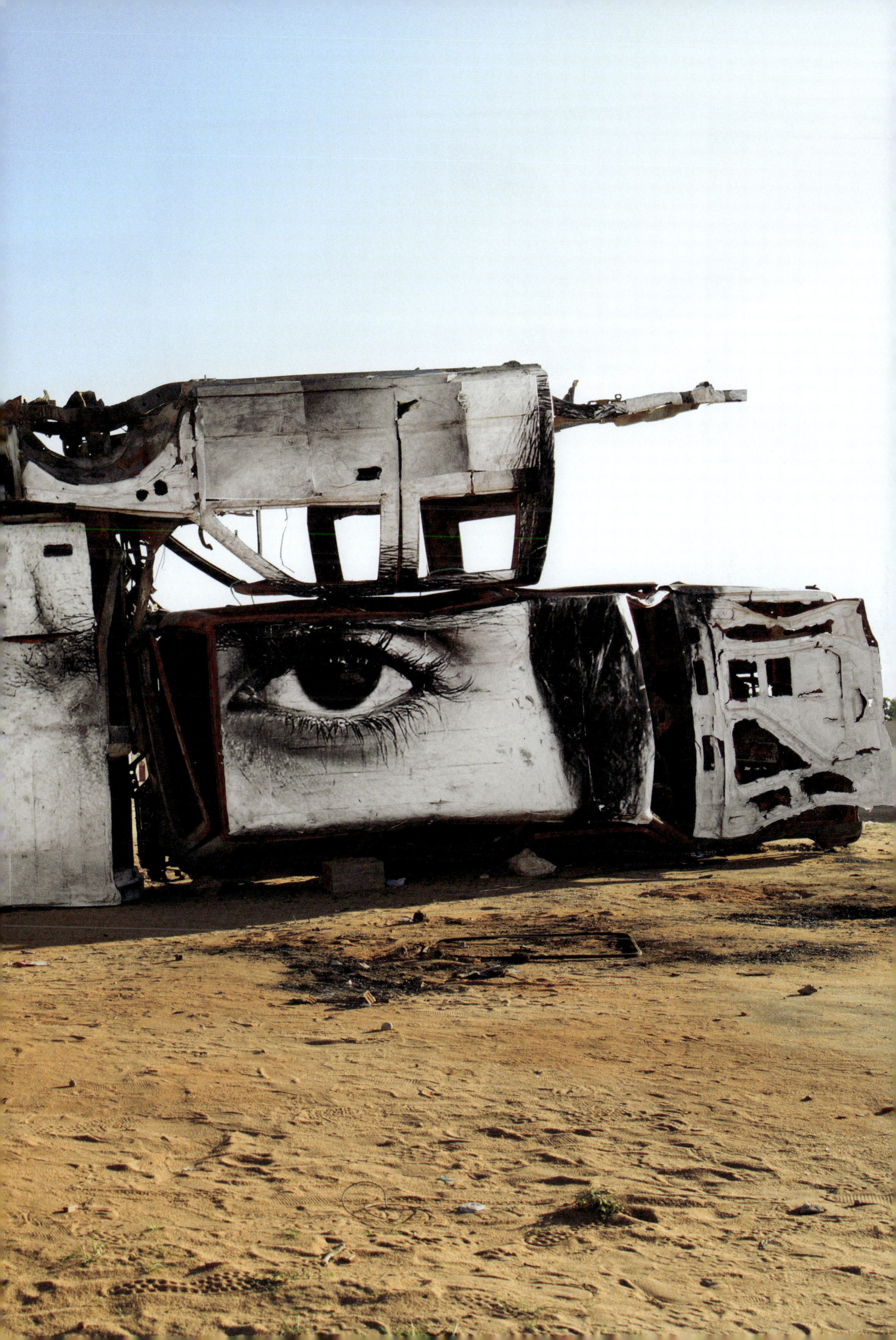

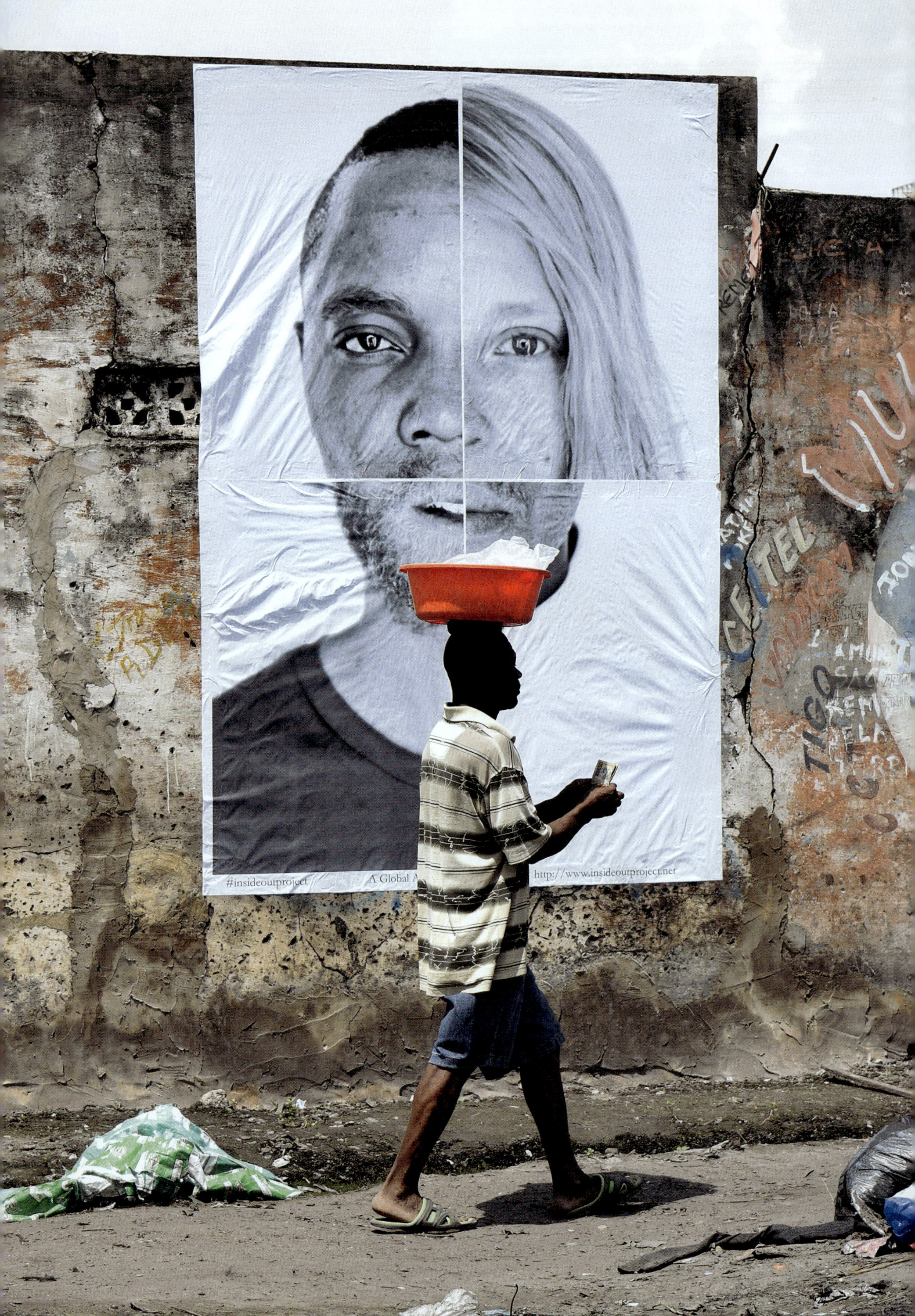
#insideoutproject
http://www.insideoutproject.net

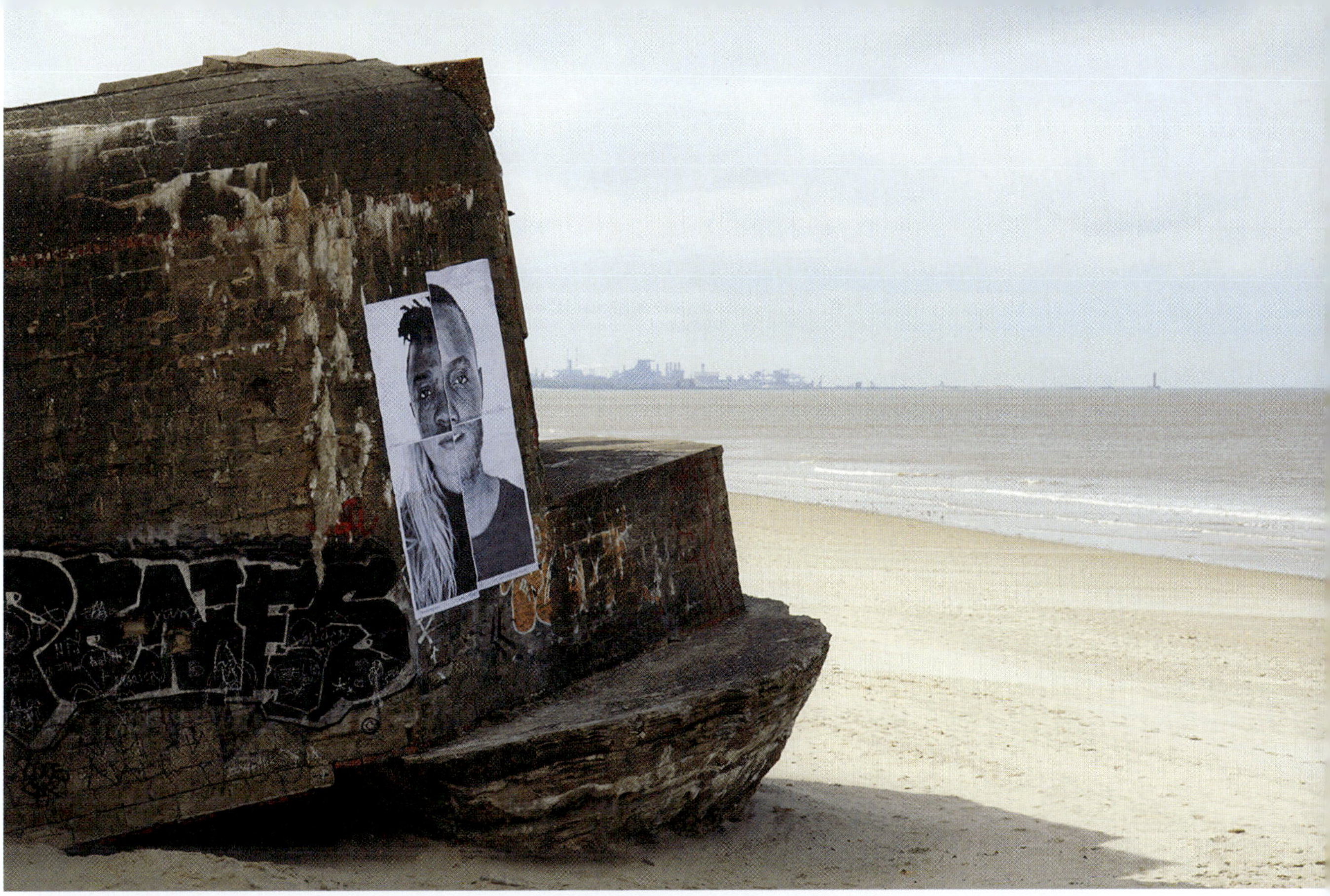

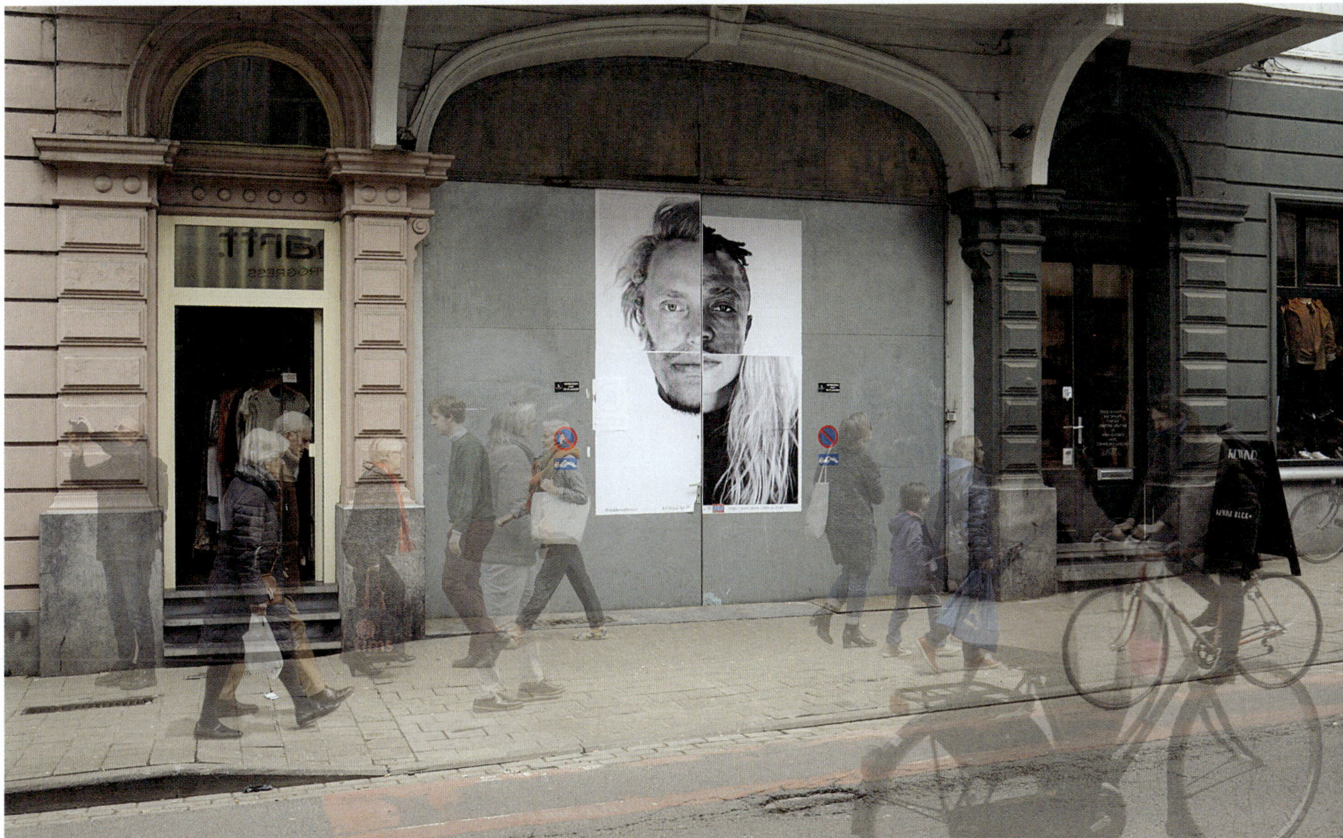

"To declare that there are no frontiers or borders when it comes to brotherhood and love, and to give a face and story to the so-called refugees; for these reasons, Biso Na Biso (Among Us) was created."

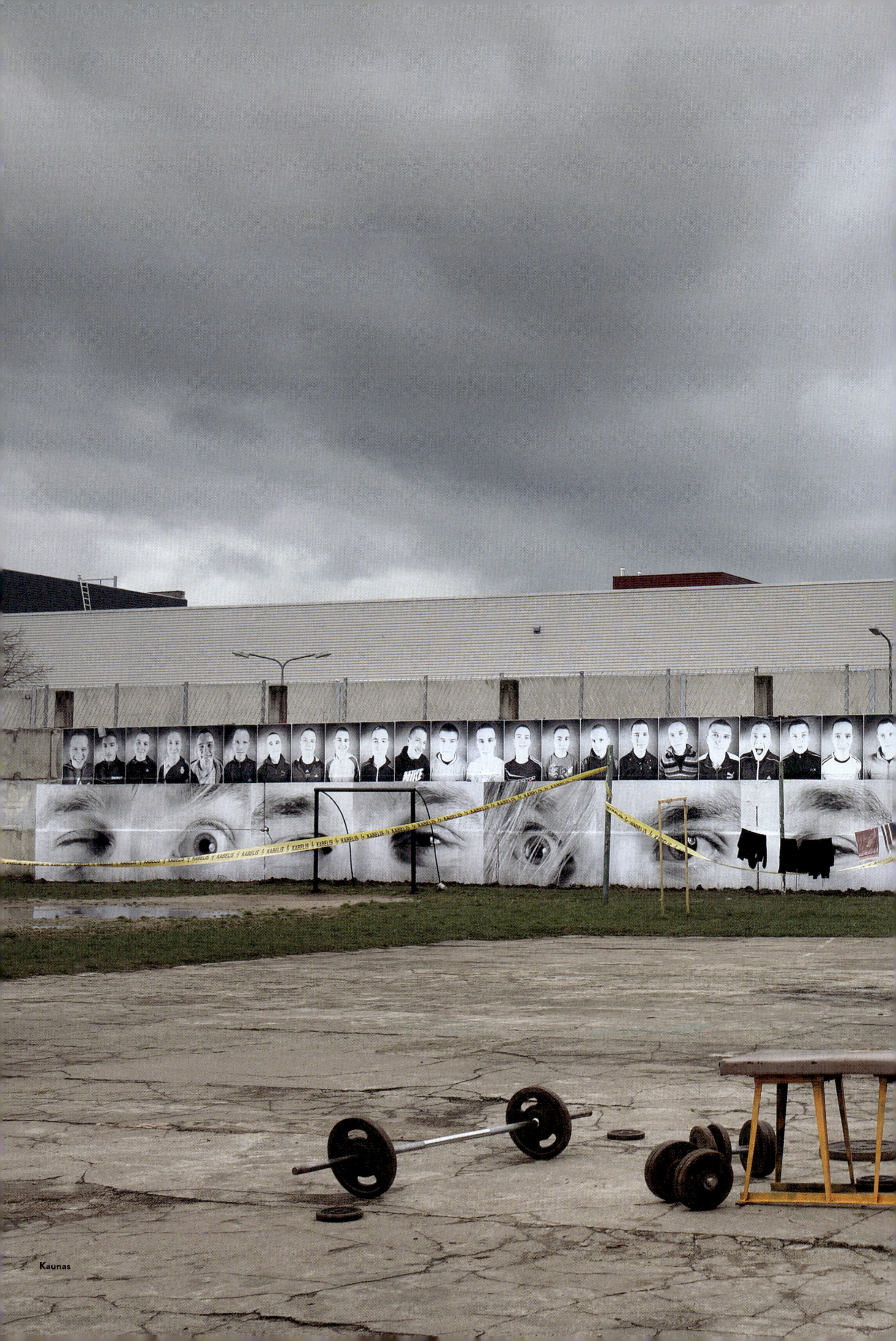

Kaunas

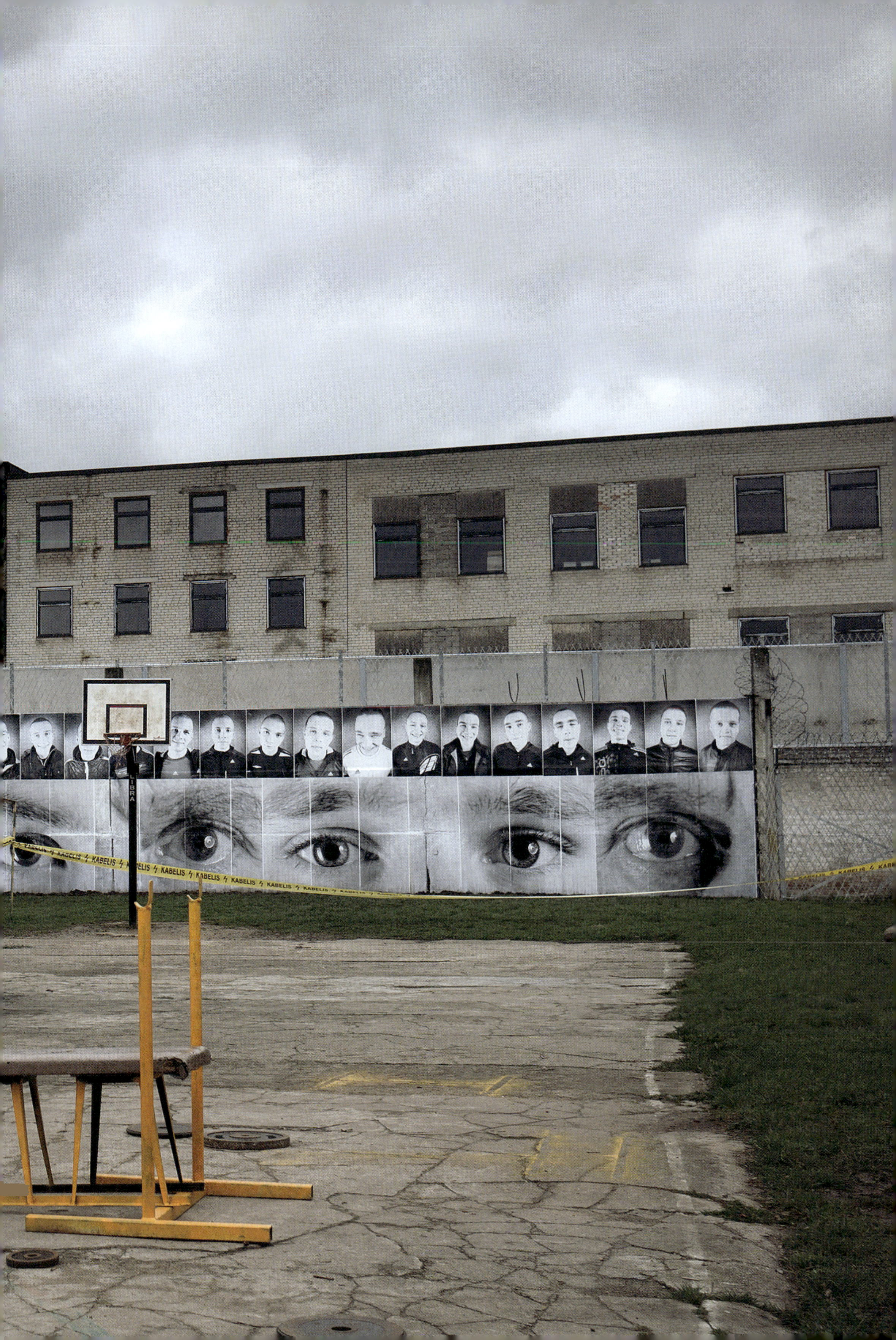
KABELIS
LIBRA

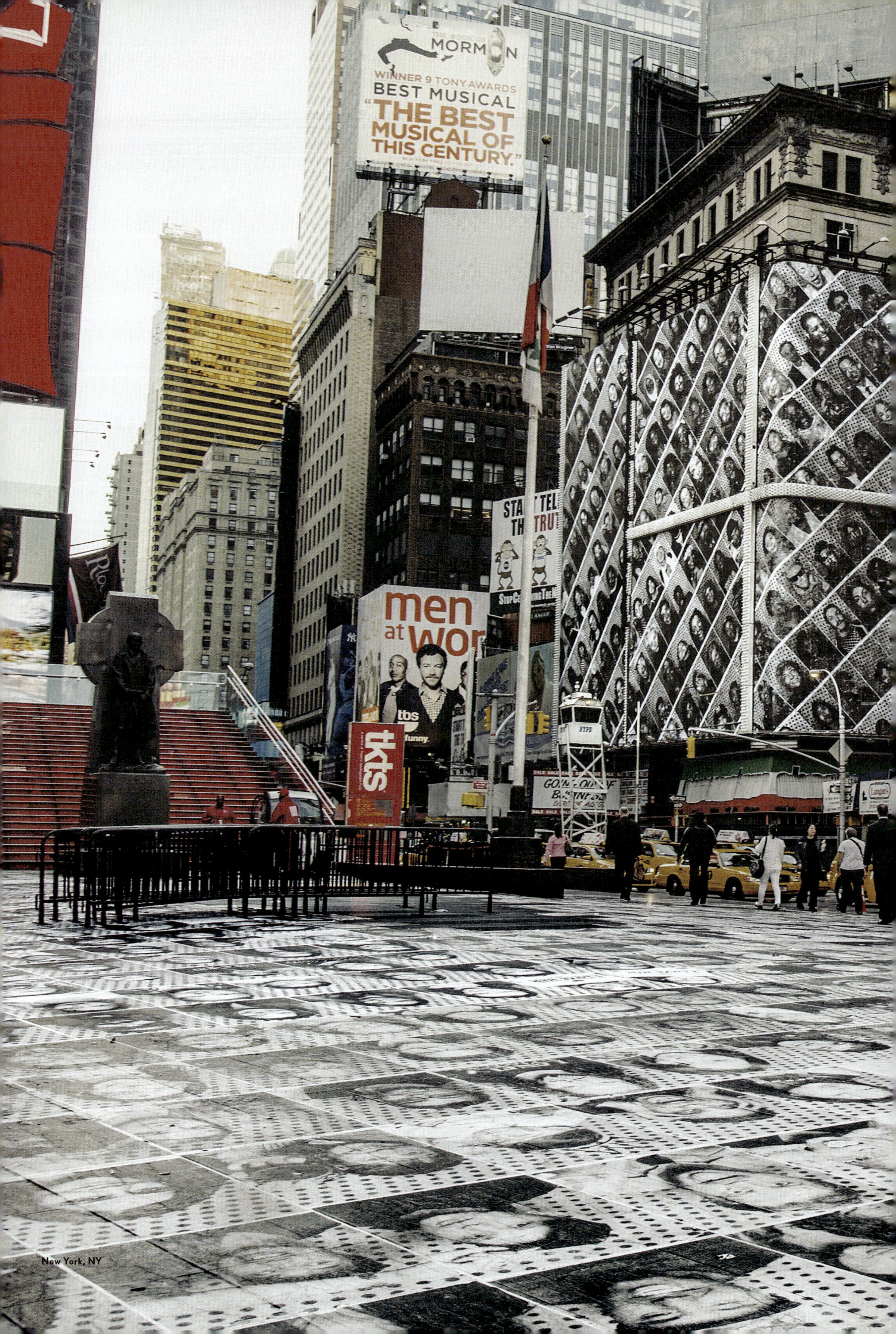
MORMON
WINNER 9 TONY AWARDS
BEST MUSICAL
"THE BEST MUSICAL OF THIS CENTURY."
tkts
tbs
funny.
NYPD

New York, NY

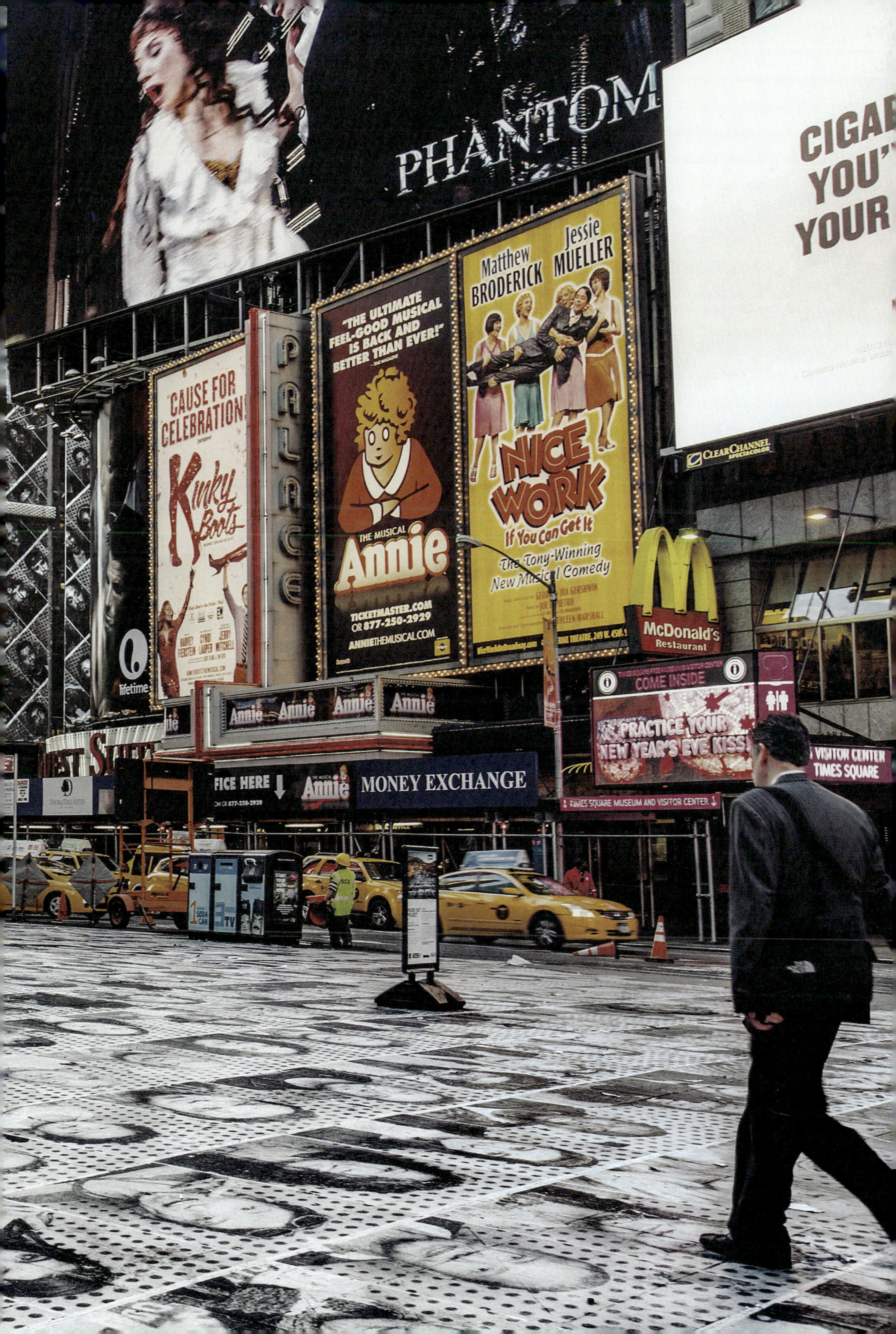
PHANTOM
CIGA
YOU'
YOUR
CLEAR CHANNEL SPECTACOLOR
CAUSE FOR CELEBRATION!
Kinky Boots
HARVEY FIERSTEIN CYNDI LAUPER JERRY MITCHELL
lifetime
PALACE
"THE ULTIMATE FEEL-GOOD MUSICAL IS BACK AND BETTER THAN EVER!"
THE MUSICAL
Annie
TICKETMASTER.COM OR 877-250-2929
ANNIETHEMUSICAL.COM
Matthew BRODERICK
Jessie MUELLER
NICE WORK
If You Can Get It
The Tony-Winning New Musical Comedy
McDonald's Restaurant
COME INSIDE
PRACTICE YOUR NEW YEAR'S EVE KISS!
VISITOR CENTER TIMES SQUARE
Annie Annie Annie Annie
FICE HERE
MONEY EXCHANGE
TIMES SQUARE MUSEUM AND VISITOR CENTER

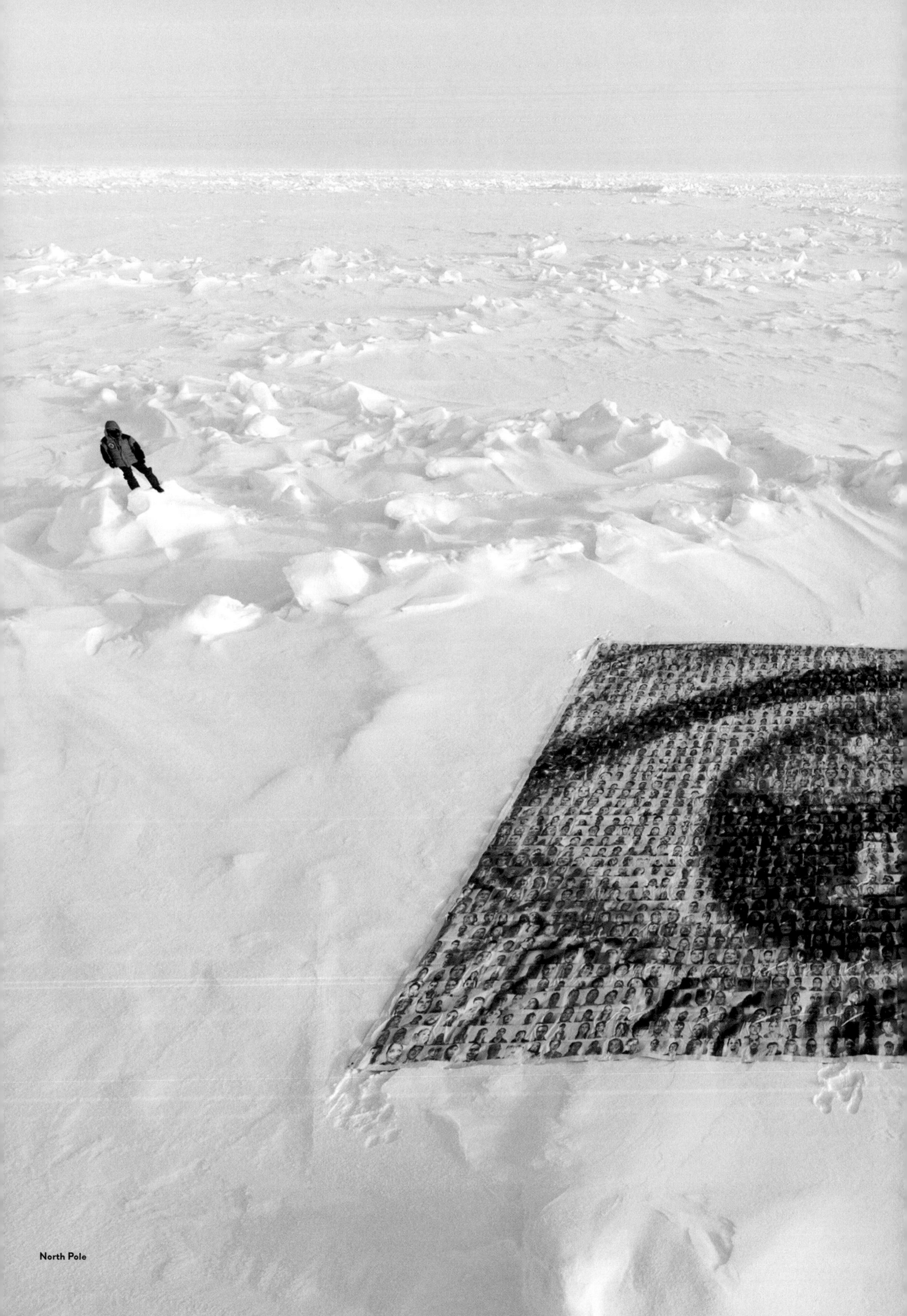

North Pole

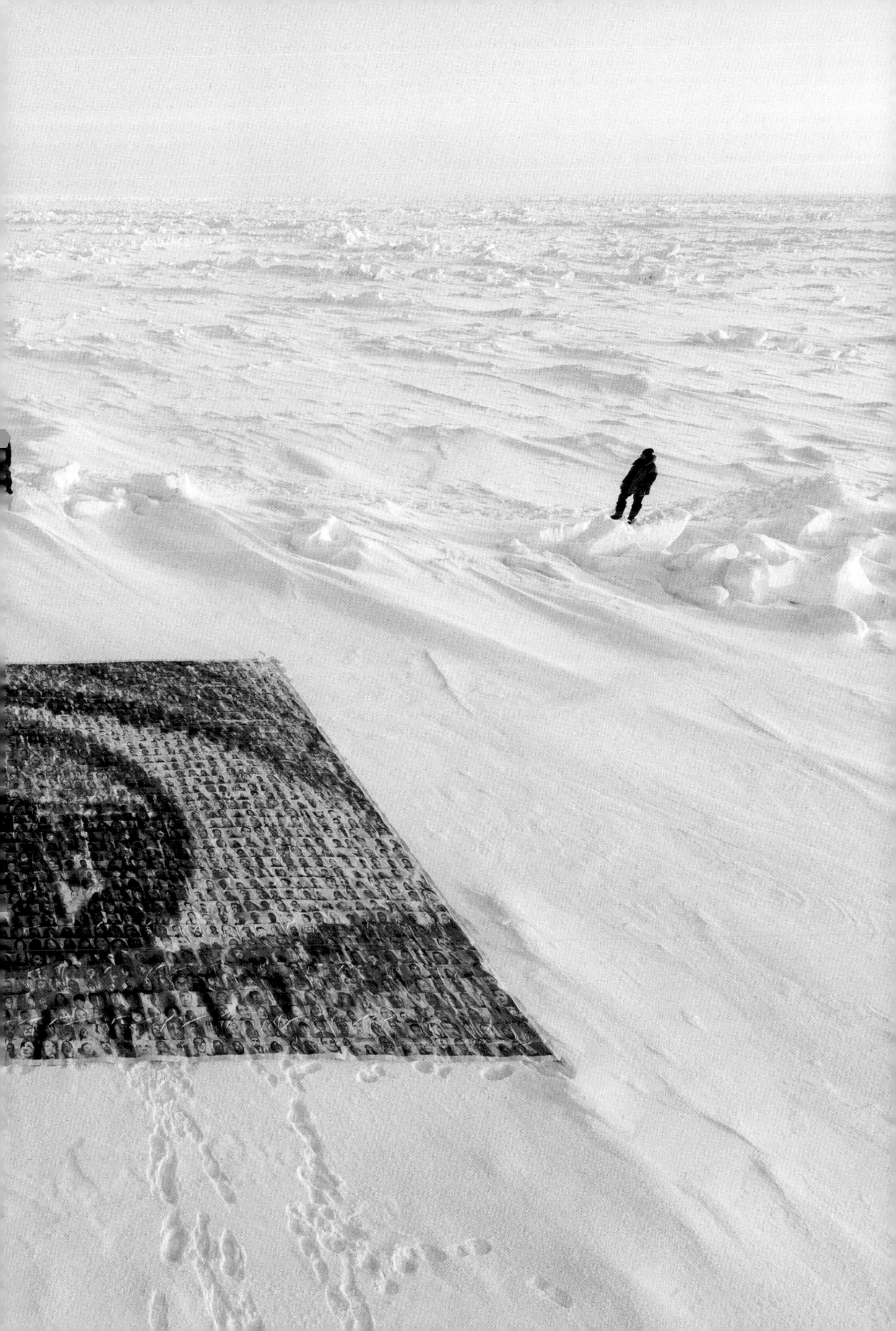

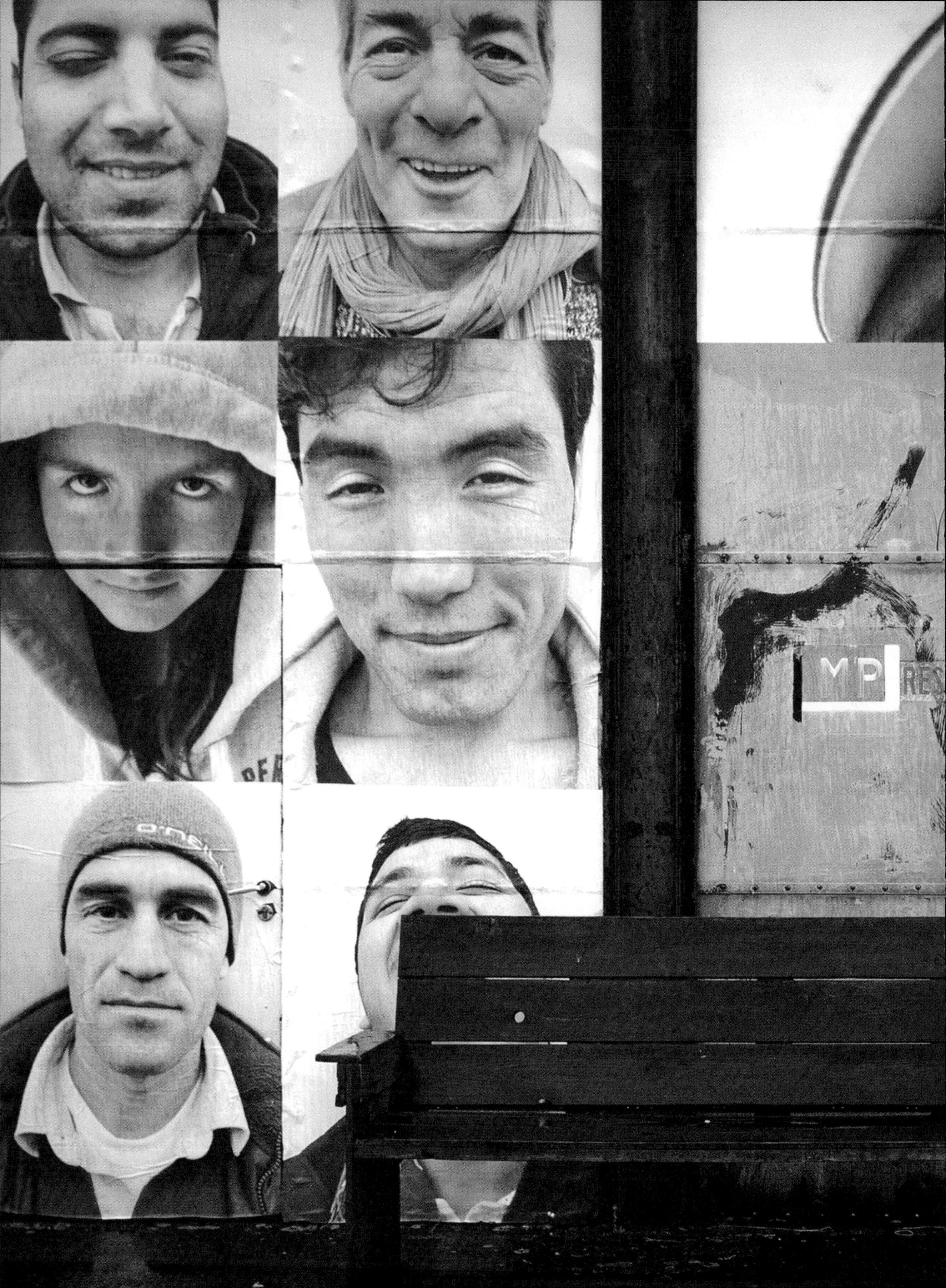
MP
RES

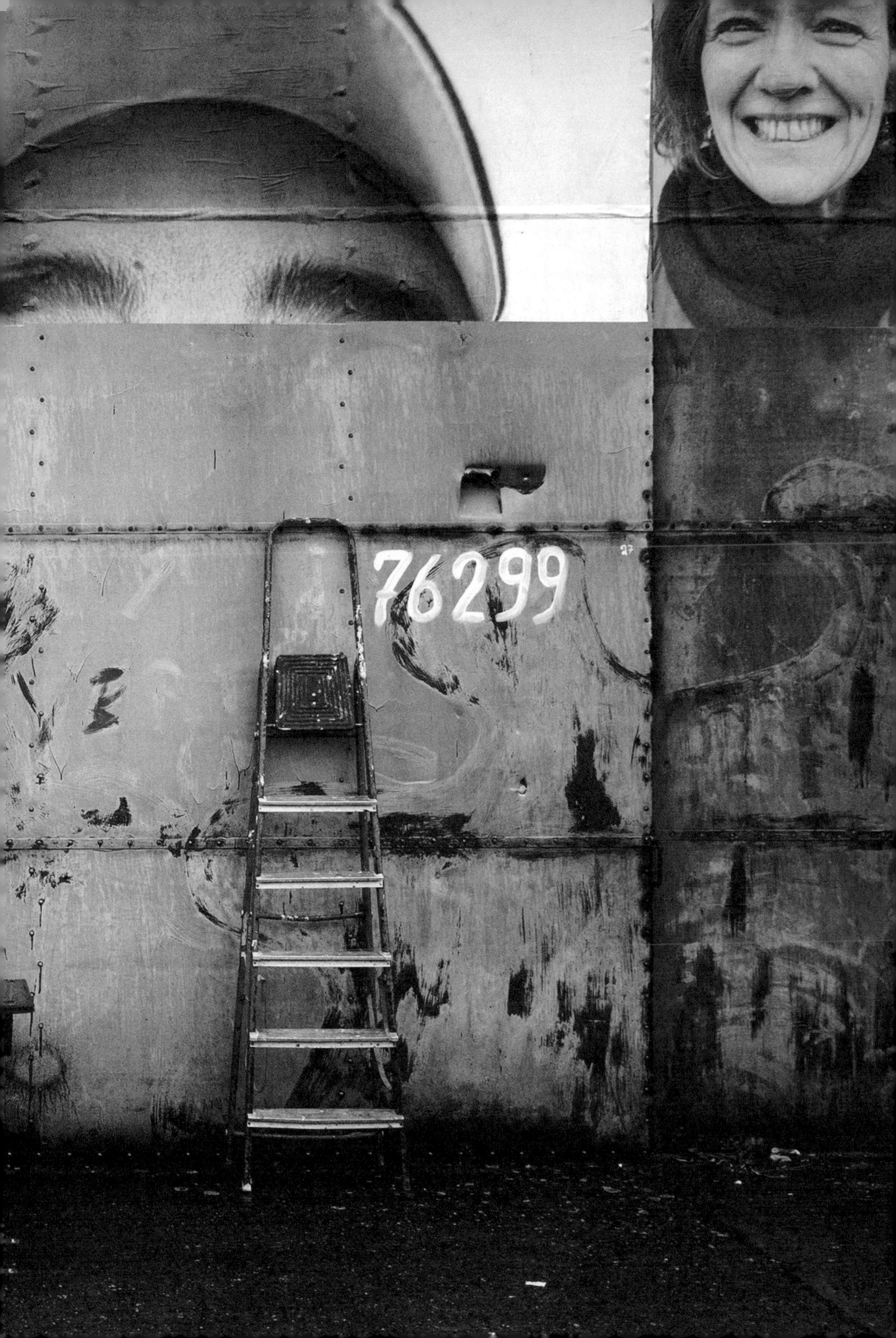
76299

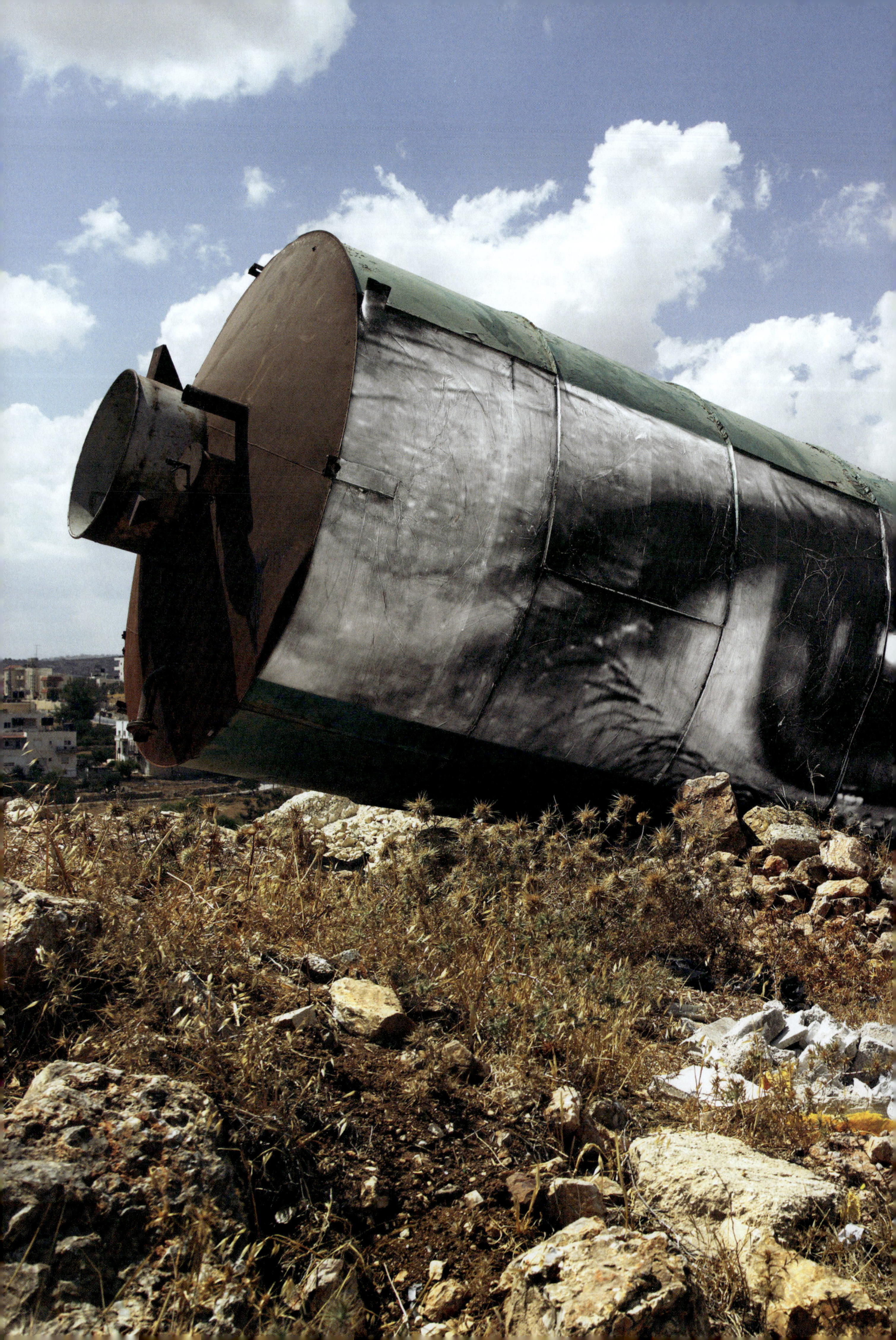

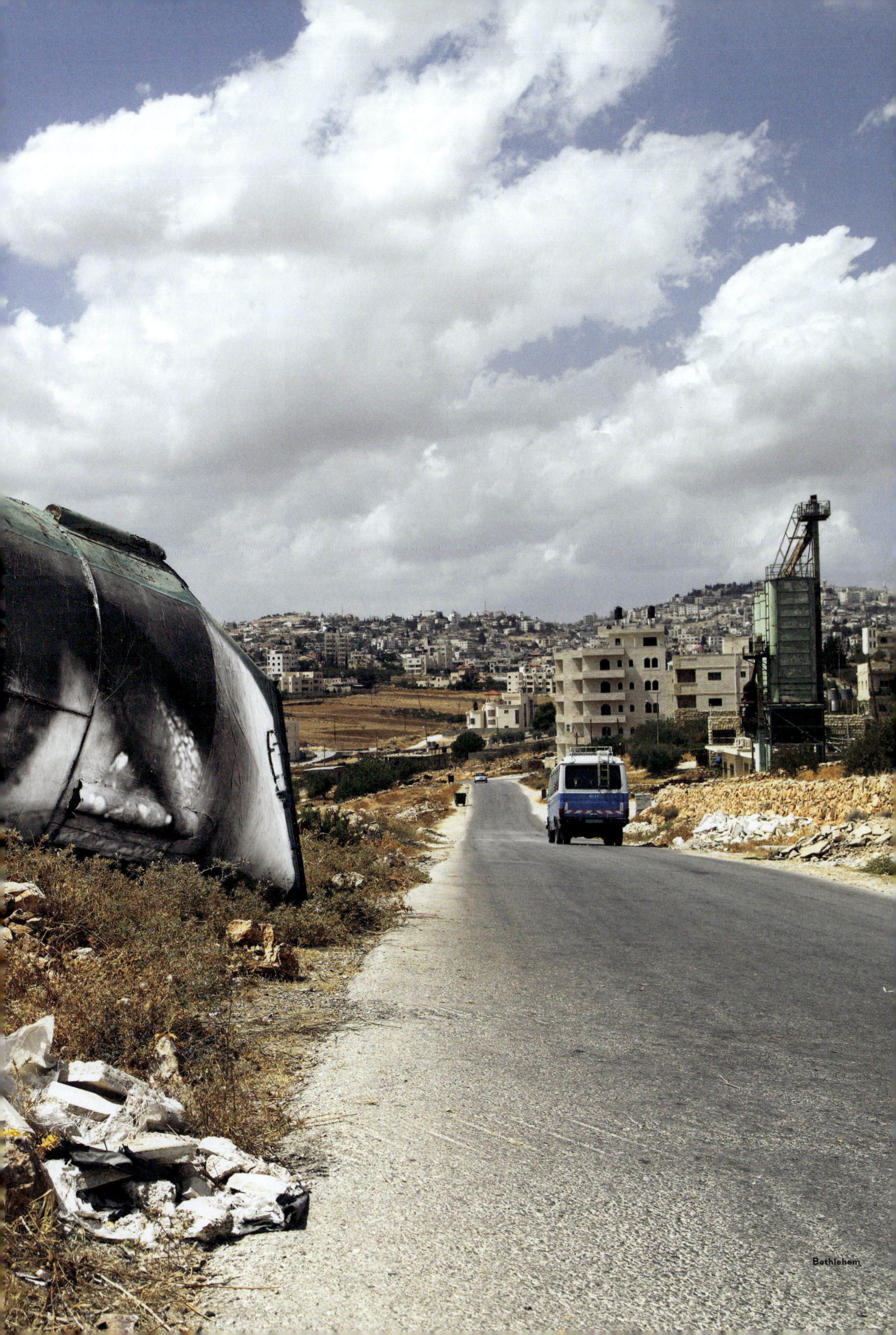

Bethlehem

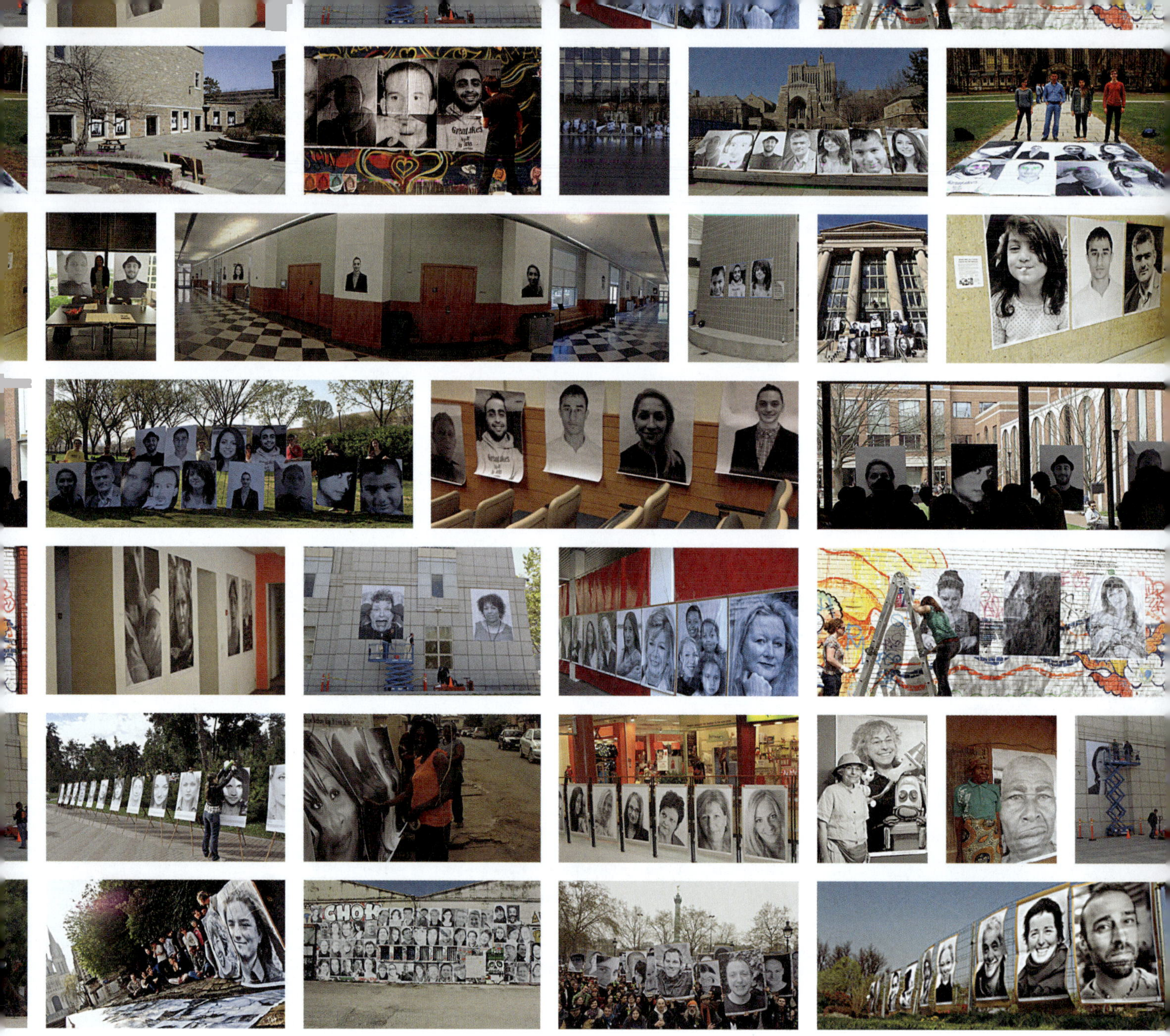

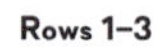

Rows 1–3 — Iraqi Refugee Assistance Project To raise awareness about the Iraqi refugees situation.

Rows 4–5 — Making Mothers Visible (MMV) is an eleven-country collaboration between the International Museum of Women and global artists and volunteers. It was presented in San Francisco, Lagos, Barcelona, Ottawa-Gattineau, Cameroon, Kiev, Baku, Buenos Aires, Latvia, Bonn, and Puerto Vallarta.

Row 6 — Colibris: I'm the Candidate MMV Colibris

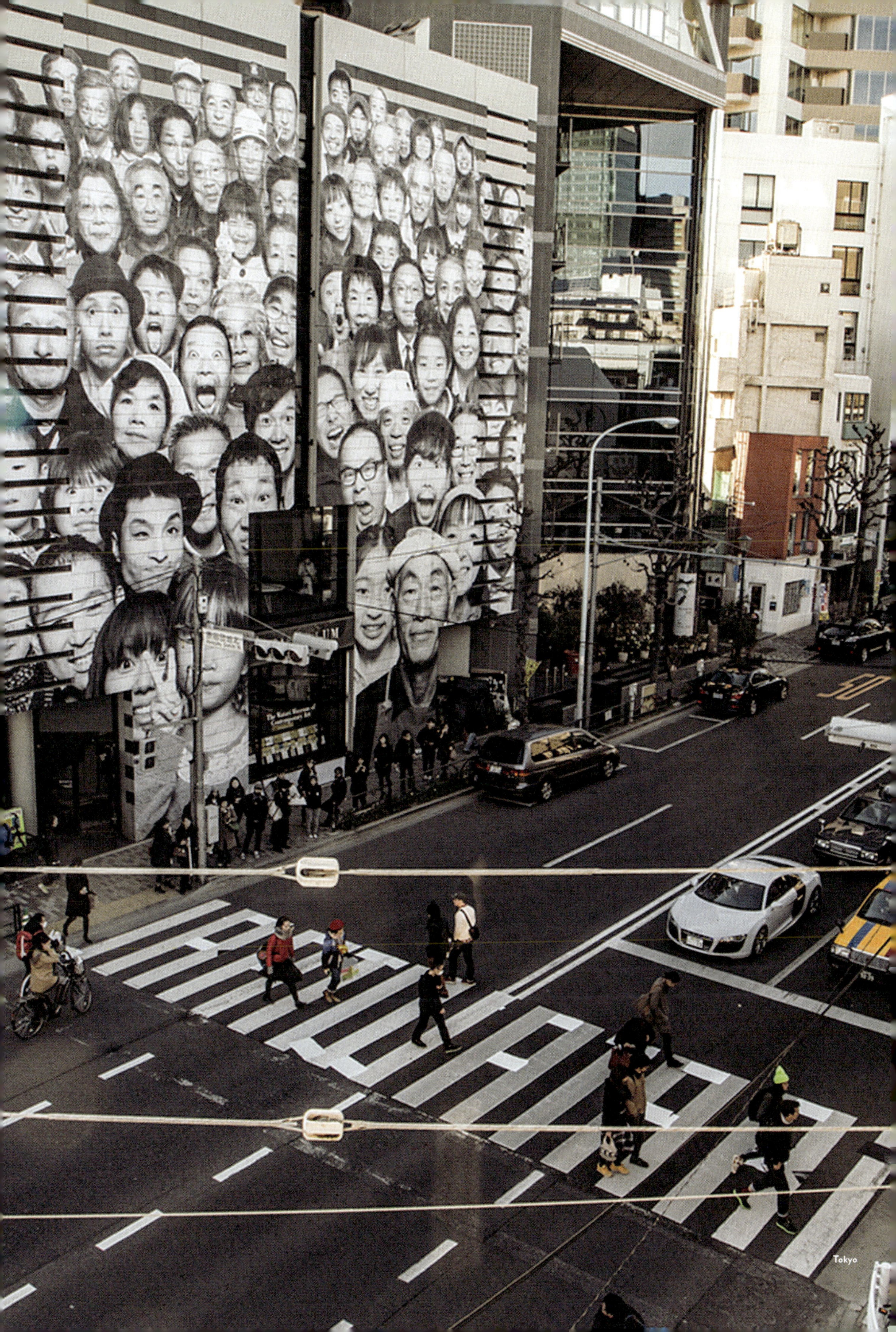

Tokyo

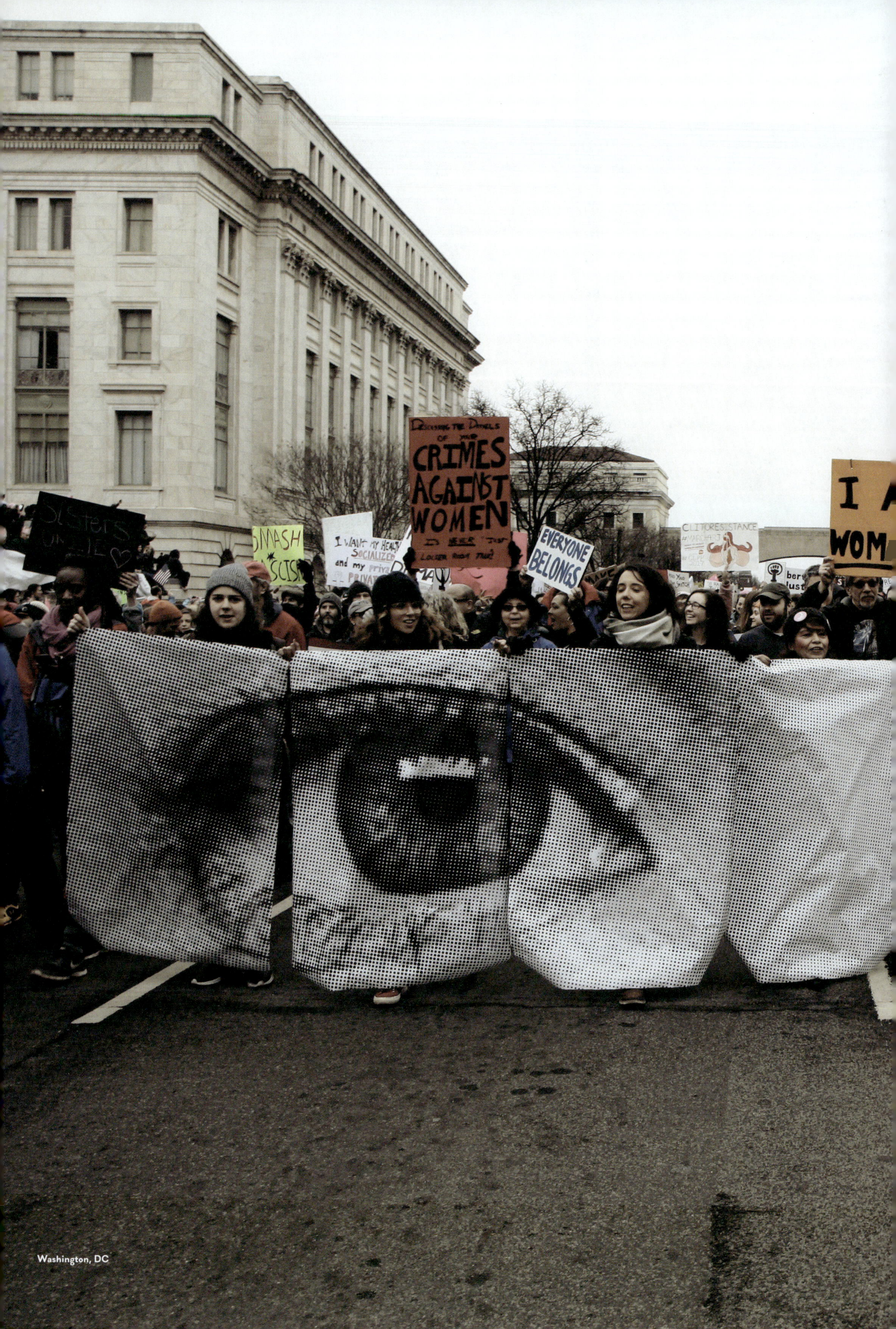

Washington, DC

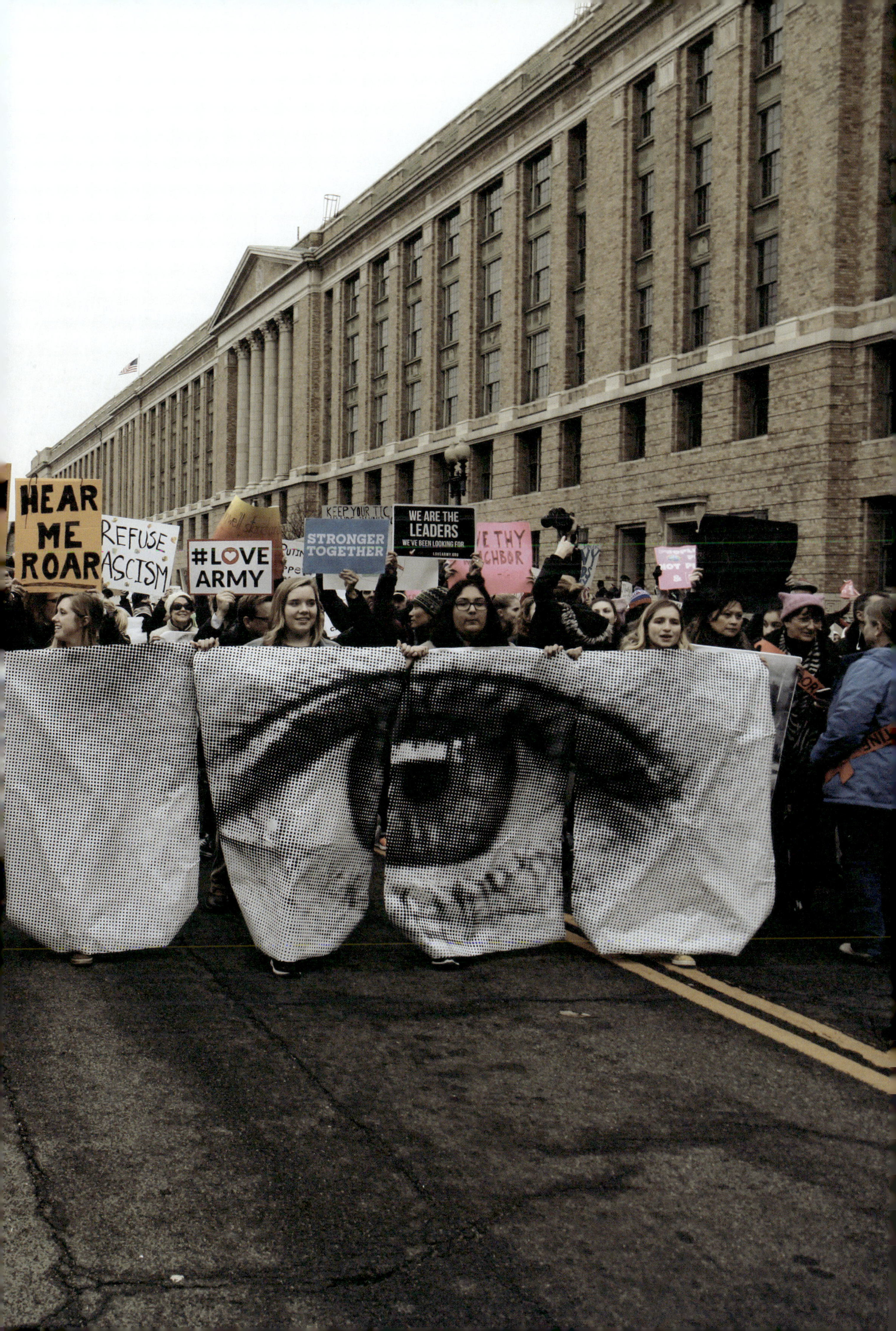
HEAR
ME
ROAR
REFUSE
ASCISM
#LOVE
ARMY
STRONGER
TOGETHER
WE ARE THE
LEADERS
WE'VE BEEN LOOKING FOR
E THY
GHBOR

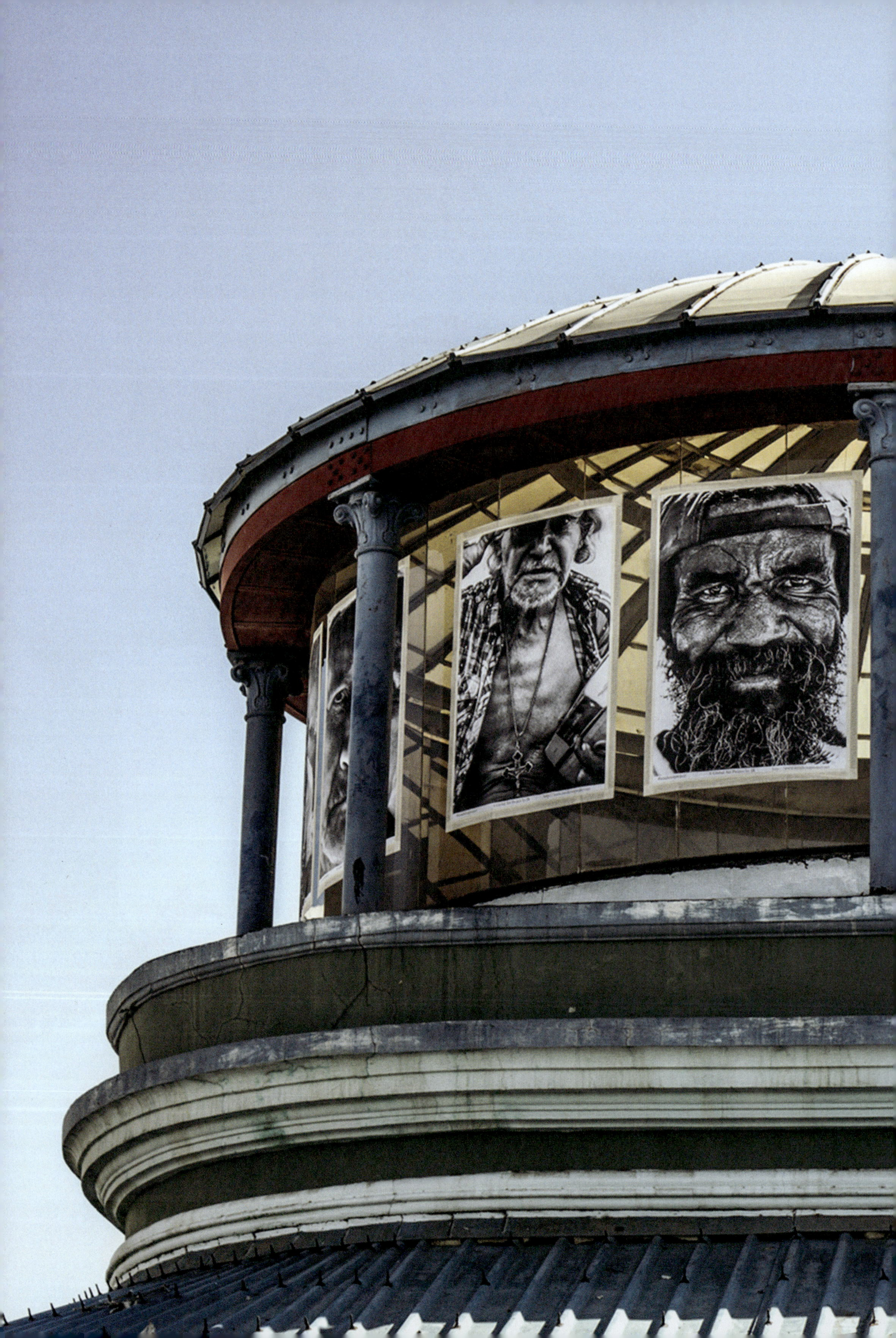

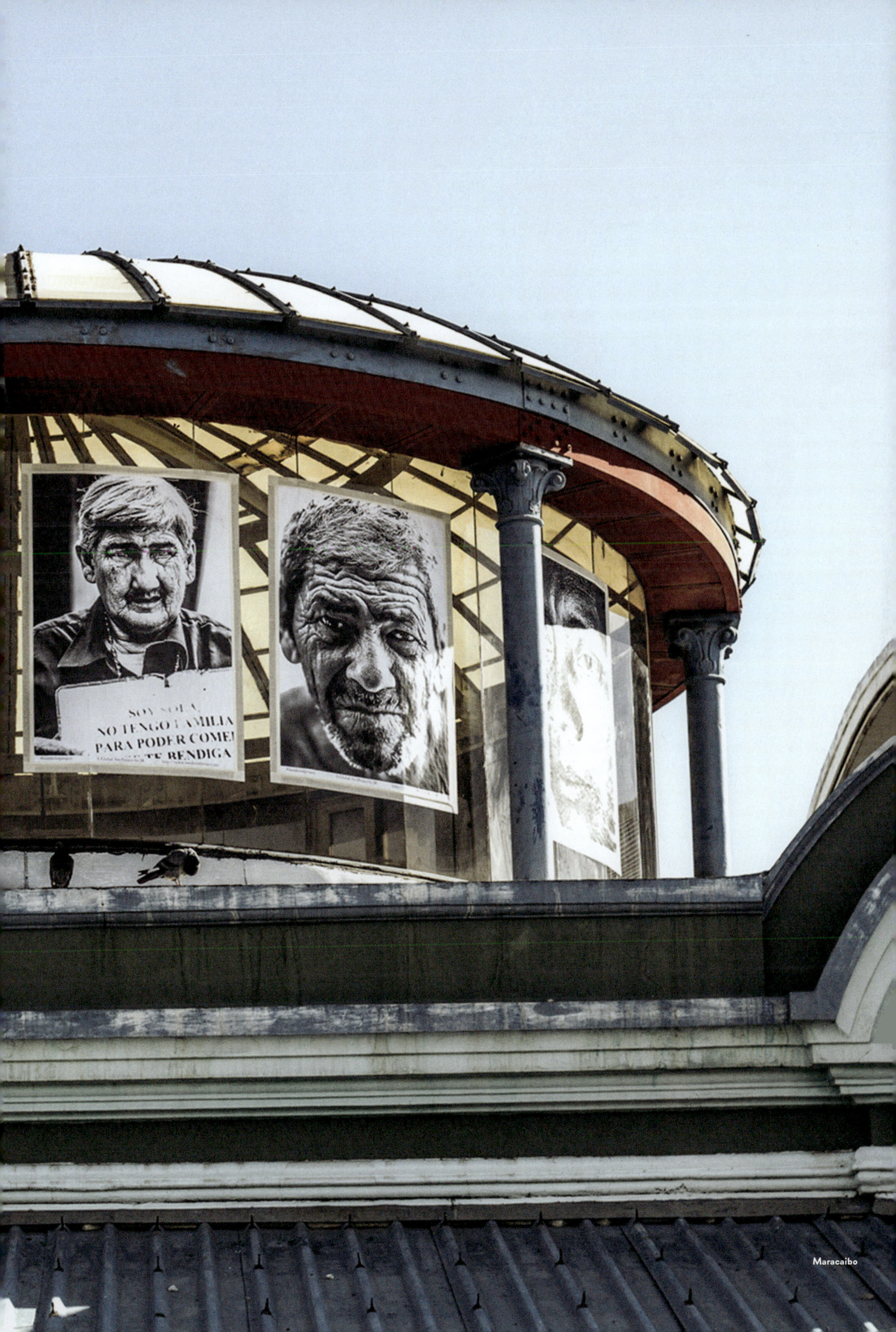

Maracaibo

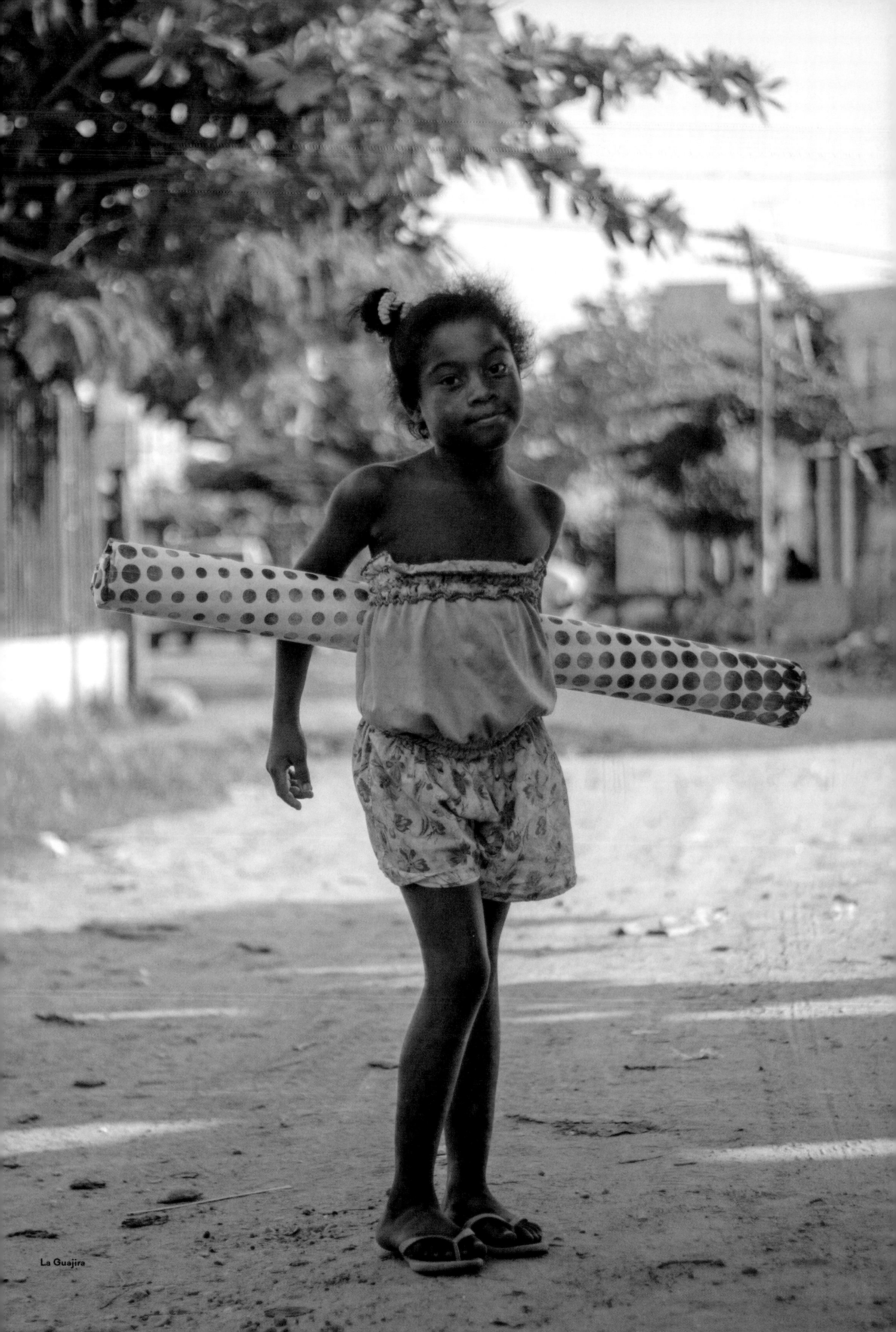

La Guajira

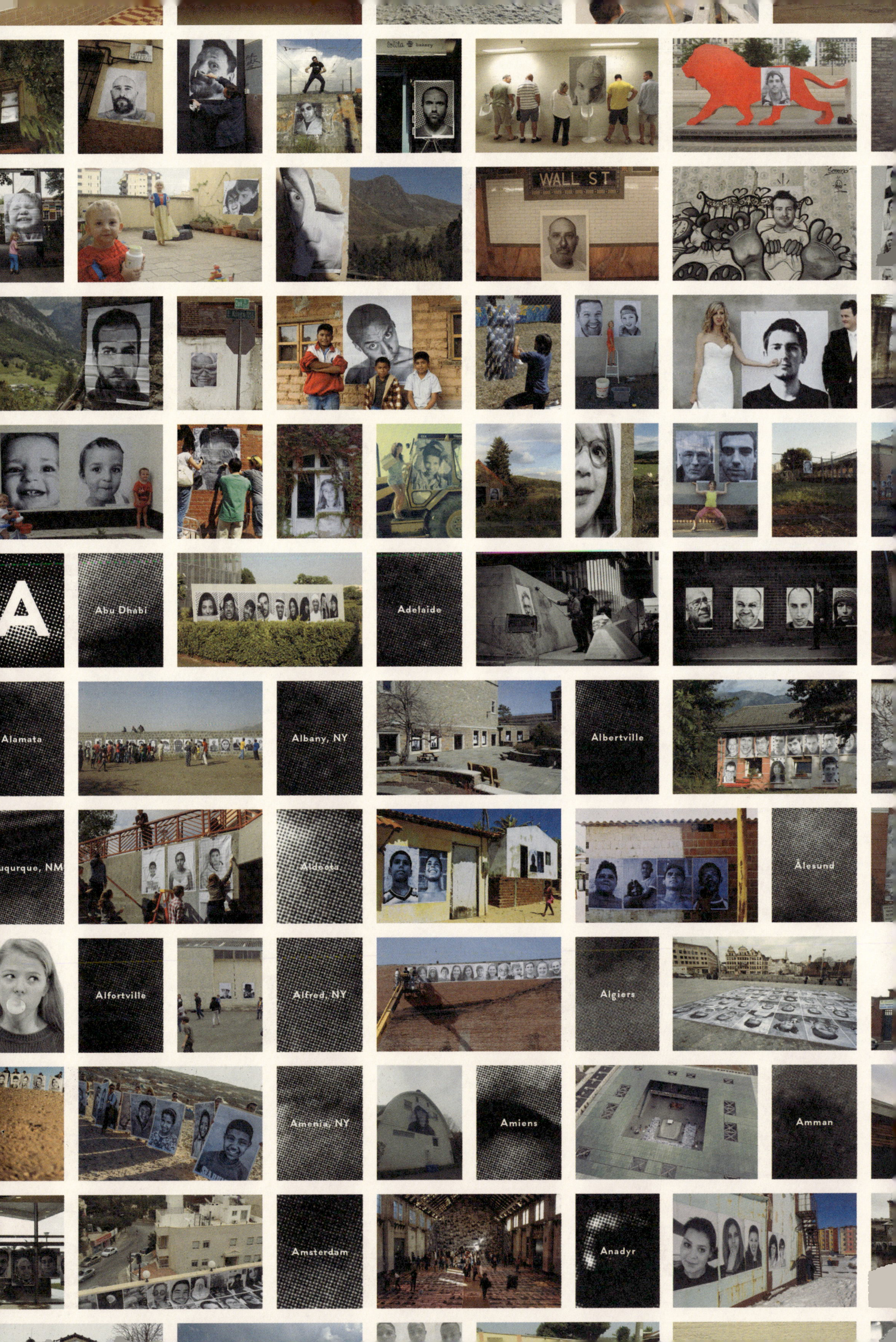
WALL ST
A
Abu Dhabi
Adelaide
Alamata
Albany, NY
Albertville
uquerque, NM
Aldeota
Ålesund
Alfortville
Alfred, NY
Algiers
Amenia, NY
Amiens
Amman
Amsterdam
Anadyr

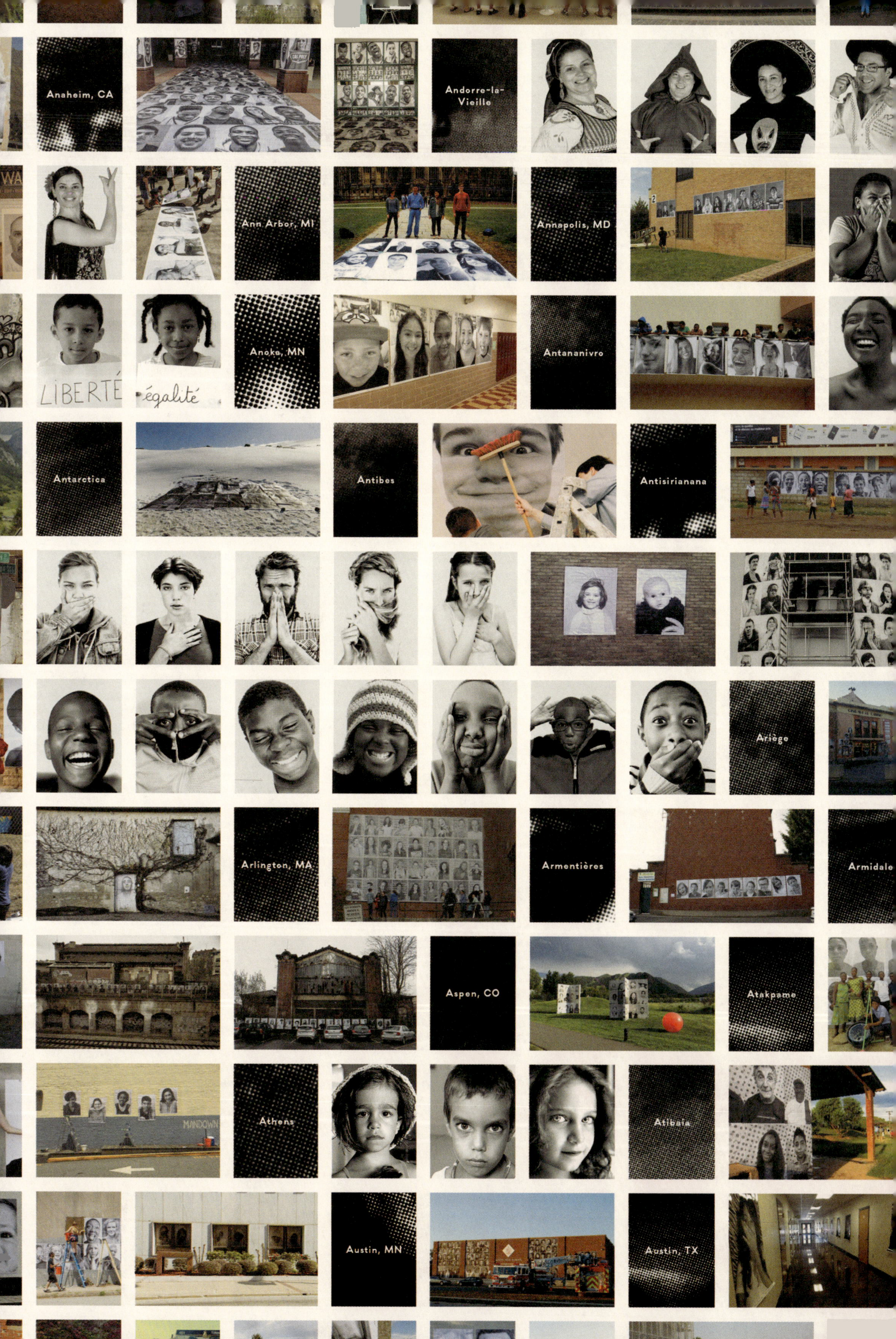
Anaheim, CA
Andorre-la-Vieille
Ann Arbor, MI
Annapolis, MD
LIBERTÉ
égalité
Anoka, MN
Antananivro
Antarctica
Antibes
Antisirianana
Ariège
Arlington, MA
Armentières
Armidale
Aspen, CO
Atakpame
Athens
Atibaia
Austin, MN
Austin, TX

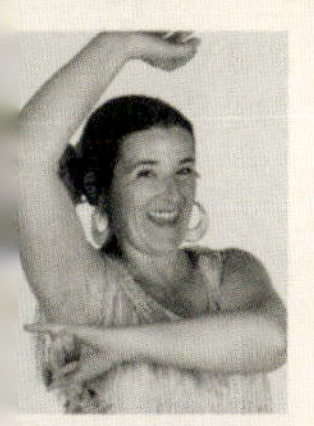
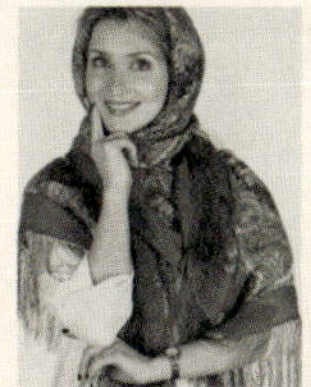
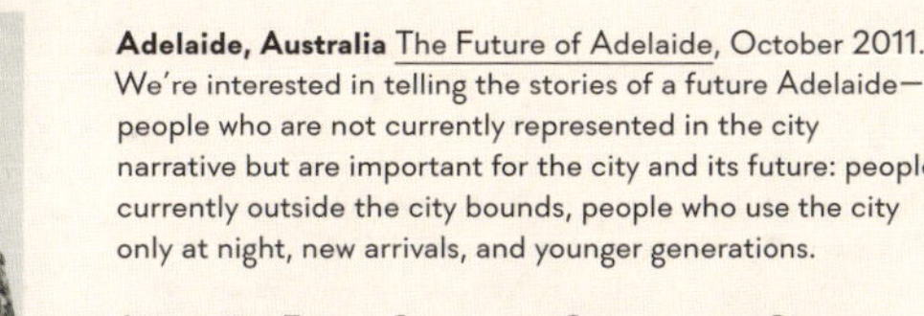
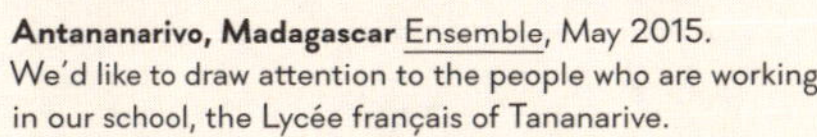
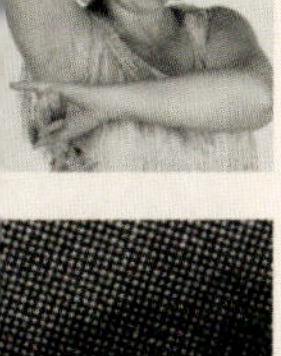
Annecy
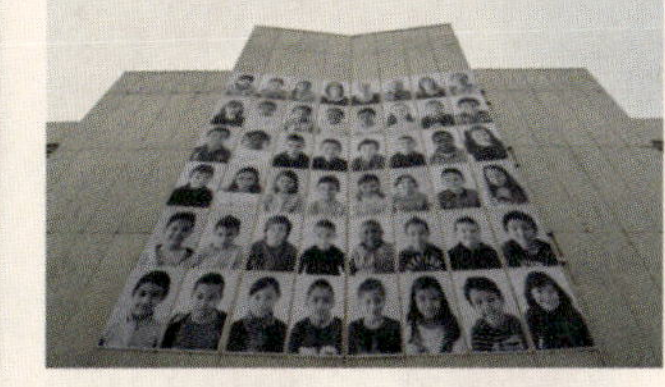
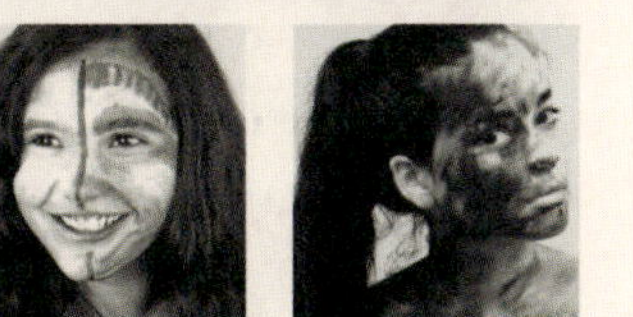
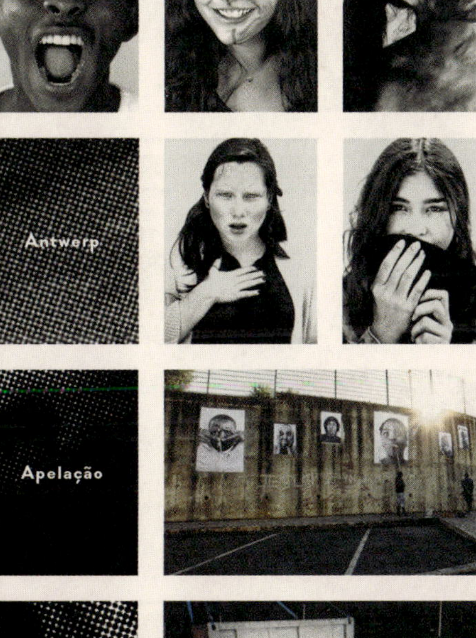
Antwerp
Apelação
Arles
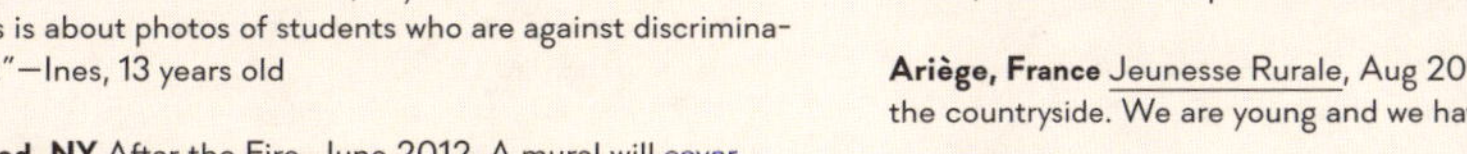
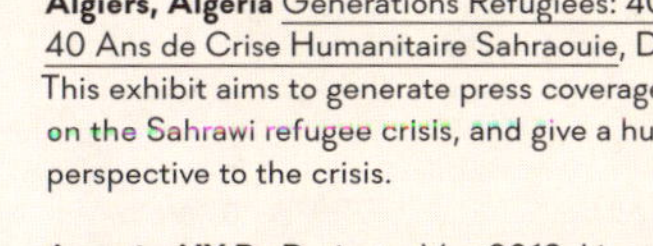
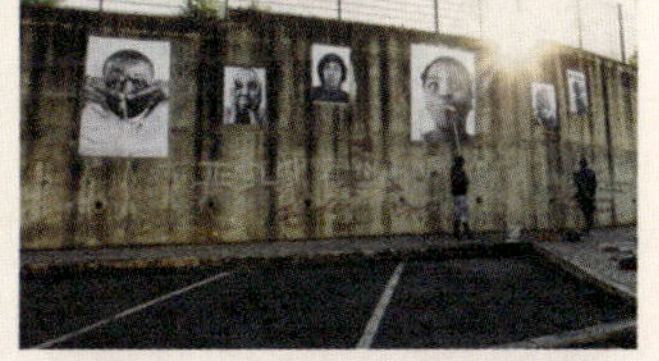
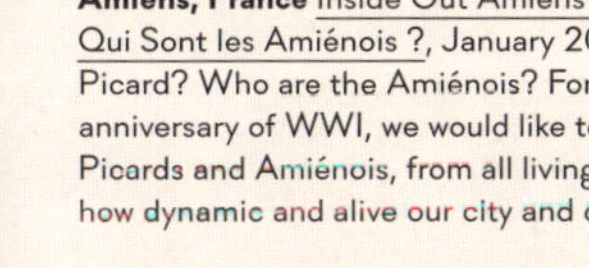
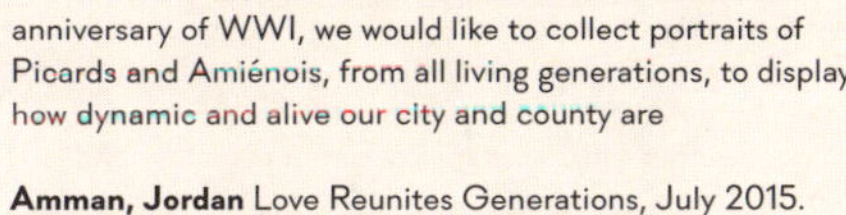
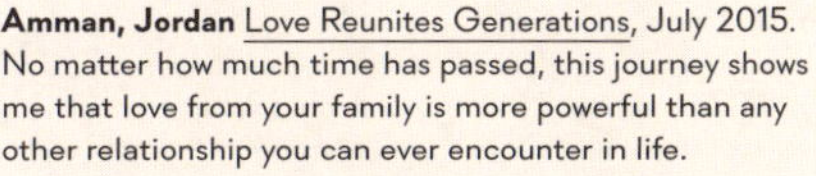
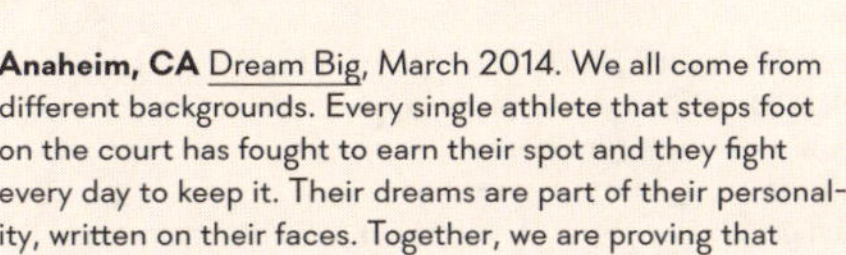
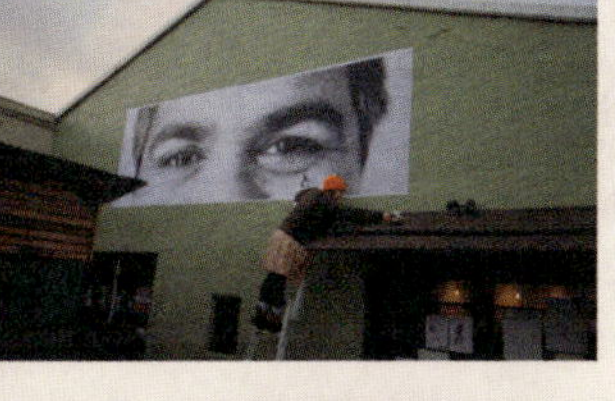
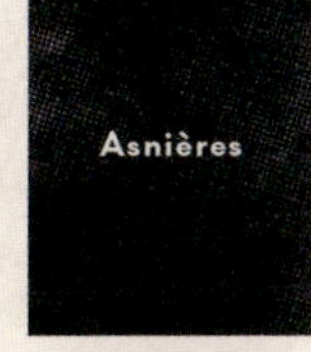
Asnières
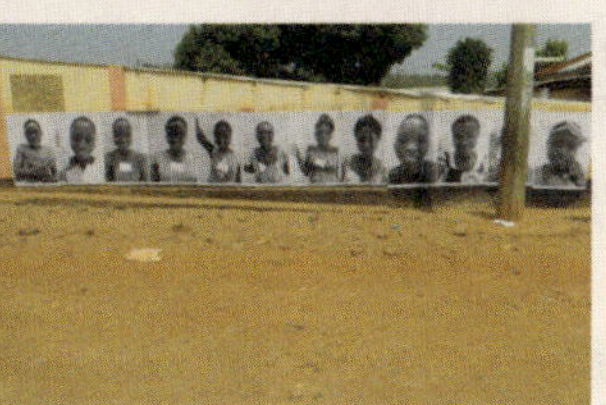
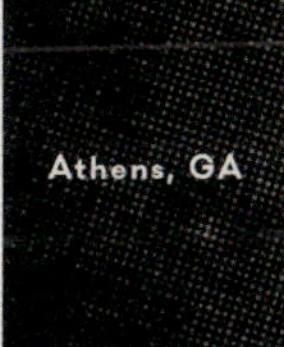
Athens, GA
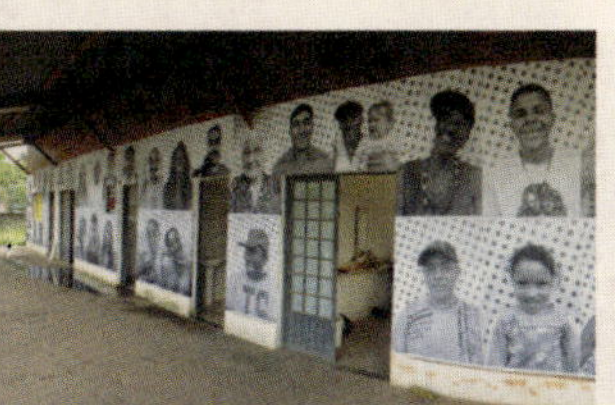
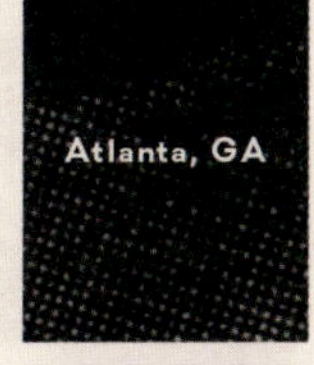
Atlanta, GA
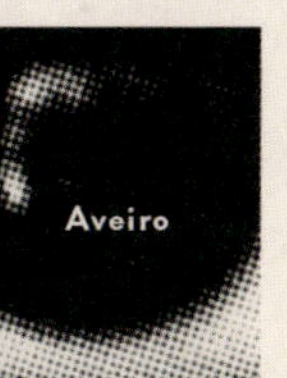
Aveiro
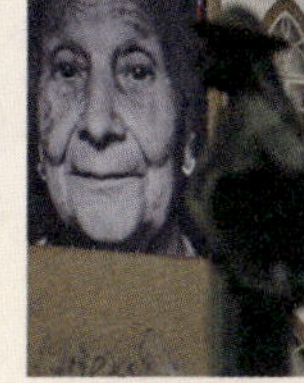
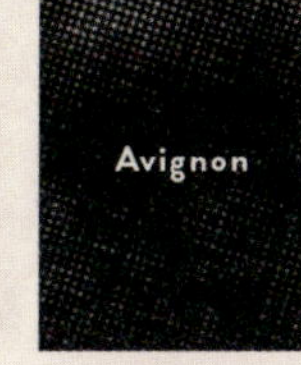
Avignon

Adelaide, Australia The Future of Adelaide, October 2011. We're interested in telling the stories of a future Adelaide—people who are not currently represented in the city narrative but are important for the city and its future: people currently outside the city bounds, people who use the city only at night, new arrivals, and younger generations.

Albertville, France Citoyens du Quartier, pour Changer les Regards, May 2014. This project is aimed at shedding light on the autistic people living in Sainsmont, Albertville, who few people know. "We have differences but we all share a place of residence. It is therefore important to share, to know, and to recognize."

Albuquerque, NM Universal, March 2016. In response to the sexual attacks on the University of New Mexico campus, students in our honors course wanted to shed light on this issue and show our solidarity with the victims. Whether victim or supporter, all students on UNM's campus are part of a caring community.

Aldeota, Brazil Contramunde, August 2012. The goal is to have a new jobs perspective and to develop sustainable incomes for the fishing community, which suffers from unemployment and an insecure future due to lack of regulations on artisanal lobster fishing. These fishermen want to insure a future for their children.

Alfortville, France Des Clichés pour l'Égalité, December 2013. "Whatever the color of our skin, we can have any profession we want."—Valens, 11 years old
"This is about photos of students who are against discrimination."—Ines, 13 years old

Alfred, NY After the Fire, June 2012. A mural will cover the scene of a downtown fire.

Algiers, Algeria Générations Réfugiées: 40 Visages pour 40 Ans de Crise Humanitaire Sahraouie, December 2015. This exhibit aims to generate press coverage in Europe on the Sahrawi refugee crisis, and give a human-centered perspective to the crisis.

Amenia, NY Be Dyslexic, May 2013. I have learned that I can succeed in academics, and that I have several strengths and interests that will carry me through life. Dyslexia is something that I live with every day.

Amiens, France Inside Out Amiens—Qui Sont les Picards? Qui Sont les Amiénois ?, January 2015. Who are the Picard? Who are the Amiénois? For the one hundreth anniversary of WWI, we would like to collect portraits of Picards and Amiénois, from all living generations, to display how dynamic and alive our city and county are

Amman, Jordan Love Reunites Generations, July 2015. No matter how much time has passed, this journey shows me that love from your family is more powerful than any other relationship you can ever encounter in life.

Anadyr, Russia April 2013. The project sums up the basic social meaning of contemporary art: allowing a person to speak for themselves to the world, and a way to see a hometown and its community from a new perspective.

Anaheim, CA Dream Big, March 2014. We all come from different backgrounds. Every single athlete that steps foot on the court has fought to earn their spot and they fight every day to keep it. Their dreams are part of their personality, written on their faces. Together, we are proving that no dream is too big.

Andore la Vieille, Andorra La Diversité Nous Enrichit, May 2015. Andorra, as any other country, can't be understood without all its immigrants who worked and contributed to the development and society in which we're living today.

Annapolis, MD Unity is Not Conformity, August 2015. Annapolis High is a culturally, ethnically, and academically diverse community and we celebrate our differences. We want to celebrate our unity and display how we are accepting of who people are.

Annecy, France Ecole Élémentaire les Romains, June 2015. We want to display the diversity of the origin of our children in our school and show to everyone that it's a great opportunity. We want to reaffirm the French motto: freedom, equal rights, and brotherhood! (Liberté, Égalité, Fraternité!)

Anoka, MN Celebrating Life in Anoka, September 2012. We are taking a pledge against bullying, and to celebrate life.

Antarctica Antarctica, January 2015.The picture was taken on Deception Island, an active volcano in the Antarctic Peninsula and also the site of a former whaling station.

Antananarivo, Madagascar Ensemble, May 2015. We'd like to draw attention to the people who are working in our school, the Lycée français of Tananarive.

Antibes, France Fersen College Students Action for Education, May 2014. Because we live in France, and we have great access to education, we understand that everyone around the globe might not be as fortunate. Although this project was led exclusively by students, we also decided to include portraits of our great teachers!

Antisiranana, Madagascar Viavin'ny Diego—Femmes de Diego, March 2015. The Alliance proposes, through the use of the art of photography, to honor the women of North Madagascar of all ages, diverse backgrounds, and experiences.

Antwerp, Belgium Clean Air—The Right to Breathe, March 2014. We are asking for clean air in Flanders, Belgium.

Inside Out 2060, August 2011. We want to make a statement about children's hopes, dreams, and attitudes so clearly visible on the faces in the streets and parks and squares!

Apelação, Portugal, We Are Much More Than We Think, October 2013. This action was made by a group of students that wanted to change the negative perception that society has about Apelação's kids and community, specifically as the reputation pertains to video footage of a gun shootout in 2008, which later was proved to be a fabrication.

Ariège, France Jeunesse Rurale, Aug 2011. We are from the countryside. We are young and we have things to say!

Arlington, VA Ottoson: This Is Who We Are, October 2016. After dealing with some terrible racist graffiti and racist verbal interactions at our school, our students came together to celebrate our differences—who we are and where we come from. We are coming together as one to show that we do not tolerate any kind of hate toward one another at our school.

Armentières, France Ecole Renan Buisson, June 2015. We, children of l'école Renan Buisson, proved that we were able to create an art project without the help of adults.

Armidale, Australia Life, Love, and Happiness, June 2011. Historically, indigenous people have been culturally shamed and this has dramatically changed their lives! They are so proud of who they are. The alley we postered has been branded with hurt; a young indigenous man with mental health issues was shot and killed by police 10 meters from where the posters were. It was our way of bringing life, love, and happiness back to the alley.

Asnières, France Un Nouveau Visage pour la Gare Lisch, February 2015. The Lisch Station in Asnières is falling into ruin because of a lack of concern from the relevant institutions and complex bureaucracy. It is time for citizens to intervene in order to prevent the loss of this beautiful building.

Atakpame, Togo Pathways Togo, January 2014. Young women! Leave behind your insecurity; have confidence in yourself and do good work.

Athens, GA Pictures of Us, April 2016. We are the next wave of thinkers, inventors, and astronauts; the ones who will make Athens proud. We are curious, brave, active, smart, shy, busy, loving, daring, and different in many ways. We are the quiet ones with books under desks, the bold ones who stand up for what's right; some of us aren't quite sure who we are yet. Together, we add life to the Athens community.

Atibaia, Brazil Reciclagem, February 2014. The Imperial de Atibaia Samba School works with communities most in need in Atibaia, where a large number of the population work at the town recycling facility and live in substandard conditions. The Carnival is one of the few artistic and cultural activities they take part in, and our project's goal is to promote themselves through their identity portraits, as well as to reinforce their community bonds. Only with everyone's help can this group put their samba school in the Carnival parade.

Atlanta, GA 45 x 45, August 2014. It was about connecting and showing the many faces of Atlanta—what makes us all different, but even more importantly, what makes us all the same.

Martin Martyrs (#MartinMartyrs), February 2014. February 26, 2012, in Sanford, Florida, an unarmed teenager named Trayvon Martin was fatally shot by George Zimmerman on the basis of that state's Stand Your Ground law. The individuals in these portraits allowed me to "shoot" them with my camera as a show of support for the unnecessary death of Trayvon Martin. The purpose of this project is to view various people who are willing to "stand their ground" against multiple unethical laws that affect their own communities; but a group of people who still willingly come together for a common cause.

Austin, TX Austin High School, March 2013. The students of Austin High School!

Austin, MN Austin High School, April 2014. We want to see a change at Garcia Middle School because of the existence of bullying. We want our voices to express the way we feel about it. People should treat people how they themselves would want to be treated. People shouldn't be judged on the way they look. School should be a safe environment where students feel comfortable and can learn without being judged by their fellow students.

Aveiro, Portugal Love Your City, May 2011. Love your city. Take care of it. Love your people. Live together with them and take care of them.

Avignon, France Les Étudiants en Art d'Avignon se Battent Contre la Fermeture de Leur Ecole!, April 2016. We are the art students of Avignon: don't let us down! This action was to peacefully protest the shutdown of the first-year entry exam and budgetary reductions.

Just Friends, May 2016. We are not family; we are only friends. Regardless: this is love!

Solidarité, November 2015. To defend and remember the values of solidarity on the occasion of Social Security's seventieth anniversary in France.

Avignon Patrimoine, June 2015. We would like to raise awareness of the risk of destruction of Avignon's cultural heritage sites.

Baghdad, Iraq TED X Baghdad, October 2011. To celebrate life in Iraq, with its varied complexities, from genuine and simple folk.

Balaban, Turkey The Forgotten Refugees of Balaban, October 2014. More than 780 refugees are living in Balaban on the Syrian-Turkish border right now. No international NGO is caring for them. Because of the fighting in and around Kobane at the Syrian-Turkish border there is a looming a humanitarian disaster for all refugees. For weeks, tens of thousands of civilians fled from the advancing ISIL fighters into the safety of the bordering country of Turkey.

Baltimore, MD Black Lives Matter, April 2015. Organized by Morgan State University's Visual Arts Department, Black Lives Matter is a visual response to the #BlackLivesMatter movement. Created in 2012 after the murder of Trayvon Martin, the movement "[broadens] the conversation around state violence to include all of the ways in which black people are intentionally left powerless at the hands of the state." Our group action aims to shed light on the presence of invisible boundaries and limitations placed on black people throughout different facets of our lives.

2nd Set, February 2015. Milford Mill Academy is a creative, high-achieving, and outstanding high school with diverse and determined students. We want to change the outlook of the school in our community.

Favorite Colors, June 2012. Favorite colors: personal, intimate, connecting.

Bangalow, Australia Bangalow Primary School, August 2011. Bangalow Primary School, in conjunction with the local preschool, holds a biannual art show where students produce artworks to be exhibited at our local community hall. This year the theme is "Bangalow Alive" and is about the people and buildings that bring our close-knit community to life.

Bangkok, Thailand Bangkok, Thailand World Up!, March 2012. World Up!

Bangkok, July 2012. A group of factory workers just outside of Bangkok with around 140 participants. Their action represents their survival from the Bangkok floods of October 2011. This area of the city was badly flooded (more than 2 meters of water) for one month.

Banja Luka, Bosnia and Herzegovina Banja Luka, January 2014. Every facial expression of an individual portrait tells their opinion on the subject: "Educational system and ability for youth to express themselves in our society." This is the problem that affects every person in our society; either students, their parents, teachers, social workers, etc. The main aim of this project is the ability for youth to express their opinion on the subject, which directly affects them.

Barcelona, Spain Vivim Aqui, January 2015. Ciutat Vella is increasingly becoming a tourist destination, where the "Barcelona Model: the Best Store in the World" is turning into a literal reality, leaving citizens by the wayside in public spaces and the neighborhood shops that have been designed exclusively for tourists. This is why we proclaim the following: 1) The area should be returned to its people, and should return to the era when it was a friendly, livable neighborhood; 2) To participate in building neighborhood public spaces for the local community's use; and 3) That the city should consider the needs of all its neighbors, including children, who should be able to meet, play, and run. This is why we call for a participatory process in the forthcoming reform of the walk from the old Roman city walls, so that our sons and daughters can run and play safely next to their school.

Learning Together in Barcelona, March 2014. Living together begins with learning together. We want to share our differences, which should be seen as a great cultural wealth.

Solidarity with the Resistance in Turkey, October 2013. We're a group of people from Turkey living in Barcelona and we would like to show our support and solidarity for the fight for real democracy in our country.

TED X Barcelona Women, March 2013. Women Empowerment. Starting conversations about the strength of women and most of all showing that Mediterranean women are changing their world.

The Real Protagonists of Our History, March 2012. We claim the construction of our children's public school.

Bastrop, TX We Stand for Hope, January 2012. We stand for the hope, strength, and resilience of the people of Bastrop as they rebuild after the US's most destructive wildfires in 2011.

Baton Rouge, LA All Walks of Life, March 2013. We are celebrating people from all walks of life who make up the diverse community of Baton Rouge.

Beaucourt, France Collège Saint-Exupéry, June 2015. This project expresses the diversity inside the high school's life: each person owns his difference.

Beijing, China I Also Wish My Photo to Be Shown, February 2013. In a country often noted for its lack of self-expression, together we create a unique narrative that illustrates that possibilities for individuality inhabit our world within the boundaries of national culture and political realms.

ME/WE, September 2012. Youth is the future. Through the eyes of the young adults from Taiwan and the mainland, we may see the possible future relationship across the strait.

Belgrade, Serbia Voices of Belgrade, March 2012. Everybody has a voice, a desire, or something they care about, and the world should hear it.

Belo Horizonte, Brazil Olhar Coletivo (Collective Look), November 2011. We want our students to see their reality from a different perspective, through art and photography.

Beloit, WI Barriers at Beloit, January 2013. This group brings students together from all parts of campus to meet weekly in small groups to discuss issues on Beloit College's campus, including race, gender, Greek life, stereotypes, and personal identities. The initiative is built on a social justice framework, in an effort to reach solutions for these issues through dialogue. We wanted to use these photographs as a way to share the small group conversations with the rest of the campus community.

Benicàssim, Spain We Are Boys and Girls and . . . We Demand Peace!, July 2014. This project was conducted in a middle school where kids were driven to talk about peace, not only as it pertains to wars, but also as it pertains to daily problems that occur in the playground, within their families, with friends; and how to solve those problems in a peaceable manner.

Bergamo, Italy Giovane Italia, April 2014. As young students in a vocational school, behind the walls of these buildings we're working hard, studying, and learning a career to grow up as an accountable and lively part of our country.

Berlin, Germany Time to Muse, January 2016. We want to give a face to the community that is rising from the migration "crisis," rather than marginalize refugees as a

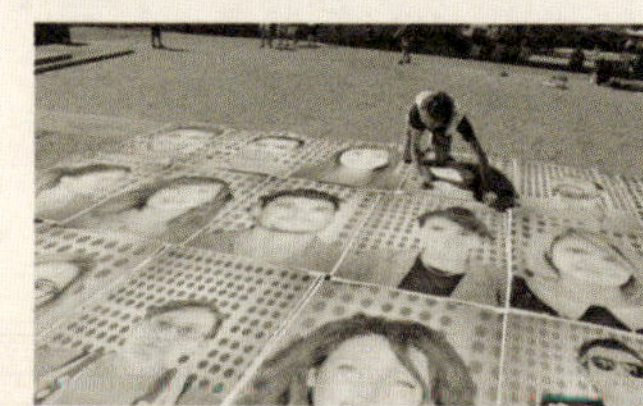
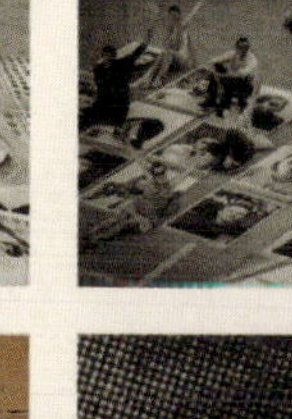
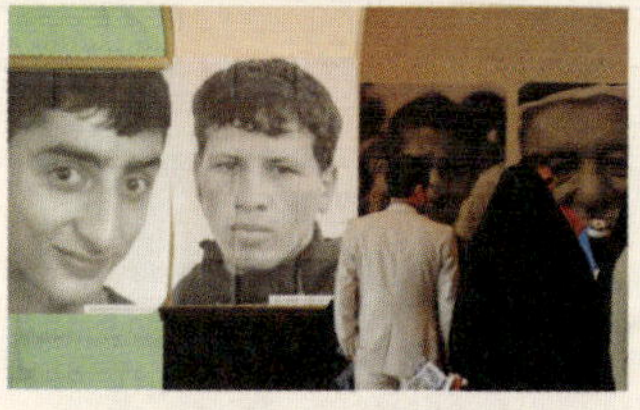
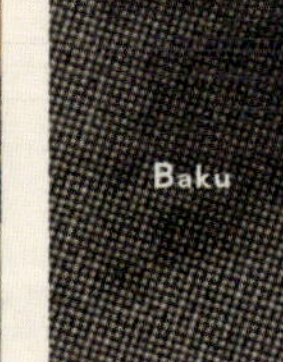

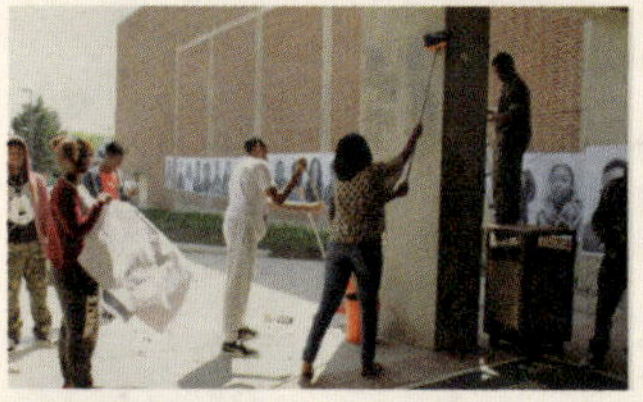
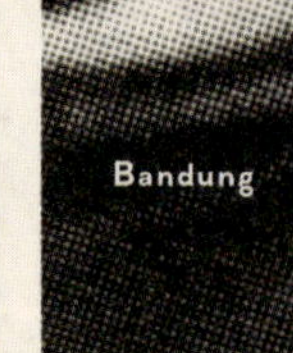

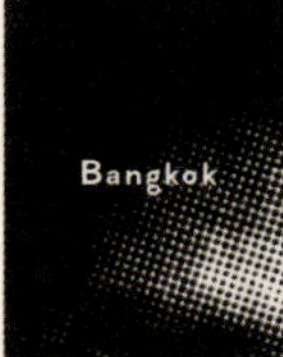

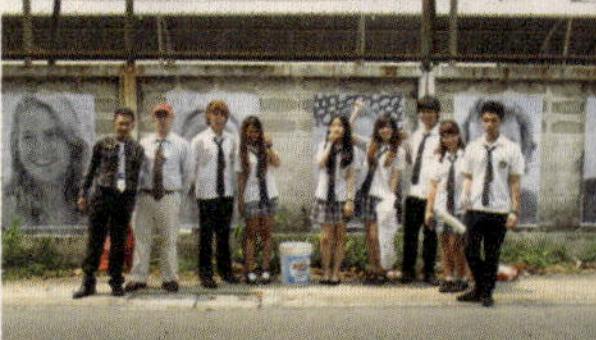
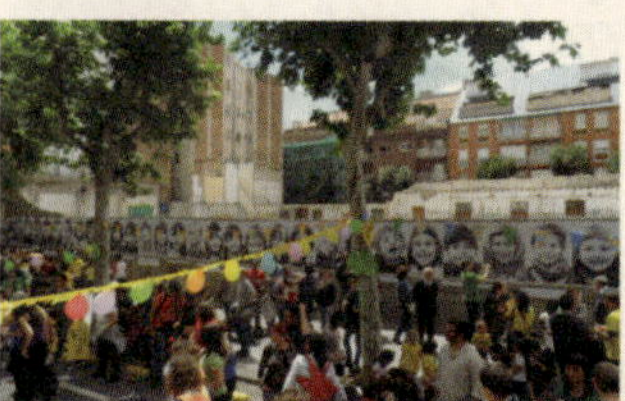
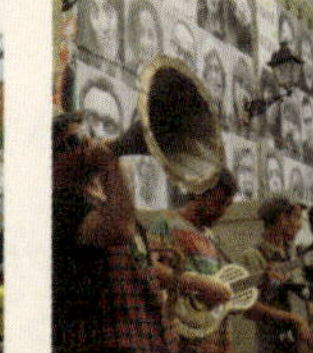
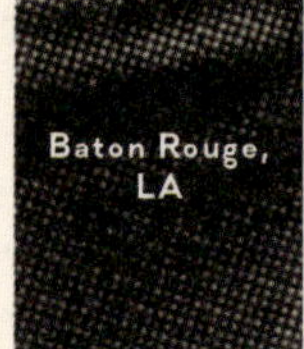

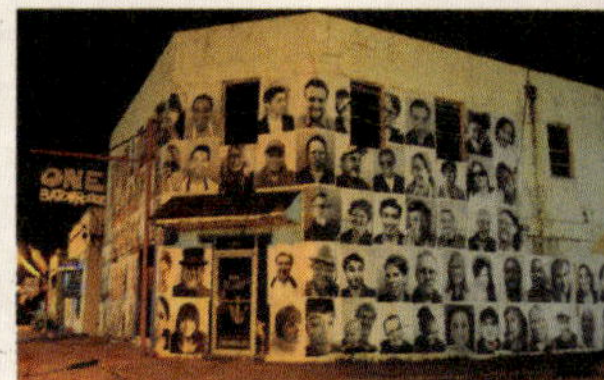
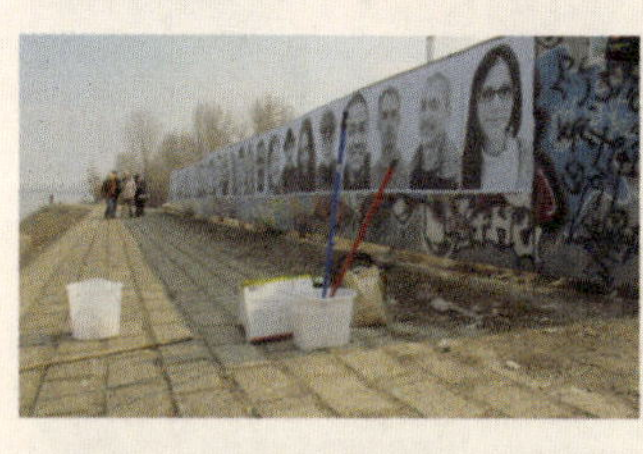
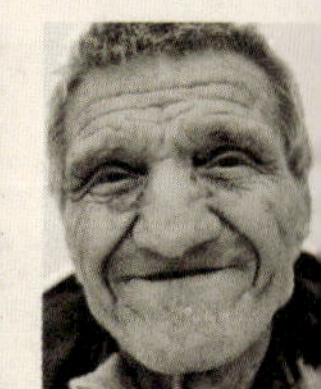
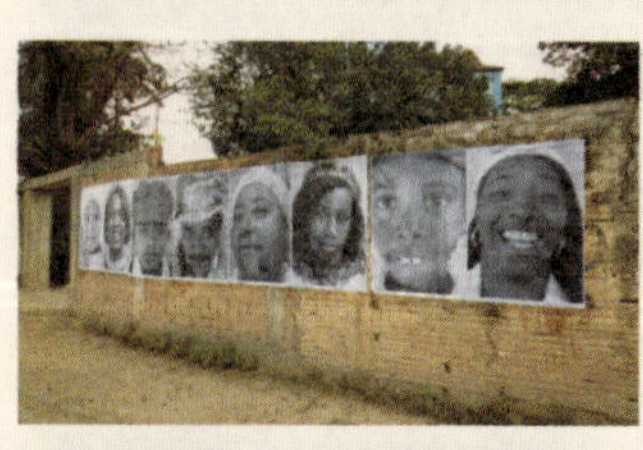
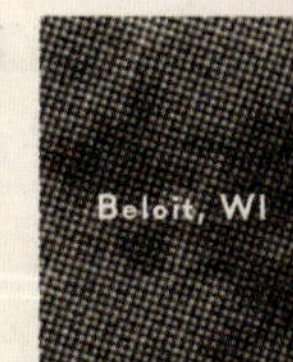

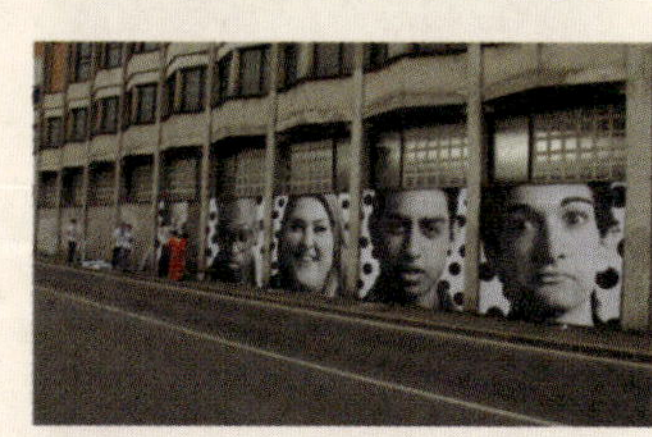
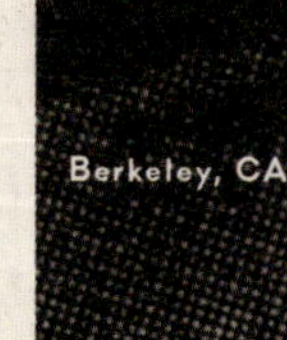

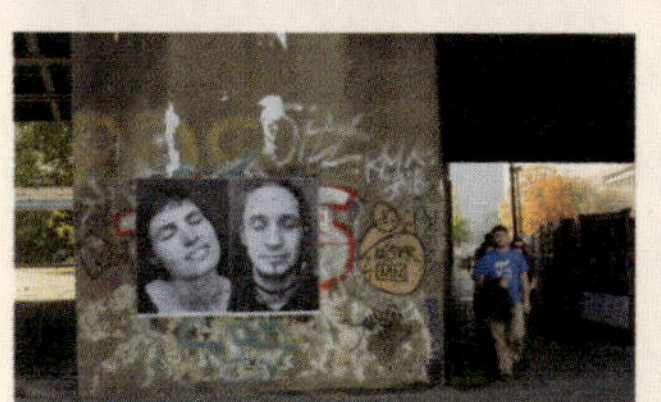
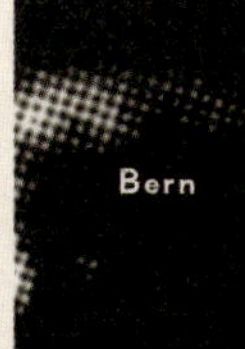

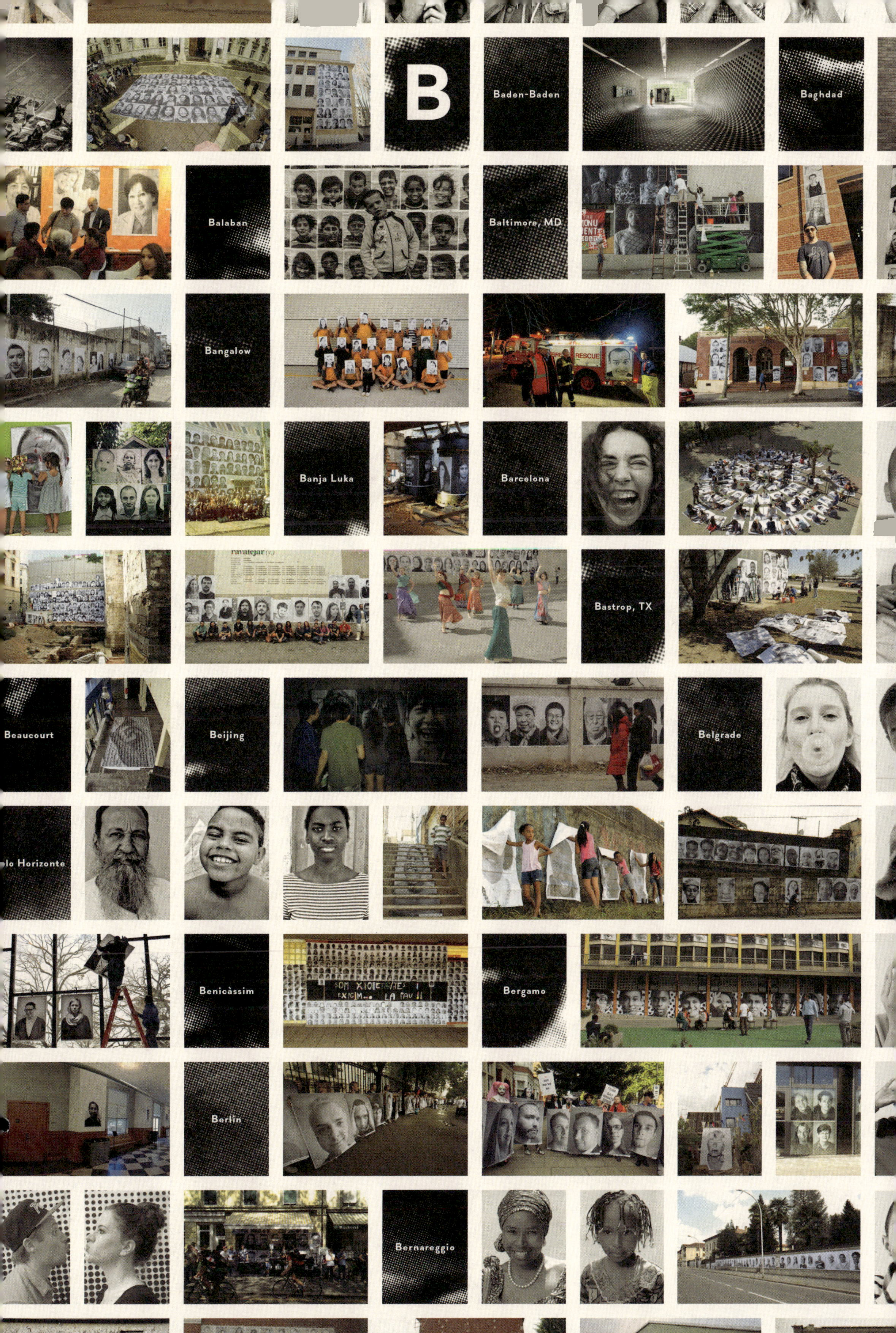
B
Baden-Baden
Baghdad
Balaban
Baltimore, MD
Bangalow
Banja Luka
Barcelona
Bastrop, TX
Beaucourt
Beijing
Belgrade
lo Horizonte
Benicàssim
Bergamo
Berlin
Bernareggio

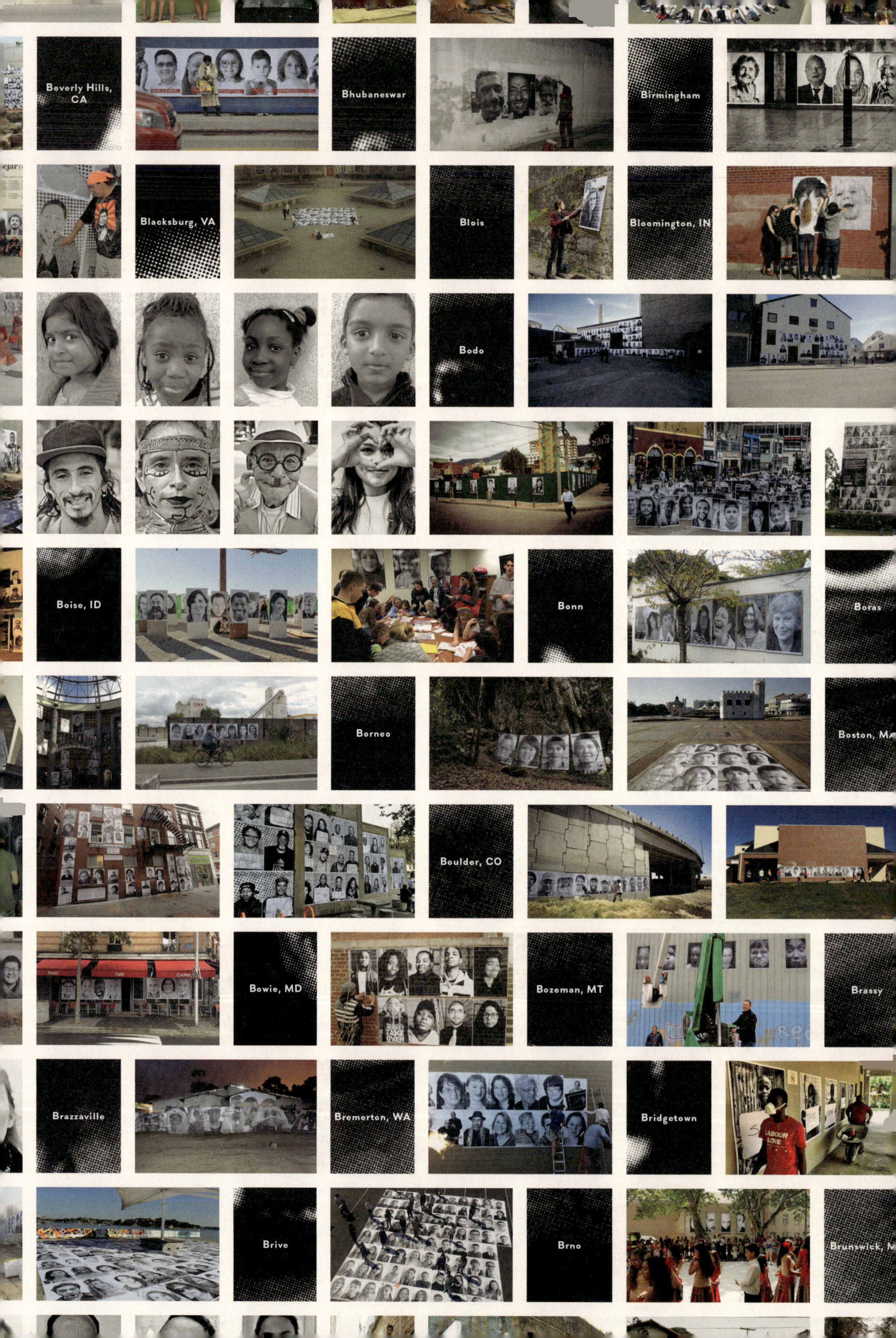
Beverly Hills, CA
Bhubaneswar
Birmingham
Blacksburg, VA
Blois
Bloomington, IN
Bodo
Boise, ID
Bonn
Boras
Borneo
Boston, M
Boulder, CO
Bowie, MD
Bozeman, MT
Brassy
Brazzaville
Bremerton, WA
Bridgetown
Brive
Brno
Brunswick, M

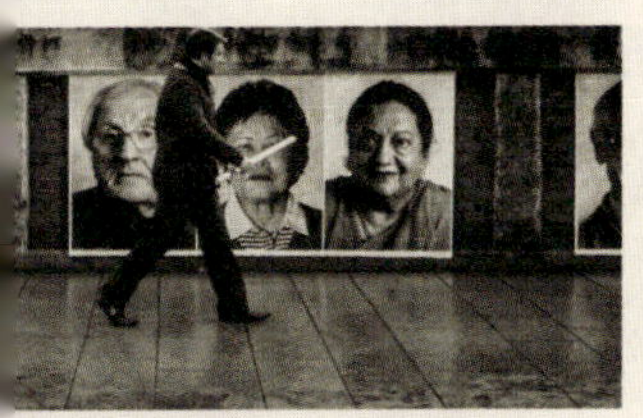
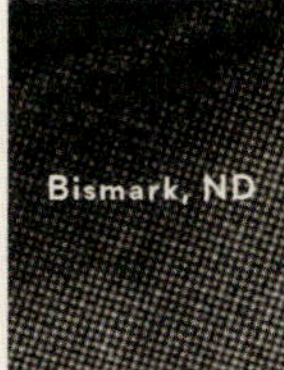

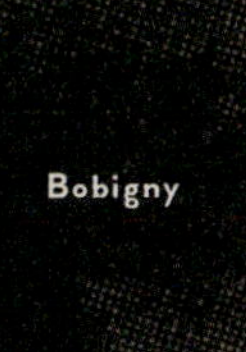

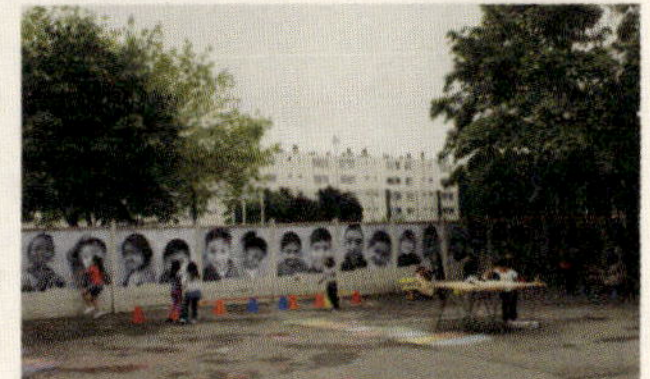
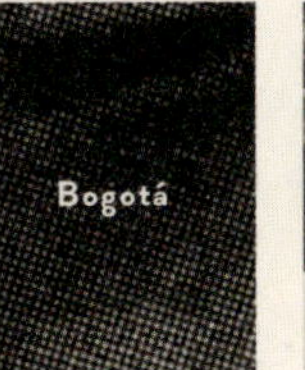

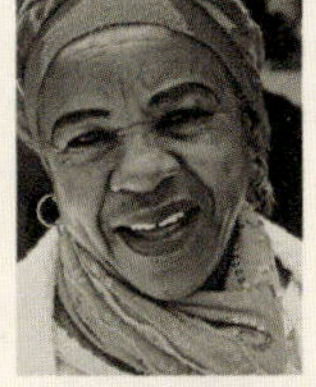
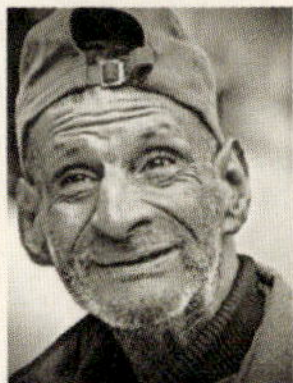
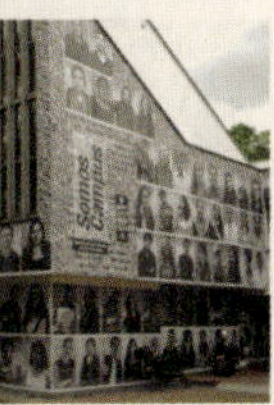
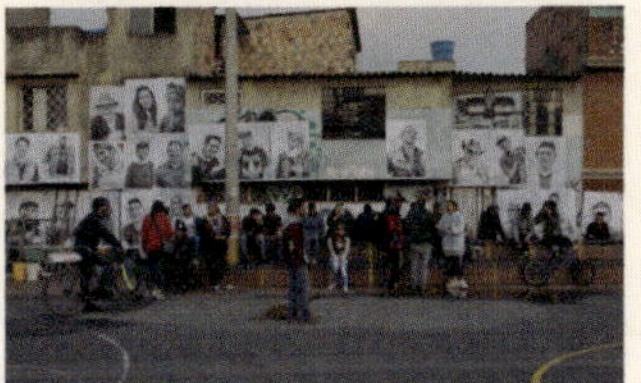
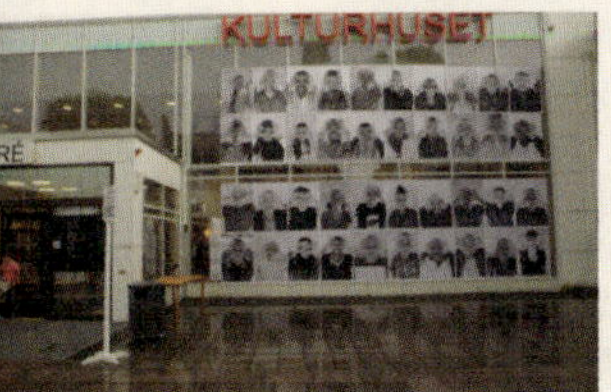

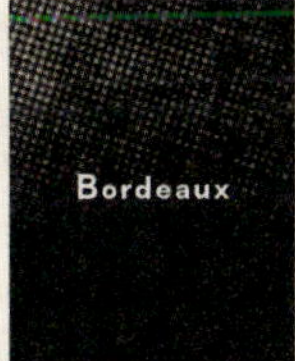

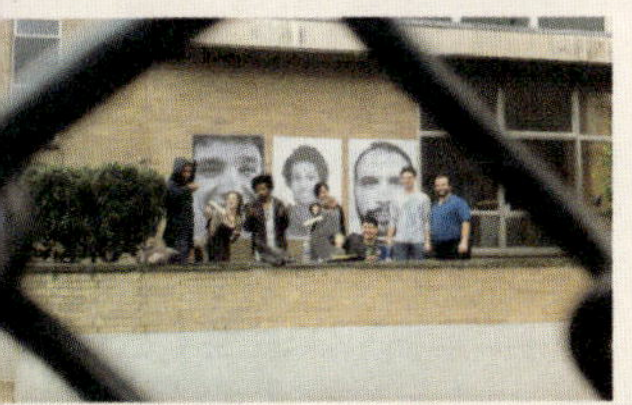
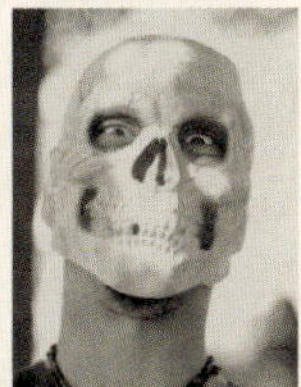
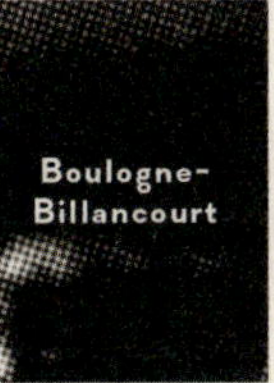

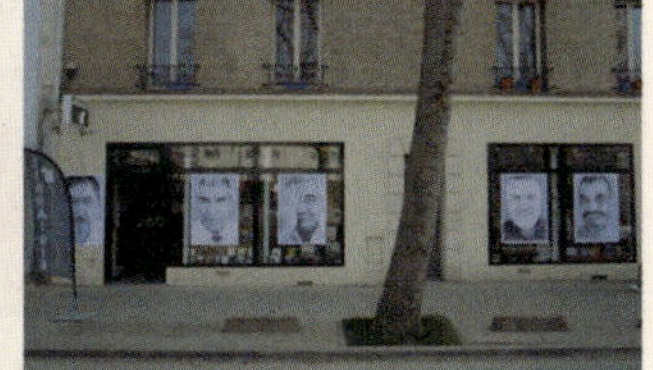
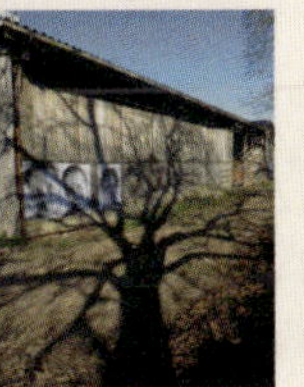
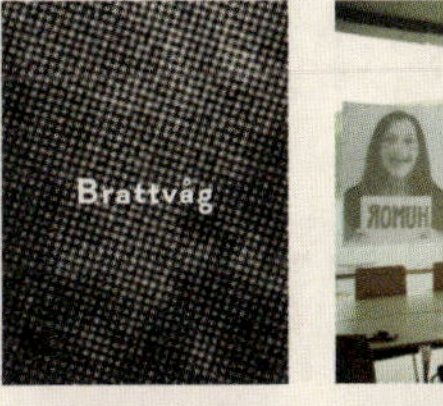

Brighton
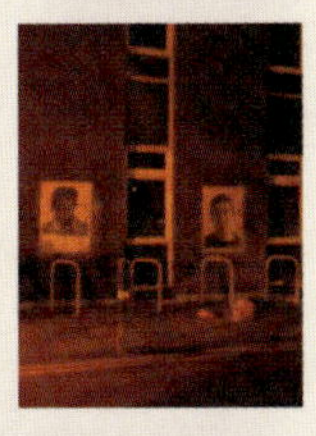
Brisbane
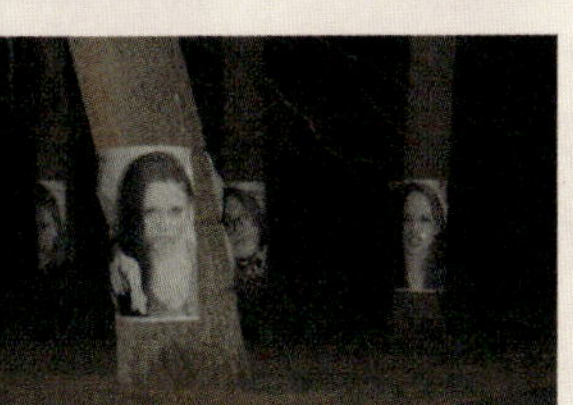
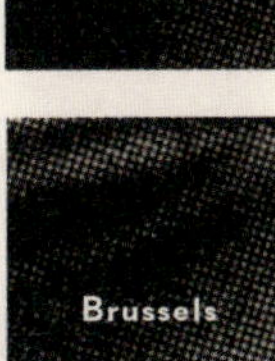

separate entity. The portraits are installed in symbolically meaningful public spaces around Berlin in order to raise awareness about this matter and to become part of the fabric of the collective consciousness.

LGBT Rights in the Berlin Russian Embassy, June 2011. They have been met with violence and discrimination from their governments, religious leaders, and right-wing skinhead groups. This year, I will once again be living with these activists in Minsk, Moscow, and St. Petersburg documenting their fight for the very human right of just being who they are.

Love Your Wrinkles, September 2012. Close your eyes and think about love or the happiest moment in your life. It will transform your day!

Bern, Switzerland Delivery Cycling, June 2013. The posters illustrate the stories of clients from my hairdressing salon, which was a checkpoint for cyclists to get their stamps during a delivery cyclists European Masters event.

Bernareggio, Italy Everyone Can Be a Work of Art. Here We Are!, September 2014. Our portraits represent our community: women, men, girls, and boys together with our richness of culture, traditions, and habits. We want to affirm that we are a community, we are together, and we can do more for one for another.

Beverly Hills, CA Inside Out Korea Town, April 2013. This is our home: our sun, our stars, our sky. This is our call, this is our storm. This is our progress, our distance, our gift, our challenge, our potential, our responsibility, our today, our tomorrow. This is our "right now." Let's face it together.

Bhubaneswar, India Showing Faces, September 2011. To have the opportunity to display Indian faces in a public place and question about these faces!

Birmingham, England Lost Stories, November 2013. The city of Birmingham has more than one million inhabitants and is proud to be one of most ethnically and culturally diverse cities in the UK. However, the proportion of people who make up the older generation is low, with only 12 percent of the population being aged 65 and older. Most of those in this aging demographic have gone through major events in their lives: childbirth, war, migration, retirement, long-term illness or disability, and bereavement, to name a few. Many of these people will still lead happy and healthy lives, others may be isolated and vulnerable, no longer having a voice within their families or communities. Whatever their backgrounds are, they all have a story to tell.

Blacksburg, VA We Are Designers!, November 2013. "Good Design Brings People Together." We are Virginia Tech students and faculty members from different design majors: architecture, graphic design, industrial design, landscape. We all came together to say that design matters. Design brings all these different majors and different people together.

Blois, France La Culture Fait Feu de Tout Blois: les Arts Plastiques ne Sont pas Facultatifs pour les Lycéens du Loir-et-Cher, April 2016. We want to show through this artistic manifestation, which displays the cultural vitality of the Dessaignes high school, that the decision of closing the fine arts option is nonsense.

Bloomington, IN Bloomington High School South, December 2011. We would like to express the acceptance of diversity in our town of Bloomington.

Bobigny, France Malgré Nos Différences, Nous Nous Ressemblons Tous Beaucoup, May 2011. Primary school students worked on similarities and differences.

Bodø, Norway I'm Momentous, April 2016. The project "I'm momentous" aims to celebrate the people who make Bodø city! The project focuses on how a society is made up of people of different backgrounds, and that all people are of equal value, regardless of social status and their own resources.

Bogotá, Colombia Memorias del Parche, October 2016. Memorias del parche is a project that is looking for an action to reconcile generations, giving a new meaning for our popular neighborhood spaces and empower the young people of our city of Jardín Norte.

The Story Behind our Wrinkles, October 2016. In Colombia, my country, we have been living a war for the past fifty years. Finally, after four years of dialogues between the guerrilla FARC and the government, we have a chance to fight for a different future by voting to "give peace a chance." However, some, filled by the bitterness and pain that war has left behind in their hearts, refuse to accept that in order to form a society as equals, we must first forgive and respect those who think different from us. We want to remind ourselves and our country how the "enemy" is only one because of the uniform or label they wear.

#SomosCampus, November 2015. The Somos Campus initiative seeks to ensure that each member of the university community is recognized as an active agent of change and acquires a real and tangible commitment to the care of the campus of the National University of Colombia—Sede Bogotá, leaving its image as a signature of acceptance of this commitment. The portraits of teachers, students, graduates, and administrators will reflect their commitment to the care of one of the largest campuses in Latin America and the most important public academic center in the country.

Faces in the City, February 2013. We stand up for peace and tolerance in Bogotá, Colombia.

Boise, ID Organization Assisting the Homeless Student (OATHS), September 2014. OATHS provides whatever homeless students need to help them enjoy, succeed, and stay in school. We want to put a face on homeless students who stay at the shelter.

Without Us, March 2012. What would you do without us? The idea is to identify twenty or more professions that are essential to our social well-being but seldom acknowledged.

Borås, Sweden We See You, September 2015. We want our project to be called "We See You" for two reasons: 1) It means that we see each other; 2) Also we see our politicians. The plan was to paste the pictures on the outside wall of our City Hall (we had to change to the "Kulturhuset," the house of culture and art in Borås), the display what the people of this city look like, and what we see going on in our streets. The people are the foundation of any city, but in ours it feels like many of us are forgotten by the local politicians.

Bordeaux, France Les Seniors Actifs de Bordeaux, September 2014. We want to pay tribute to the elderly population of Bordeaux, which represents a dynamic generation, full of vitality and joyfulness.

Femmes, April 2014. The strength and solidarity of women.

Borneo, Indonesia Preserving the Penan Culture, November 2011. We would like people to know more about the Penan. The Penan are living in the Borneo forest and are in great danger because of logging companies that are cutting down the Borneo forest, and palm oil companies that are replacing the forest with palm oil plantations. There are fewer than one hundred nomadic Penan left in Borneo today and many specialists state that their culture will disappear in the next twenty years because of deforestation.

Boston, MA Outside In for Homelessness in Boston, May 2013. Youth are homeless for three reasons: home doesn't exist; home isn't safe; home isn't supportive. It only takes one courageous person to make a difference in these lives. We are dedicated to helping communities dig deeply into conversations around how they will end the experience of homelessness.

Music Can Change the World, March 2012. We're a group of musicians passionate about how music has changed our lives and how it can transform the lives of others. We want to explore the impact that music has had on the lives of musicians in Boston who care about having an impact on their communities through music by showcasing their faces.

Boulder, CO Boulder Rebuilds, October 2013. As Boulder rebuilds its community after the flood, we are reminded that our community is made up of diverse people who work together in the face of adversity. We are all Boulder, and we are resilient.

Eat Your Art Out, March 2013. Paying tribute to local farmers in my city!

Boulogne-Billancourt, France Renault Billancourt, Mémoires Vives, August 2014. Through this project, we would like to shine a light on all the people who worked in these factories. Behind the outstanding industrial progress that took place were tens of thousands of employees who have witnessed this history.

Bowie, MD Bowie State University, December 2013. We want to stand in solidarity and share our own visual expressive support to those students who feel they don't have a voice. The project was a way for them to explore their own personal identities and to feel empowered.

Bozeman, MT Snap Out of It!, September 2012. I want to successfully represent my neighborhood correctly by installing the images all over a 4-block radius.

Brattvåg, Norway Inside Out HVS, June 2014. The Inside Out Project is a collective effort, but it is also about individuality and what makes each and every one of us unique. To combat the negative ideas of the Law of Jante and to promote individuality, we want our Inside Out project to create positivity and confidence.

Brazzaville, Republic of the Congo Inside Out Brazzaville, April 2013. We want to foster artistic creation in the Congo.

Bremerton, WA Artists of Kitsap Part 2, June 2013. Bremerton, WA is a town where the local economy is driven by a military base, the health care industry, and a community college. Through Inside Out, the Artists of Kitsap County will introduce themselves and bring public art to the community. We hope the community will grow its support for local art and local places where people of all ages can practice creative expression.

Bridgetown, Barbados Barbados 50 Independence Project, July and November 2016. 2016 marked the fiftieth anniversary of Barbados's independence from Great Britain. We asked each subject to chose a word that they thought represented themselves, their country, or Barbados's independence.

Brighton, England Behind the Scenes, January 2014. This project is to show appreciation for everybody who works at the university: the dinner ladies, cleaners, technicians, cooks, caretakers, students, and lecturers that make the place function.

Brive, France The Difference, May 2016. The difference is the way we are seen by the others, but does it reflect what we are inside our body and our mind? We would like people to think about it when they will look at the school wall where these posters will be displayed.

Brno, Czech Republic Ghettofest 2013, March 2012. We stand for our home, the place we live in Brno; "Bronx" is not merely a dangerous place or socially excluded Romani location. We invite everyone who wants to share positive change with us. Come to the Ghettofest festival and help us open the gates of the "ghetto" to the minds of the people of the city!

Brooklyn, NY Through the Lens of Freedom: Redefining Ourselves and Inventing a New World, October 2016. We envision ourselves as inventors, building a community that values our views and supports a world free from bullying.

Broward, FL Mirror Lake Elementary, December 2015. "Future Leaders of Mirror Lake"

Brunswick, ME Take Back the Night, May 2015. Sexual violence happens at Bowdoin College and on other college campuses. It can take place inside any building, at any field, in any parking lot, and at any time. Research suggests over 80 percent of sexual assault survivors know their assailant. On a campus our size they are likely to come into contact with their aggressor after the event. Today, these women are taking back this campus, where many students have become survivors of sexual violence.

Brussels, Belgium Inside Out for Belgium, April 2016. To fight conflations after the terrorist attacks in Brussels in March, and to show that we stand united in the face of adversity.

MEPs are Like You, September 2015. "MEPs #LikeYou" aims at creating a virtual meeting between members of the European Parliament and citizens.

Générations Réfugiées: 40 Visages pour 40 Ans de Crise Humanitaire Sahraouie, December 2015. 2015 is the fortieth anniversary of Sahraouie's humanitarian crisis. We want to attract the media's attention in Europe, and make them aware.

Justice for Afghan Refugees in Belgium, January 2014. The 2013 Amnesty International report states that in Afghanistan thousands of people have endured indiscriminate attacks from the armed opposition's group. As the Declaration of Human Rights says, everyone has the right to life, liberty, and security of person, and the right to seek and to enjoy asylum from persecution in other countries. They are asking to have the chance to live in peace, to work, and to give their children a better future.

Inside Out Brussels: We Are All Photographers, March 2013. We are all photographers.

University of Medicine—Silly Faces, December 2011. We are a group of friends, students at the University of Medecine, and our project is pasting portraits of students, professors, and administration staff making faces. We want to paste them in pairs, to eliminate the inevitable differences that may exist between them. We also want to show the cultural diversity on campus.

Búdardalur, Iceland Respect for the Elderly . . . Respect Life . . . Respect Everyone's Happiness . . . Just Respect, July 2016. In elderly people's faces we see a respectful story of life. They have lived through different times and experienced every possible emotion. Support them if needed and respect their story of life. It's all right to forget if you remembered enjoying life.

Buenos Aires Argentina Mate—Activists, June 2014. Volunteers come by on a daily basis to share moments of love and help the prisoners encourage the vision that contributes to a more peaceful life. Love is the only medium that allows us to feel the freedom of life, wherever that may be.

World Up!, April 2012. World Up!

Buffalo, NY Buffalo Schools Stand Against Bullying, October 2011. My students wish to take a stand against bullying and discrimination through participation in this project.

Butteaux, France Butteaux's 50th Anniversary, June 2012. This year the rural home village of Butteaux celebrates its fiftieth anniversary. Here are portraits of people of all ages who live together, a symbol of decades of solidarity.

Cagliari, Italy stampaxi+, February 2013. This project consists of a big poster of photos of urban actors in order to strengthen the identity and sense of community, and to break down the wall of mistrust due to a lack of knowledge of new residents.

Cairns, Australia The Power of Resilience, February 2012. Empowering young people who are at risk of becoming homeless or are homeless. Highlighting resilience rather than risk.

Cairo, Egypt Cherishing Our Differences, March 2016. To show the people that even the most serious people have their quirks, and to encourage people to loosen up and stop judging others on their differences.

TED x Cairo, September 2012. Our statement is that you need to look around—especially in megacities—to understand how different yet similar we all are.

Calgary, Canada Southwood Community, July 2012. Community building and revitalizing community spaces. We want to build on the sense of community and well-being in Southwood.

University of Calgary—We Have a Story to Tell, March 2012. The students of University of Calgary's Story and Happiness classes are uniting with the Taylor Family Digital Library to send a message about story and community.

Callan County Kilkenny, Ireland KCAT We Are!, December 2014. "We Are! We are artists! No other labels please." (This action addresses the issue of how the artists portrayed are continually defined as Artists with Disabilities rather than the simpler label afforded to able-bodied artists.)

Cambrai, France Inside Out Cambrai, May 2014. For this first joint project, we chose to highlight the market traders of Cambrai. Merchants of our cities are direct social links with the people. We want to pay tribute to them by displaying their portraits in their place of work.

Cambridge, MA My Vulnerability=My Humanity, April 2014. Inviting members of our community to contemplate their vulnerability—a charged notion resonating with one's identity as an individual, group member, or global citizen—Inside Out Harvard encouraged participants to transform this perception, which potentially drives us apart, into a creative expression of our shared humanity.

Cannes, France Les Visages de Ranguin, May 2015. This action is to reinforce the relations between the population and the workers of the city.

Cape Town, South Africa Diamonds, May 2013. On the surface, these guys might be a lil' bit hardcore (hard-living), but they are diamonds in the streets, people I believe God is busy shaping, polishing up so that they can shine from all angles when He is smiling upon them, and they do shine already! Just look at them when they are smiling! It's all about the heart at the end of the day! And these people almost cry when I tell them they are diamonds and amazing . . . But they believe it, because they know their value and potential deep inside.

Inside Out: South Africa, June 2011. High school students in Cape Town, South Africa, participate in an Inside Out project that explores and fosters a dialogue about racism.

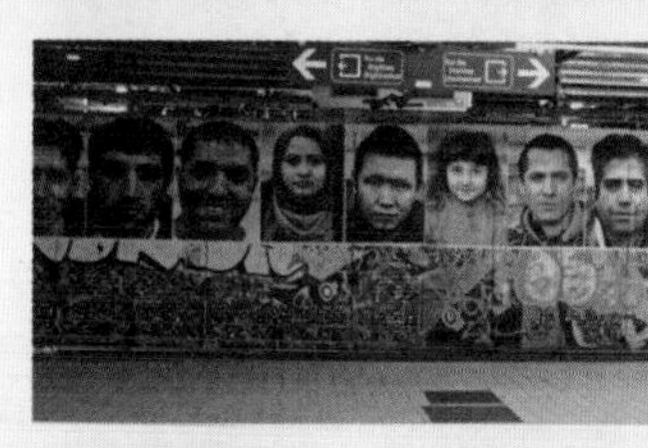
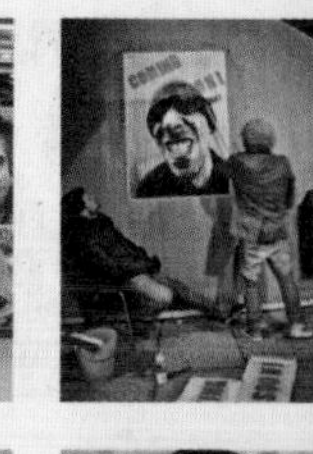
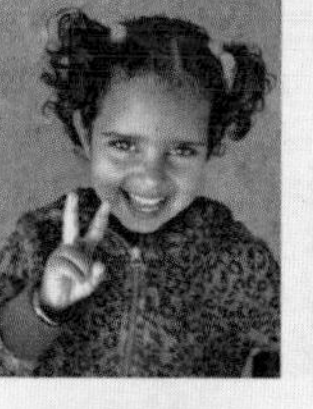
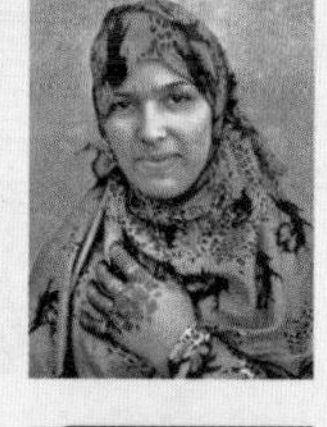
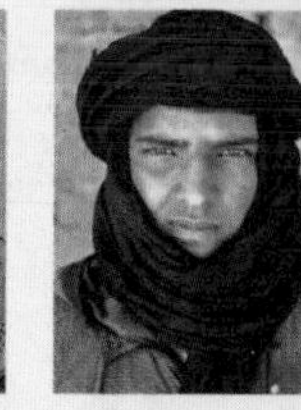
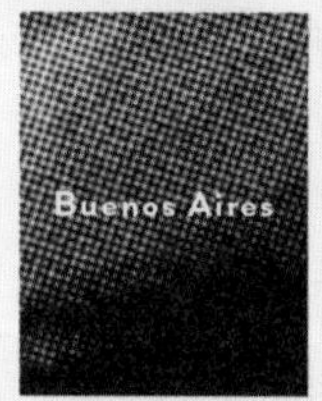

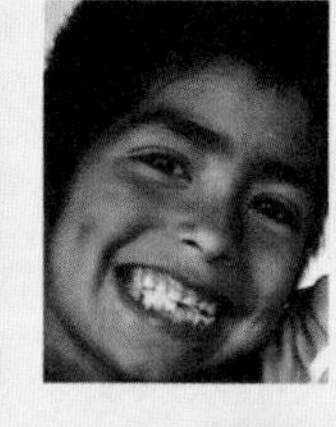
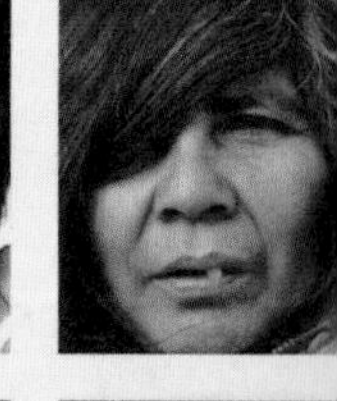
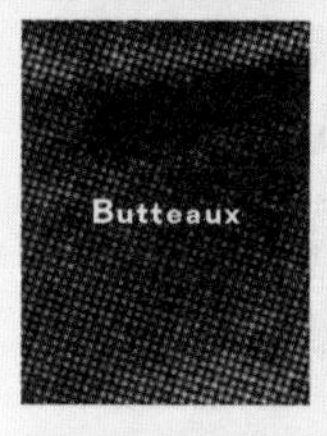

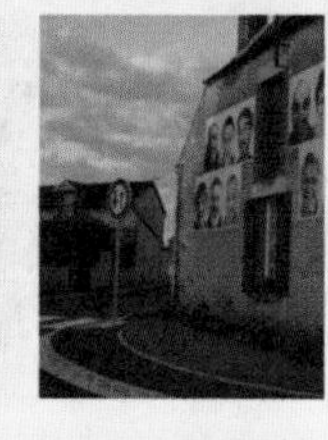
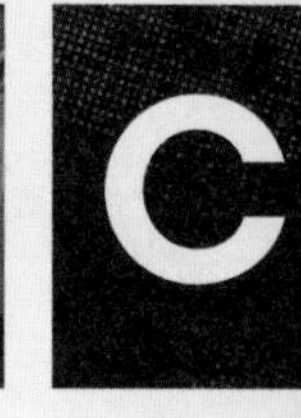

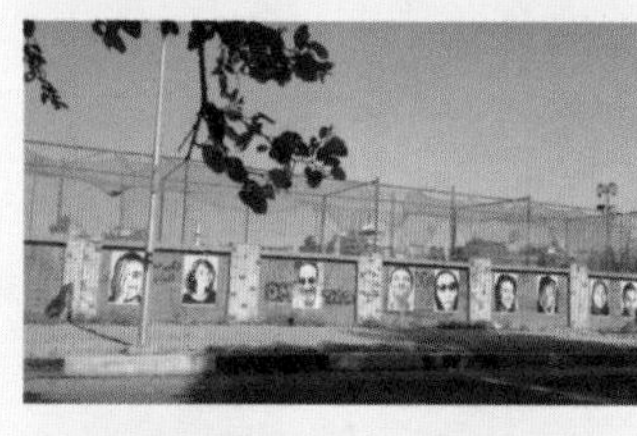
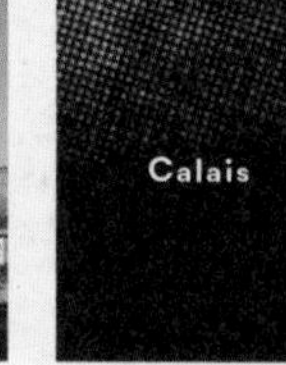

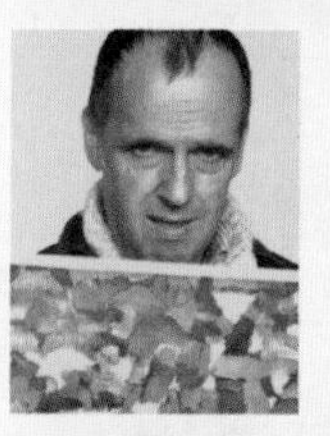
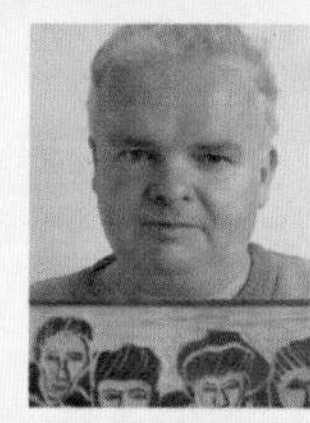
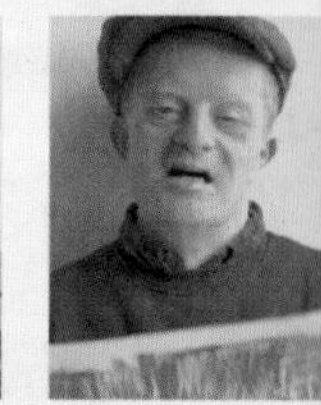
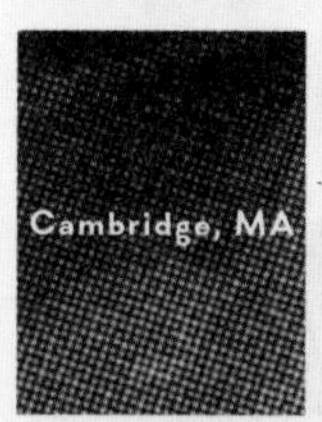

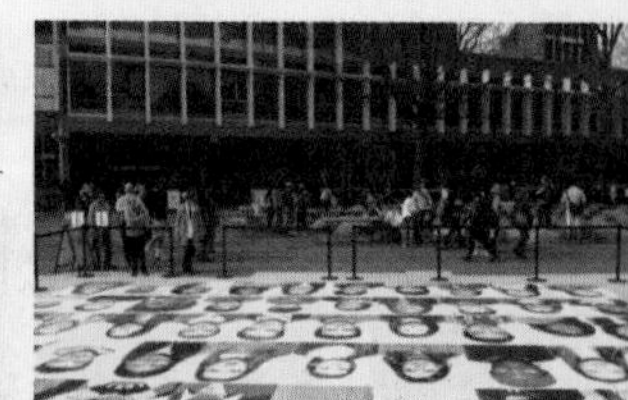
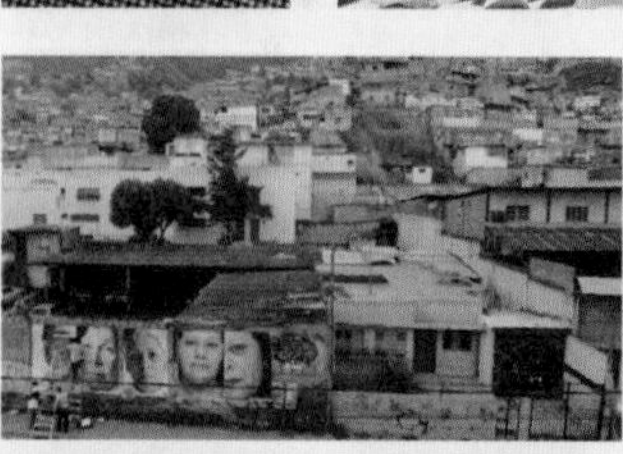
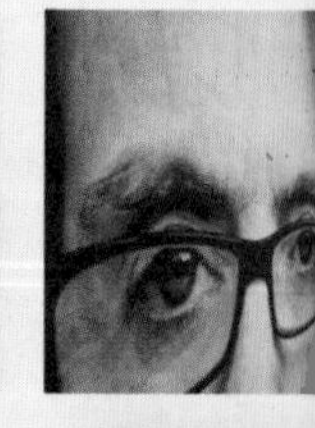
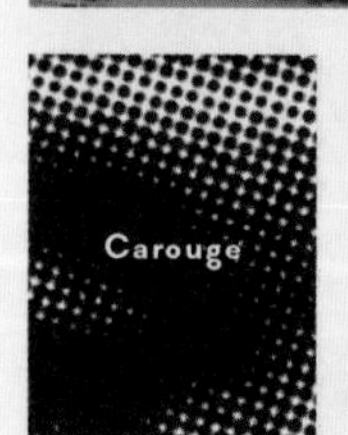

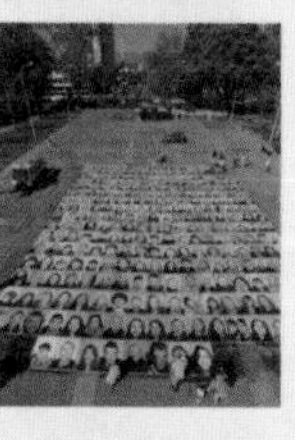
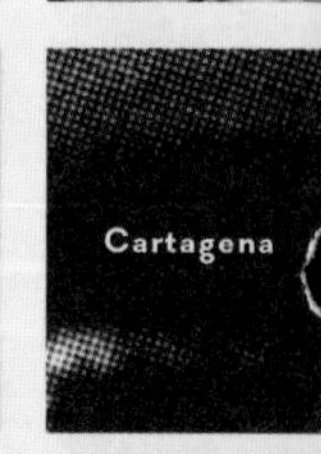

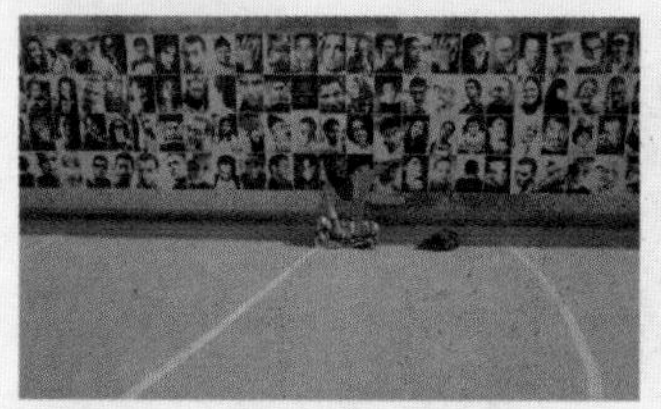
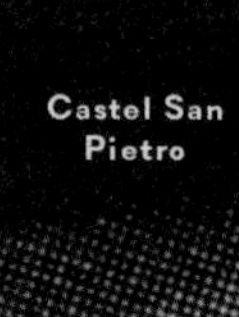

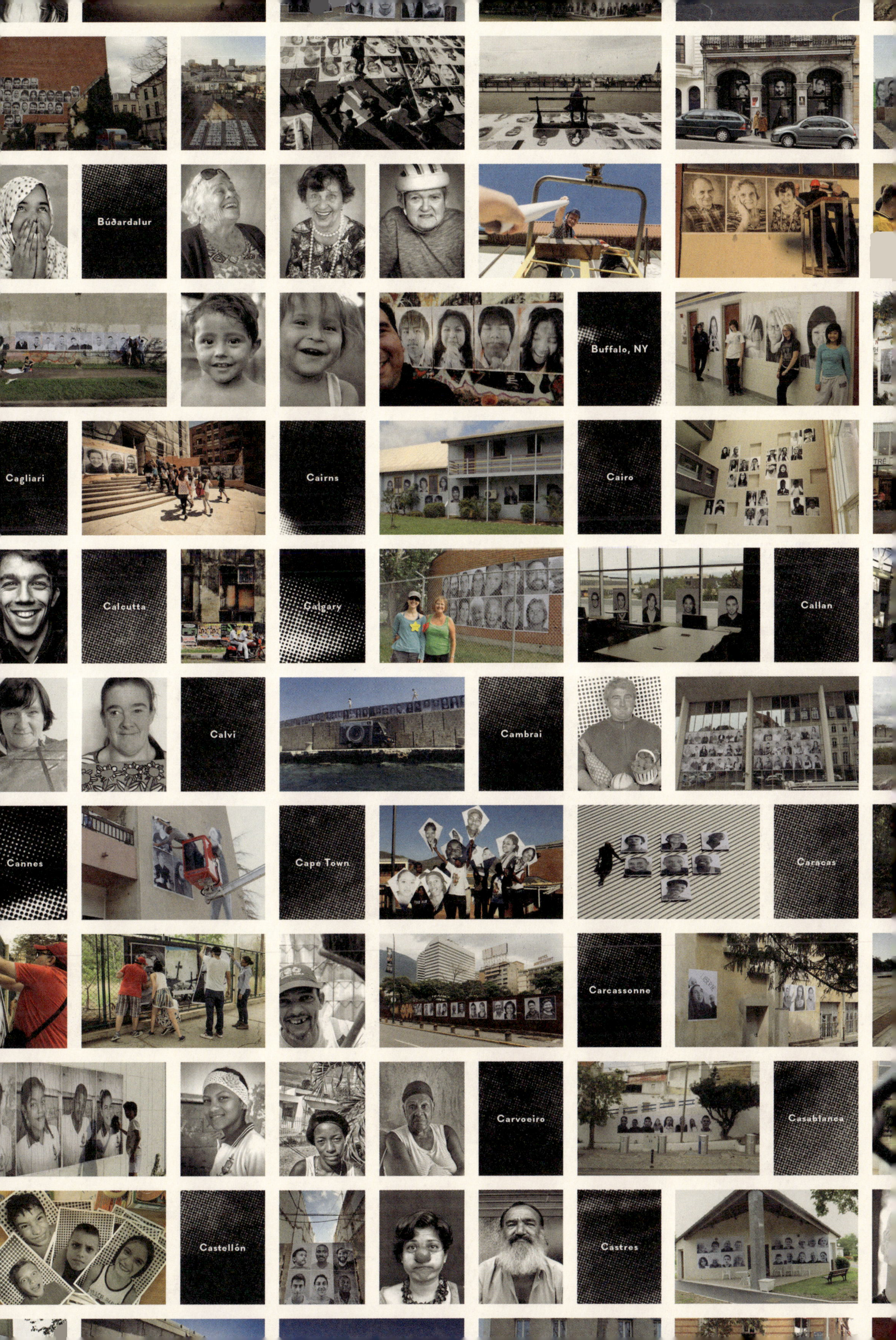
Búðardalur
Buffalo, NY
Cagliari
Cairns
Cairo
Calcutta
Calgary
Callan
Calvi
Cambrai
Cannes
Cape Town
Caracas
Carcassonne
Carvoeiro
Casablanca
Castellón
Castres

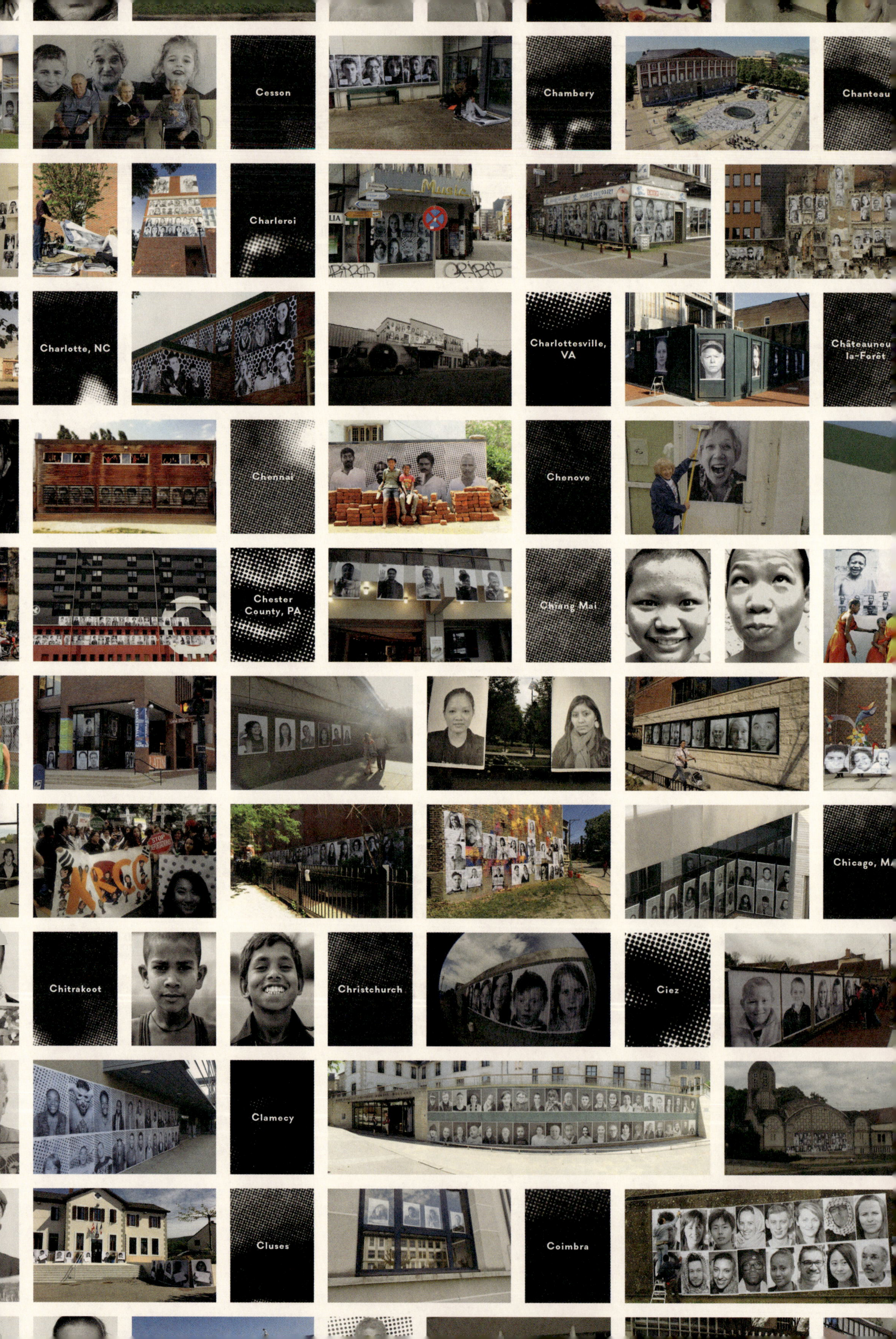
Cesson
Chambery
Chanteau
Charleroi
Charlotte, NC
Charlottesville, VA
Châteauneu la-Forêt
Chennai
Chenove
Chester County, PA
Chiang Mai
Chicago, M
Chitrakoot
Christchurch
Ciez
Clamecy
Cluses
Coimbra

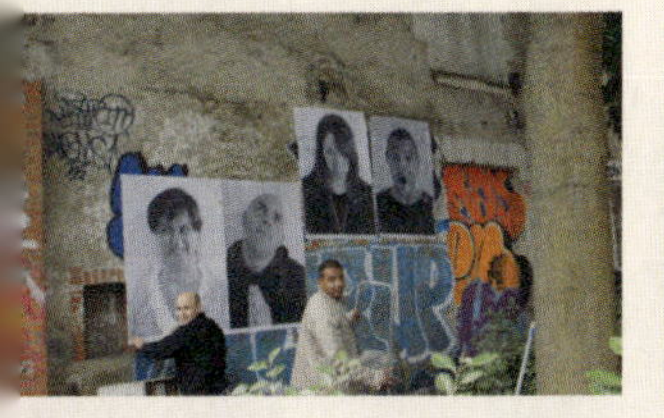

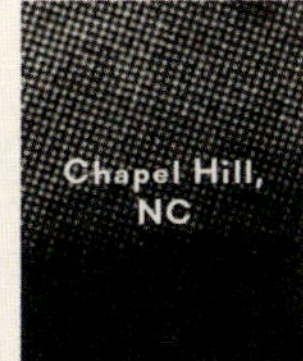

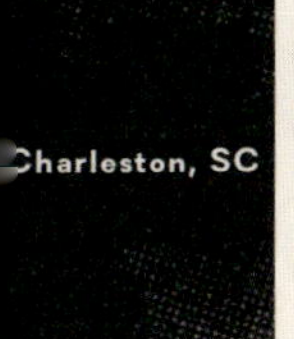

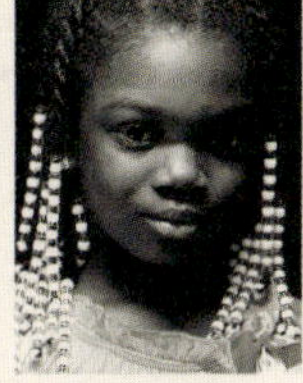

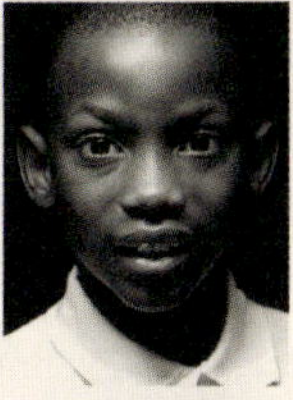

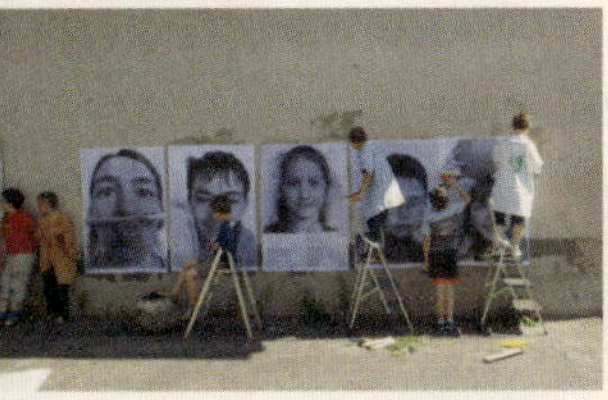

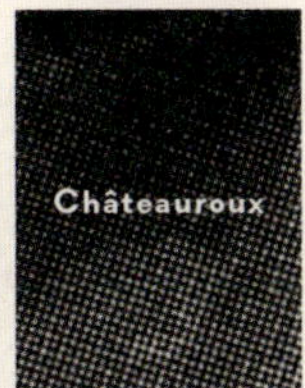

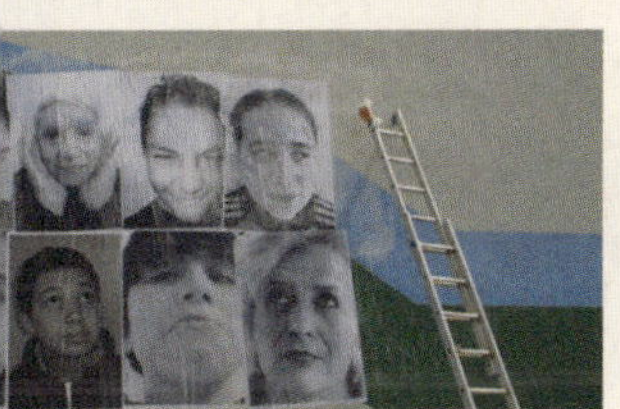

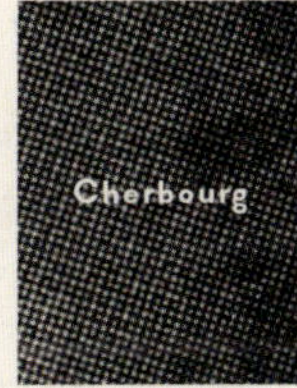

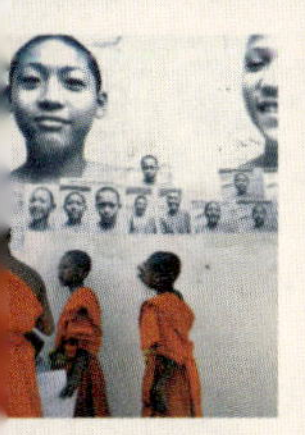

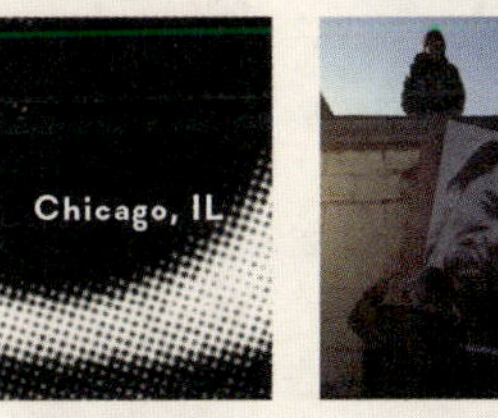

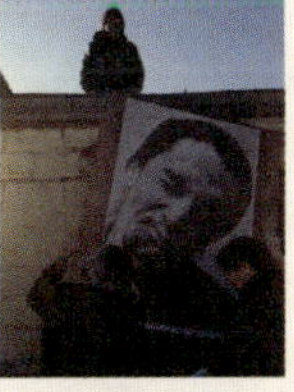

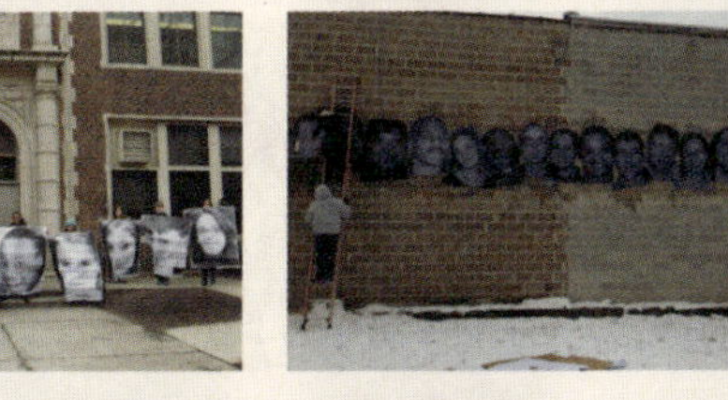

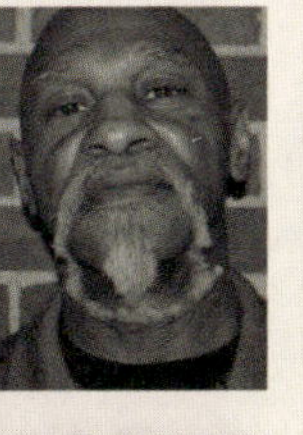

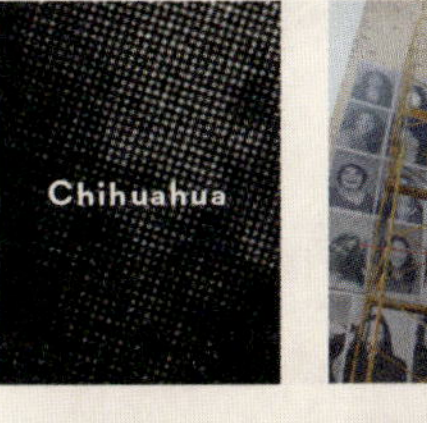

Cincinnati, OH

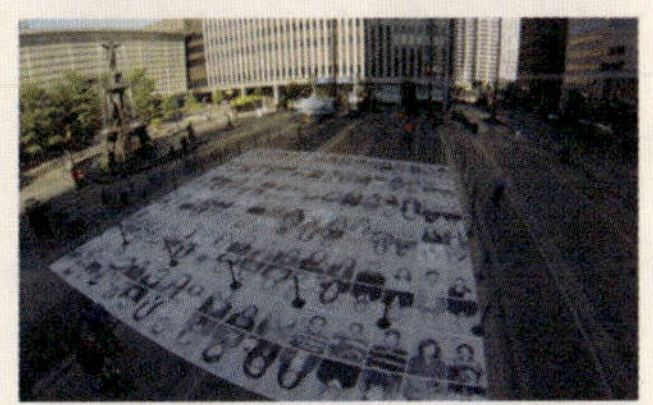

Clarafond

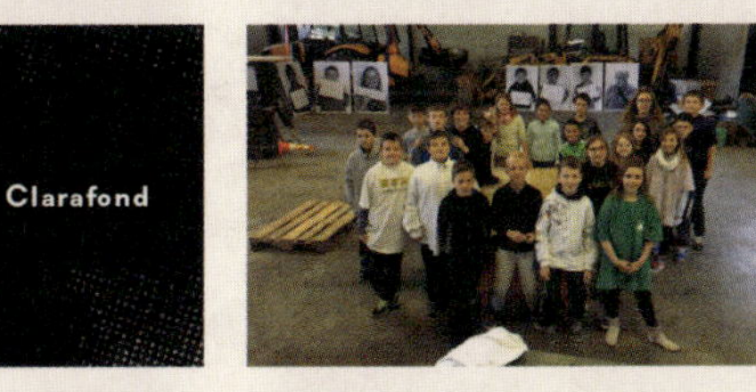

Cologny

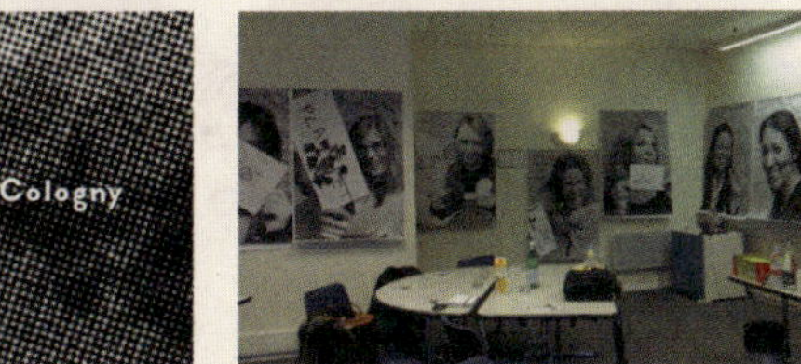

Caracas, Venezuela Somos Uno, November 2015. Since 1999 in Venezuela the people have tried to make a difference between those who support the government and those who are against. In the end we are all Venezuelans. We all want to live in peace, equal opportunities, and prosperity.

The Faces of Luis Brito, November 2015. Luis Brito died earlier this year; he was one of the most important photographers of the country, award-winning, and a leader of social causes. Brito's work was devoted to creating awareness. His close-up portraits of ordinary people delivered the message of the importance of the history of a country from the perspective of the ordinary people. They confront us with the necessity to recognize and accept each other, with the goal of building a community.

Never Forgetting, November 2011. When your child is murdered, you become branded, like cattle. When you lose a child you are uninterested in the sun; and the sun rises every day, even if you prefer staying in the dark. One thing that has helped with this process of grieving is updating my blog in his memory. The blog became a little window for me to talk to people without being seen. When I am at the computer I have to appear courageous because they think I am brave. I do it all because I need my son's name everywhere. No one should forget about him. There are a lot of Taners in this country.

Carcasonne, France "Vivre Ensemble #InsideOut au Collège Varsovie", April 2015. The goal of this action is to express the idea that each middle school student can live without adversely bothering other students and shouldn't let other students bother them.

Carouge, Switzerland Reflets, April 2015. "An open city at the crossroads of destinies and diversity."

Cartagena, Colombia Inside Out Cartegena, December 2013. We aspire to celebrate a series of identities that offer a unique perspective through which the community sees itself reflected.

Carvoeiro, Portugal P. P. Family, December 2014. The reality is not what people say. The bad reputation of the Poço Partido community is not what people generally believe. If you need help, there is always somebody who is there for you to give you a hand. Our unity is our strength.

Casablanca, Morocco Expressing What's Inside, August 2011. We made people smile and express their feelings. It was interesting to discover that in Morocco people have a huge need to express what they feel inside, and it is not as easy at it sounds. They have so much to say but they keep it inside.

Castel San Pietro Terme, Italy Finding Emotions—Emozioni Cercasi, September 2016. All children know what emotions are, but sometimes it is difficult for them to explain them.

Castellón, Spain Faces of an Intercultural City, October 2012. Faces of an Intercultural City aims to raise awareness of the deep cultural diversity present in this small town of the Mediterranean coast of Spain, which resides in a highly conservative political environment.

Castres, France Inside Out Castres, January 2016. "Lifelines Castres" (Lignes de Vies) aims to combat the loneliness and isolation of the elderly in nursing homes and to foster exchanges between different generations.

Cesson, France Identité Collective / Identité Personnelle, May 2016. How to exist and assert oneself when individual liberties are rattled.

Chanteau, France No Religion Too, July 2013. A reflection on the negatives of organized religion.

Chapel Hill, NC Water in Our World, February 2013. At UNC, we celebrate water and its central role in giving, sustaining, and enhancing life, knowing that with water we thrive.

Charleroi, Belgium Inside Out Smile, May 2012. To show the smiling faces of the Charleroi people during the Urban Art Biennale.

Charlotte, NC Faces of Myers Park High School, May 2014. To celebrate the diversity of our student body at Myers Park High School. We have approximately 3,000 students on our campus, from all over the world. This project is in honor of them.

Charlottesville, VA Protecting Mountains from Mountaintop Removal, April 2012. The individuals portrayed here are active in the movement to end mountaintop removal (MTR). MTR is a rapidly growing industry that affects central and southern Appalachia: Kentucky, West Virginia, Virginia, and Tennessee. These activists are defending their homes and their very lives.

Châteauneuf-la-Forêt, France S'ouvrir au Monde et à la Connaissance pour Mieux se Respecter, June 2014. Open yourselves to the world and knowledge in order to know yourselves better. Because culture, art, and sports help us understand ourselves better, live in society, and therefore respect ourselves.

Châteauroux, France On Voit Loin! June 2014. We want to send a message of support to children from all countries who don't have the same opportunities as we do in France, and who fight to get the most basic rights respected, the way Malala fought for the right to go to school.

Chennai, India Inside Out India, September 2014. In Chennai, Gopi and a group of embroiderers have decided to pay tribute to their craft. The message is: "We are proud to be embroiderers."

Chenove, France Affichez-Vous!, December 2013. Our neighborhood is deeply changing and the face of our city evolves. We want this change, we want to live better, together. We re-appropriated our environment peacefully, to state: "We are here."

Cherbourg, France Tous Humains?, April 2016. The goal is to get children to analyze and compare their lives to the lives of children from the 1930s, child workers, and today's migrant children—by linking their portraits with pictures of these other children.

Chester County, PA You Don't Need a Label / Legacy of Arts / Inspiring Lions, February 2014. Never give up on a talent but use it to make God proud.

Chiang Mai, Thailand The Faces of Monastic Life, January 2012. Showing new faces of the monastic life through portraits of samaneras (monk novices).

Chicago, IL Embracing Cultural Heritage, June 2016. We are more than just Americans, more than just kids, more than who you think we are. In a school community where thirty-five languages are spoken, we represent current and past immigrant cultures. We are a country, a city, a school that strives to honor and accept cultural heritage.

KRCC Supports CIR! August–September 2013. The Korean American Resource and Cultural Center supports comprehensive immigration reform because it affects our families and immigrant communities across the country.

Chicago Teachers: Inside Out, March 2012. The project aims to turn Chicago schools inside-out and present a positive view of teachers in the community.

Undocumented and Unafraid with the Jane Addams Hull-House Museum, August 2012. To share our stories publicly, as undocumented members of this country, bringing forth our existence and realities.

Inside Out Common Cup, February 2012. Common Cup, artists' group.

Latin School of Chicago, January 2011. Celebrating and affirming our community members who were born outside the United States.

The Post-Industrial City, January 2012. Putting pictures of people around neighborhoods may produce the effect of social reflection; a reflection that will challenge people to question our current state of apathy and the "stranger" state. It will reinvigorate that impulse that we all have had within us since infancy: empathy. The best way to conjure up that feeling is to see another human face. To look in their eyes and analyze their expressions. To realize that they are you, with a different set of experiences and memories and a different perspective that is just as valid to them as your experiences are to you. The realization that we are one. All of Chicago is one!

Aware Chicago Students, November 2011. We care about making positive changes in our world, our environment, our community, our school, our space. We value where we have come from and where we can go, the opportunities we have to express ourselves, the people that care, and every day we live.

Chihuahua, Mexico Se'Wa'Chih—New Strong Generation Women, March 2014. In recent years, Chihuahua has gone through a strong wave of violence in which a large number of women were victims of femicide, which left a hole not only in their families' worlds, but also in their communities. This concern has generated a revolutionary attitude, driving us to bring out our best: we, the women.

Christchurch, New Zealand Faces of a Bright Future, November 2012. After two years of deadly earthquakes that resulted in the displacement of thousands of people, many losing their homes as well as a central city, which was demolished. We were inspired to fill the massive voids of destruction.

Clamecy, France Visages en Fête, June 2016. Visages en Fête is a gift to our city to show its diversity, its identity, and its vitality.

Clarafond, France La Mémoire pour Faire le Lien, May 2016. To commemorate the Second World War, we want to create intergenerational interactions around the themes of the duty of remembrance, peace, and solidarity.

Cluses, France Projet Inside Out au Lycée Charles Poncet, May 2015. Each participant chose a value he wanted to represent and wrote it down on his face or his arm in order to demonstrate that we all share the same essential common values necessary to a thrinving community.

Coimbra, Portugal Eu Sou Saharaui, April 2014. "Freedom means the supremacy of human rights everywhere. Our support goes to those who struggle to gain those rights and keep them. Our strength is our unity of purpose. To that high concept there can be no end save victory." —Franklin D. Roosevelt

Cologny, Switzerland Transformation, February 2013. Our group is composed of fourteen pictures with a letter on each picture that, when posted together, spell "transformation."

Columbus, OH Columbus Inside/Out, November 2011. While the city leaders aim to position Columbus as "Open and Smart," to be competitive for jobs, the Columbus Inside/Out project aims to reinforce the central core that makes up this dynamic city: the diversity of its citizens and their contributions to our Midwestern values, sensibilities, and explorations.

Compiegne, France Preconceptions in Compiegne, January 2012. To fight against preconceptions about students in Technical High Schools.

Cordoba, Argentina The National Museum of Fine Art, October 2012. We pasted on an enormous abandoned art museum that only operated for four months back in 2000! It is destined to become a new area of lots for fancy apartments and we want to remind people about its history and what it promised: for construction jobs, most times the budget of the actual construction is reduced to less than 30 percent by the time everyone in the chain takes their cut of the money.

Cork, Ireland Gamer's United, July 2011. The clear common ground in the area is gaming. These different groups of people are all united by this passion. It's time to stop judging people based on appearance, and think about what unites us.

Cormeilles-En-Parisis, France Dernière Année au Collège, April 2014. This group action helps us keep alive the memory of this past year spent together and show the links that unite us all.

Cosne-Cours-sur-Loire, France Visages de Quartier—Face Cachée, July 2013. Show and Hide: hidden faces of the neighborhood.

Cournon D'Auvergne, France Environmental Awareness, March 2013. To make other students and the school staff aware of societal and environmental issues that we wish to denounce.

Cúcuta, Colombia Cúcuta con la Frente en Alto, October 2015. In Cúcuta we are more than a border. I raise my voice because #CúcutaEsMiCasa. And you, what do you stand for? I am from the land where Colombia was born, the cradle of coffee, the place where the border receives the whole world, where the encounter of culture enriches the Cúcuta. I belong to the place where the green of the trees intertwines with the breeze and human warmth. Today more than ever we are a soul because we declare ourselves proud Cúcutans of our land and our people; this is the pearl of the north, the "house of elves:" Gran Colombia.

Cuges-les-Pins, France Passages Nomades, December 2013. We wish to reveal exchanges and sharing between wandering artists and the residents of Cuges, who discover artworks: the encounter between those who give to see and those who see, between those who give to perceive and those who perceive.

Culver City, CA Different & Proud, April 2014. Culver City High School, is an amazing school. Our school is unique because it is filled with different races and cultures, which enables students to learn and understand each individual's differences. There is no racial tension and racial divides is the last thing a student here has to worry about. We want to celebrate diversity, appreciate the variety of cultures, and value the differences in race here at Culver City High School.

Dakar, Senegal, and Paris, France Sur le Chemin de l'École, April 2014. School access in Senegal should no longer be a gamble but a right, for all.

Darkhan, Mongolia The Power of Cooperation, July 2013. A person can't do everything alone. People always do things together. This is called the power of cooperation. There's a Mongolian proverb that says, "A single twig cannot become a bonfire. A single person cannot become a family."

Dayton, KY Art Building Communities, April 2012. We are making changes through art to help bring life back to our inner cities.

Debar, Macedonia The Eyes of Hope, July 2013. We, the youth of our city. We, the future of our city want to emit hope into the hearts of our fellow citizens. We stand here in our city as figures of promise that our city can move on, after twenty devastating years. We are here to say, and say it loudly, that there is hope in our town.

Delta, Canada "We Are People Too"—Students for Syrian Refugees, April 2016. Through anonymous portraiture, capturing just the eyes of our affiliate volunteers, we are using the power of art and photography to transcend cultural barriers, differences, and misrepresentation in hopes of reaching people's inner humanity allowing them to realize that "WE ARE PEOPLE TOO!"

Denver, CO Not Exactly Homeless, July 2013. We are a group of six artists in Denver, Colorado. Homelessness is a pervasive condition that has affected each of us. The intent of our group is to put a familiar, friendly face on a homeless person. To bring humanity to the issue. It has been through the creative process that we have elevated ourselves and raised community consciousness. We want to stimulate dialogue and bridge the gap in our city.

Derby, Australia My Face, Our Place, October 2013. My Face, Our Place cuts through social divisions and celebrates diversity and humanity in our city. There are deep social divides in Derby, and because of its remote location there is a large population of fly-in, fly-out workers. This action developed out of a desire to see positive community messages being communicated through public art.

Des Moines, IA Harmony Within Diversity, April 2016. Recognizing Mount Rainier High School as a place where different people from various ethnicities come to create one singular community, and by portraying young individuals and their messages, we wish to create one singular and understanding community.

Devon, England Identities Through Art, April 2012. Creating art which expresses the way we each construct and build our identities, often through strategies we develop to overcome our fears and obstacles in life—the result being strength in adversity and self-belief.

Dhaka, Bangladesh The Soulside Out, May 2013. The Bangladesh action is in honor of the millions of women working in the Bengali garment industry: leading the struggle for socio-economic justice in one of the world's poorest, and most densely populated countries now synonymous with sweatshops.

Donzy, France Who is Donzy?, February 2012. Who am I?

Dresden, Germany World Picture, July 2013. One hundred artists participated and used their notes as carriers of personal thoughts and/or questions about the economy. The notes were sent May 20, 2013 via helium balloons and witnessed by an Inside Out Project group action photo installation. These pictures went though the earth's atmosphere and into the stratosphere.

Dreux, France Des Chibanis et des Ados, November 2016. "Les Chibanis" of Dreux are Moroccan war veterans who have put their lives on the line for France. Today, they live in precarious conditions, isolated and forgotten. Our students have met them to tell their stories, so they do not fall in oblivion. Memory lives through different generations.

Dronero, Italy Build Up Your Future While Laughing, May 2013. Our project mirrors the day-to-day realities of many Italian small towns and villages. There, there aren't all the possibilities that big cities offer, but despite this young people react and try in every way to carry on with their passions and their projects for the future. Our project is specifically dedicated to them; in particular, to those who are resolute

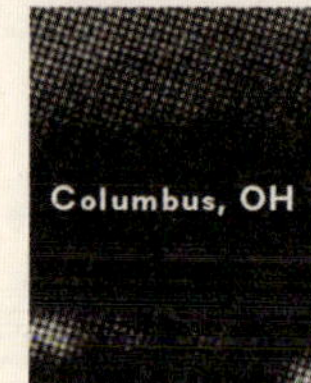

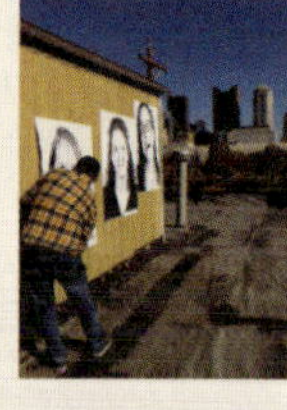
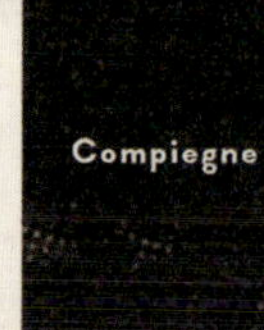

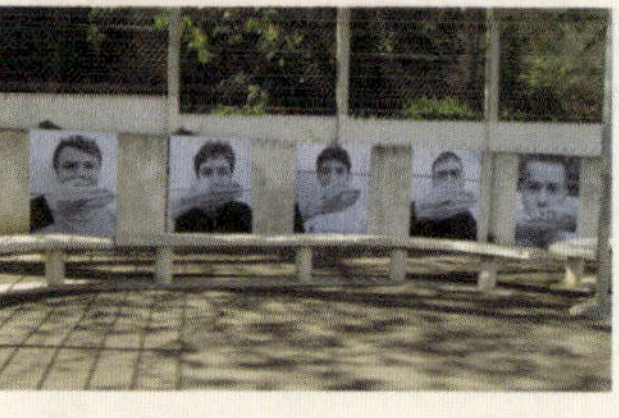
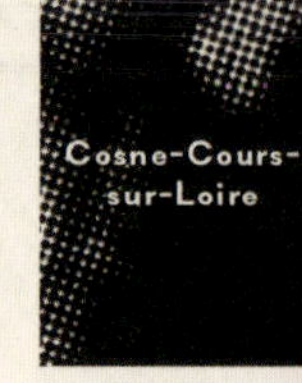

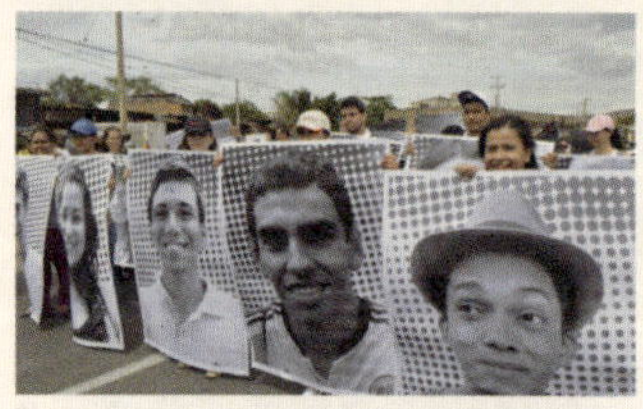
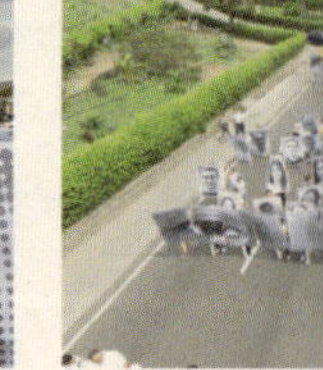
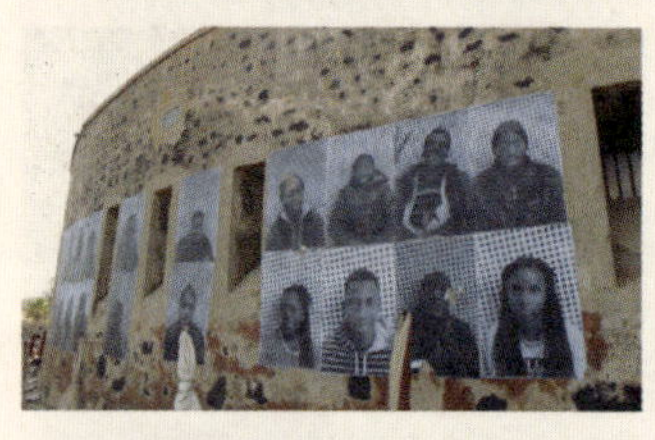
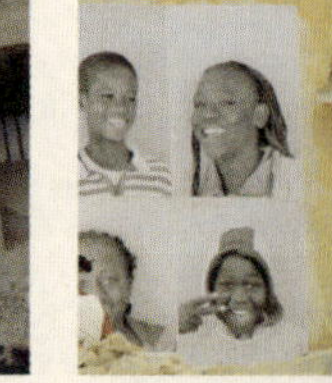
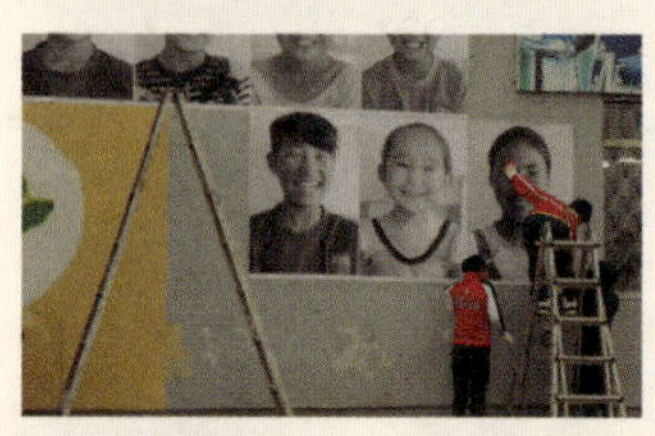
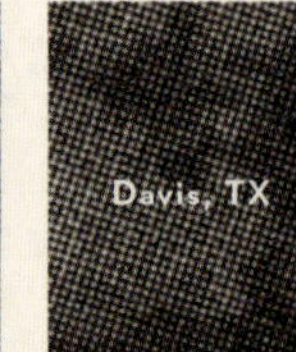

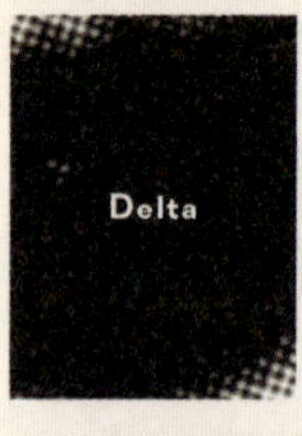

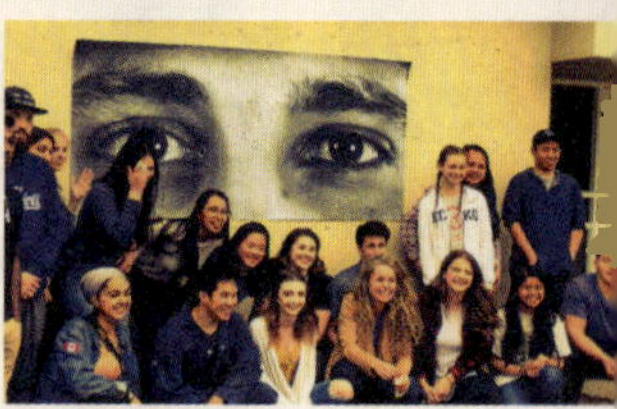
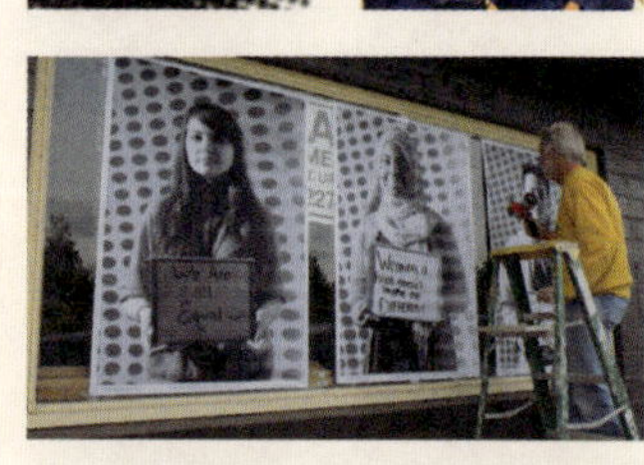
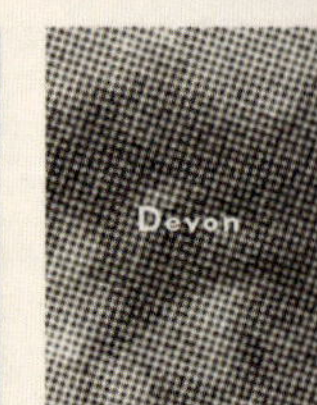

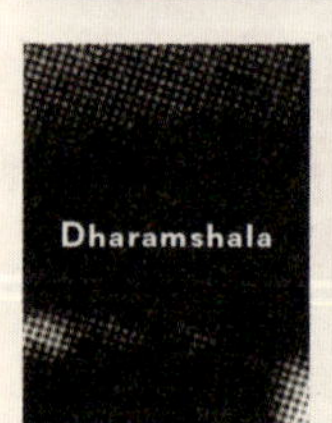

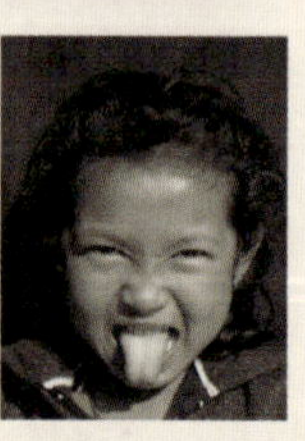
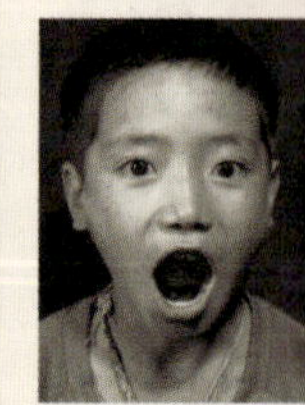
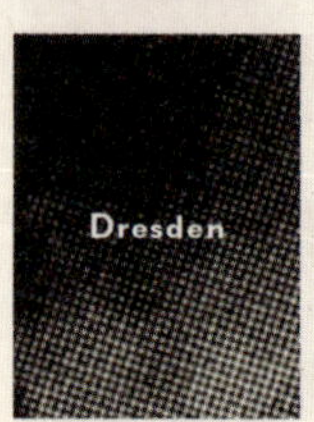

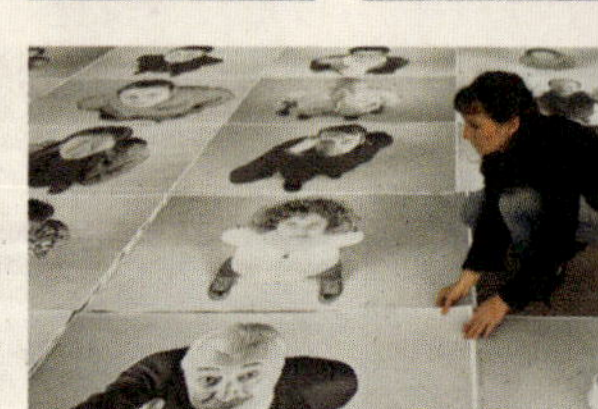
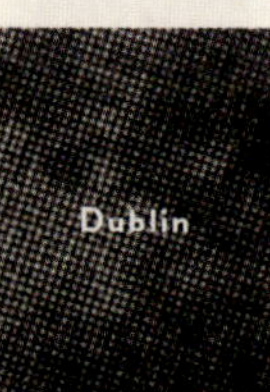

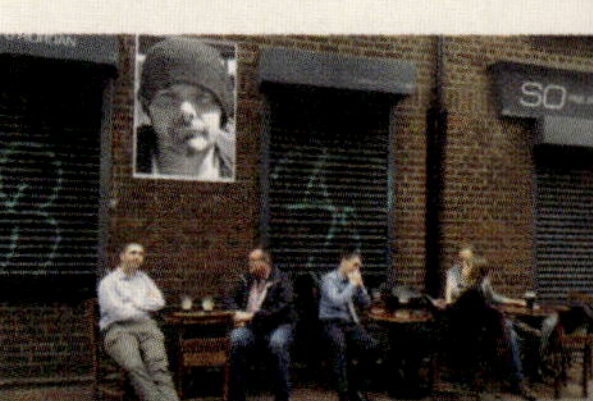

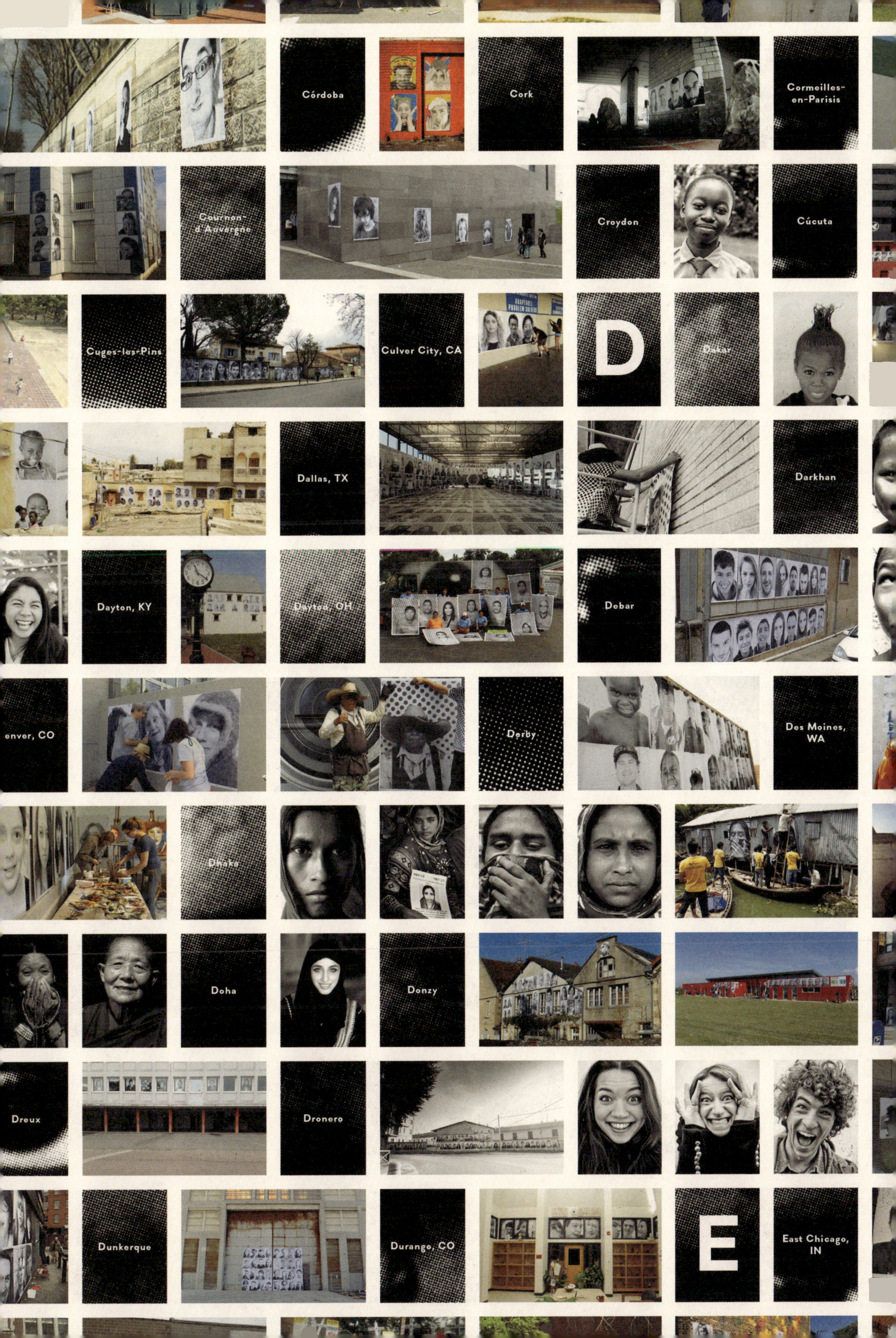
Córdoba
Cork
Cormeilles-en-Parisis
Cournon-d'Auvergne
Croydon
Cúcuta
Cuges-les-Pins
Culver City, CA
D
Dakar
Dallas, TX
Darkhan
Dayton, KY
Dayton, OH
Debar
enver, CO
Derby
Des Moines, WA
Dhaka
Doha
Donzy
Dreux
Dronero
Dunkerque
Durango, CO
E
East Chicago, IN

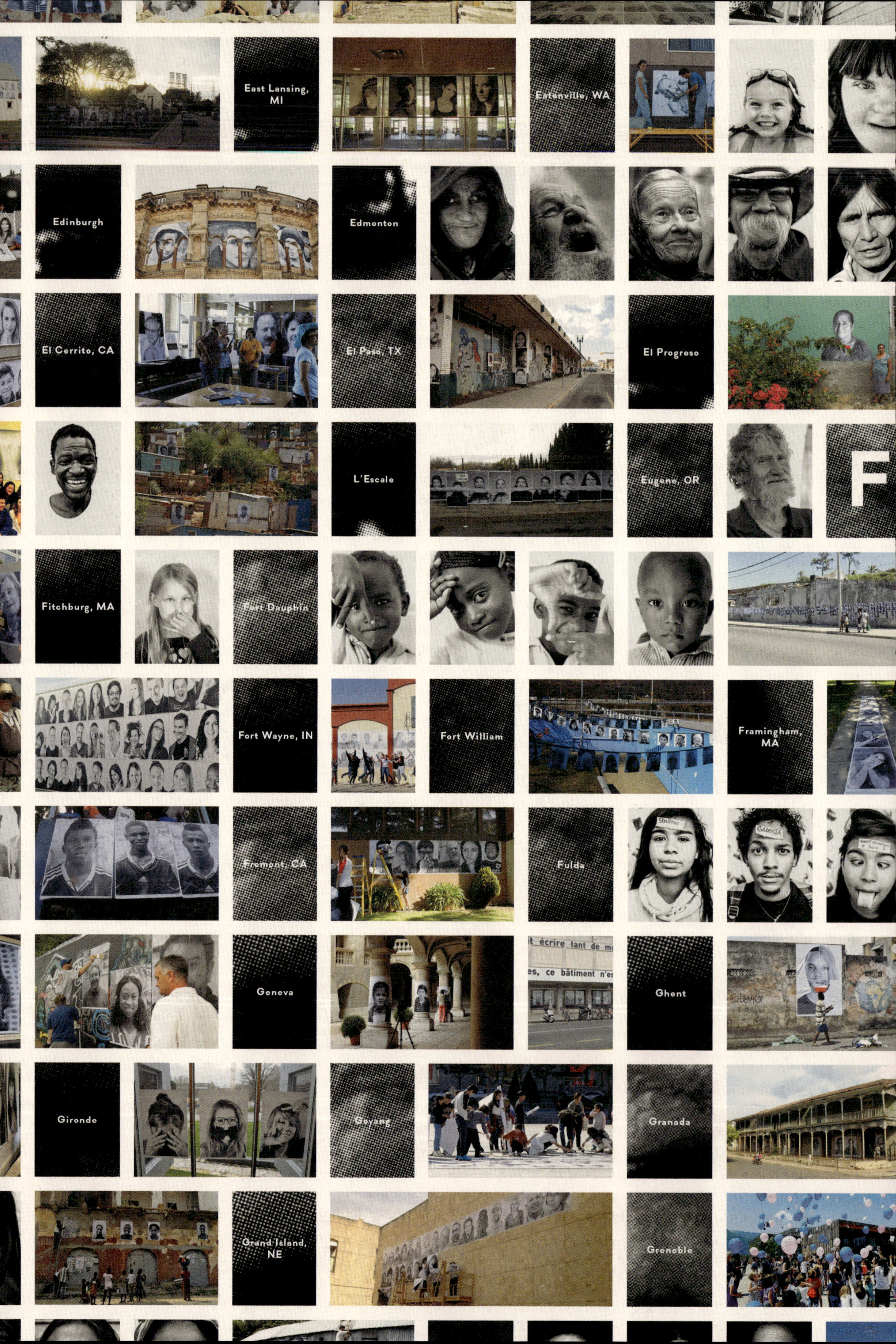
East Lansing, MI
Eatonville, WA
Edinburgh
Edmonton
El Cerrito, CA
El Paso, TX
El Progreso
L'Escale
Eugene, OR
F
Fitchburg, MA
Fort Dauphin
Fort Wayne, IN
Fort William
Framingham, MA
Fremont, CA
Fulda
Geneva
Ghent
Gironde
Goyang
Granada
Grand Island, NE
Grenoble

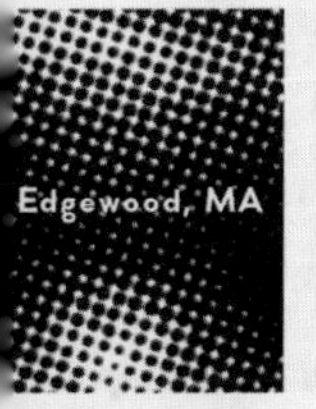

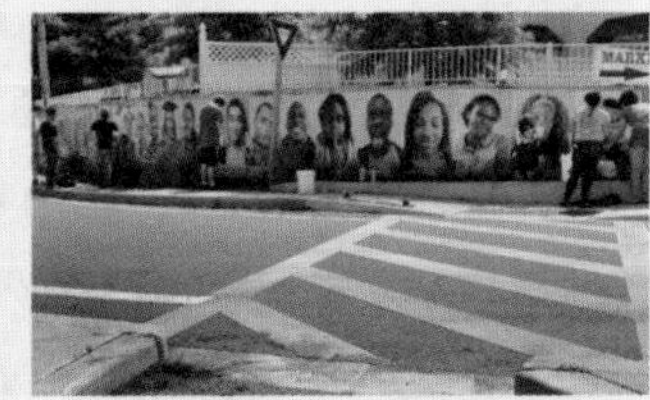
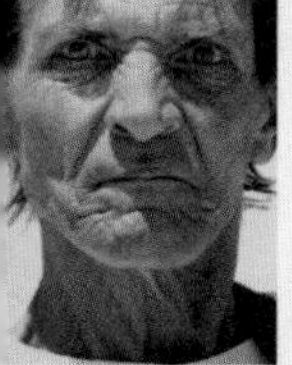
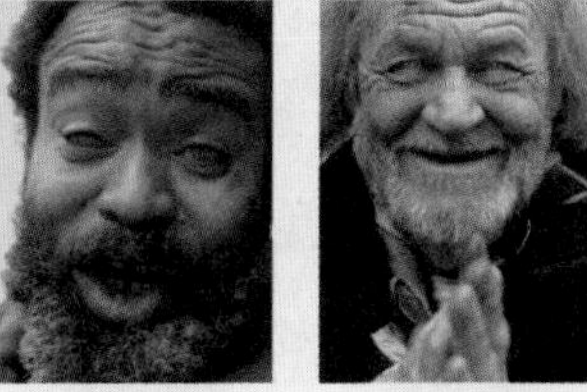
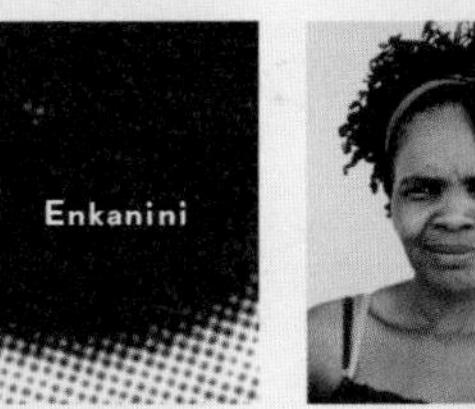

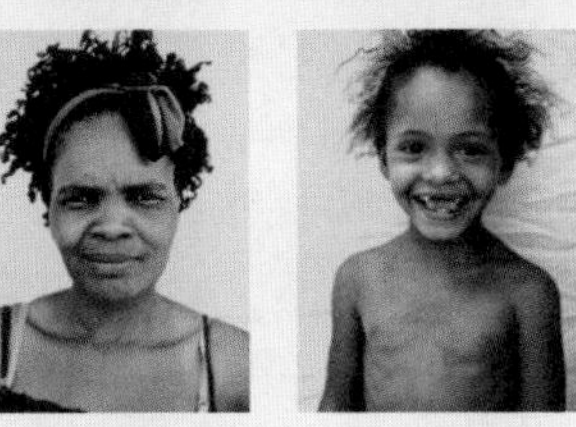
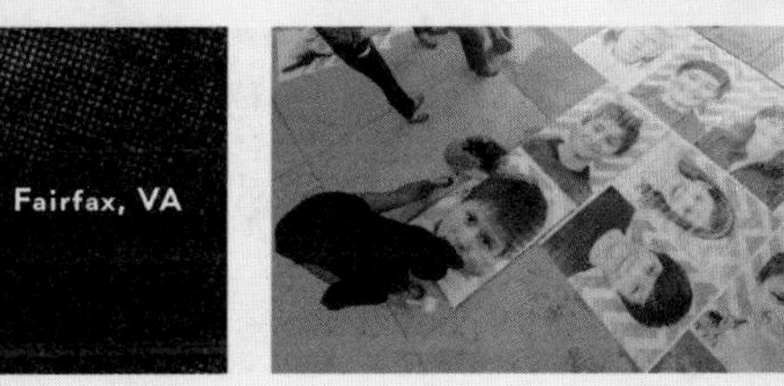

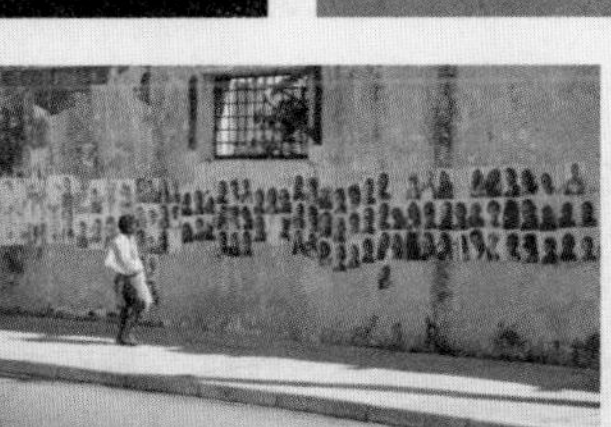
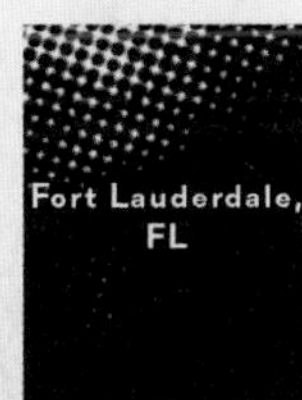

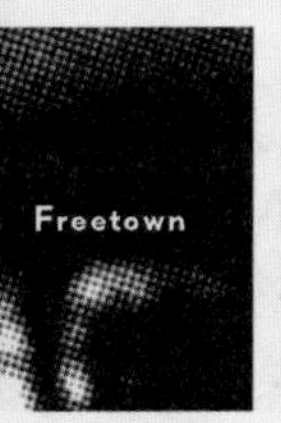

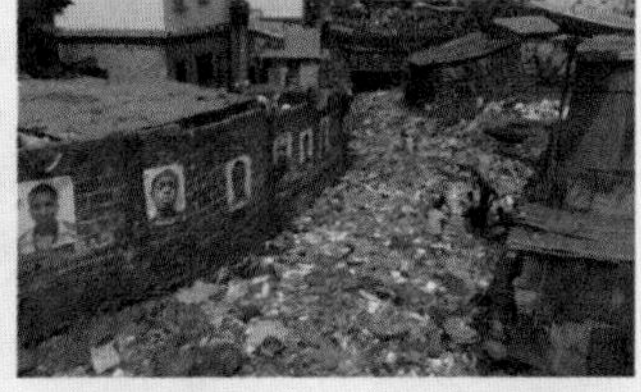
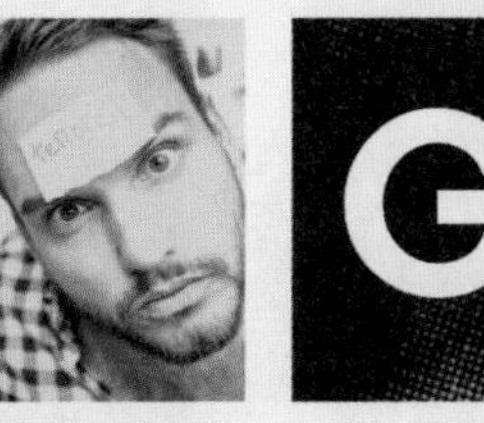
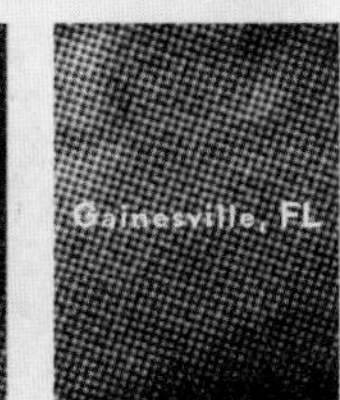

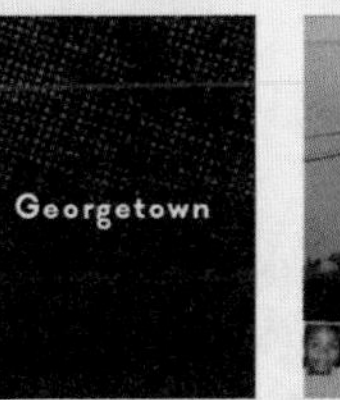

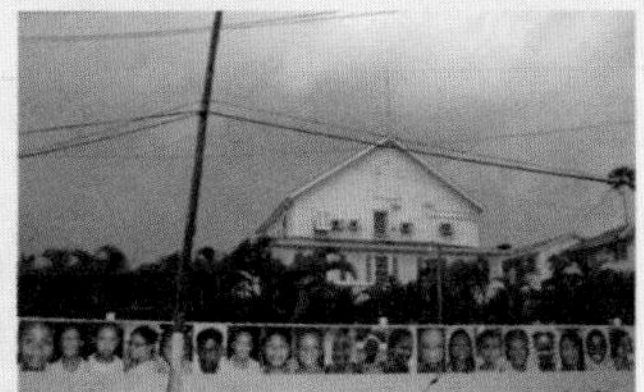
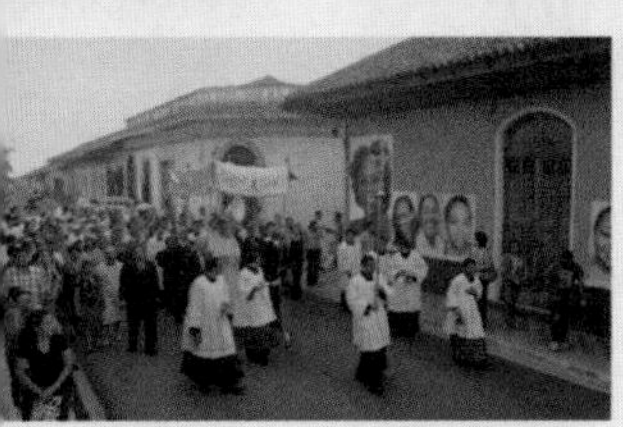
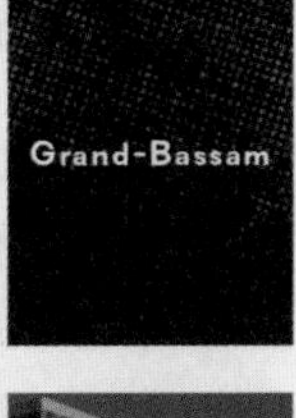

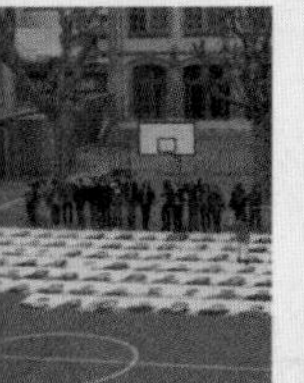
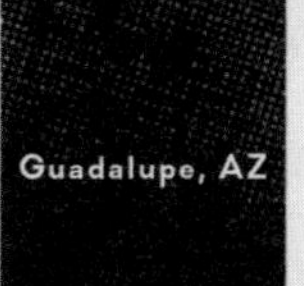

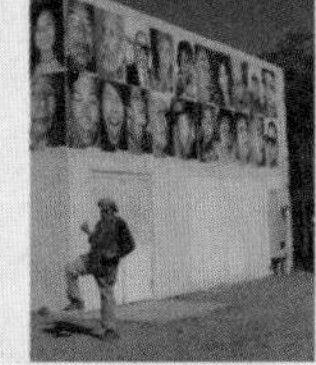

and joyful and don't allow themselves to be unduly influenced by what surrounds them.

Dublin, Ireland Faceless, August 2015. The subject matter is people who have come to hard times and ended up living on the streets in my community. I approached these people and explained what I was doing, then sat with them for a while and heard their stories of shattered homes, addiction, jail, emigration, and hope.The title of this project reflects on how we pass these people by around the world and not see them.

A Shared Passion, February 2013. We are a group of students from Dublin. Coming from different age groups, nationalities, and paths of life we want to express the passion for photography and art that connects us and other people in this city and all over the world.

Dunkerque, France Une Jeunesse Heureuse à Dunkerque, May 2014. I would like to prove that it's possible to be young and happy in Dunkerque, because a lot of young people leave my city to a bigger one where they can have a good job and more cultural facilities.

Durango, CO Getting Out of the Box, October 2011. Students are so often contained within the confines of a desk, a classroom, a school, and the general education system that does not necessarily fit their identity. We wanted to make a statement about how these confines can limit their creative abilities.

East Chicago, IL I Am Marktown, June 2015. We are the faces of Marktown, a century-old workers' community nestled between steel mills and an oil refinery in northwest Indiana. Though on the National Register of Historic Places, the neighborhood's future is in jeopardy as British Petroleum—our neighbor—continues to purchase and demolish our homes.

East Lansing, MI The Curator as Artist, April 2012. We were really interested in portraits as a way of seeing and sharing different perspectives.

Eatonville, FL In Spite of the Rain, July 2011. We want to showcase some of the identities of the people who normally stay indoors because of the rain.

Edgewood, MD This Is Edgewood High School, May–July 2013. As individuals, and more importantly, as a community, the goal of this project is to pull back the veil of misconception that plagues the mindset of the students at Edgewood High School and the surrounding areas. With our heads held high, we say with pride; "I am Edgewood, we are Edgewood, this is Edgewood!"

Edinburgh, Scotland Fringeee, August 2011. Narrative of old and new theater-goers . . . engineers . . . actors . . . the local community.

Edmonton, Canada Souls of the Street, May 2016. This project is to give a voice to the homeless, people who often are ignored, forgotten, and unnoticed.

El Progreso, Honduras Portraits Missing, December 2011. We would like to create a group to photograph these women and paste them up in their communities and town centers to give homage to their strength and struggles.

Enkanini, South Africa Embedding Character and Leadership, June 2012. Marginalized Muslim students at an Islamic school in an afterschool project using art as a vehicle for embedding character and leadership.

Fairfax, VA Bonnie Brae Community, April 2016. The term "Bonnie Brae" means "pleasant hill" in Gaelic. This project exemplifies the pride and love we have for our community and one another.

Fort Dauphin, Madagascar Tolagnaro Izahay, September 2014. Even on the other side of France, people live and add a contribution to the world. Madagascar, the Red Island, the Continent Island is not left behind.

Fort Lauderdale, FL Inside Out Fort Lauderdale: Faces of Art, September 2013. The objective of our group action is to celebrate the creativity of our city, and to encourage the community to support local art.

Fort Wayne, IN Heroes Among Us, April 2014. We believe that there are heroes everywhere, from the local firefighter to the small-town veteran to the five-time cancer survivor to the smallest boy scout with dreams of accomplishing great things. We urge the community to broaden their definition of hero.

Fort William, Scotland Vibrant Fort William, March 2013. The aim is to portray the vibrancy of local life and in doing so promote solidarity, equality, and community spirit through the portraits.

Framingham, MA The Advocates Community, July 2014. We believe everyone is entitled to the blessing and freedom of self-expression and to live peaceful lives.

Freetown, Sierra Leone Rendering a Helping Hand to the Lost Generation of Sierra Leone, September 2013. To make Sierra Leone a place for all, in all aspects in our lives; and to cultivate a productive nation building toward the transformation of our beloved country by educating the minds of all by offering a change of their circumstances.

To Be or to Have?, September 2012.

Fremont, CA California School for the Deaf, April 2013. Students will have healthy deaf identities through shared experiences, language, culture, history, and society.

Gainesville, FL Get to Know Me, October 2015. Get to Know Me seeks to explore the amazing possibilities that exist when you take the time to get to know someone, rather than making assumptions on just on how a person looks.

Geneva, Switzerland SWAP—Habitat Geneva 2012, August 2012. We are waiting for an automatic system that allows everybody to give their speech from a distance to the Bank of Oaths.

Banque des Serments, September 2016. Banque des Serments is an artistic process to spark new human behaviors.

Il n'y a pas de Murs Entre Nous, March 2014. Claiming new visibility in public spaces for asylum seekers so they are not forgotten.

Ghent, Belgium Lobi c'est Lelo / Biso Na Biso, April 2016. To state that there are no frontiers nor borders if it comes to brotherhood and love, and to give a face and story to the so-called refugees, "Biso na Biso" was created.

Georgetown, Guyana We See Guyana, January 2012. Photos taken by children of other children and adults sending the message "We See," and you must stop violence against our mothers, sisters, aunts, and neighbors.

Gironde, France Advertising IUT Michel de Montaigne Bordeaux III, July 2012. Promoting the sector Advertising IUT Michel de Montaigne Bordeaux III.

Goyang, South Korea You Are the Hope, October 2015. You are our hopes and dreams. You are precious beings. Look at yourselves and build self-confidence.

Granada, Nicaragua Celebrating the Strength of Nicaruaga Women, May 2013. The action is a tribute to the strength and perseverance of the generations of Nicaraguan women, who have always been and continue to be the heart and soul of their country.

Grand Bassam, Ivory Coast Grand Bassam, Januay 2017. We want to give a second wind to Grand Bassam, which has been hurt by several crises and the 2016 terrorist attack. Our aim is to rebuild the historical monuments and bring back tourism.

Grand Island, NE The Faces of Grand Island, May 2014. We are a community of 50,000 people in central Nebraska. Our project is a celebration of the people who live in our city. The portraits will represent every age, gender, and ethnic neighborhood.

Grenoble, France Art to Remember, February 2015. We want to show how art can help memory. We want to show pictures of a man and a woman who survived concentration camps, one picture is from the past, and the other from today.

Art to Educate, March 2013. We can help growing children thanks to art, and expose a positive image to each student and each member of education community.

Guadalupe, AZ August 2011. Throughout time from thousands of years ago until the present these desert people (Yacqui) have celebrated life via their customs, dances, and a desire to rise above the situation to endure.

Guangzhou, China Global Friendship, September 2015. We want to share with the world that despite our borders, we are all human beings.

Guatemala City, Guatemala De Cara à Cara—From Face to Face, September 2015. We are looking to put the candidate's face in front of ours, in order to confront what's imposed alongside the genuine. The parties' propaganda deals with our authenticity.

Guayacan, Venezuela Los Niños de Guayacan—The Guayacan Children, October 2011. Guayacan is a small village that still keeps its traditions, even being surrounded by the most touristy beaches of the island. We took pictures of the kids and will paste them on the boats and on the village's walls and stairs to support the subject: "preserving the innocence."

Hamilton, Canada The Many Faces of Crown Point, October 2016. From business people, to artists, to activists, Hamilton's east end has a vast array of people that all deserve a place in the spotlight. We believe their faces should be remembered, because they all contribute to the neighborhood's identity.

Hanover, Germany The Right To Save, February 2014. We want them to change the financial state of handicapped citizens, to express to the government that things have to change. We want our community to think about this problem.

Hanoi, Vietnam Lullaby of the Streets, March 2015. We wish to launch an art project in the hope of embracing the compassion within our community towards these underprivileged children.

Harare, Zimbabwe Inside Out / The Guardians of Stone—Harare, May 2014. The Guardians of the Stone is a tribute to artists who, despite economic challenges, keep their spirit intact and make the stone alive through their hammer and chisel. The portraits were made in Tengenenge, an African village in the north of Zimbabwe. The village is an open-air gallery, the particularity is that the inhabitants are all stone sculptors of all ages.

Harare, Zimbabwe Untold Stories, April 2013. We seek to inspire some positive change by sharing a few powerful untold stories of hope and compassion. The five mothers featured are dedicated, hardworking, and through their love for their communities have become pillars of strength, worthy of celebration.

Hartford, CT Raising Our Voices to End Gender Injustice, March 2016. We hope these images will encourage and inspire people to raise their voice against gender injustice.

Haryana, India Women of India, September 2015. We chose to photograph only women because being a patriarchal society, women in India are generally relegated to the background of society and not seen outside of their homes as much as men are!

Hautes Bruyères, France Juif—Dignity in Villejuif, June 2012. This is intended to restore dignity to the residents of the neighborhood Hautes-Bruyeres Yvan Guibert.

Havana, Cuba Influencers, May 2015. This project encouraged people to make a difference by helping their community, or offererd something new to people they share common spaces with. The people in the portraits have been involved in projects and activities that reflect the idea of contributing within their community, thus becoming influencers.

Cuba Linda, February 2016. "The cry of the poor is not always just, but if you don't listen to it, you will never know what justice is."

Haverhill, MA Inside Out Haverhill Spirit and Souls, June 2015. Our goal is to celebrate the rich talents of our community. These folks are business owners, children, elderly, artists, chefs, waitstaff, teachers, civil servants, and public officials. No one is excluded. We all contribute to our community.

Hendaye, France Mange Ta Soupe!, June 2016. Through a face, an expression, we want to enlighten the unreasonable comportment of some students.

Hereford, England Herefordshire Farmers: Guardians of the Soil, June 2016. The faces behind the products they buy, and landscapes they see. Supporting the local trade and small business of Hereford, UK.

Hesperia, CA This Is Us, December 2013. Our goal is to break the stereotype that HHS is an old, battered, low-performing campus by highlighting the programs, students, and teachers that make HHS a dynamic, energetic campus.

Holland, MI The Holland Inside Out Project, March 2012. Our goal was to display images depicting the wide range of colorful and vibrant people who live in our area with compassion, sensitivity, and flair.

Homer, AK Homer Rights and Responsibilities, August 2011. Celebrating our fishing culture and working towards a collaborative conversation in Homer about fishing rights and responsibilities.

Hong Kong, China Happy Mother's Day with the French International School in Hong Kong, May 2015. This action was a surprise to all MUMS for the French Mother's Day. The message was clear and simple: MUM I LOVE YOU . . .

Horb am Neckar, Germany The Face of Horb's Youth, July 2013. We are a group of students who want to draw attention to the lack of leisure facilities in our town. Since the cinema closed a few years ago the situation grew even worse, and there are very few places for us and our friends to hang out. With this action we hope to reach a lot of people and draw attention to the limited possibilities young people can have for their free time.

Hudson, NY Children's Rights in Hudson, October 2012. They are watching you. The way you act. The things you say. We want children to know their rights.

L'Île-Saint-Denis, France Projet Babel, March 2016. We want to put forward the diversity and cultural richness of our middle school and town in the context of the annual "Week against racism and discrimination."

Iloilo City, Philippines Inside-Out Iloilo: "What We Stand For", March 2015. The purpose of our project is to be an example of positive change in our community. By reworking expressions and looking outside yourself through this project, we believe that helping to change people's perception about how they look to others could mold and transform them into better people.

Ipswich, MA Perceptions of Beauty, April 2012. Society has shaped women and girls into its own perception of perfection and sadly, most of we "average" females do not meet those standards. With these portraits, high school students challenge perceptions of beauty.

Iquique, Chile Precaria, November 2013. This project seeks to show that whoever sees these faces will be persuaded to reflect on poverty, hope, and social inequality.

Irbid, Jordan We Are Arabs. We Are Humans., January–June 2015. We are thankful for the somewhat calm situation we have today but are sending a message to the world in memory of all the fallen babies, children, parents, and grandparents in the Arab world.

Ishøj, Denmark Empowering Neighborship and Sense of Community, June 2015. Vejleåparken is what you would consider a true modern melting pot. The goal of our group action is to salute the people who live here. By proudly exhibiting the broad variety of people, we seek to raise awareness on neighborship and encourage dialogue as a means to strengthen community engagement and empowerment.

Istanbul, Turkey The Laughingbox, October 2014. We fight for women's rights in Europe!

We Are the Same While We Are Smiling (Smilearity), December 2013. We want to end discriminatory policies in our country. They lead to a societal separation with regard to religion, ethnic origin, and even leads to a gender-based segregation of people, which helps create rampant homelessness.

Be Inspired, November, 2015. All participants were introduced to a long list of creative geniuses, personalities who mastered artistic creation throughout history, and shown how they inspired us.

Ivanhoe, NC North Carolina Artists, April 2014. This gesture aims to bring artists together to create outside of studio spaces, in a public expression of esprit de corps!

Jerusalem, Israel Gifted Students in Jerusalem, December 2016. The Jerusalemite gifted students can sing out of the tune of occupation, and follow their dreams and inspire many others of their ages.

Johannesburg/Rosettenville, South Africa I Wish . . ., October 2014–May 2015. We want to show that Rosettenville has a face made of many faces, and a future made of many wishes that deserve to be seen and deserve to be heard.

Orphans with HIV/AIDS, November 2011. Ubuntu Theatre is creating a play with thirty street children with HIV/AIDS to help remove the stigma that they live under with having AIDS, and to portray them as the heroes they are.

Juárez, Mexico October 2011. We stand for peace in our city, our country, and the world!

Justinópolis, Brazil June 2013. The goal is to show artistic movements' traditions and their diversity among the Brazilian people.

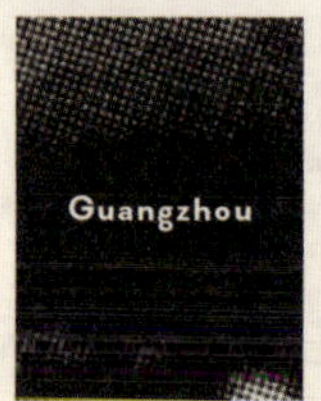

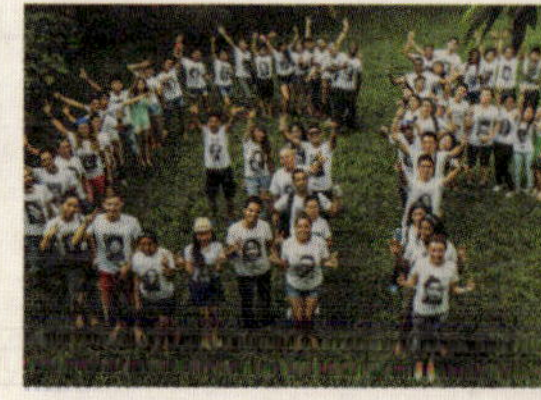
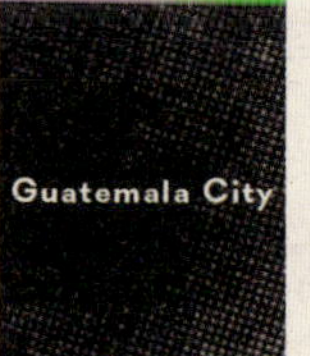

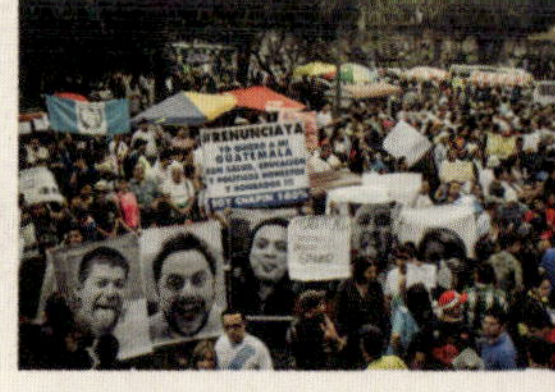
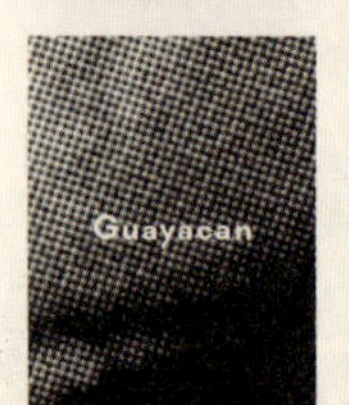

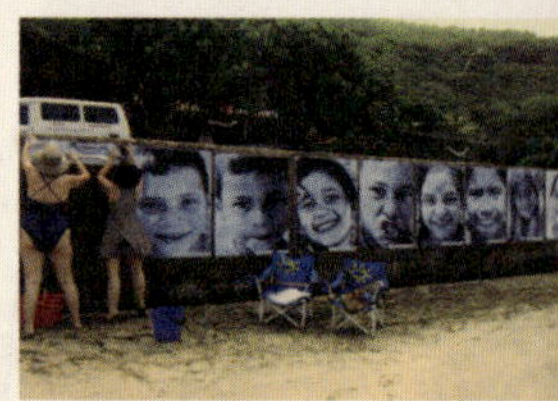
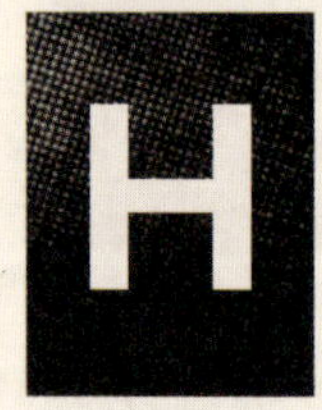

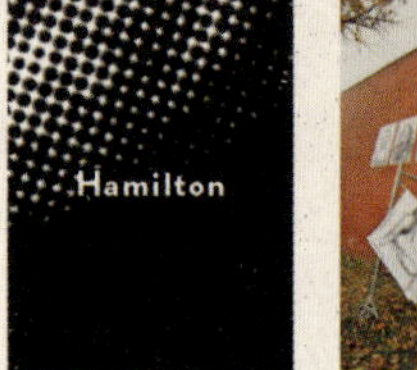

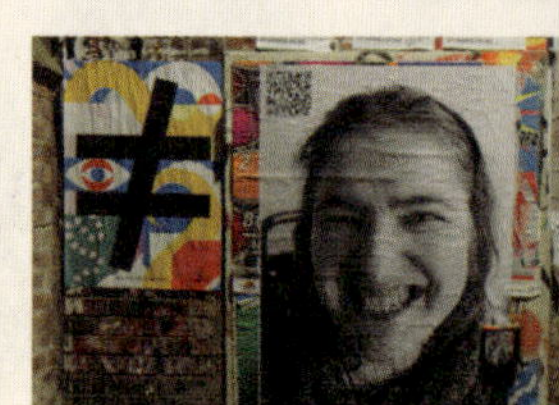
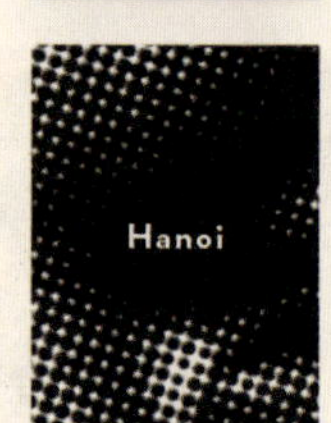

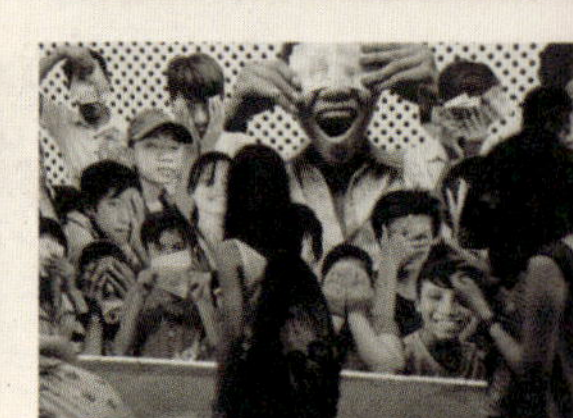
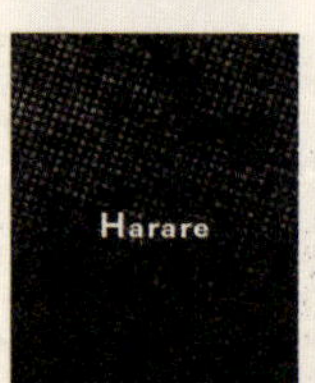

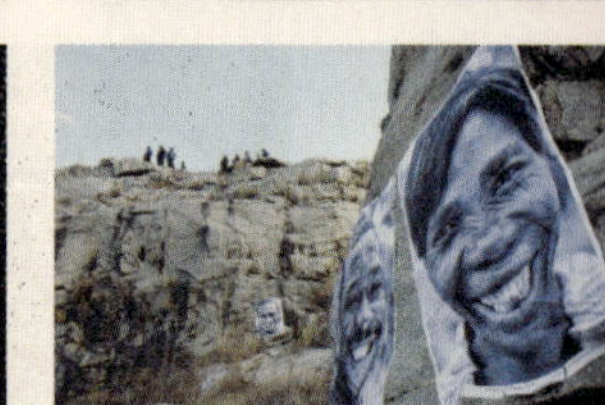
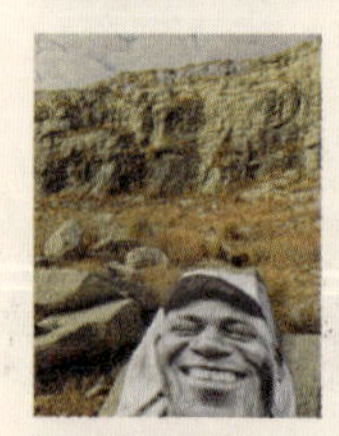
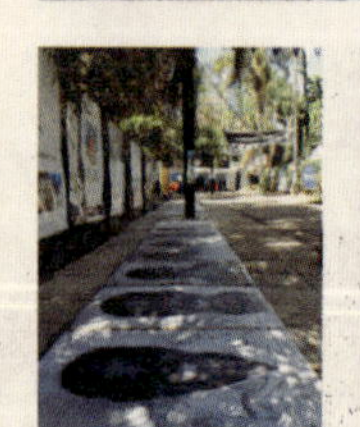
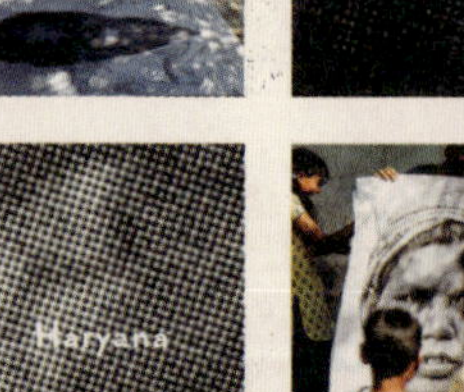
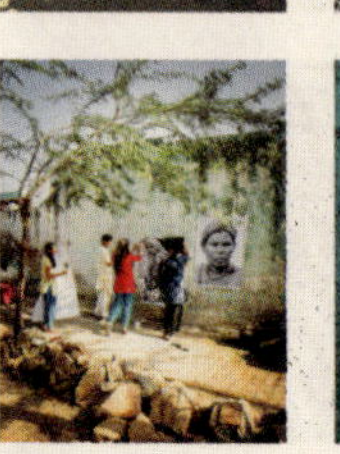
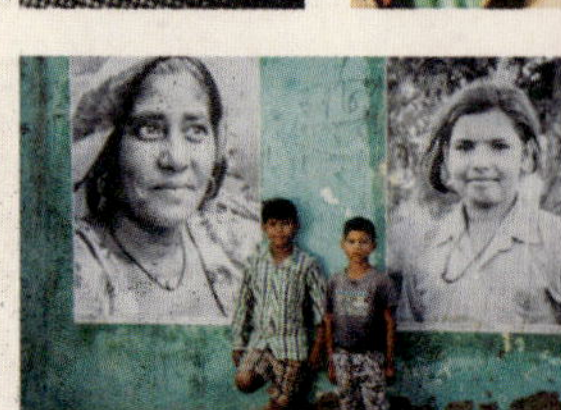

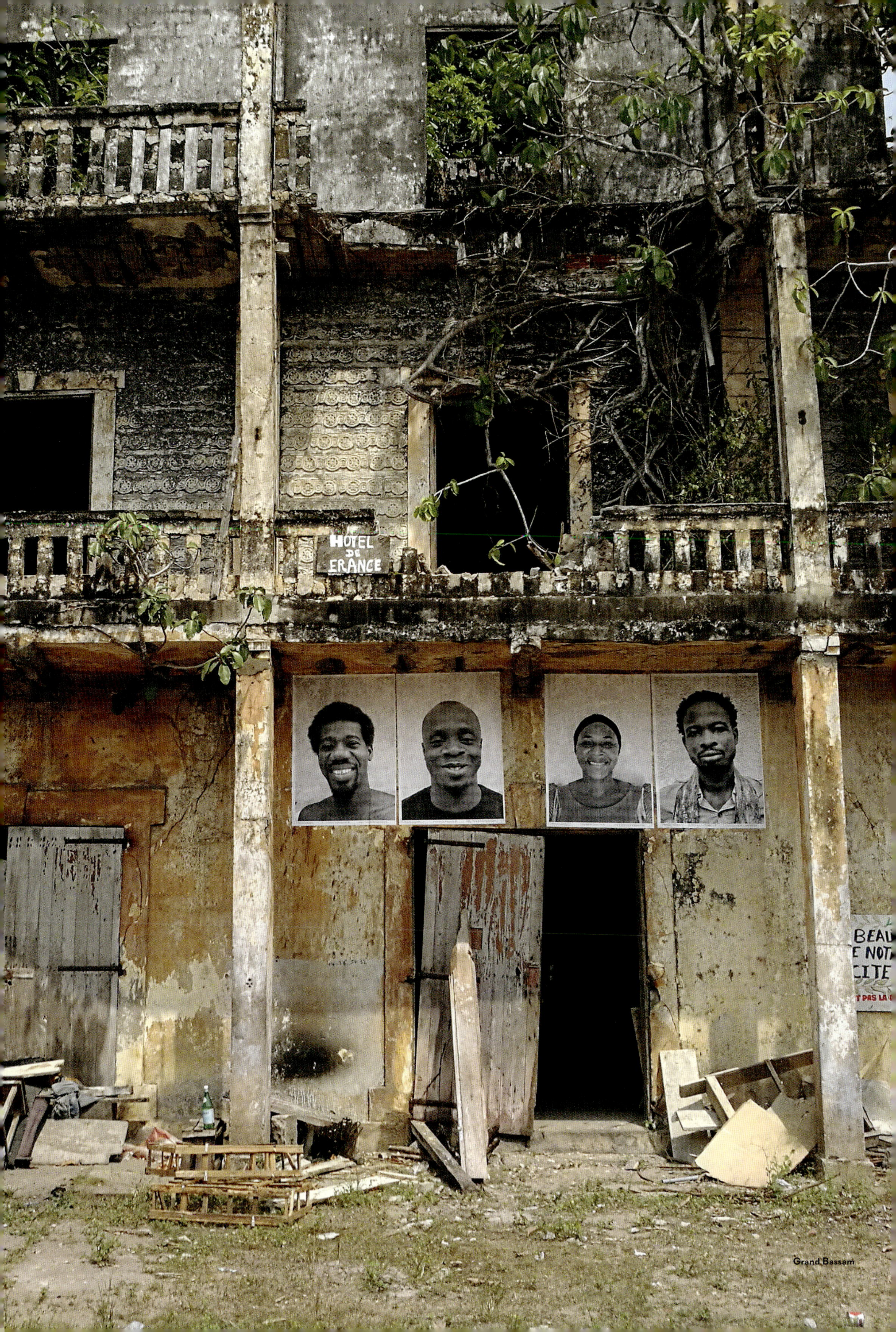

Grand Bassam

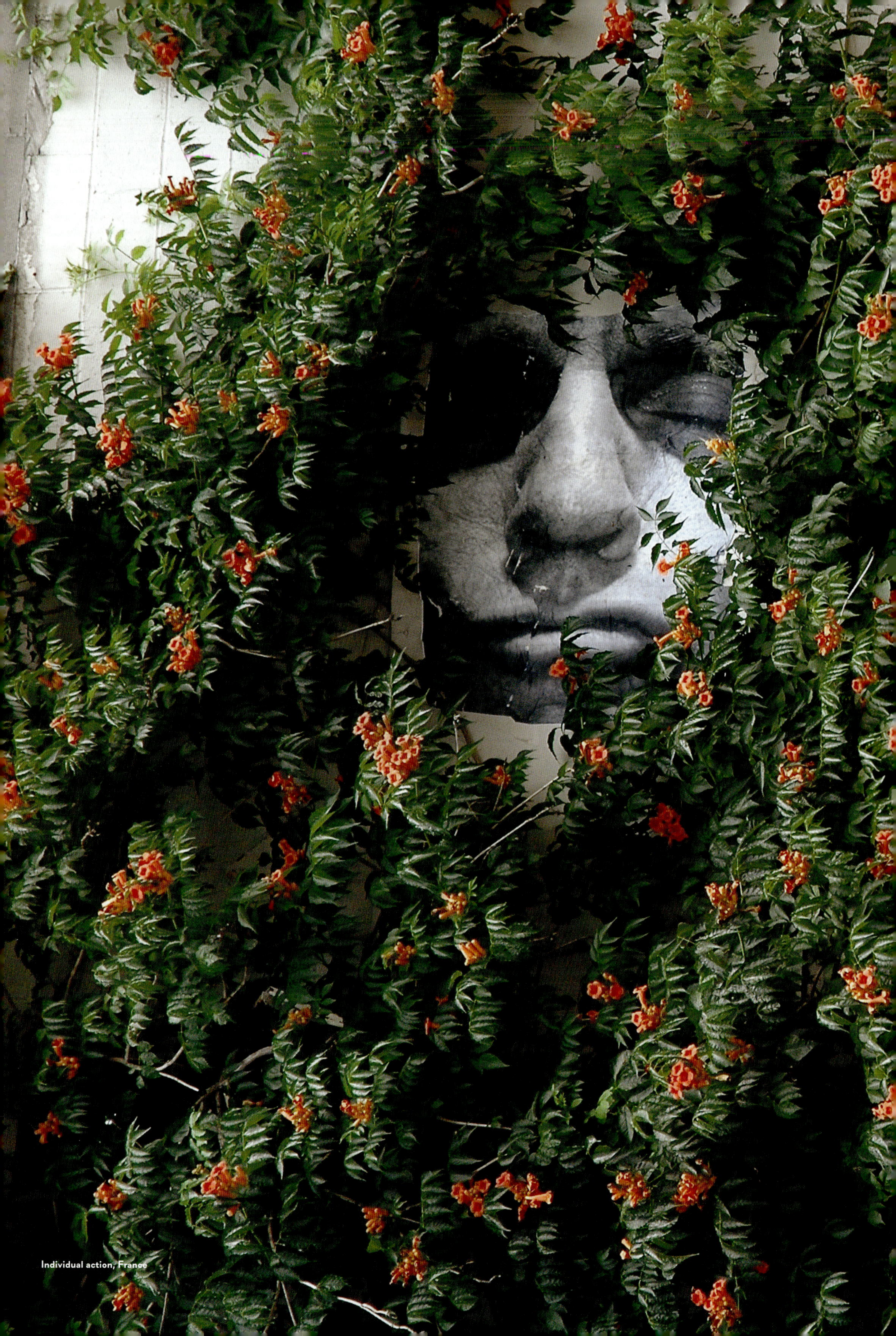

Individual action, France

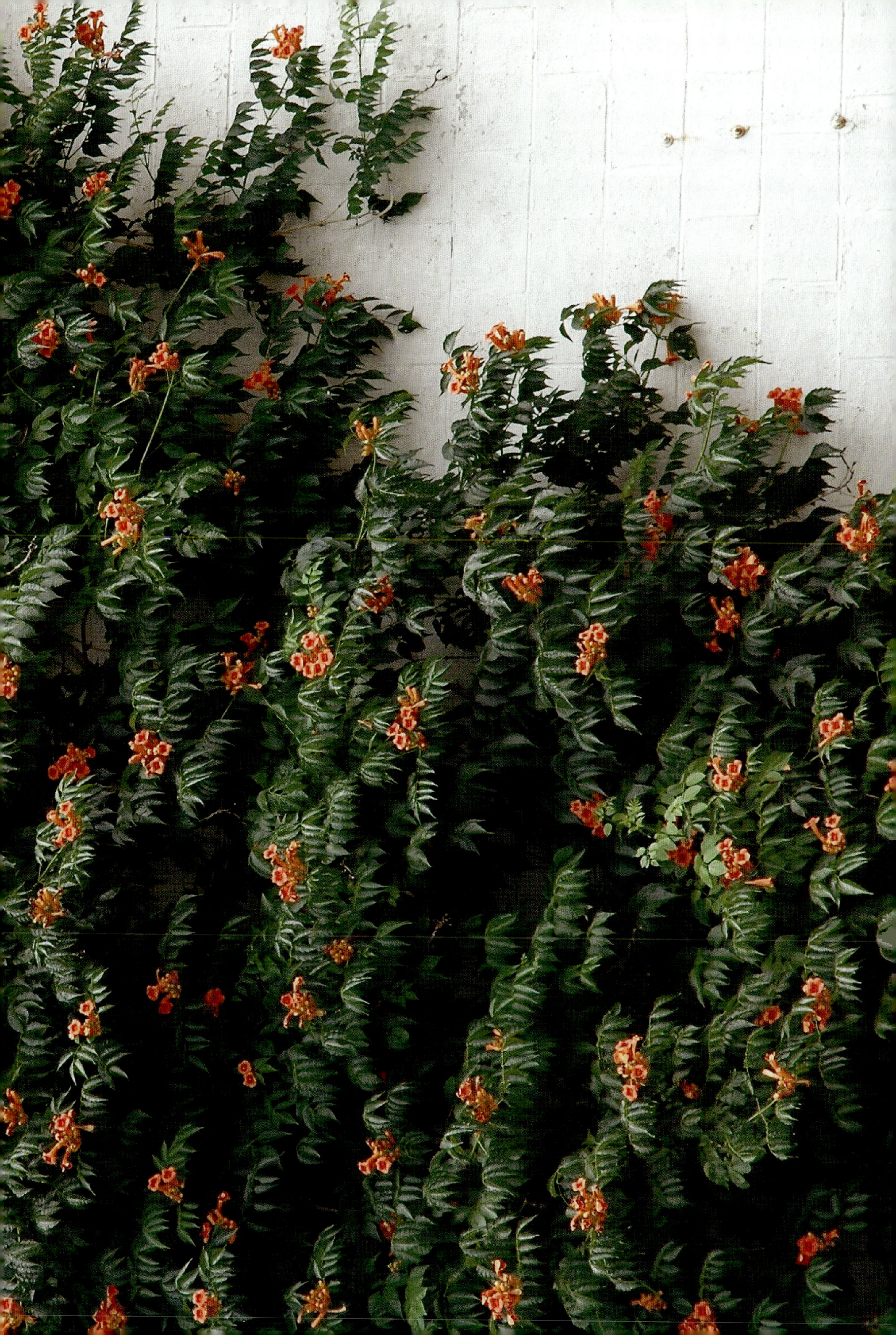

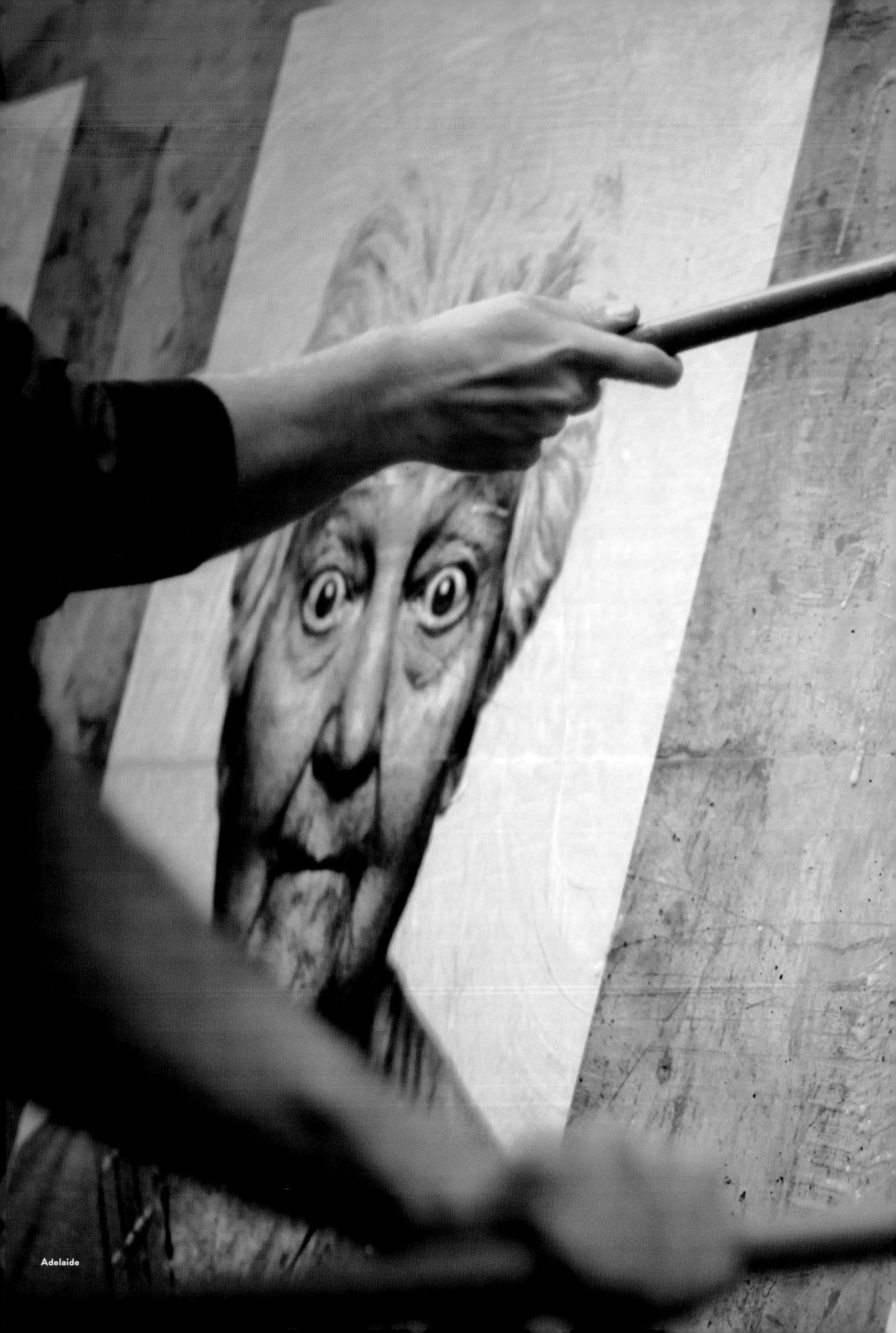

Adelaide

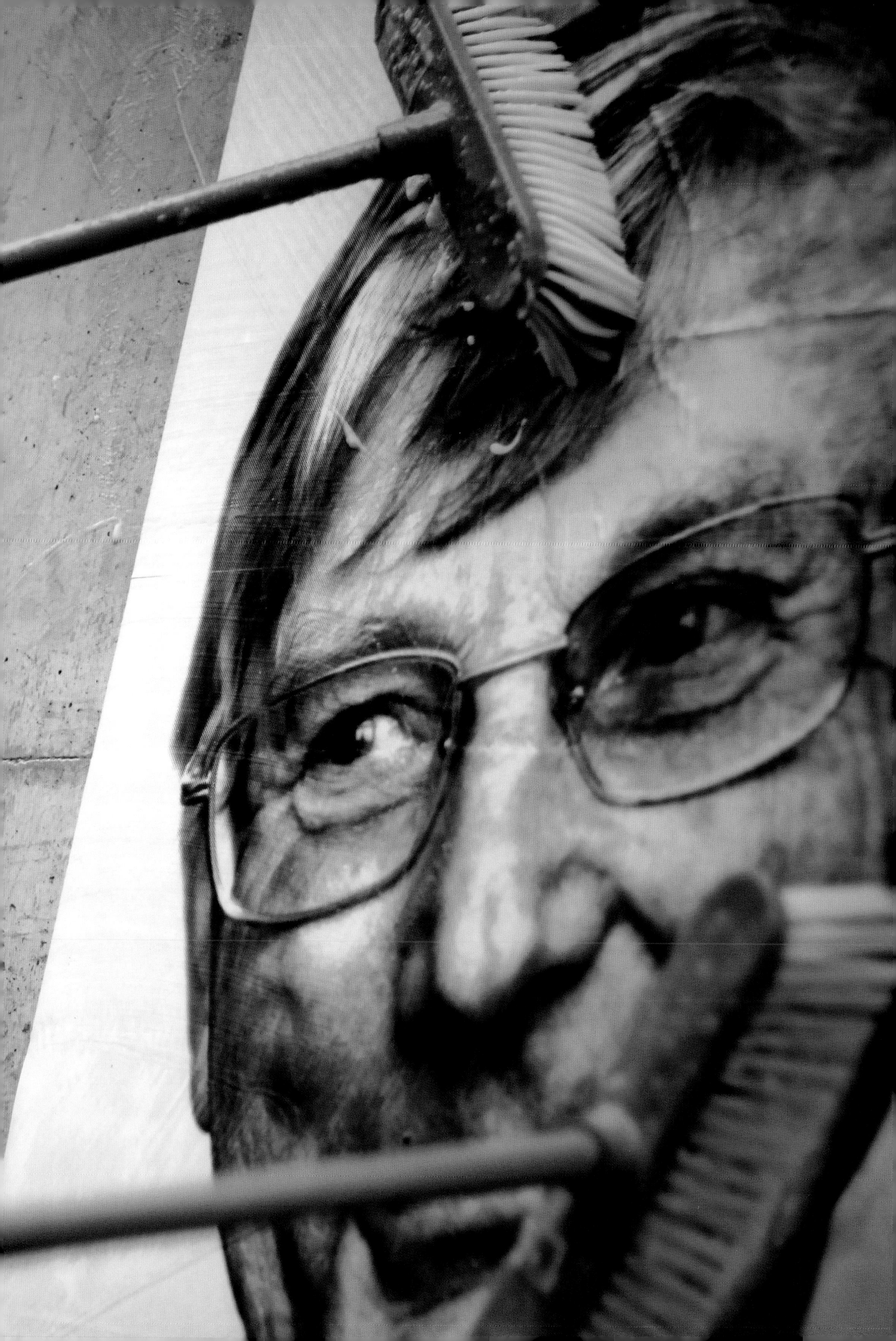

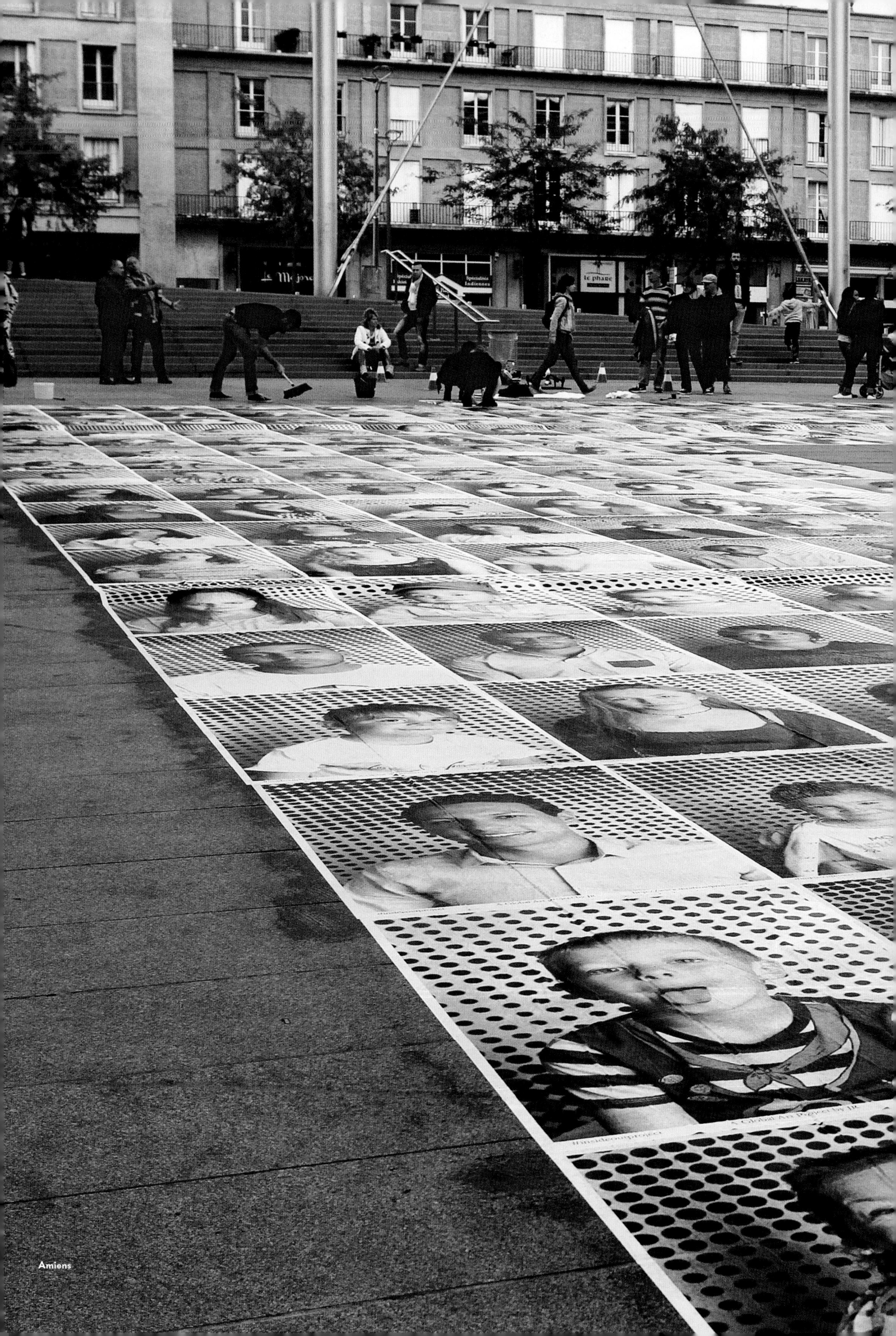

Amiens

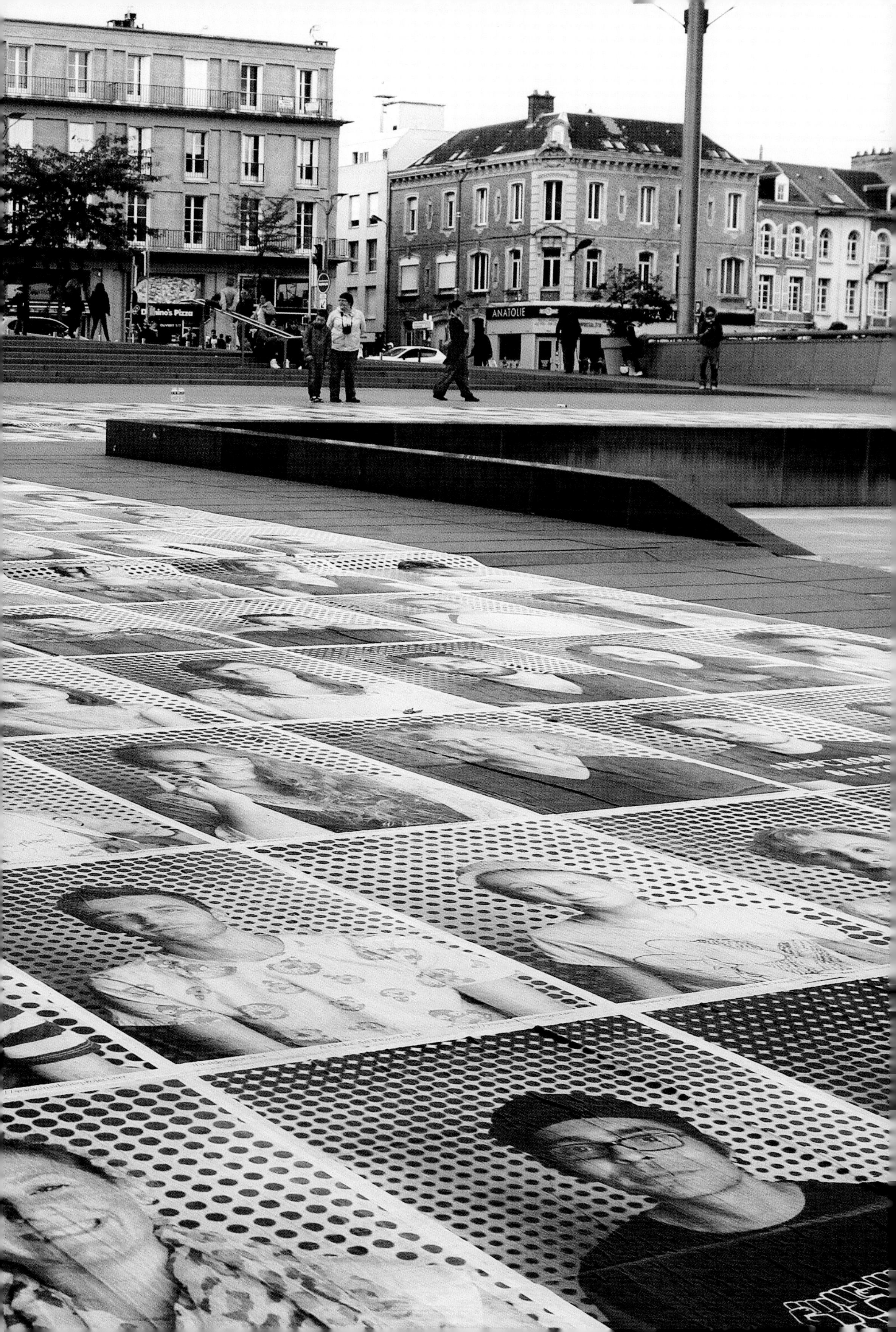
ANATOLIE
Domino's Pizza

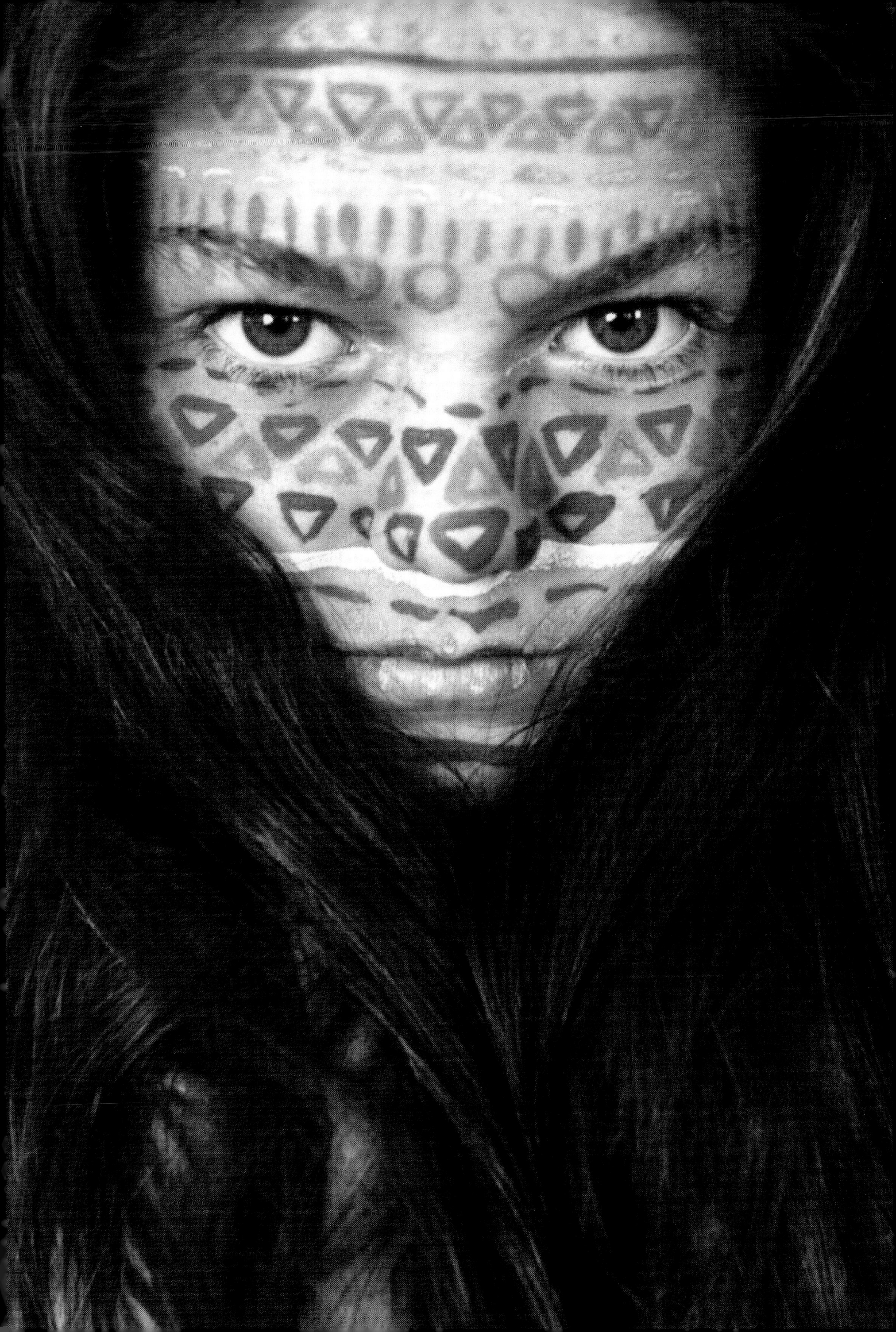

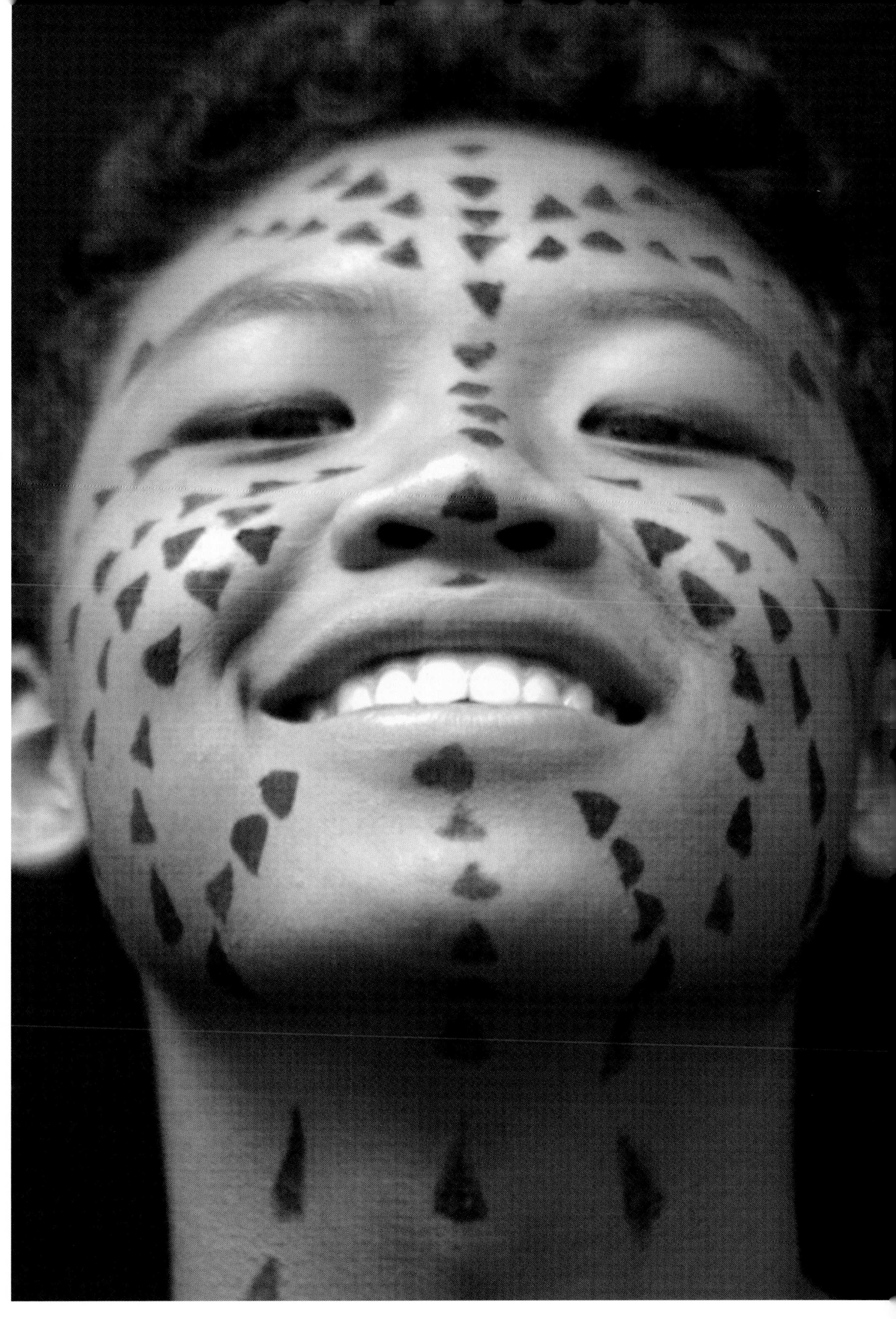

"We'd like to enlighten the people working in our school."

Antananarivo

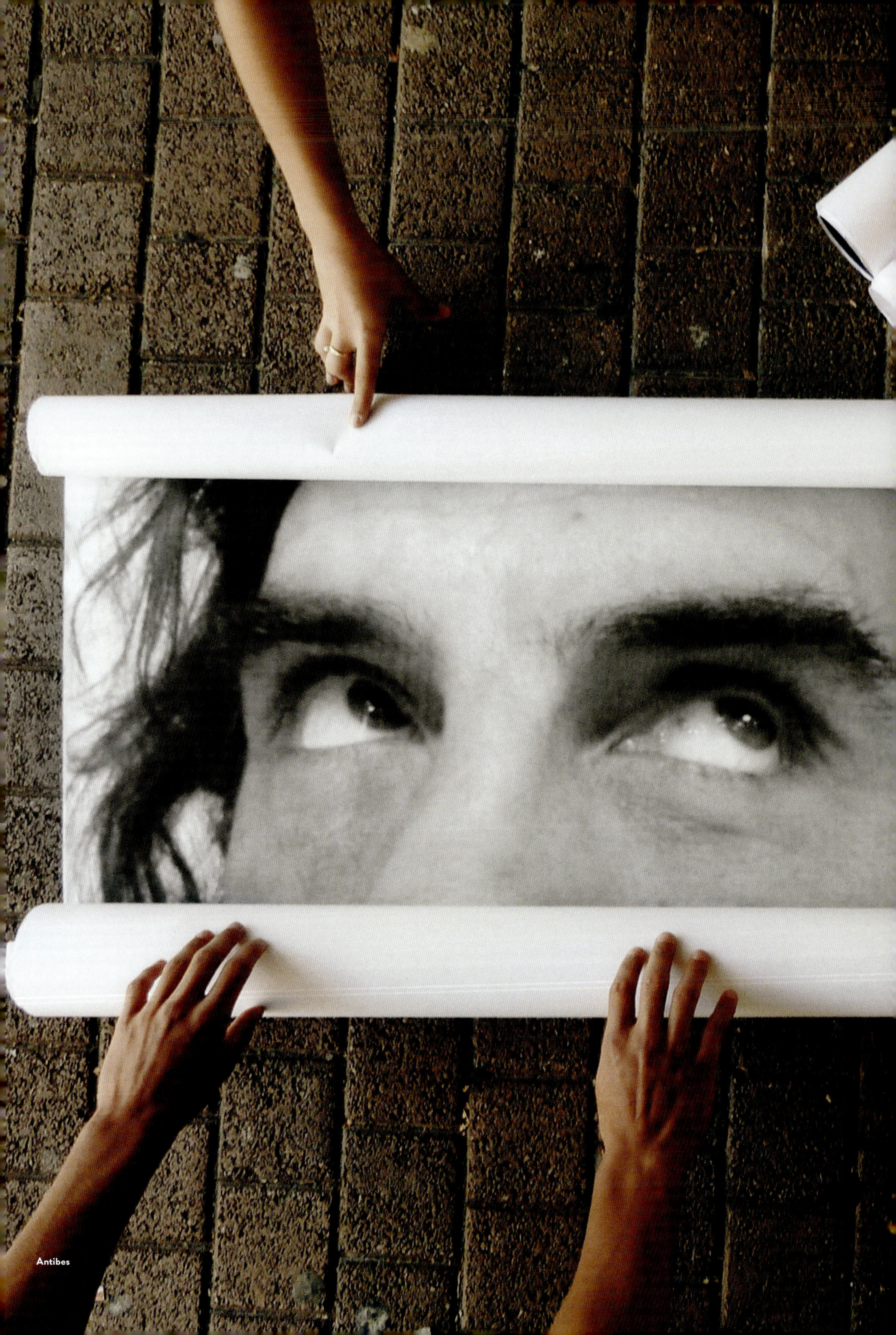

Antibes

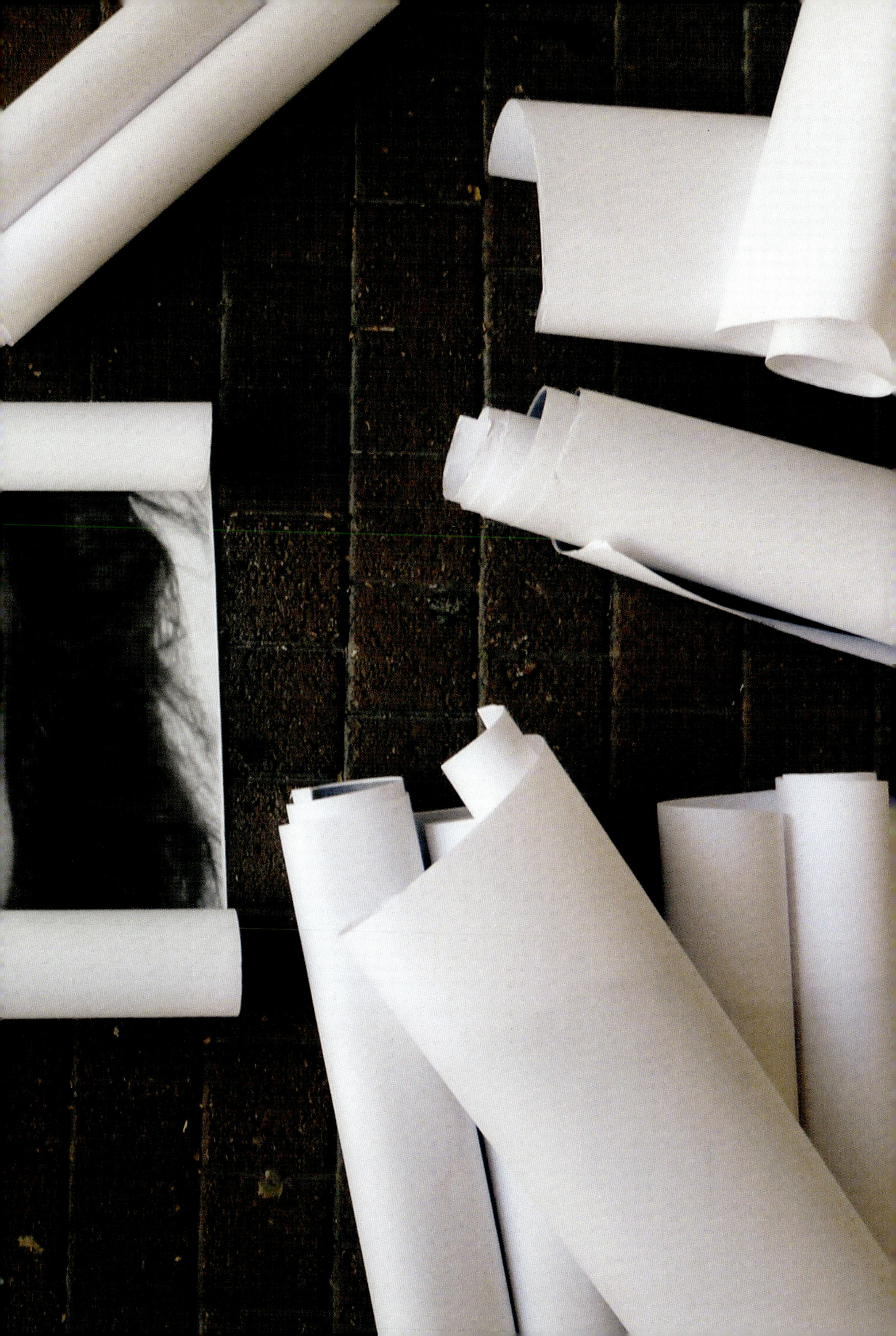

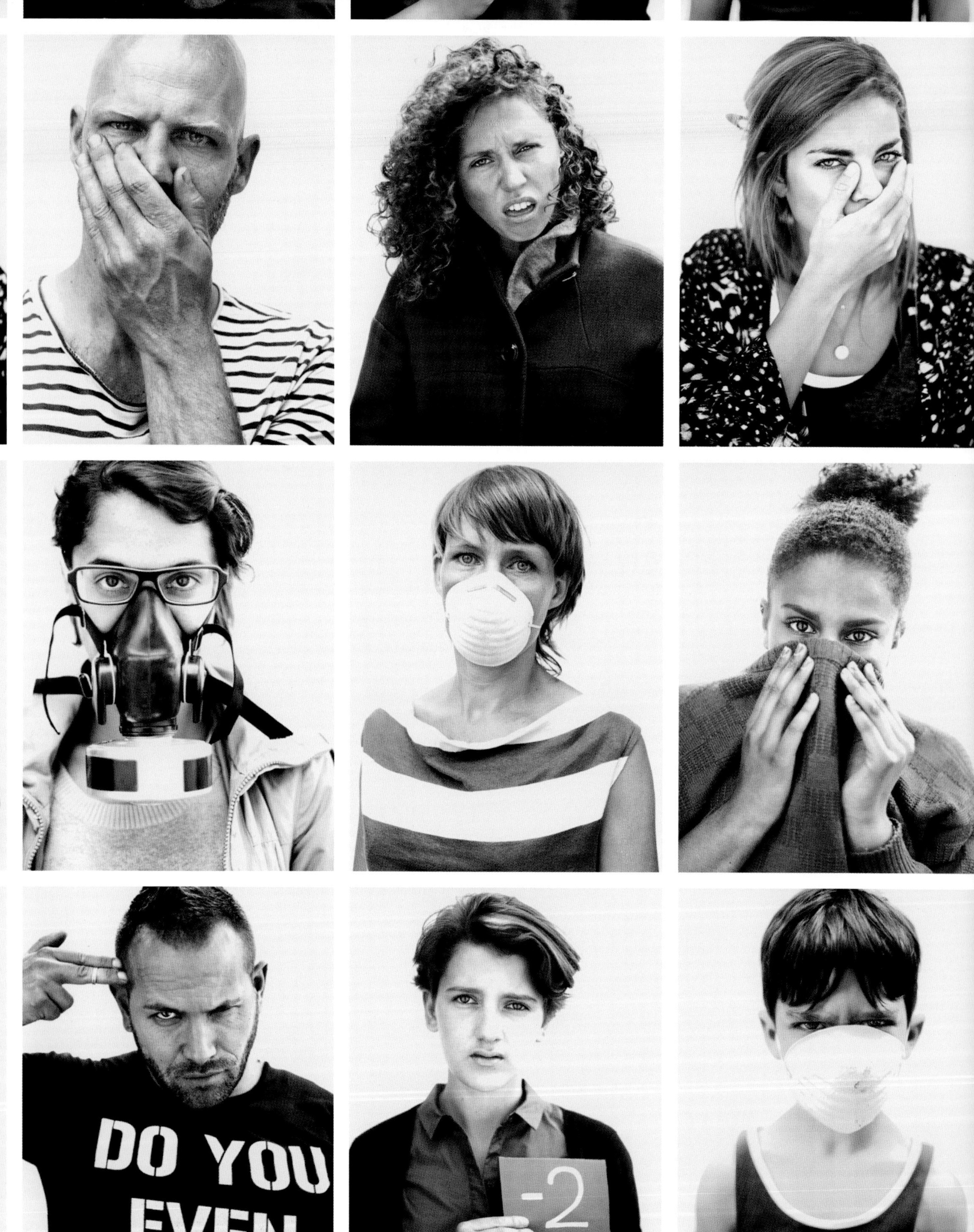

"We're asking for clean air."

Antwerp

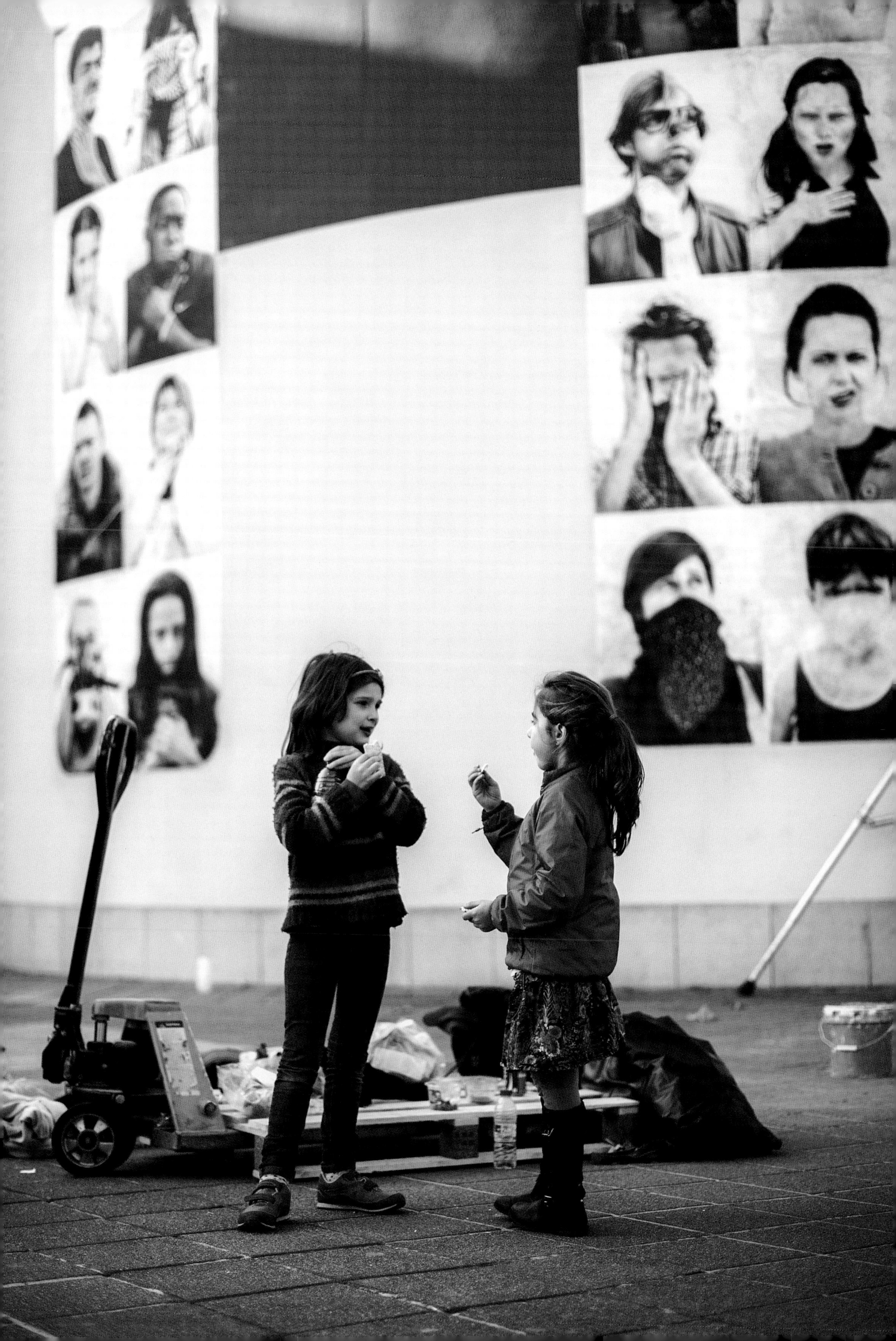

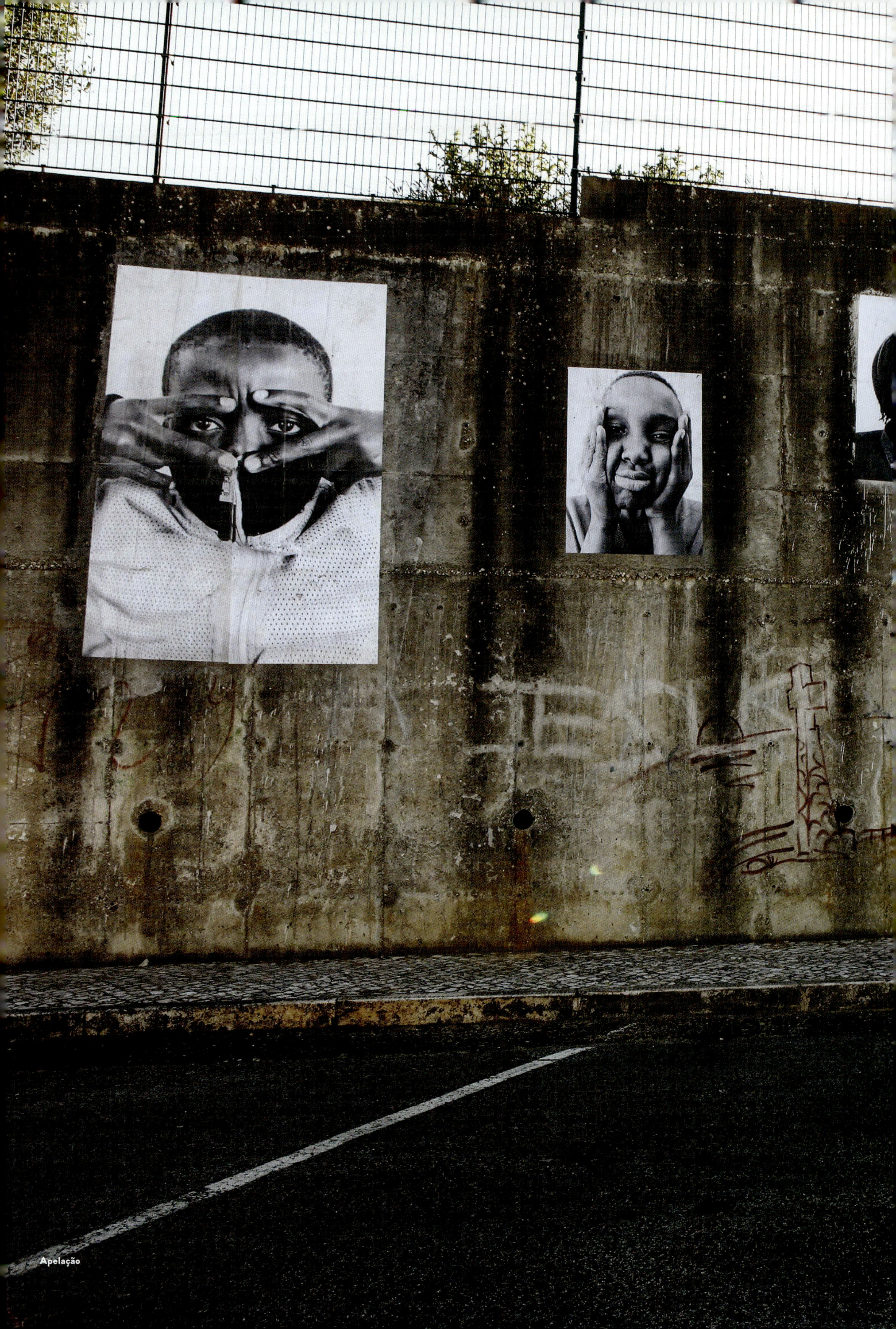

Apelação

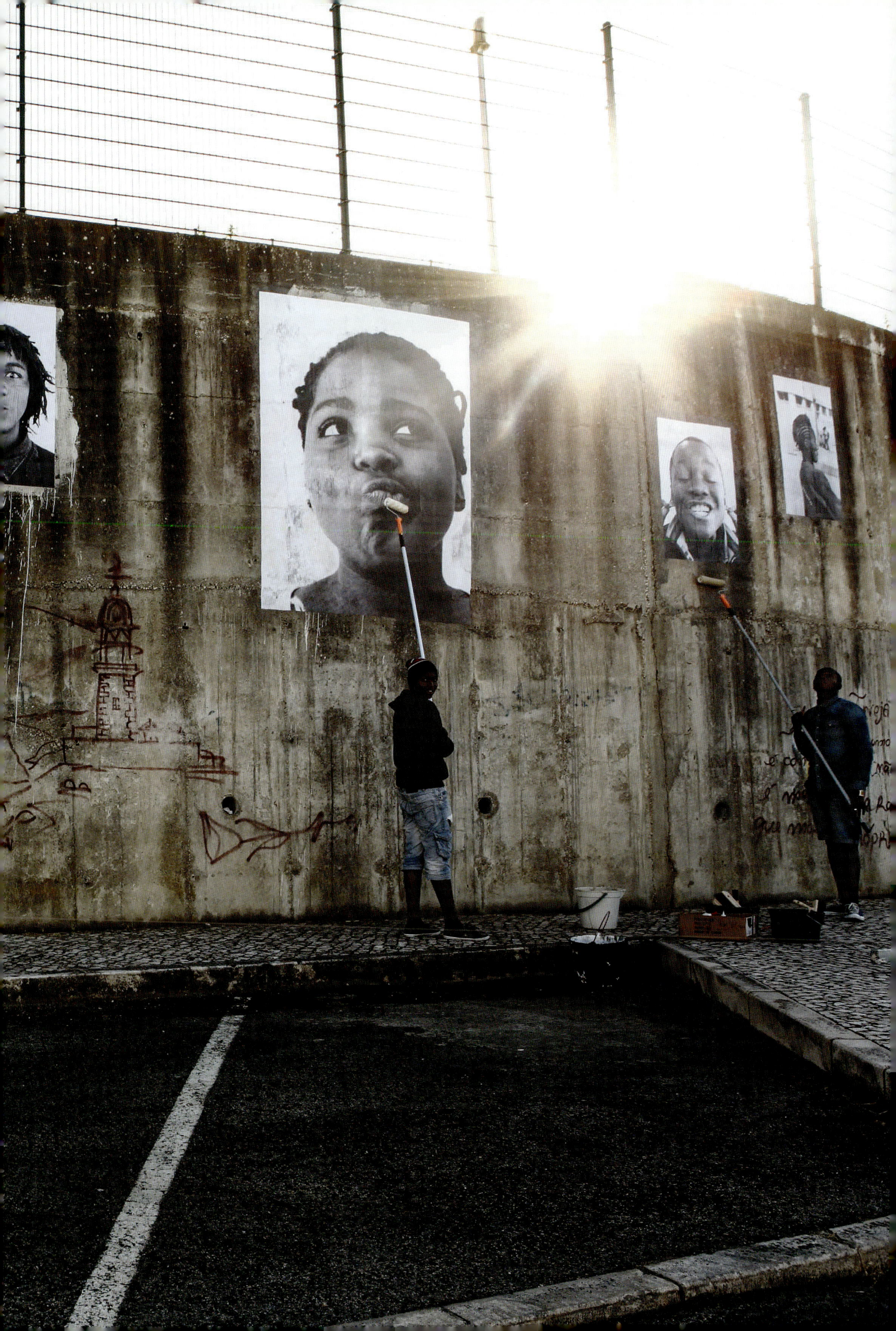

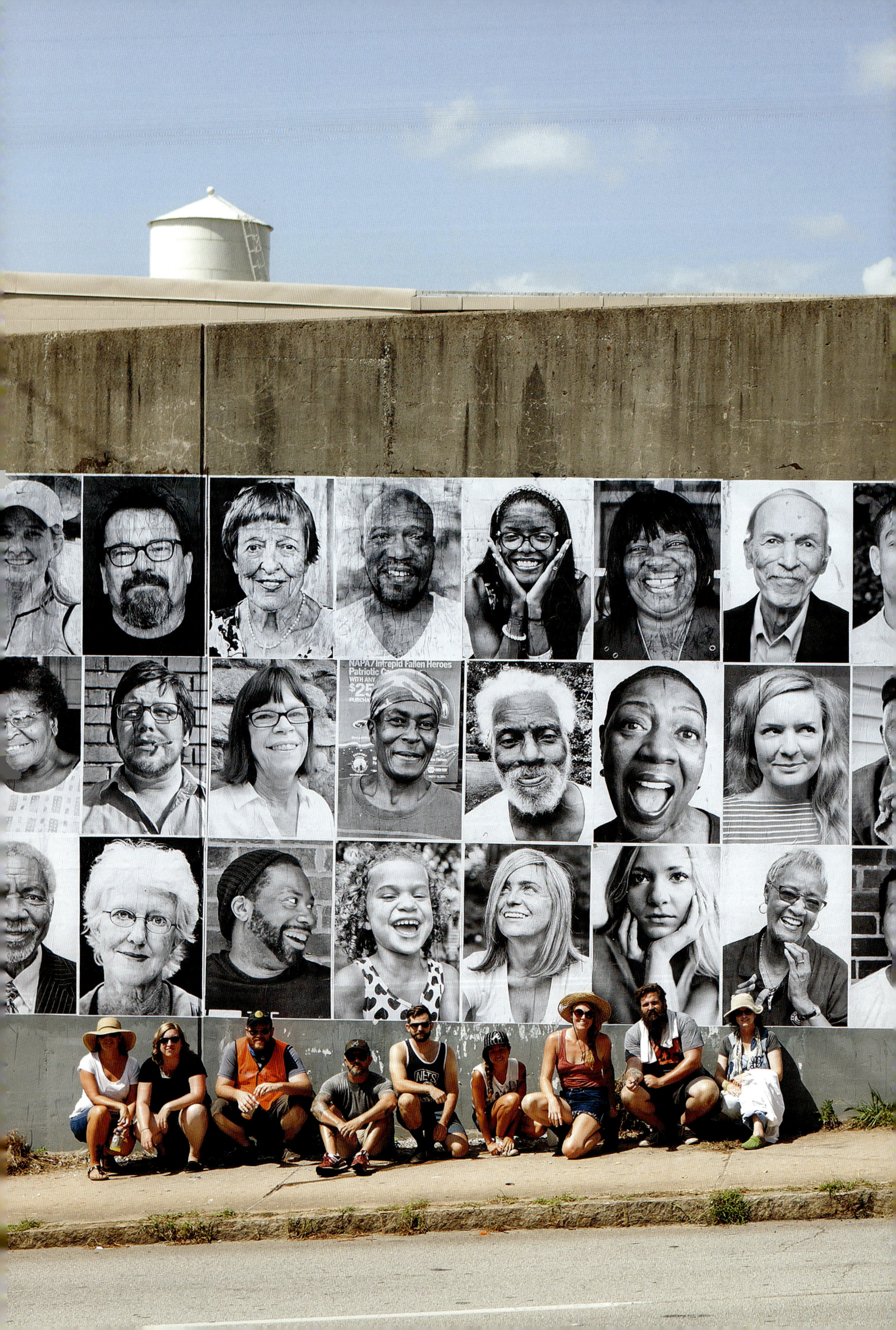
NAPA / Intrepid Fallen Heroes
WITH ANY
NETS

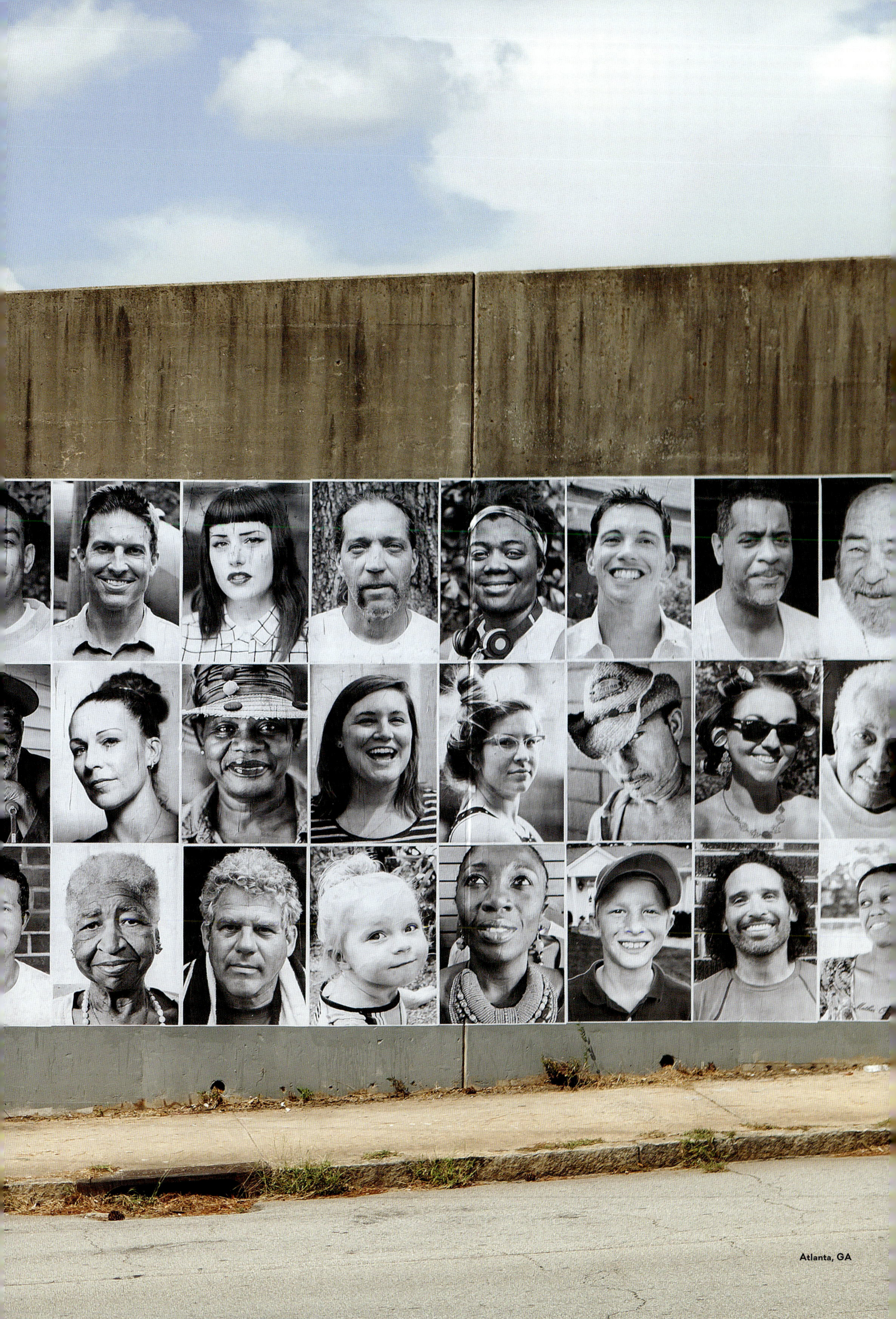

Atlanta, GA

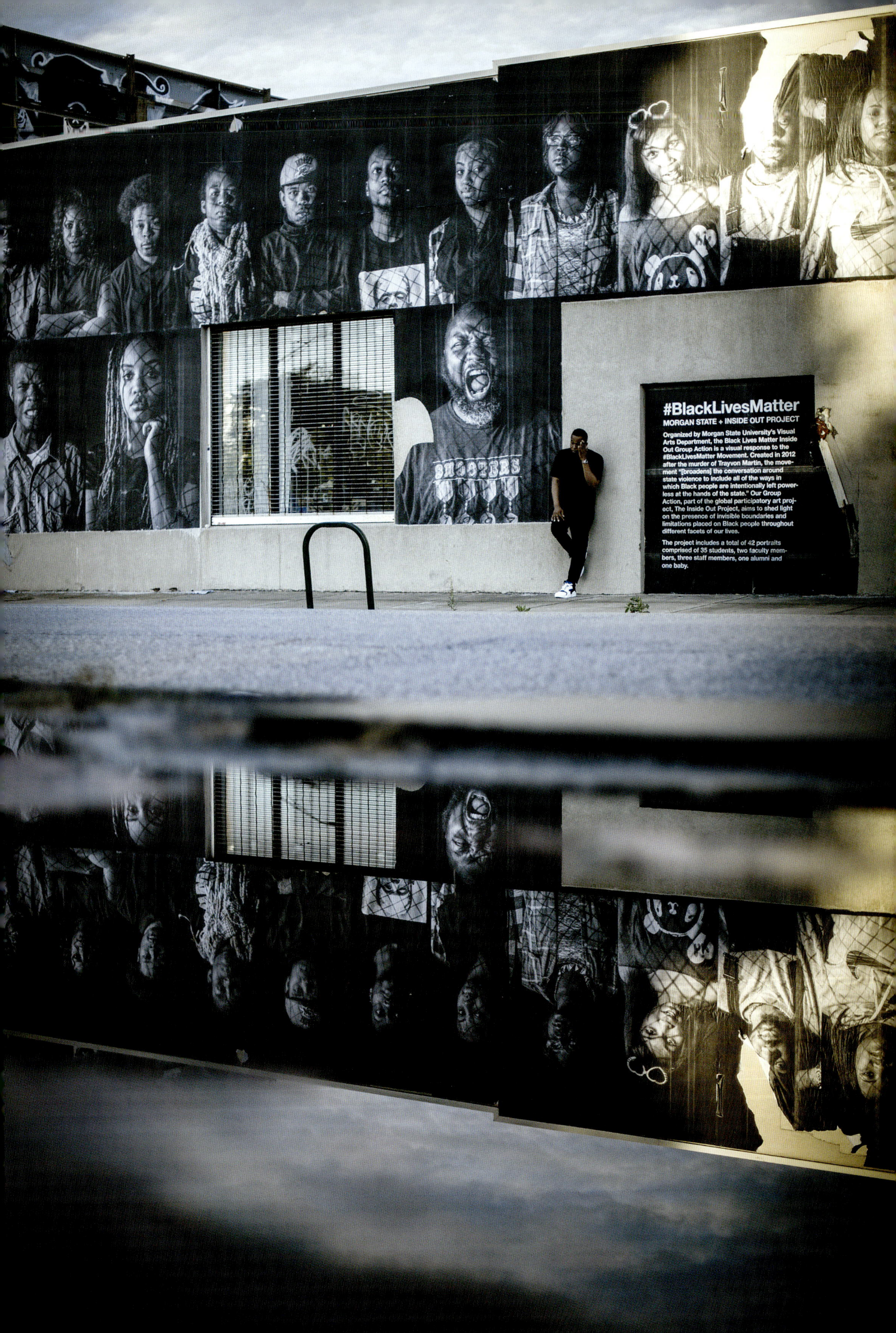
#BlackLivesMatter
MORGAN STATE + INSIDE OUT PROJECT
Organized by Morgan State University's Visual Arts Department, the Black Lives Matter Inside Out Group Action is a visual response to the #BlackLivesMatter Movement. Created in 2012 after the murder of Trayvon Martin, the movement "[broadens] the conversation around state violence to include all of the ways in which Black people are intentionally left powerless at the hands of the state." Our Group Action, part of the global participatory art project, The Inside Out Project, aims to shed light on the presence of invisible boundaries and limitations placed on Black people throughout different facets of our lives.
The project includes a total of 42 portraits comprised of 35 students, two faculty members, three staff members, one alumni and one baby.
SHOOTERS

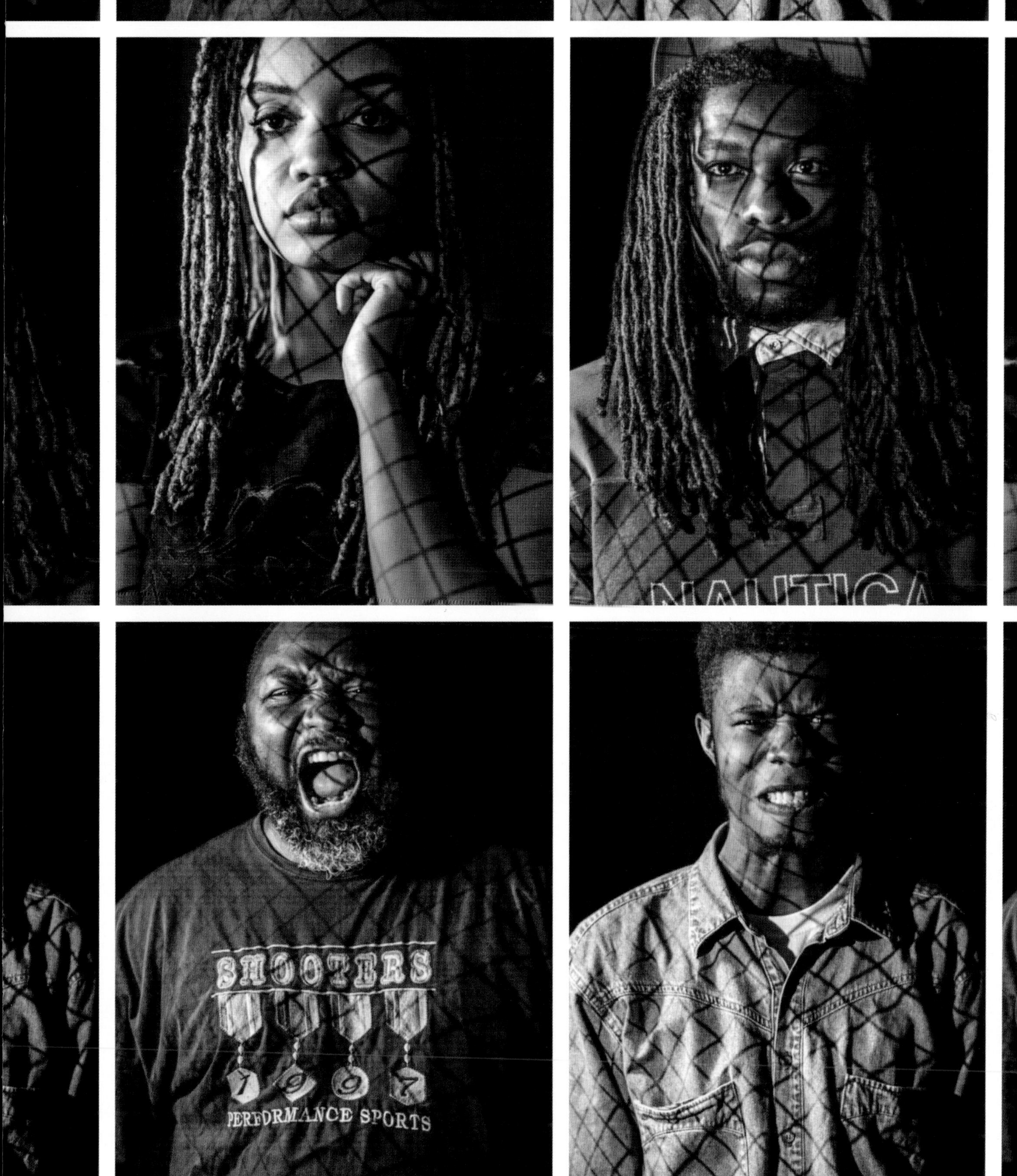

"Created after the murder of Trayvon Martin, the movement broadens "the conversation around state violence to include all of the ways in which Black people are intentionally left powerless at the hands of the state." Our group action aims to shed light on the presence of invisible boundaries and limitations placed on Black people throughout different facets of our lives."

Baltimore, MD

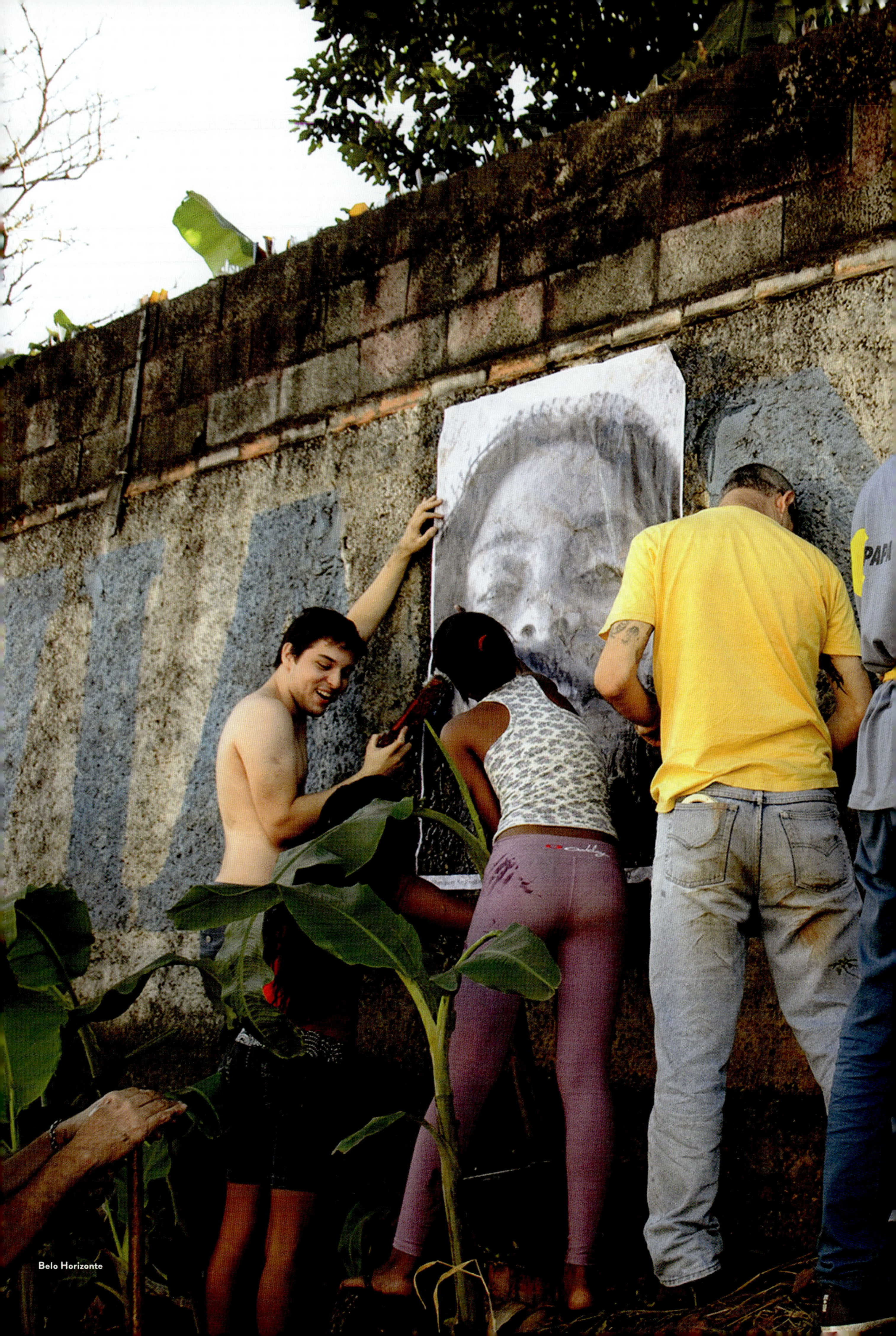

Belo Horizonte

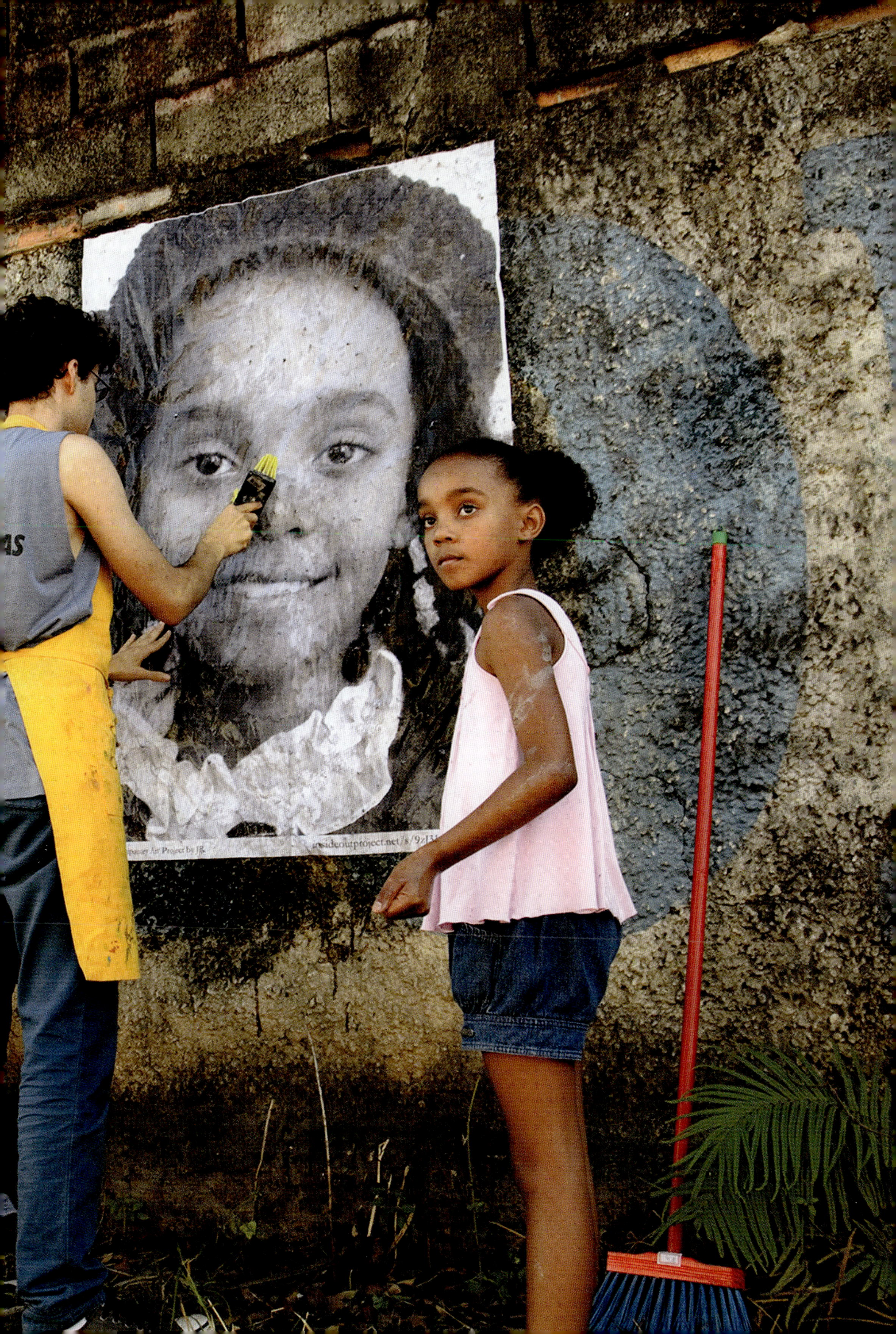
Art Project by JR

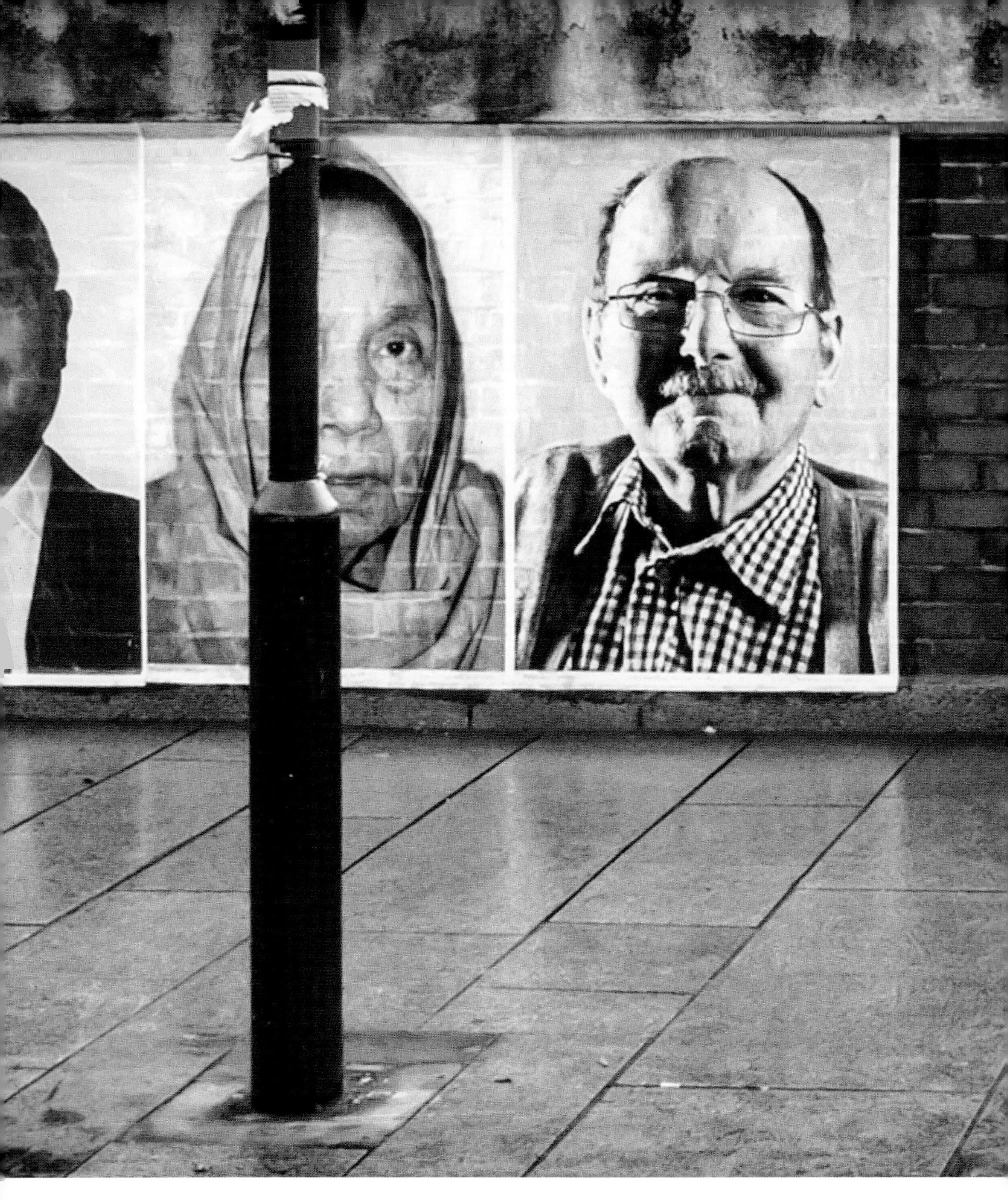

Lost Stories, November 2013. "The city of Birmingham has more than one million inhabitants and is proud to be one of most ethnically and culturally diverse cities in the UK. However, the proportion of people who make up the older generation is low, with only 12 percent of the population being aged 65 and older. Most of those in this aging demographic have gone through major events in their lives: childbirth, war, migration, retirement, long-term illness or disability, and bereavement, to name a few. Many of these people will still lead happy and healthy lives; others may be isolated and vulnerable and no longer have a voice within their families or communities. Whatever their backgrounds, they all have a story to tell."

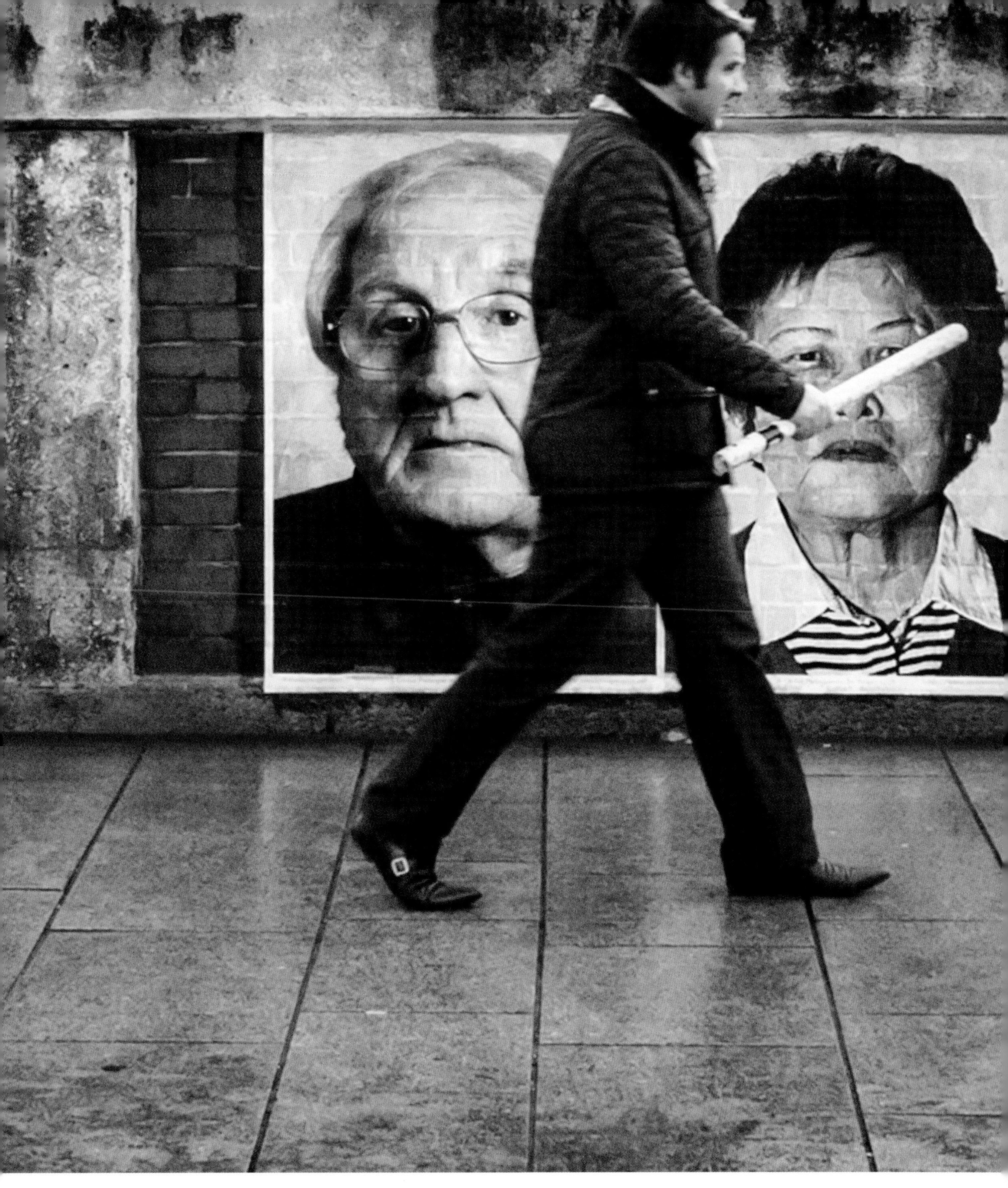

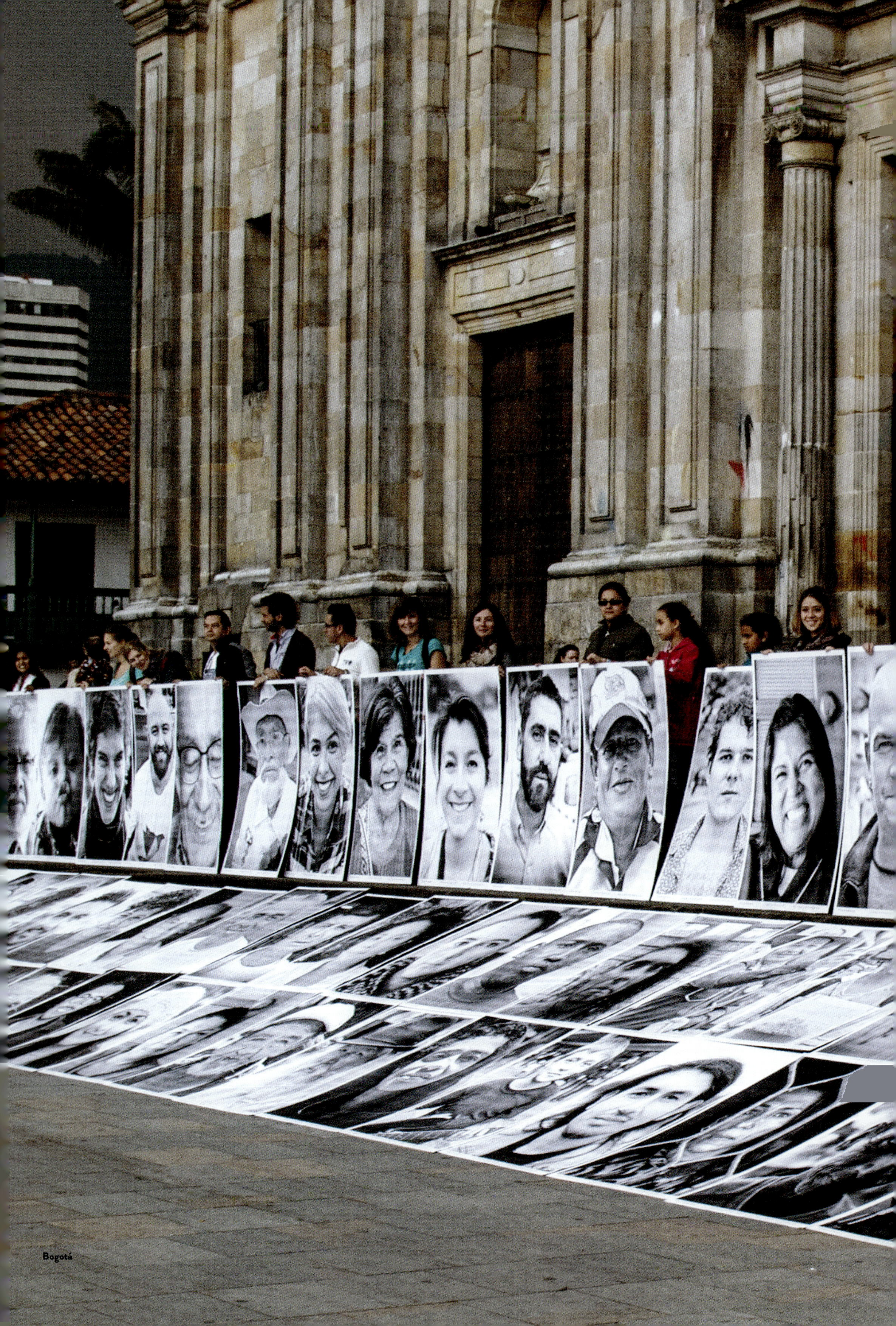

Bogotá

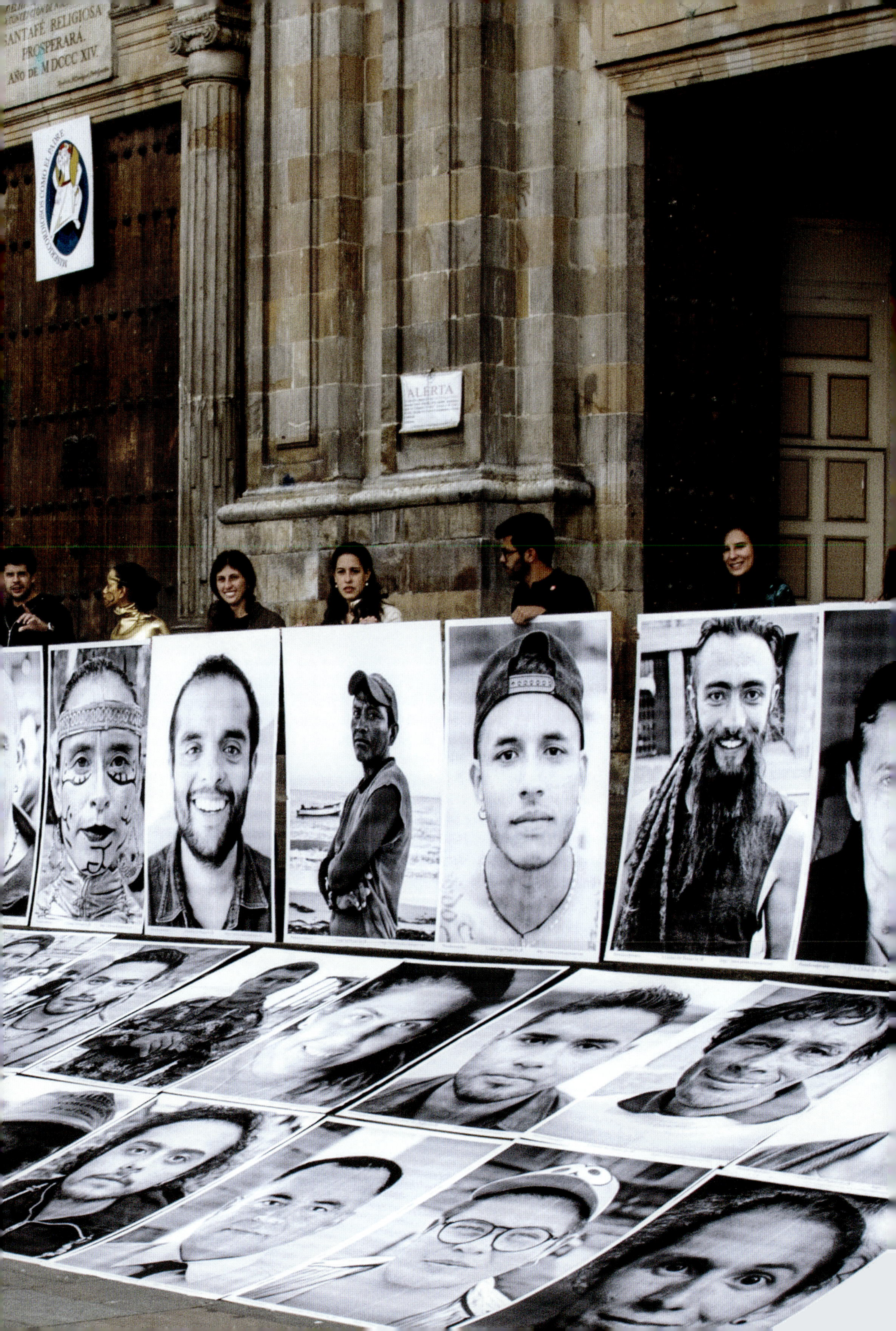
SANTAFÉ RELIGIOSA
PROSPERARÁ.
AÑO DE MDCCC XIV.
ALERTA

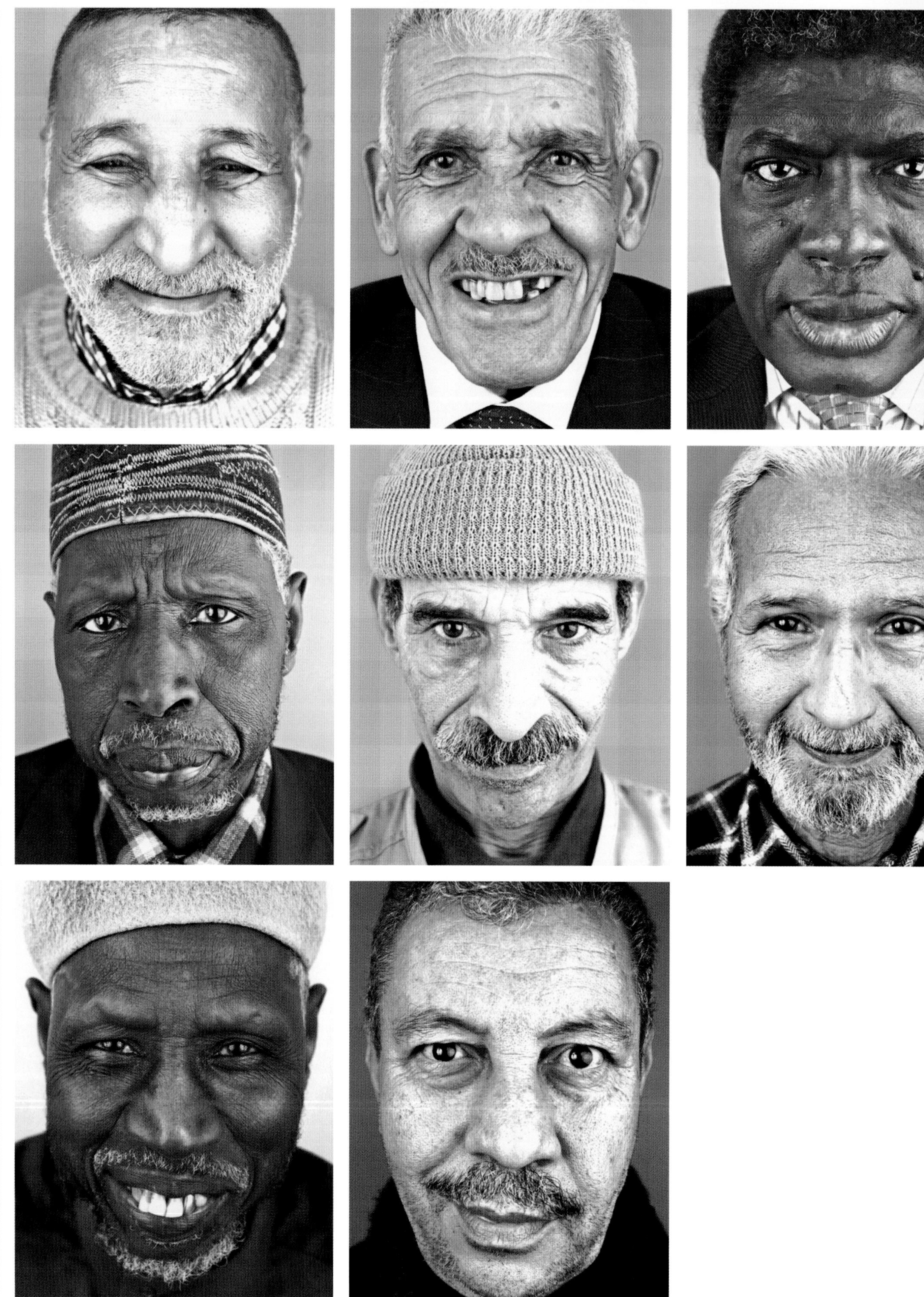

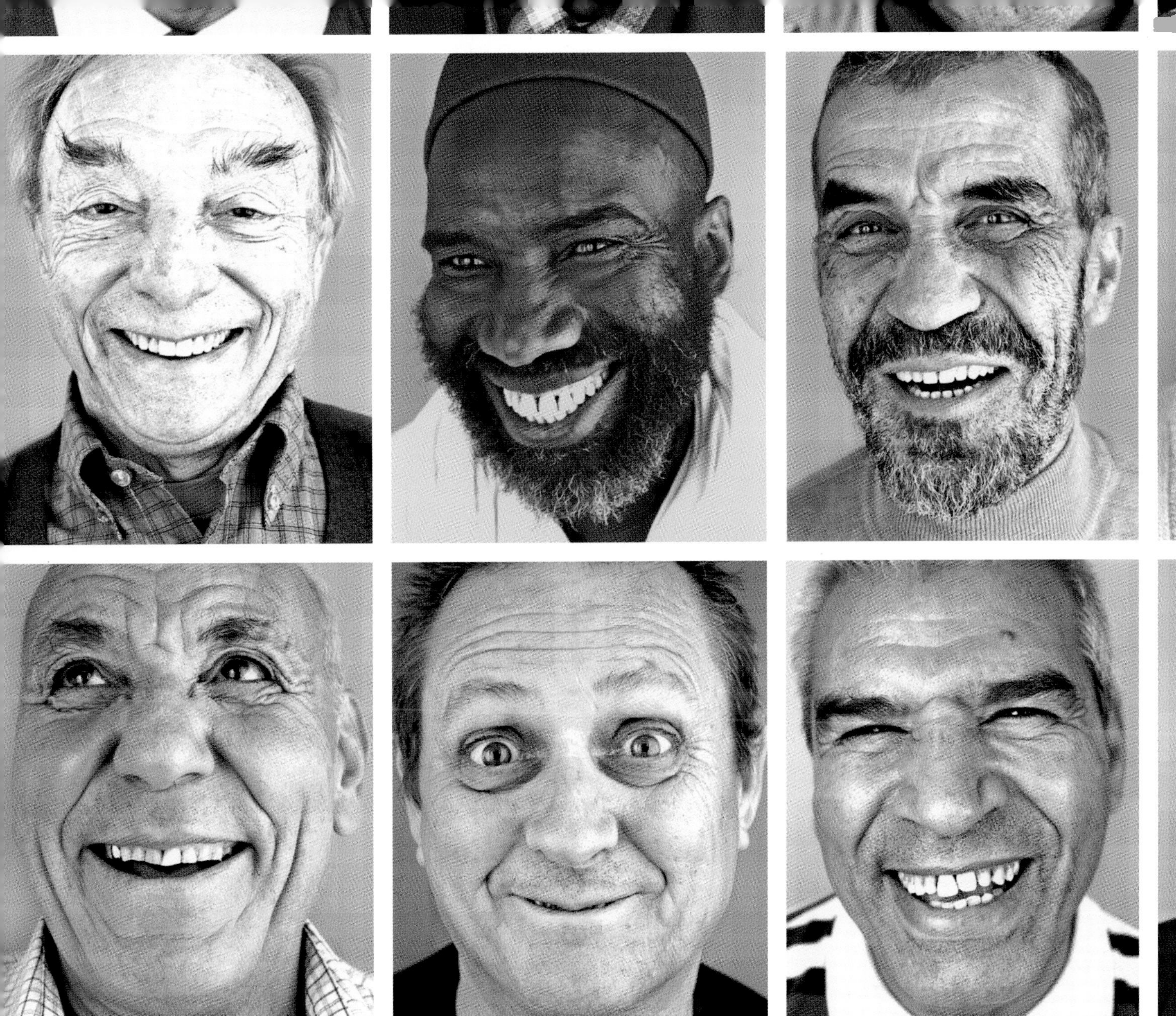

"Through this project, we would like to shed light on all the people who worked in these factories. Behind the outstanding industrial progress that took place were tens of thousands of employees who have witnessed this history."

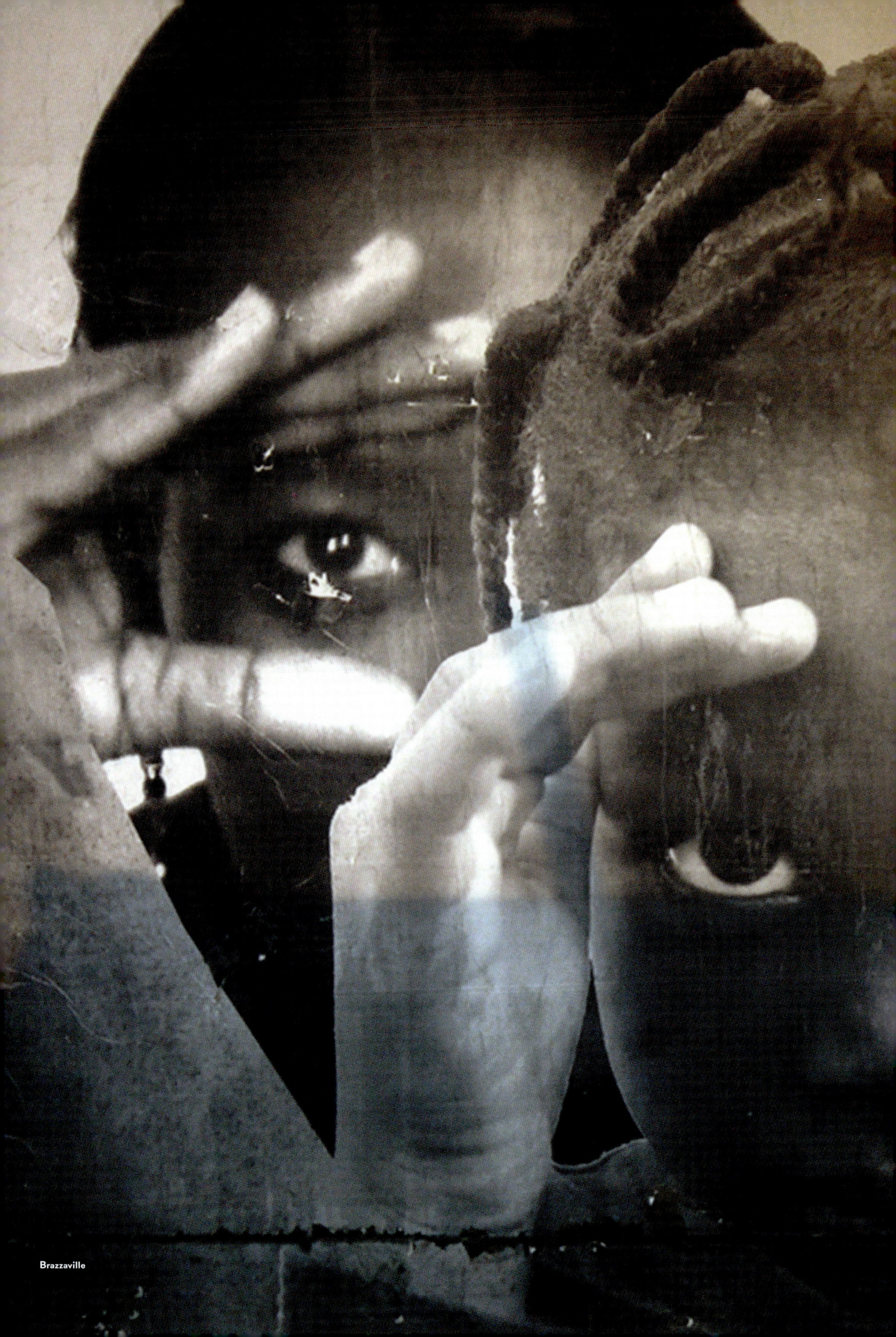

Brazzaville

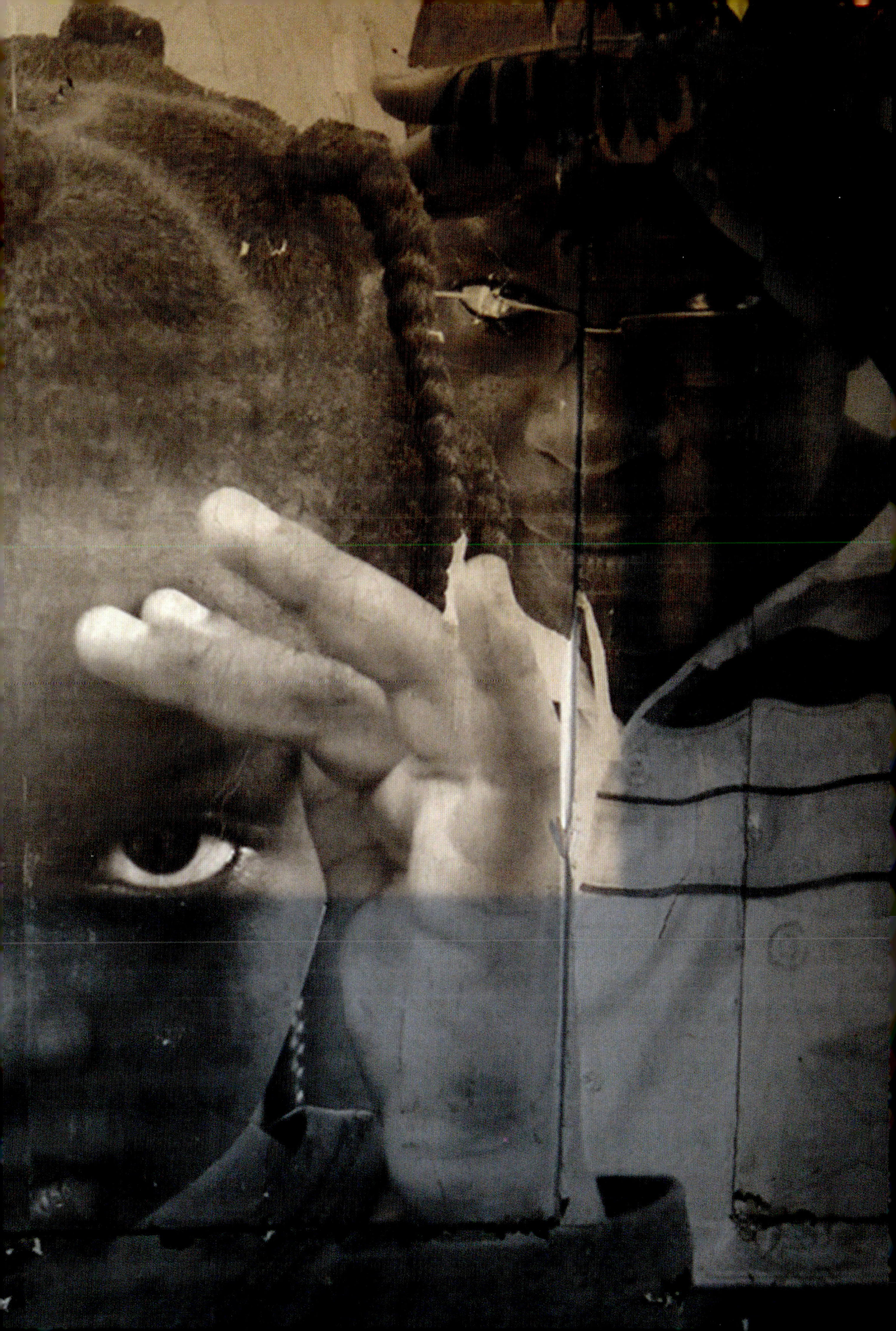

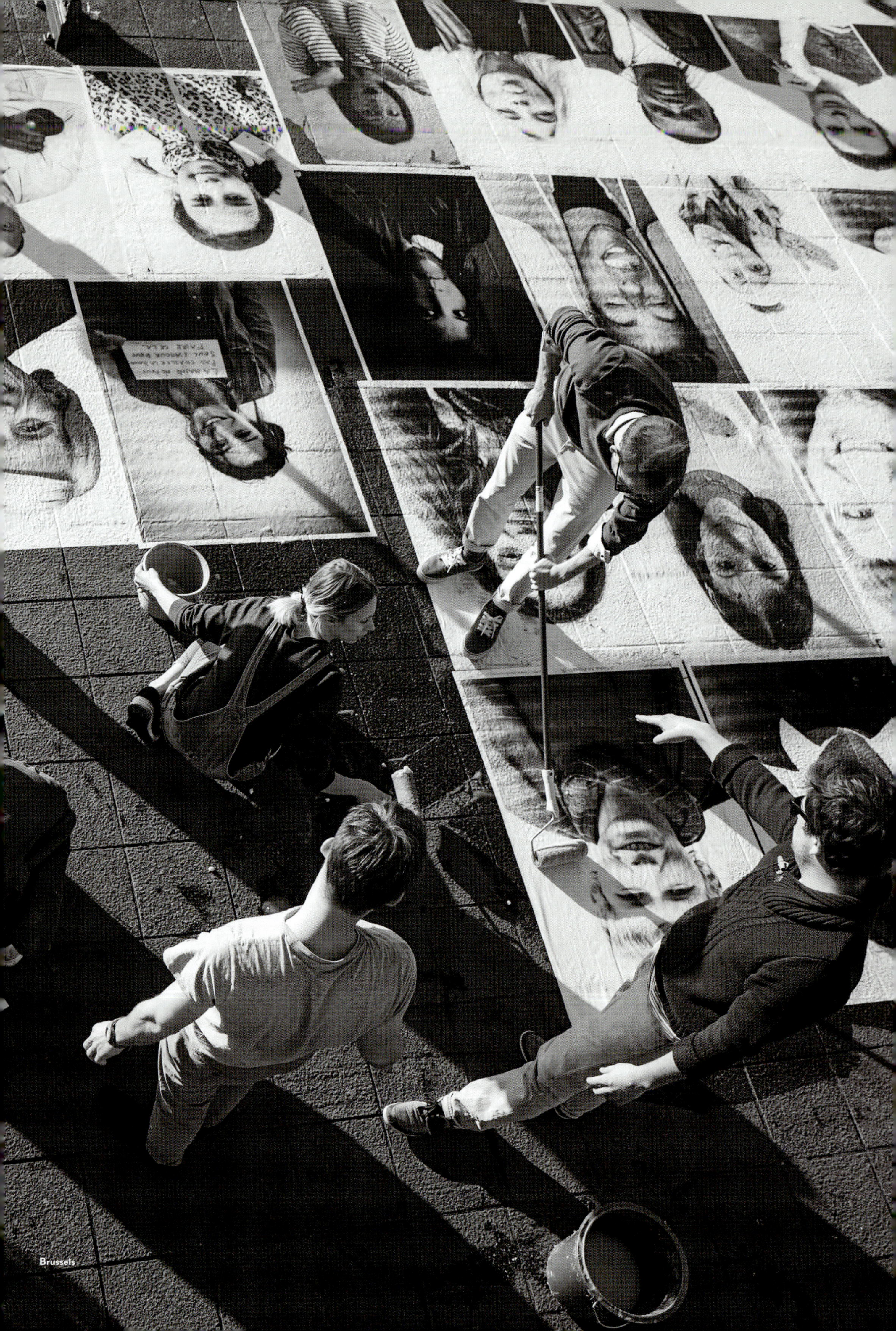

Brussels

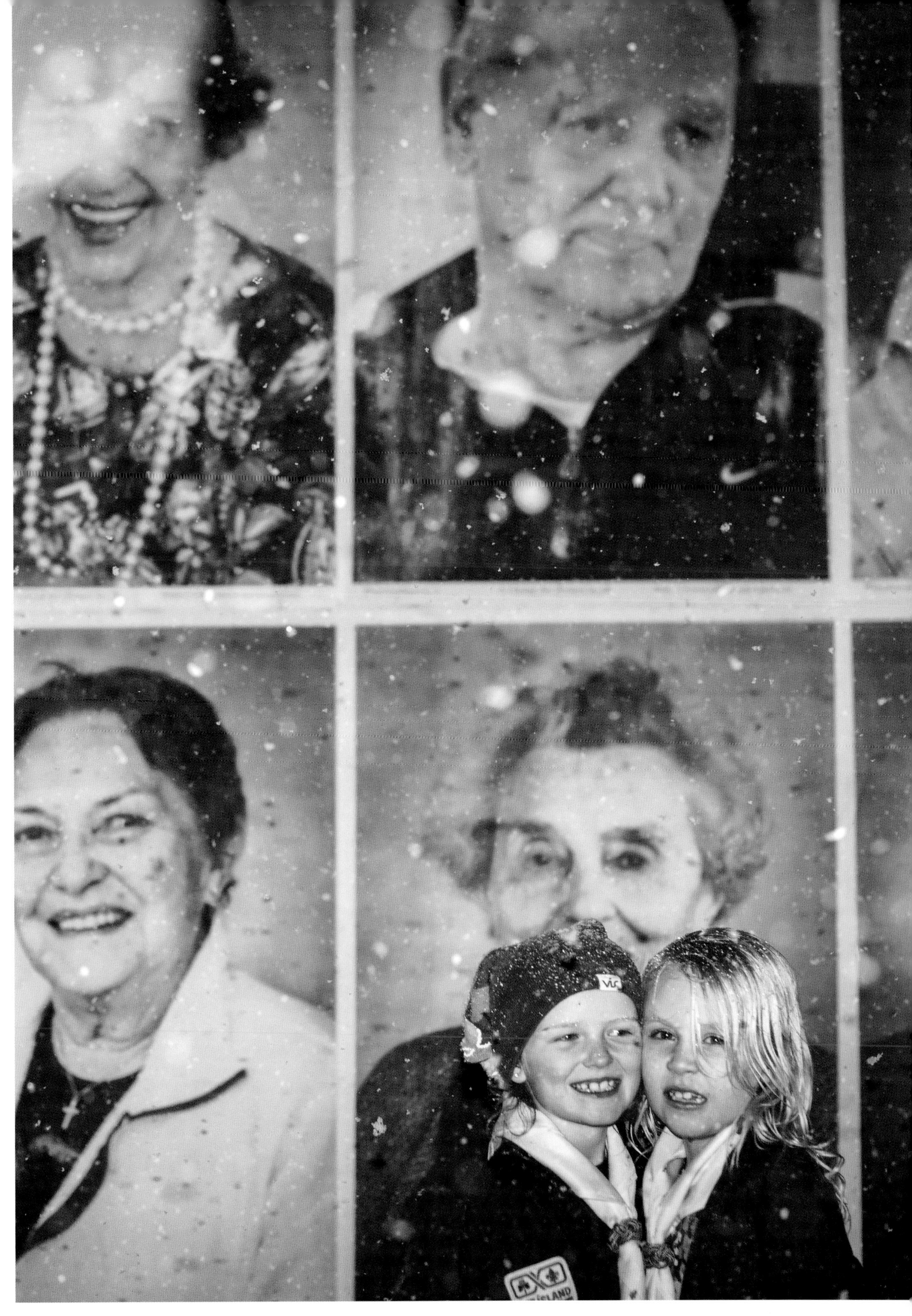

"To fight the perception that grew after the terrorist attacks in Brussels in March 2016 that all Muslims are extremists or terrorists, and to show that we stand united in the face of adversity."

Búðardalur

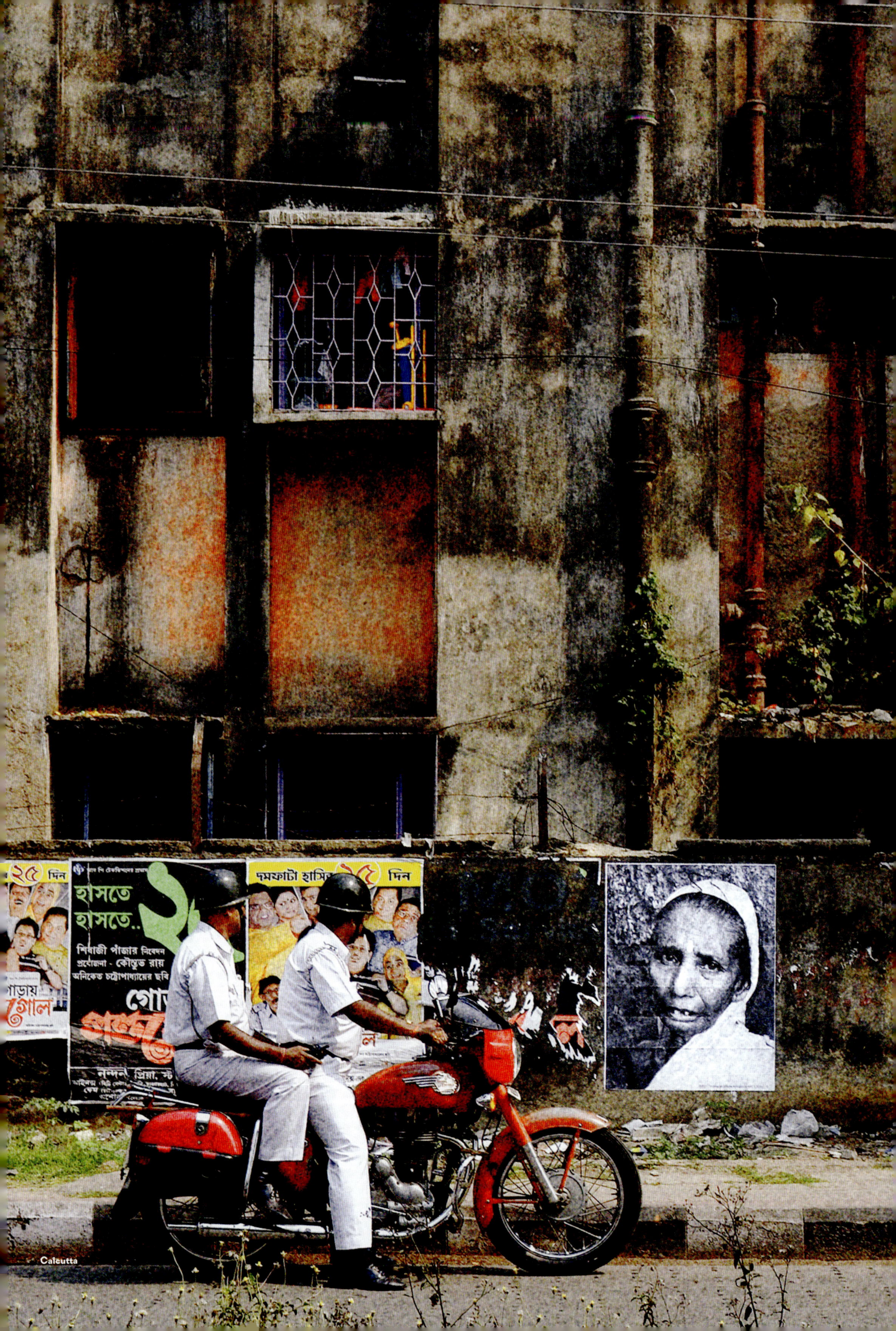

Calcutta

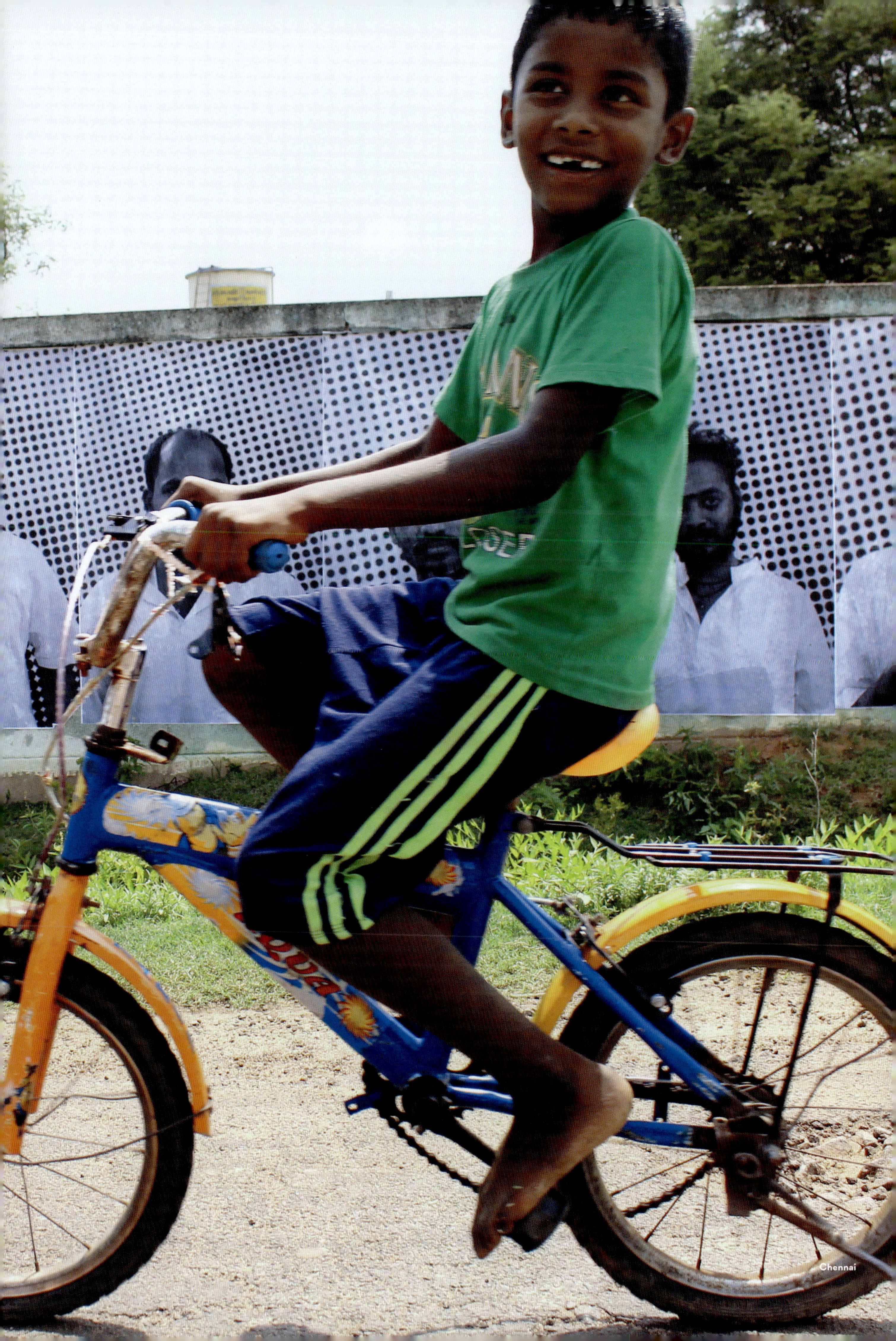

Chennai

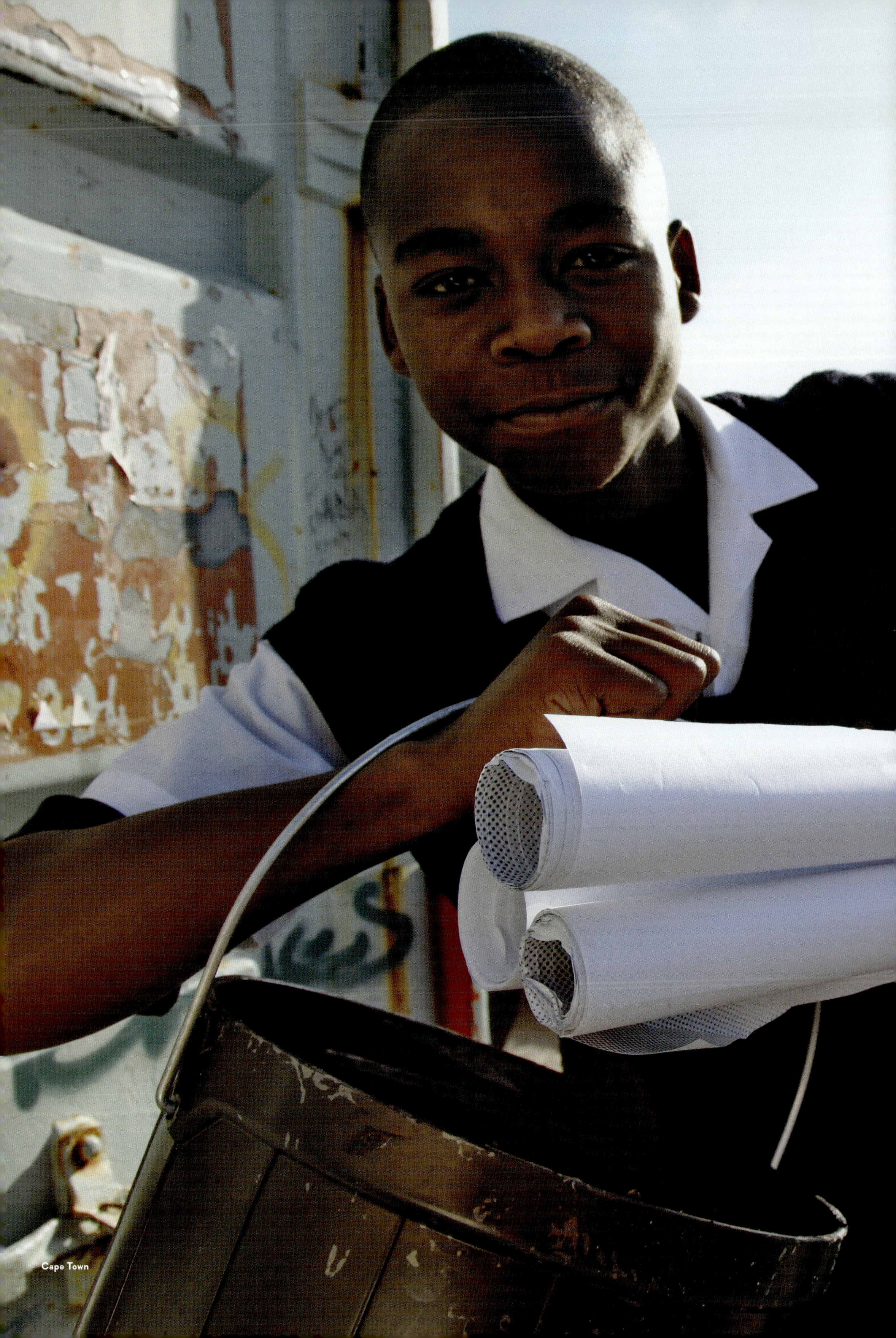
Cape Town

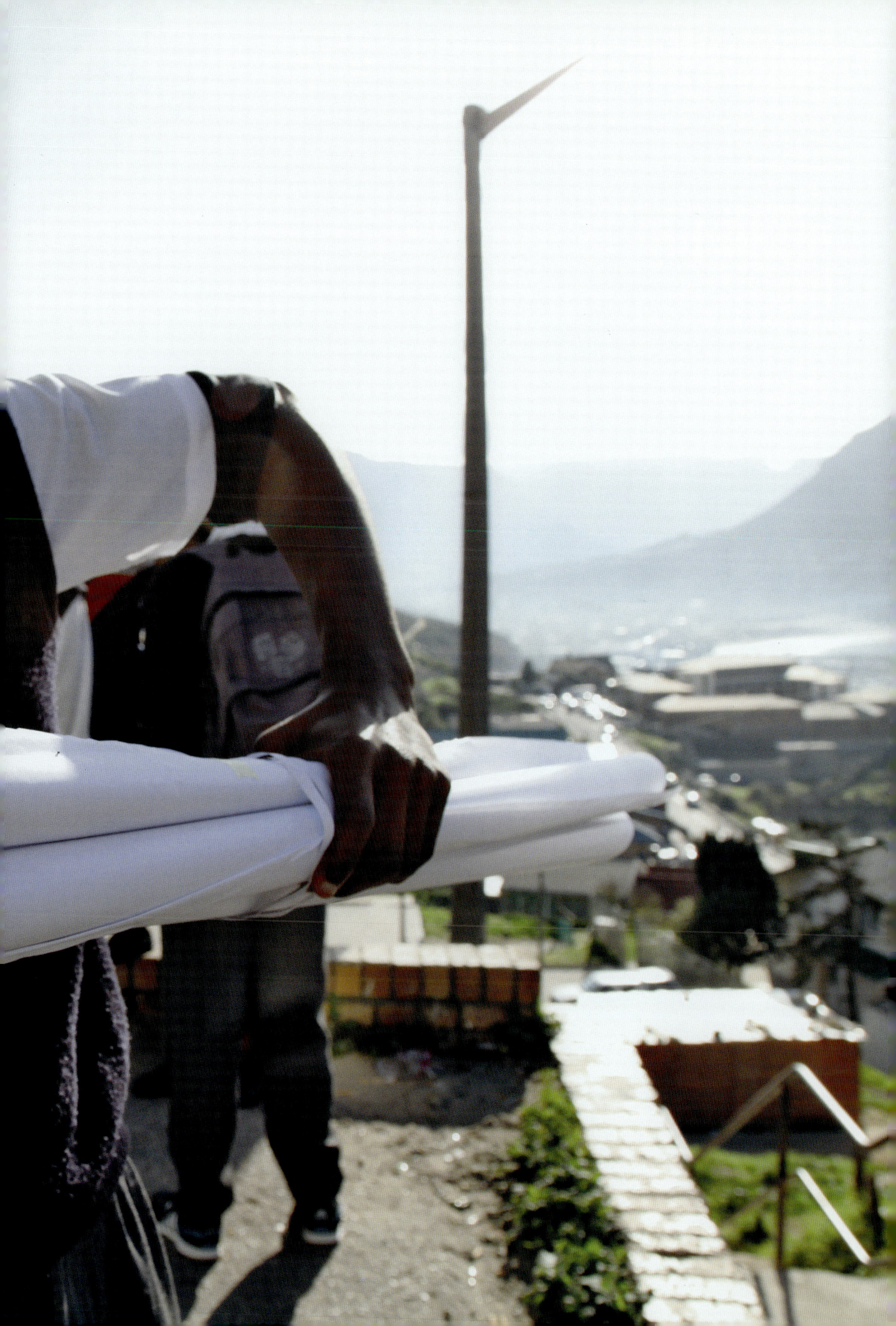

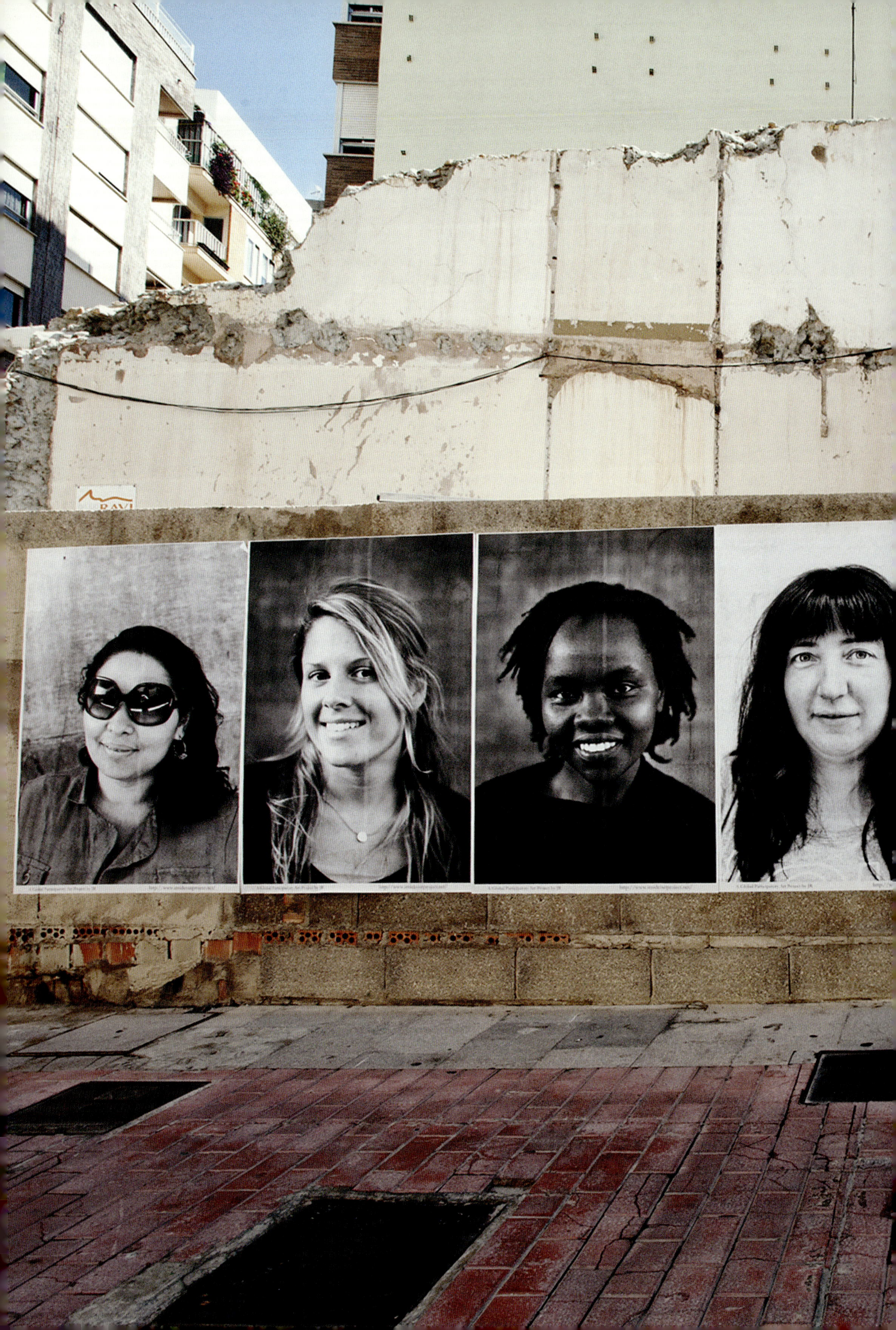

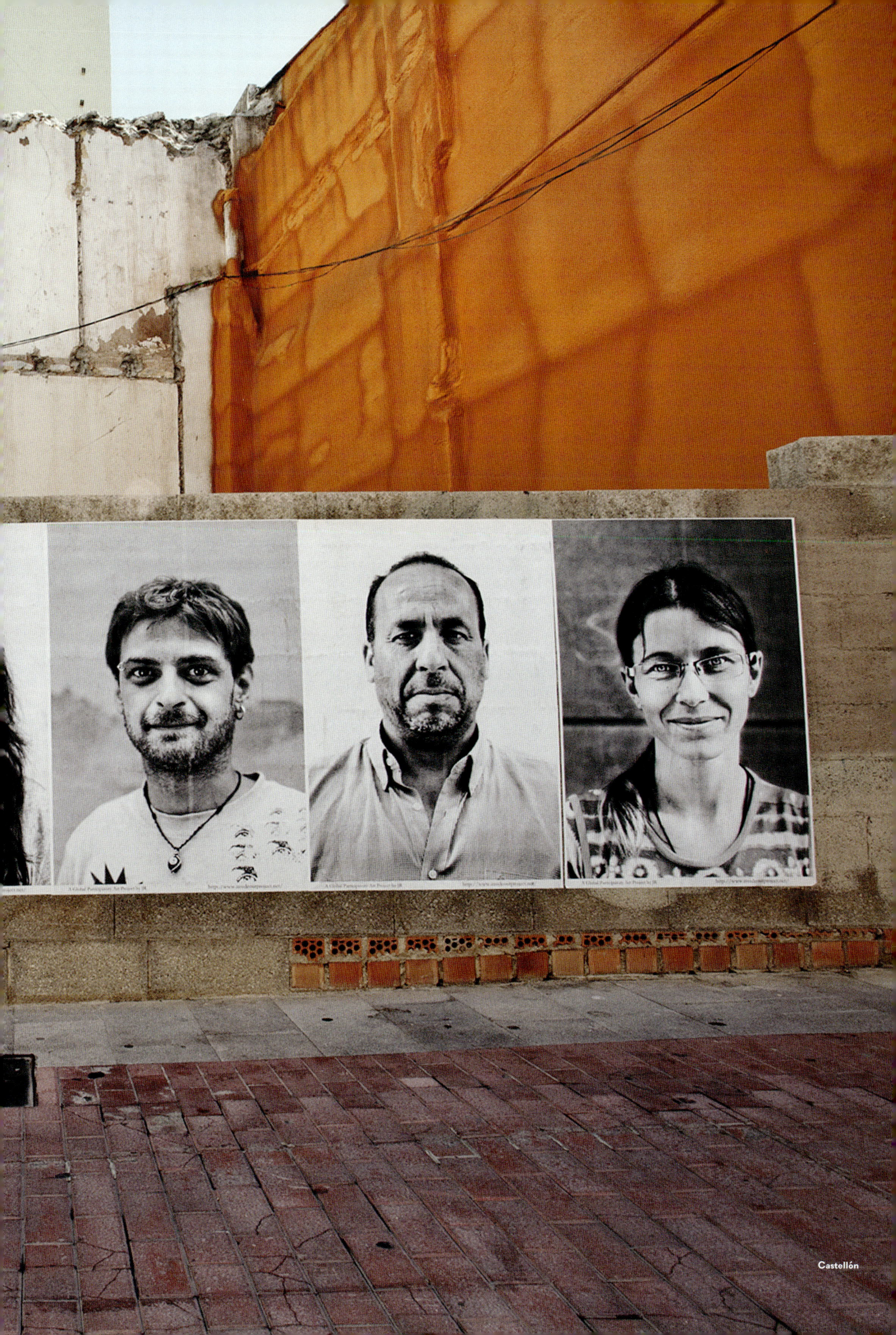

Castellón

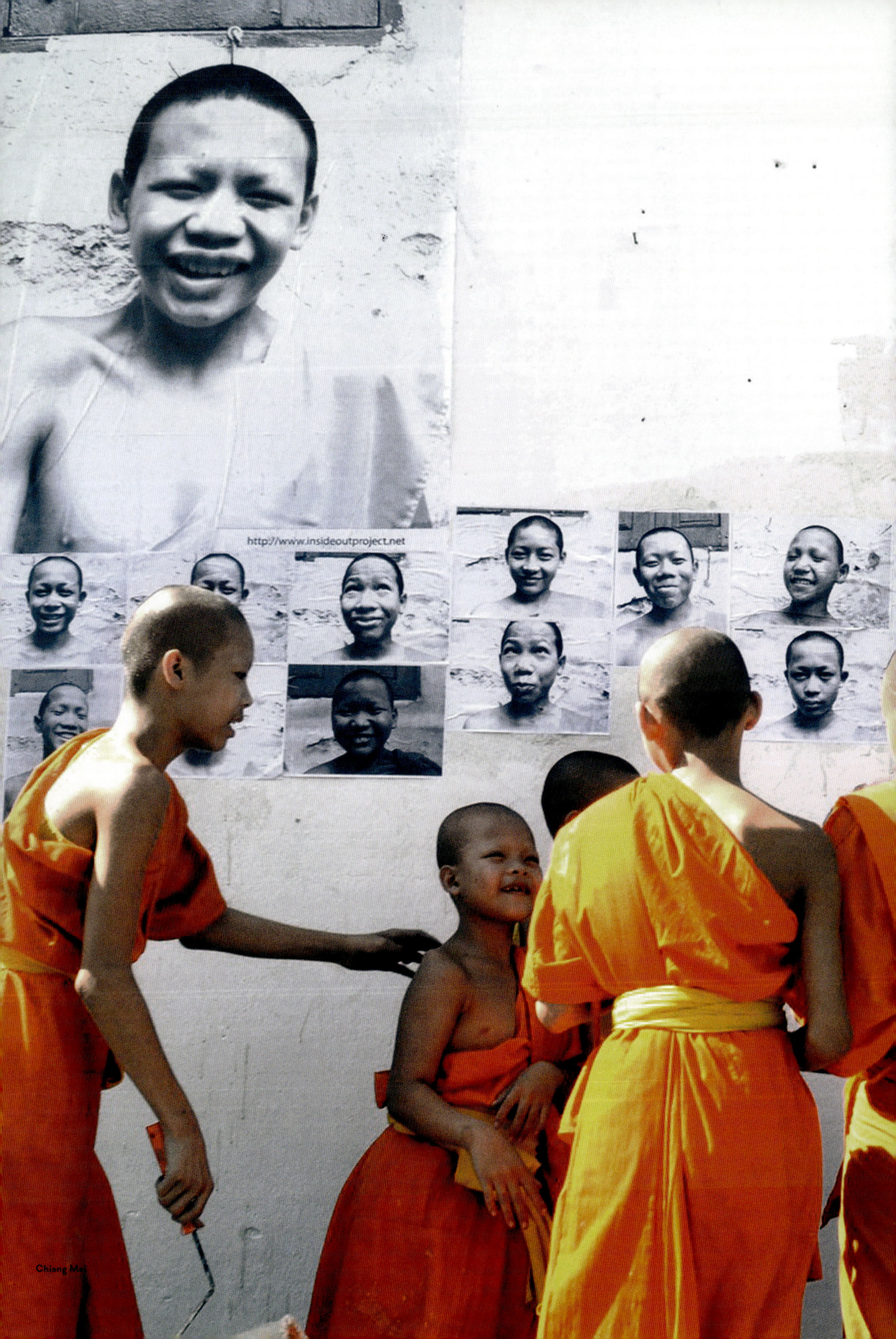

Chiang Mai

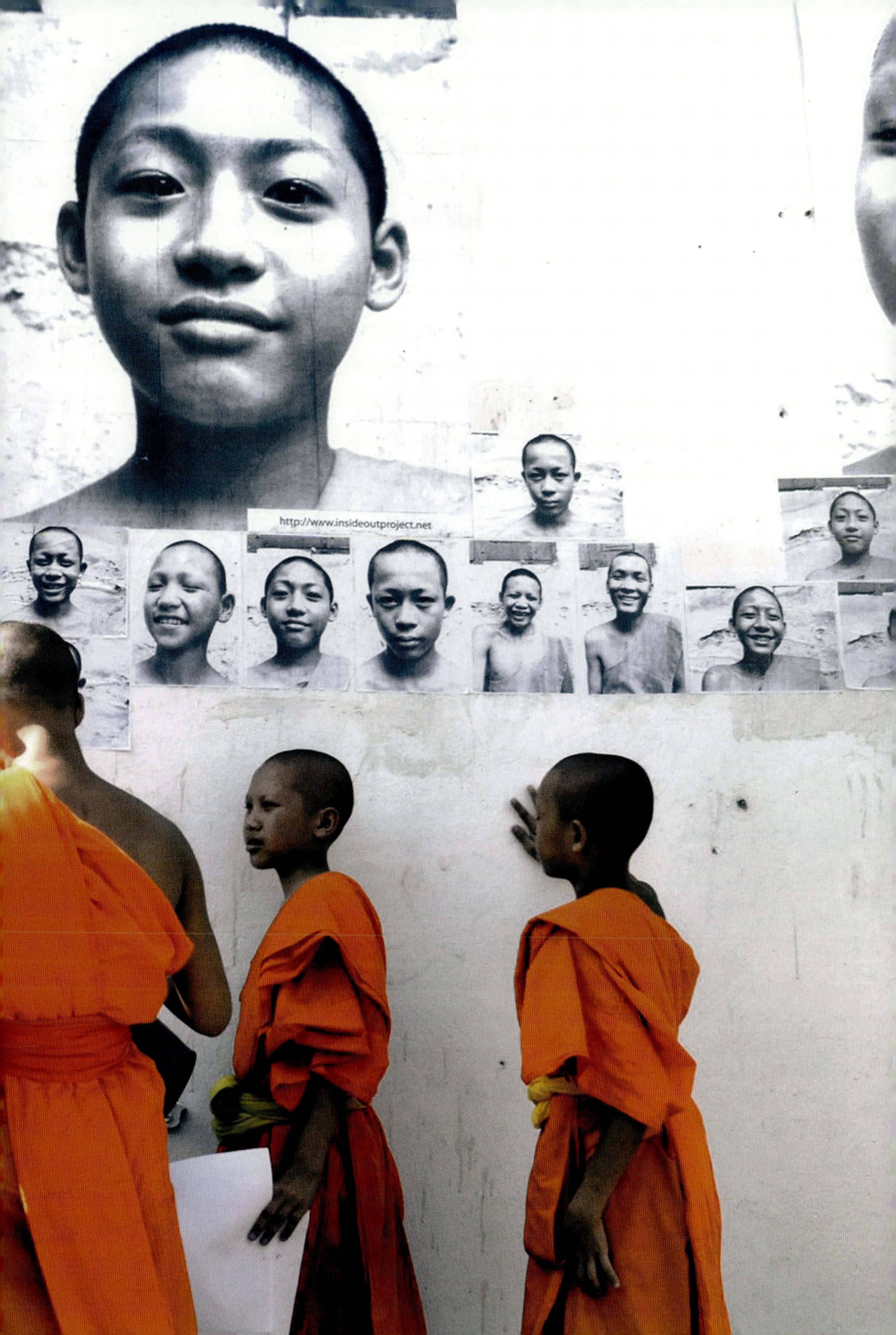
http://www.insideoutproject.net

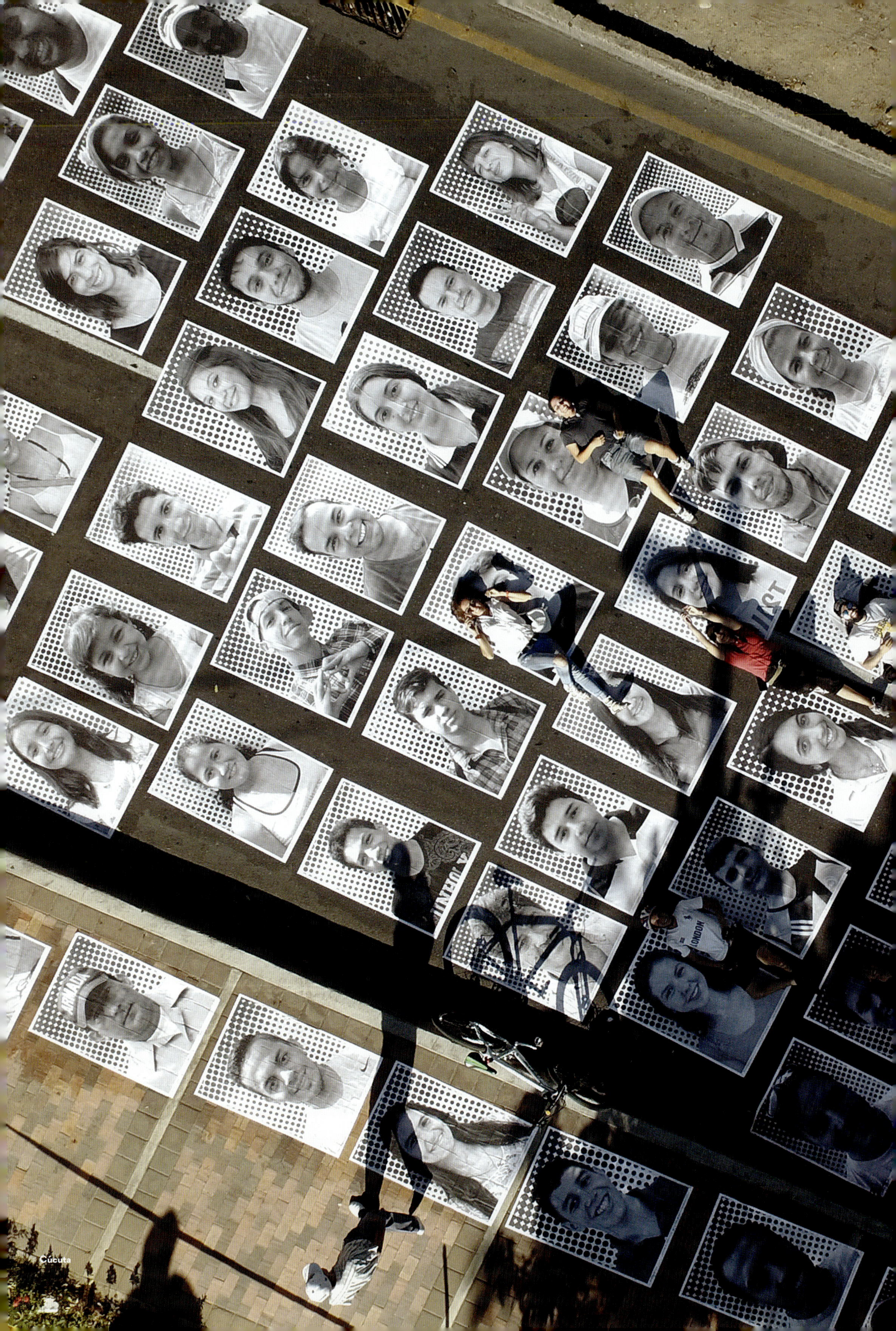
Cúcuta

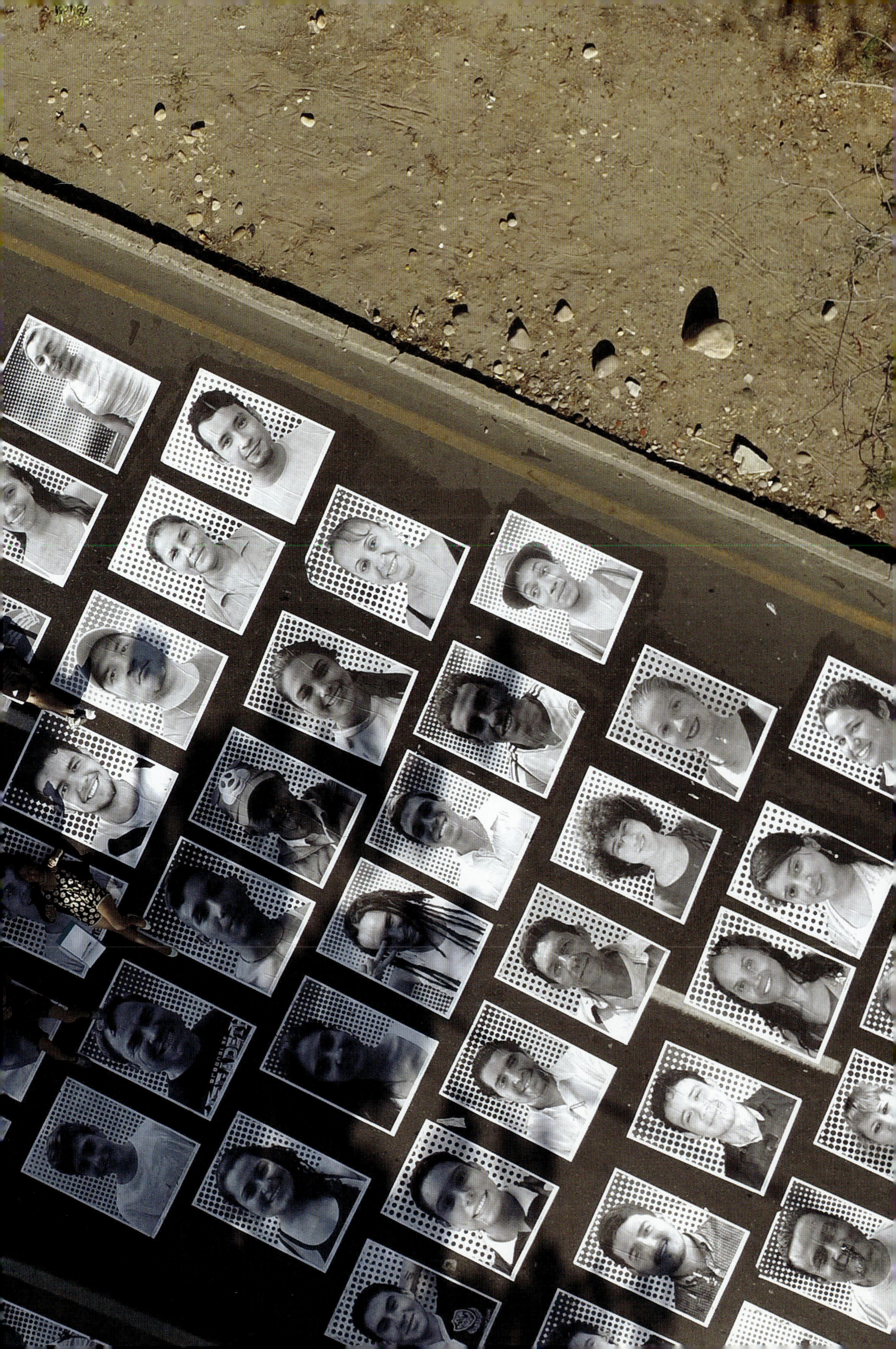

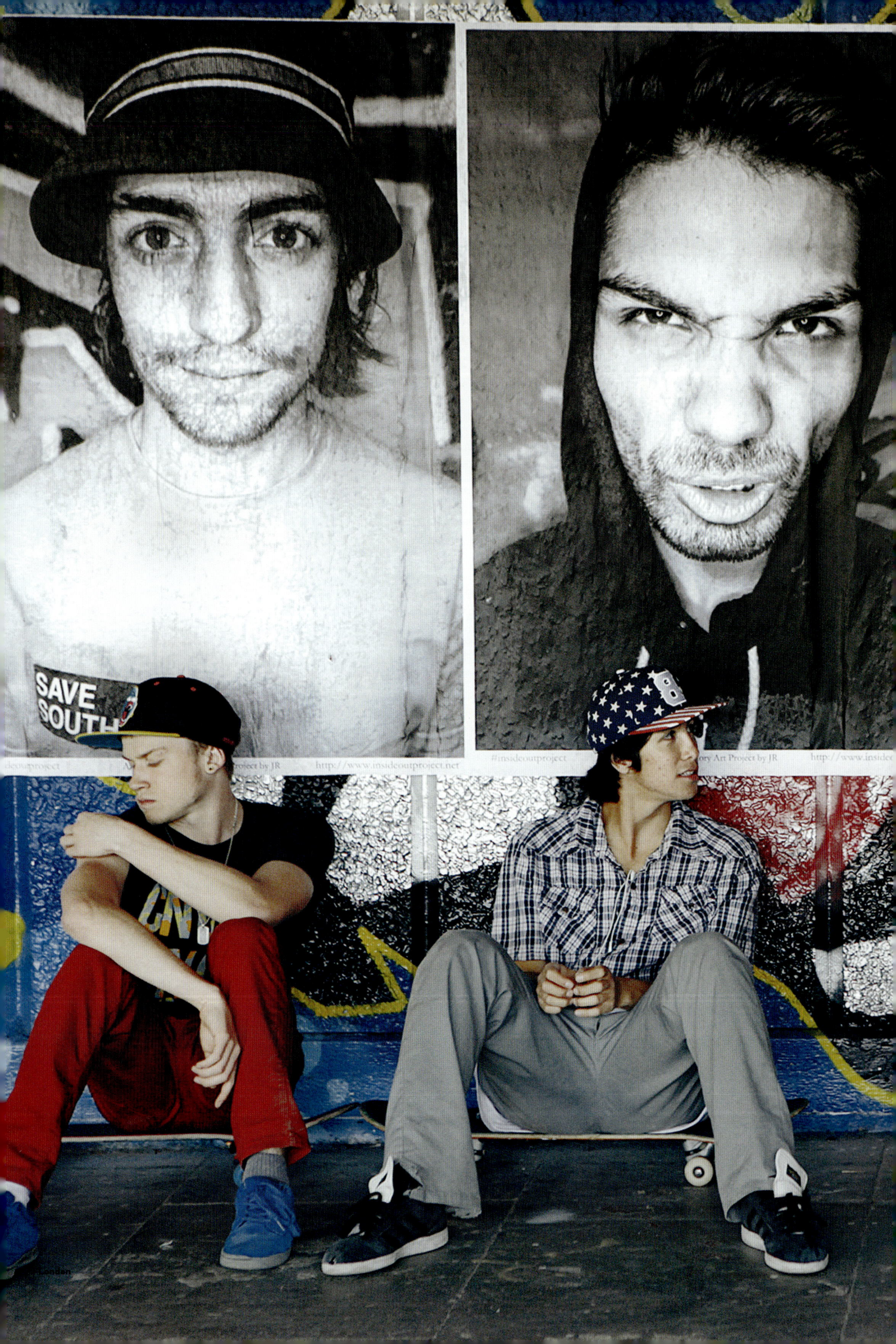
SAVE
SOUTH
#insideoutproject
Project by JR
http://www.insideoutproject.net
#insideoutproject
Art Project by JR

London

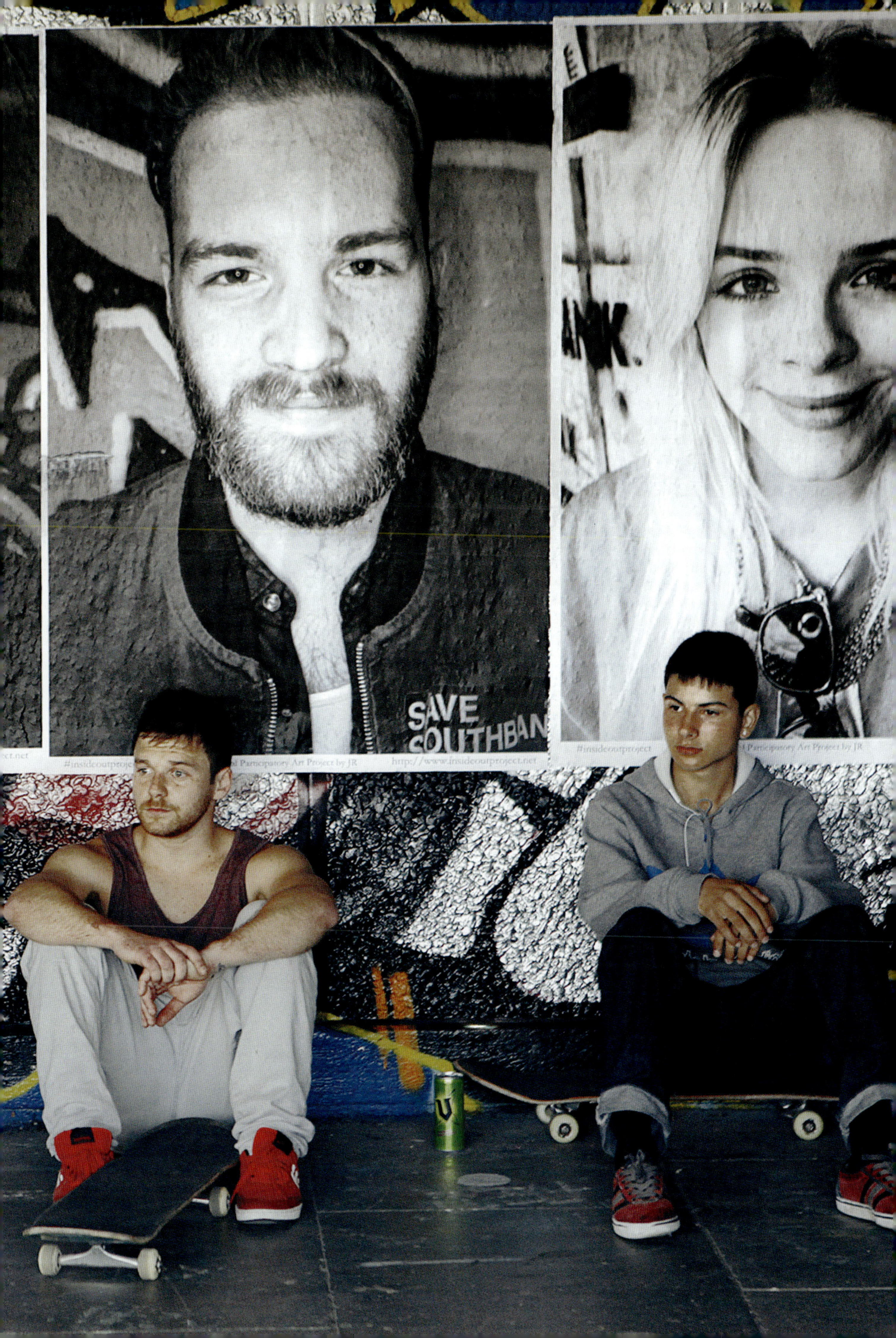
SAVE
SOUTHBAN
http://www.insideoutproject.net
#insideoutproject

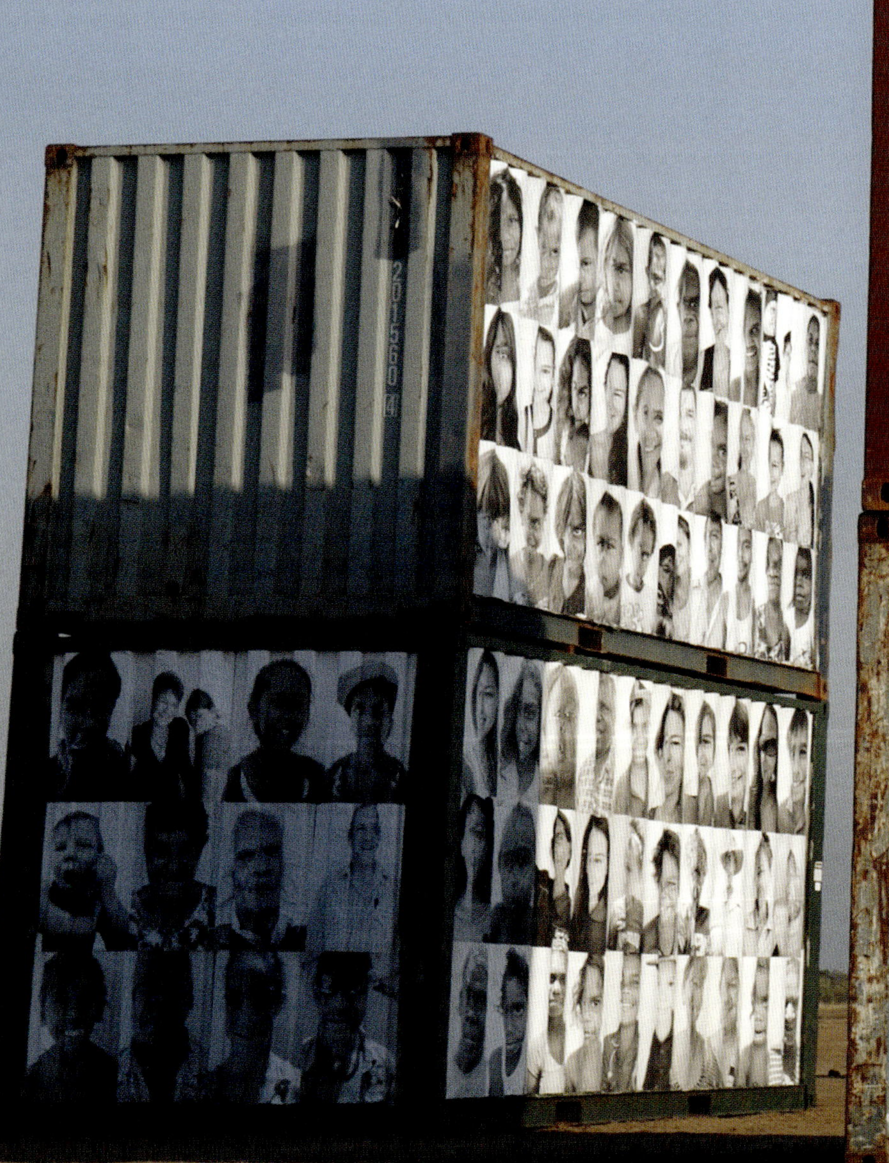

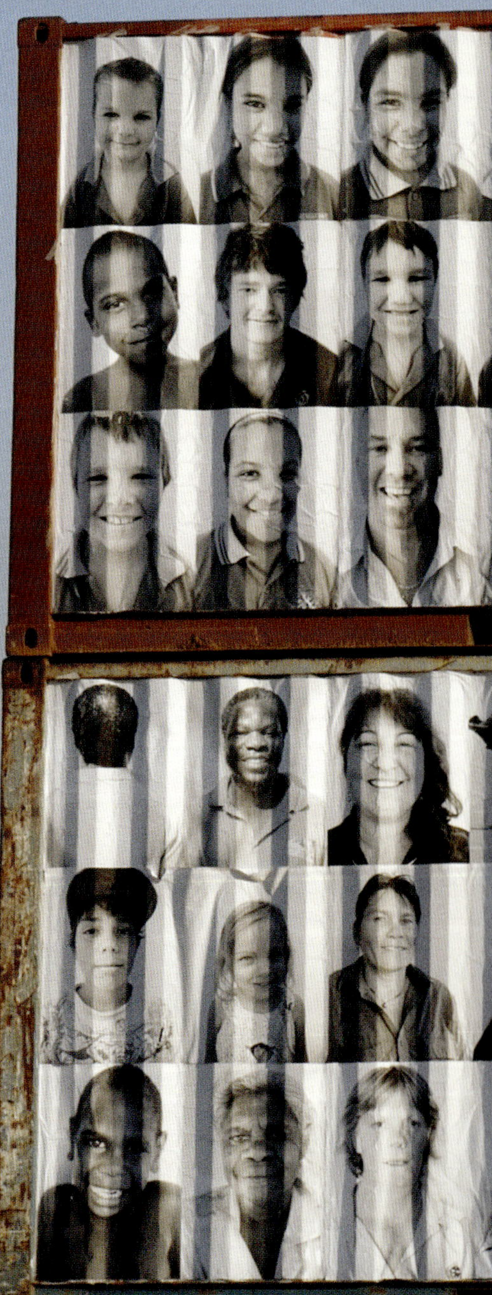

Derby

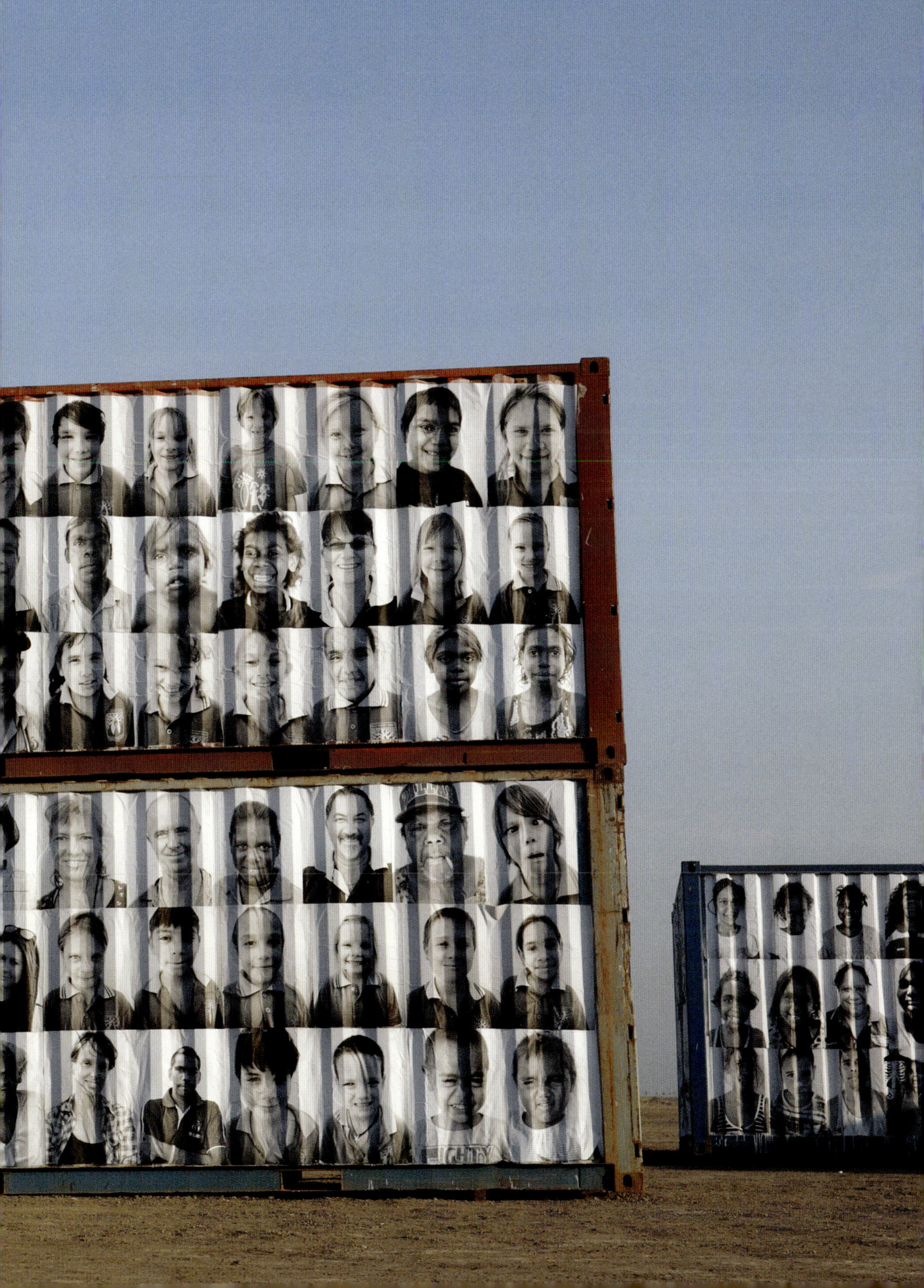

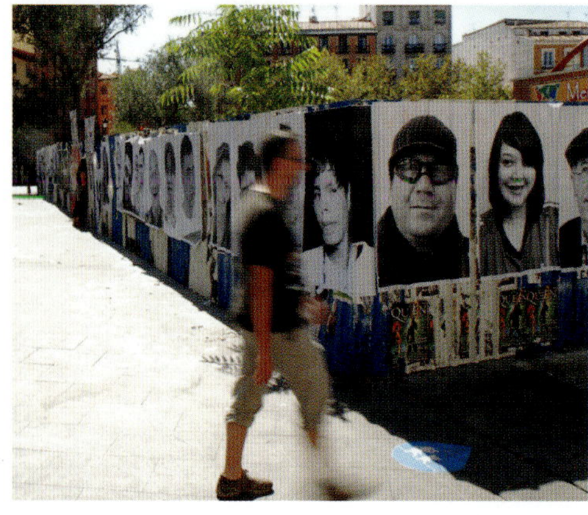

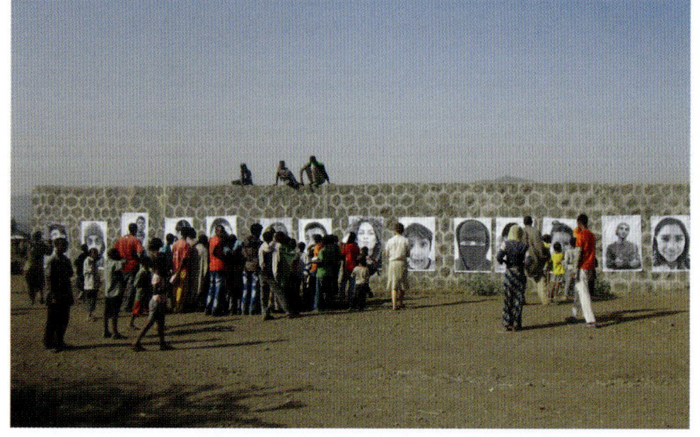

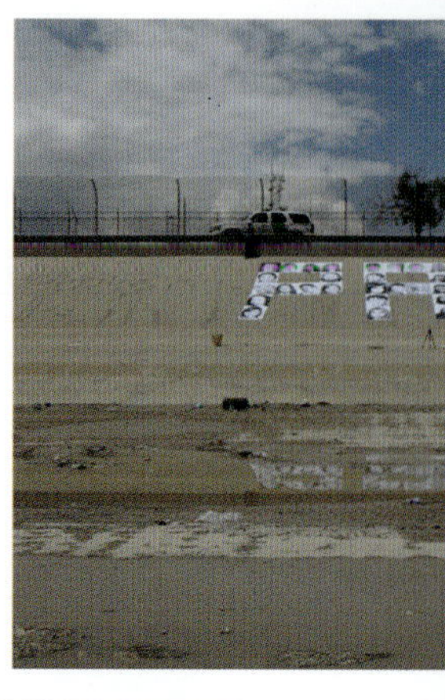

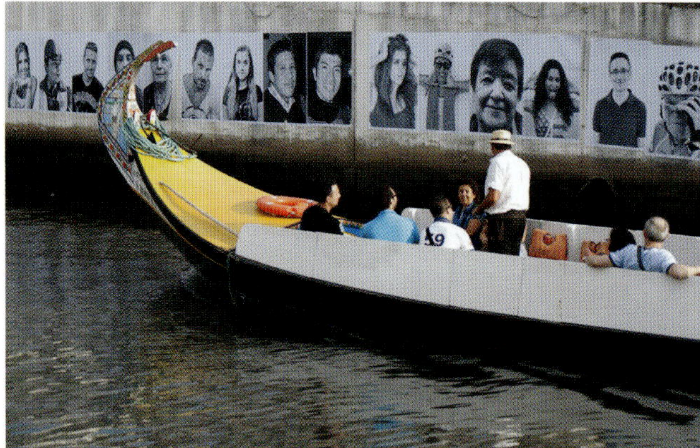

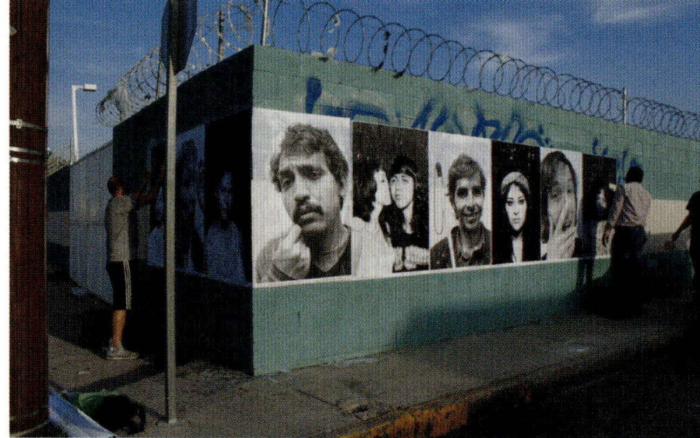

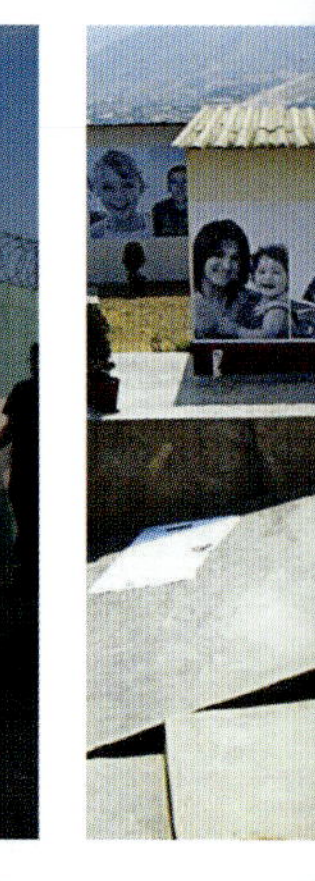

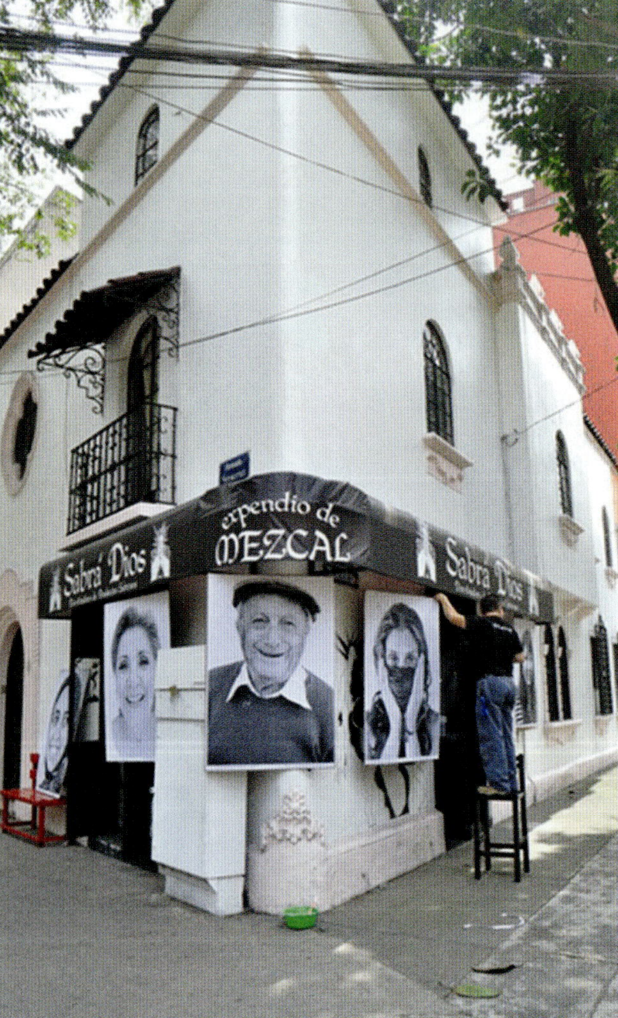

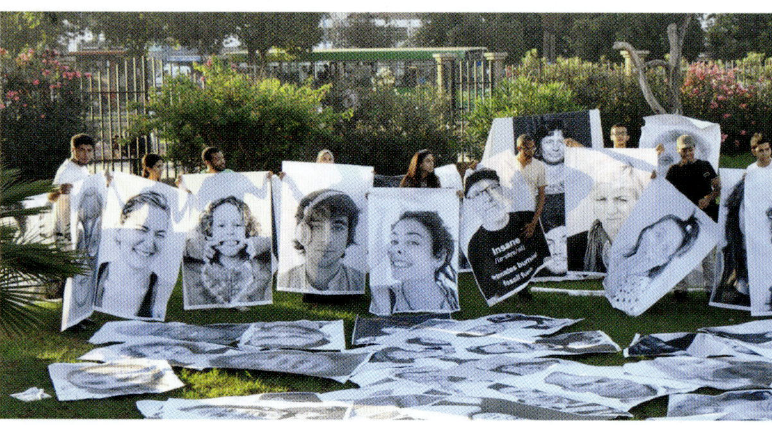

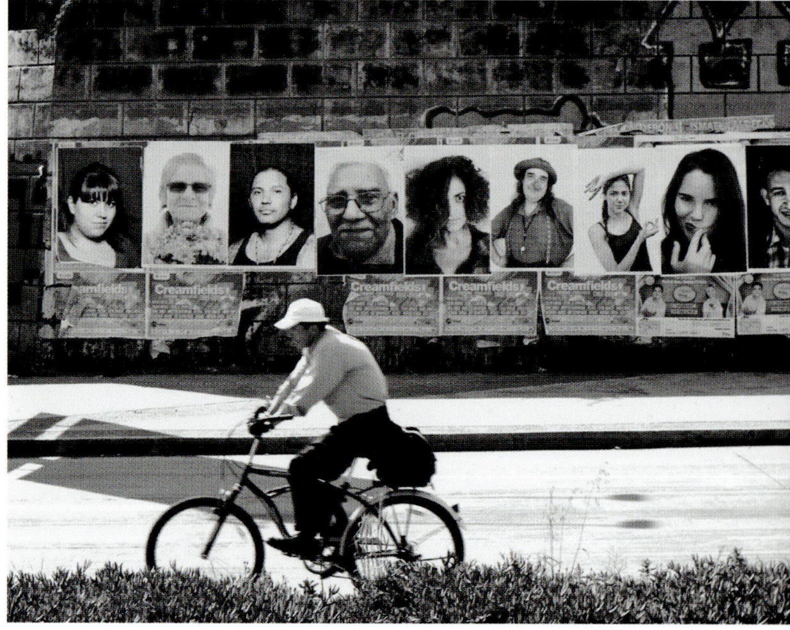

Be the Change: Alamata / Athens / Aveiro / Austin, TX / Bandung / Brisbane / Casablanca / El Paso, TX / Juárez / Lima / Madrid / Mexico / Mulhouse / New York / Nicosia / Tunis / Santiago / Seoul

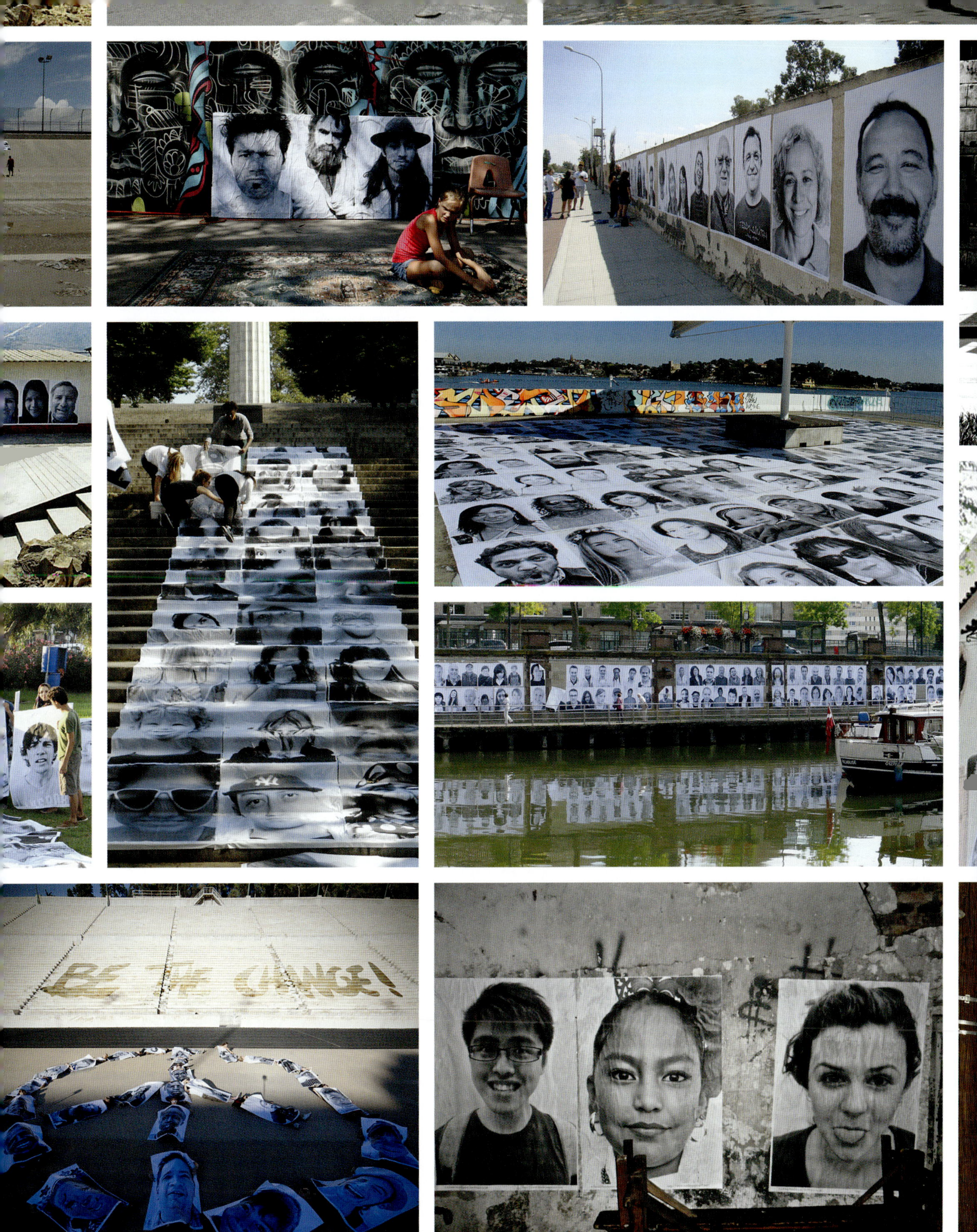

"We stand for peace in our city, our country, and the world!"

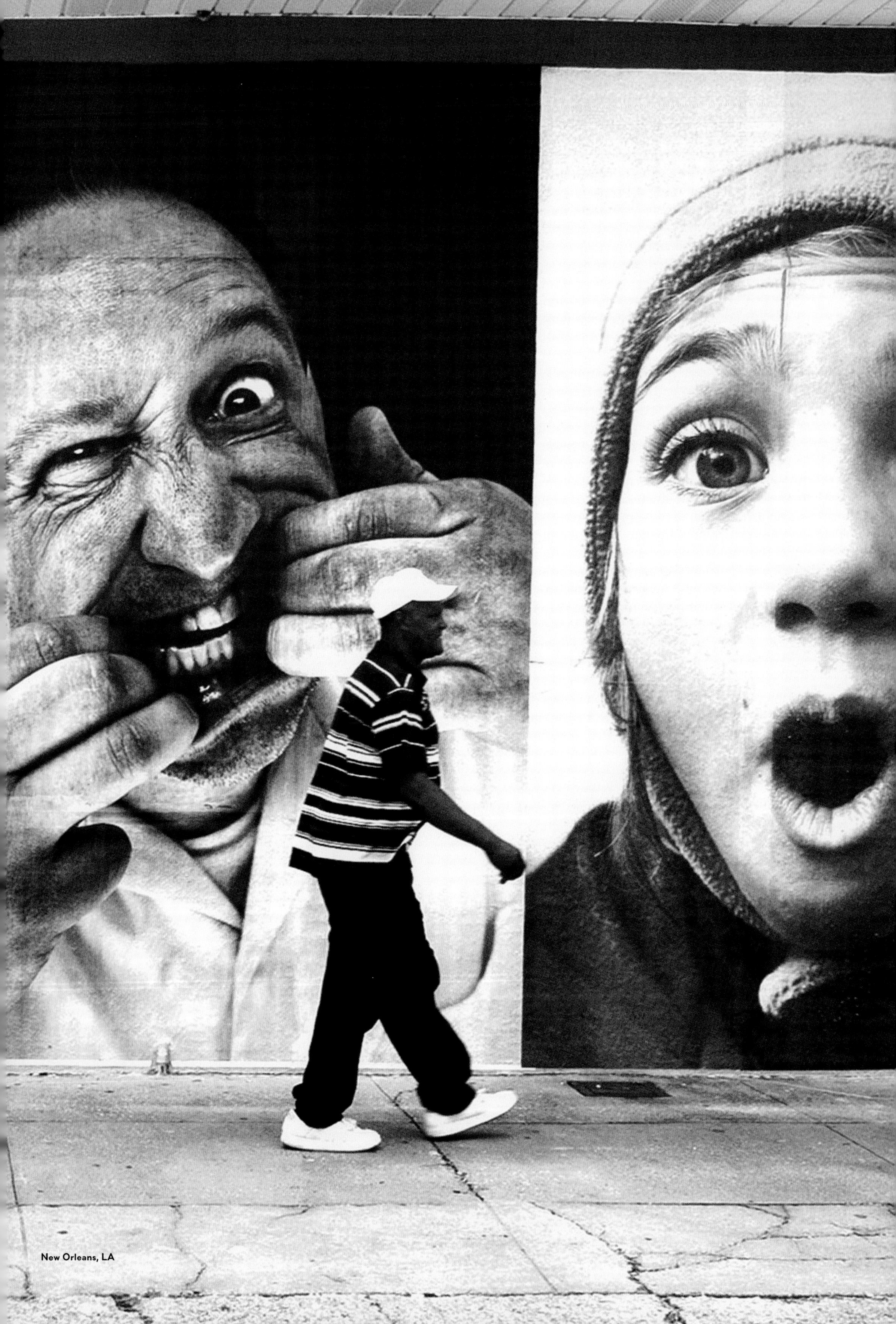

New Orleans, LA

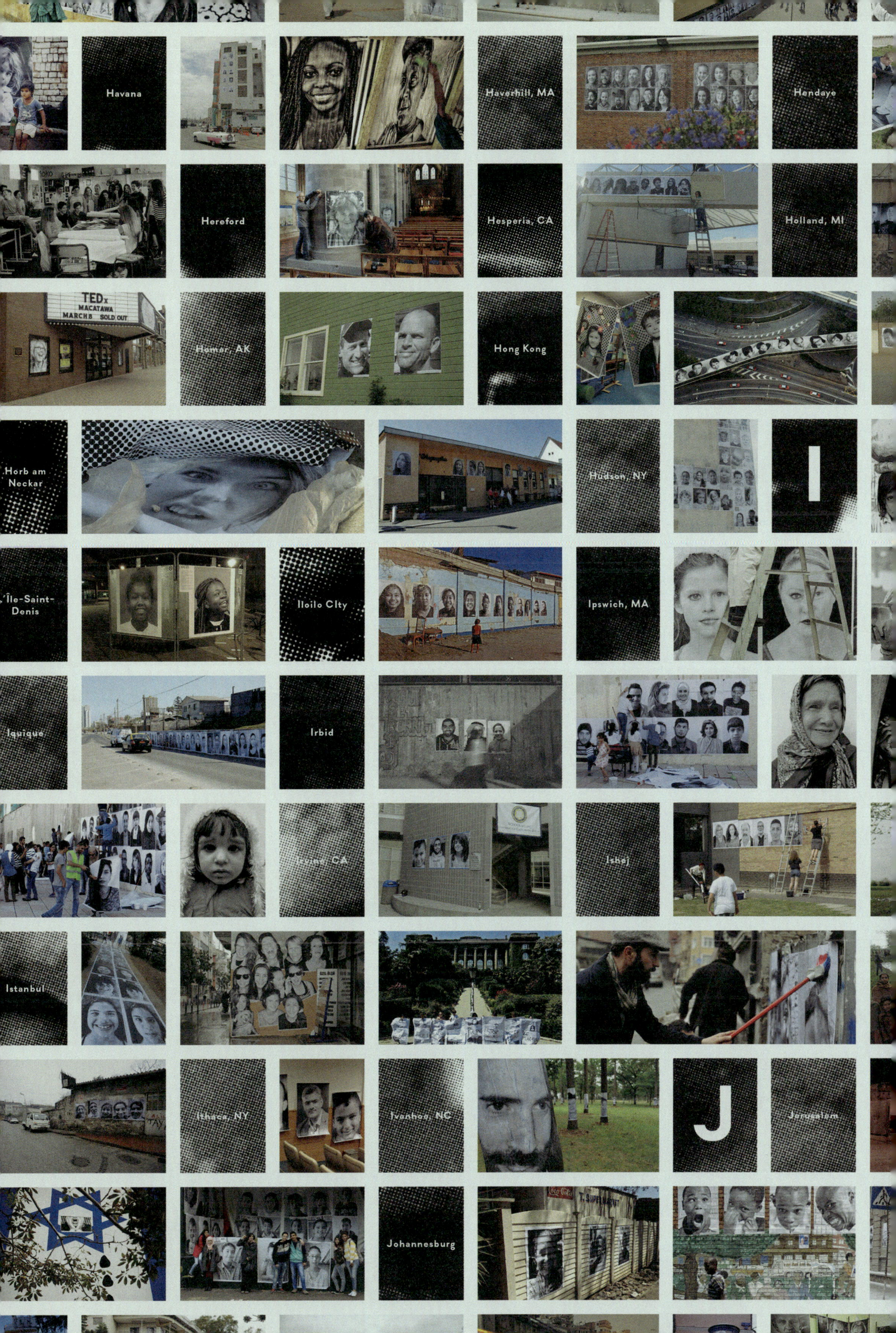
Havana
Haverhill, MA
Hendaye
Hereford
Hesperia, CA
Holland, MI
TEDx
MACATAWA
MARCH 8 SOLD OUT
Homer, AK
Hong Kong
Horb am Neckar
Hudson, NY
I
Île-Saint-Denis
Iloilo City
Ipswich, MA
Iquique
Irbid
Irvine, CA
Ishøj
Istanbul
Ithaca, NY
Ivanhoe, NC
J
Jerusalem
Johannesburg

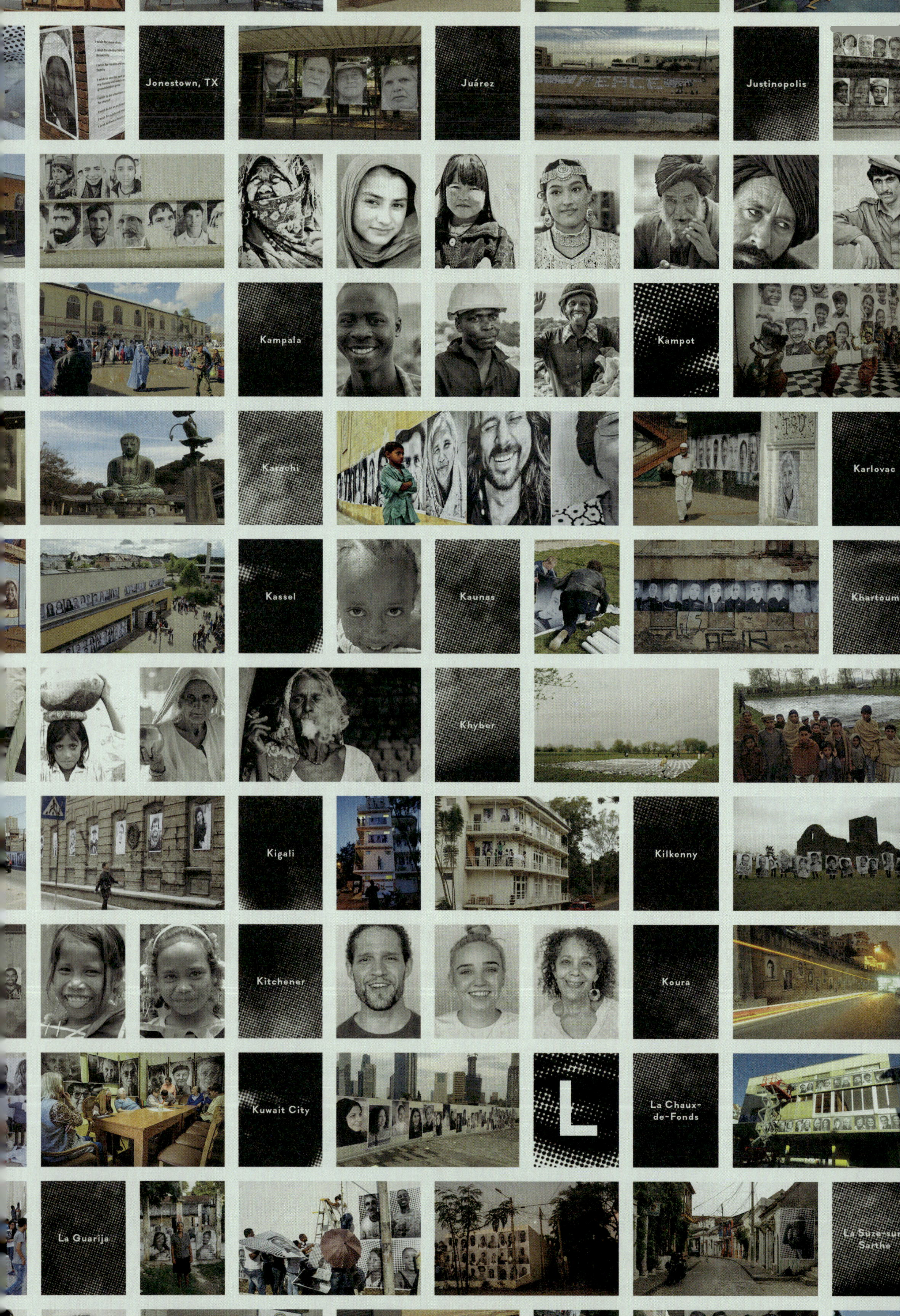

Jonestown, TX
Juárez
Justinopolis
Kampala
Kampot
Karachi
Karlovac
Kassel
Kaunas
Khartoum
Khyber
Kigali
Kilkenny
Kitchener
Koura
Kuwait City
L
La Chaux-de-Fonds
La Guarija
La Suze-sur-Sarthe

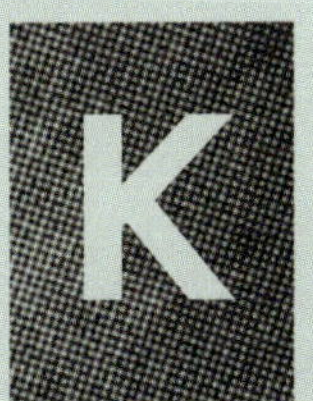

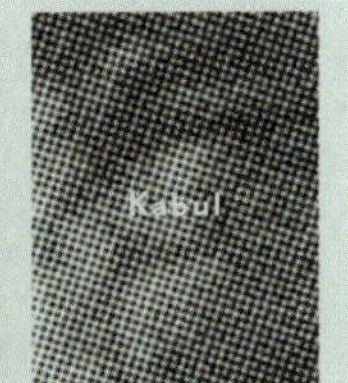

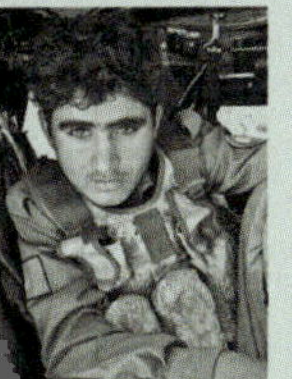
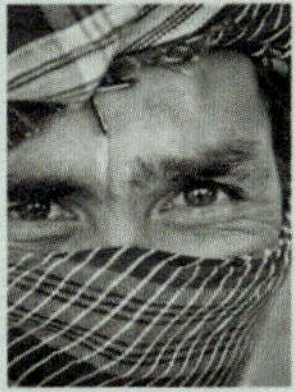
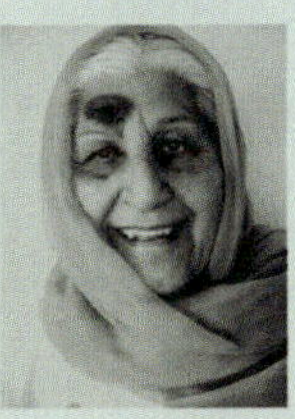
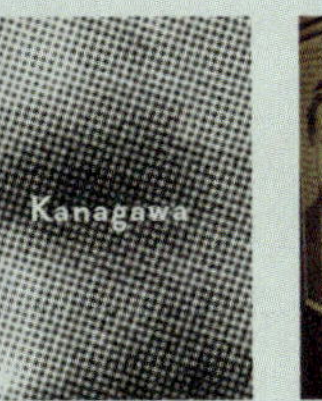

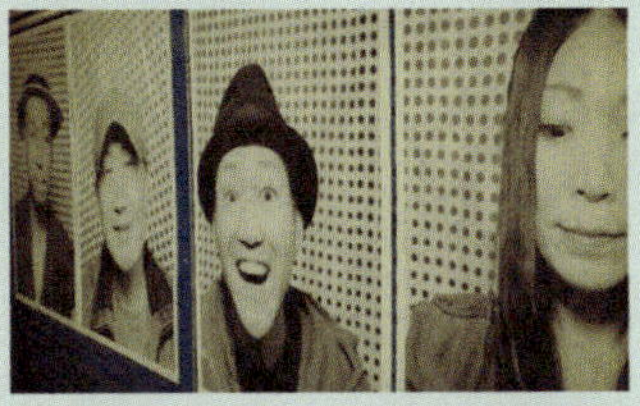
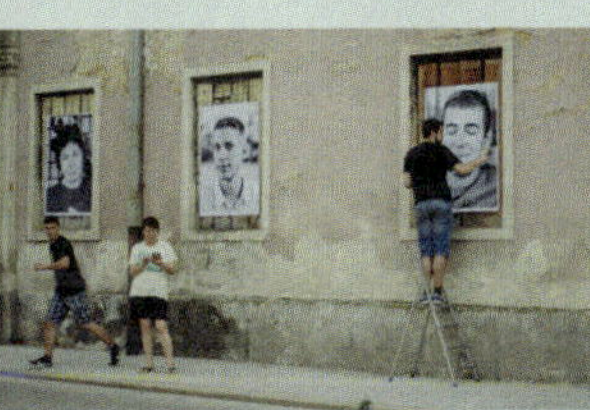
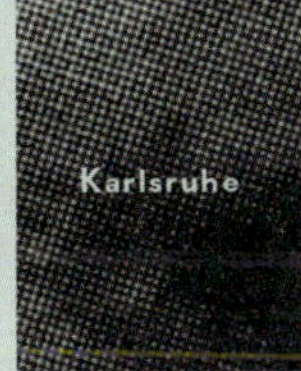

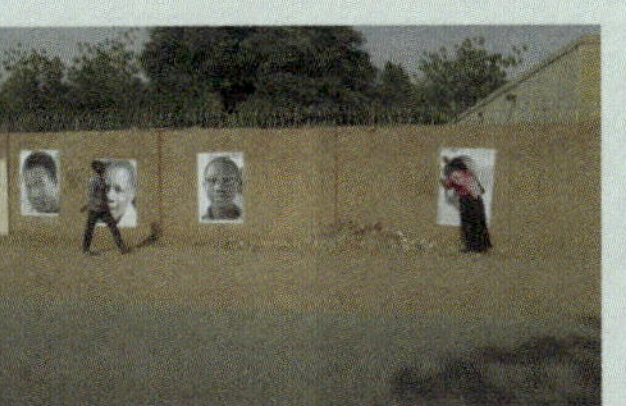
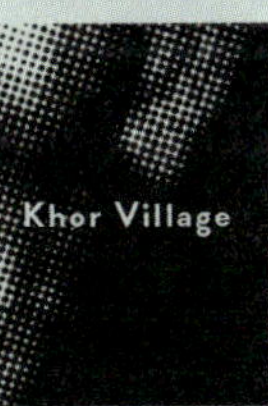

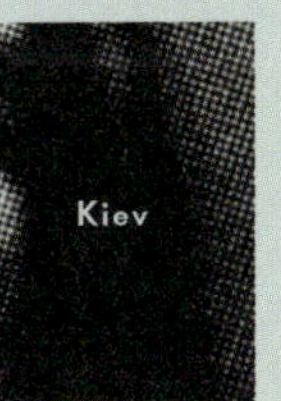

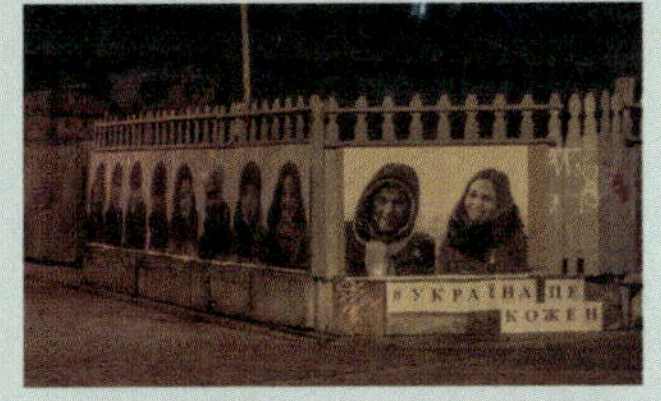
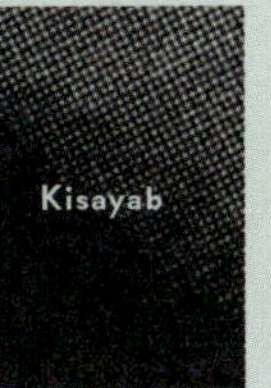

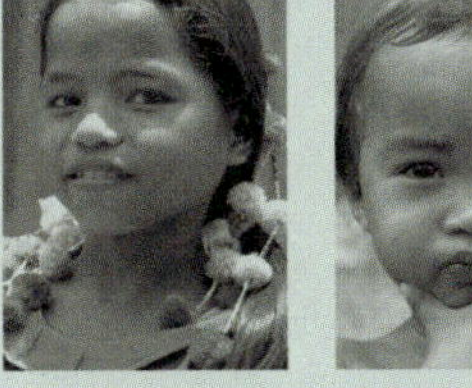
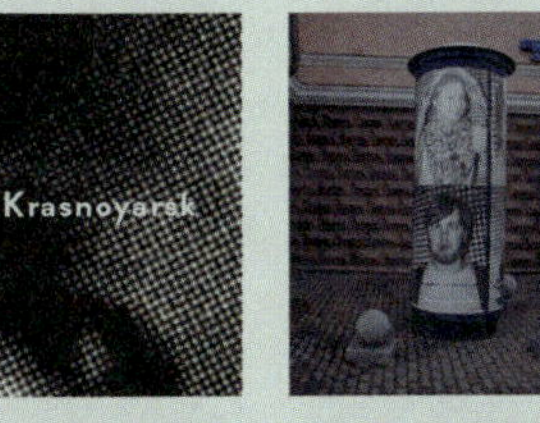

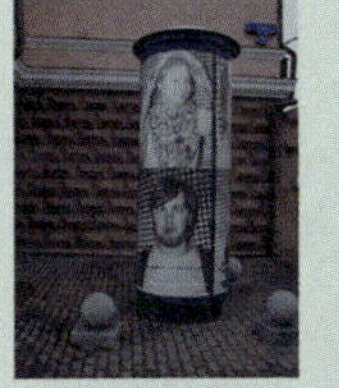

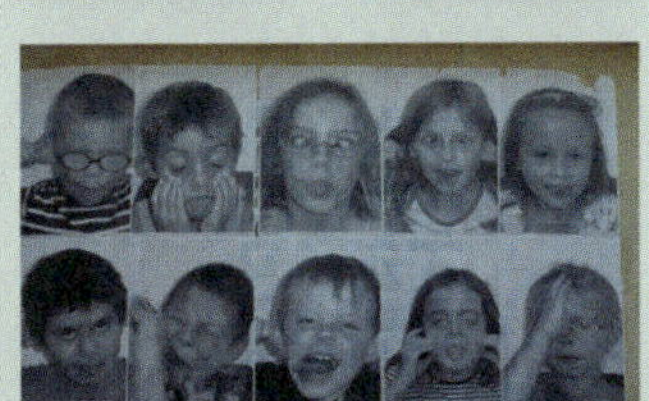

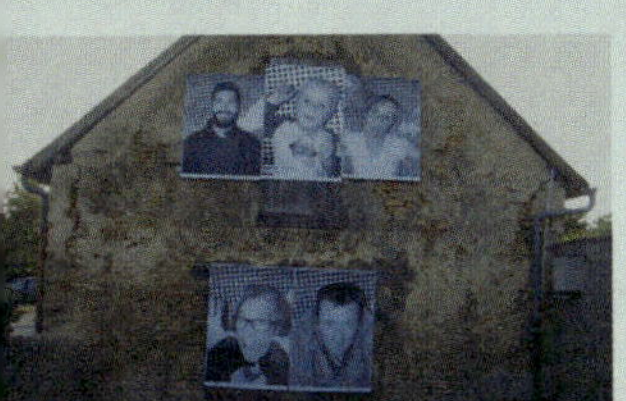
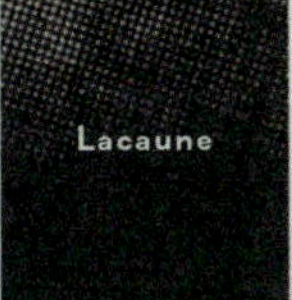

Kabul, Afghanistan The Celebration of the Real Afghanistan, September 2012. Afghanistan is not only the story of Khalid Hosseini portrayed in the media. There is hope and joy here, and we want to celebrate it.

Kampot, Cambodia Move Cambodia, May 2014. With energetic, smiling, and open faces, these children represent the present-day Cambodian people: heads up, eyes straight ahead, poised to move their nation forward.

Karachi, Pakistan TED X Karachi, May 2011. To expose the persecution of minorities in Pakistan.

Karlovac, Croatia The Pursuit, June 2015. We believe in art. We believe in creativity. We believe that culture makes the world worth living in. We gathered inspiring people that give their all to make the town better.

Karlsruhe, Germany Ludwig-Marum-Gymnasium: The Senior Year, June 2015. This group action will be the last mark we leave at our school before graduation: we grew up together, shaped each other's characters and became a strong, outstanding community of classmates.

Kaunas, Lithuania Made Corrections, April 2014. We hope the boys will be inspired to do better, not only for themselves but for their families and have a better sense of wellbeing because of it.

Khartoum, Sudan Khartoum International Community School, March 2013. Students wanted the kids at the orphanage to feel recognized and show their humanity through their faces to members of the community.

Khyber, Pakistan Not a Bug Splat, April 2014. Since 2004, drone strikes in Pakistan have killed an estimated 3,000+ people. While some of these were high-profile targets, a large number were civilians. Including 160 children. The people who operate the drones describe their casualties as "bug splats", since viewing the body through a grainy-green video image gives the sense of an insect being crushed.

Kiev, Ukraine Ukraine Is Everyone, February 2014. These are typical Ukrainians of different social status, ages, and genders. They all gathered around one idea: for the government to see that hundreds, thousands, millions of Ukrainians want change.

Smile Power, December 2013. A project to spread the image of a unified country and a generation centered around values of forgiveness and positive attitude.

Kigali, Rwanda Rwanda: Positive, Negative, Equal, May 2013. We want to challenge ignorance and share the message that HIV stigma is harmful to the community.

Koura, Lebanon Paving the Way for a Better Future, May 2013. We promote equality and pave the way for a better future, by embracing the diversity in Lebanon in an attempt to push aside political differences.

Kremnica, Slovakia Unnoticed, May 2015. The word "gratitude" best describes the primary emotion experienced during visits to the mental hospital.

Kuwait City, Kuwait #WeCanDoIt, September 2015. The campaign's aim is to spread positivity and raise awareness about women empowerment in the Middle East (GCC)!

La Chaux-de-Fonds, Switzerland Shake Our Interior, January 2012. This series of portraits aims to shake our interior walls through very different faces. We examine the political divisions that are tearing apart our region. We also want to question the generation gap and the real or fantasized tensions between here and elsewhere.

La Force, France Child, November 2013. We want to show children that are welcome in our center while their parents are working is a true chance; it is not a punishment.

La Guajira, Colombia Atrapar un Sueño, April 2016. You and I build illusions, sowing love and hope, opening doors to make our dreams come true.

La Suze-sur-Sarthe, France Pourquoi pas Nous, June 2014. Arts and culture play an important role in the lives of all people, however, not all people are able to engage with it equally. As deaf and disabled artists, we can face physical, attitudinal, and communication barriers that exclude us from full participation.

Lacaune, France Recognizing the Elderly, June 2013. "Lifelines Castres" (Lignes de Vies) aims to combat the loneliness and isolation of the elderly in nursing homes and to foster exchanges between different generations, and to create a more compassionate society with kinder and healthier ways of caring for the elderly within our villages and cities so that they are not hidden away behind nursing home doors. The project is also about reclaiming the public space, which has been taken over by advertising. We question how the singularly young and photoshopped images, which dominate our public space, reinforce our dissatisfaction with ourselves.

Lalitpur, Nepal Hope for Tomorrow, October 2015. The terrible earthquake of April 25, which took the life of approximately 9,000 people, brought a lot of tragedy and fear to people's hearts. It also showed the wonderful spirit of resilience of the Nepalis. "Hope for Tomorrow" shows the story of a united community, the inhabitants, and the people connected to Swotha square in the old Patan, Kathmandu Valley.

Langres, France Quand les Bénévoles s'y Collent, les Associations s'Envolent, August 2013. We want to pay homage and support associations and their volunteers, in their efforts to sustain the arts and culture in the face of rural exodus.

Las Palmas, Spain Mujeres, Femmes, Donne: el Futuro Está en Ellas, December 2016. Inequalities between men and women have no place in our future. The future is a part of our bodies; it's ours.

Las Vegas, NV Kaleidoscope of Cultures, October 2015. How can we serve as instruments of peace if we don't see or understand each other? If our countries are enemies, must we too be enemies? What is possible when we look deeper—beneath the headlines, beyond the wars and prejudices—and into each other's hearts?

Laudio, Spain A Face That Looks Back at You, September 2011. A face that looks back at you can say so much without even speaking a word. We want for people to find out what our expressions say to them. We want them to look at us and have something stir inside of them. From the outside we want to get into their inside.

Lauris, France 1000 Sourires de Lauris, June 2016. We want to show the smiling face of our town Lauris and welcome others to come visit!

Lausanne, Switzerland Let's Celebrate Diver "City" of Lausanne, September 2016. Switzerland has been a welcoming country for many immigrants . . . and Lausanne is embodying this tradition. The city is really diverse and we wanted to celebrate it by walking through the city and taking random pictures of people.

Lawrence, MA Lawrence Inside Out, April 2015. This project invites participants to celebrate Lawrence's thriving artistic community and encourages everyone to see themselves as artists.

Le Barp, France Manifeste des Cp et Ce1, May 2015. Elementary school students' declaration: "You should never be sad, we are adorable, we're angry against the school on Wednesdays, the bad people that attacked Charlie Hebdo, the polluters and the thieves; we care about nature, we want peace in the world, we aren't afraid of anything and we will never give up, thanks to the world and the people who love us."

Le Crès, France Liberté d'Expression: Autoportraits de Groupe, April 2015. This project is important for the students because they realize the importance of freedom of speech. They debate and affirm their position.

Le Havre, France Mouvement de l'Economie Solidaire, September 2012. Faces of the people who are developing the Positive Economic Movement.

Le Mans, France Coexister Dans Notre Quartier, June 2016. To show the diversity of our neighborhood.

Le Pont de Claix, France Affiche Ta Différence!!!, June 2016. Differences provoke unkind looks, hurtful judgments, violent reactions . . . All this prevents us from being ourselves. With this action we want to express our differences, while enjoying it.

Le Pouliguen, France Ayez Confiance!, May 2014. To ask questions about portrait, identity, people's perspective, and engagement.

Leiden de Meelfabriek, Netherlands Inside Out, March 2015. De Meelfabriek Inside Out is a photography and film project that unites multiple stories of the people who have shaped the history of this place.

Leon, Nicaragua "No" to Violence, "Yes" to Love, July-November 2013. The youngsters want to make a statement against violence and abuse: through better communication within relationships, we can create an environment of trust, in which love prevails and violence and abuse lose.

Levier, France Close Your Eyes, February 2013. Change your way of seeing; close your eyes; open your heart.

Liège, Belgium Inside Out St. Gilles: My Fun Area, April–August 2016. The aim of this action is to rediscover our neighborhood through the eyes of the people who inhabit it and make it a very lively place.

Lightbourne, Bahamas Faces of Bahamians, November 2012. Bahamians, like many peoples in the Caribbean, are of an incredibly mixed descent. While many foreigners—and even some Bahamians themselves—think "real" Bahamians are only the descendants of African slaves—true Bahamians are of many colors and ethnicities.

Lilongwe, Malawi Lake of Stars, November 2014. This project is dedicated to Malawi and the world talent it is brewing. In a country that falls in the top 5 poorest in Africa, it is right to raise awareness to the creativity and the talent of the individuals that must live with such harsh realities and still manage to shine some light onto the world.

Lima, Peru ComunidArte, August 2013. Political and economic pressures displaced the Shipibo from their land in the Peruvian Amazon in 1999, when Cantagallo was a landfill site. The children from this community are growing up far from their land and identity in an impoverished shantytown with very few resources and in unsanitary conditions. ComunidArte engages the children in art-making activities in the hope of contributing to a better future for their community.

LGBT Cause, May 2011. Against LGBT tensions.

Lisbon Portugal Inside Out Alfacinha, June 2014. Every year, Lisbon is regarded by tourists as one of the best cities in the world rankings. But what about the real Lisbon locals, the so-called "Alfacinhas"—does the world know about them? We decided to bring the most typical Alfacinhas (from the Sé neighborhood potter to the flea market vendor), to downtown Lisbon, to welcome tourists in one of its oldest city entrances.

Eating for the Planet, June 2014. For food equality for all, and the end of the north/south gap. For the lessening of meat-eating for 3 reasons: ecological, health, and violence against animals. A stance against the meat industry, against the actual way of growing, raising, and killing animals.

Little Rock, AR Inside Out—Be Nice, April 2014. The North Pulaski High School diversity club, located in Jacksonville, AR wants to bring a voice to all students who have ever felt shameful, embarrassed, or bullied for being themselves. Everyone deserves to feel safe, and when we are accepting of each other no matter our race, sexuality, appearance, culture, religion, etc., then we can grow as a peaceful world.

Livingstone, Zambia Young Faces in the Agriculture, September 2012. Diversity is wonderful and to embrace the young faces in agriculture is inspiring as well as motivating: Our main goal is to showcase the young faces in agriculture. It is because we are connected that agriculture will continue to grow as an innovative industry.

Ljubljana, Slovenia Inside Out—Slovenia, March 2014. Through our portraits we want to show that fatalism is not the only choice, that active involvement filled with positive attitudes and a sense of togetherness can make a great difference. One active, positive person can change his/her own future; many can change the future of a whole generation.

Lodz, Poland We Are All Workers, September 2016. Through hard work our grandmas and grandpas built the foundations of contemporary Lodz. We need to remember them. We would like to honor and thank you. We wish to know your history so we can get to know ourselves better—the young inhabitants of Lodz. Stand up! Your history is our history. We are all workers!

London, England Demolition Party, September 2013. The NHS was created from the ideal that quality healthcare should be available to all. It was launched by the then Minister for Health, Aneurin Bevan, on July 5, 1948. We believe this government's policies of marketization, privatization, and funding cuts are fatally undermining these principles and we are demonstrating our opposition to this.

Young People Also Have a Lot to Express and Demonstrate, July 2013. We decided to put our project on one of the famous Bricklane's walls, Buxton Street, East London, because this place represents the freshness of ideas, some kind of free thinking, and a perfect creative hub for the youth culture.

Skate South Bank Forever, June 2013. This is our creative space, where we learn and practice. We want to let the world know that we love this space and it is special and unique to us. It is this space which makes us share, grow, communicate, and be unique. This is where we ride!!

Free to Play, April 2013. Free to Play is the utopia we wish for—where our children can get fresh air and develop a sense of fair play, sharing, and genuine human interaction.

Passing Clouds, March 2013. "Living By the Wall" is an arts-based project that aims to broaden understanding and challenge preconceptions regarding the lives of Palestinians living in the occupied territories of the West Bank, Gaza, Palestine.

Untitled, August 2011. We stand together for reopening, rebuilding, and moving forward with a new understanding.

London's Local Artists, March 2013. We believe in supporting our local community, artists, and traders

Longmont, CO Wide Angle: The Artist in All of Us, March 2013. Our group would like to support the local art of our city, by recognizing the artist in all of us.

Los Angeles, CA Da FUNction, June 2015. Da FUNction celebrates the creation of a community garden, gathering space, food, education program center, and retail container cafe. The main goal of this garden is to activate each individual to revitalize a collective consciousness that leads to an empowered self-reliant community.

Not Up Yet, November 2014. We aim to call attention to the women who make theater, and how their work intersects with their lives. In capturing the cast, crew, and administrative team of a play about an actress and theater impresario from the Belle Epoque whose work was well ahead of her time, we are championing a woman whose remarkable story was almost lost to history—as many women's stories are. They have committed to continuing to tell the stories of the under-represented, including women, in modern day theater.

Empowering the People, October 2011. Empowering the People.

Louvain-la-Neuve, Belgium Photokot, March 2013. In our house, called PHOTOKOT, we are working on the promotion of photography on the Campus of the University of Louvain-La-Neuve.

Luanda, Angola Kick Out the Violence!, March 2013. "Violence is not okay with anything" is the central theme of the project in Luanda, where people were asked to show a facial expression against violence, an evil that unfortunately has manifested itself in many ways in our society, hence the interest of all in combating it.

Lugano, Switzerland Retirees in Lugano, June 2012. Arte Urbana Lugano dedicates this project to people who live in retirement homes and have little say in the context of the city.

Lyon, France College Alain, Différents Mais Egaux, April 2015. In Saint Fons, students and staff work together for respect and tolerance. Five hundred portraits, mingling adults and teenagers alike, materialize an openness to the world and reflect the idea of a successful community: we live together, different and equal.

Marchers of Lyon, December 2013. This action commemorated the thirtieth anniversary of the walk for equality and against racism that began in 1983 in Lyon. The walk was motivated by a police riot in the suburbs of Lyon and a tense political climate, which inspired people to walk five hundred miles from Marseille to Paris in protest.

Macquarie Fields, Australia Thank You!, August 2013. To create this project, we choose to photograph a member of our school community who has made a positive impact on our journey as students. These people include other students, administrative staff, teachers, our canteen ladies. We wanted to take the time to say thank you.

Madison, WI Up Close, October 2015. Students from Morgan County Crossroads School explore their place in the community: "We come from all over the world and we carry our heritage with strength and dignity, but we are all human. We all have feelings and face different challenges, and together our diversity is strong. We can be self-confident and equal. We are who we are."

Madrid, Spain We Like Art, June 2017. Art is fundamental in the emotional and educational development of any human being.

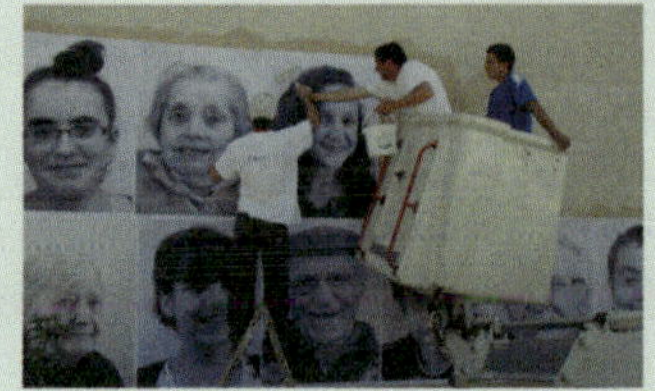

Lagos

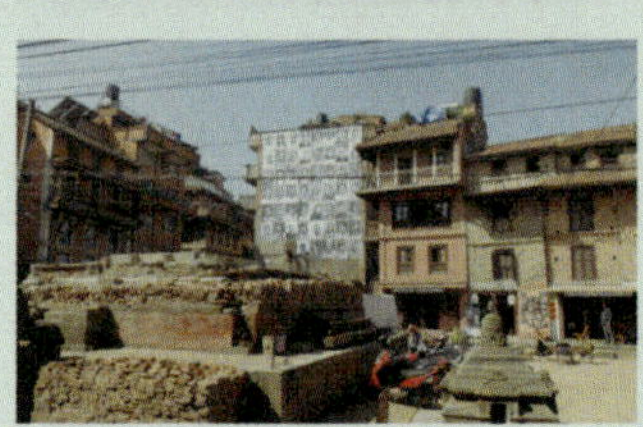

Langres

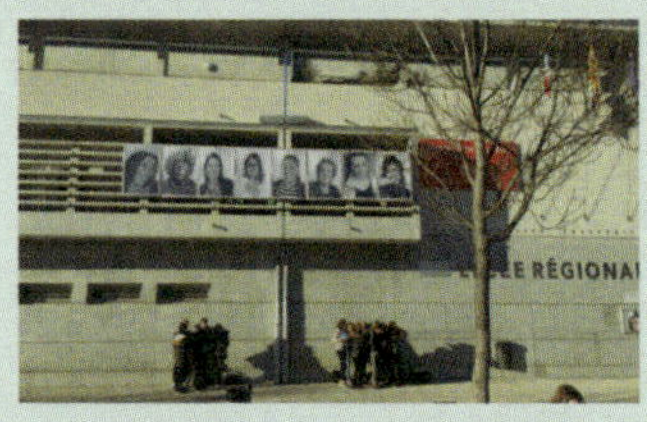

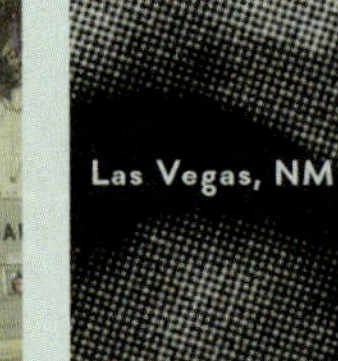

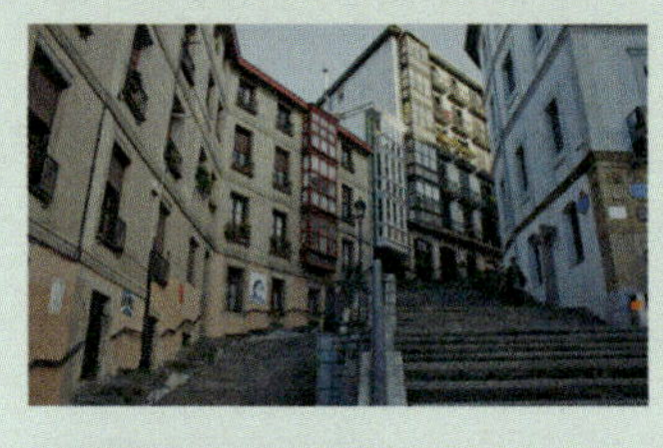

Lauris

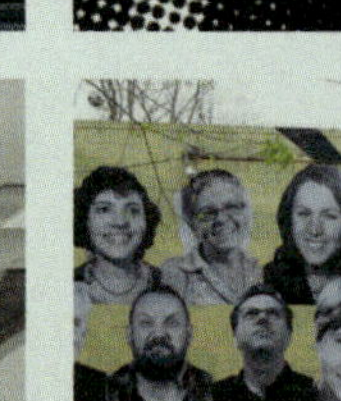

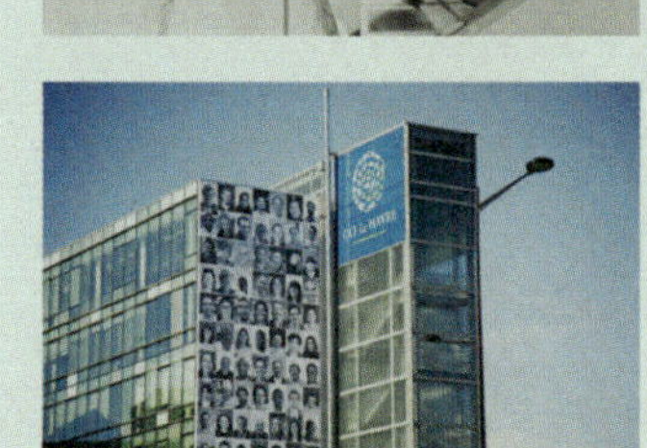

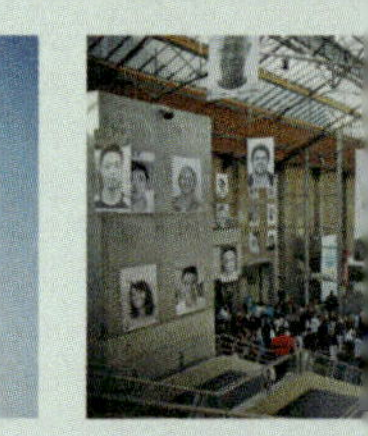

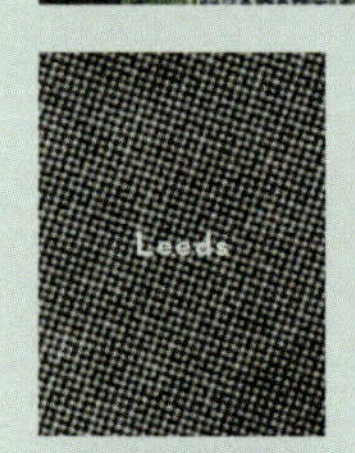

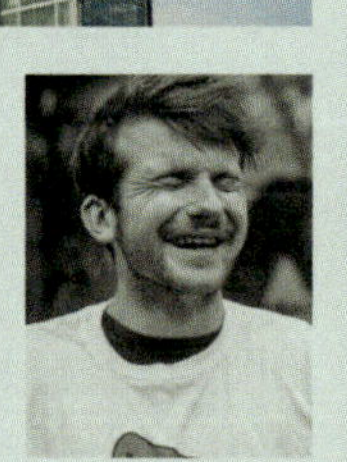

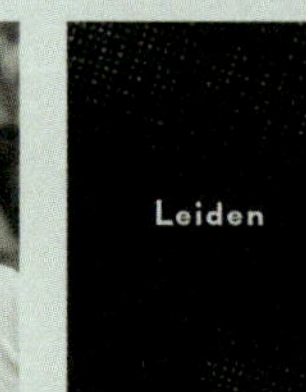

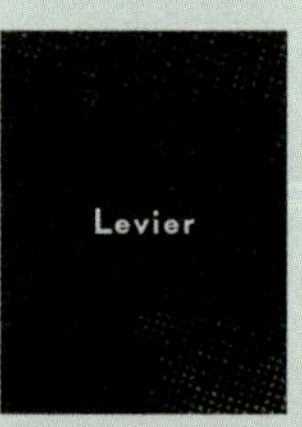

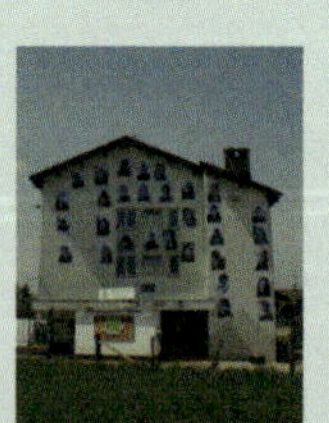

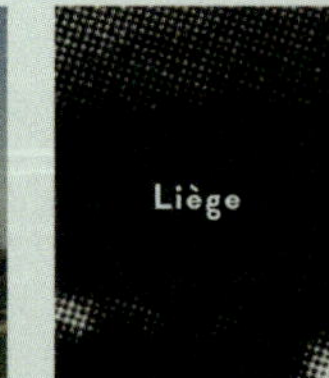

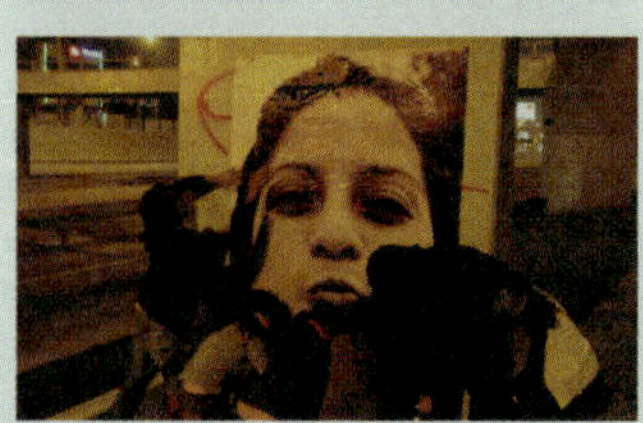

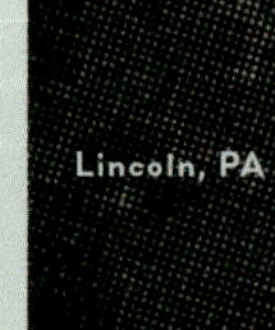

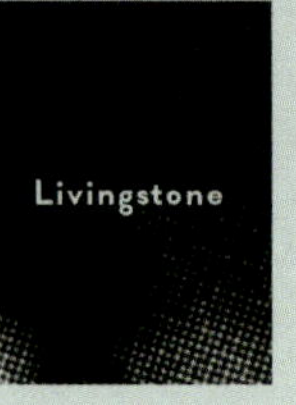

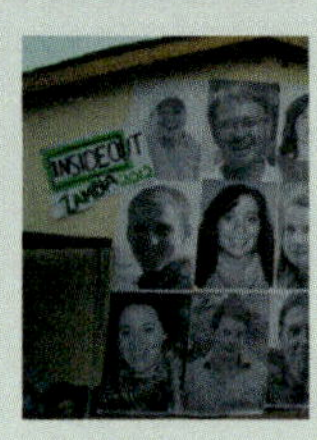

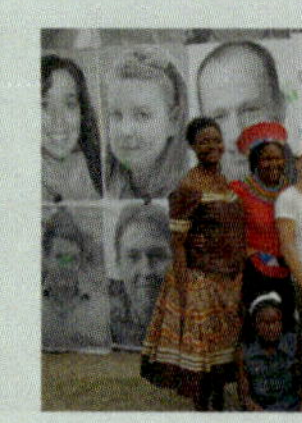

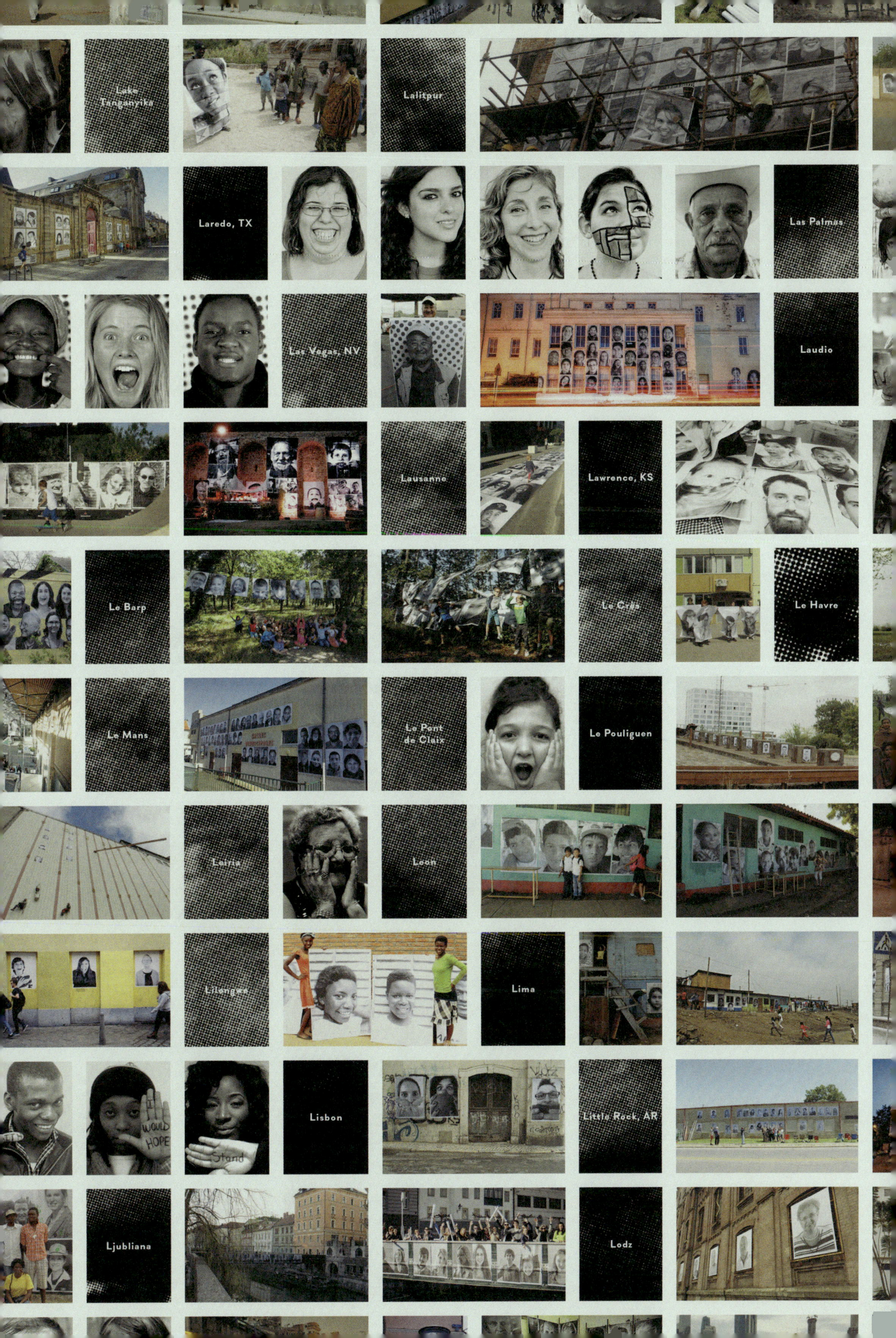
Lake Tanganyika
Lalitpur
Laredo, TX
Las Palmas
Las Vegas, NV
Laudio
Lausanne
Lawrence, KS
Le Barp
Le Crès
Le Havre
Le Mans
Le Pont de Claix
Le Pouliguen
Leiria
Leon
Lilongwe
Lima
Lisbon
Little Rock, AR
Ljubliana
Lodz

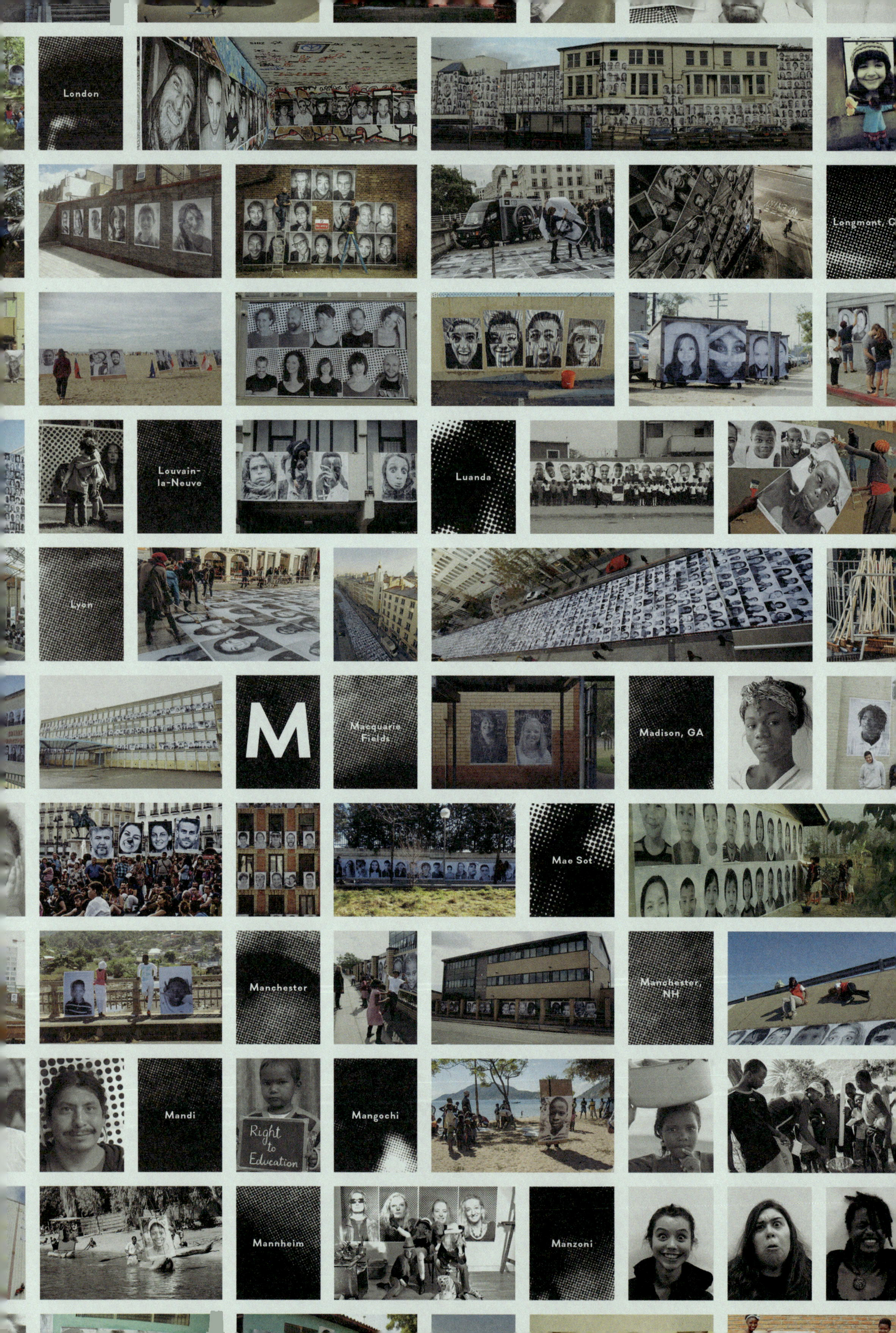
London
Longmont, C
Louvain-la-Neuve
Luanda
Lyon
M
Macquarie Fields
Madison, GA
Mae Sot
Manchester
Manchester, NH
Mandi
Right to Education
Mangochi
Mannheim
Manzoni

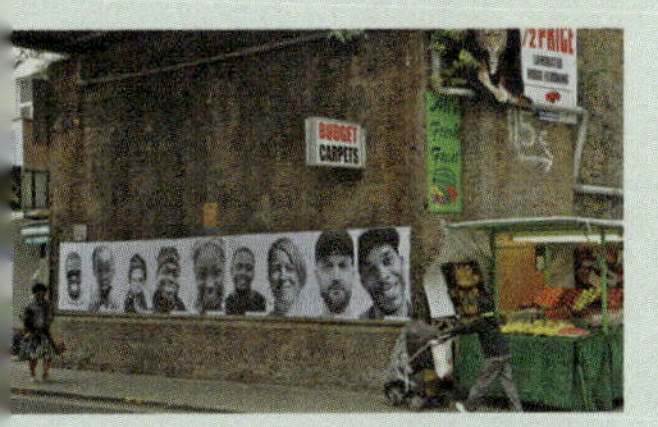
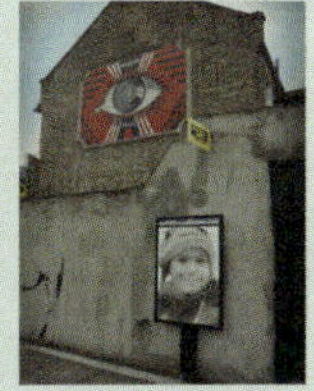
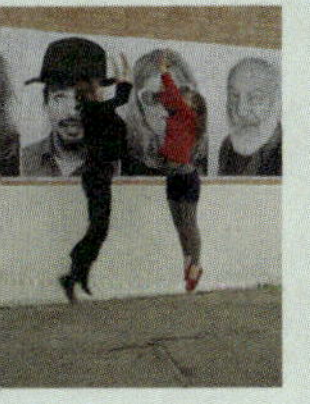
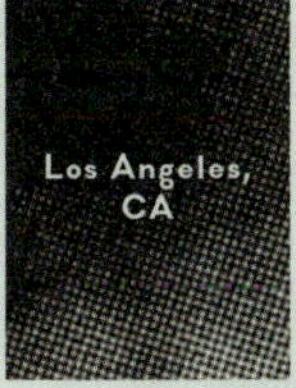

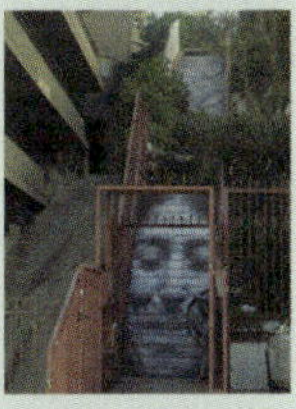
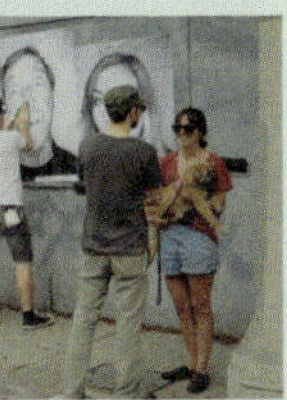
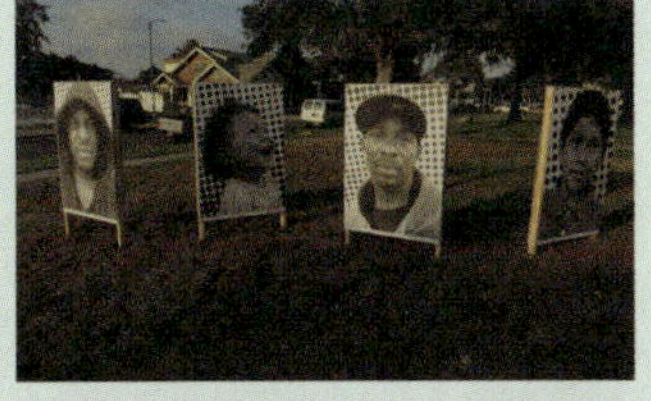
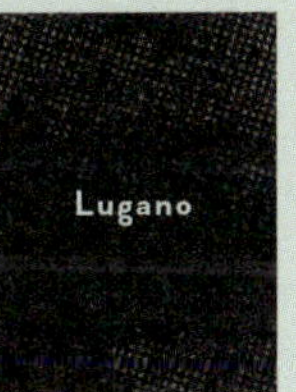

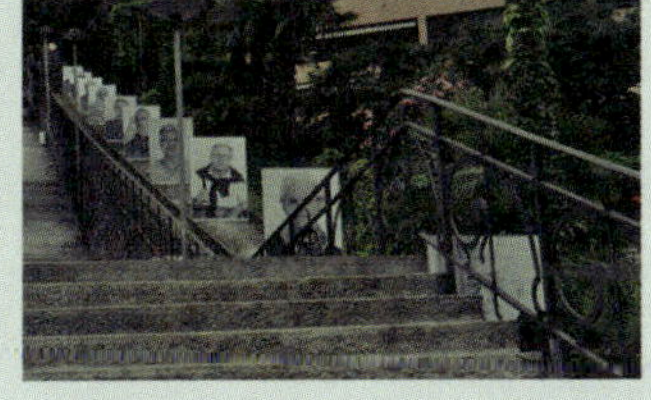
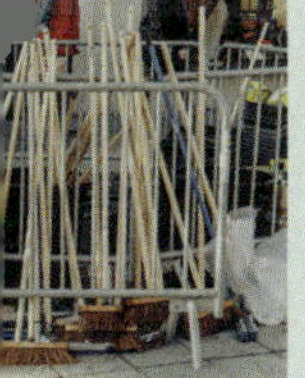
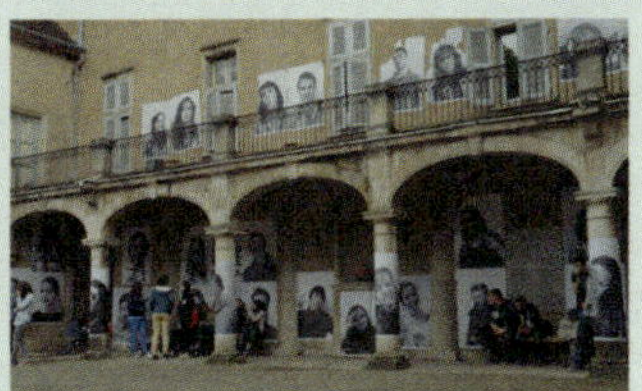
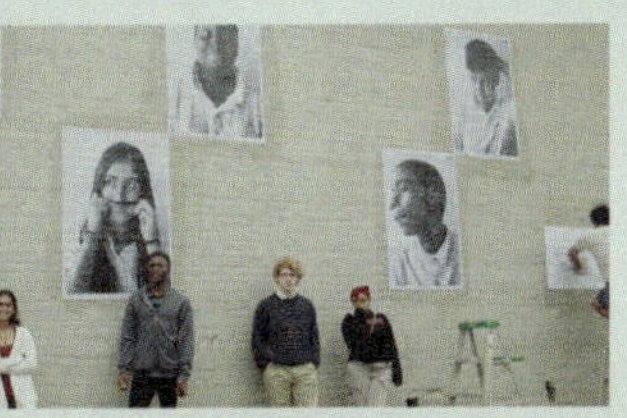
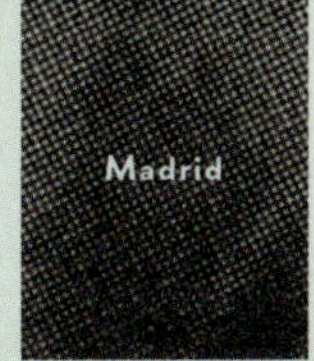

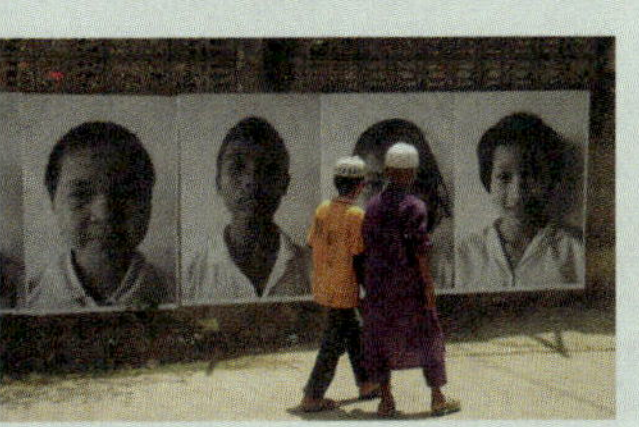
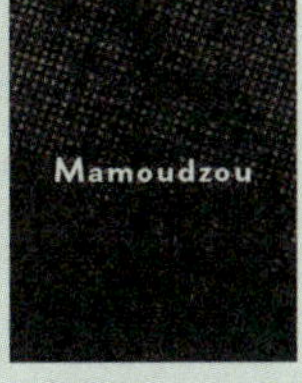

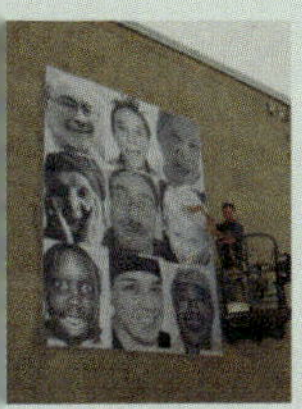
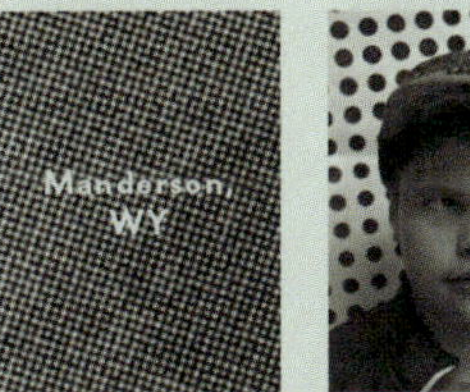

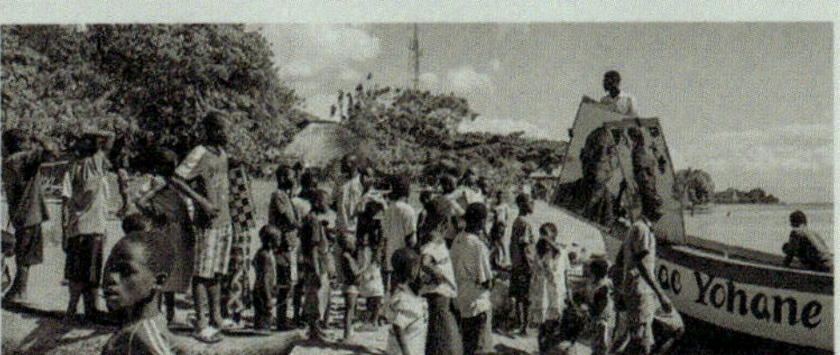

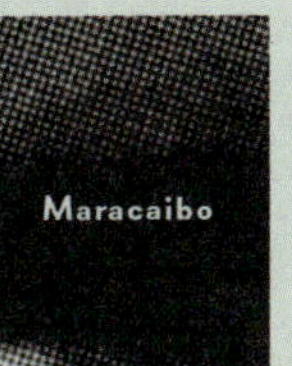

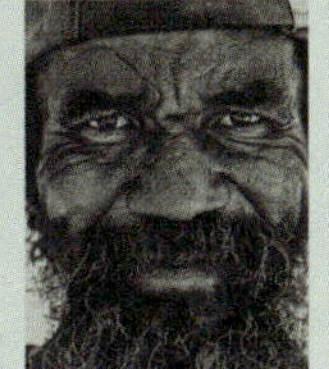
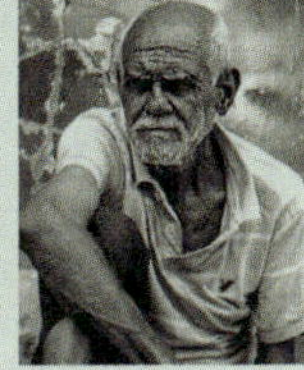

El Rastro, September 2012. We live in a very charming and traditional neighborhood in Madrid. Our neighbors are old people, young people, of different nationalities, with different jobs. Every window has a special story behind it.

True Democracy, June 2011. People are camping in the squares of every Spanish city. We are demanding a true democracy, the separation of powers, and to stop the corruption in politics. We want to saw out indignation in a non-violence way.

Mae Sot, Burma Voices for Migrant Schoolchildren, March 2012. Inside Out on the Thai-Burma border promotes a positive identity and provides a voice for migrant schoolchildren in Mae Sot, Thailand.

Mamoudzou Doujani, Mayotte Quand Nos Regards se Croisent, May 2016. Thanks to paper and glue, we want to change the way people perceive Doujani middle school and youth generation.

Manchester, England Inside Out Moss Side, May 2011. We want to encourage humanity to realize that healthy relationships between people and landscapes are as important in the city as anywhere else.

Manchester, NH Manchester Arts Commission, October 2011. The statement we hope to make is that irrespective of national origin, skin color, or socio-economic status, Manchester must live and love as one community.

Mangochi, Malawi The Faces and Stories on the Frontline, May 2013. To reveal the faces and stories of the people working on the frontline in Malawi's food and fishing economies. To highlight some of the challenges faced by these workers at a time of change in the country.

Mannheim, Germany Talking with Tigers Meets Inside Out Project, June 2015. Wake up, keep your mind open, and act for peace, justice, humanity, and democracy!

Maracaibo, Venezuela Hornocity, February 2015. I want to create a perfect collage of the heart of America, where the majority of people don't look like they stepped out of the television. I like to think that I treat everyone here with such honorable respect.

Margate, South Africa Changing the Kids' World, June 2011. I aim to change the world through art, or at least change the kids' world.

Marrakech, Morocco Blown Glass Factory, September 2016. We are men who recycle glass to create glass for other men.

Marseille, France Vive les Arts, January 2015. We want to promote plastic arts in our high school and in Marseille.

Massiac, France We Only Like Peace! 2014–2018 Memories Shared by Generations: Focus Upon the First World War, October 2014. The idea is that people could share the memories of WWI and make it pass through generations.

Mazatlán Sinaloa, Mexico Hope for Sinaloa, July 2013. Sinaloa is a rich land where people work hard and are also very friendly and passionate. We want the world to know that in Sinaloa, there are good people, we want to show photos of them smiling, enjoying, loving what they do, laughing . . . people with HOPE.

Medellín, Colombia No Boundaries, Bigger Dreams, December 2011. Children have to dream big in order to raze imaginary boundaries.

Medfield, MA Visions and Voices, September 2013. We are sharing ideas to inspire change and shape our community's future.

Meiganga, Cameroon Meiganga's Star Athletes: Inspiring Youth Engagement in the Community, January 2015. We believe that youth athletes serve as great role models and inspire their peers to participate and excel. By sharing photos of our student leaders on the walls of our town's stadium, we hope that other students will see them, be inspired by them, and be motivated to have an impact themselves.

Melbourne, Australia Youth Action at the End of the Line, December 2015. We want to make positive images of youth at the end of the train line and post them in the Melbourne CBD to change peoples' perception of youth in today's society, particularly suburban youth coming into the city.

One Hundred Years of Community Spirit at CJC, November 2014. Our community wants to celebrate the diversity of cultures and languages of our students and we want to share what it means to us to be part of this multicultural school by portraying students and former students who learn(ed), play(ed), and grew in this part of the world for the last one hundred years.

Artists in Our Community, July 2013. Our intention is to raise awareness about artists in our school community and to strengthen participation in the visual arts. We believe that visual art plays a significant role in the development of a diverse and creative community.

Visibility, October 2013. We are for the understanding and appreciation of all people. We want to be visible in the city of Yarra.

Inside Out Melbourne, April 2012. We want to share faces of the refugees who live in Melbourne.

Memphis, TN Finding Awareness Through Process, March 2016. Society has lost itself to a culture of hyper-reality, a search for perfection, and has become nothing more than a culture of instant gratification. The effect of this is the loss of our identity, which is becoming a singular mass that is defined individually by a label created by society. People no longer take the time to interact with each other and enjoy the journey of process.

Art Saves Lives, June 2015. As artists/teachers, we believe that art saves lives. We support quality art education in our public schools and will advocate strongly for it. Every student deserves an education that includes a place for thinking and personal expression in the visual arts.

Metz, France Portrait de Résident, March 2014. We would like to show the diversity and cultural richness of our neighborhood's population, while embellishing the "Boite à Musique" construction site.

Mexico City, Mexico Fundación Renacimiento, June 2016. All kids have the right to a life with dignity.

Facial Tattoos, June 2015. The project reflects the trustworthy voice that exists behind the fake visualization of the urban tribes as a synonym of vandalism, when youth faces segregation and discrimination in their social groups or outside them.

Unemployment in Mexico City, March 2013. This project represents those individuals who have been marginalized from the formal employment market and have had the need to create their own "office space" within the streets of Mexico City.

Milan, Italy Fight Violence Against Women, October 2013. Women are often abused. It's time for them to fight back.

Dude Chefs, June 2012. We are throwing a big food event with "dude chefs" coming in from all over the world.

Milwaukee, WI Urban Eden, September 2014. We come from around the block and around the world. Together we are growing food, flowers, and goodwill in an abandoned city lot.

Missoula, MT Big Sky High School, May 2014. Some students spend high school secluded, leaving the face of our school defined by the most popular students, keeping the other half completely unrecognized. We want to bring these unrecognized students to the face of our school!

Mitsuhama, Japan We Will Be Living in Mitsuhama, August 2013. We want to show that this city is not dead; that we're a part of the society. We declare that we exist.

Monaco Dare to Be You, April 2016. Dare to be you: Show the world all the anonymous people who really make Monaco as it is (teachers, nurses, doctors, waiters, sweepers, bar tenders). To all the hidden souls working in the shadow of the city, it's time to come in the light and express yourself.

Montclair, NJ Montclair Cooperative School, June 2015. The seventh and eighth grade students of the Montclair Cooperative School are very concerned by the significant gap between those who are actively making better choices to protect our environment and others who don't want to be inconvenienced by changing their comfortable and ingrained behavior.

Monroe, NC Piedmont High School Diversity United, January 2017. Our objective is to show our students that though we are all different inside and out, we are a part of the same Piedmont High School Community.

Monterey, CA TED X Monterey, April 2013. A celebration of the collective power of individuals in our community.

Montevideo, Uruguay Inside Out Montevideo, December 2013. This action is for the rights of the handicapped in Uruguay!

Wastepickers, June 2012. We want to honor the cooperatives of waste pickers, who work in the streets, with dignity, for the recycling system.

Montigny-le-Bretonneux, France Mannequin d'Un Jour, March 2013. To put forth the work of an organization that takes care of the handicapped.

Montpellier, France Je Suis Moi-Même. I Am Who I Am, March 2015. In our school, many races are represented: Caucasian, Asian, Arab, African. But as well as different religions: Muslims, Christians, Atheists.

Faire Face, September 2013–June 2014. Everyone suffers from pain, which is often hard to express or share. Patients, hospital staff, and doctors decided to put their faces on the walls to fight these difficult moments together.

Montreal, Canada Québec Education, September 2016. We want to take the issue of tuition increases, budget cuts, and their effect on education quality and turn it into a very approachable project: in the form of photography. We intend to voice the students' concerns though an artistic and more human approach. Quality education should remain accessible to all.

1MTL, June 2014. We want to resume and reaffirm Montreal's motto and tradition of harmonious living and coexistence by showing that our cultural, religious, ethnic, and linguistic differences are not a reason to divide us, but rather to enrich us. We are all one Montreal!

What it Means to Be 18, June 2013. Turning eighteen years old is special, with new opportunities and new experiences. It's an age of longing to achieve when you are younger, and reminiscing when you are older. We want to know what it means for them to be eighteen.

Ayotzinapa: Crise de Droits, Complicités d'État, April 2015. This action presents the faces of the 43 missing students of Ayotzinapa.

Montreuil, France Downfall, Demain C'est Loin . . . !, June 2013. Last year, a building in construction collapsed. We wanted to show that the people in our neighborhood stand in solidarity when a dramatic event happens.

Moshi, Tanzania The Importance of Education In Kilimanjaro, July 2014. These pictures come from the school of Rogerville (a small village near Le Havre in France) and the school of Mbokumu (a small village near the Kilimanjaro). They symbolize the right of all children to quality education regardless of their origin or condition. They show the children the importance of going to school every day and remind the adults of the need to get involved to defend education for a better world.

Mount Pleasant, NJ Psychological Disorders, April 2014. The project's goal is to encourage discussion and to bring light to psychological disorders in their many forms. We want to emphasize that these disorders are not uncommon and individuals who are burdened with them are not alone, and therefore must not suffer in silence.

Racial and Cultural Diversity, April 2014. Our goal as students of Central Michigan University is to bring light to the cultural and racial diversity found here on campus that is oftentimes dismissed or overlooked by those who attend the school. We want to communicate that diversity should be more celebrated by youth than it is currently.

We Are All Capable, April 2014. Disabled or abled, we are all capable.

Working Class Heroes, April 2014. We believe in the necessity of a mobile working class and aim to bring attention to their dedication and function in our society. There are many jobs in America that are forgotten about, especially the ones that involve day-to-day transportation. These workers have to brave the weather, endure rush hour, and deliver to those of us who are unwilling to do the same. We respect their jobs and feel they deserve recognition for their hard work. We installed the portraits of mobile workers at covered bus stops as a way to bring attention to the mobile working class.

Homelessness, April 2014. Our mission is to bring awareness to homelessness and those who assist the homeless in the Mount Pleasant, Michigan, community.

Victims of Violence, April 2014. These portraits demonstrate what violence can do to an individual not just physically, but emotionally, reminding everyone that sometimes people cannot see violence just by looking at someone. As a group, we have not experienced this kind of violence, but we took it upon ourselves to do our makeup to replicate real bruises, and to take these pictures to raise awareness about violence, more specifically, violence against college females. Before you can take a stand on an issue, you have to be aware of it, which is exactly what these photographs are for.

MTzamboro, Mayotte No Violence! En Mai, Fais la Paix, May 2015. We want to fight against violence, to pass on a message of tolerance and peace. The goal is to show people's equality in their expressions in the face of violence or a peaceful situation.

Mukono, Uganda Together We Can, Empower the Youth, May 2014. Education and love are two powerful ingredients when combined to give youth a future, especially when these youths are orphans with no relatives or future. Komo Learning Centres is a grassroots community development initiative in Uganda that puts an emphasis on youth through education sponsorships, mentoring and youth job training.

Mulhouse, France La Jeunesse Mulhousienne s'Exprime, June 2016. On September 28, 2016, the Place de la réunion in Mulhouse became a giant piece of art thanks to the participation of 750 students, giving the people of Mulhouse a huge space of tolerance, reunion, and diversity.

Murcia, Spain Suma de Individualidades para una Educación Rica y Plural, September 2014. With Inside Out UM, these students and their teacher look to highlight the importance of the individual potential of each person that each community consists of, where differences are accepted and the contribution of each individual is seen as a collective benefit.

Nablus, Palestine We Stand for Ourselves, May 2012. We are a group of teenagers who want you to know who we are and what we can do.

Nampa, ID Love and Loss: A Celebration of Día de Los Muertos in Black-and-White Imagery, November 2015. The goal of this project is to educate the community on the history and traditions of the Mexican holiday of Day of the Dead (Día de los Muertos).

Inside Out Nampa (Self-Empowerment Through Self-Expression), May 2015. Our group action has come together to highlight the power of self-expression that lies within each of us and to celebrate the uniquely magnificent beings that we are!

Naperville, IL Authenticity, November 2016. To portray "the gap between art and life" and to investigate our identity as a community, through the physical, emotional, cultural character of the locals.

Nashville, TN Seeing Nashville, October 2012. "The World Hears Nashville, Now They See Us"

Nassau, Bahamas Faces of Bahamians, November 2012. Bahamians, like many peoples in the Caribbean, are of an incredibly mixed descent. While many foreigners—and even some Bahamians themselves—think "real" Bahamians are only the descendants of African slaves. True Bahamians are many colors and ethnicities.

Nazareth, Colombia Yo Soy WAYU 2, March 2014. Through art, we want to tell the world about the identity, cultural richness, and needs from our indigenous WAYUU community in Colombia's Guajira to improve our basic living conditions.

Neuchâtel, Switzerland "Nous Sommes Là" École Supérieure Numa-Droz, September 2016. Our high school is going through a tough period because it has to move into new buildings. Its identity until now was characterized by its location. It's in crisis. We need to find our bearings in this new location.

New Bedford, MA Secret City Reimagined, September 2015. New Bedford, once deemed the "Secret City" for its alleged silence toward street crime, has been home to some of history's most vocal proponents for social justice, such as Frederick Douglass, Ezell A. Blair, Jr. (aka Jibreel Khazan), Marie Equi, and Benjamin Tucker. Today, this tradition lives on. We aim to shed light on the citizens, social workers, legal professionals, advocates, artists, and community leaders who continue the fight against injustice and inspire the hero in all of us.

New Brunswick, NJ The Faces of the Future of Theater, March 2013. We embrace the fact that we are the next generation of great theater-makers. We promise to remember the love we have for this community of artists, in this moment, and call upon those feelings in our futures—wherever we may be in the world.

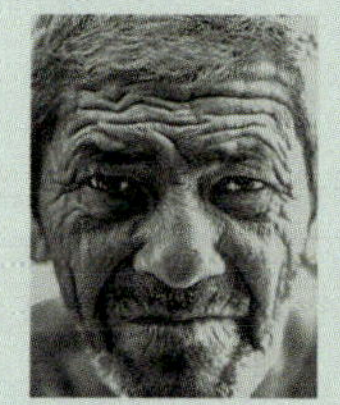
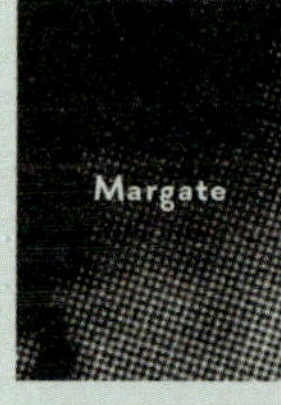

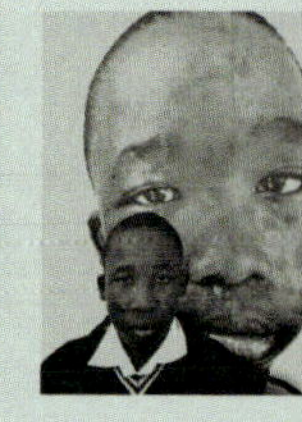
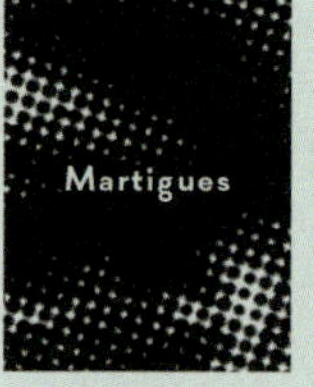

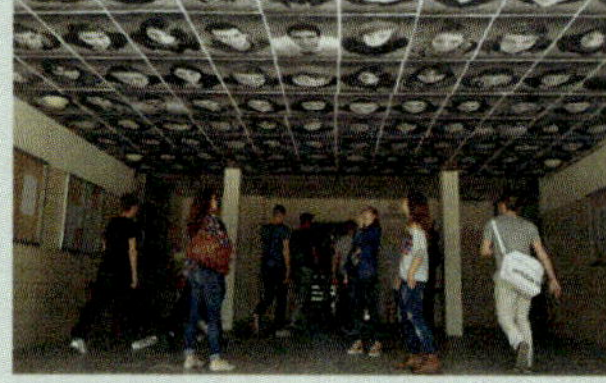
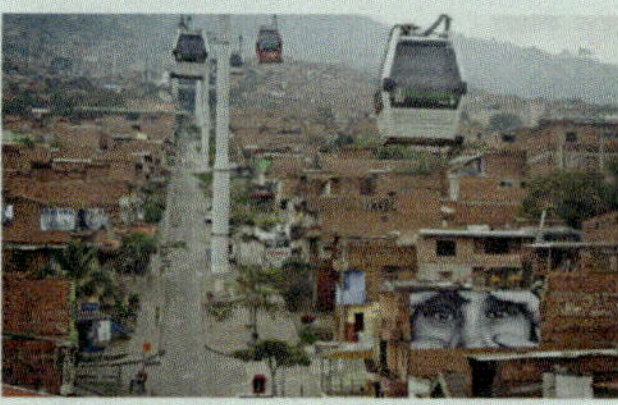
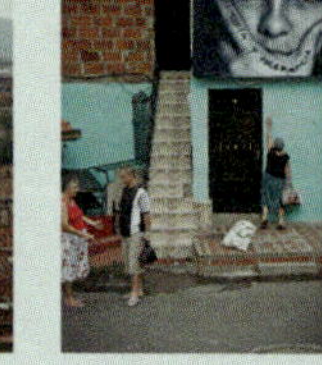
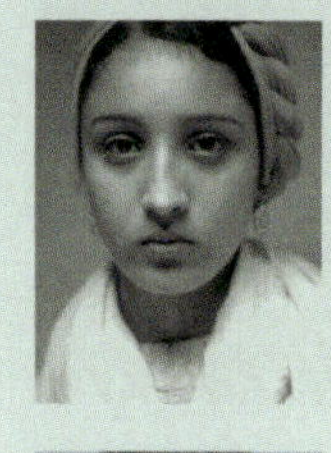
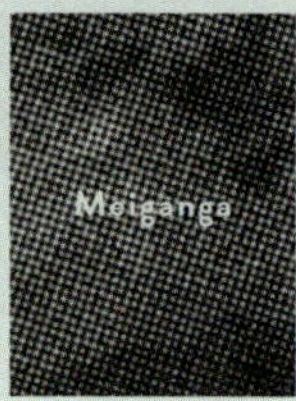

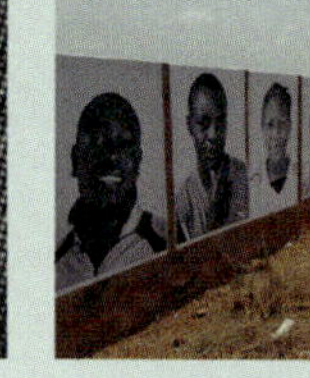
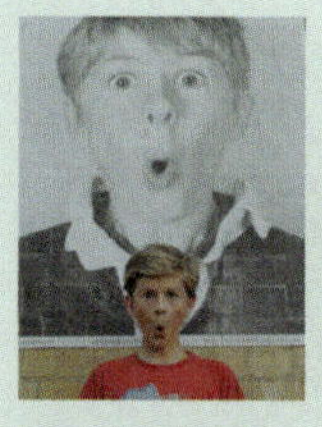
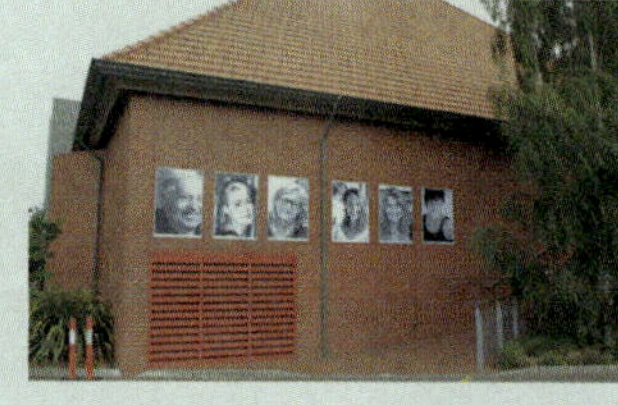
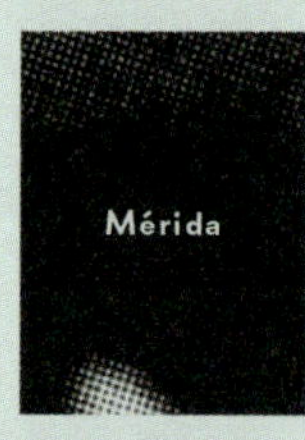

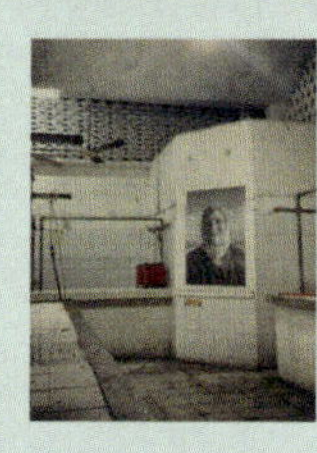
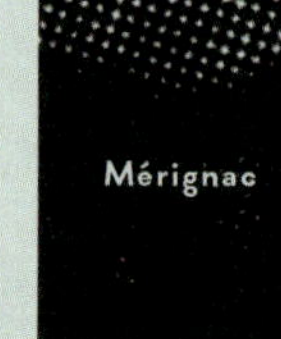

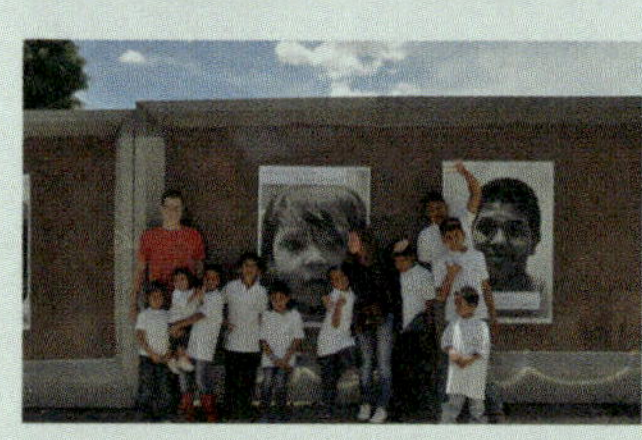
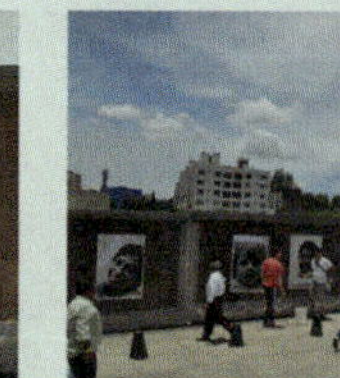
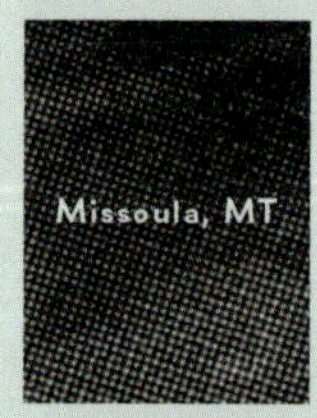

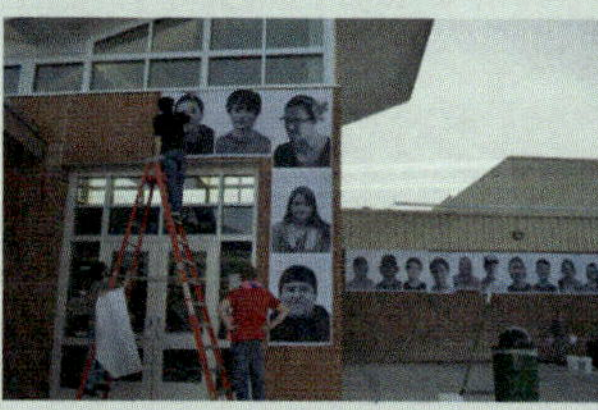
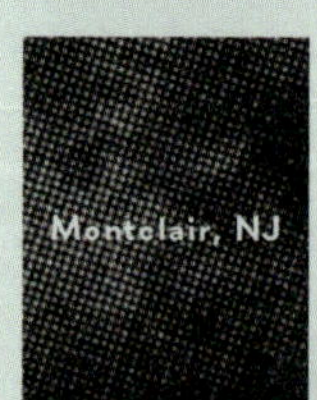

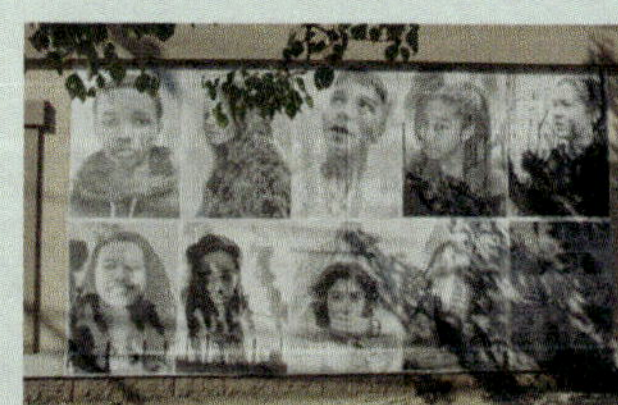
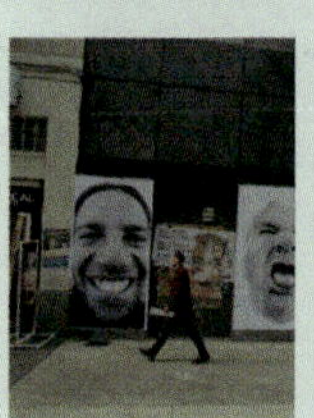
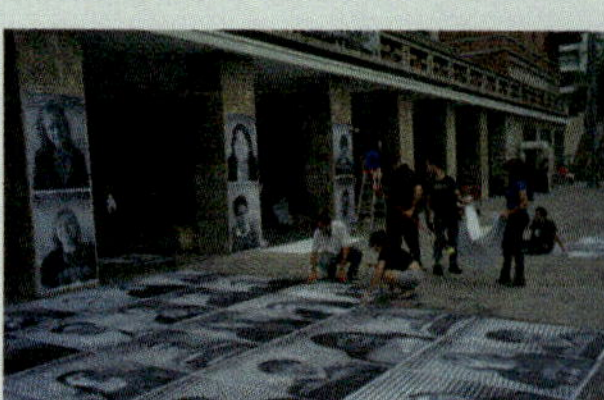

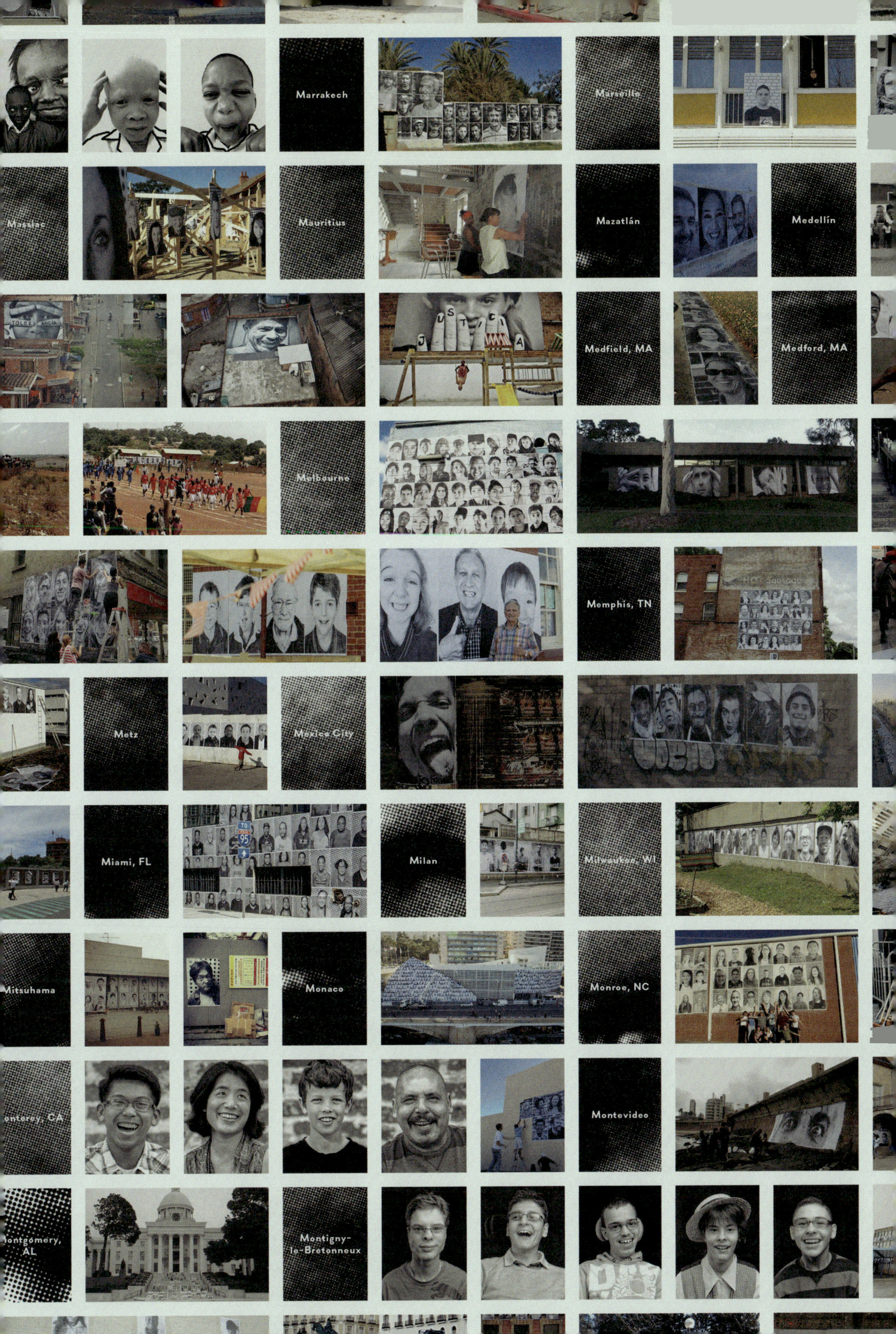

Marrakech
Marseille
Massiac
Mauritius
Mazatlán
Medellín
Medfield, MA
Medford, MA
Melbourne
Memphis, TN
Metz
Mexico City
Miami, FL
Milan
Milwaukee, WI
Mitsuhama
Monaco
Monroe, NC
onterey, CA
Montevideo
ontgomery, AL
Montigny-le-Bretonneux

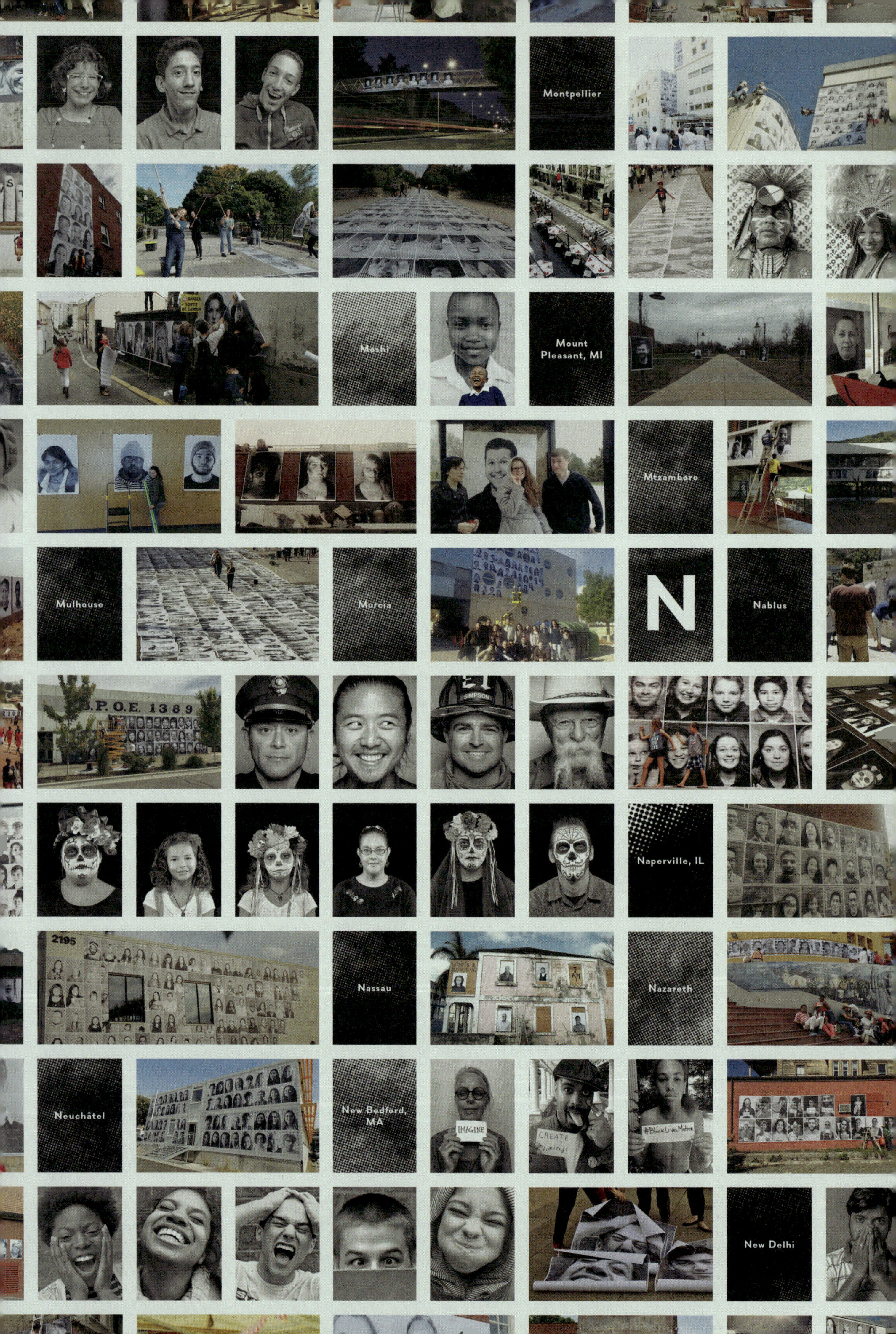
Montpellier
Moshi
Mount Pleasant, MI
Mtzamboro
Mulhouse
Murcia
N
Nablus
B.P.O.E. 1389
Naperville, IL
2195
Nassau
Nazareth
Neuchâtel
New Bedford, MA
IMAGINE
New Delhi

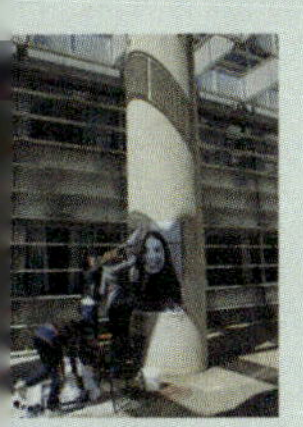
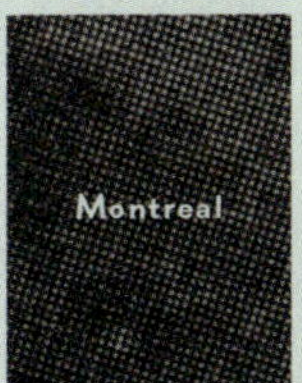

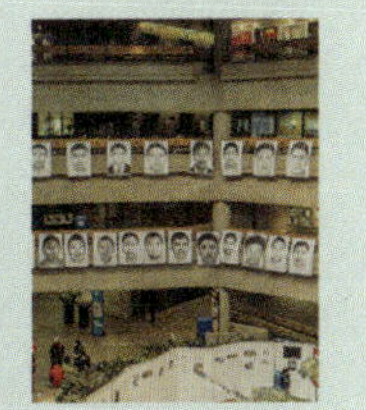
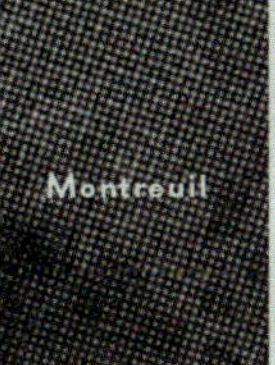

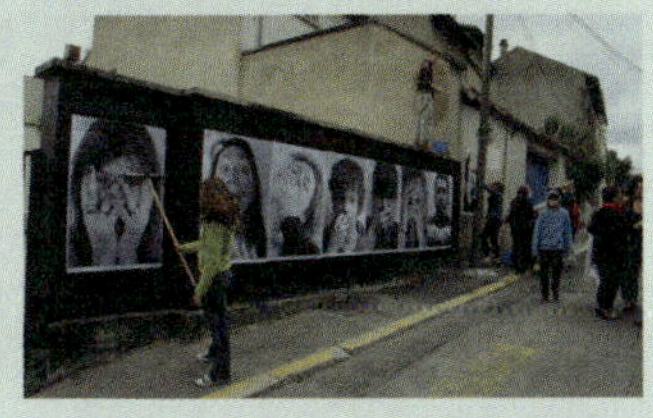
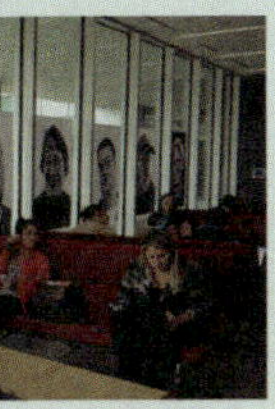
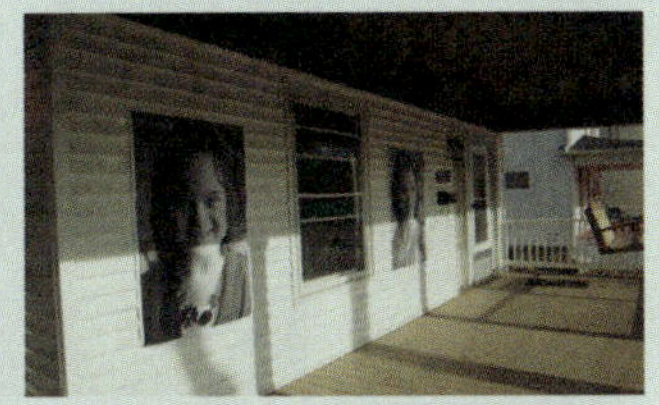
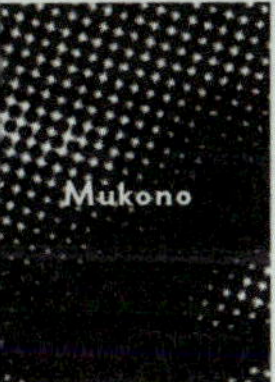

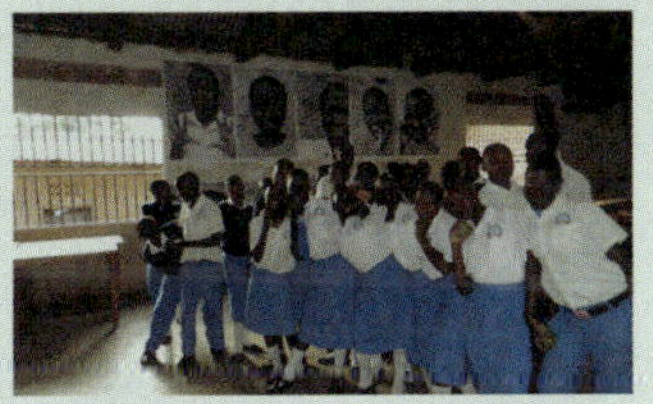
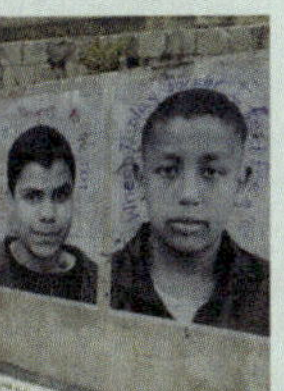
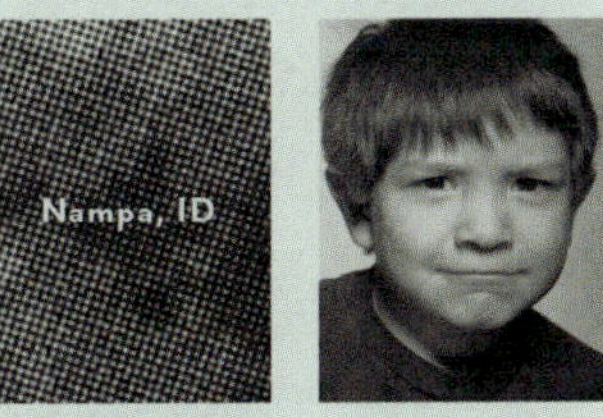

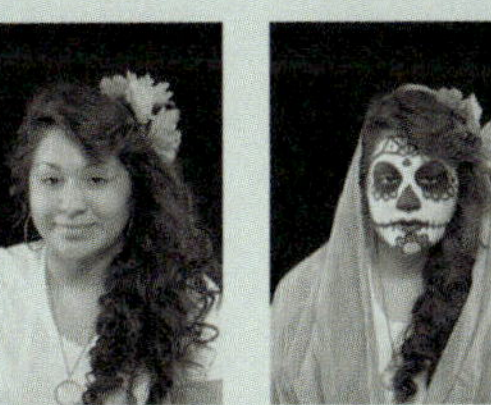
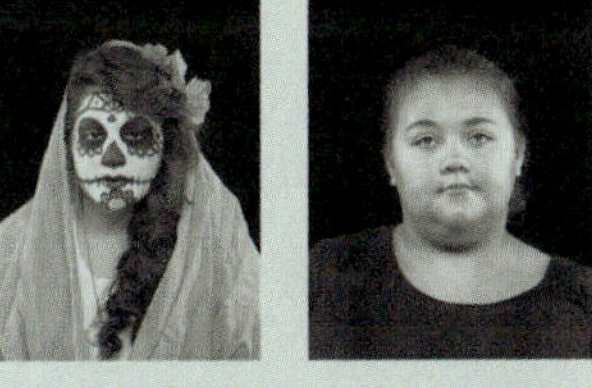
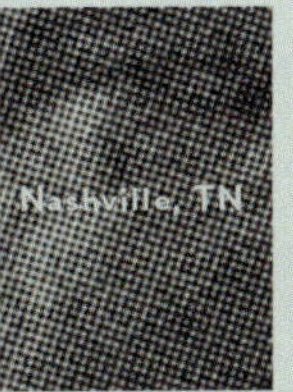

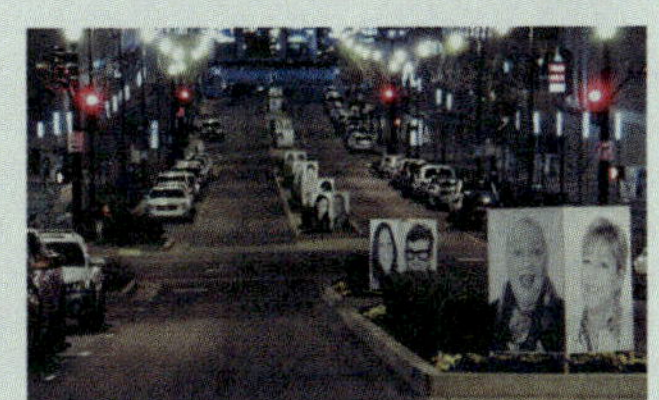
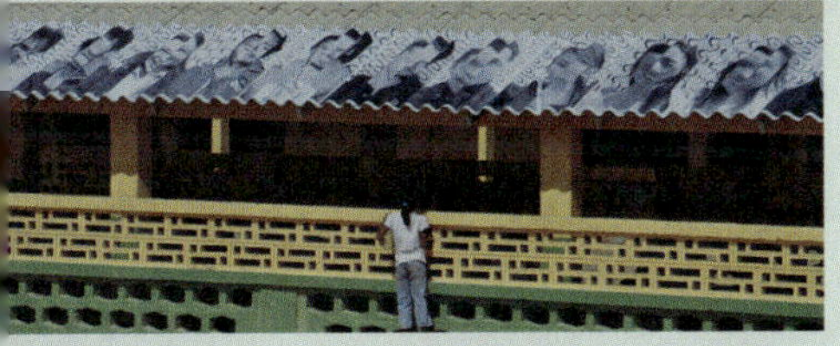
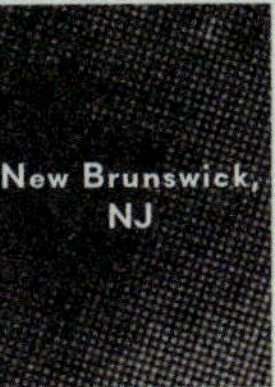

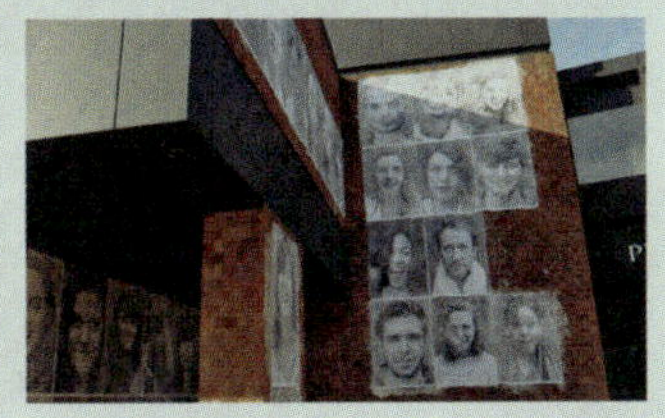
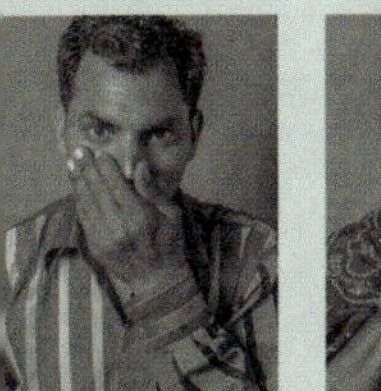
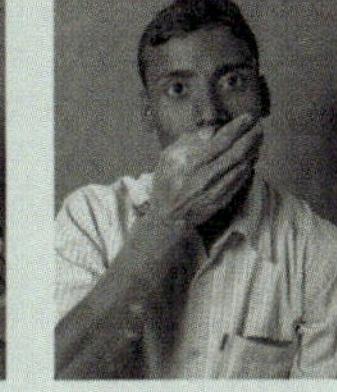

New Delhi, India Help Delhi Breathe, April 2016. Air pollution in Delhi has reached crisis levels. Air quality monitors have repeatedly shown hazardous levels of pollutants in the air, however there are no real health advisories or information disseminated to the people who live and breathe Delhi's air every day. Delhi's government has put in place some positive measures, however, there are many more that need to be implemented in order for Delhi's air to be healthy again.

New London, NH Be Gritty!, April 2014. Winners never quit and quitters never win. Be Gritty!

New Lynn, New Zealand Celebrate Diversity, June 2013. What started as a small gesture to celebrate diversity in an unloved and unappreciated urban town has exploded into community interest and involvement. Diversity is good and celebrating it is empowering!

New Orleans, LA Get Busy Living, April 2013. The idea of the project is to inspire others to put on their best face and to "get busy living."

New South Wales, Australia A Look Into the Tent Embassy And Its Mission, December 2012. Photos of Aboriginals and non-Aboriginals who support the embassy. To provide greater dignity, respect, and understanding for the Tent Embassy and its mission (which is to protect a 5,000-year-old grave and protect sacred relics in the area) amongst the broader local community.

New York, NY Orensanz, August 2011. Love, of course. From Tunisia to Iran, from Paris to Great Neck.

Haiti's Cholera Victims, October 2015. As we mark five years since cholera broke out, we are calling on the UN to stop ignoring victims and the harm they have suffered. It's time for the UN to live up to its own ideals of human rights and the rule of law, and face Justice.

Resilient Community, March 2015. We, as an Asian-American community, would like to make a statement that we matter in the making of the community, be it our school, our groups of friends, our families, or our neighborhood. We would like to have a voice and in this case in the form of portraits to show that we exist and are a huge part of the resilient community we are helping to build every day

Inside Out—New Design High, November 2014. Inside Out New Design documents portraits of students and staff of New Design High School to show its unique culture.

Diversity United, June 2014. The mission of the New York French-American Charter School is to develop bilingual global citizens who will be the leaders of tomorrow.

Youthful, May 2014. We are teenagers in an incarceration alternatives program, and we want to share with our community that we feel childhood is a special time.

We Walk With Jane Jacobs, May 2014. Jane Jacobs fought for walkable neighborhoods and engaged communities. On May 4, we took to the streets and led one hundred-plus neighborhood walks of communities in all five boroughs across New York City in the spirit of her urban activism.

True Conviction, November. 2013. We are teenagers in an incarceration alternatives program in the East Village. We invited all kinds of community leaders: housing activists, educators, arts organizers, city council members, fitness experts, gardeners, and even the lady on the block whom everyone talks to. Everyone who came to visit with us told their true story and shared their true face, without any mask. We were surprised to learn that many of them had faced obstacles in their youth, just like we are now, but they made their way through it. They were not ashamed of their past, and it even inspired them to have an impact on their community. Here's what we learned: regardless how troubled your past may have been, it doesn't determine your future.

Park Slope, Brooklyn September 2013. To honor the longtime, largely immigrant small shop owners in our neighborhood.

Freedom of Voice, June 2013. We want to ask every person we photograph what is their calling in this life, what is the purpose they have, their dreams, and what makes them happy. Principally to have freedom of voice, respect and accept.

Onten Iran, June 2015. While Saman Arbabi was working on a video report about JR's Inside Out Project for "OnTen," a weekly Persian-language political satire show, he learned that although thousands of people worldwide have participated in JR's project, only one of them was from Iran. Saman decided that the best way to illustrate his story, which aired on the day of the Iranian elections, was to create his own group action. Saman and the OnTen production team used pictures of forty of the people who were killed in the uprisings following the Iranian presidential elections in 2009. The images occupy a 20 ft. x 50 ft. area on the well-known Bushwick Art Park in Brooklyn. Colored television bars were used to enliven the black and white photos of the deceased.

Why I Rise, February 2013. "Why I Rise" seeks to raise awareness about violence against women around the world.

Freedom of Voice, December 2012. We students want to inspire freedom of voice and share positive inspiration for humans in search of their calling in life.

South Bronx Community Gardens, October 2012. These are the portraits of the participants/gardeners in a community garden in the South Bronx, built and managed by a New York City–based non-profit called Leave It Better, which builds community gardens, holds farmers' markets, and teaches documentary film production to its young members.

New York City Stands Against Bullying, August 2012. To take a stand against bullying and to make peoples' day better.

Golden Rule NYC, June 2012. It doesn't matter what group you are part of or where you are from, we are all the same, we all need friends, so don't judge others—treat all people with the respect you want for yourself.

Tribeca Film Fellows: Harlem, April 2012. "If they shoot, and they don't know who they are shooting at, and they see us young kids outside of Minisink Townhouse, they'll think twice about shooting." —Sixth grader Christian Houston

Diversity In South Williamsburg, December 2011. I was teaching an after-school enrichment digital photography class at Williamsburg Collegiate Charter School. My students were primarily black and Latino and ranged in age from ten to fourteen years old. The neighborhood where the school is located in South Williamsburg, Brooklyn, is primarily Hassidic and many of my students also live nearby. They often expressed that they don't feel very welcome in their own neighborhood, and I thought it would be interesting and empowering to create this project with them.

Occupy. Inside. Out., October 2011. Occupy. Inside. Out. is an effort to document the people behind the Occupy movement and to share their stories; an opportunity to paint a positive portrait of the face of change.

Art Education Changes Lives, October 2011. Arts education changes lives.

Real New Yorkers, September 2011. In New York City, all we see on the walls are corporations' ads. We want to celebrate real New Yorkers, those who are the essence of our city.

New Sudanese Communities, September 2011. New Sudanese Communities is a focus on the Sudanese people now living in Brooklyn who have been displaced as a result of the ongoing conflicts in Sudan.

Celebrate Dumbo, September 2011. Celebrating Dumbo!

Seniors in East Harlem, August 2011. Showing faces of seniors in East Harlem.

Hepatitis B Awareness in Chinatown, August 2011. To raise awareness of Hepatitis B.

Tagai Mentorship Program, May 2011. The Tagai students and the communities that they live in are often overlooked in New York. There is poverty, violence, and a lack of opportunity that don't exist on the other side of the East River. This is the perfect way for New Yorkers to see their fellow citizens in a different light.

South Bronx (S)Heroes, June 2011. South Bronx (S)Heroes celebrates Bronx mothers and community members by depicting Bronxites looking through mothers' eyes.

True Selfie, June 2014. In an era when self-branding is becoming more and more common, we think it is important to be yourself. Peer pressure to fit in can be very strong in children and we want to create an event and environment that will help our members to feel free to express who they truly are.

Newburgh, NY Celebrate Newburgh, May 2012. We want to celebrate the people of the city of Newburgh, NY, who live with hope, determination, courage, and faith to meet the challenges of a community laden with poverty and crime, and support each other to rise above.

Nha Trang, Vietnam Same Same but Different, February 2016. In our school, we embrace the challenges of a multicultural community, recognizing that we are "same but different."

Nieuwpoort, Belgium 6HS Basisschool Go!, June 2012. Showing the diversity within our school by making photos of two children of each class.

Noisy-le-Roi, France Violence + Injustice=Je Réagis!, June 2015. Violence and Justice: two words that create echoes every day, in a world where inequality is deep. This action reminds us of the necessity to become indignant and to contribute every day to changing the world.

Norcia, Italy Faces from Norcia, December 2013. Living in a small town does not have to become a synonym of a narrow mentality despite the limited opportunities of a non-metropolitan reality. We believe that social cohesiveness represents a neverending stimulus to open up to the surrounding world and support cultural and artistic activity.

Norfolk, VA Start a Chain Reaction, January 2014. We seek to share our story through art in the hopes that we can develop a culture of kindness, integrity, and peace through raising awareness for Rachael's Challenge.

North Lake Tahoe, NV Wanderlust, July 2012. What would you do if you were President? What do you stand for?

North Pole Save the Arctic, July 2012. The eyes of the world, at the top of the world, watching over the world: over a thousand portraits of members of the #savethearctic movement make up a giant eye on the North Pole, in a statement of defiance against destructive industry in the Arctic.

Nottingham, England A Normal Pakistani, February 2015. "A Normal Pakistani" celebrates the identity of contemporary Pakistani men choosing to highlight their normality. The portraiture, led by a Pakistani woman, questions the Western labeling of "other" for the men of her society.

Nouméa, New Caledonia InsideOut—New Caledonia, July–October 2014. The gaze is a common language.

Multiculturalism and the Common Destiny, October 2011. We would like to convey through this project a simple message: the richness of multiculturalism and the "common destiny" that unites all communities that make up the Caledonian society.

Sur les Murs des Maisons Coloniales, October 2015. We want to incite the Nouméan population to face the destruction of colonial houses by pasting their portraits on the ruins.

Nova Gorcia, Slovenia TED X Slovenia, July 2013. Each and every one of us is a unique individual—however, we are all unified with a pulse.

Oakland, CA You Matter!, June 2016. I want the community to have an awareness of the unknown people who care about our kids' safety and well-being. I want to appreciate the unappreciated.

Occupy Oakland, February 2012. This project focuses on Occupy Oakland, and the individuals that make up this widespread movement. The movement belongs to thousands of people with different backgrounds and concerns. It is anything but homogenous, despite common perceptions of narrow interests and narrow demographics. The strength of Occupy lies in the fact that a professor, a laborer, a student, an immigrant, the unemployed, and a business owner can stand together demanding change. This project will be a visual testament to the diversity of Occupy and will provide faces/images that might replace and personalize events and activities that otherwise fall prey to media characterization.

Park Day School, December 2011. As fifth-grade students, we can make a difference by raising awareness about issues of discrimination and social injustice.

Oaxaca de Juárez, Mexico Diversity in Colonia Ex-Marquesado, January 2015. Students from the underserved community of Col Ex-Marquesado in the city of Oaxaca de Juárez took photos of the diversity in the neighborhood in which they live.

Ojinaga, Mexico Assumptions, April 2013. As a school with students from around the world, our community holds a lot of assumptions about one another and we have a unique opportunity to break down barriers.

Ongole, India Educating India, December 2013. Education is such an important part of someone's life. We take it for granted some of the time but here in India it is so valuable. These children strive to better their lives and they need an education to do that. With this education, their ambitions can turn from mere dreams to reality.

Oslo, Norway Independent Oslo, May 2015. Here are inspiring stories from passionate business owners. What gets them up in the morning? How do they manage to succeed next to big capital? We have visited nineteen places and taken thirty-two portraits of people who: add flair to the urban landscape, care about the local community, and have an active and engaged ownership.

Otranto, Italy A Tribute to Authenticity, August 2012. We want to show the people who live here, and remind everyone they are the essence of that place and not the masters of economy and tourism.

Ottawa, Canada Facing Each Other, April 2013. We are two classes: Ottawa, Canada, and Oaxaca, Mexico, that have been reaching out to each other all year over the Internet. We were able to visit with each other for one week and we put up our posters together. This project represents a whole year of learning about another culture, sharing ideas, and seeing how we are now a larger community as a result—one that spans the continent!

Open Our Eyes, April 2013. "Open Our Eyes so We Can See." This action grew out of students discussing what things in their lives/culture might be preventing them from seeing themselves or others clearly.

Ouagadougou, Burkina Faso Inside Out Project: France–Burkina Faso, September 2014. We want to organize a cooperation, and solidarity between two cultures through photographs (France and Burkina Faso). We want to denounce racism, and the differences of opposite cultures; we are all the same. Black or white, children or adults, we are all human beings.

Combattons Ensemble la Faim au Burkina Faso, October 2013. More than one hundred portraits of young graduates, farmers, and figures in the rural world invite the Burkinabe population, its youth, and its leaders, to join the #CULTIVONS movement to combat hunger and poverty through: the promotion of entrepreneurship within young graduates (men and women) in agriculture and farming; the modernization and support of familial agricultural farming through better investment; and the consummation of local products.

Owen Sound, Canada Bridge: Ahzhogun, September 2013. The Festival aims to represent cultural richness and diversity of our region through the celebration of the arts in all forms: visual, music, literature, dance, film, and culinary.

Oxford, GA We Are Oxford, February 2014. In the era of increased globalization, diversity can be found everywhere but there are still pockets of homogeneity. At Oxford College of Emory University we break that cookie-cutter mold of homogenization and pride ourselves in diversity from all aspects. Everyone is included in our pool of smart and talented students who have decided to call Oxford home. From rich to poor and international to domestic students, Oxford has students from all walks of life.

Paducah, KY Girls Who Have Been Bullied, August 2013. Kentucky leads the nation in teen suicide attempts. A teen is bullied every 7 seconds and kids as young as seven are now self-harming as a result of the stress of bullying. We want to raise the faces and the voices of those who have been bullied. These ten girls have shown their courage by their willingness to participate. We learned that kids are often afraid to admit having been bullied and it was these ten girls who raised their hands to say they wanted to make a difference and to stop the violence.

Palermo, Italy There Were Others, Here We Are, May 2014. The installation consists of seventy-two large, black-and-white posters, laid out in six rows and representing students from the Amari-Roncalli-Ferrara school (and others also living in the area).

Palo Alto, CA Not in Our Schools, May 2011. "Not in our schools" is a campaign against bullying and promoting acceptance.

Pantin, France L'Ourcq Mon Amour, August 2013. Whether in giant formats or smaller formats, more than three hundred faces occupied the walls of Ourcq's canal with a common trait. Every one of them works here, or has worked here at some point in time: workers in a concrete central, ancient millers, bank employees, dancers, high school students, restauranteurs, boat captains, writers . . .

Paramus, NJ It Takes a Community College, September 2013. What does it take to create a truly educated citizen? It

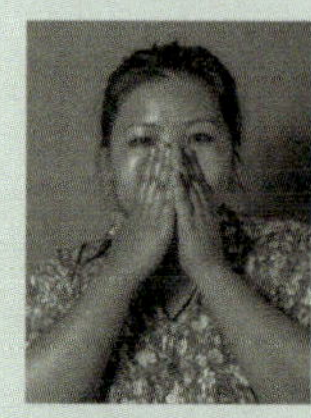
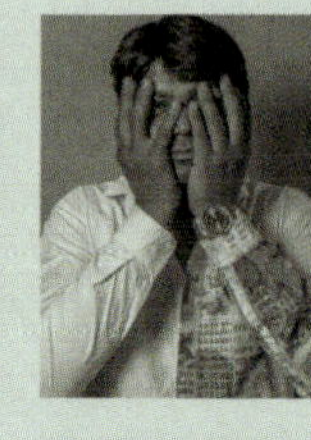
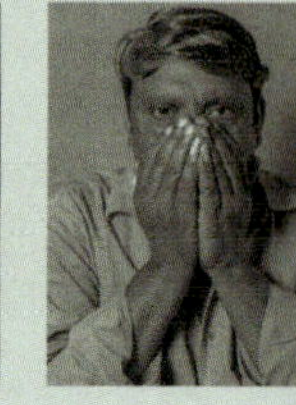
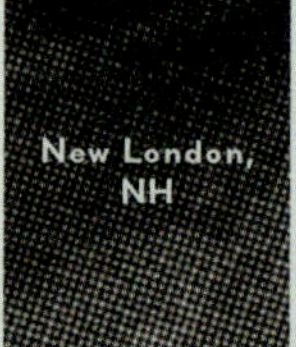

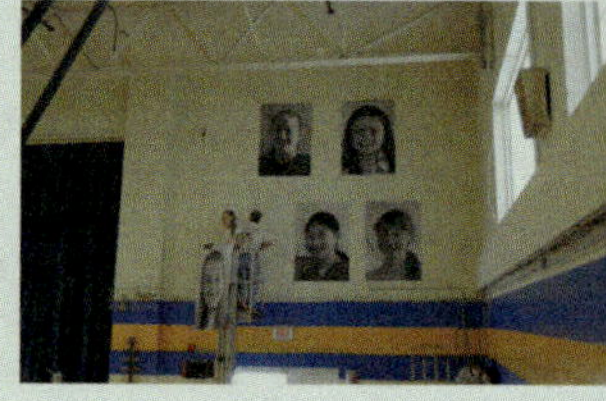
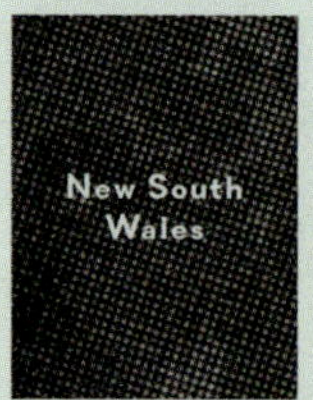

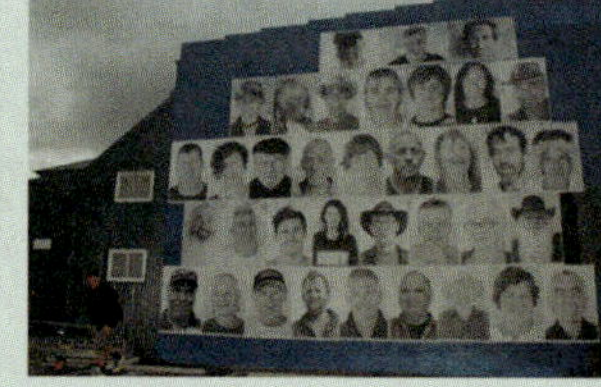
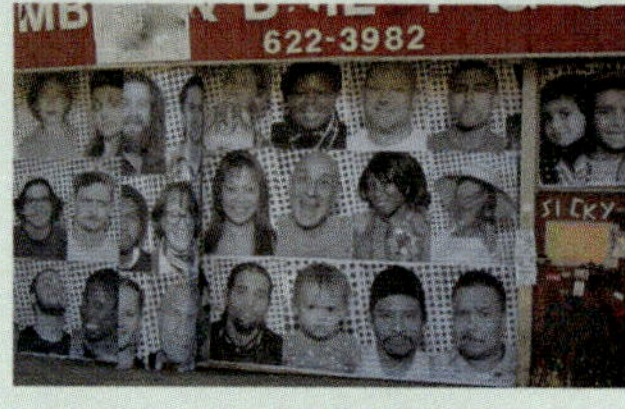

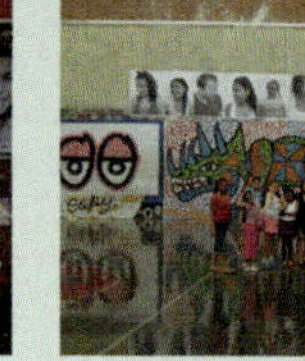
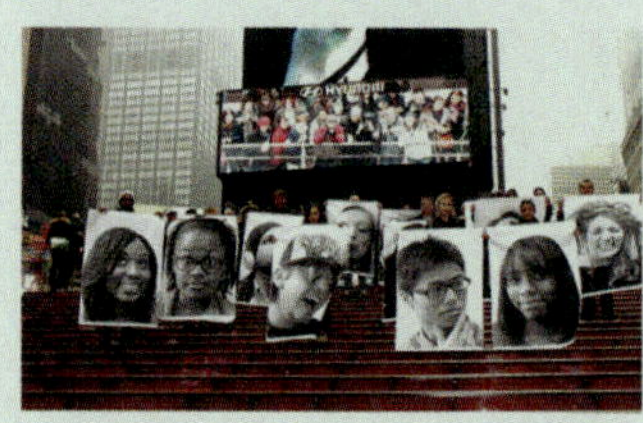
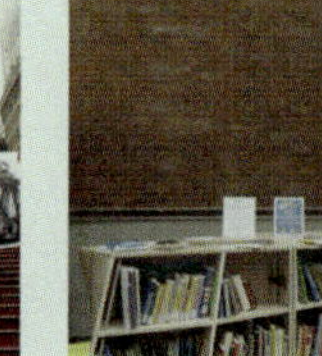
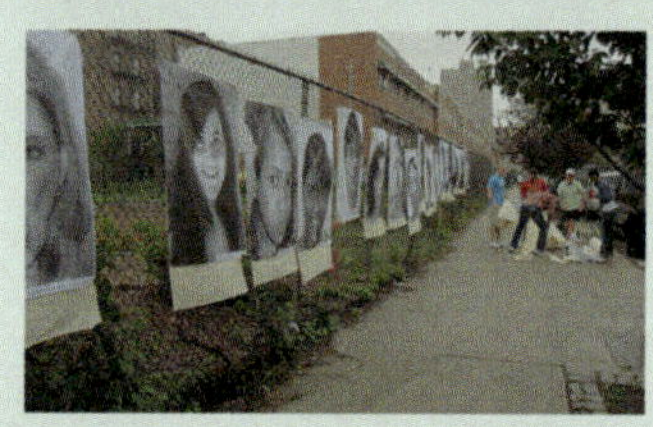
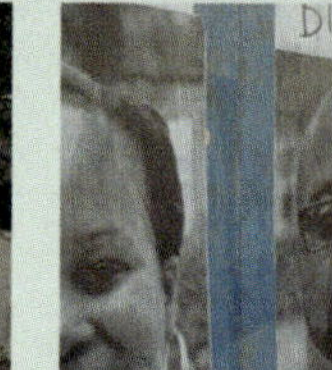
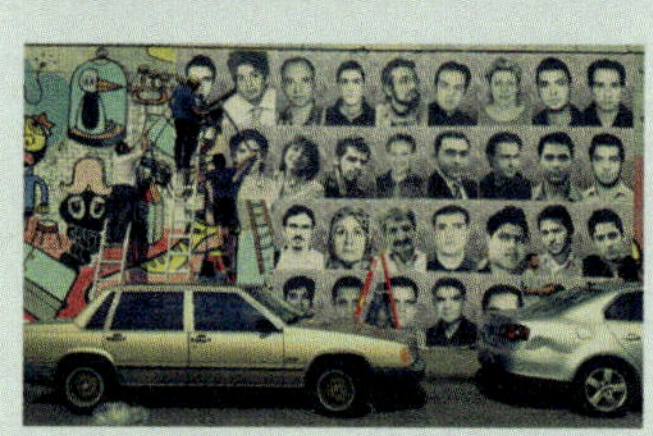
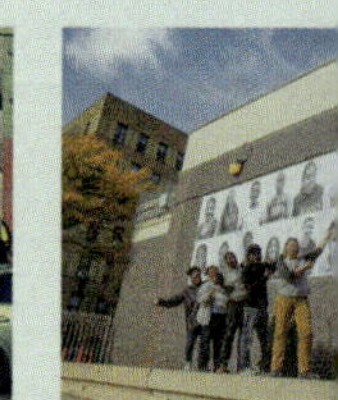
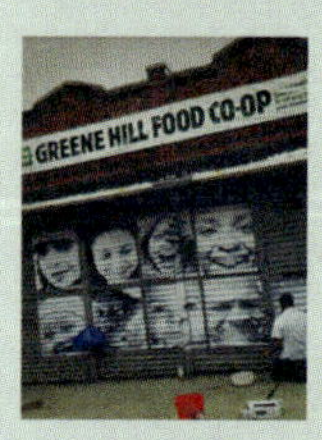

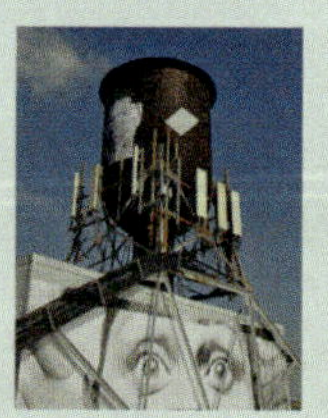
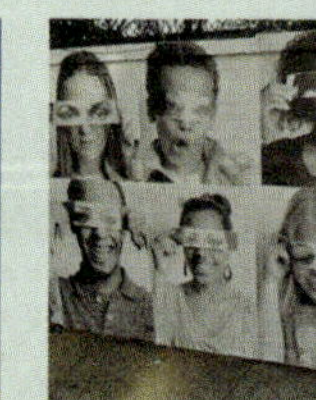
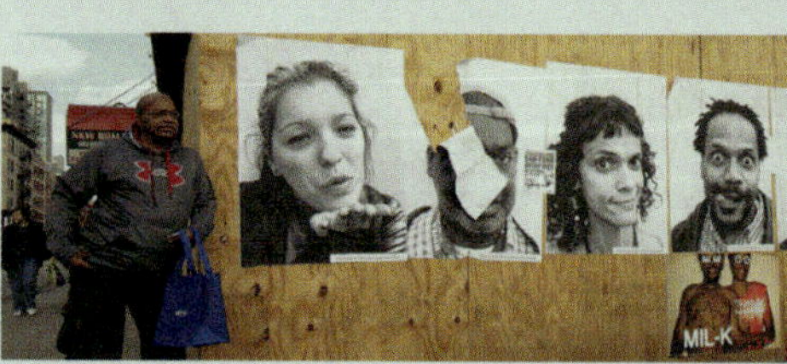
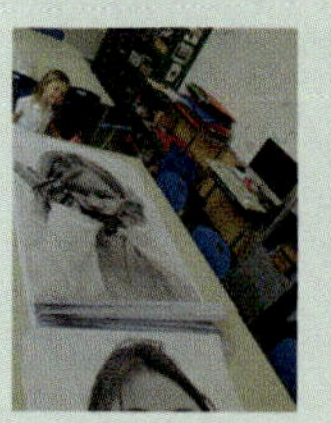
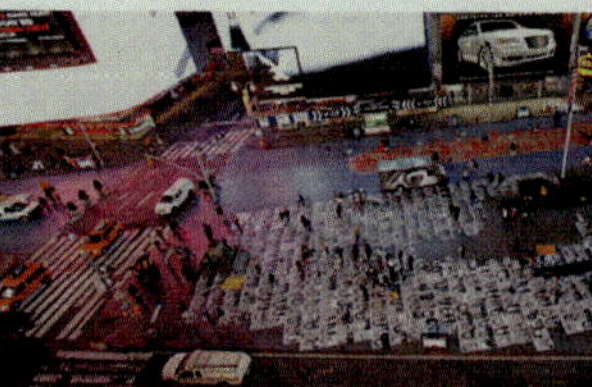

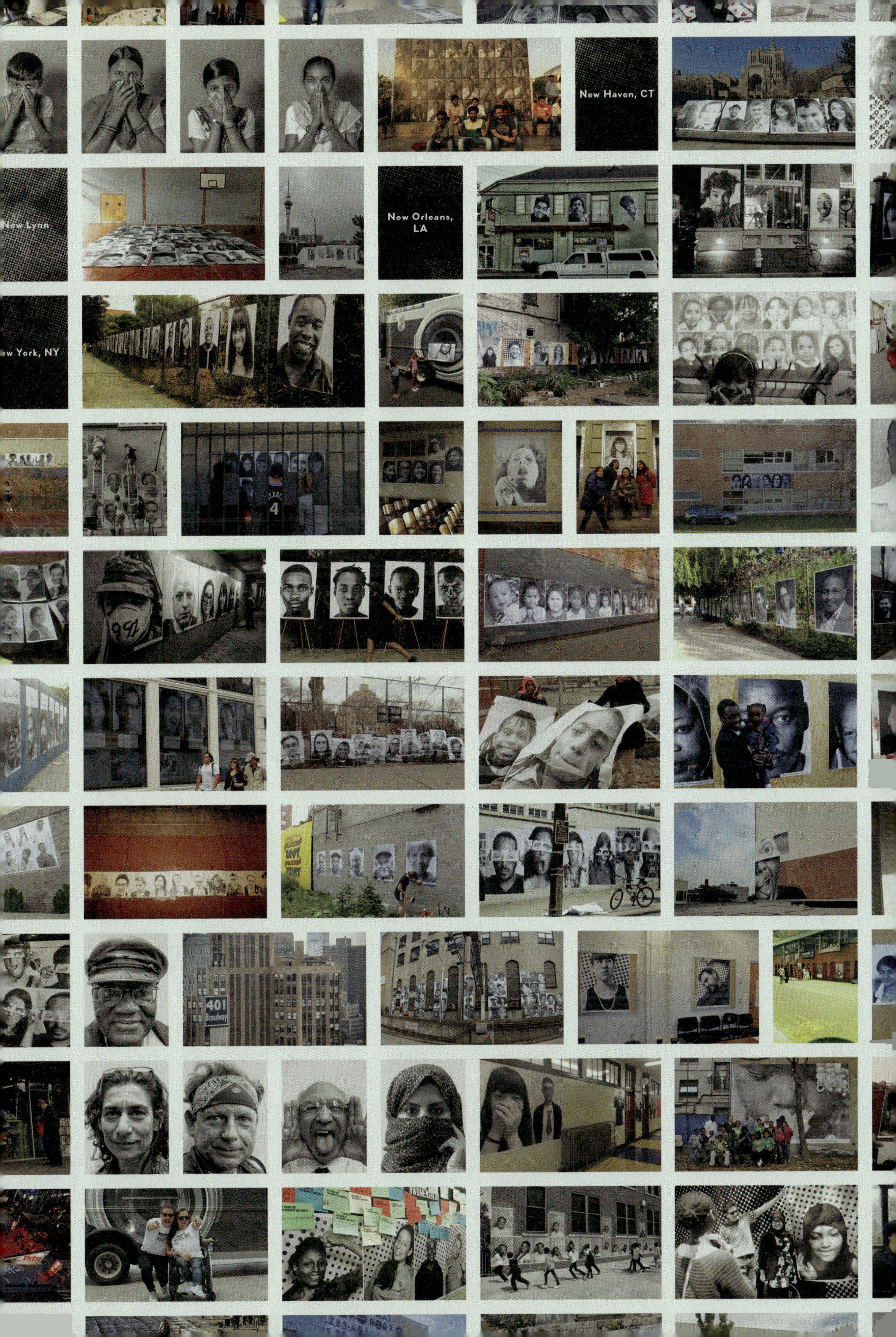
New Haven, CT
New Lynn
New Orleans, LA
401
Broadway

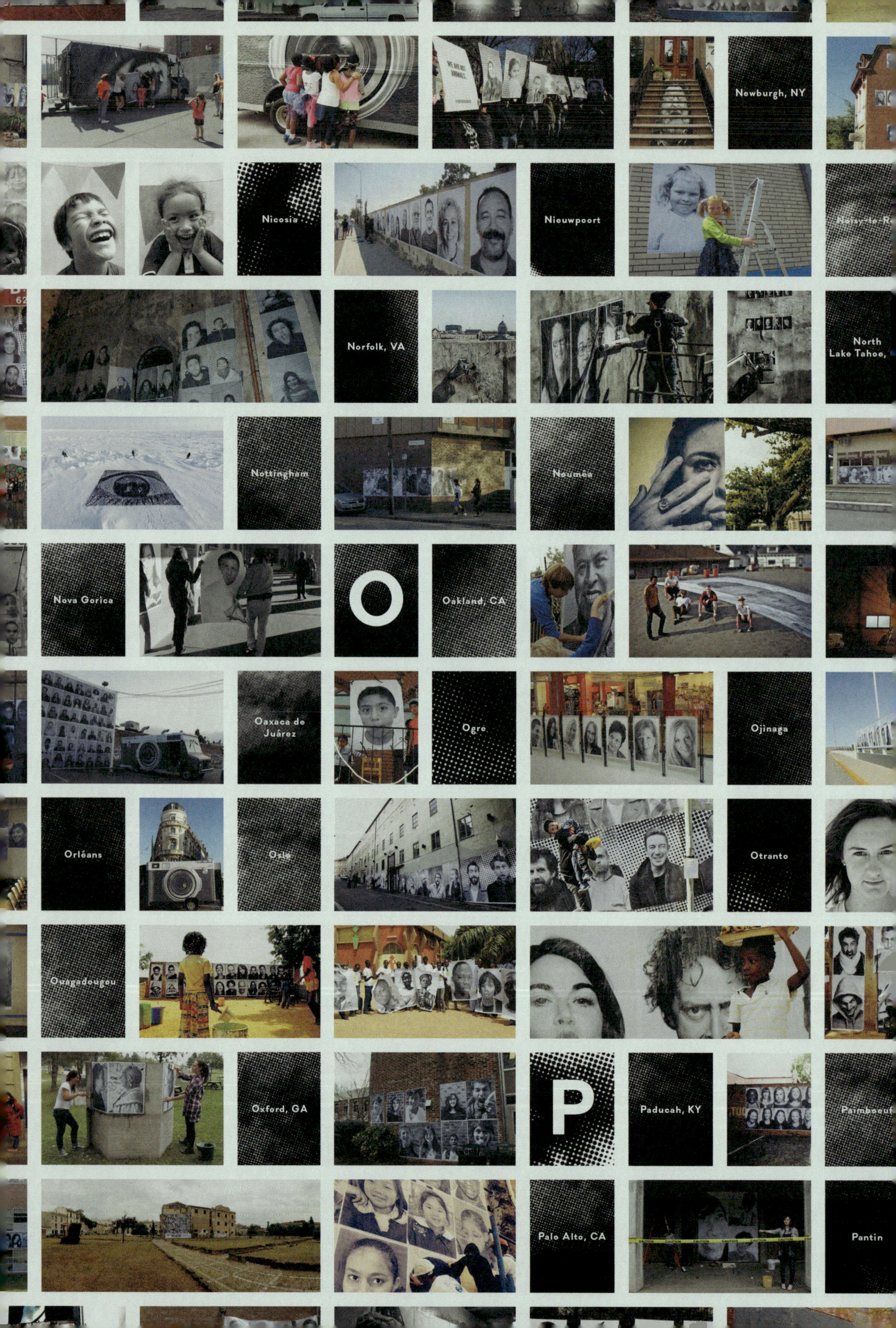

Newburgh, NY
Nicosia
Nieuwpoort
Norfolk, VA
North Lake Tahoe,
Nottingham
Nouméa
Nova Gorica
O
Oakland, CA
Oaxaca de Juárez
Ogre
Ojinaga
Orléans
Oslo
Otranto
Ouagadougou
Oxford, GA
P
Paducah, KY
Paimboeuf
Palo Alto, CA
Pantin

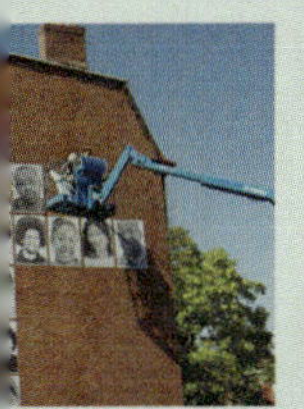
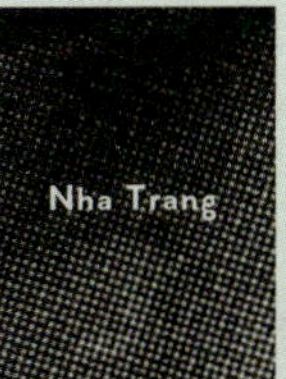

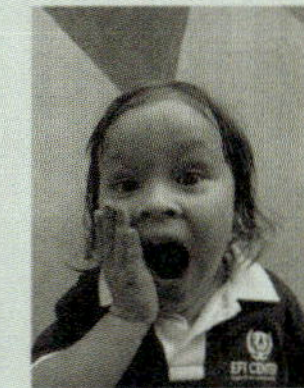
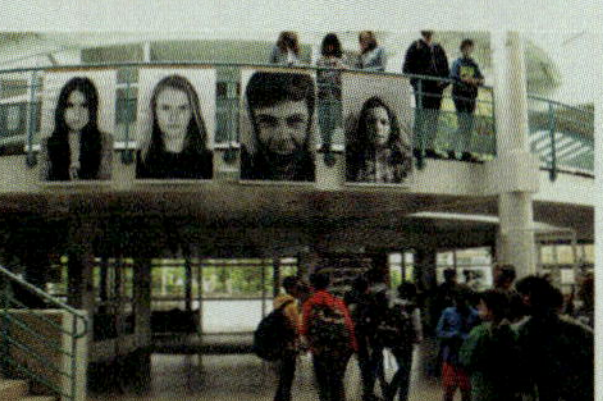
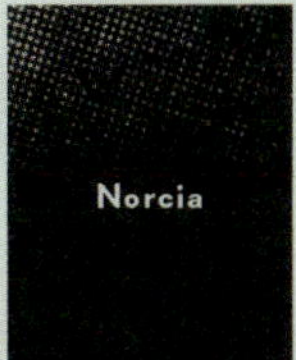

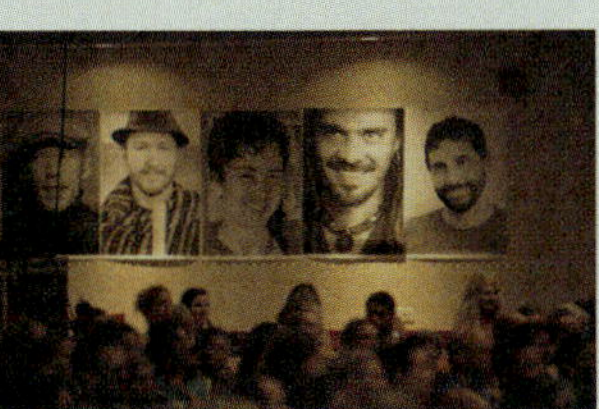
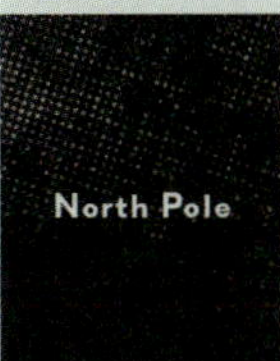

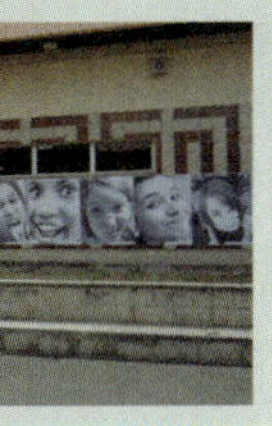
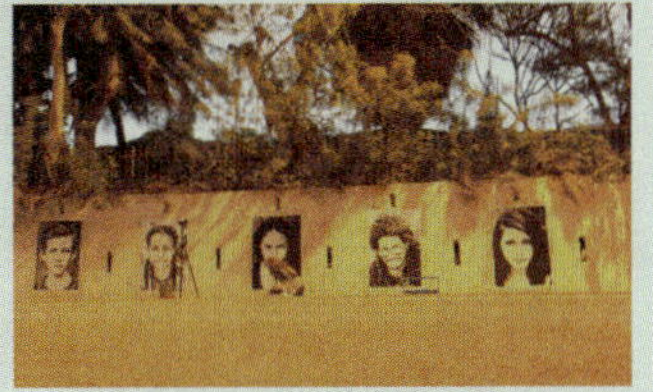
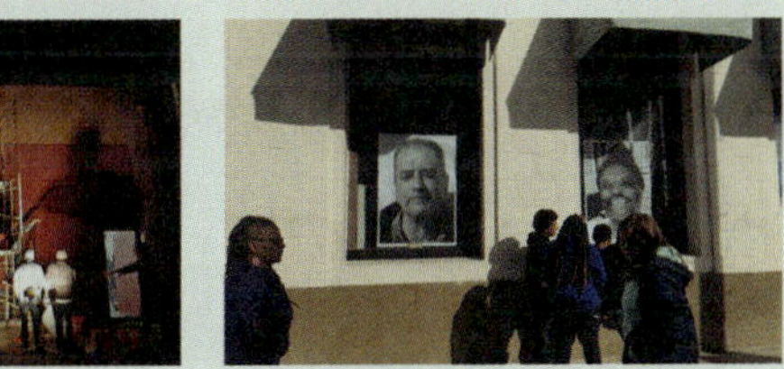
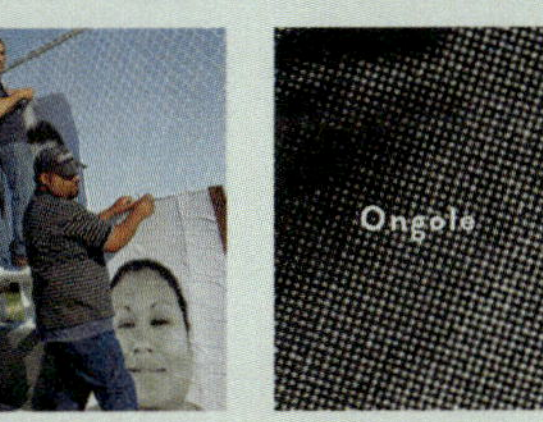
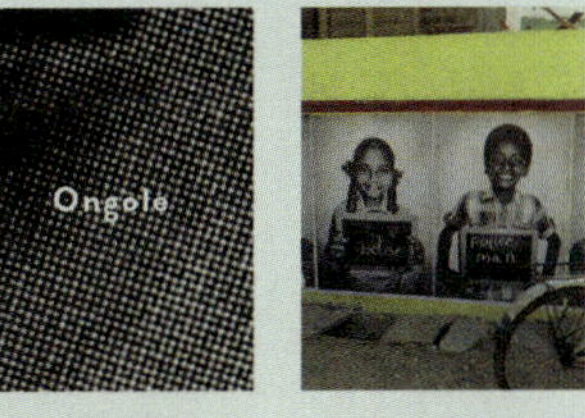

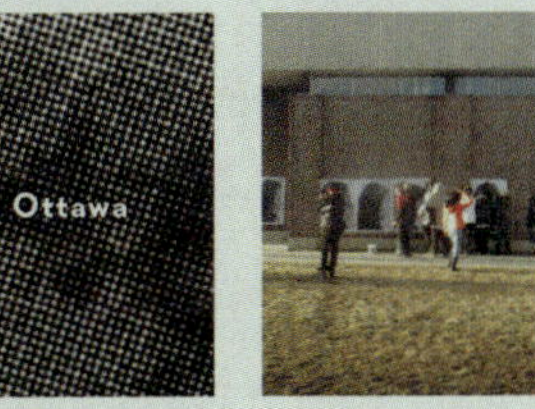

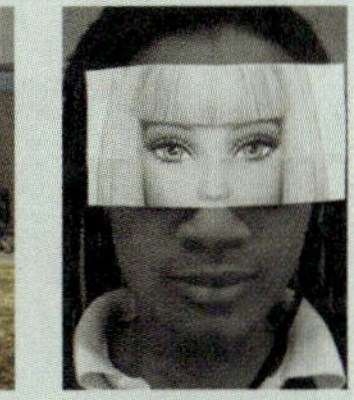
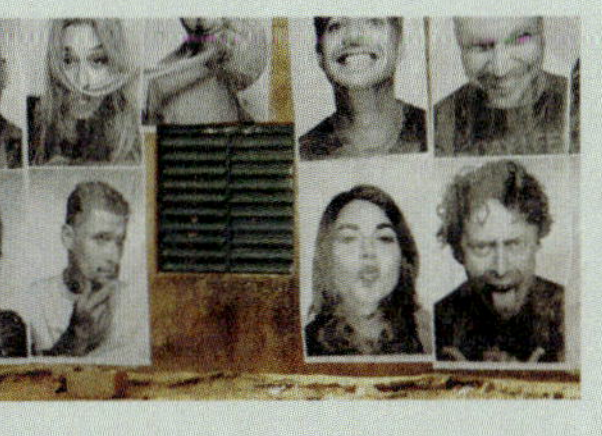

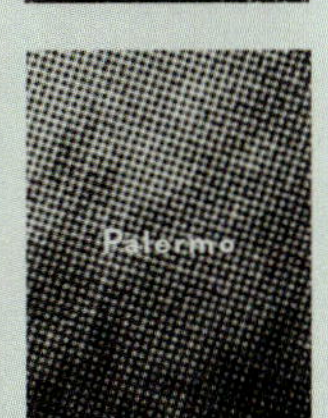

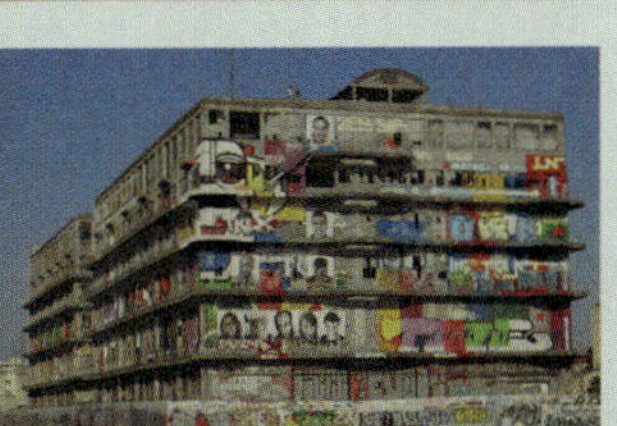
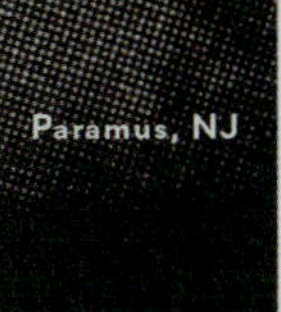

takes an entire community of faculty, staff, and administrators to put aside their distrust or resentment and focus on their students. The entire community of Bergen Community College will come together for a Day of Community where we will engage, interact, and learn from and with one another. Let's showcase our commitment to one college through our portraits.

Paris, France Inside Descartes, October 2016. Our university is losing its humanity. We'd like to gather all the students and remind them that they're not alone in these infinite corridors.

Why Ayotzinapa?, January 2015. On September 26 in Iguala, Mexico, forty-three students were kidnapped by the local authorities, and according to the official declarations, killed. Since then, a massive social movement has burgeoned, driven by the claim of justice. Many groups have gathered all over the world to show their support to this emerging movement. We want to do the same. We are people living in Paris who are deeply concerned about this situation. And we want to show why. Through our pictures expressing our feelings and thoughts, we want to show all the people directly affected by this political conflict over drugs that they are not alone. We believe it is crucial to raise international awareness about the democratic crisis that the country undergoes today. We cannot allow these massacres to continue to happen. We want justice!

#LibertéEgalitéMobilité, September 2015. We want to invite a dialogue between drivers of taxis and chauffeur-driven vehicles, soothing tensions between these two groups that, in the end, have the same goal: earn a living and change the way people go around in their country.

Nous Sommes l'Avenir, October 2014. We want to show that the future is in good hands with today's youth.

Portraits d'Habitants: Cité Curial, July 2013. The Cité Curial is populated by approximately 4,500 people. It is incredibly diverse in terms of communities. The aim of the Portraits of Residents action is to help the inhabitants get a hold of the renovation and make it their own, because the place can only become peaceful and citizen-friendly if the inhabitants take care of it. This means they must love it and feel at home, as a community. Whether they are Jewish, Asian, Muslim, African, from Eastern Europe, or other parts of the world.

Women Leadership, March 2012. Traditionally inside, women are coming out! When getting visible, women change the way they are looking at themselves and at the others.

Celebrating Art in Nateau, March 2012. Celebrating how we love art and nature, especially in Nanteau.

The Veiled Men, May 2012. Veiled men on Beauboug street: a sacred idea!

Dernière Année au Collège, June 2012. This group action helps us keep alive the memory of this past year that we spent together and to show the links that unite us all.

Parisian Theater, July 2012. Aspiring actors take over some iconic places to spread art across Parisian theaters.

A White Wave for Syria, April 2012. A White Wave for Syria is a Solidarity Action organized on the occasion of the sixty-sixth anniversary of the independence of Syria, under the patronage of the International Federation for Human Rights and the League for Human Rights.

Face to Face—Inside Out Sorbonne Nouvelle, June 2016. We aim to create a wall of expression, representative of our intellectual, human, and artistic curiosity. This project is going to transmform an crossroads into a place of sharing: professors, staff, and students from every walk of life will gather together in the name of art.

Park City, UT Inside Out Park City, July 2016. (I)dea+(E)ffort=(O)utcome is an Inside Out Park City group action installed in an area with a high concentration of vacant buildings. In direct contrast to the empty storefronts, we placed photographs celebrating those in our community who have embraced the entrepreneurial spirit—those who have taken an idea and made and effort to build something from scratch in order to make a difference.

Parroquia Guangaje, Ecuador The Inclusion of the Kichwa Indians, March 2012. The Kichwa Indians that live in Parroquia Guangaje, an indigenous parish in the Ecuador highlands are largely excluded from the wider cultural and political dialogue that occurs in the country. Most have never seen photos of themselves. The only photos posted publicly are those of the Mayor and other public office holders who pay little attention to the indigenous population of the area.

Patlekhet, Nepal Women and the Soil, December 2011. This is a group of women—mothers, grandmothers, wives, daughters, and sisters— all who are farmers in the rural village of Patalekhet, Nepal. Together we are exploring the deeper sense of fertility; the physical, cognitive, emotional, and spiritual bonds between women and the soil. Our focus is women's health and food security, inspiring them to take pride in their connection with the soil.

Pati, Indonesia Anggora Farming Project, March 2015. We (Class of '83, Faculty of Veterinary Medicine, Bogor Agriculture University, aka the ANGGORA) believe that inspiring the students of SMK Farming Pati to be aware, become engaged, and be passionate about the field of agriculture and farming in particular, by sharing our achievements and success stories will help them plan, organize, and shape their future.

Pau, France Sourire, May 2015. Smile to share the future, to live, to prove that we exist.

Pennsburg, PA Perkiomen School, May 2013. We need the stories of others. As a school with students from around the world, our community holds a lot of assumptions about one another and we have a unique opportunity to break down barriers. Additionally, students do not often interact in a meaningful way with the neighborhood. Both the school community and the larger community could benefit greatly from the other.

Perth, Australia Reconciliation and Equality, July 2011. To bring about change for our indigenous people and work together toward reconciliation and greater equality.

Pertuis, France Une Génération Pro s'Affiche-Lycée Val de Durance, April 2016. We want to present the students of the "professional" section of the Val de Durance high school in order to highlight this section.

Philadelphia, PA Grow Through High School, March 2013. The purpose of our action is to explore the importance of growth through the high school years. Graduating seniors have a lot of useful guidance to share with students who are just finishing their first year of high school. Our photos would transition from the school's youngest students to those graduating seniors.

Young Philly Lives—Science Leadership Academy, January 2012. We want to represent our students, their diversity, their fears, and their hopes for the future.

KIPP Dubois Collegiate Academy, January 2012. Art students will be taking pictures using pin hole Holga cameras of a family member that means the most to them/pushes them to pursue their education.

Phnom Penh, Cambodia Inside Out Phnom Penh, July 2012. Faces of the neighborhood near the traditional Catholic church.

Piatra Neamt, Romania Testimonials in Piatra Neamt, September 2012. The concept is that every photo will be a testimonial, a promise that every person makes to themself. The promises will be written on the back of the photos so nobody but the writer will know them.

Pisa, Italy Vita Tua, Vita Mea, December 2015. We want this project to help many people realize that society's growth no longer depends on individual success at the expense of others. On the contrary, we should use individual success as inspiration for the whole community to do better.

Pittsburgh, PA Propel Schools, September 2011. Portraits of a diverse student population.

Plerin, France Tous Citoyens?!, April 2016. Being a citizen means having rights and duties for yourself and others; it means being held accountable for one's opinions and free to express them, while remaining respectful of all.

Ploermel, France All Volunteers Against Exclusion!, March 2015. We are a class in a high school in France. Our message is "all volunteer against exclusion" because we wanted to put forward the work of the volunteers in different charities. We also wanted to say "no" to all kind of exclusions.

Podgorica, Montenegro Essentially Equal, March 2013. A project in Podgorica focusing on the coexistence of the native population with a nomad Roma population that lives on the outskirts of city. The goal was to show that although we are culturally, economically, and socially different, even in a legal sense, we as human beings are dependent on each other and in essence equal.

Pont-Péan, France Inconnus Connus, June 2016. Reflecting on the notions of acceptance and openness to others regardless of our differences: "What if directly engaging the stranger that we would normally disregard or ignore was easy and constructive?"

Pontevedra, Spain Remember Sonia, June 2011. Soon it will be a year and a half since she disappeared. We want to remind everyone that Sonia has not returned to us, that we will probably never see her again, and that the one responsible for her disappearance will not tell us where she is.

Poolesville, MD The Humanities Seniors, January 2014. The Humanities seniors of Poolesville High School are an intelligent, creative, and diverse group of individuals who deserve to be recognized for their hard work over the last four years. This group action serves to celebrate not only their achievements at school as members of the Humanities "family," but also their unique personalities as they embark on their futures at college and the world beyond.

Porches, Portugal STOPRacismo, December 2014. We are in the twenty-first century, we live in a democracy. We are all equal, we have the right to be treated equally. We want the same opportunities, and so we've got to endwith differences. Peace and love. No to racism.

Port-au-Prince, Haiti Rising Souls in Port-au-Prince, January 2012. Rising Souls, Haiti standing for the resilience of Haitians.

Port-au-Prince Budget Cuts, June 2011. To humanize school budget cuts by posting pictures of four teachers that are being let go due to the budget.

Powell River, Canada The Women of the Powell River, April 2012. As a rural, geographically isolated, and highly diverse community, Powell River has an ongoing shortage of family physicians and access to other health care services and facilities. The goals of our action are to give all Powell River women an opportunity to express what they need to gain and sustain good health for themselves, to strengthen their ability to express their needs, and advocate for themselves and build support with other women. Raise awareness in the community about the gaps in health care services and start a dialogue with care providers to enlist their help in addressing health care needs for women in Powell River.

Poznan, Poland Histories Against the History, December 2016. This project should increase awareness, while at the same time, decrease indifference towards the presented social problems. Perhaps this encounter shall turn into a social therapy, which shall lead to discovering each other.

Praia, Cape Verde Role Models in Cape Verde, June 2012. Cape Verde is a small archipelago off the coast of West Africa. Although the country's educational system has made great strides in recent decades, in some areas there is still room for growth in introducing creative thinking to the classroom. Our goal is to combine the efforts of the Inside Out Project with our initiative to encourage Cape Verdean youth to consider what life after high school could be.

Prince Olav Harbour, South Georgia Water for Life and Peace, November 2014. We live in transformative and rough times, faced with global challenges such as climate change, wars, extreme poverty etc. . . . But one thing is a constant: our need for water.

Princeton, NJ The Many Faces of Princeton University, October 2011. The many faces of Princeton University.

Providence, RI Together, We Are Smith Hill, November 2014. We are not separate communities living in one space; we are a group of individuals that form a diverse community. We live on different streets, and we come from different places; but, together, we are Smith Hill.

Puerto Peñasco, Mexico Helping by Non-Stop Exodus, November 2014. It is almost impossible to stop the exodus that for decades we have seen, lived, and felt. Our action is to help those immigrants to be seen by the society.

Québec City, Canada Embelissons Notre Quartier, August 2014. Let's embellish our district. There are many vacant buildings with boarded windows in Québec City's Saint-Roch district. Let's raise awareness and promote the maintenance of those buildings.

To Make a Difference, May 2012. To make a difference.

Quetzaltenango, Guatemala The Radiant Faces of Xela Locals, November 2012. Our action lit up the streets of Quetzaltenango for one night, the radiant faces of our Xela locals showing the perpetrators of these several rapes that they are not, and will not, be victims.

Quito, Ecuador Same City, Same Rights, October 2016. These eight men and women, and all the 104 million people who live in informal settlements around Latin America, deserve the same city, and the same rights. Habitat III is the most important—and almost the only occasion for us to make these voices be heard—by those who will make the decisions that will manage the fate of the cities for the next twenty years.

Sourire Avec l'Âme, October 2015. Our objectives are: to give a positive image of the "Other," to invite artistic interactions between two youth groups of different social backgrounds, and to spread a positive message: "Smile with your souls."

Rancho Santa Margarita, CA Santa Margarita High School Varsity Arts Club, February 2016. Santa Margarita High School wants to break the stereotype of the high school community by showing our individual selves and unique gifts for all to see. Our goal is to highlight the power and beauty that we each have inside of us that makes our community stronger, unique, and better when we come together as ourselves.

Reims, France Droits des Enfants, July 2015. As children, we have rights.

Rennes, France Les Mendiants Sont dans la Ville, February 2015. Our project aims to re-sensitize the population of Rennes to the situation of the homeless people that live in their city.

Be Organic, February 2014. Eating allows us to live, so eating healthy equates healthy living. Isn't it worth paying more to eat products that won't kill us?

Reston, VA We Make Reston, September 2015. What does your face stand for? How does your individuality contribute to the Reston community? WE MAKE RESTON featured large-scale portraits representing the diverse faces of Reston.

Reykjavik, Iceland Standing Together For Gender Equality!, December 2013. We would like to highlight the importance of gender equality, using art as our means. You probably won't find it surprising that women still earn less than men, are underrepresented in parliament and in the board room, but we think it's time to stop talking about it and start doing something about it.

Richmond, VA Freeman Family Unity, April 2015. We want to create art that will visually unify and celebrate the many cultures that make up our student body.

Rio de Janeiro, Brazil Connecting Two Realities, April 2014. The aim of this project was to connect two different realities that share the same neighborhood: Rocinha, the largest favela in Brazil, and PUC, the major private university in Rio de Janeiro.

PALC—Habitat Rio de Janeiro 2012, August 2012. This event will bring about change if the resolutions are passed and, especially, if the actors stick to their promises of action. Franck NA was invited by the Summit of the People to imagine and create a participatory art work. As a result, he opened the first "Office of Oaths," a moving store that incites people to give a speech on camera about the causes they are fighting for.

Mães de Igualdade (Equality Moms), September 2011. Equality Moms is a group of strong, proud Brazilian mothers fighting for the rights of their LGBT sons and daughters.

Morro da Providencia, May 2011. We don't want our houses to be destroyed.

Riyadh, Saudi Arabia Globility: Why Not?, June 2014. As students at an International School in Saudi Arabia, we are fully aware of how important it is to respect cultural, ethnic, and religious differences. We realize as individuals in society, we must learn to acknowledge and become sensitive to differences while we build communities of trust, respect, and equality.

Rockford, IL We Are the Future . . ., September 2013. We stand for peace and unity and the idea that all children are equal. We ask you to stop the violence in our community, celebrate our history, protect us, and guide us because we are the future . . . We are Rockford!

Rodez, France Accepte-Toi, Accepte l'Autre, May 2016. To fight against discrimination; to learn to understand and love our differences for what they are.

Rome, Italy Costruiamo la Comunità del XXI Secolo, May 2016. The MAXXI museum created a kaleidoscope of portraits of young students who enthusiastically express the multiethnic cohesion of the MAXXI's community!

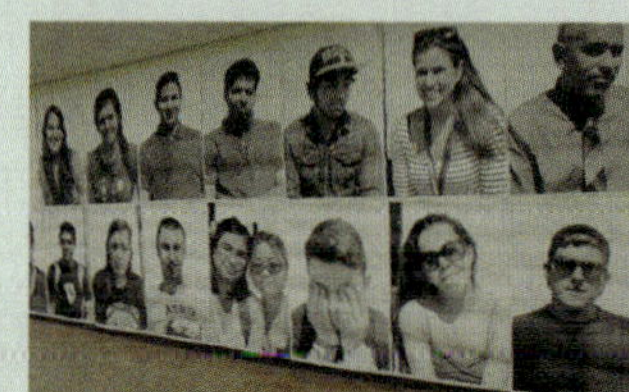
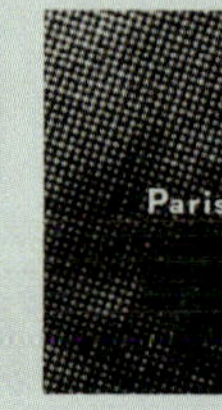

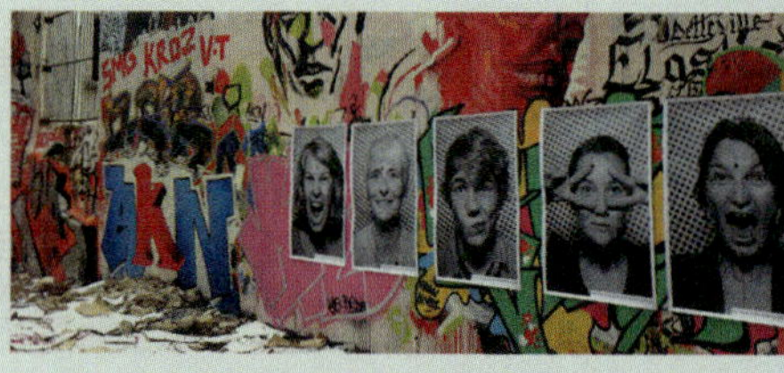
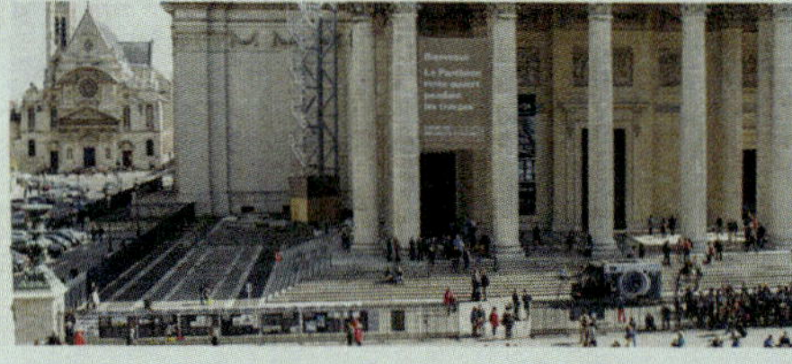
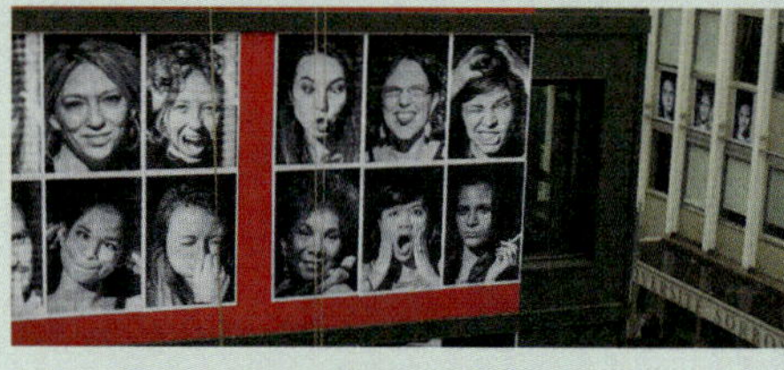
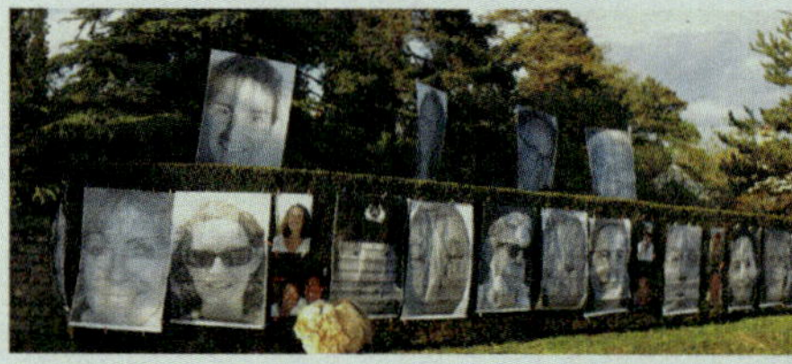
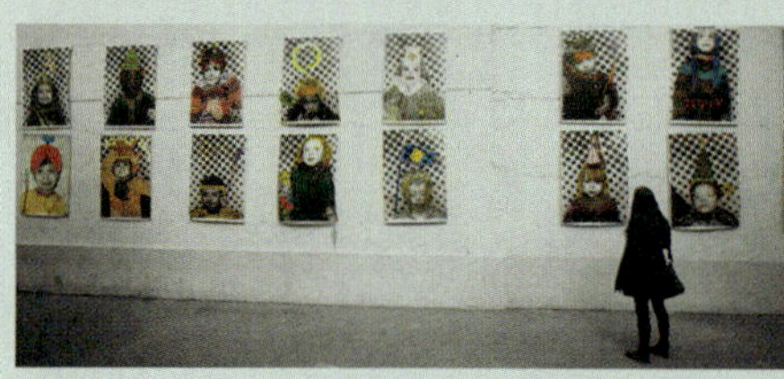
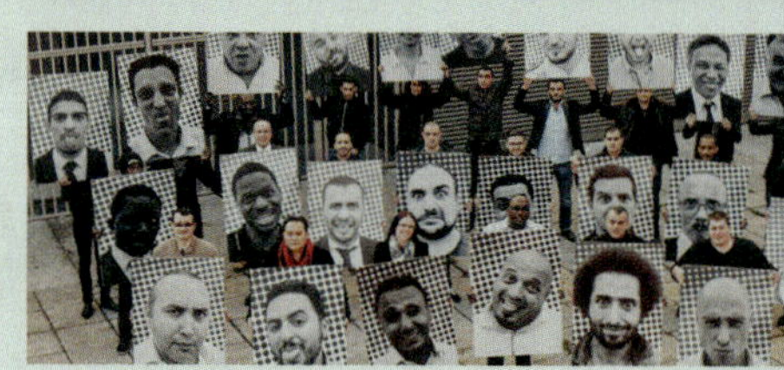
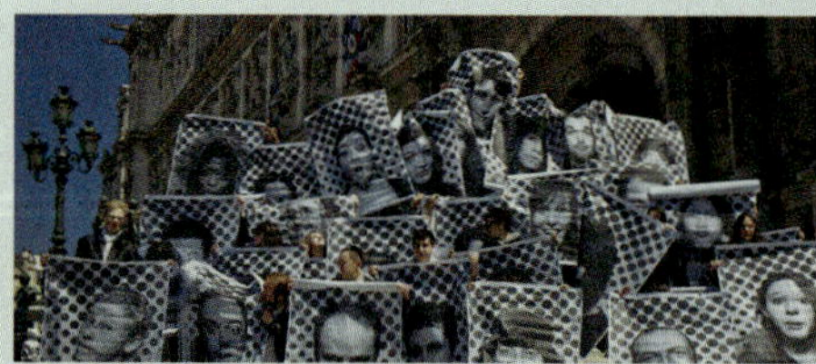
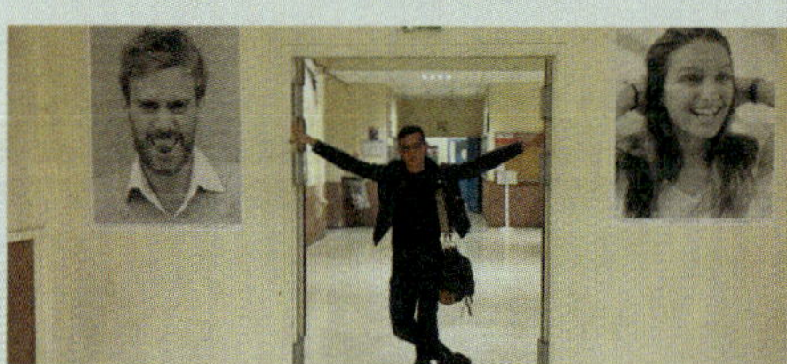
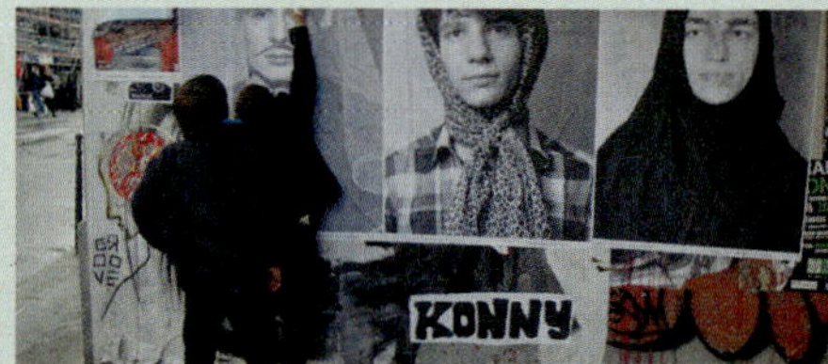

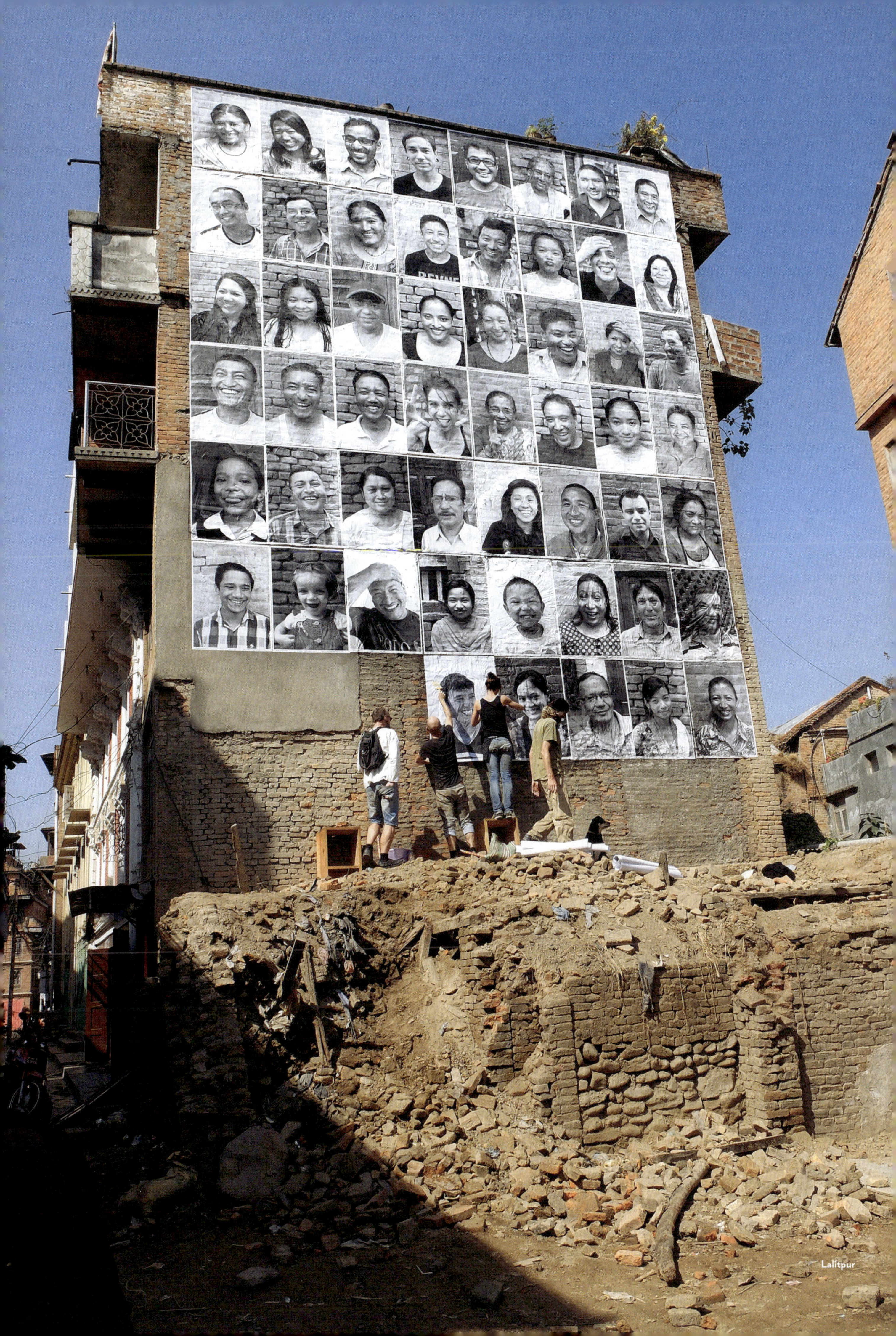

Lalitpur

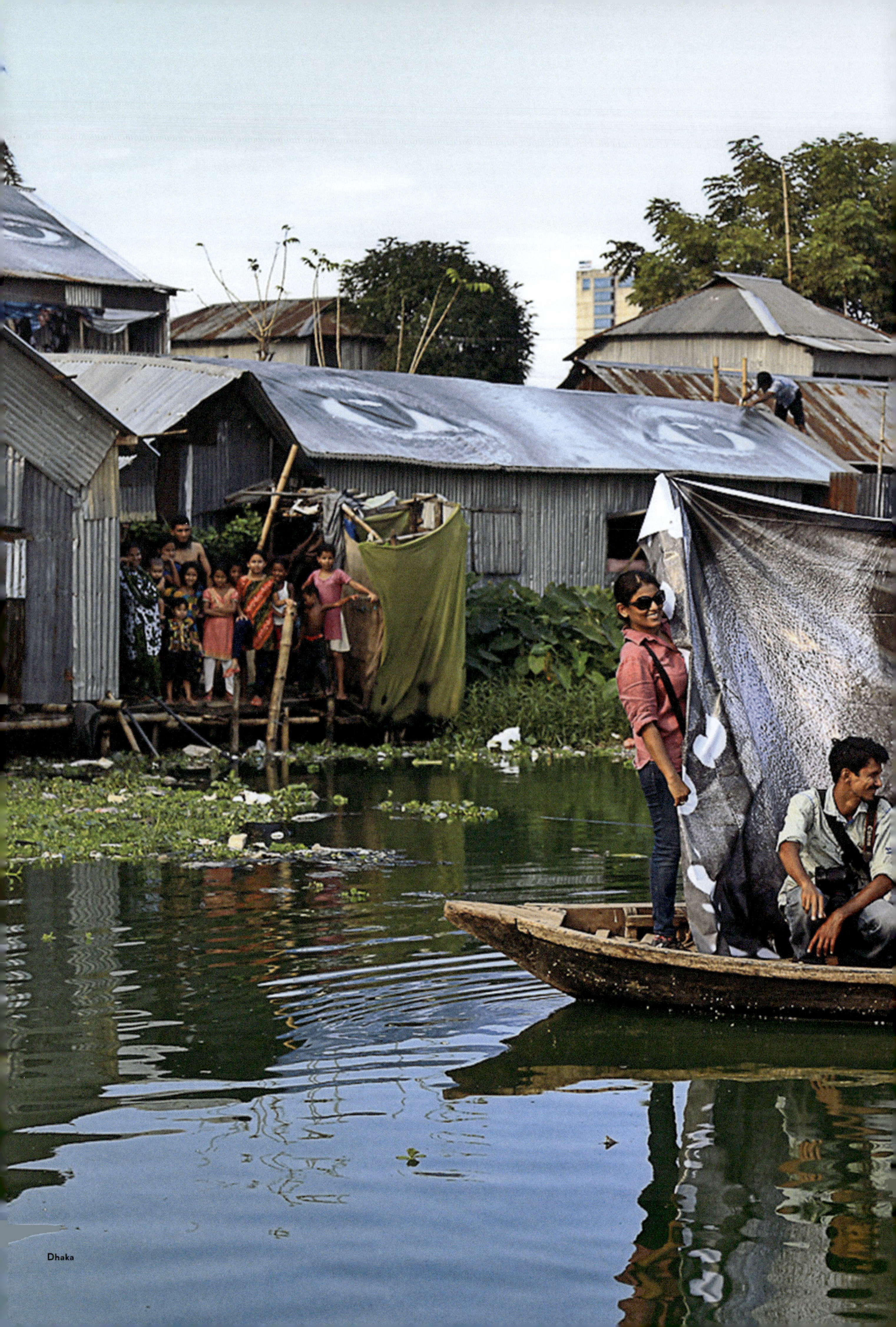

Dhaka

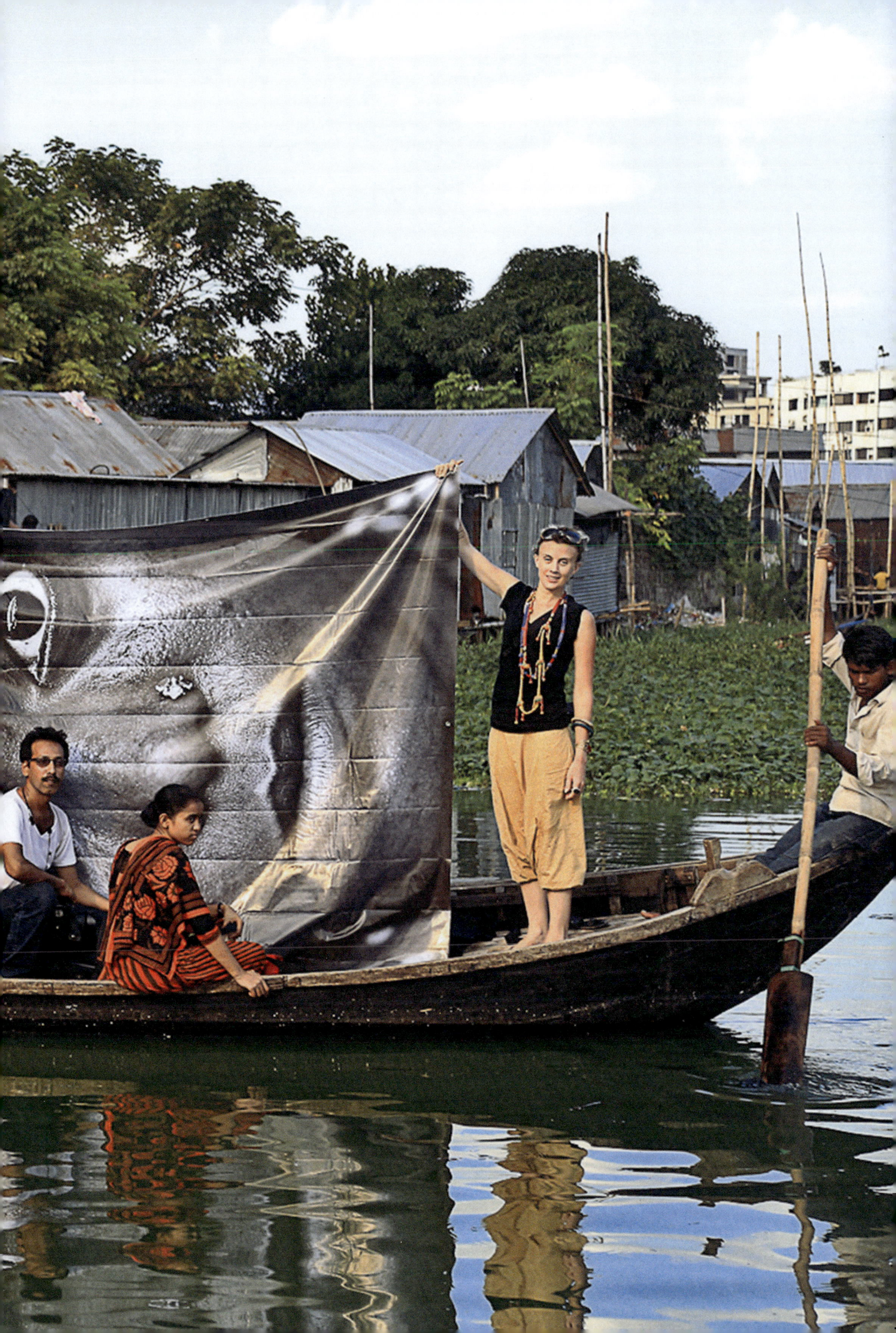

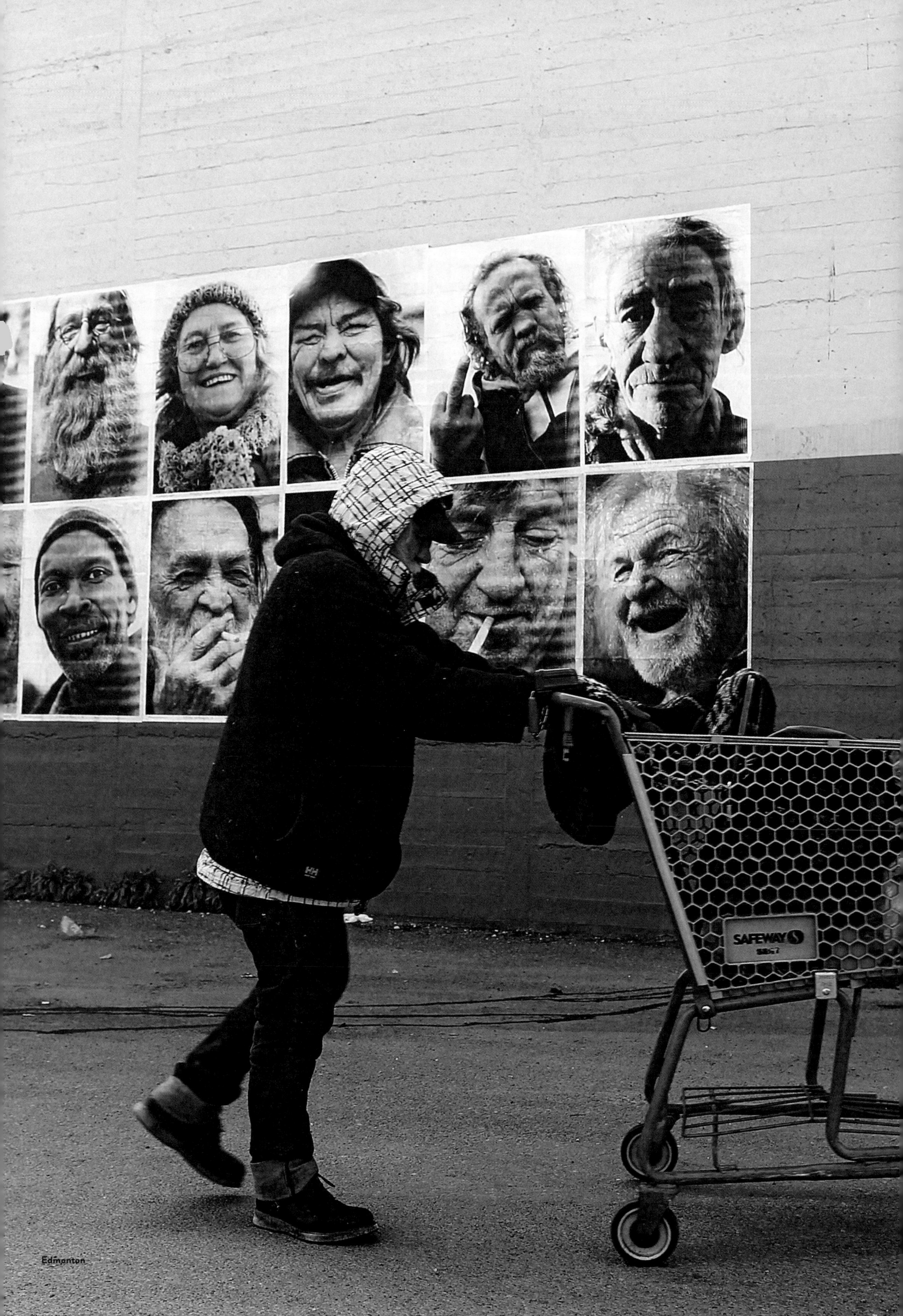

Edmonton

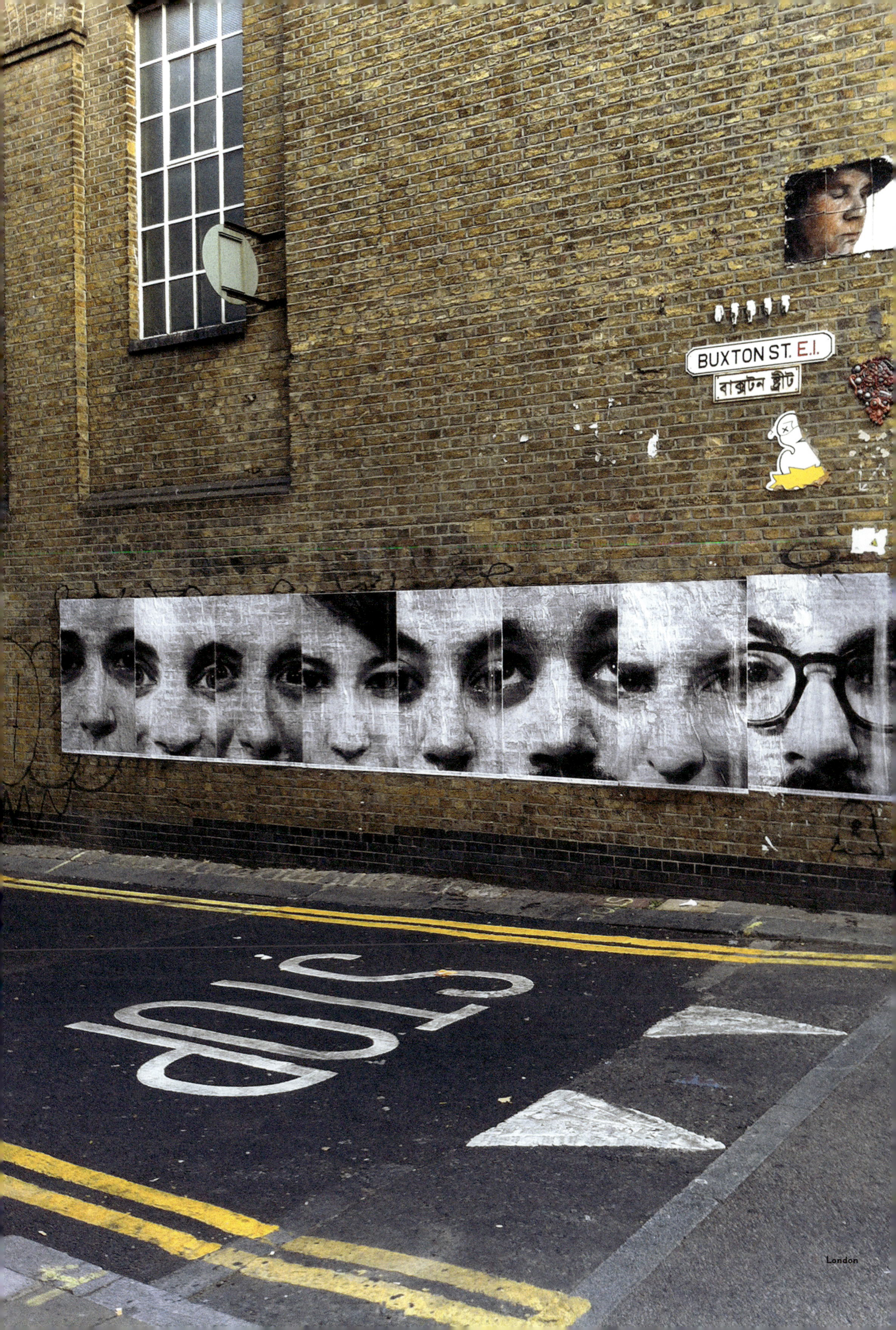

London

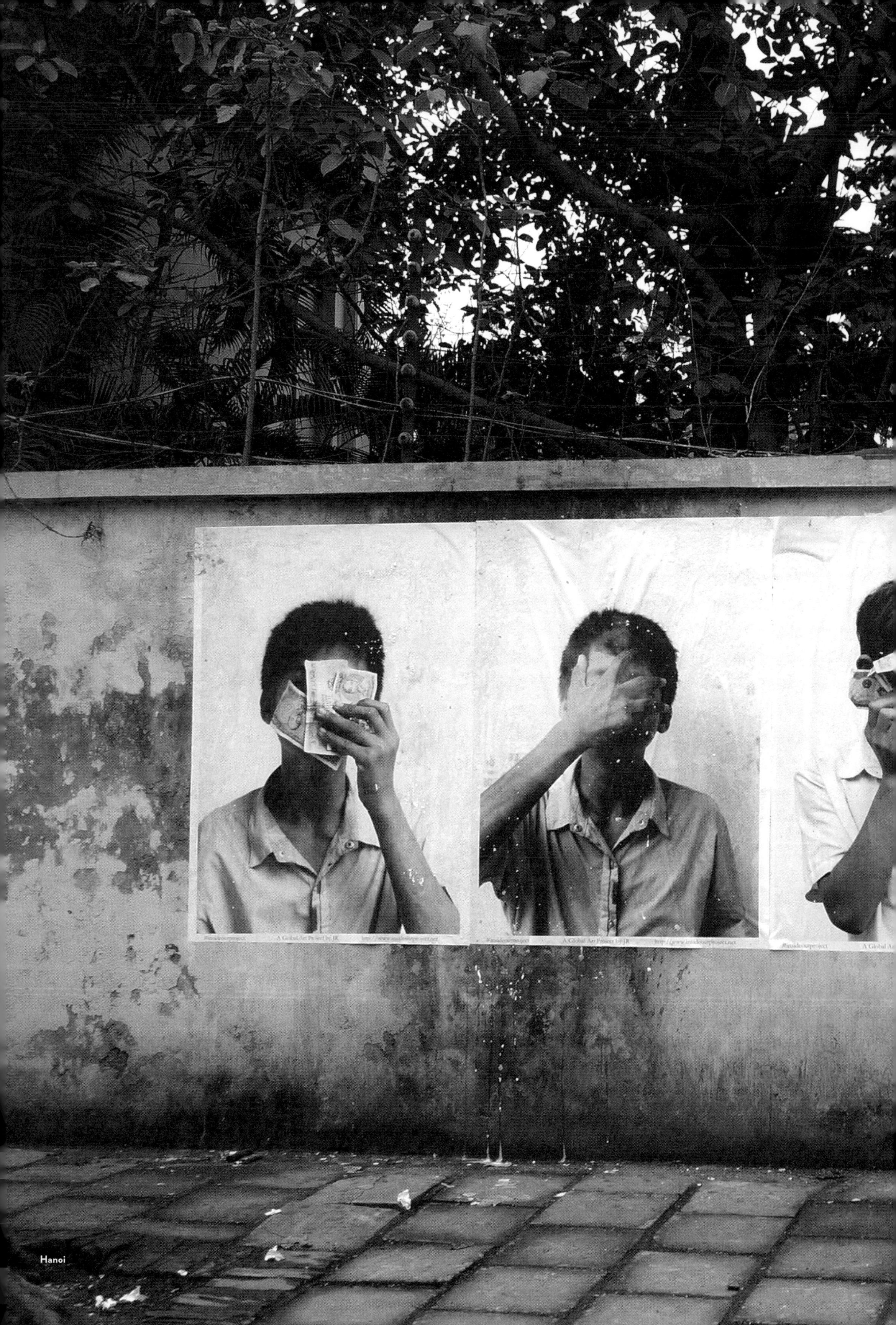

Hanoi

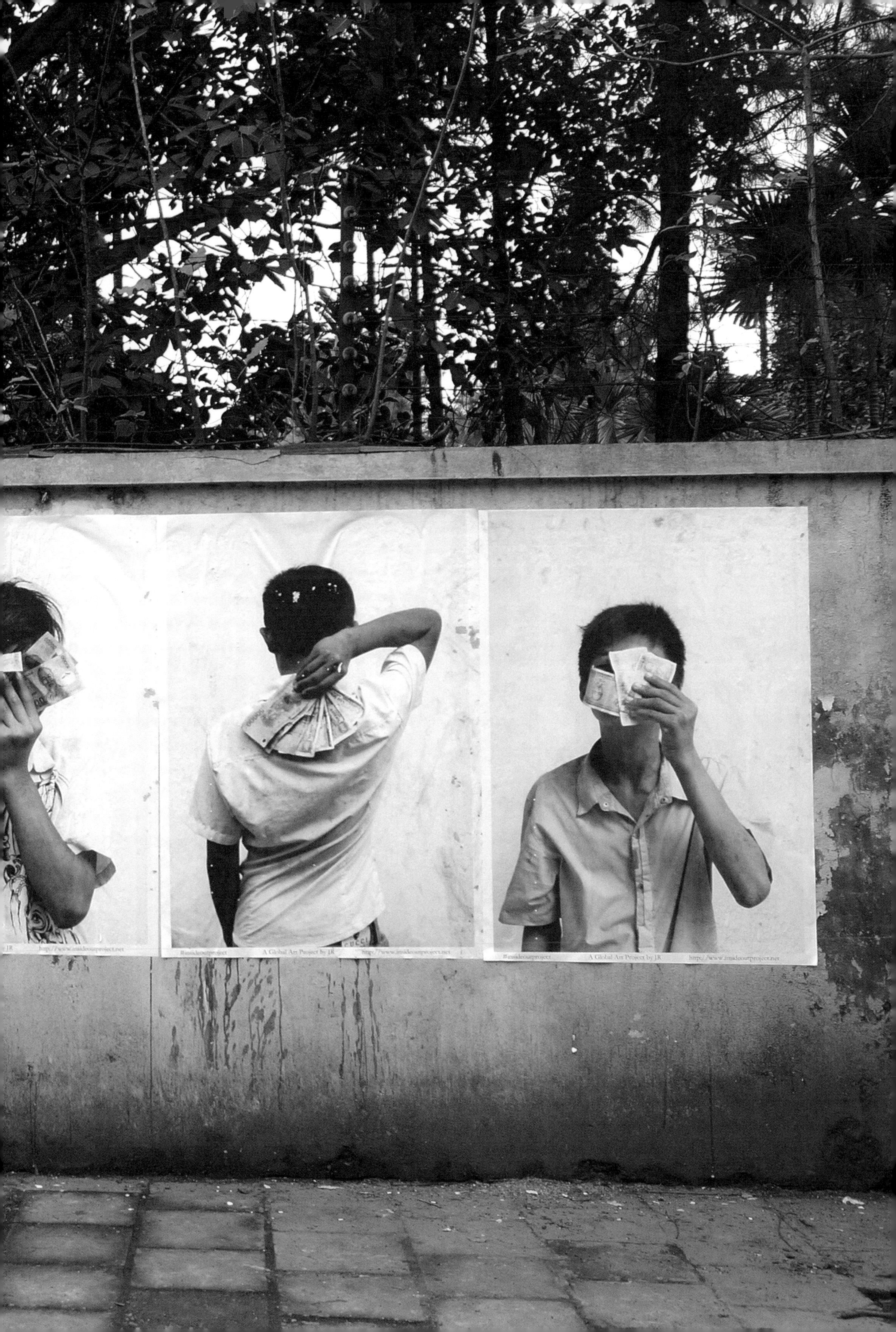
JR
http://www.insideoutproject.net
#insideoutproject
A Global Art Project by JR
http://www.insideoutproject.net
#insideoutproject
A Global Art Project by JR
http://www.insideoutproject.net

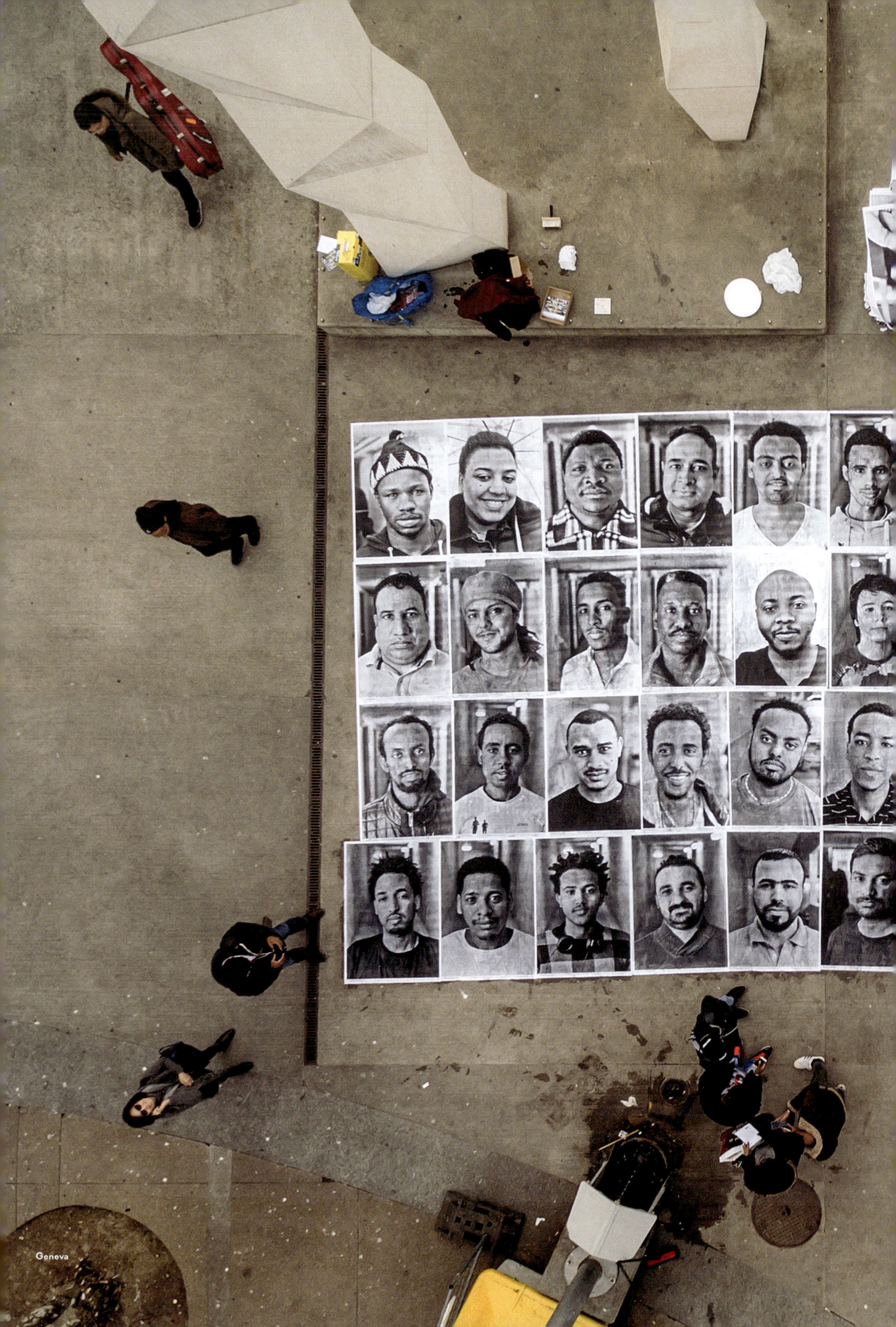

Geneva

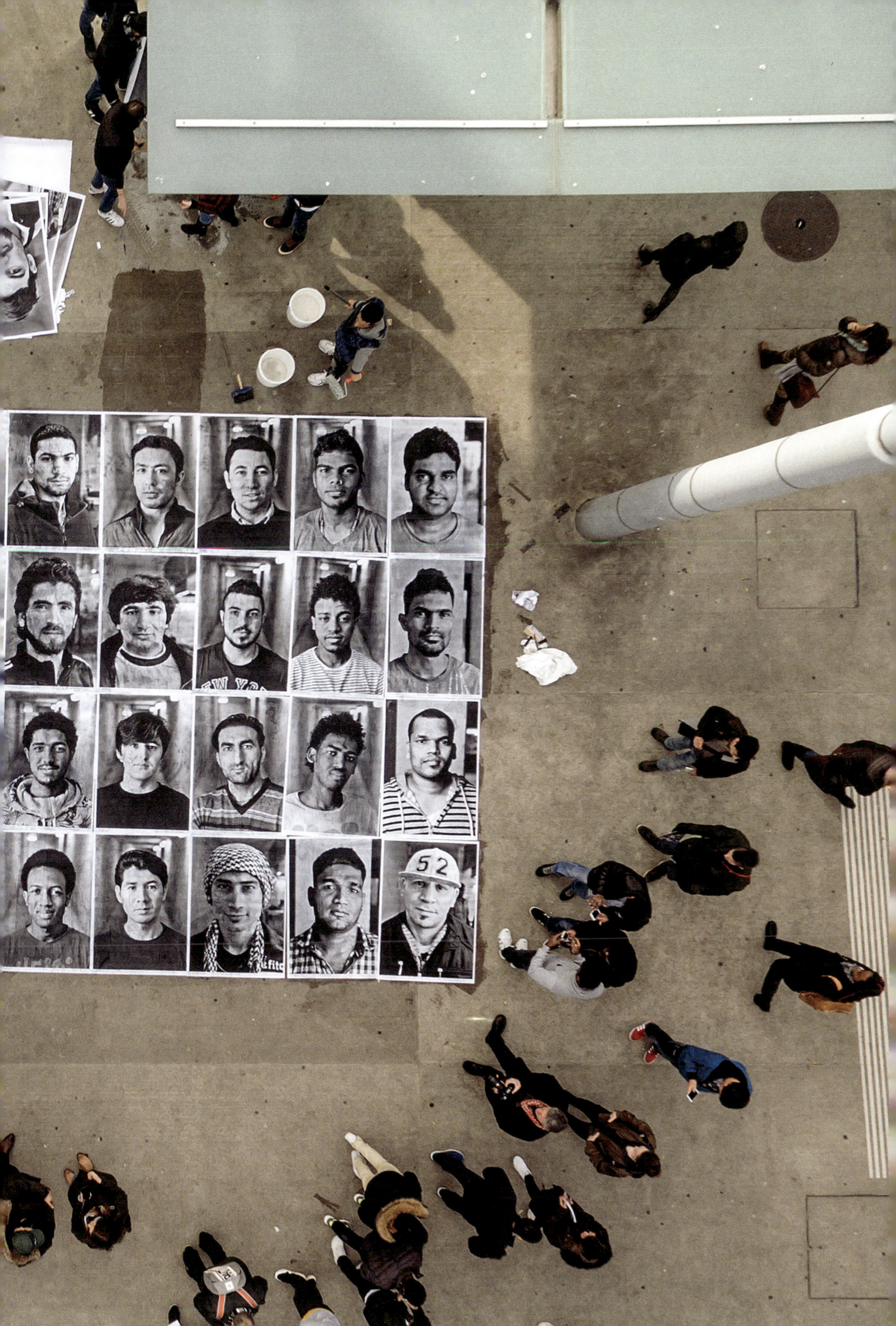
52

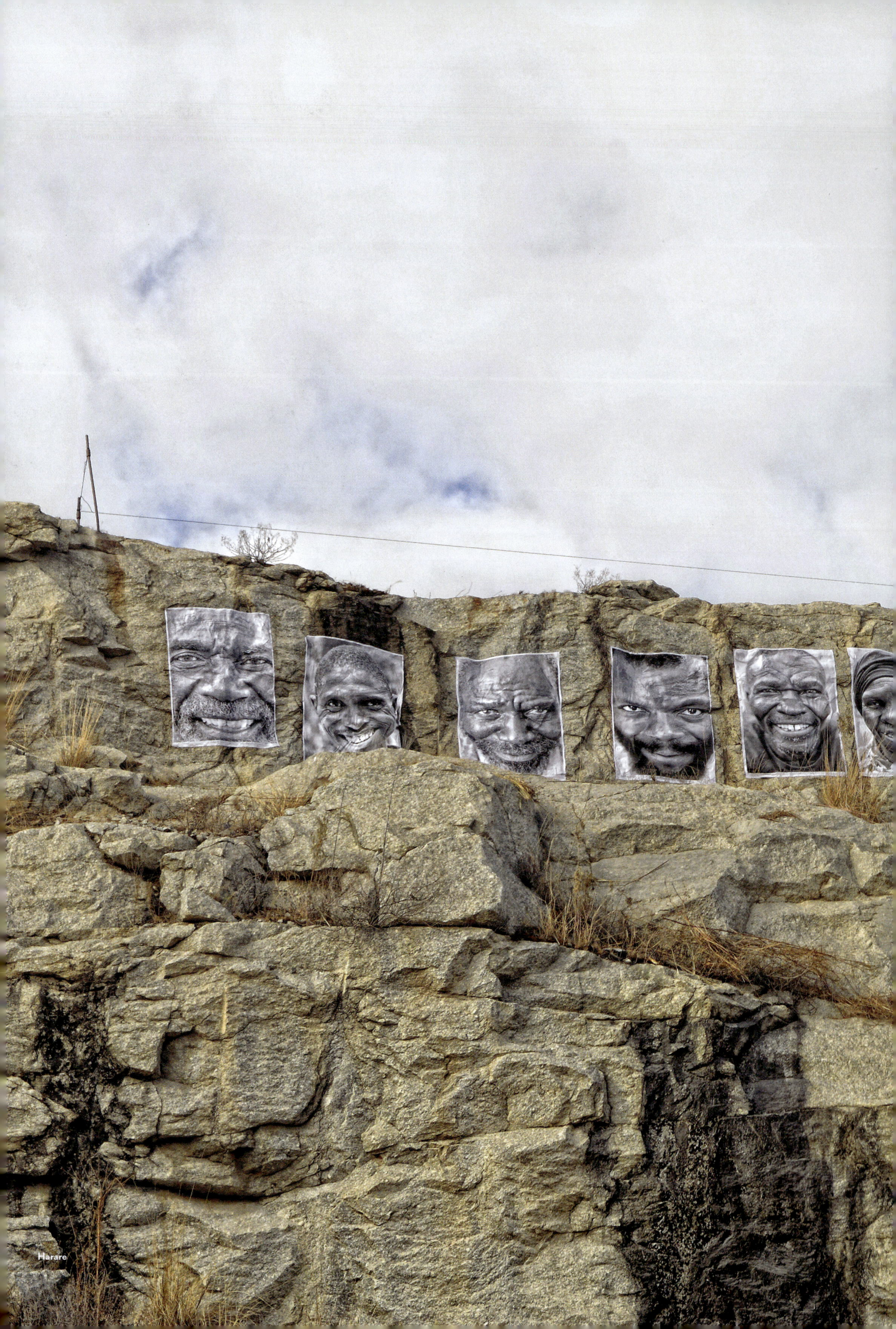

Harare

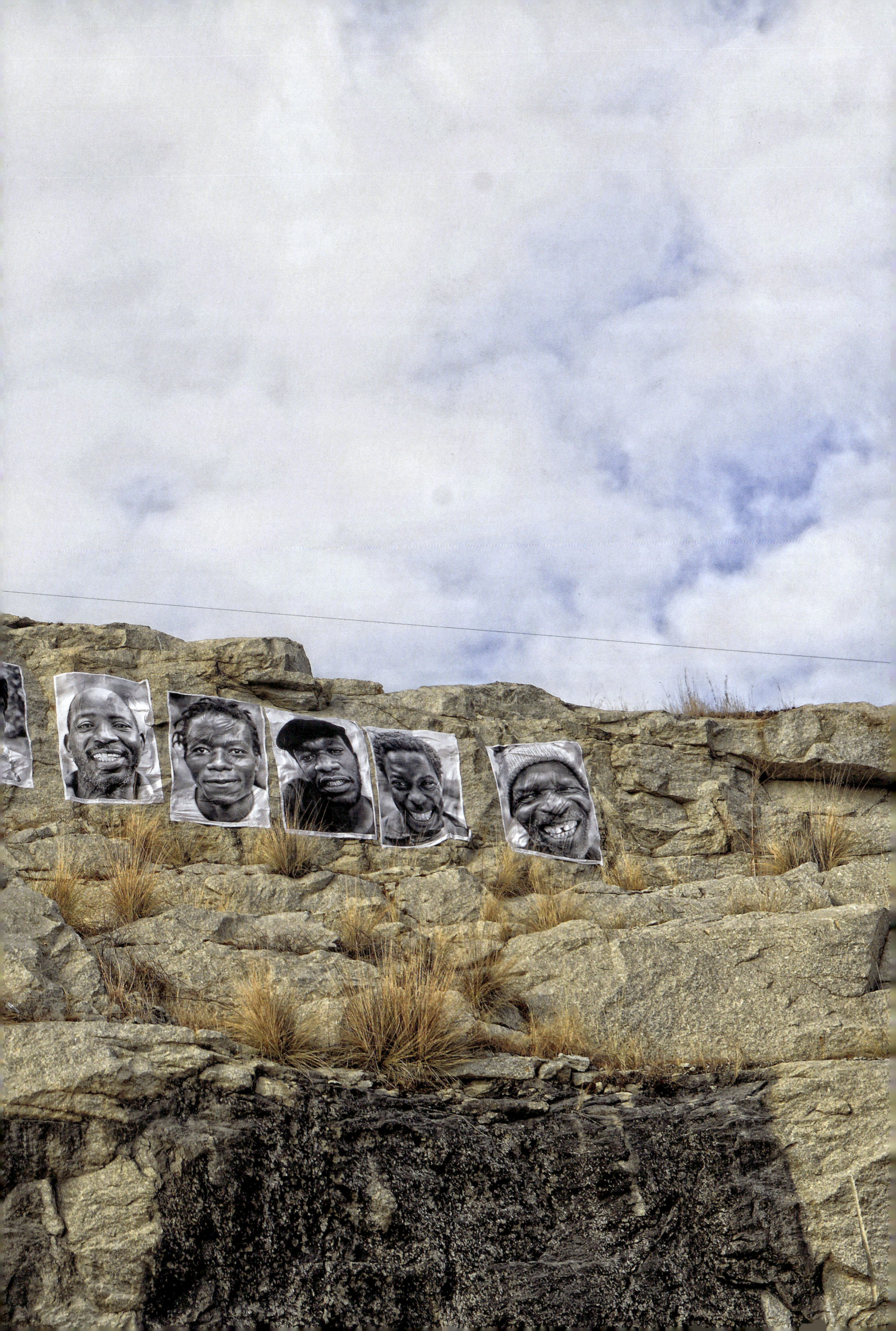

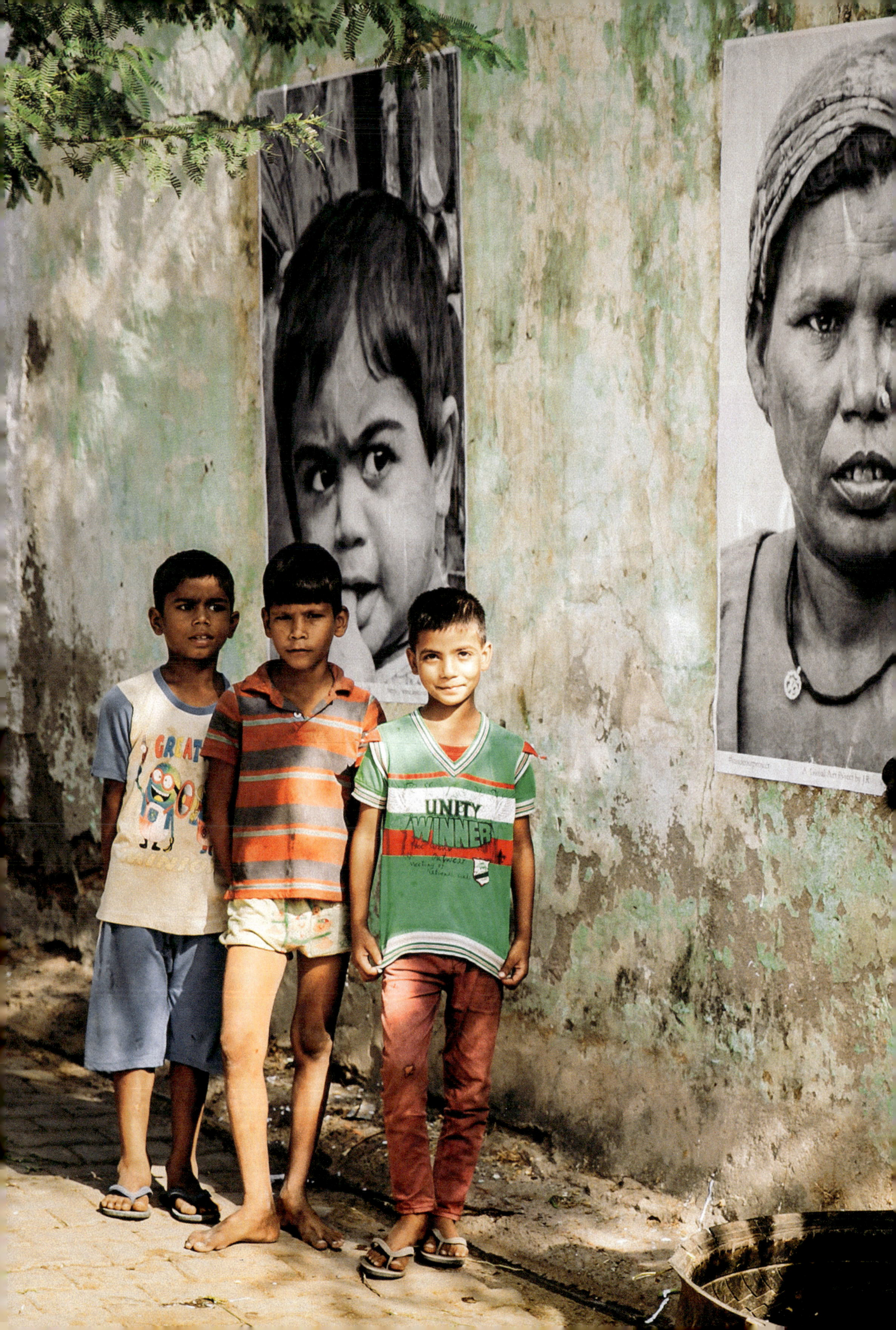
UNITY
WINNER

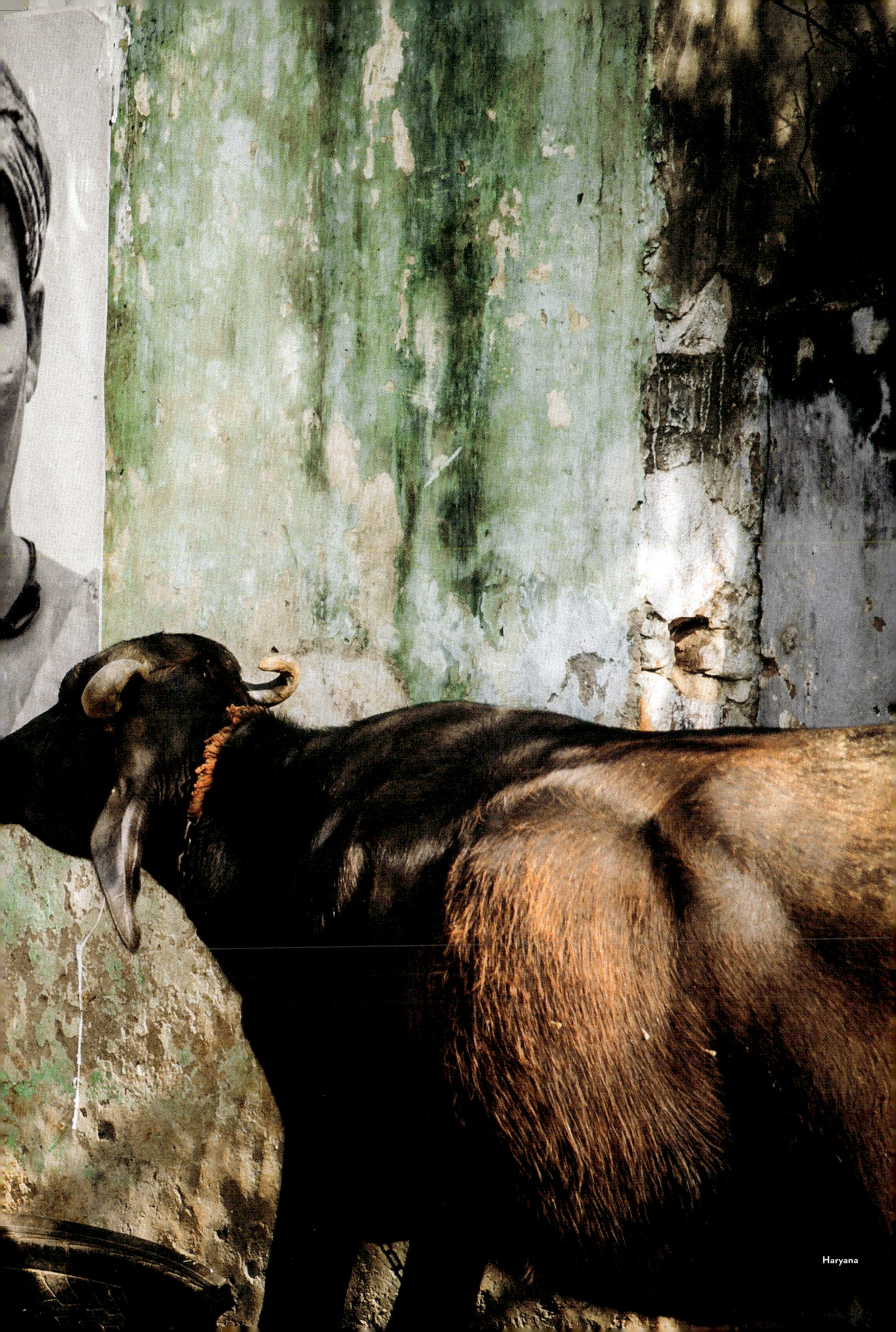

Haryana

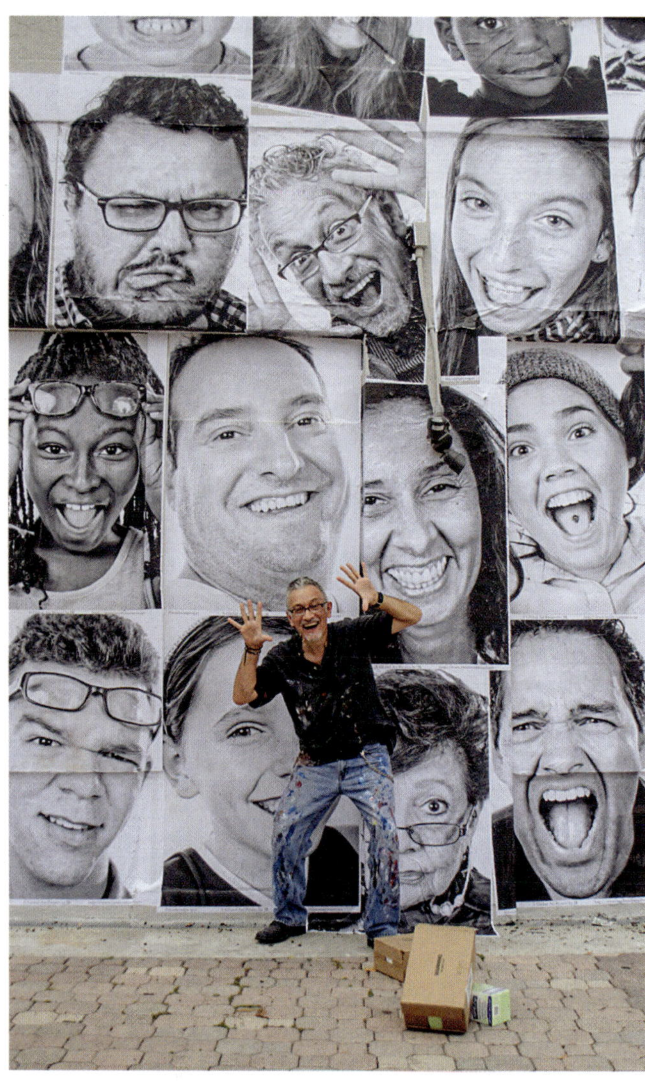

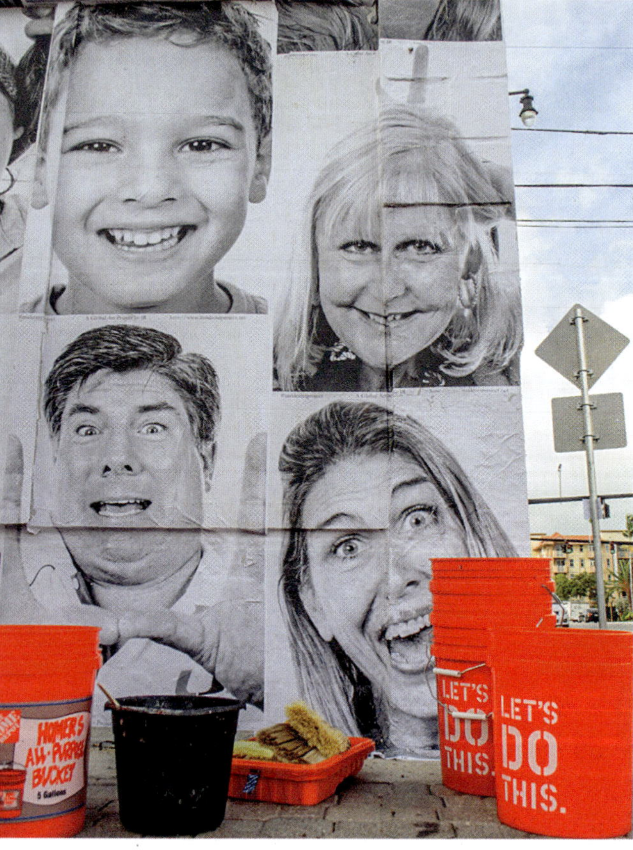

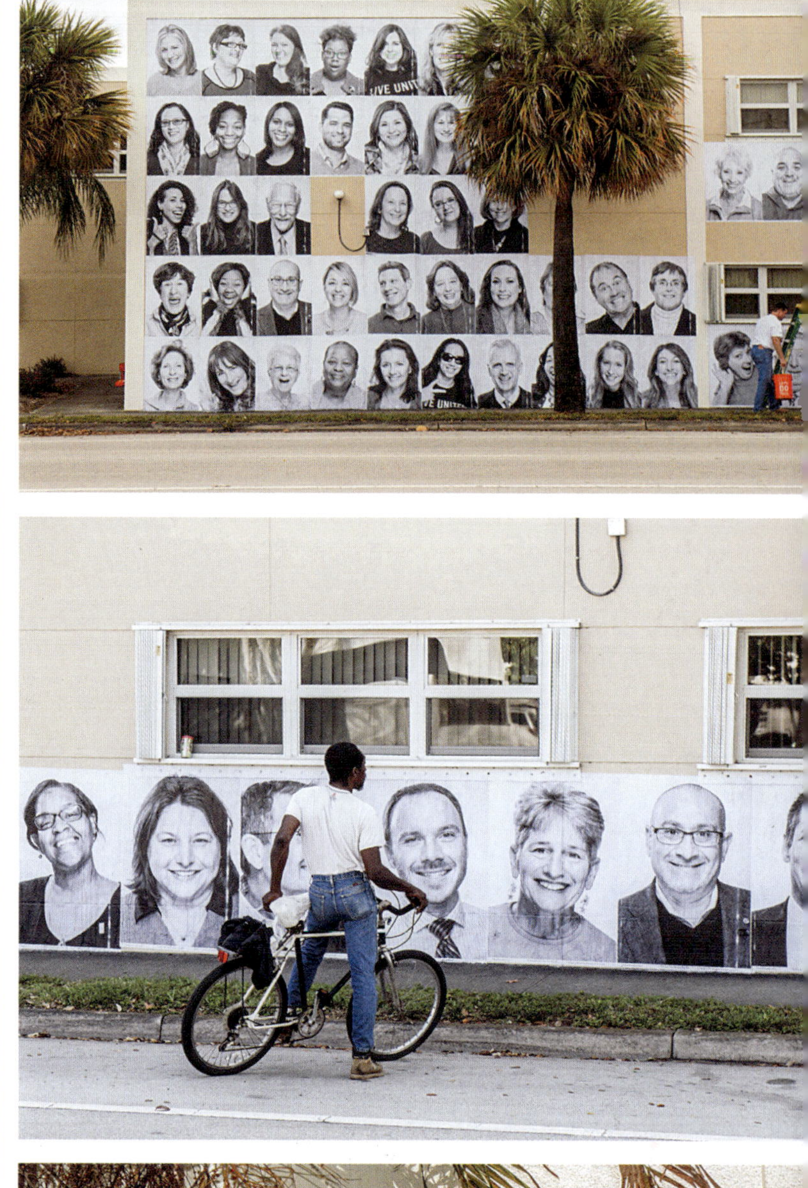

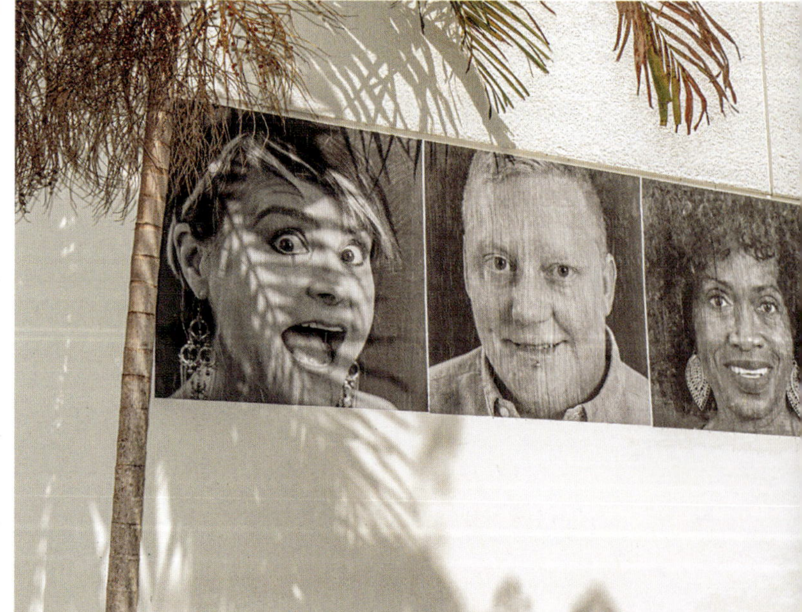

Broward 100—Celebrating the Art of Community: Broward / Davie / Fort Lauderdale / Lauderhill / Miramar / Pembroke Pines / Plantations / Pompano Beach / Tamrac / Welleby / Weston / Wilton Manors, FL

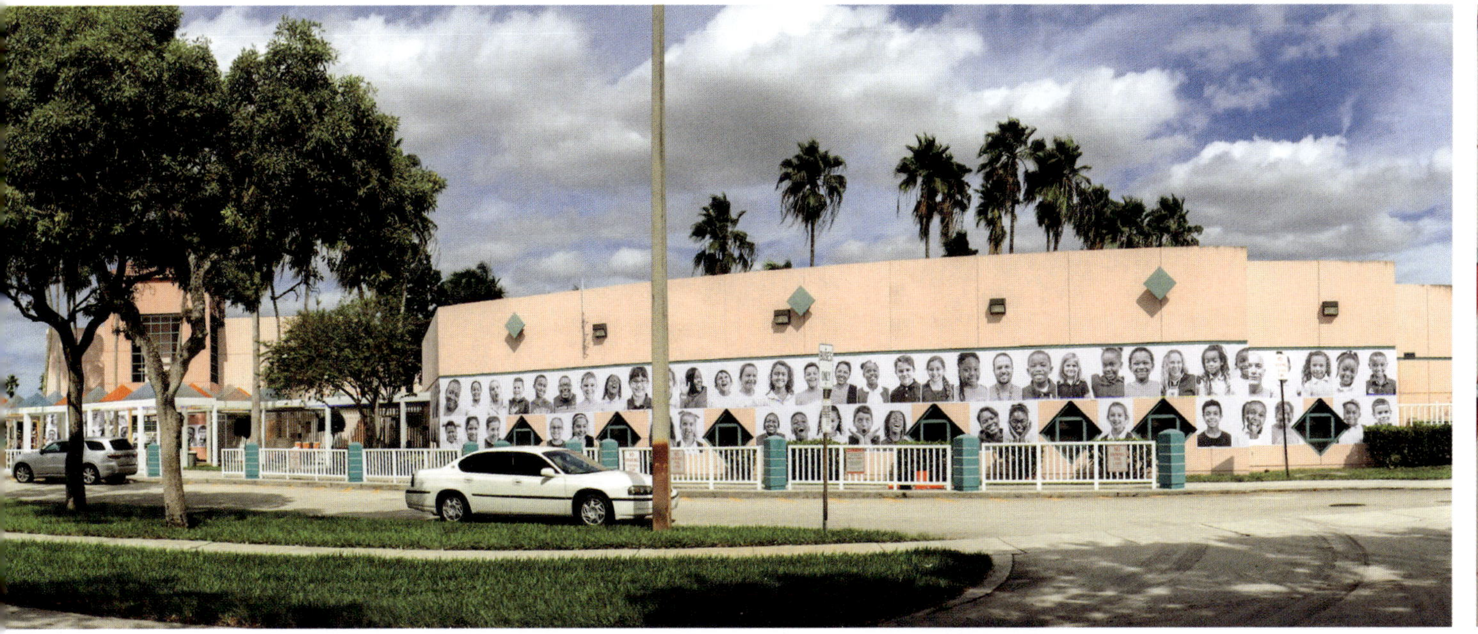

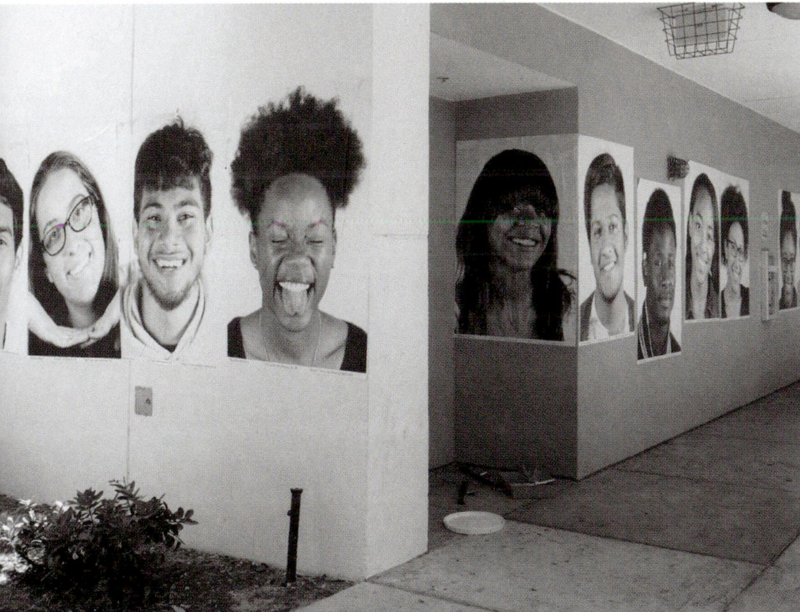

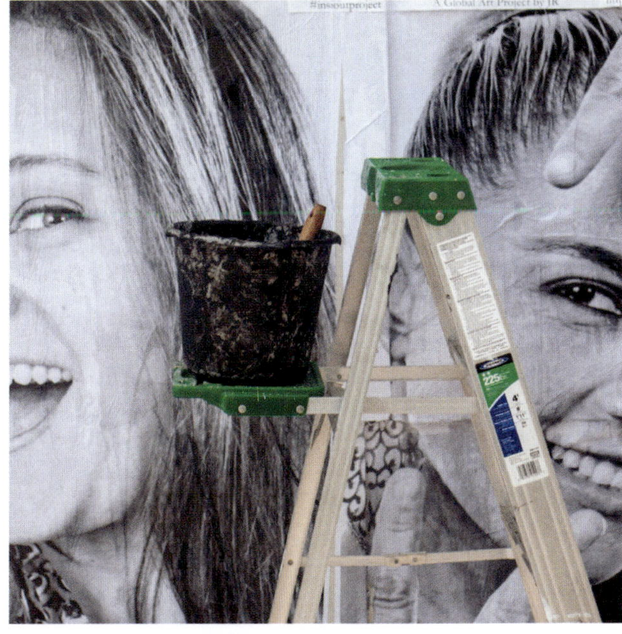

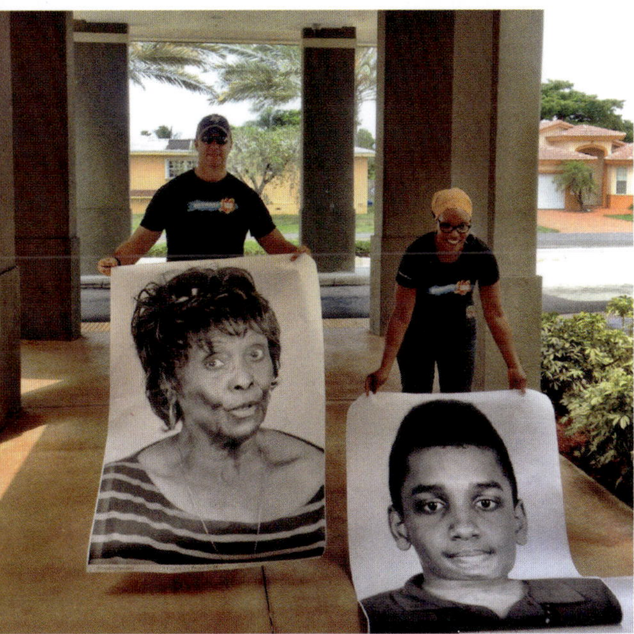

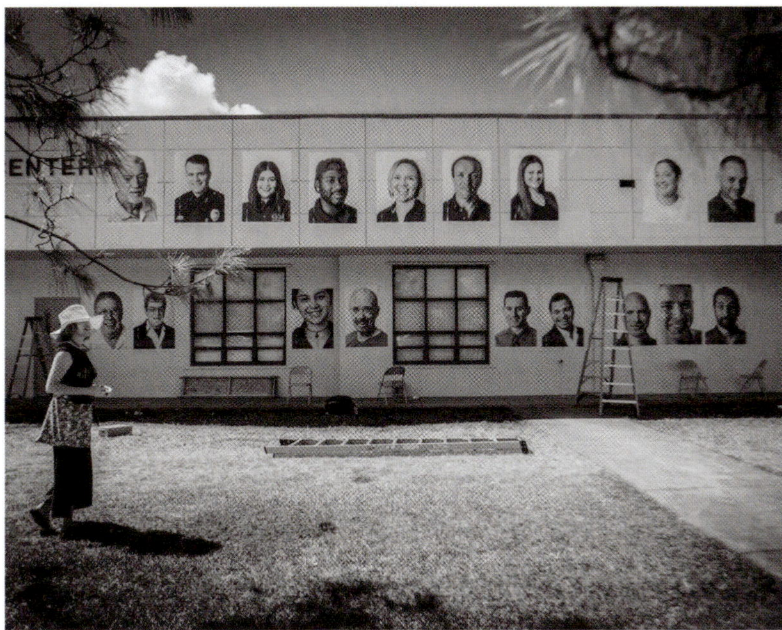

"When it came time to commemorate 100 years as a county, this powerful community project lent itself as the perfect mechanism for 1.8 million residents to creatively engage, embrace diversity and provide awareness while celebrating the milestone anniversary. Inside Out became a main component of Broward's centennial celebration, with the support from our county administrator, our Board of County Commissioners and event sponsors. Residents enthusiastically embraced the concept, echoing the message of acceptance and connection to every corner of the County. Through more than 50 projects and 5,000 images, Broward County became one of the largest Inside Out installation sites."

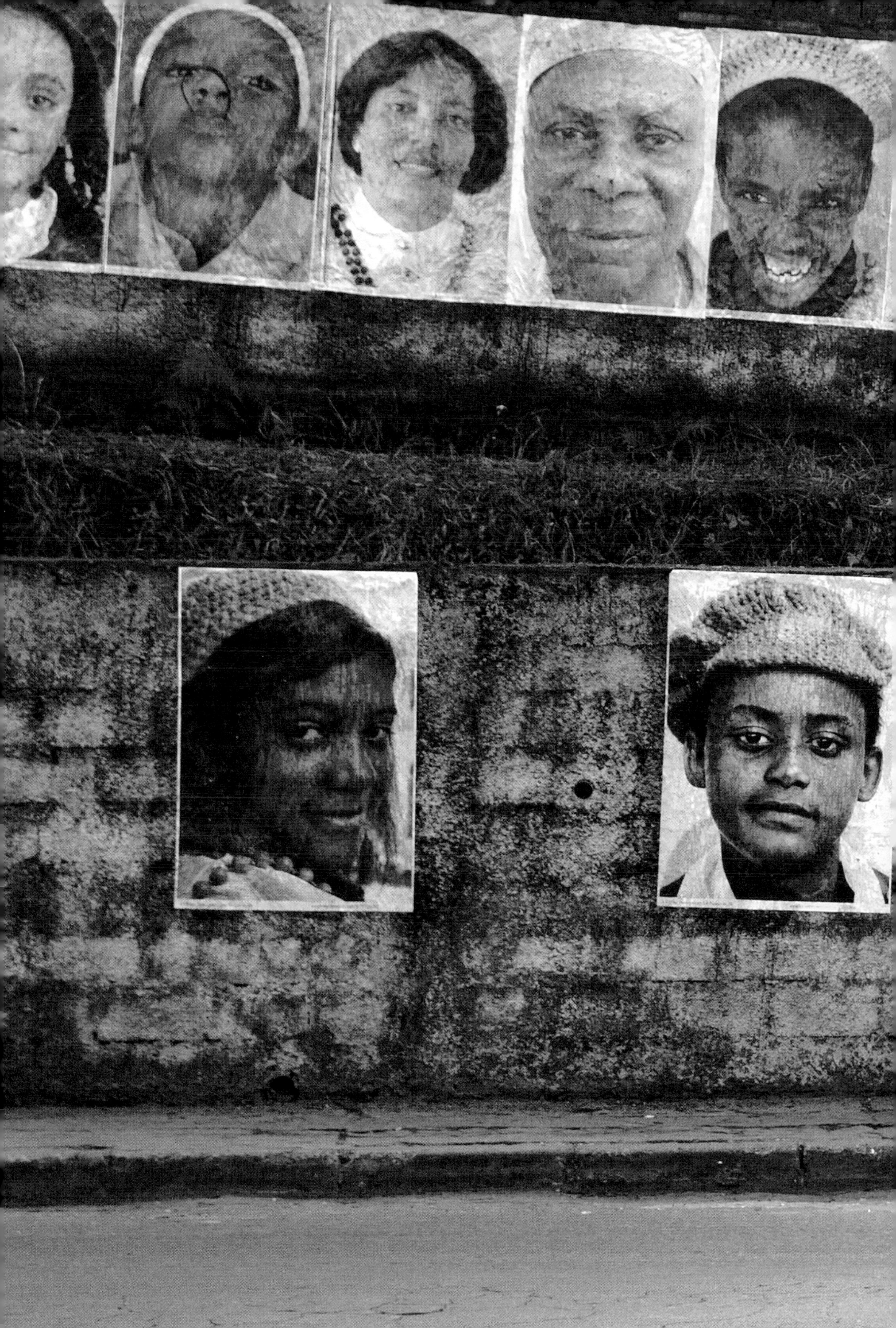

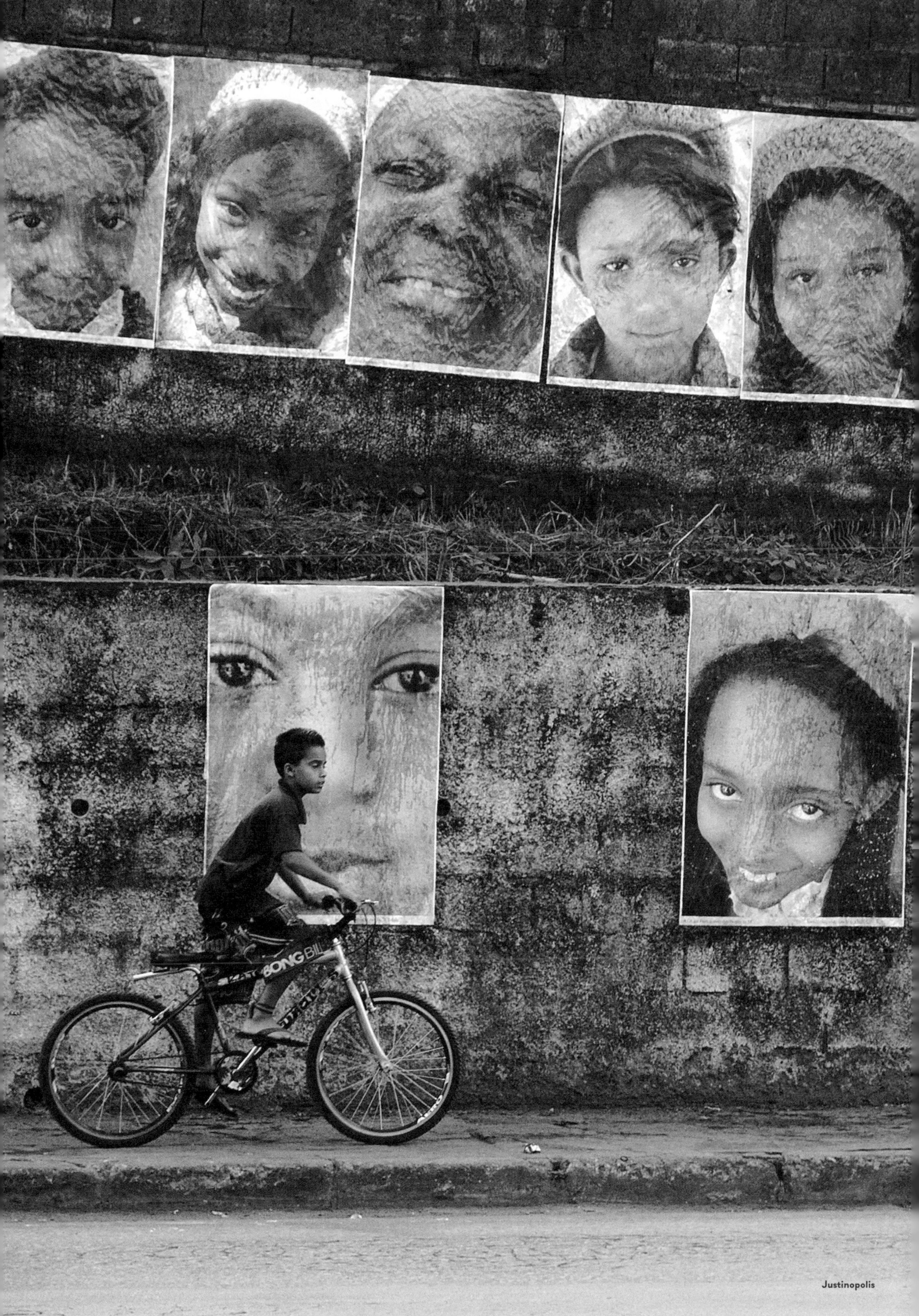

Justinopolis

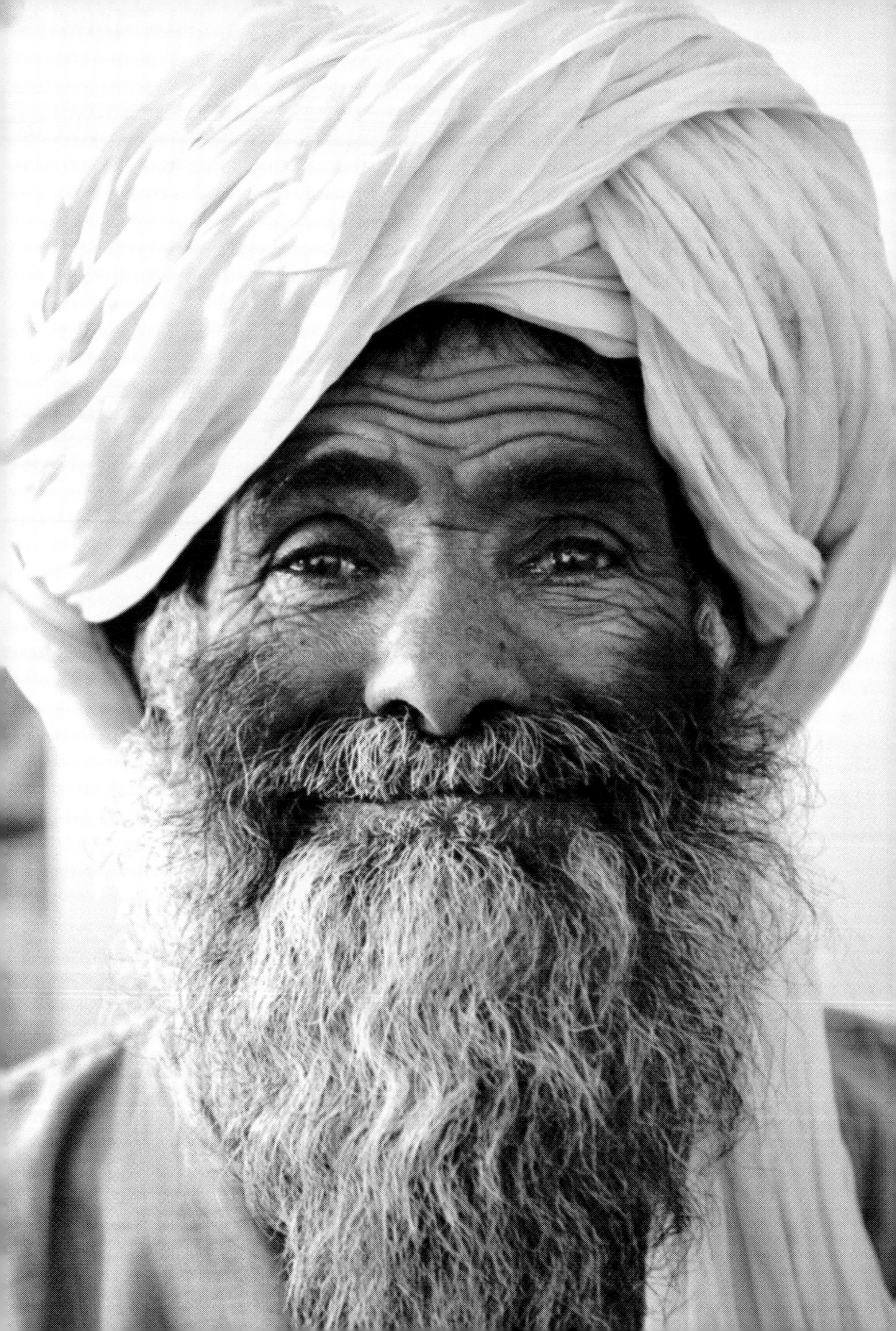

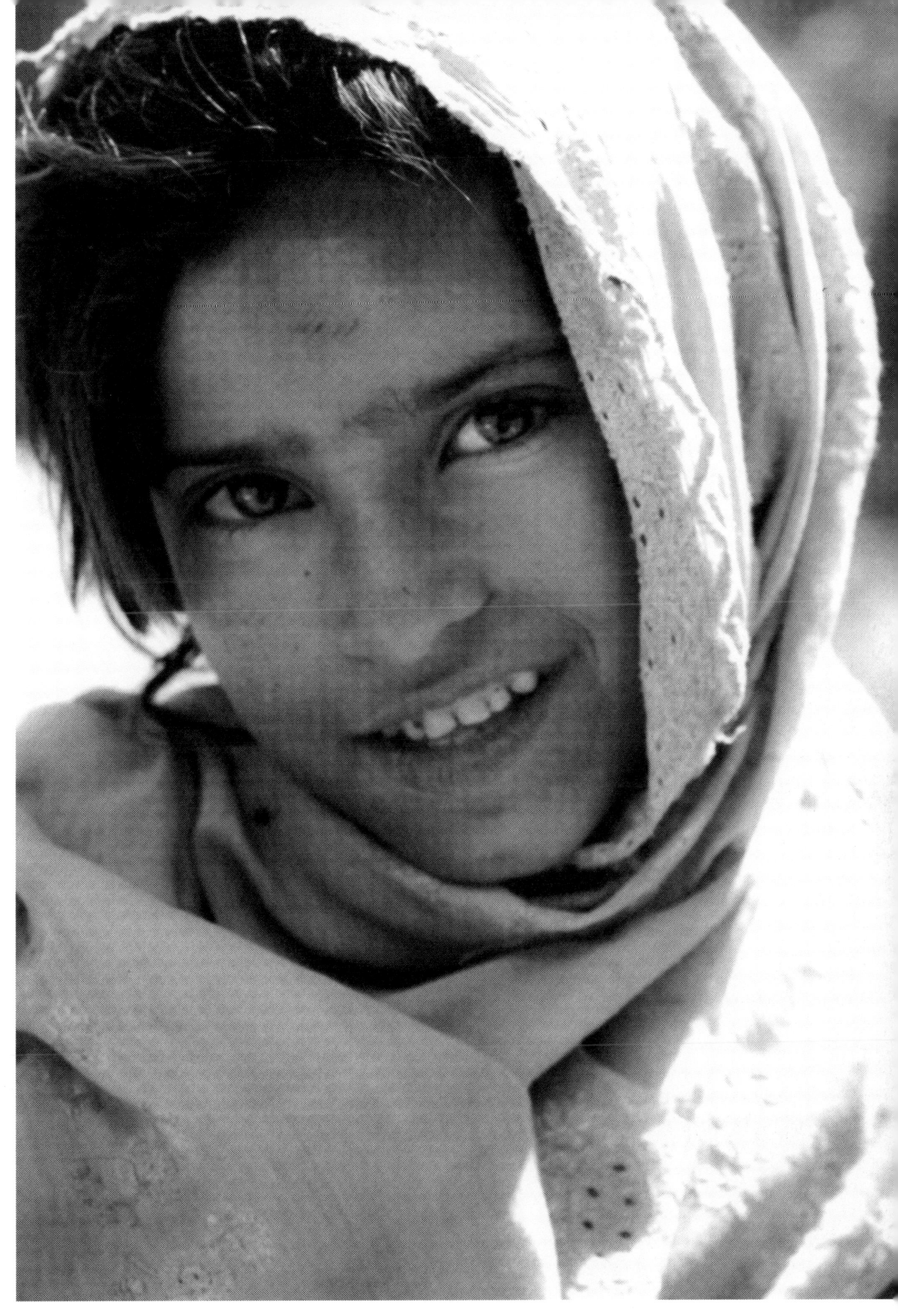

“There is hope and laughter in Afghanistan, and that should be celebrated.”

Kabul

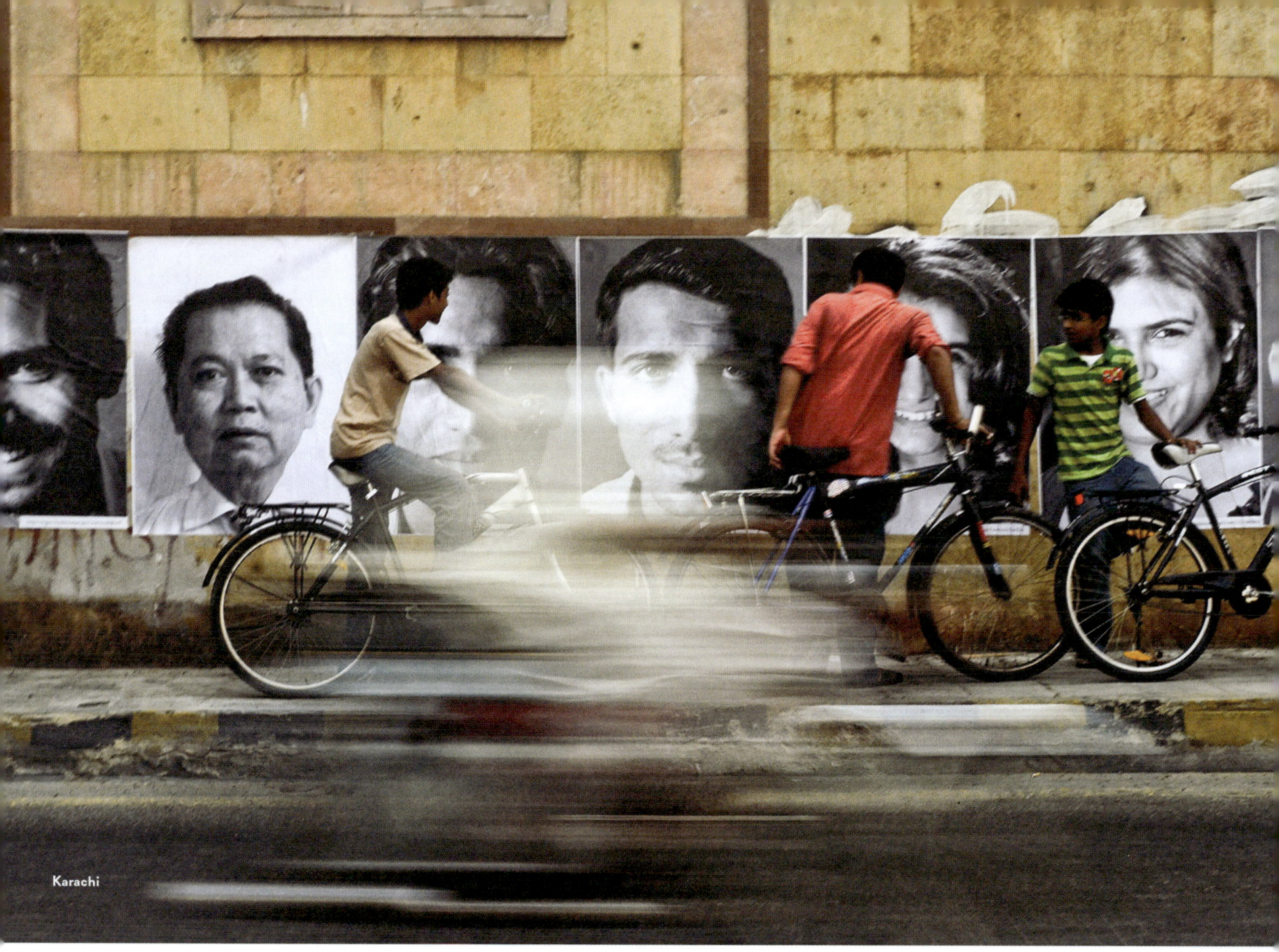

Karachi

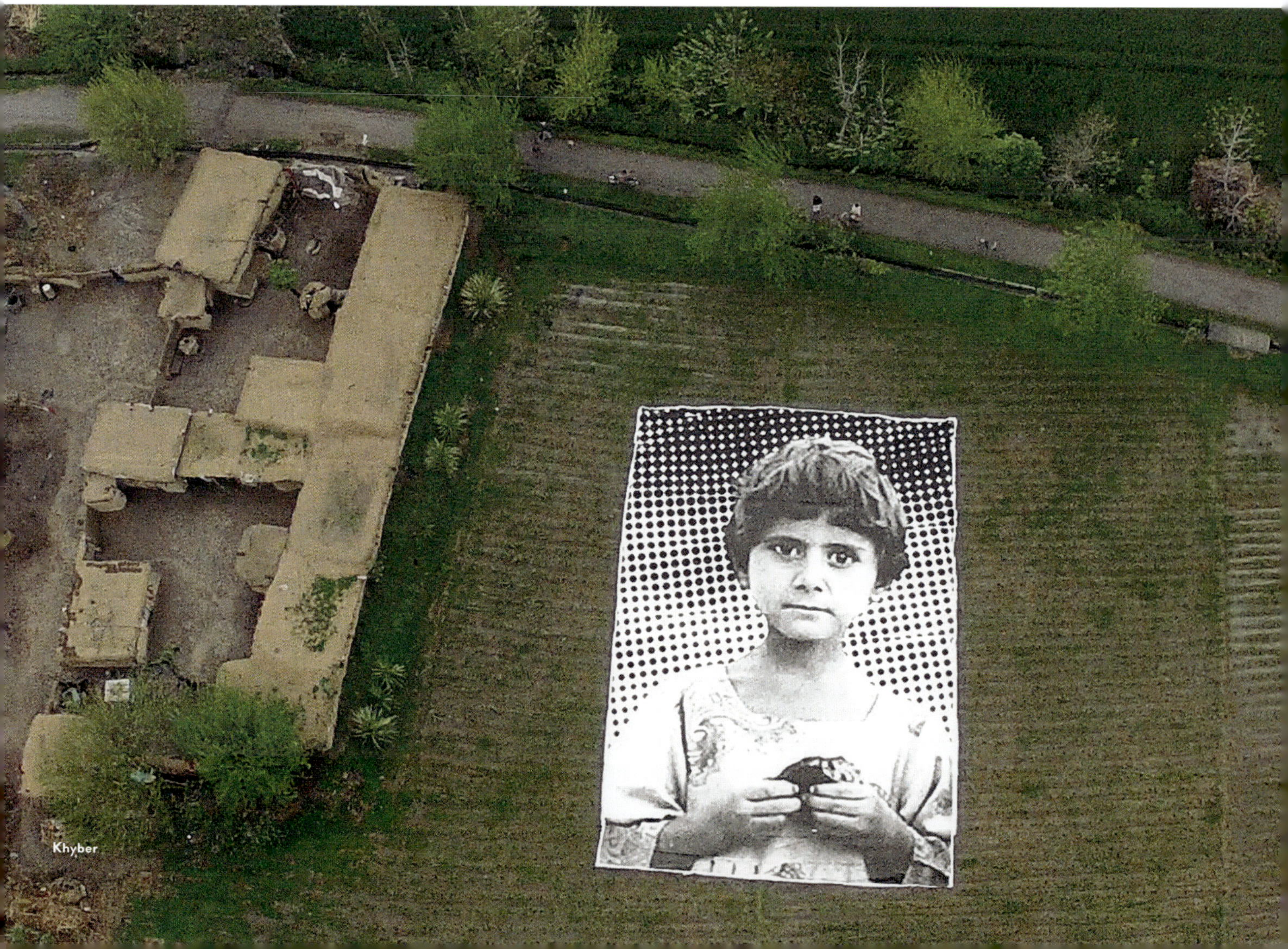

Khyber

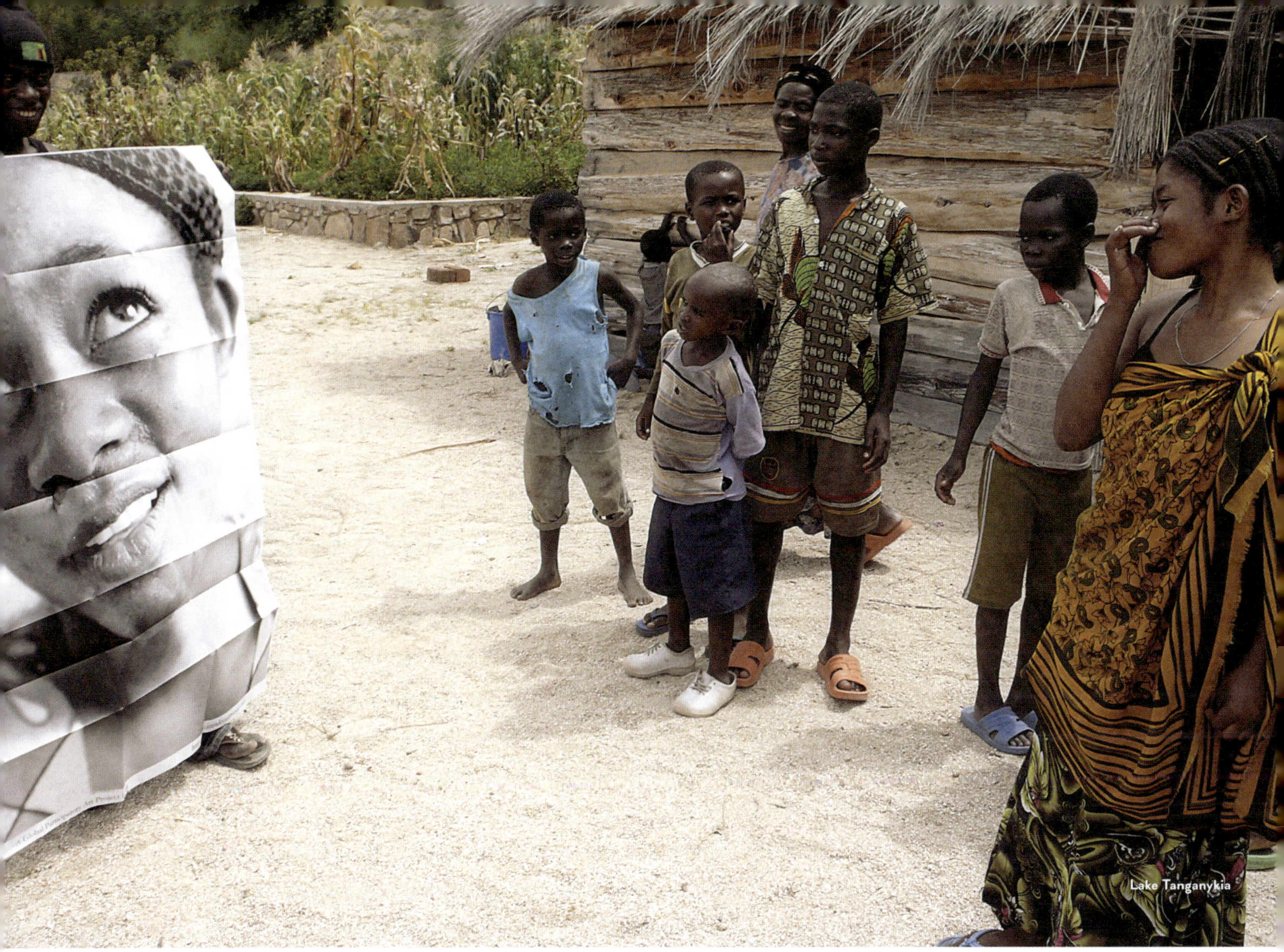

Lake Tanganykia

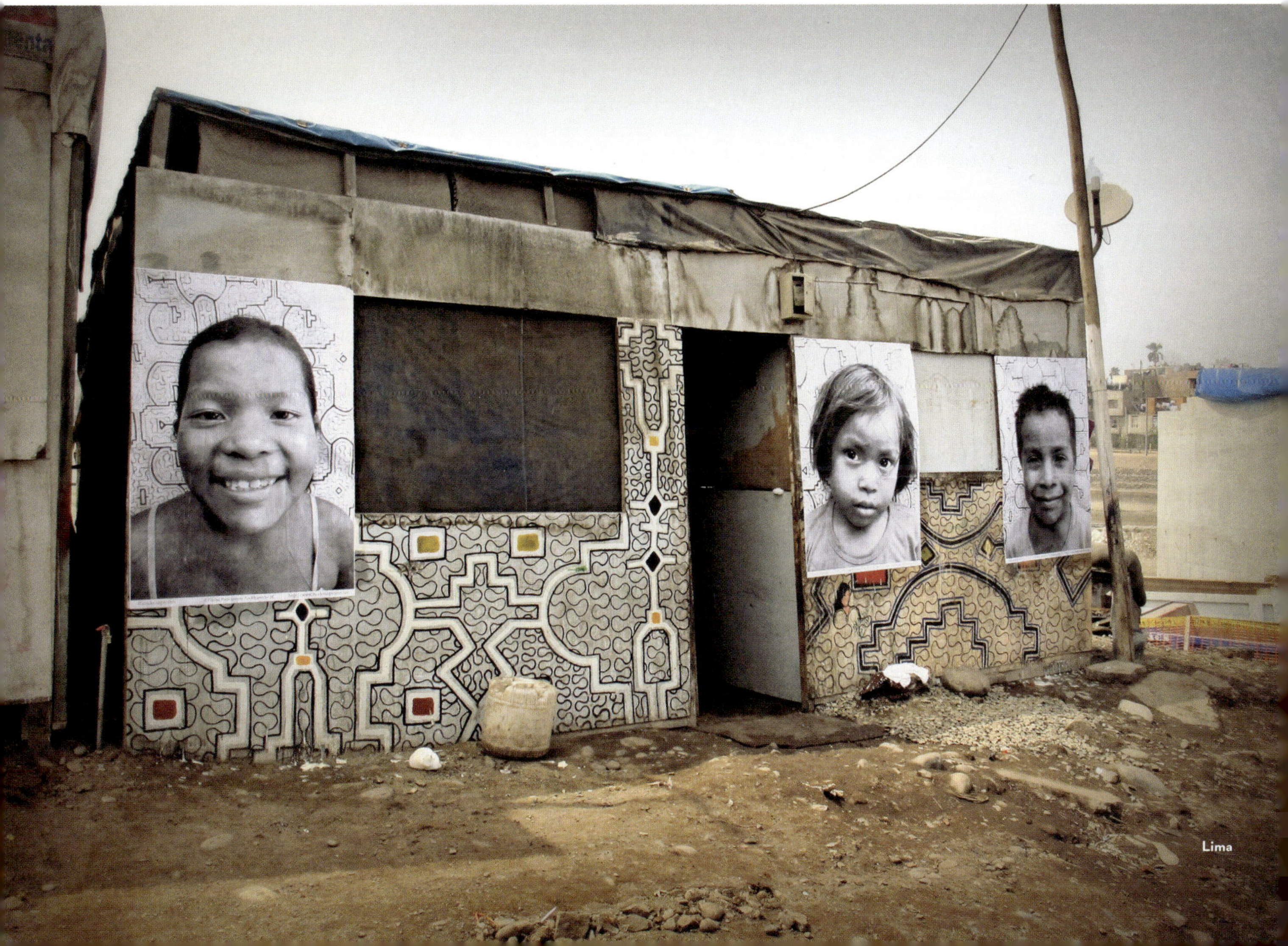

Lima

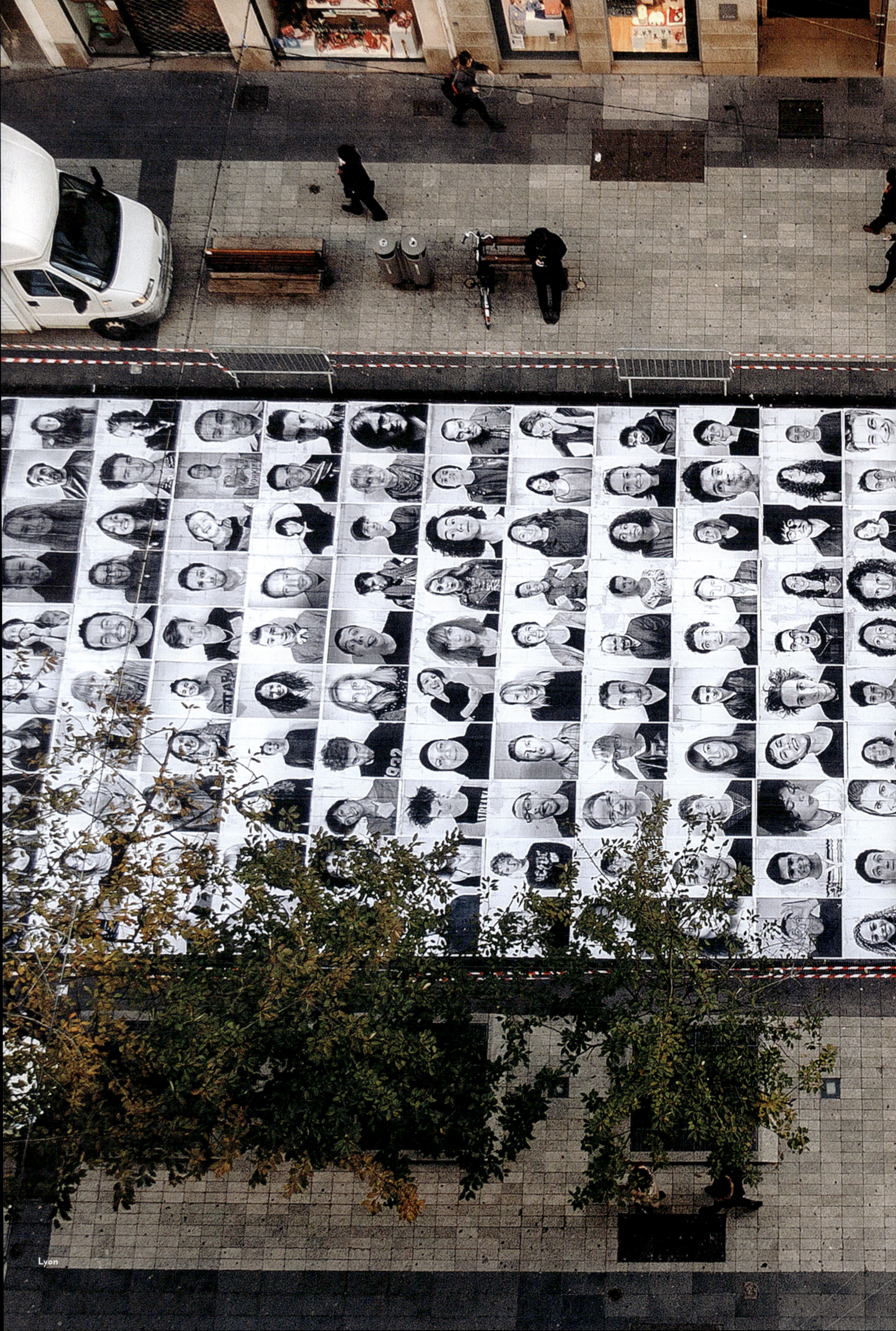

Lyon

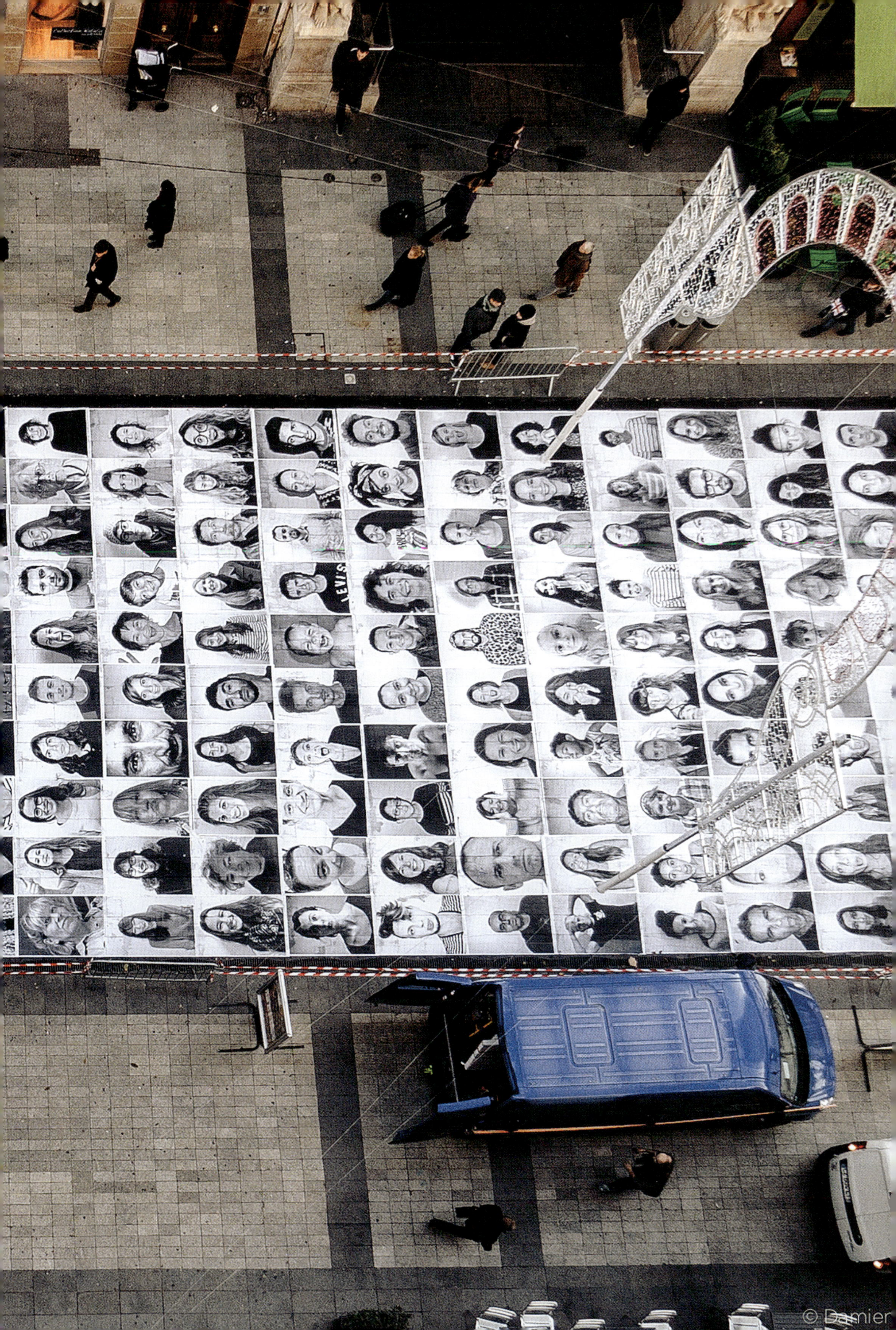
LEVI'S

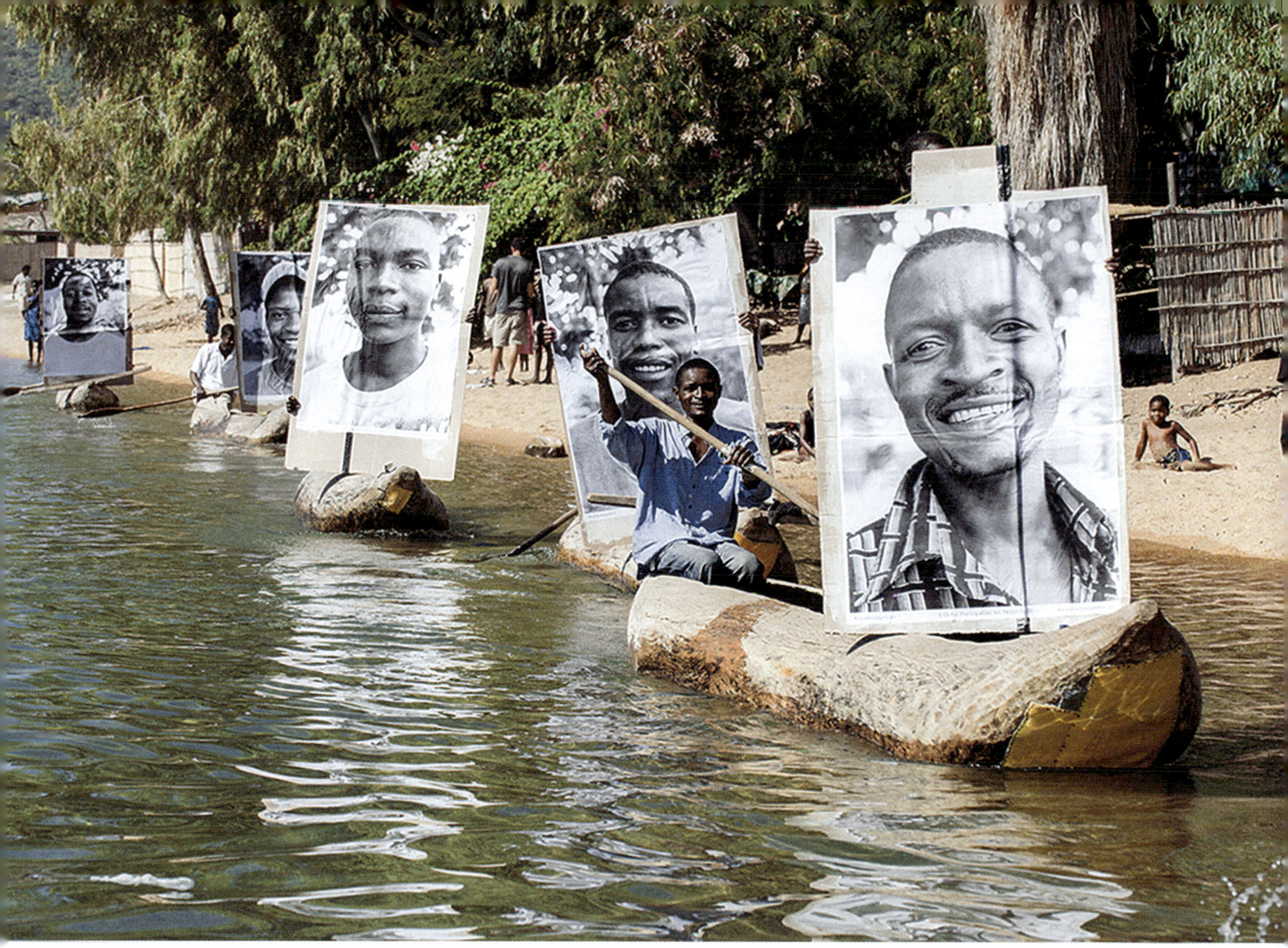

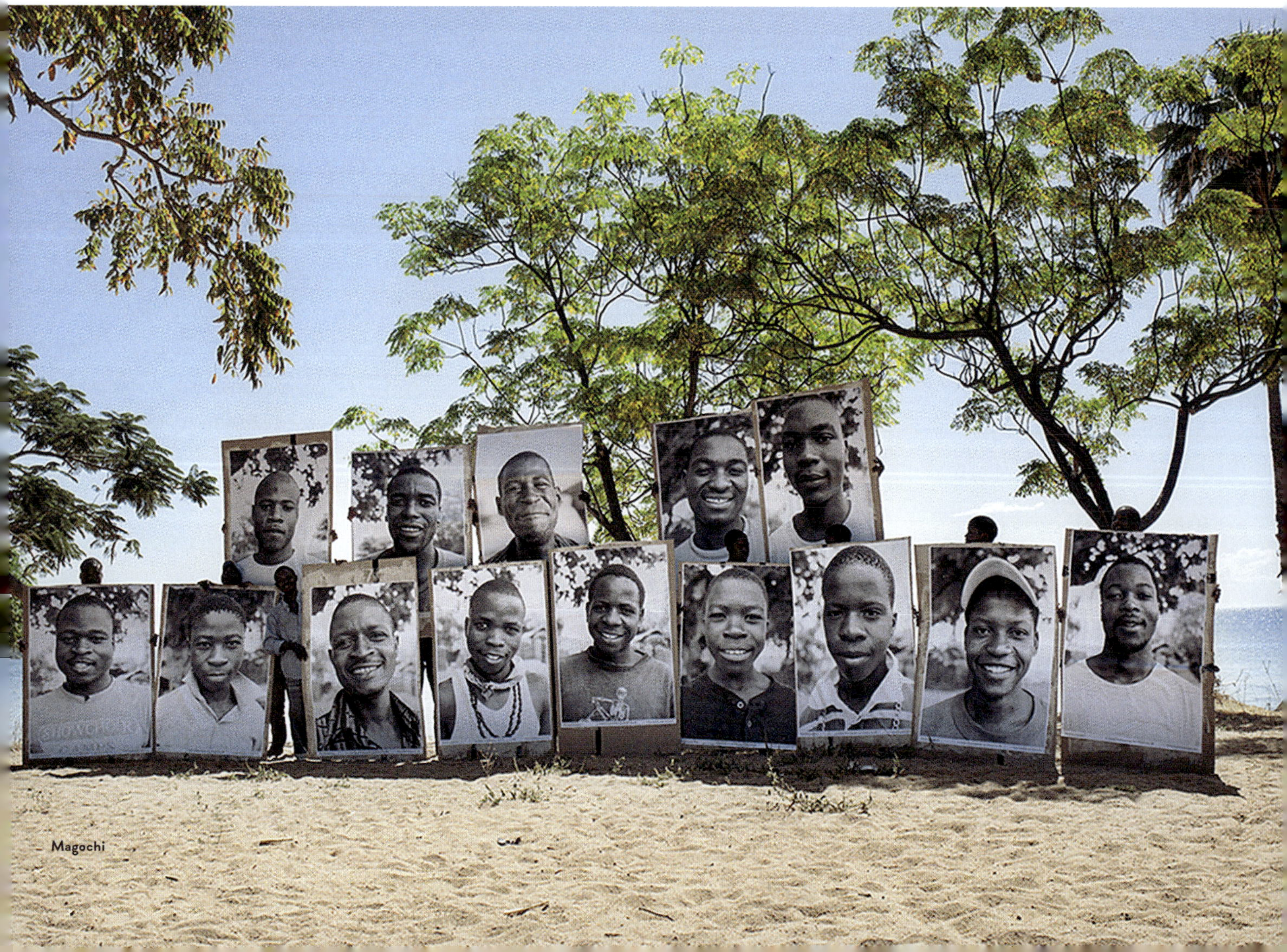

Magochi

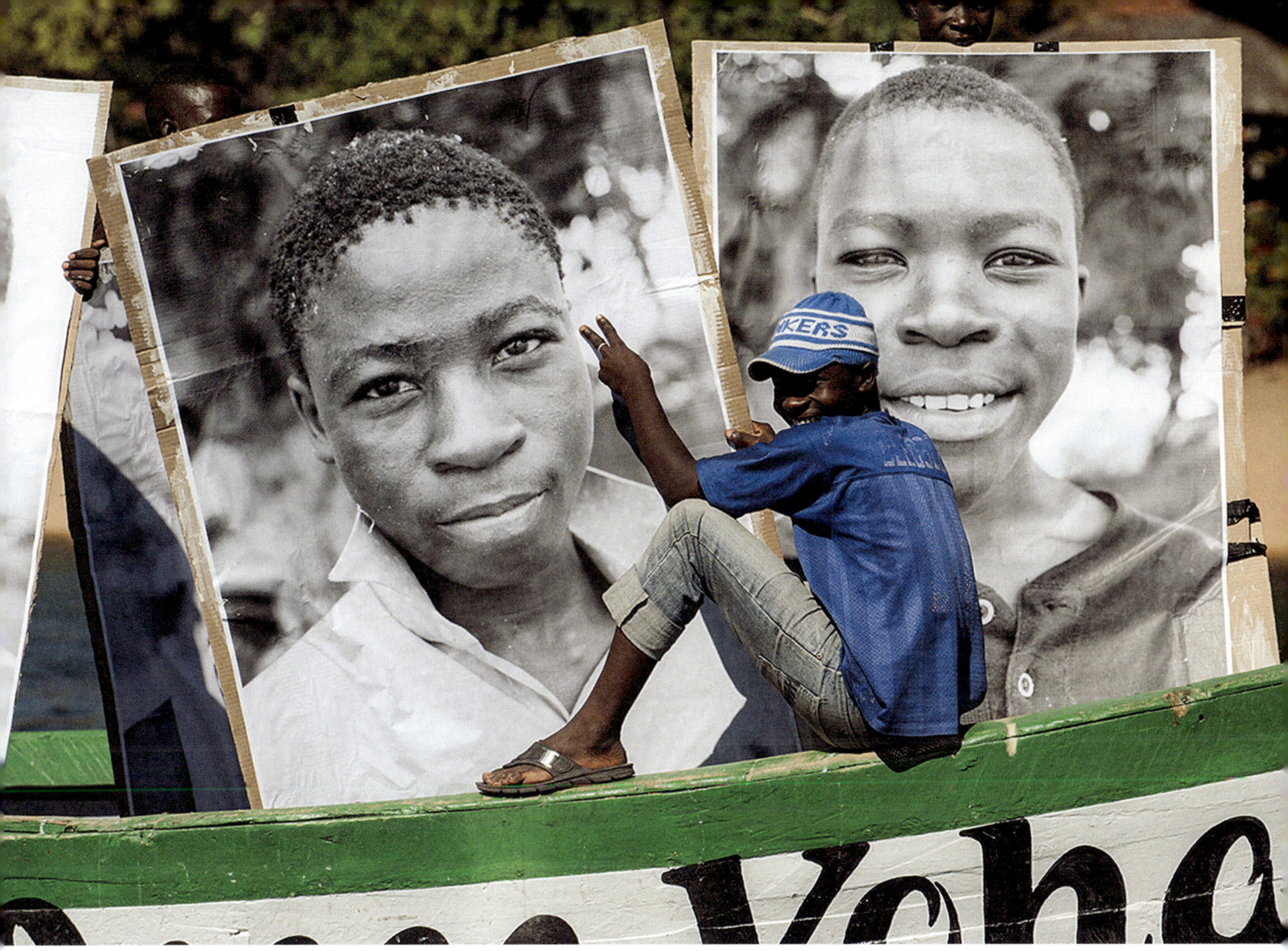

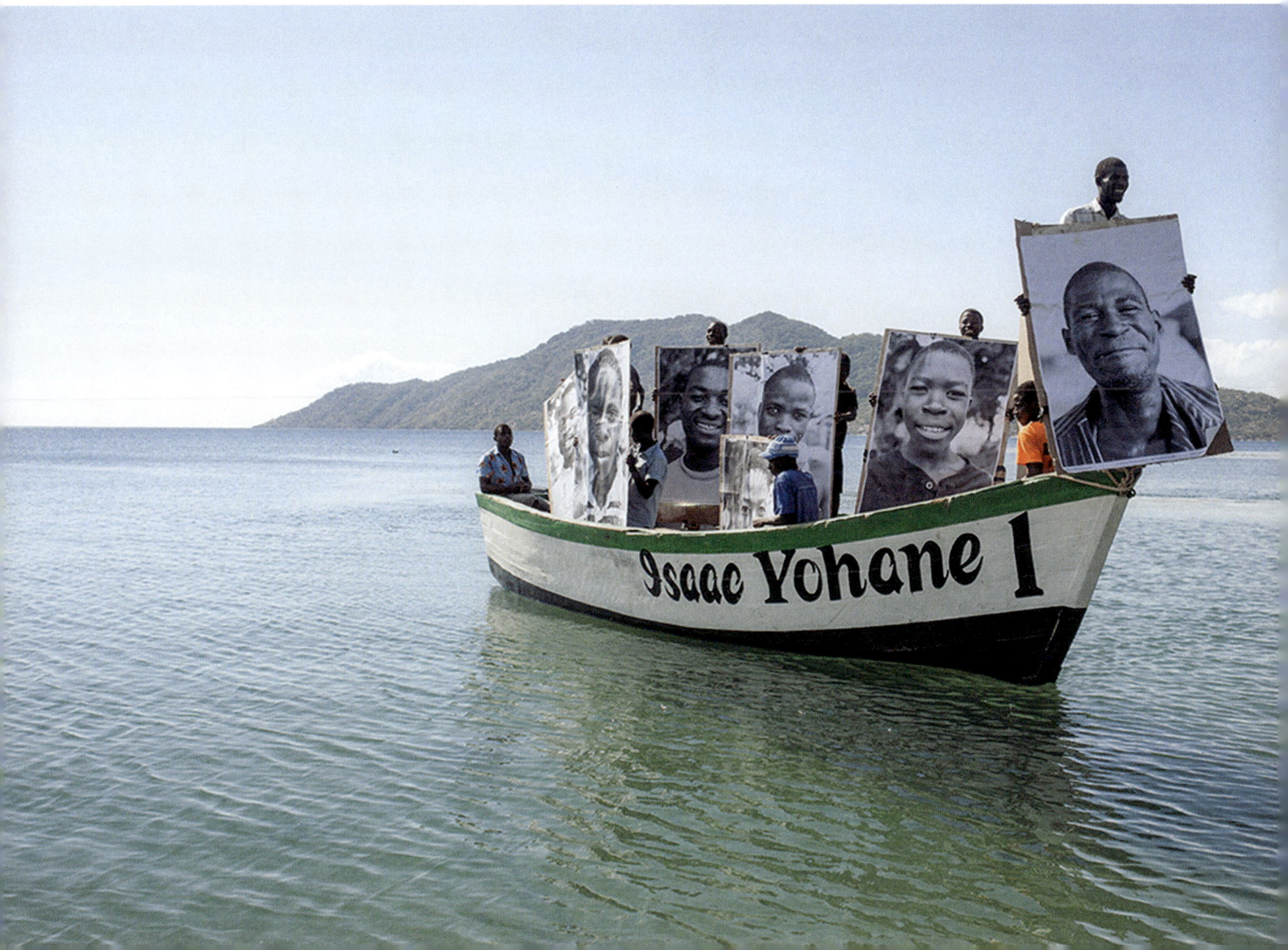

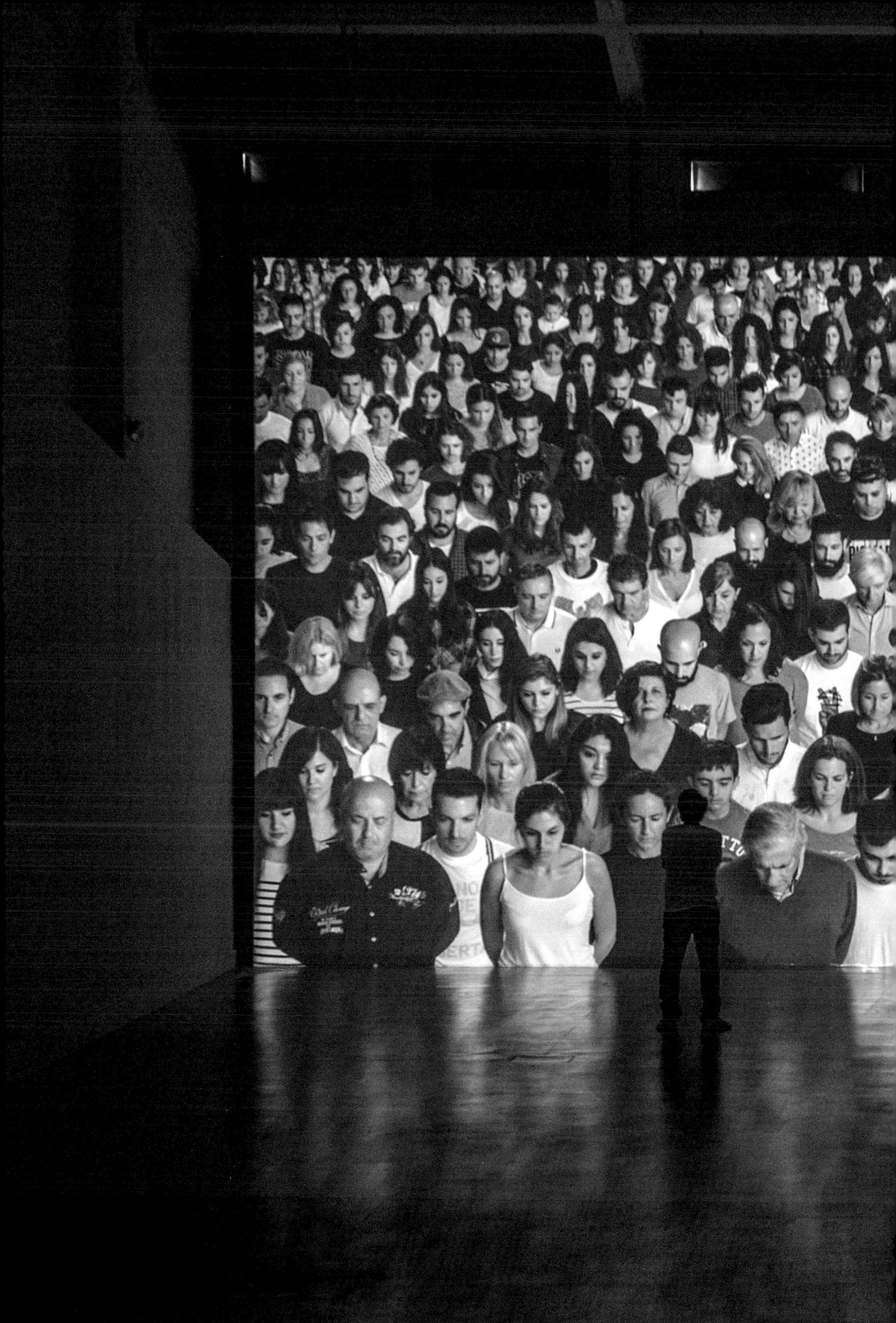

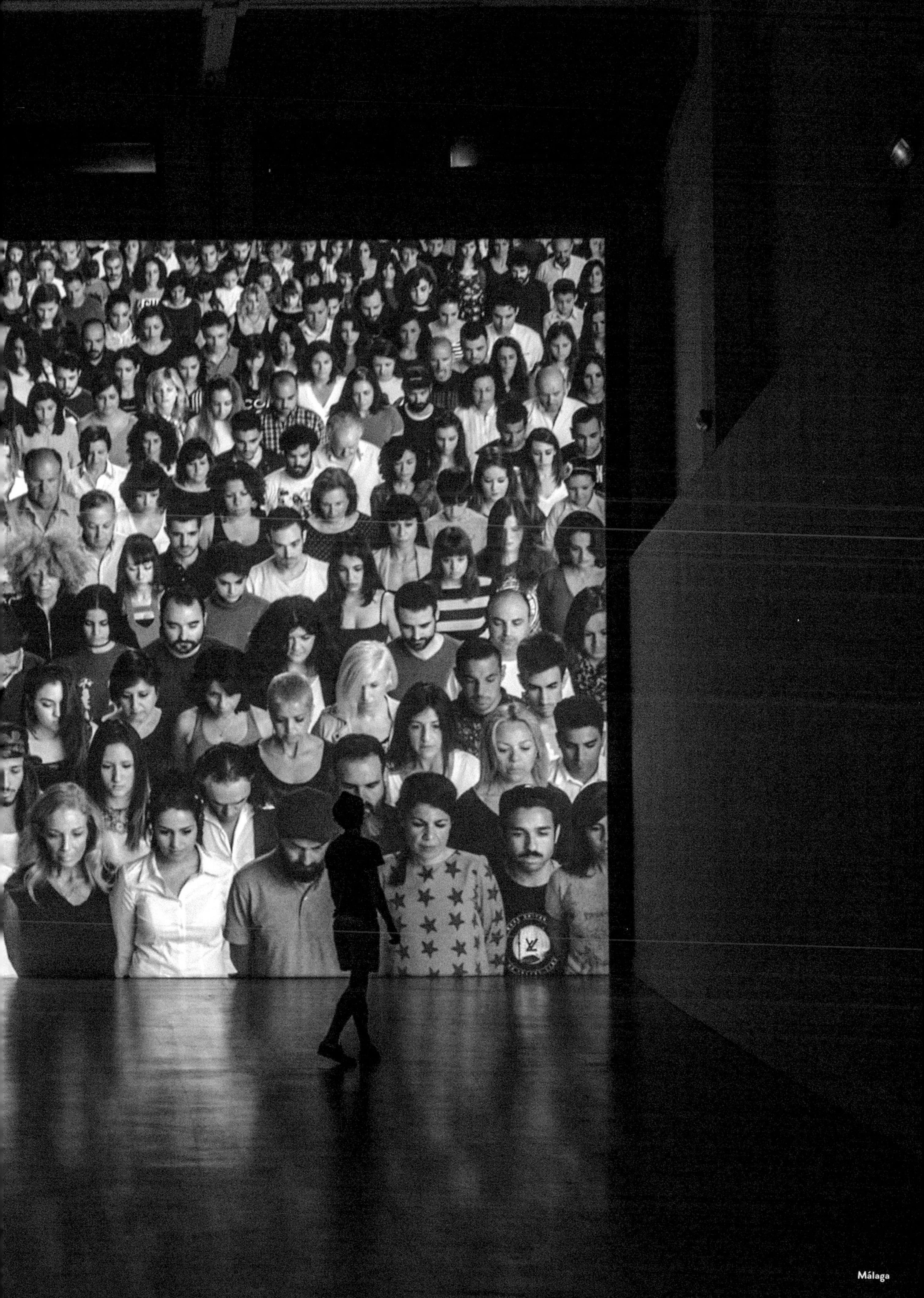

Málaga

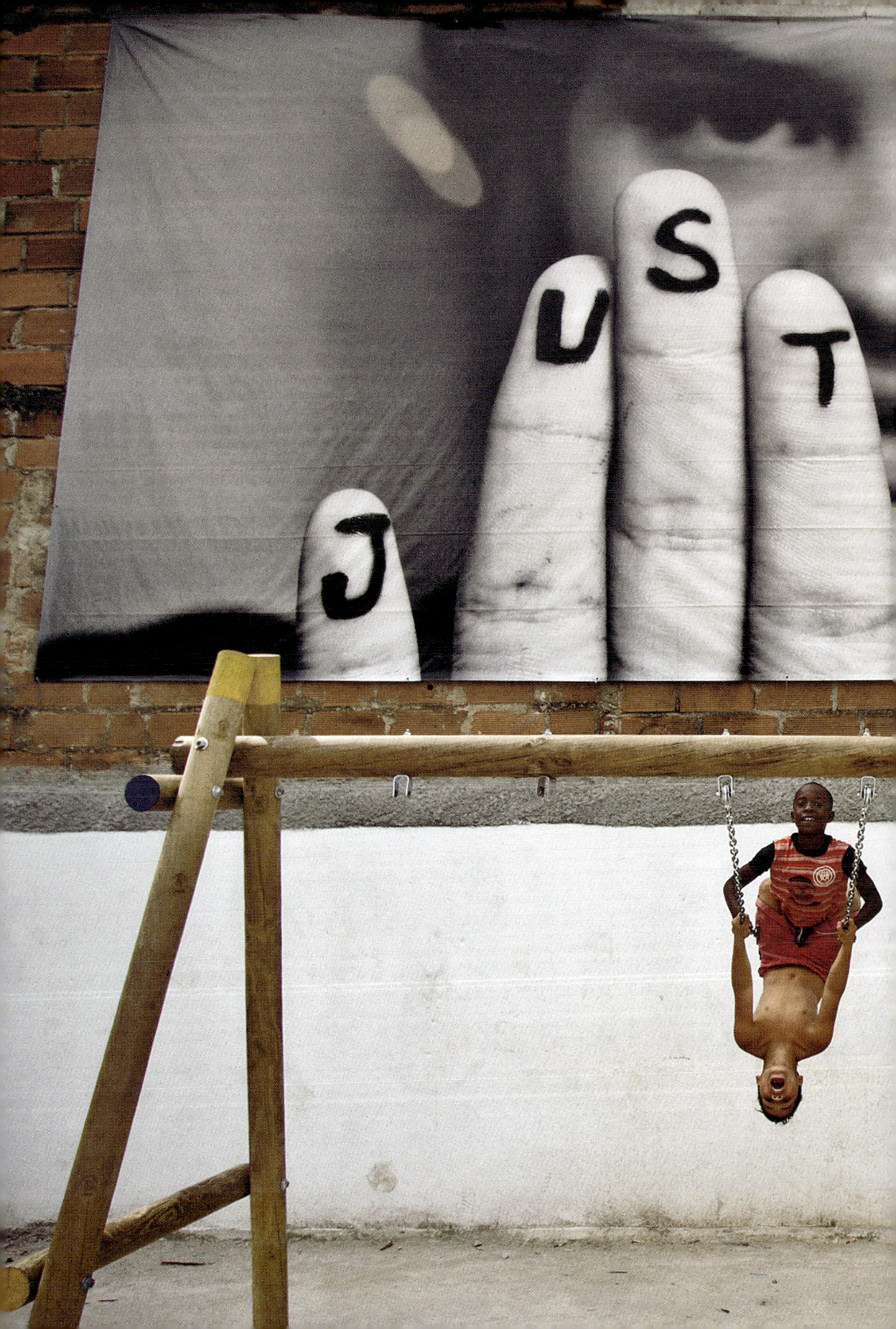
J
U
S
T

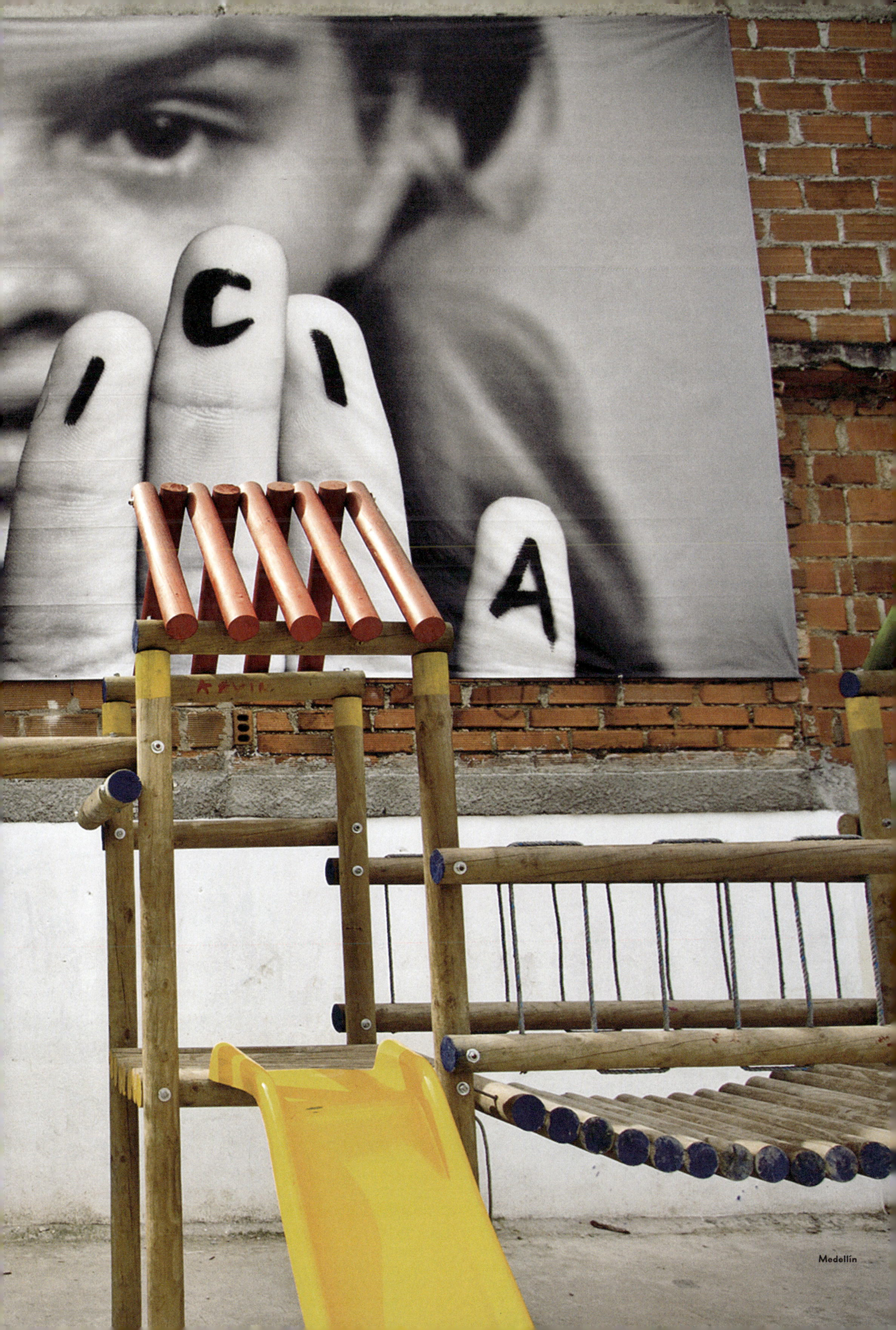

Medellín

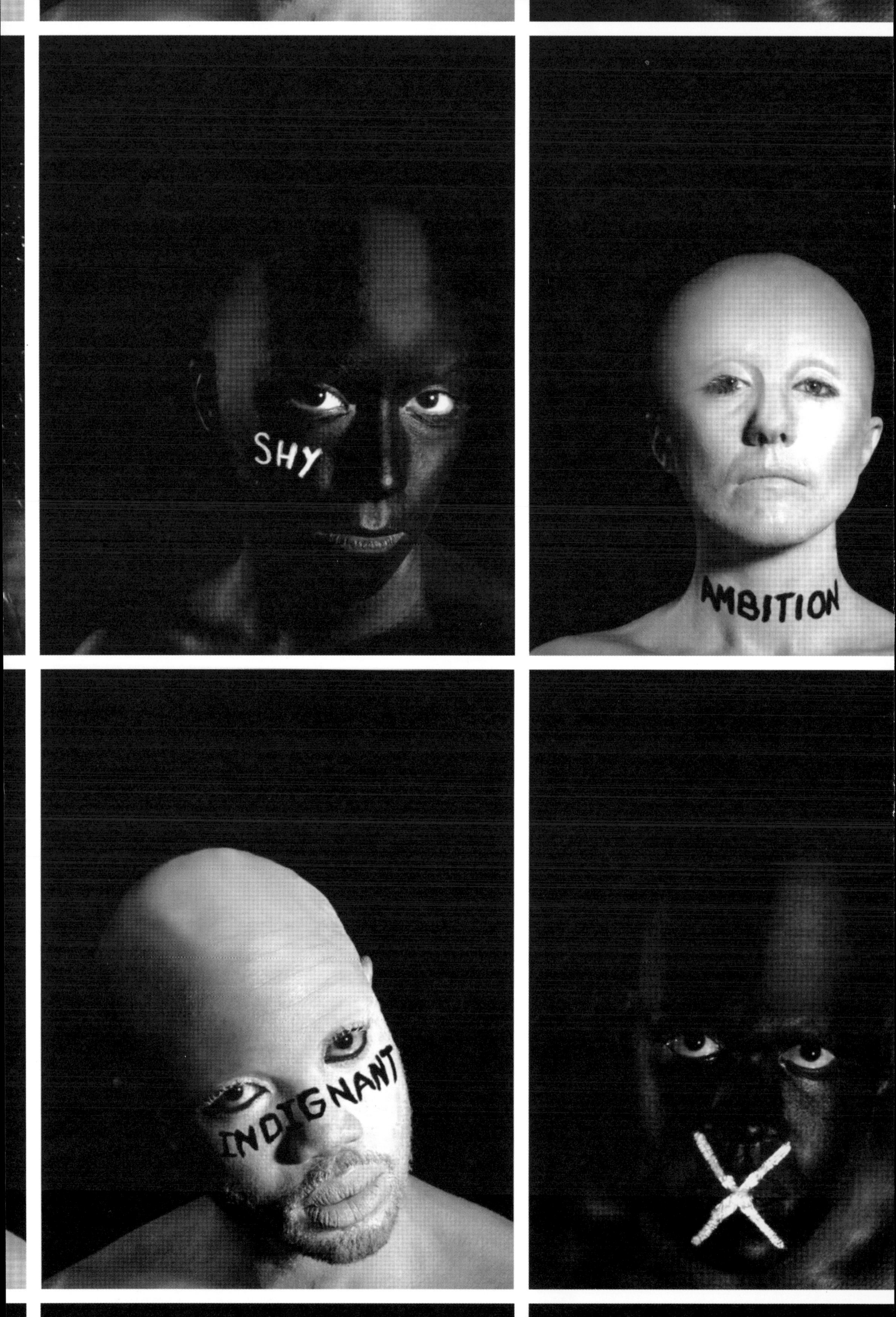
SHY
AMBITION
INDIGNANT

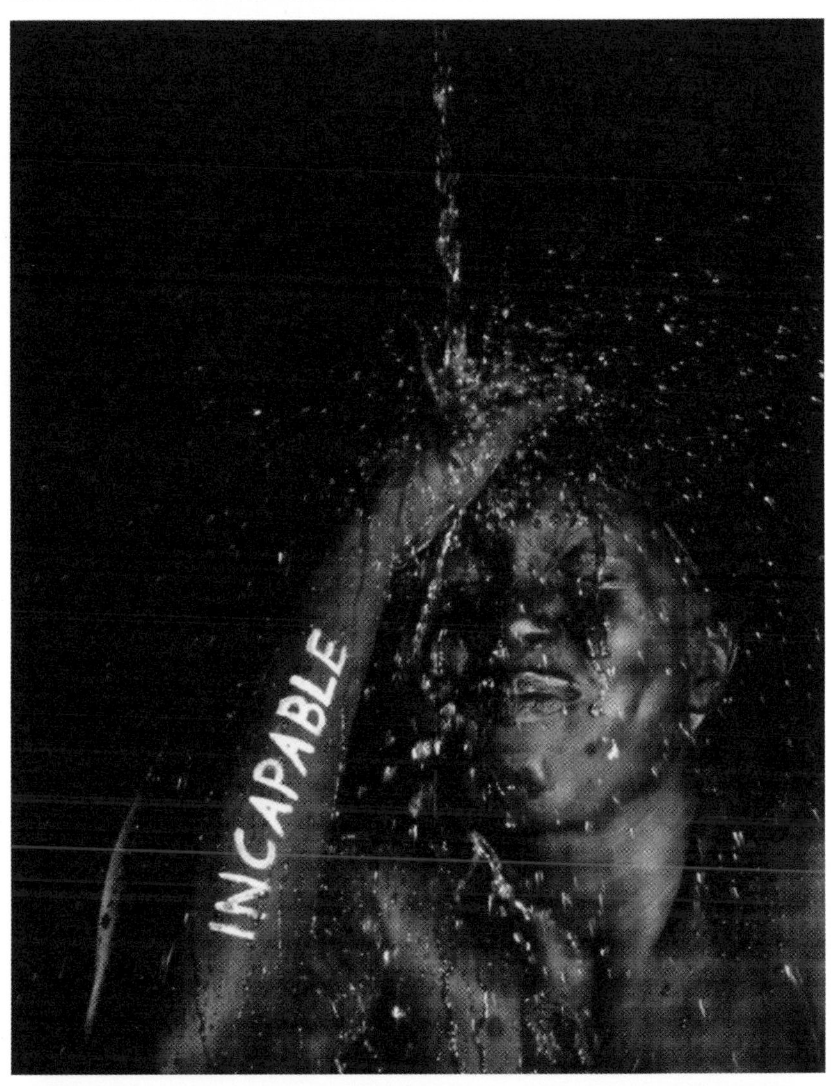

“The concept behind the portrait session is that society has lost itself to a culture of hyperreality, a search for perfection, and has become nothing more than a culture of instant gratification. The effect of this is the loss of our identity, which is becoming a singular mass that is defined individually by a label created by society. People no longer take the time to interact with each other and enjoy the journey of process.”

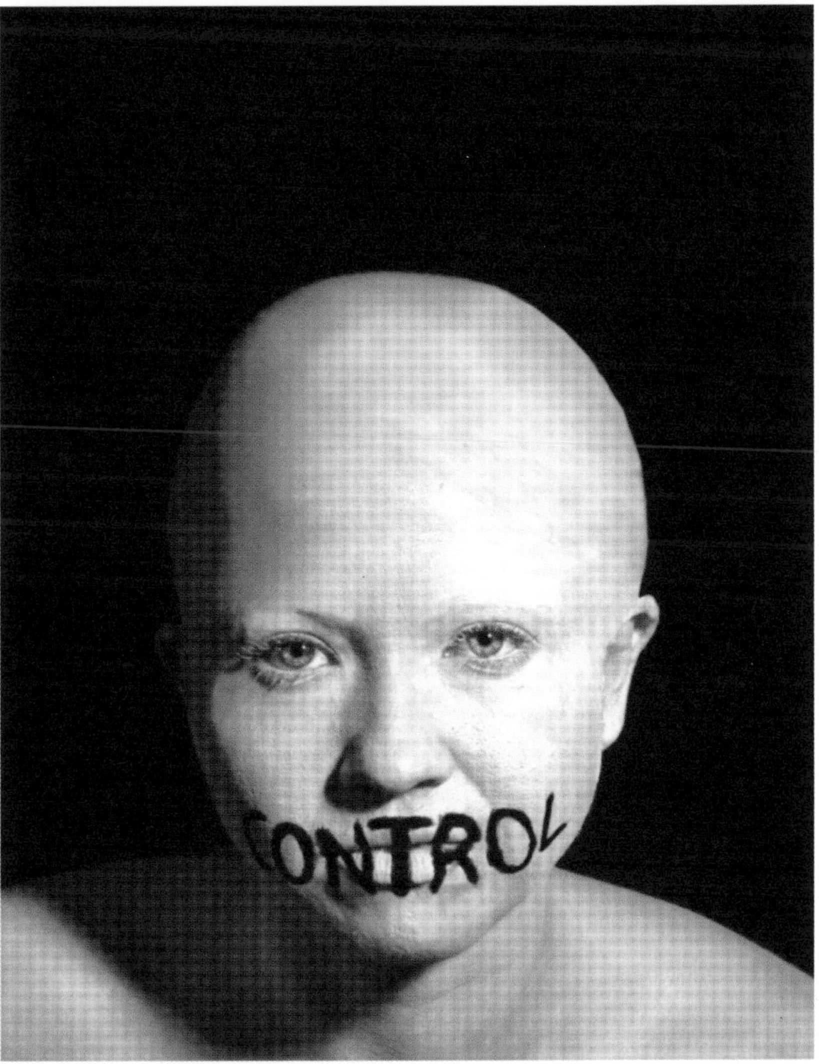

Memphis, TN

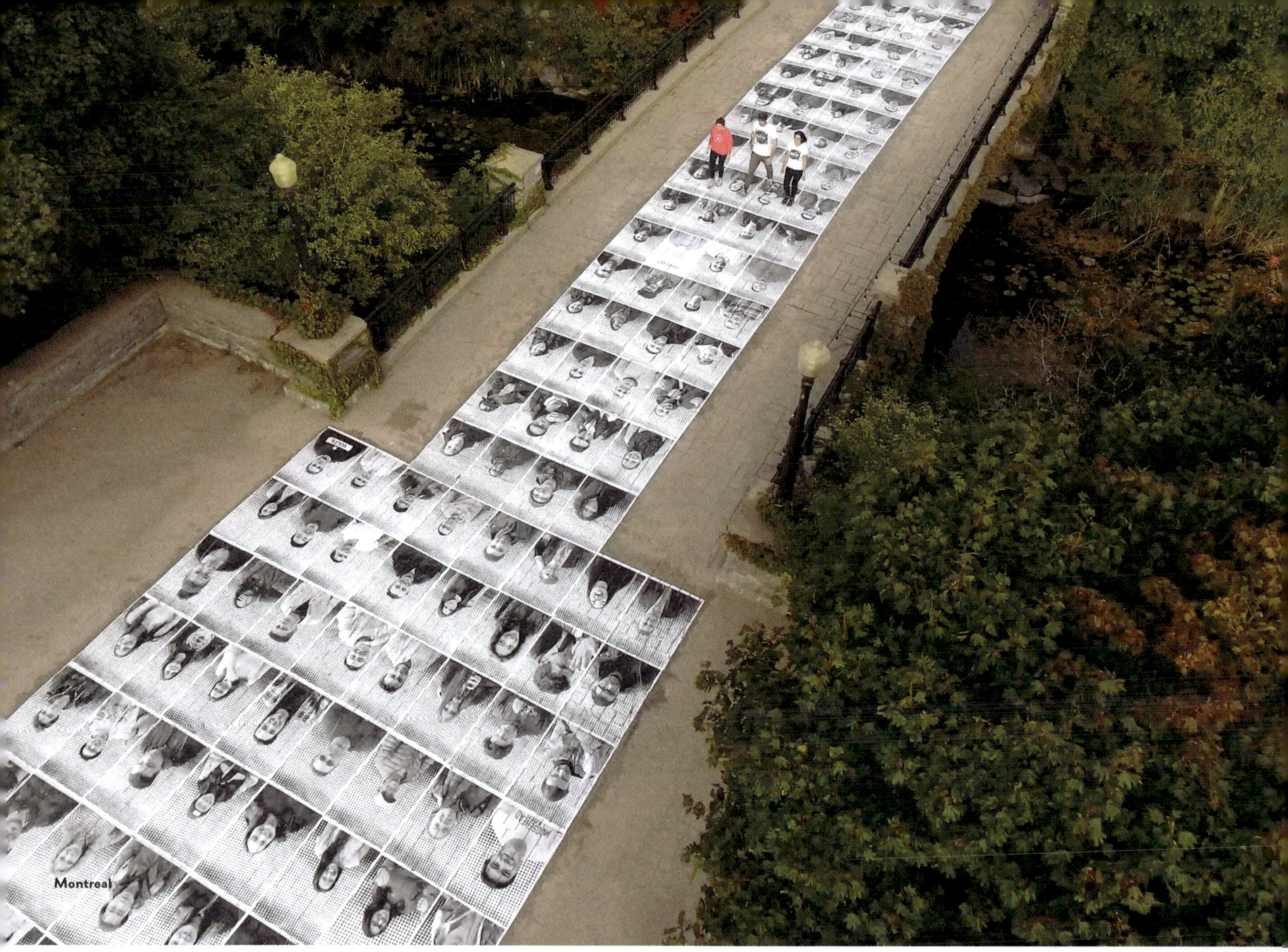

Montreal

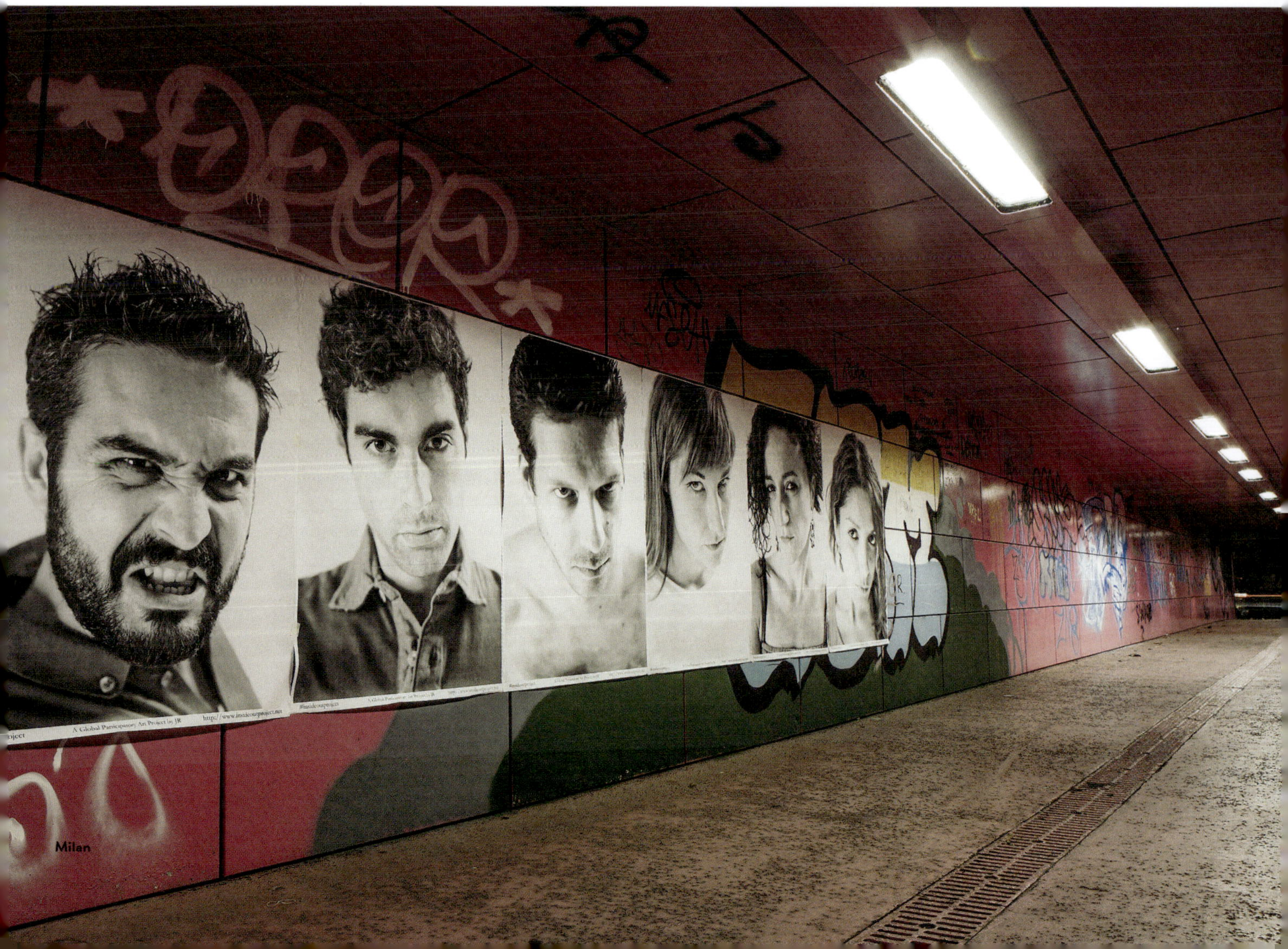

Milan

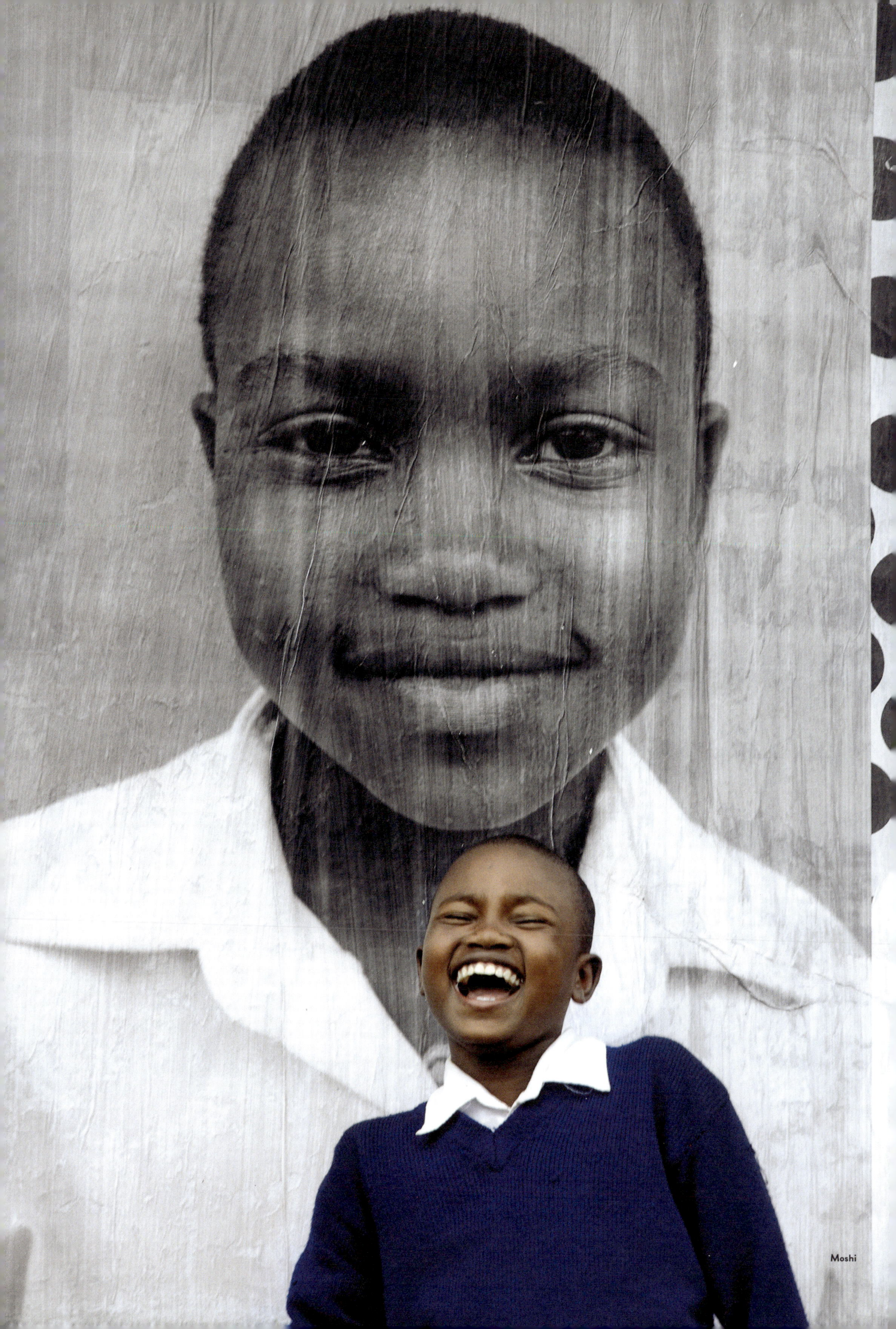

Moshi

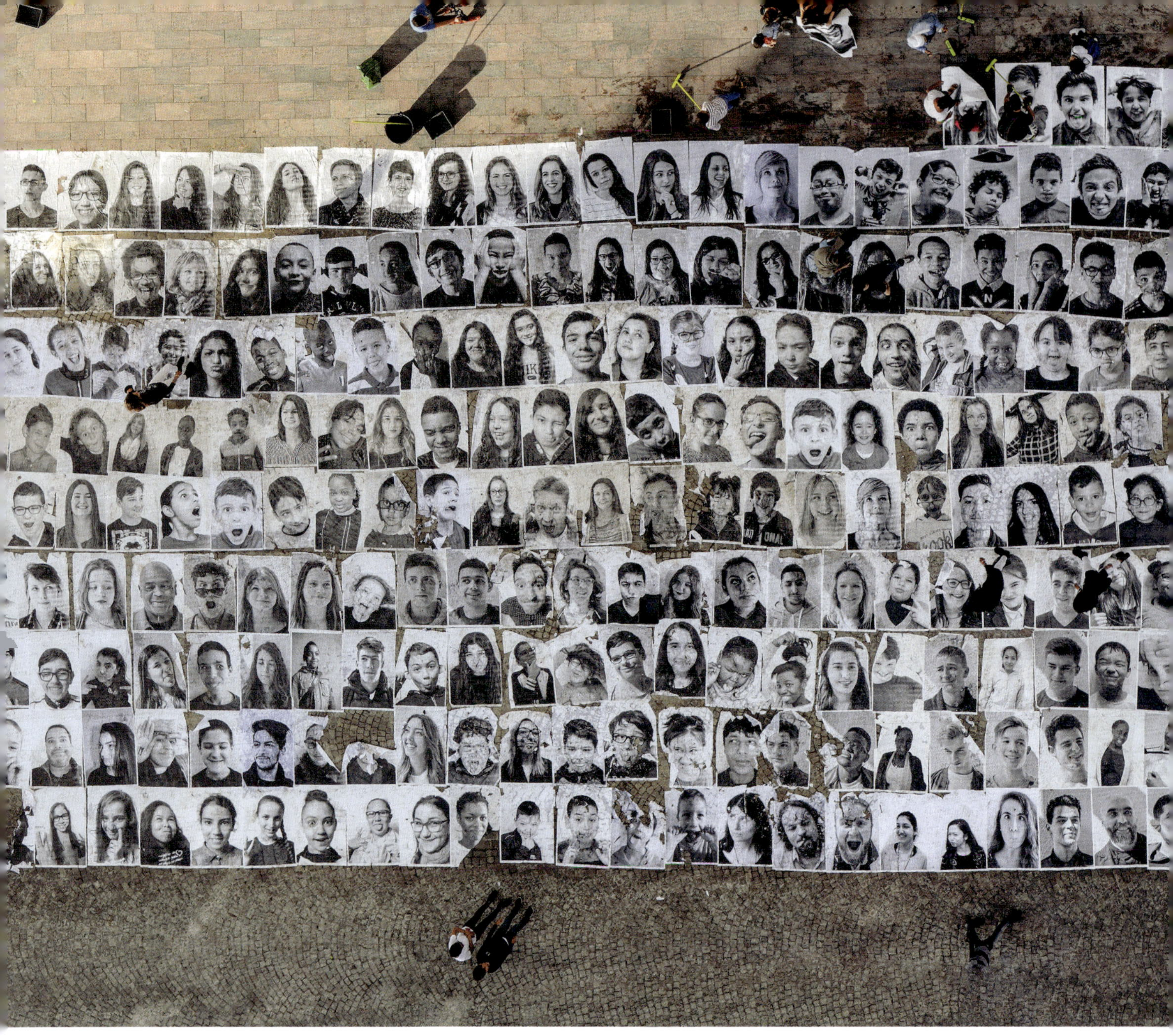

Mulhouse

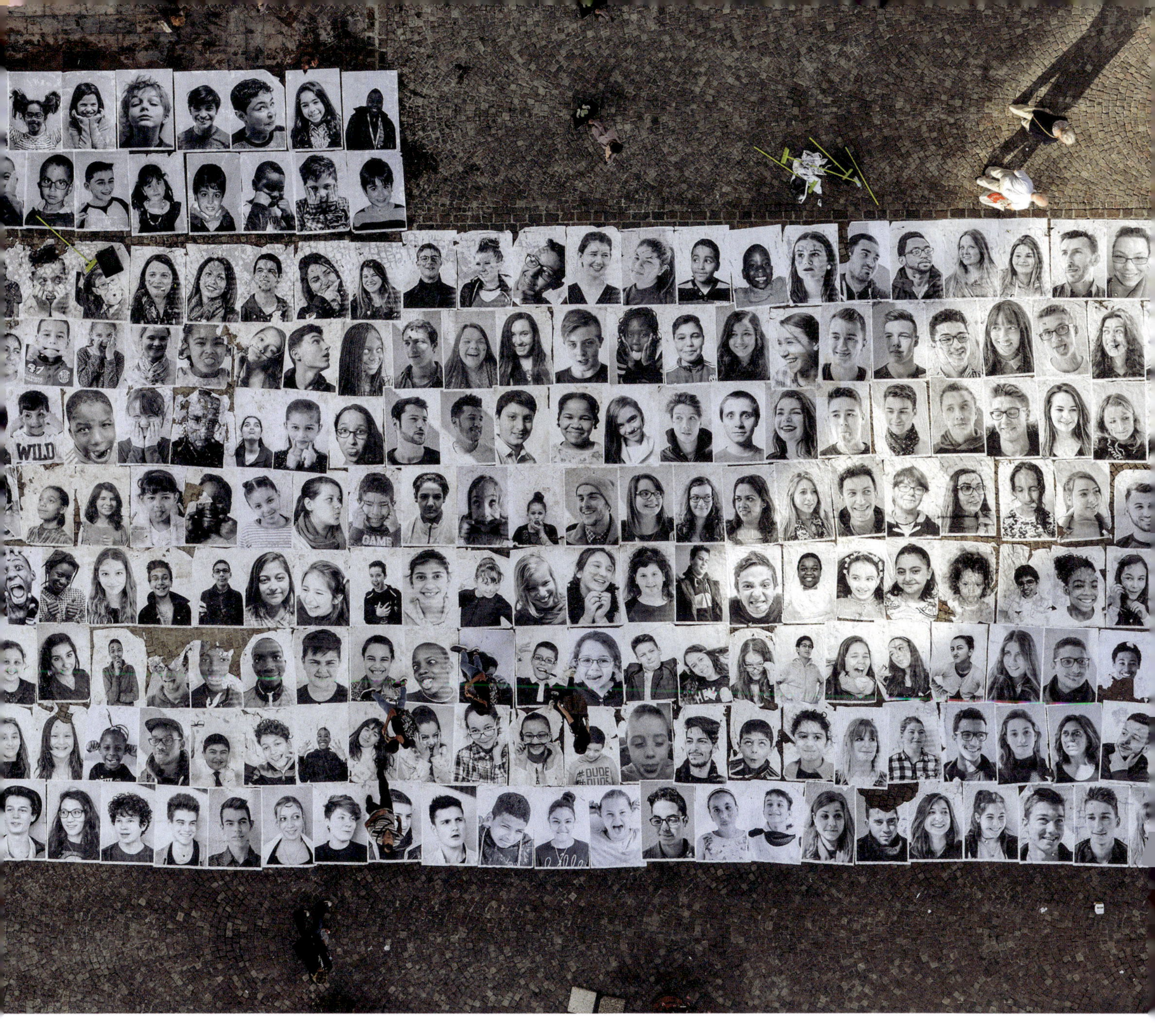

"On September 28, 2016, the Place de la Réunion in Mulhouse was transformed into giant piece of art thanks to the participation of 750 students, creating for the people of the city a huge installation of tolerance and diversity."

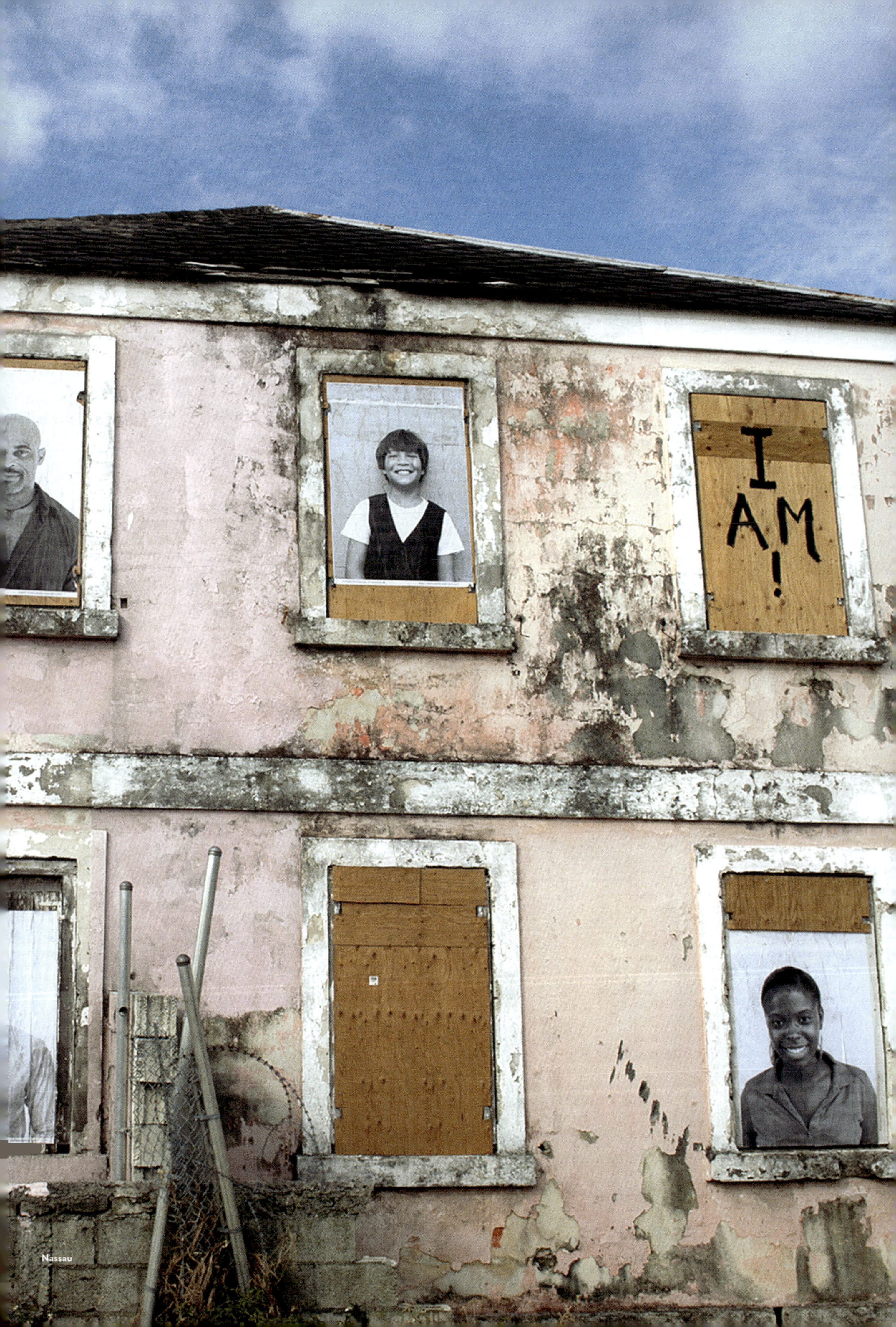

Nassau

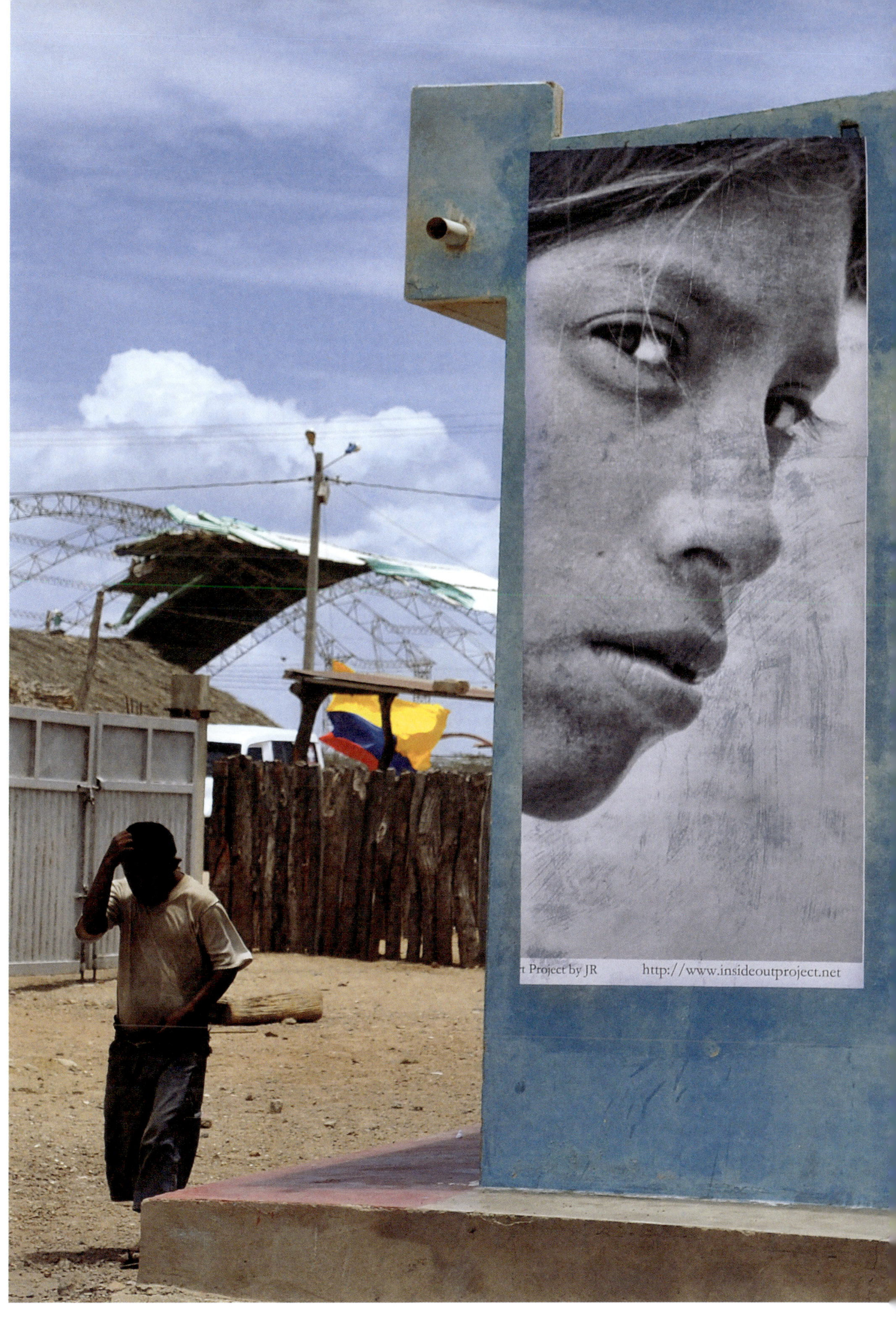

Nazareth

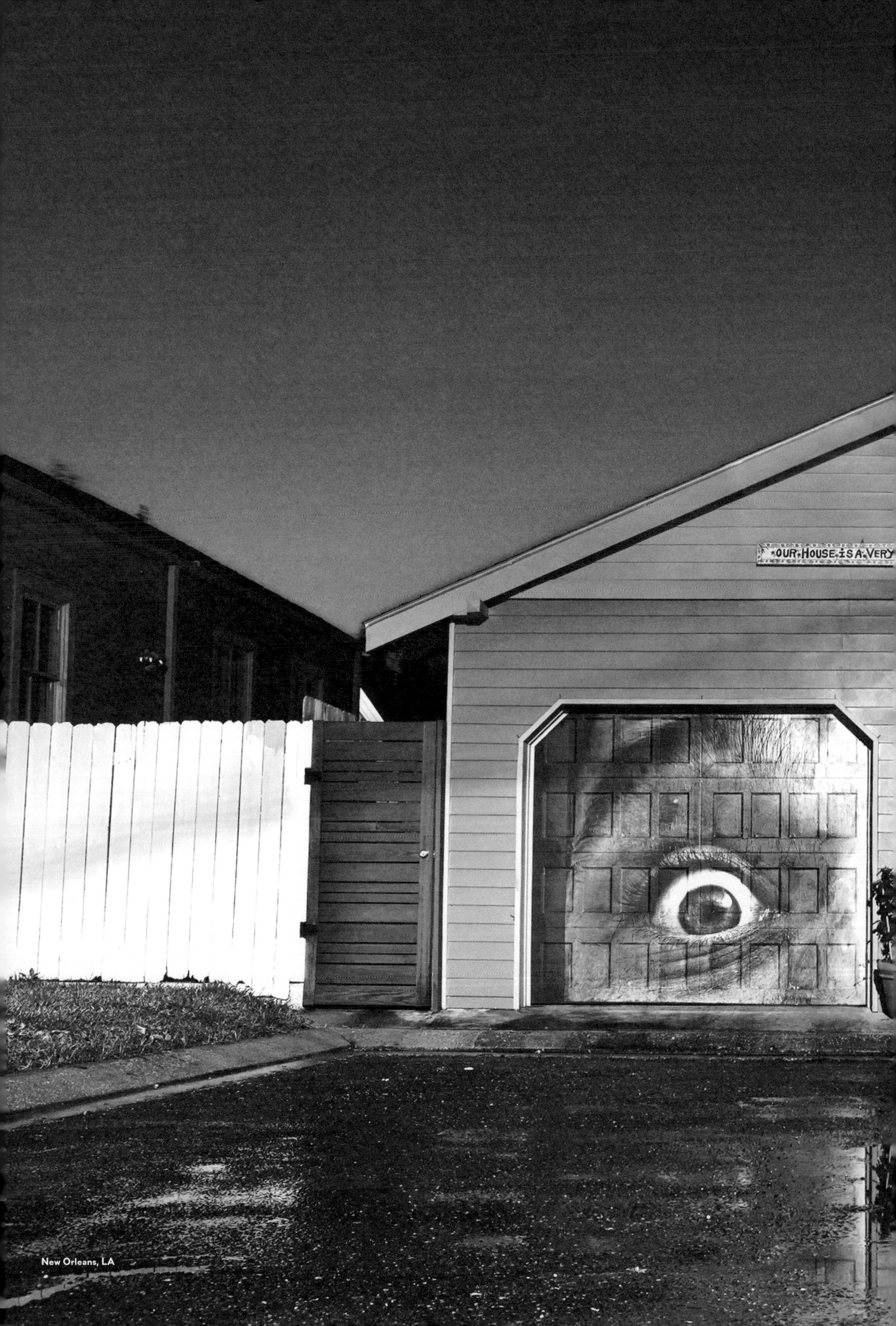

New Orleans, LA

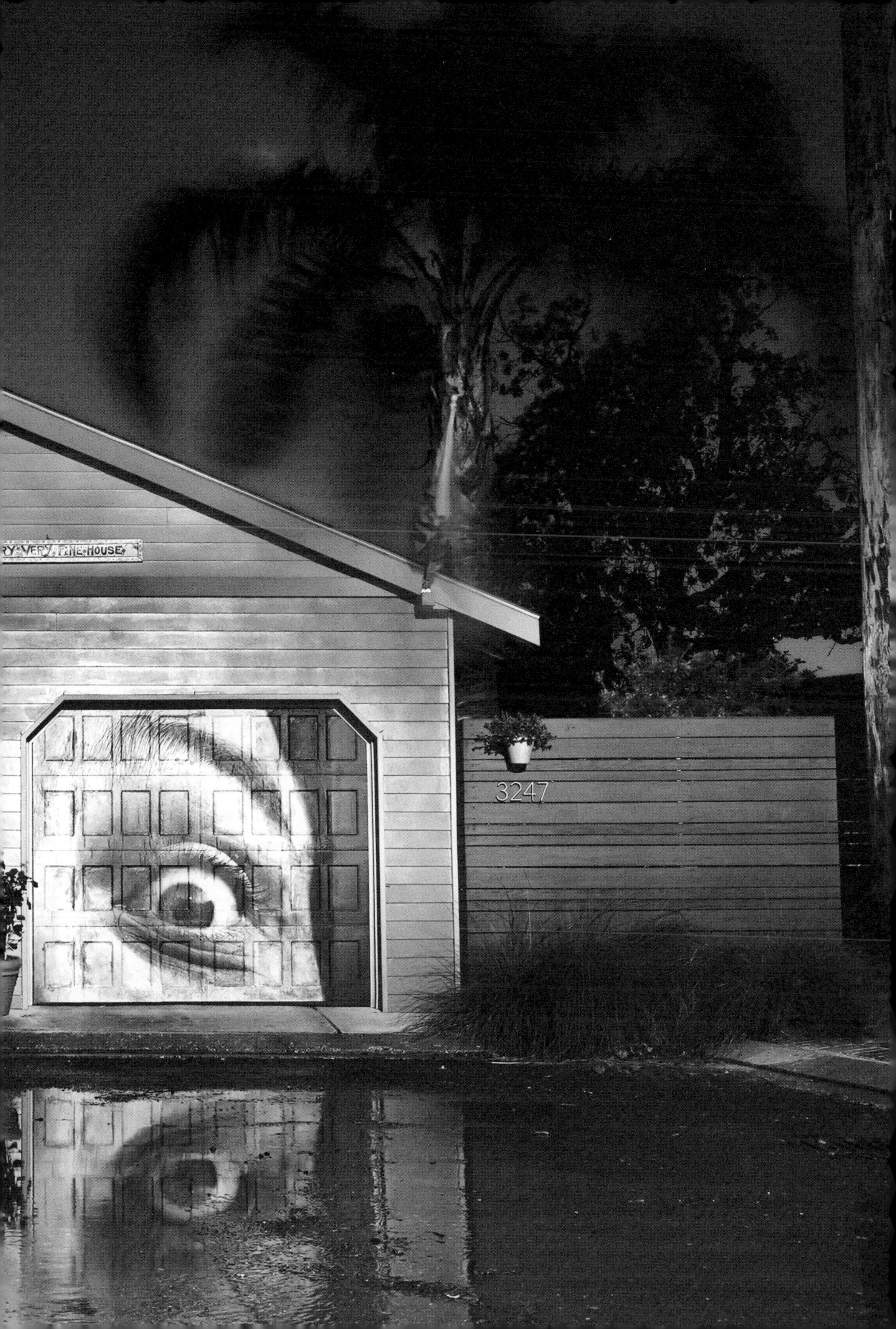
RY VERY FINE HOUSE
3247

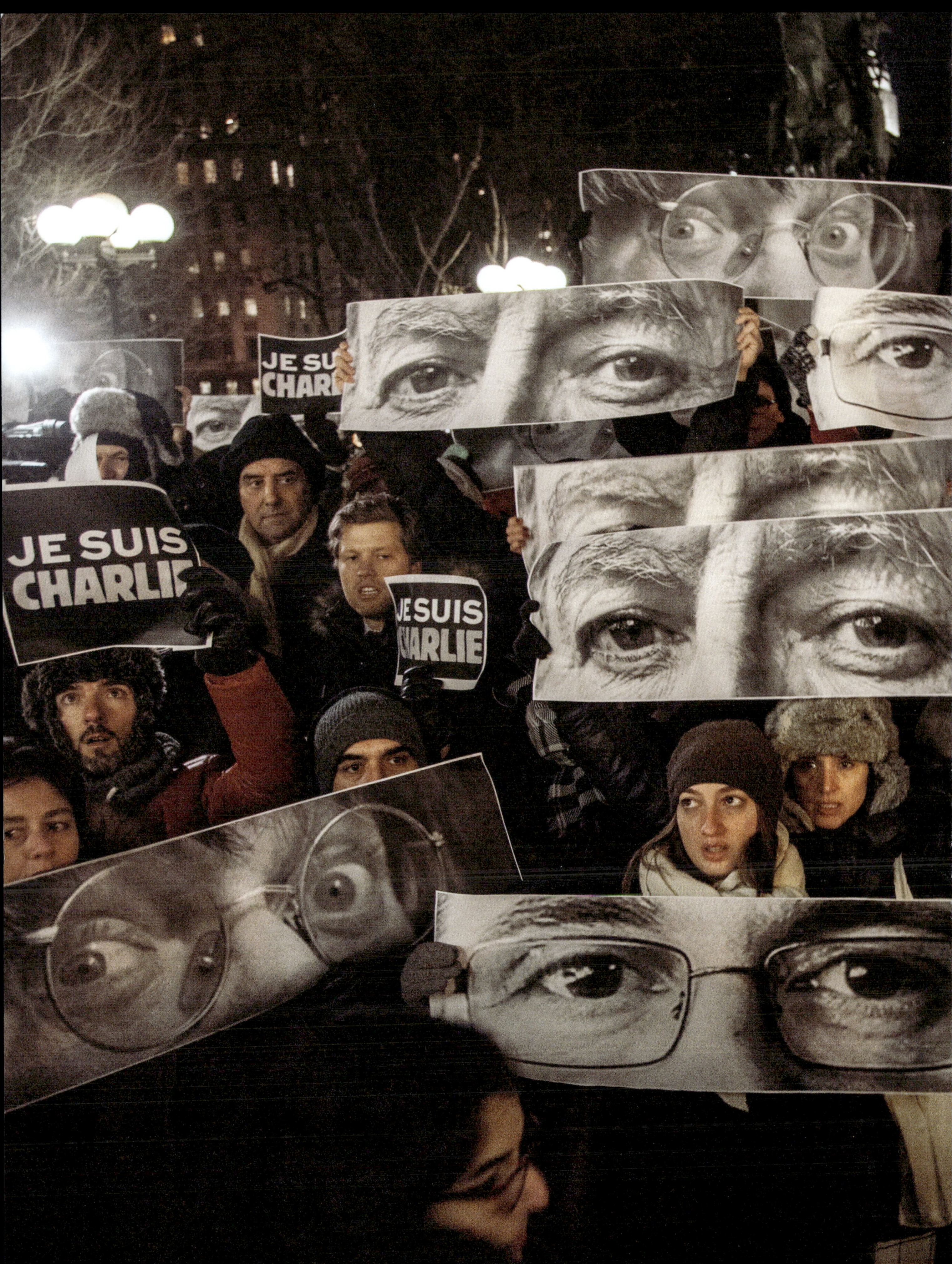
JE SUIS
CHARLIE
JE SUIS
CHARLIE

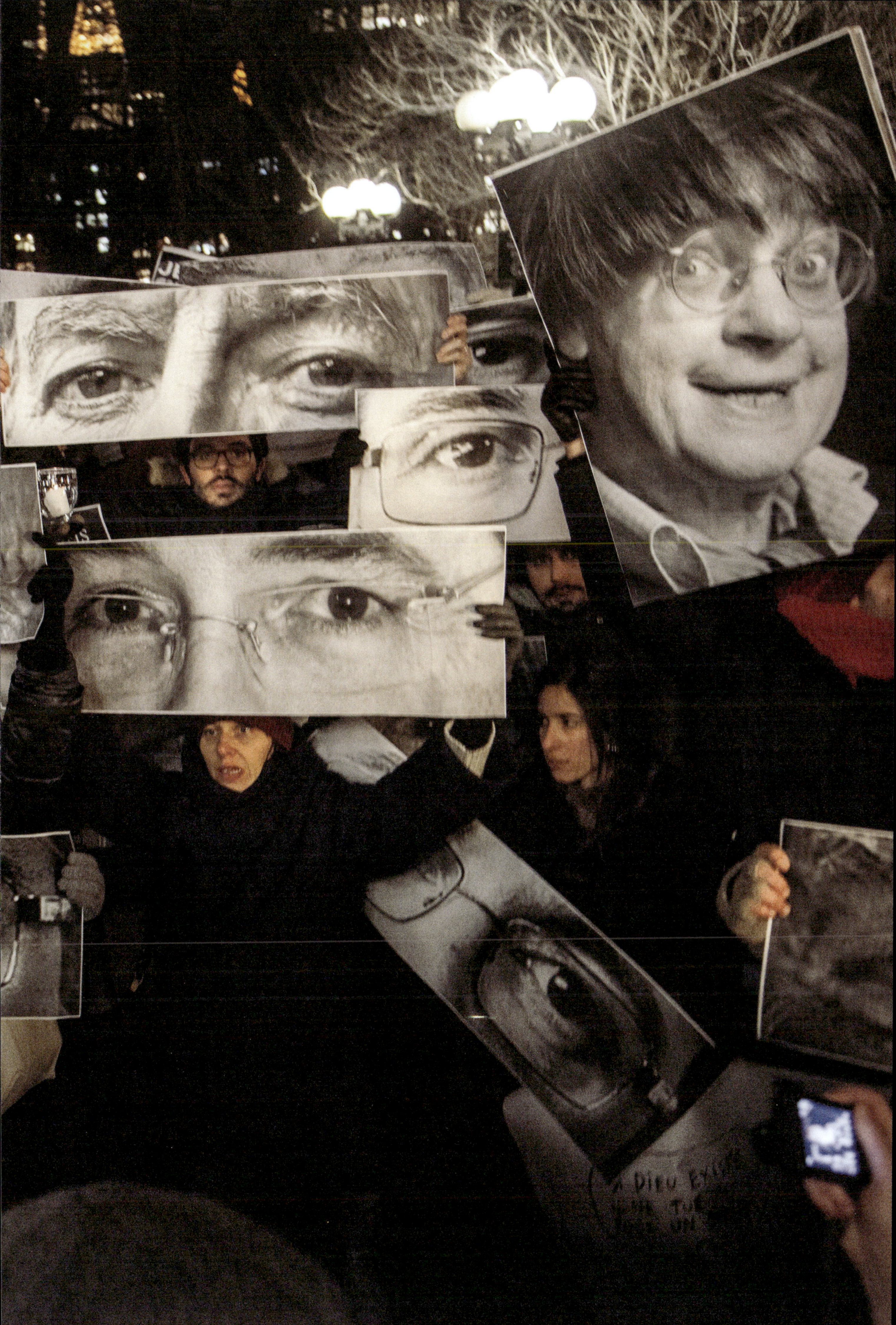

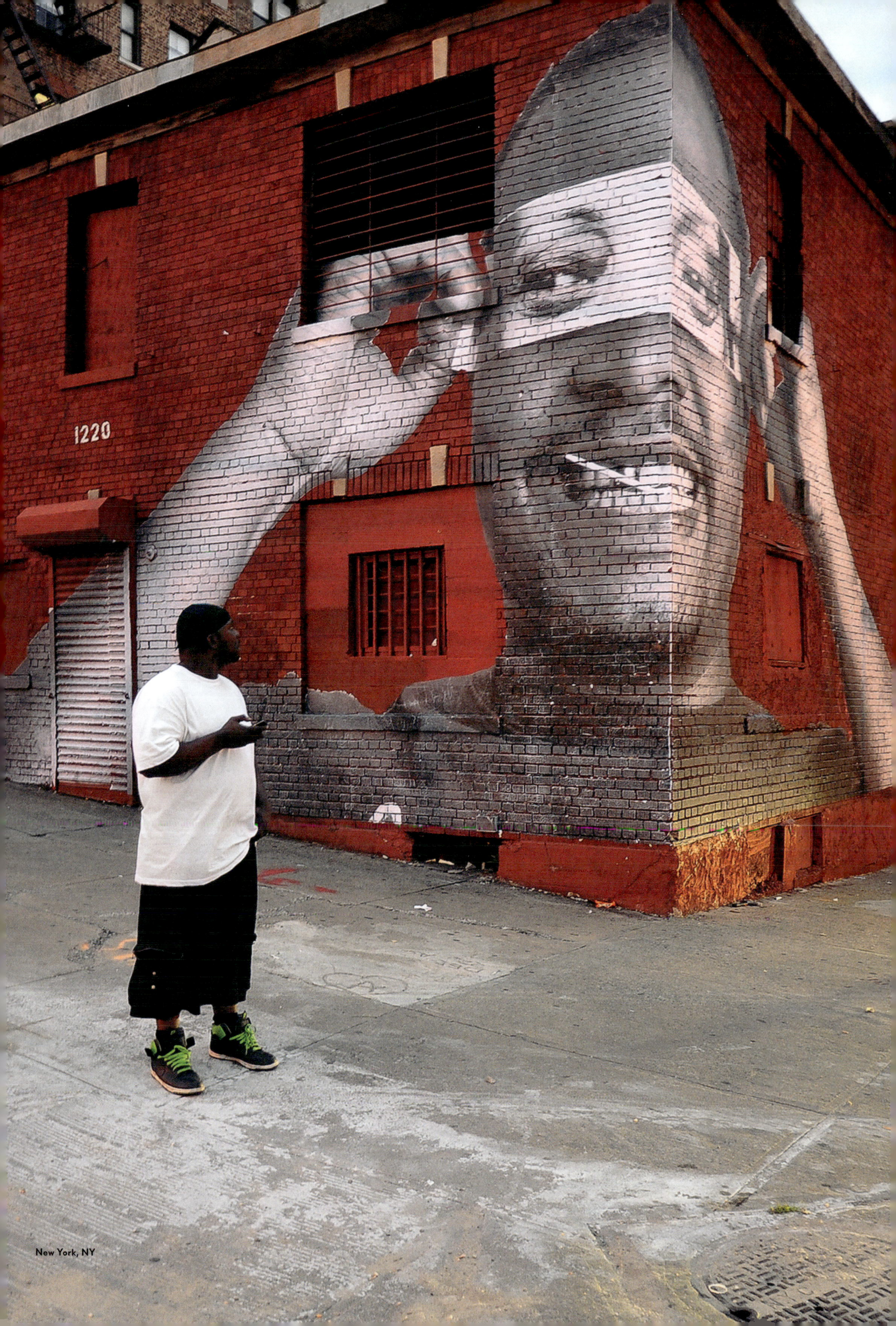

New York, NY

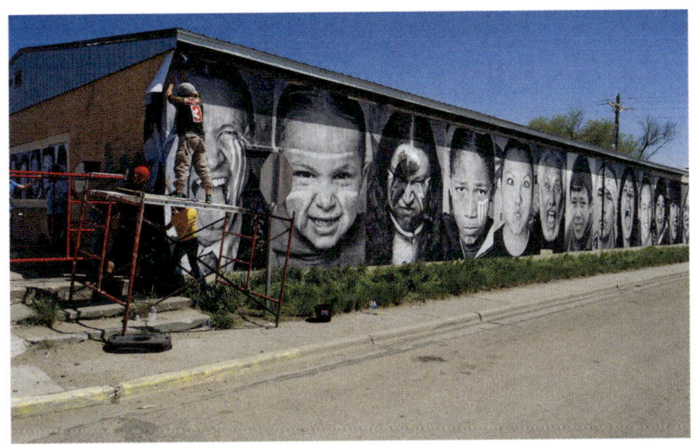

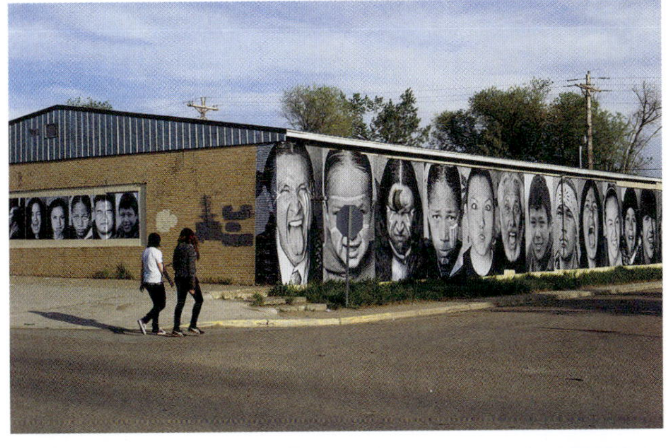

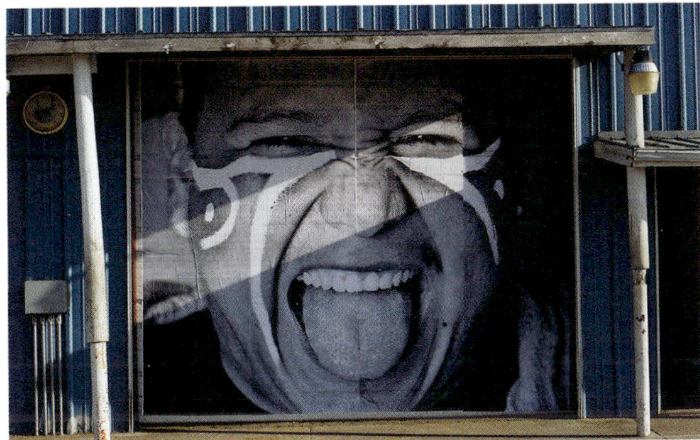

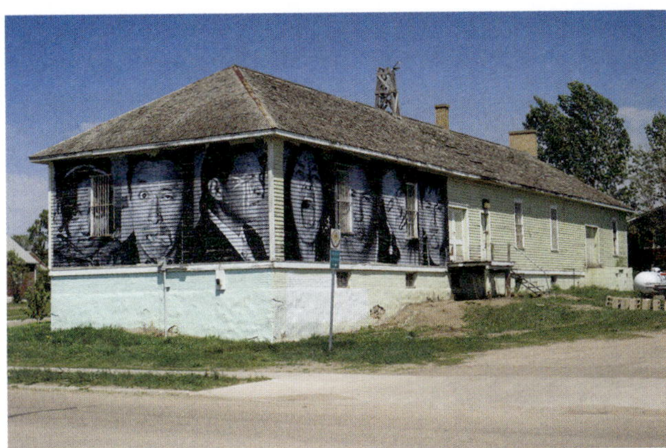

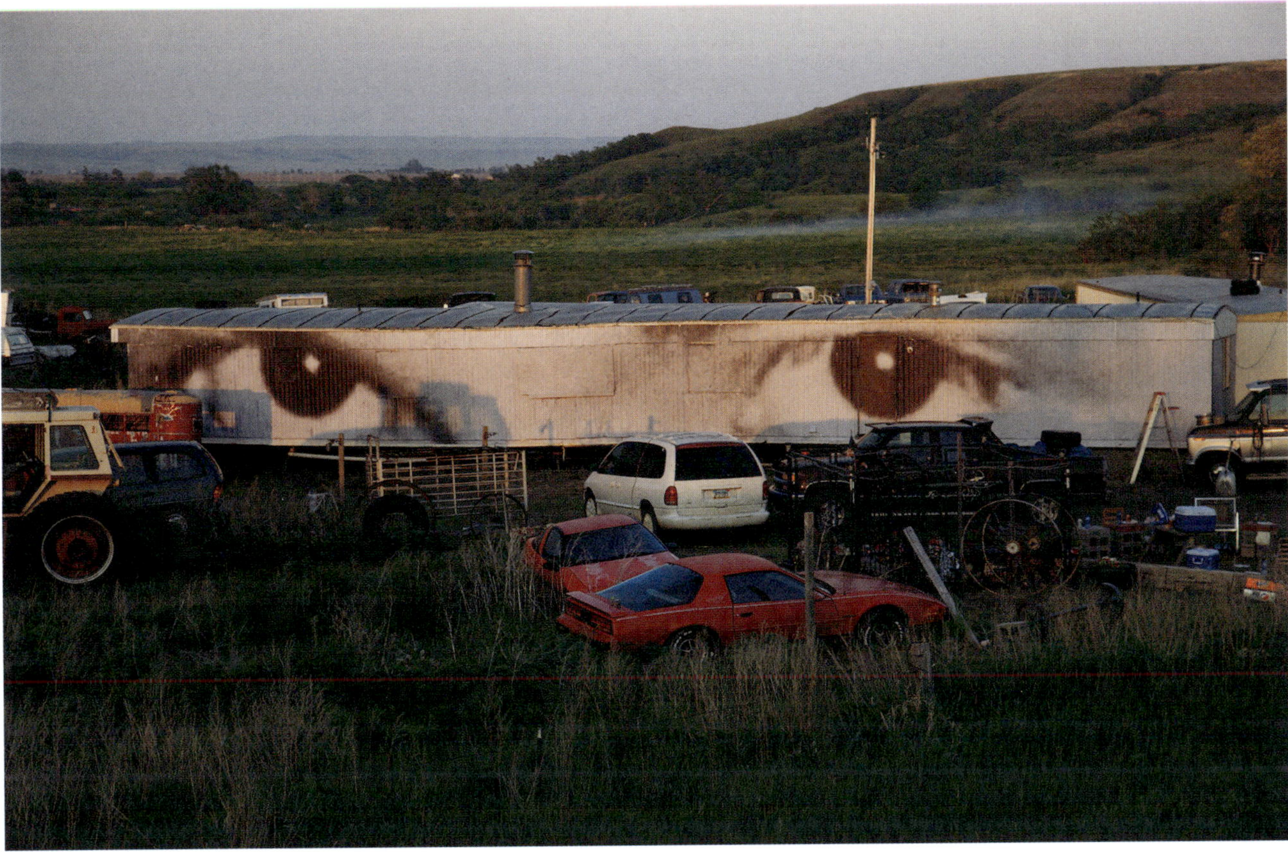

"We are the Lakota Tribe. We still exist."

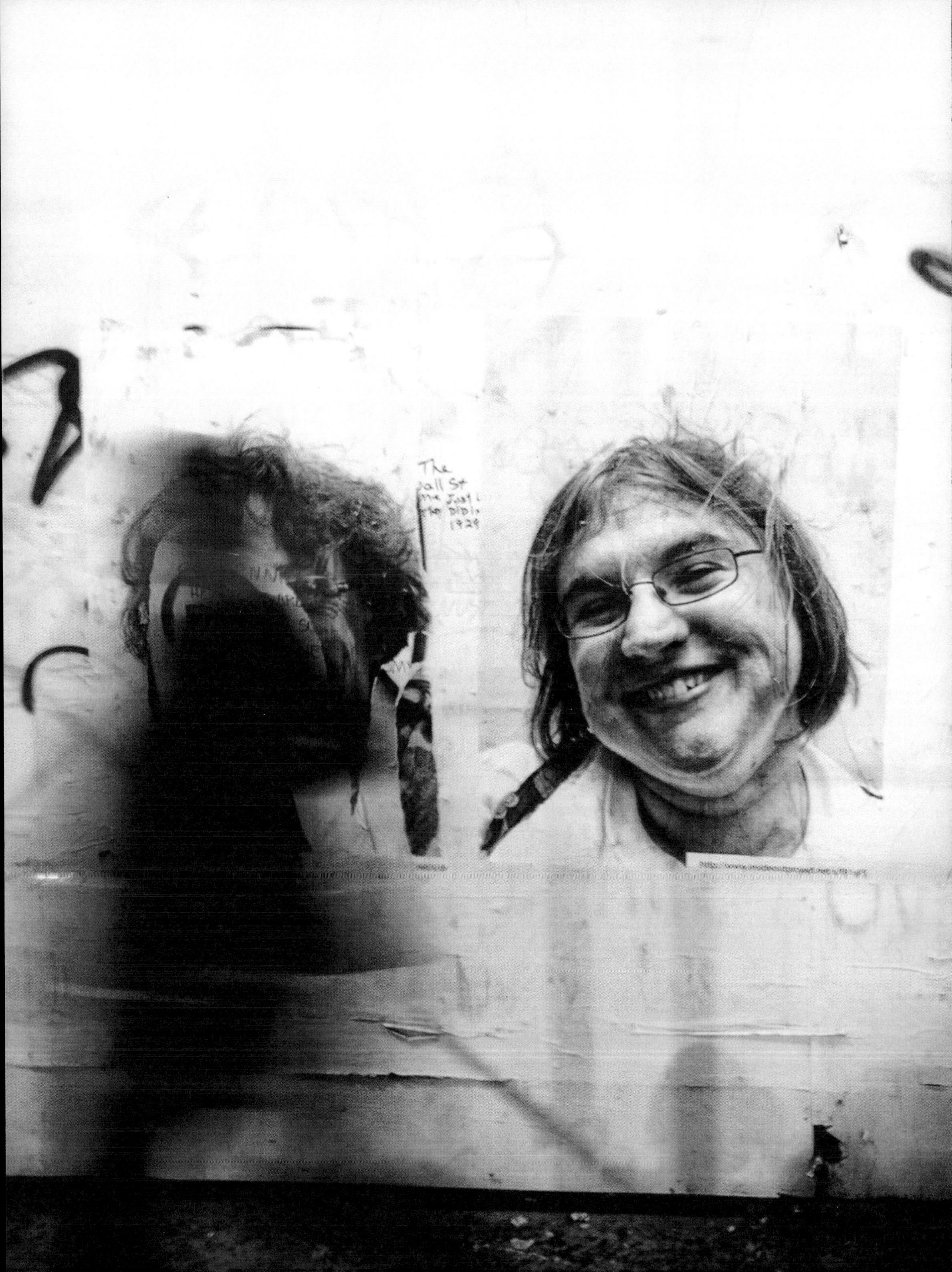
The
1929

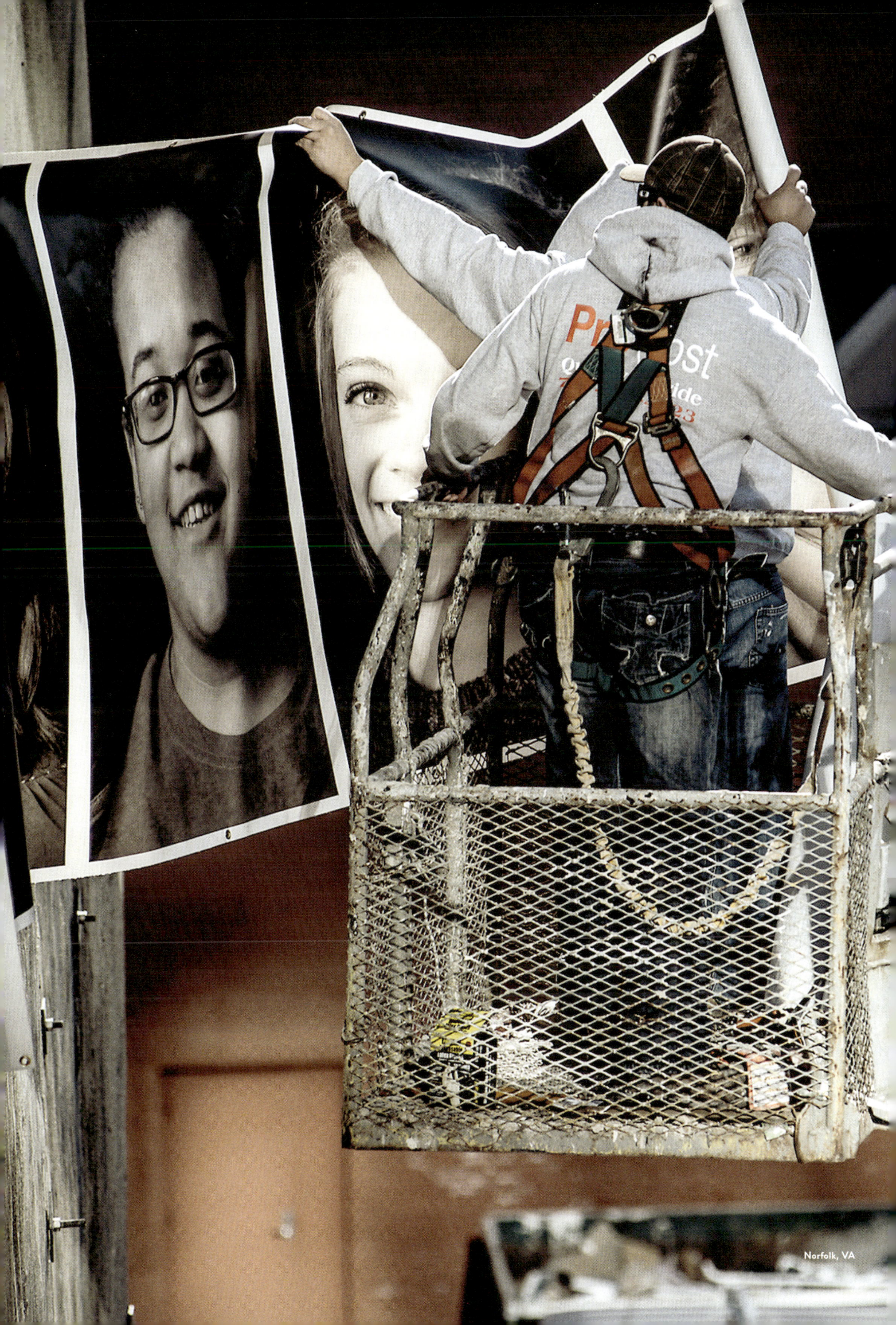

Norfolk, VA

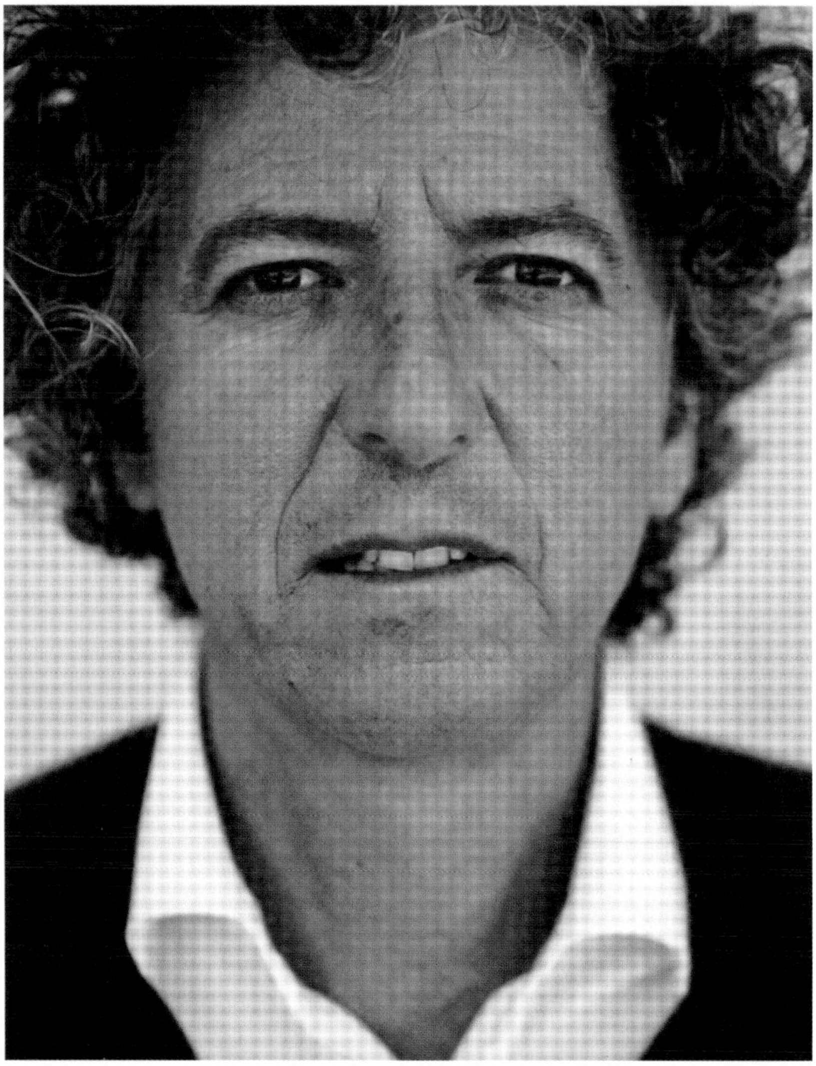

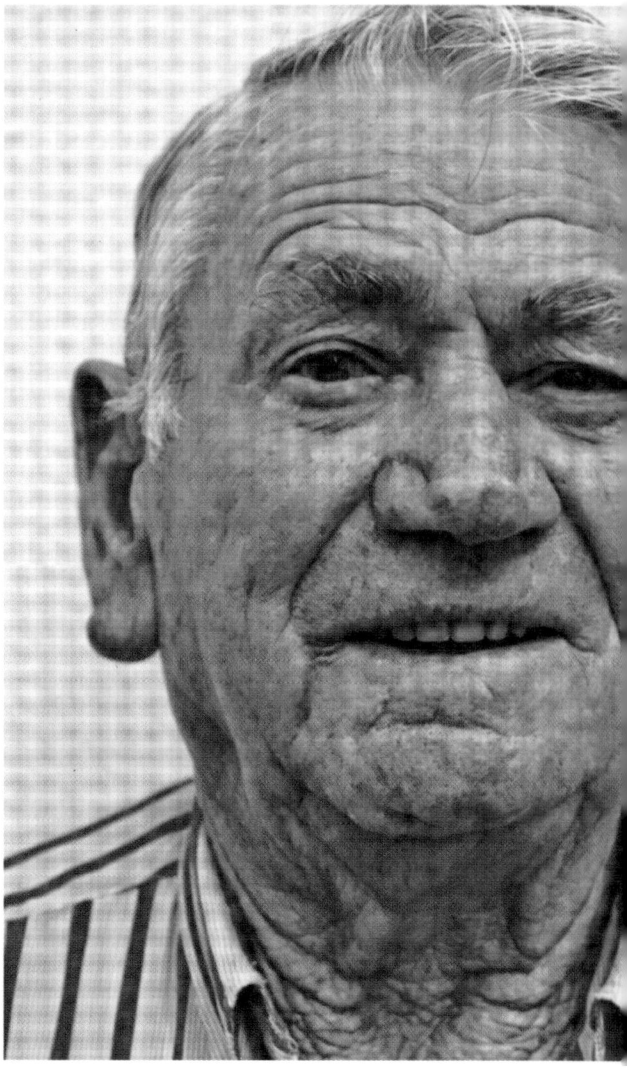

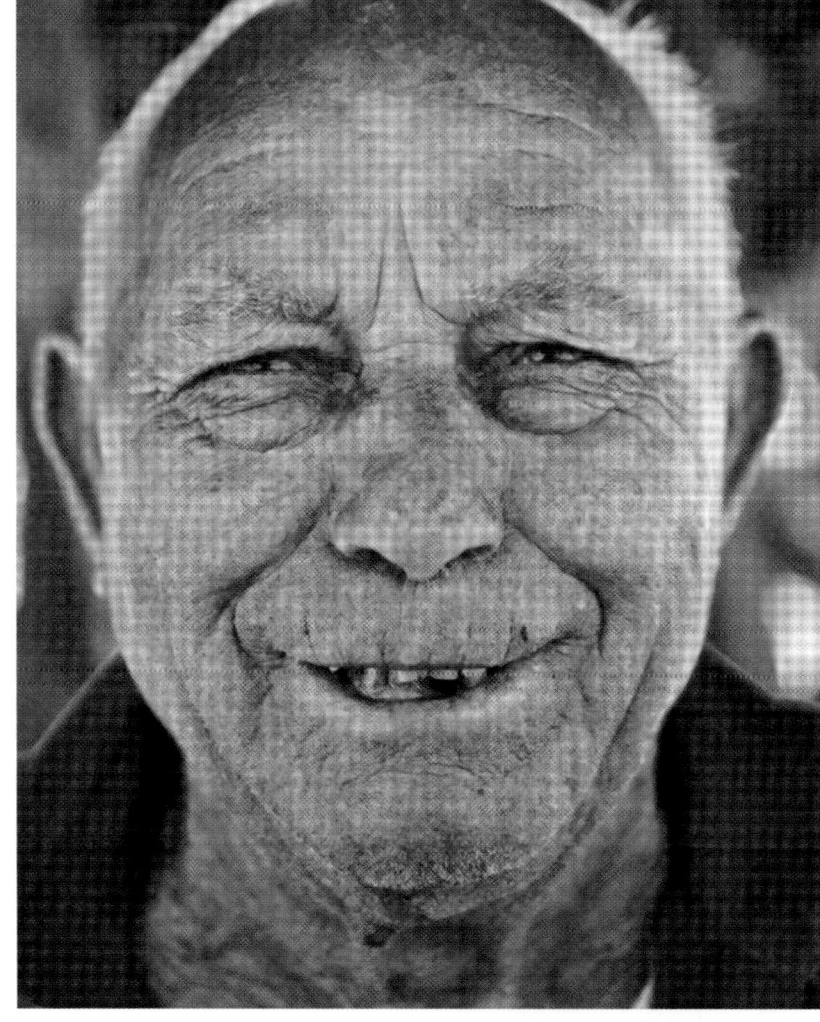

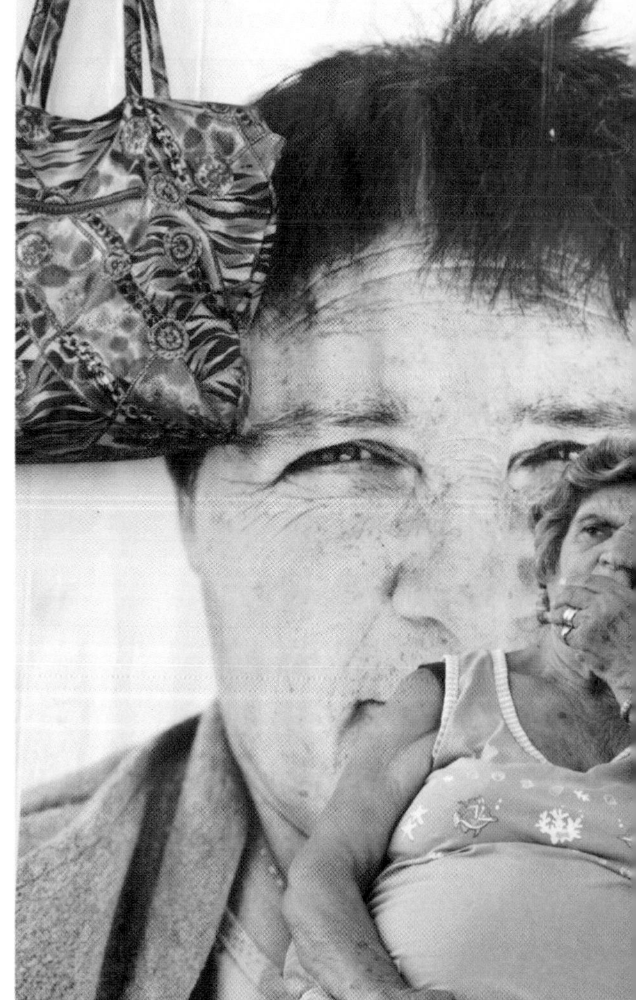

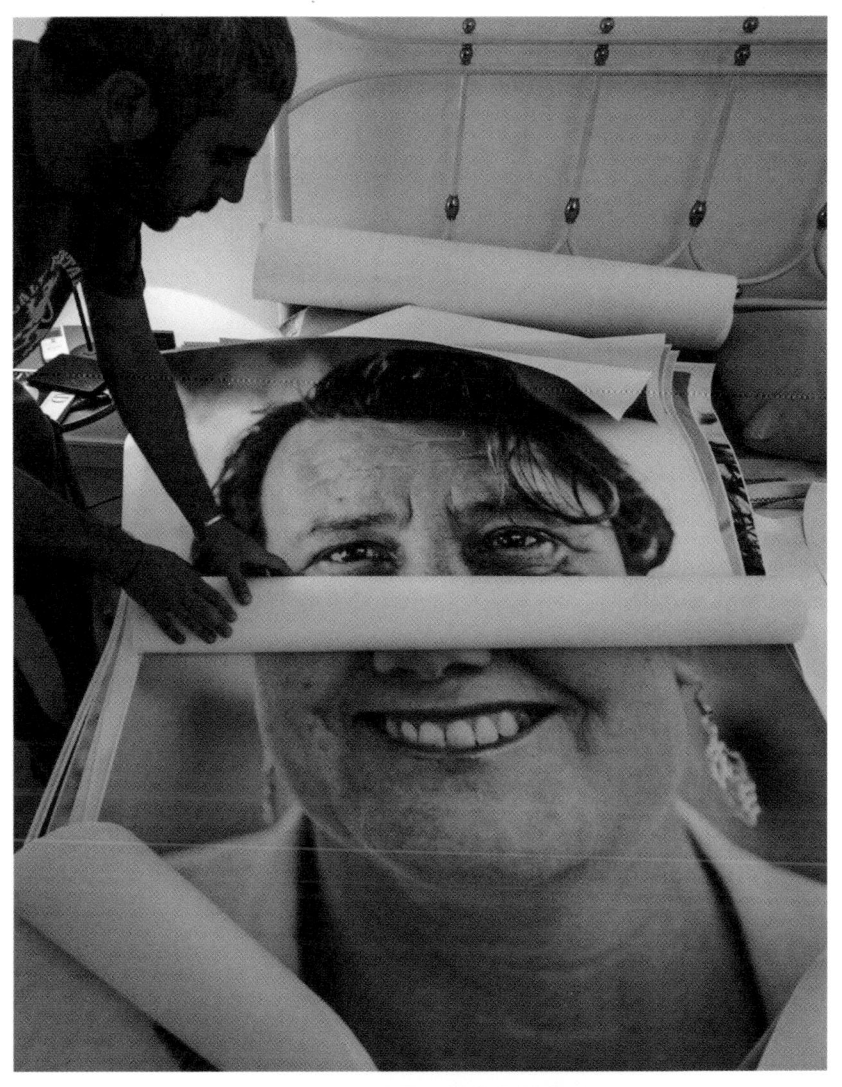

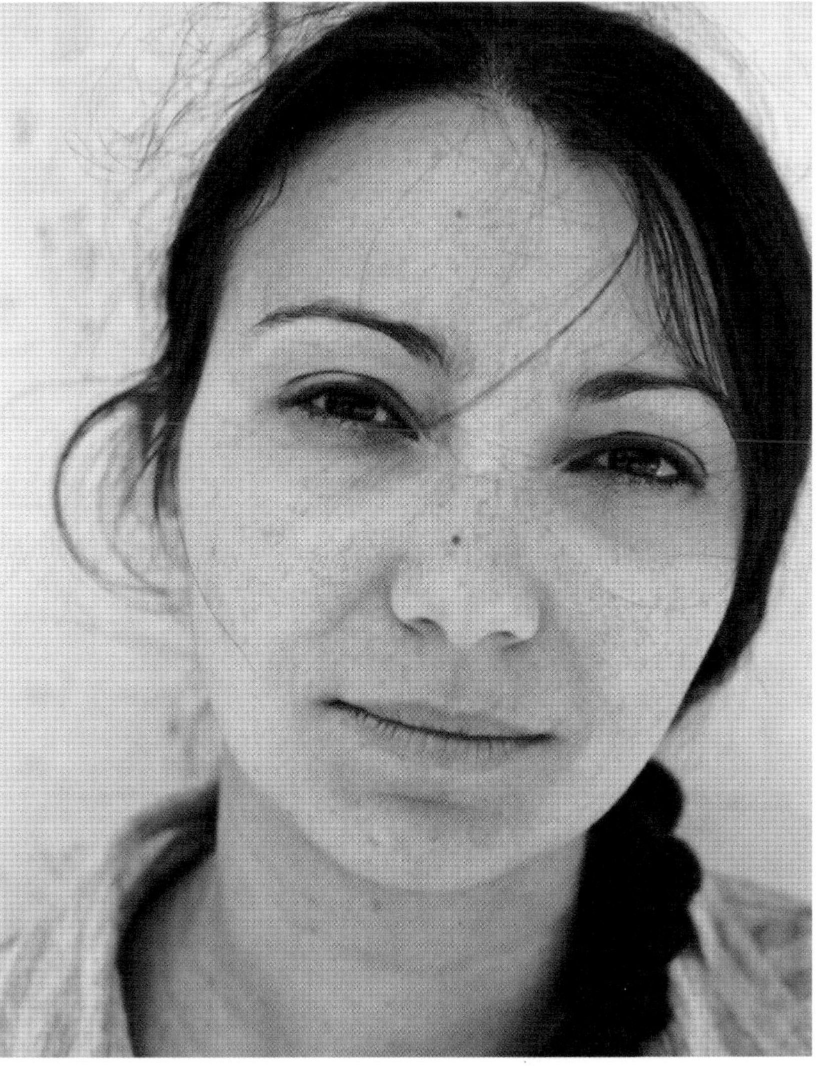

“I don’t know if our show changed anything, but I know we changed, our friends changed. They still thank us. And I thank JR.”

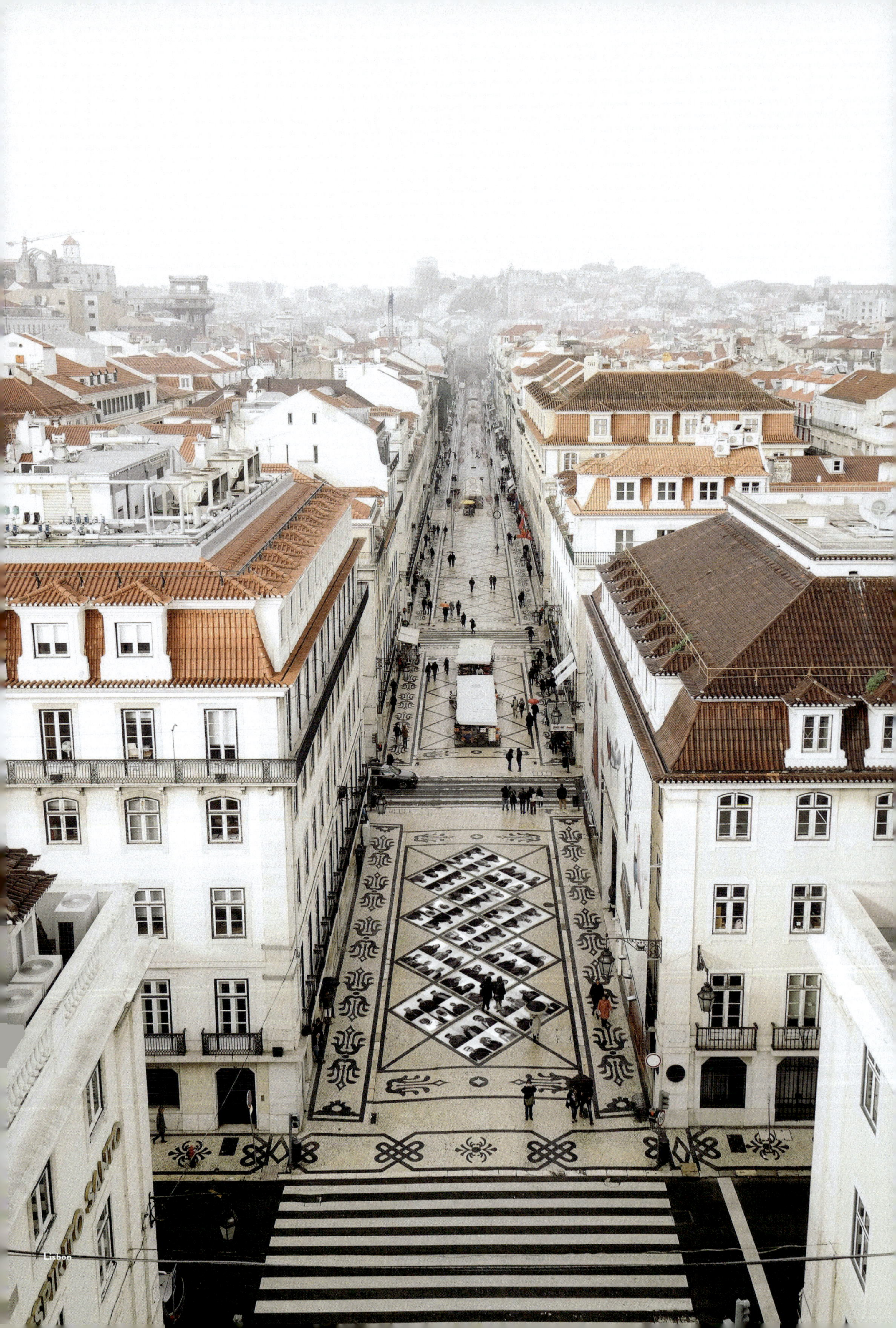

Lisbon

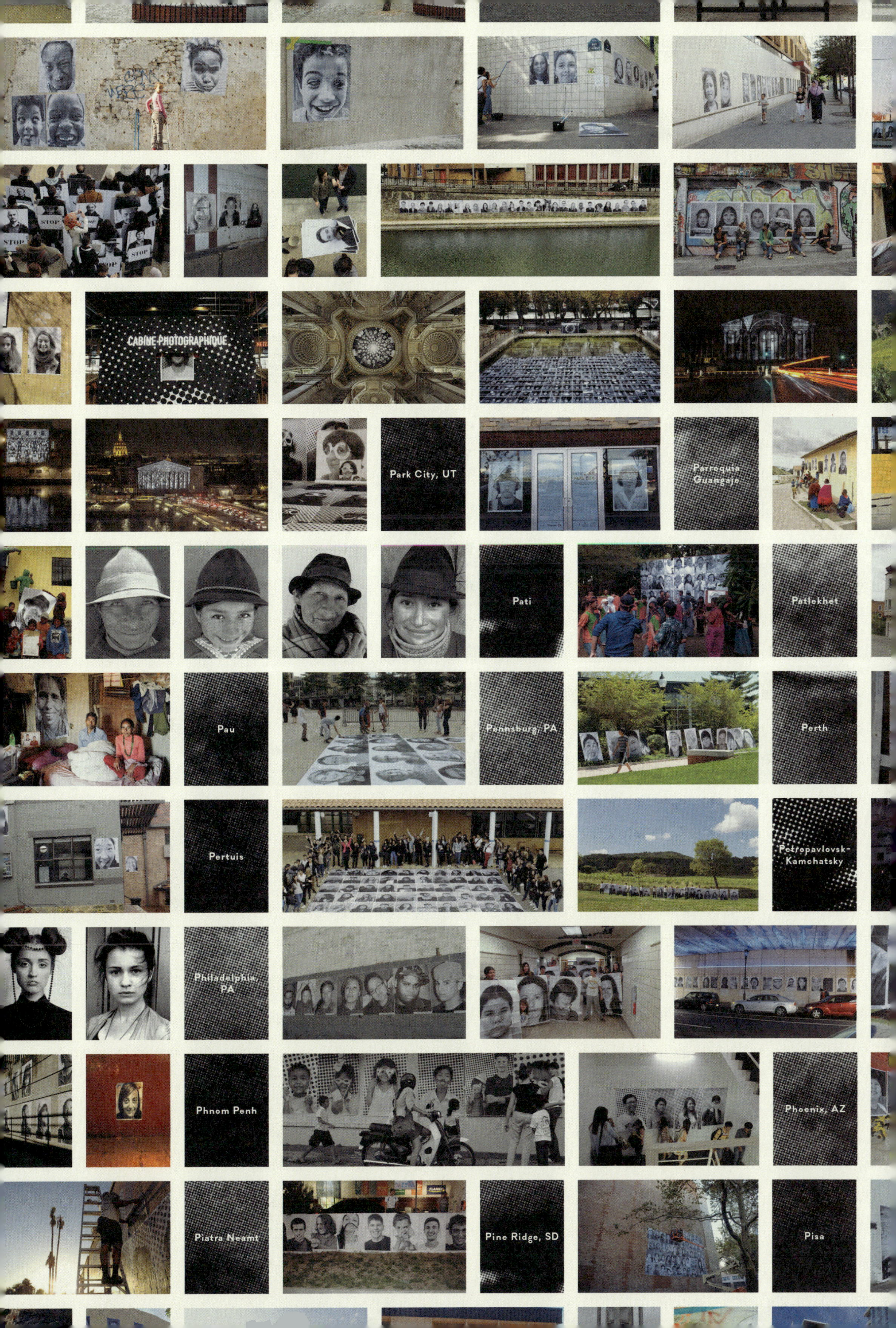
CABINE PHOTOGRAPHIQUE
Park City, UT
Parroquia Guangaje
Pati
Patlekhet
Pau
Pennsburg, PA
Perth
Pertuis
Petropavlovsk-Kamchatsky
Philadelphia, PA
Phnom Penh
Phoenix, AZ
Piatra Neamt
Pine Ridge, SD
Pisa

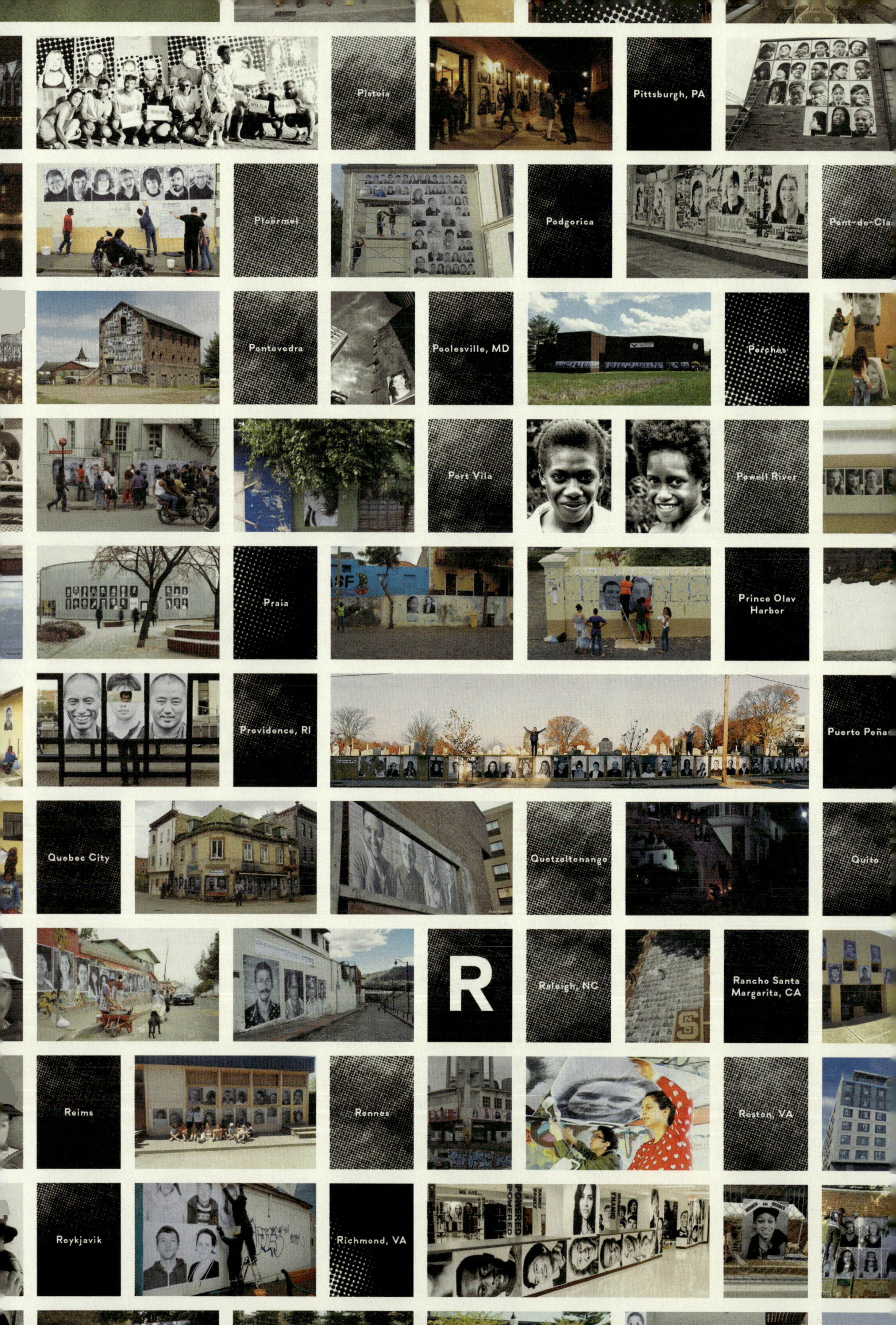
Pistoia
Pittsburgh, PA
Ploërmel
Podgorica
Pont-de-Cla
Pontevedra
Poolesville, MD
Porches
Port Vila
Powell River
Praia
Prince Olav Harbor
Providence, RI
Puerto Peña
Quebec City
Quetzaltenango
Quito
R
Raleigh, NC
Rancho Santa Margarita, CA
Reims
Rennes
Reston, VA
Reykjavik
Richmond, VA

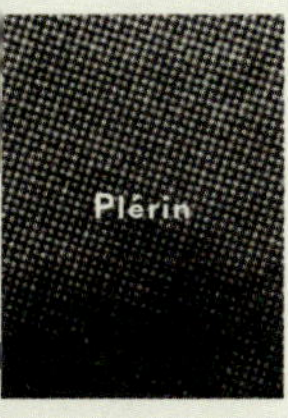

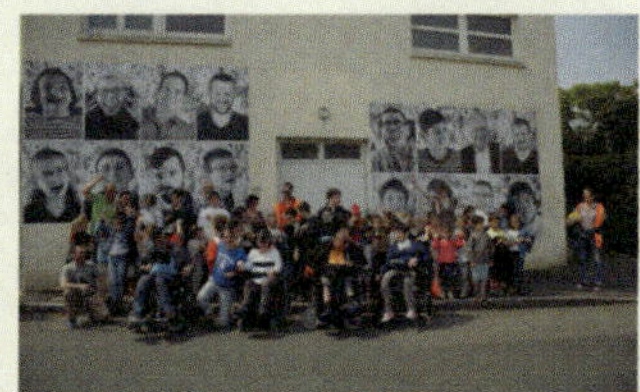

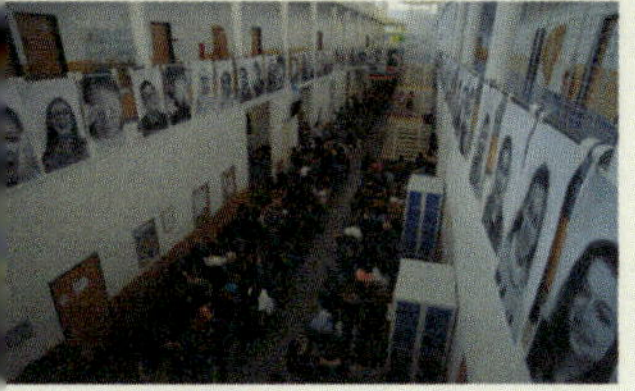

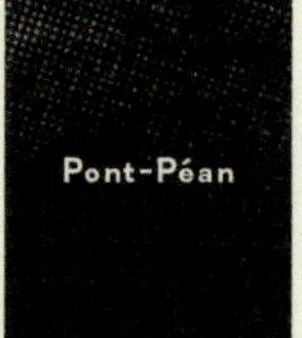

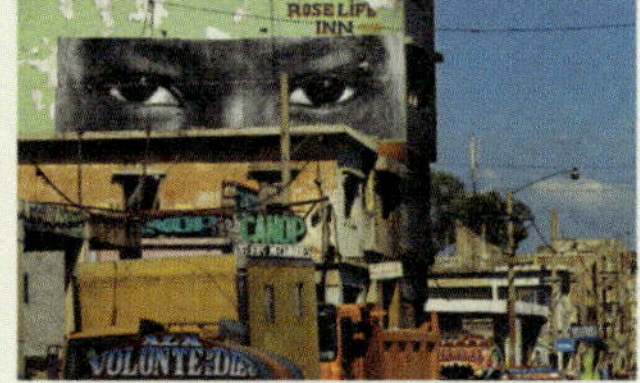

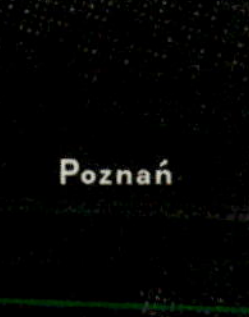

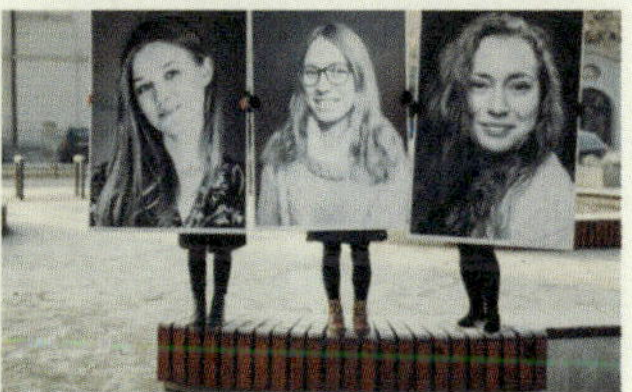

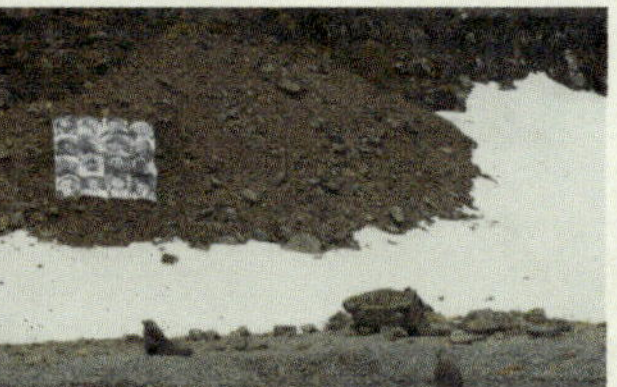

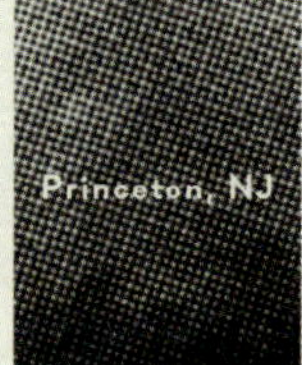

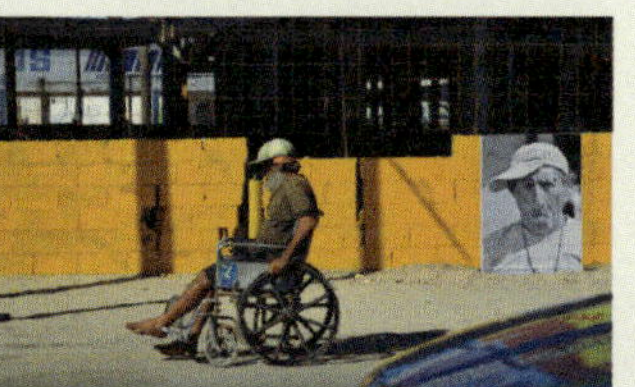

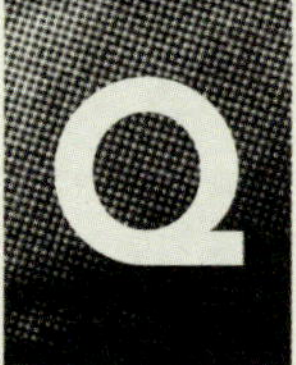

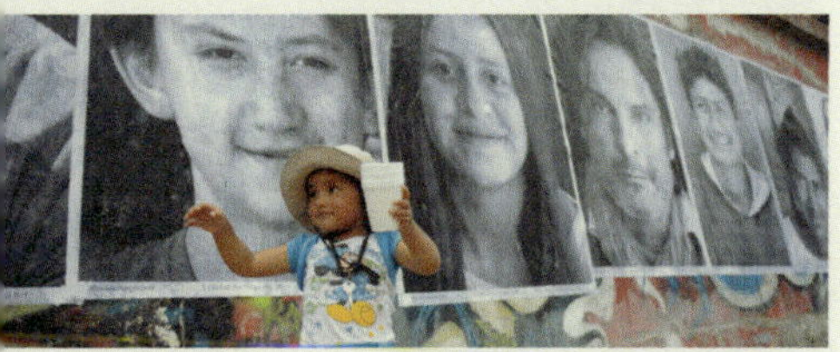

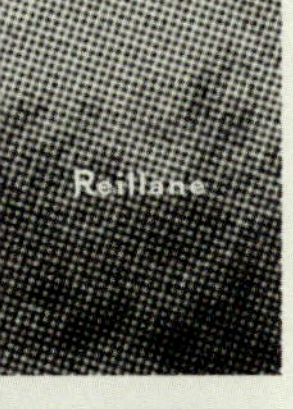

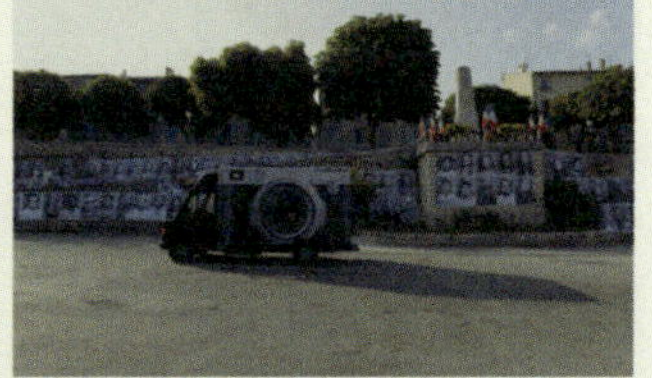

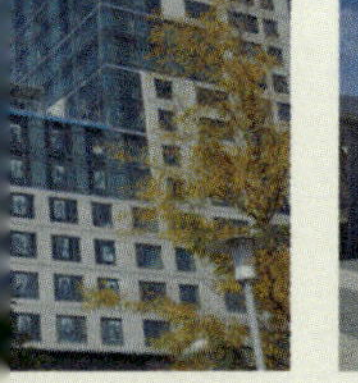

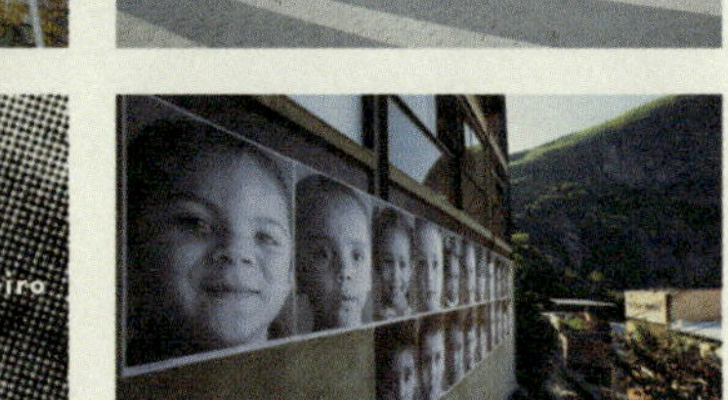

30 Days, 30 Portraits, November 2013. 30 Days, 30 Portraits is a global social initiative encouraging people to unite and say no to war. It is a photography project which began in Rome September 1, 2013, and lasted thirty days, capturing one portrait per day. This project is meant to bring people together and celebrate the power of unity and peace through photography.

Respect for Immigrants, October 2011. Respect and compassion for immigrants.

Rouen, France Si t'es Citoyen, Cité Citoyenne, May 2014. We want to show the children what art is, how it can decline, and how it's possible to create some with motivation and engagement.

Rueil-Malmaison, France Reuil-Malmaison School Stands Together, May 2011. Our work was motivated by the fact that our art school, funded largely by the city of Rueil-Malmaison, closed due to budget restrictions. As students, we wanted to reclaim these places for the last time as a definition of financial education.

Sacramento, CA Showcasing the Creative Energy of an Artistic Community, May 2013. To draw attention to and celebrate the creative energy of the artistic community in the Sacramento region.

Saint-Affrique, France Ludomino, June 2014. Inside Out helped us defend the humanist values of the Ludomino Association, defending Otherness and sensitizing a large audience.

Saint-Gilles-les-Bains, La Réunion Galerie de Portraits des Élèves du Collège Les Aigrettes, February 2014. We would like to take over the impersonal space that high school can be and make it a place for students to display their diversity. We want to create a portrait gallery to show that every student at the school has a history, a past, and that high school is not merely a waystation with a neverending cycle of faceless students who stay for only four years.

Saint-Jean-de-Moirans, France Mon Avenir, September 2016. Students from Saint-Jean-de-Moirans express their feelings towards the future that awaits them outside school. We wish them the best of luck!

Saint-Just-en-Chevalet, France L'Art à la Campagne, June 2014. Art and culture in the countryside!

Saint-Lô, France Portraits d'Aujourd'hui, May 2016. Regardless of the diversity in our ways of living, our origins, stories, social status, neighborhoods, we share the idea that culture must be accessible to all and allows us to stand united.

Saint-Marc, Haiti Ayiti Cheri: Empowering Girls Through Education in Haiti, January 2015. We are three teachers, one in Saint-Marc, Haiti, and two in New York City, who are dedicated to the education of young girls in Haiti. We would like to raise awareness of the need to educate girls in Haiti.

Saint-Marcellin, France L'Identité ne se Résume Pas à un Mot, February 2014. Every person is a part of our high school.

Salamanca, Spain Facultad de Educación Universidad de Salamanca, February 2016. "Education is the most powerful weapon you can use to change the world." —Nelson Mandela.

Salt Lake City, UT Trans*Formando Salt Lake City, May 2013. Trans*formando Salt Lake City showcases the vibrant trans-identified community and allies that live in this city. Many outside of Utah and even those living in Utah are not aware of the wonderful trans community here. We used this photo project as a way to create awareness and start the conversation about the needed resources and services, especially for trans individuals of color, and it has meant the strength to "come out" and say, "This is who I am and I am proud of it."

Neighborhood House, September 2012. We promote the understanding of community through voices, expressions, and portraits of community members, while landmarking public art.

We Are One, March 2014. Our school used to be mostly white kids from Utah but it's changed a lot over the years, and today it's filled with students from all over the world including Latino, Pacific Islander, Asian, Native American, African, African-American, European, and a lot of mixed kids.

Washington Elementary Thrives, January 2014. Washington Elementary thrives because of the people who support our children every day in a variety of ways. Our students' success hinges on the efforts of their parents, teachers, and community members, from waking kids up on time for school and creating rich classroom experiences to making sure everyday essentials are provided—such as hot meals, warm coats, and safe places for families to be together. Let this wall of photographs be a daily reminder to have conversations about how we all must engage in helping our children—and ourselves—thrive.

Salvador, Brazil Artistas que Brilham, February 2012. Artists who shine in life because of the reduction of violence.

San Diego, CA Emerging Vision, July 2016. There is no time other than the present to engage youth as storytellers and change-makers within their communities. The mission of Outside the Lens is to empower youth through photography and digital media to create change within themselves, their communities, and the world. Our group action will seek to reflect just that.

Liberty Station: Moving the Inside Out, December 2014. NTC at Liberty Station is a former Naval Training Center in San Diego that has been transformed into an arts and culture district. The artists, dancers, photographers, and painters have joined together to share their stories on the outside of these newly renovated buildings.

Reclaiming Education, July 2013. Reclaiming Education is meant to draw attention to the deficiencies of a UC education and the misplaced priorities of allocating resources by the Californian government. In San Diego, the priority of the military over the educational system is glaringly apparent. As students, we feel the effects of the accumulation of debt for a degree that is becoming increasingly irrelevant in today's economy, as it guarantees nothing. At the same time, we realize our privilege in being able to take out the loans to get this education, as there are many others for whom this is merely a pipe dream. Together our faces represent a rupture, the reality, of the spectacle of education.

San Francisco, CA Be the Voice—The Community Project, March 2015. We want to "be the voice" of the unheard of in our community and put everyone together regardless of their social status. We want to bring together the homeless and sheltered with the rest of us. We want to send a message where we look around and see individual persons and not just people.

Sandwich for a Story, August 2013. Sandwich for a Story is a documentary photography project meant to stimulate dialogue around urban poverty in San Francisco and encourage people to get to know their neighbors.

Inks of Truth, September 2012. The project is called "Inks of Truth" and uses art to bring forth social awareness and provoke critical thinking.

Homeless San Francisco, June 2011. Our aim is for the photos to act as humanizing "advertisements" for the forgotten. Ideally these portraits will give a voice to the voiceless, offering the passersby an opportunity to see the overlooked and oft forgotten in a new and dignifying light.

San Isidro del General, Costa Rica El Camino Hace La Diferencia—The Journey is the Reward, July 2015. The statement refers to the work of the founders of the community of San Andres, a neighborhood in San Isidro, Costa Rica. Forty-five years ago, people began to move here. Back then were no roads, water, electricity, a school, or a church. Additionally, a bridge was needed to connect them to the town center. How did this rural place developed into a vibrant neighborhood of 3,000 habitants?

San Jose, Costa Rica Sonrisas Jóvenes que Hacen, Felices a Corazones Viejos, October 2015. There are many stories captured in the faces of these senior citizens. There is much to learn from them, and this project is about giving our elders the respect they deserve. Many of the senior citizens there have been "abandoned" and have no children or family to live with, which is the tradition in Costa Rica. I wanted to show them that they are not forgotten and that people care about them.

San Marcos, CA The Faces of Budget Cuts, August 2011. There have been budget cuts at all of California's community colleges. We wanted to show the people who are actually being affected by these cuts. This is very diverse group, one that displays a good cross-section of the population. "Who is affected by budget cuts?"

San Rafael, CA Facing the Gap: Educational Equity in Marin County, April 2013. It is the right of all people to have access to a full and dynamic education. In Marin County, one of the most affluent counties in the country, the educational inequities are still stark. Disenfranchised youth are not seen beyond the stereotypes and the geographic barriers that divide them and their communities from educational opportunities that can stop cycles of poverty and injustice.

San Salvador, San Vicente, Chalatenango, El Salvador Mothers and Families of the Disappeared, April 2016. We hope our contribution will help guarantee that this violation of human rights will not be forgotten, nor happen again.

Santa Ana, El Salvador La Violencia Se Puede Vencer, el Arte Es Parte de la Solución, May 2016. We want my people to overcome fear and violence, we can all participate, we can all come together. The fear of expressing ourselves through art is to overcome the social problems of violence in our country.

Santa Cruz, CA Live Oak, July 2011. We live in an unincorporated and underserved part of the county and the kids will be documenting important people in their lives (perhaps themselves!) to display on the side of a huge old granary building on the train tracks.

Libraries Inside Out, August 2011. Turns out libraries have nothing to do with silence.

Santa Fe, NM Come Cry for Me, April 2011. People's tears can represent sadness, madness, or being just plain fed-up; come and express your tears.

We Are One, April 2012. We are one! Our mission is to celebrate diversity one face at a time, so take a deeper look.

Santa Monica, CA Protection, April 2012. The concept is to illustrate the concept of overreaction and clumsy attempts to "protect" young people by withholding information from them, or lying to them, or dulling down the content of their artwork/educational experience.

Santiago, Chile Security Guards, August 2011. I decided to make a tribute to those who work there but whose work is often overlooked and forgotten as a crucial part that allows the rest of the employees to work in peace: the security guards, who control the access to the building.

Santorini, Greece The Local Variable, August 2012. Santorini is a very popular summer destination for tourists but also a very harsh and lonely place to live in the winter. The elderly people of the island especially lead a very rough life because they are cut off from the rest of the country due to limited connections with the mainland. They endure the heavy jobs and the water shortage, and survive in solitude during the long winters without sufficient medical care or leisure activities.

Santurce, Puerto Rico Santurce's Community Leaders, July 2011. These thirty people are the ones making an effort and the difference for the community to survive and not be viewed as a criminal and abandoned area. They are committed and love the community and want it to prosper. Their actions show everyone it is possible to make progress.

São Paulo, Brazil Inside Out Project: Café Europa Holocaust Survivors, April 2014. Holocaust survivors are barely remembered all year long. People pay tribute and remember the millions of Jews that were killed during World War II, but today, they close their eyes to the ones who are still alive and need care and support. This action is going to be held at a symbolic date: The "Yom Hashoá" (Holocaust Day in the Jewish Calendar). Our goal is to show people in São Paulo we still have many Holocaust survivors among us (at least two hundred and fifty), and we want to show their faces to the city.

Haitians In São Paulo: The Broken Dreams, March 2014. After the 2010 earthquake in Haiti, Brazil opened its borders to Haitians, who had to leave families and friends for survival. Many migrated to São Paulo believing in the Eldorado of the financial capital of Brazil. After a difficult and risky trip via Panama, Ecuador, and Peru, they struggled with the harshness of the metropolis: an expensive city to live in, and hard low wage work in the construction business. They gather in Glicerio, where they remain invisible to most of us. Behind each of these eleven portraits, there is a unique story, a dream, an identity, and eleven artists from Brazil created their own interpretation of each portrait photographed.

Inside Out Bom Retiro, January 2014. This Inside Out project draws an anthropological cartography of the Bom Retiro, one of the most cosmopolitan neighborhoods of São Paulo, through actions on various cultural institutions of the area and connecting them for the first time.

We Can and Will Change the World—The Graded School, June 2012. We decided to take portraits of a student from each grade—kindergarten through twelfth grade, thereby showing how "ageless" our concept was—and to paint words on their foreheads that spelled out two different sentences: "We can change the world" and "We will change the world." Each student would have one word written on their face, and when their portaits were posted side by side, the viewer could read the two completed sentences together.

Dharma, October 2012. The main purpose is to give visibility to the Favela do Moinho's community—and to open new fronts of dialogue and action.

New Interactions, August 2012. This action was developed by people who live in the center of São Paulo. Participants were people who pass by and work in the Centro de Convivência É de Lei, an NGO that works to reduce risk and harm related to drug use. We conducted two interventions in town discovering new ways of dealing with other people and the city by simply walking with our posters.

Seattle, WA Flying Kites, October 2011. Flying Kites seeks to raise the standards of care available to the world's poorest children.

Segovia, Spain Disappearing Villages, July 2011. We want to make portraits of children and paste them in small villages in our area, which are disappearing due a lack of population. We're talking about places that have from two to twenty inhabitants, villages that are victims of modernity and that don't have opportunities for anyone anymore.

Selangor, Malaysia We're All Mixed, November 2011. We're a group of people who support interracial marriage. Because, in essence, we're all mixed. And the idea that we're "pure" is something purely fabricated to distinguish one another. At the end of the day, the only thing pure about us is that we're humans. All of us. So let's stop using race as an issue and embrace the basic needs of every human being.

Sélestat, France Vivre Ensemble, March 2016. We want to prevent uncivil behavior and show that the founding principles of living in a community are respect for others and the collective space. We also want to put forward all the different trades in our institution.

Seoul, South Korea Existing with A Seoul, June 2013. Republic of Korea has been a single race country, or a Dan-il minjok guk ga, for thousands of years. However, recently, the number of foreigners and different ethnic groups have been increasing rapidly. We—a group of Koreans, Filipinos, and Americans—want to raise awareness of the foreigners living in Korea. It can get difficult at times to be accepted by a society with an ethnically homogeneous history, but Korea is becoming a melting pot and we want to celebrate that with the world! All of us exist here—with a Seoul!

Education Fever, December 2012. I, as a teacher at an elementary school, wanted to divert their attention from studying major subjects to collaborating on hands-on projects.

Education Fever, July 2012. In Korea, there has been an "education fever" for a long time. This is because education records have been used as the only tool for society to evaluate people. For example, universities select applicants for their grades and the companies in turn select graduates from top-ranking universities. Under this educational system with current methods of assessment, students are forced to focus primarily on high-stake exams such as the SATs. Thus, students are becoming so passive at schools that they do not initiate their own projects or apply their own interests.

Breaking Down Stereotypes, April 2012. I hope to stage a virtual reunification between South and North Koreans and break down the stereotypes of North Koreans.

Sevilla, Spain Decentrados, January 2013. The goal of this action is to "de-centralize" the cities, taking advantage of the cultural offers that normally are centered in downtown, spreading them to other neighborhoods. Rebuilding abandoned places, giving them a new use, making them axes of social and cultural life, injecting dynamism and activities on the hoods.

Sevran, France Les Habitants Font le Mur, April 2016. Decorating the fences that surround the future social center and creating, during the action, a big street art studio.

Siem Reap, Cambodia Dreaming Big Dreams, November 2011. Most Cambodian children are not given the privilege to dream big dreams. My hope with this project was to use a creative medium to show these children how big they can be. For many, it was the first time they'd seen a photo of themselves. By building awareness through organizations like Inside Out, those less fortunate might soon be given opportunities to live their own dreams. In turn, we might learn their amazing perspectives.

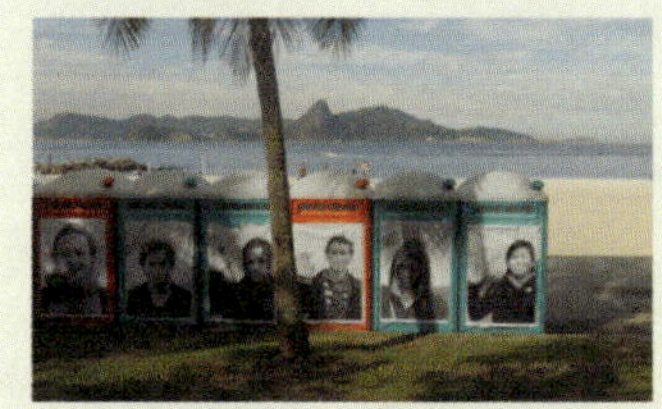
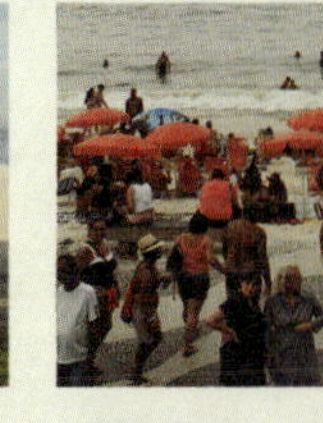
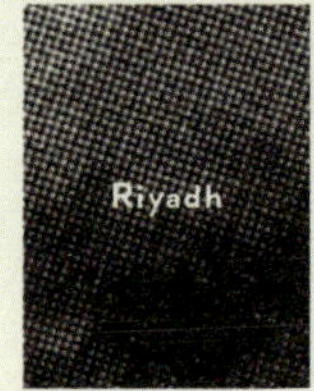

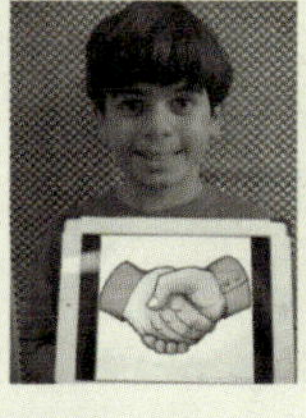
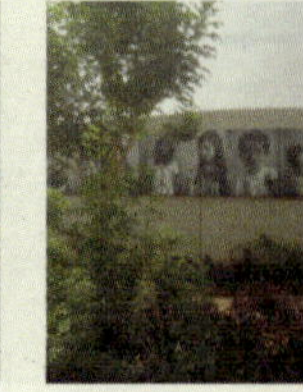
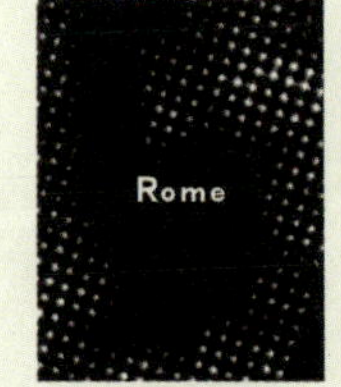

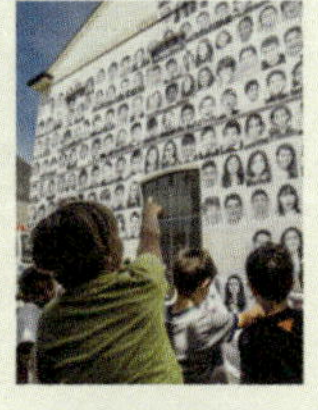
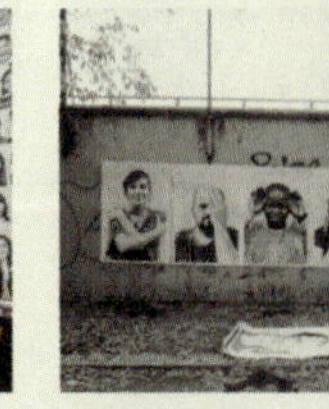
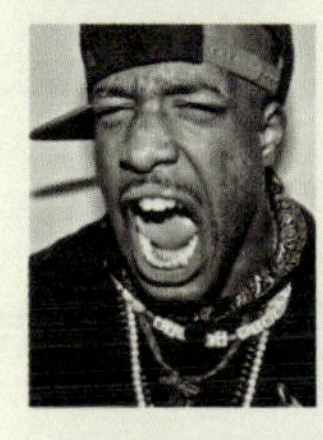
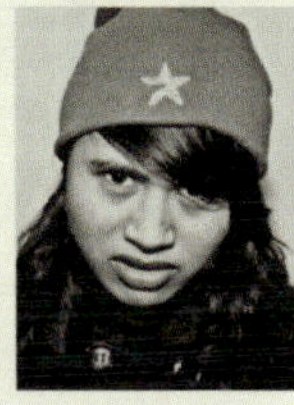
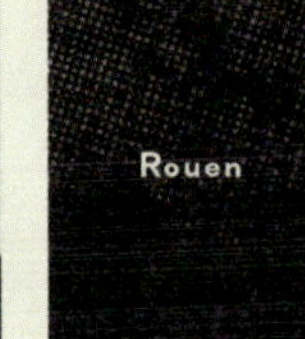

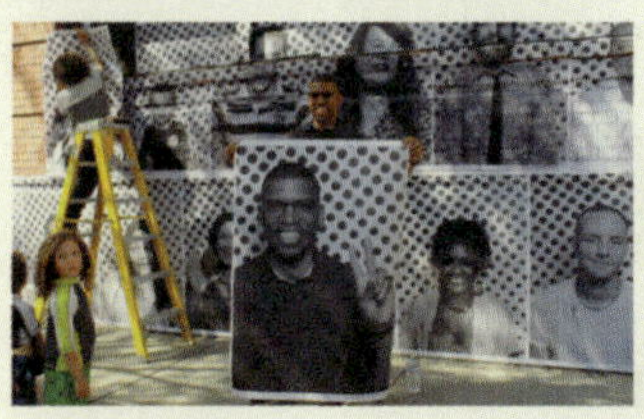
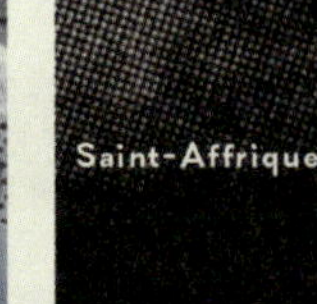

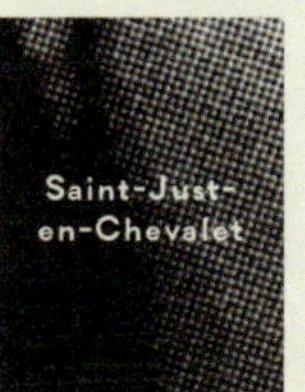

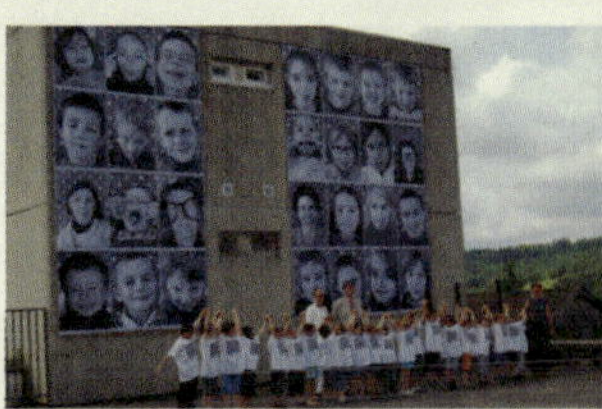
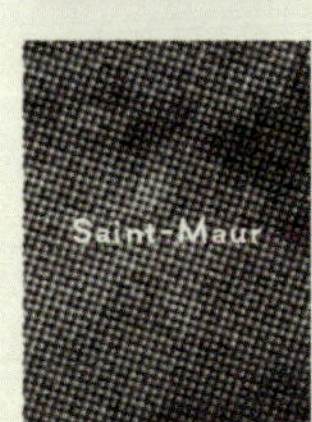

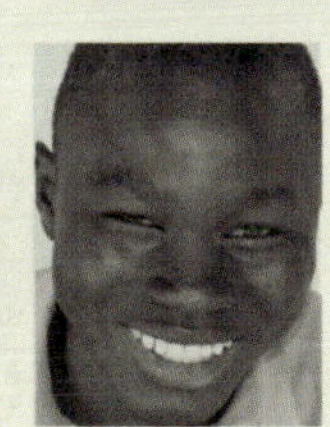
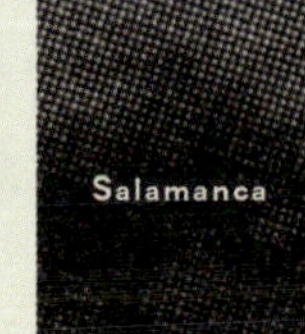

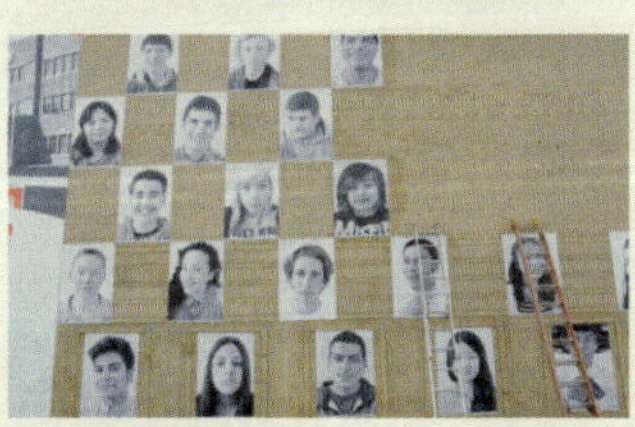
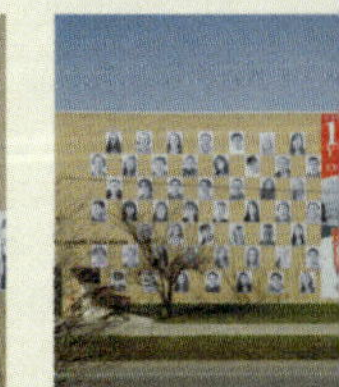
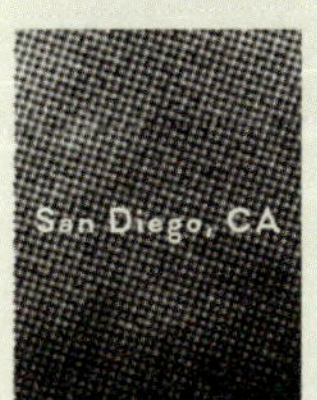

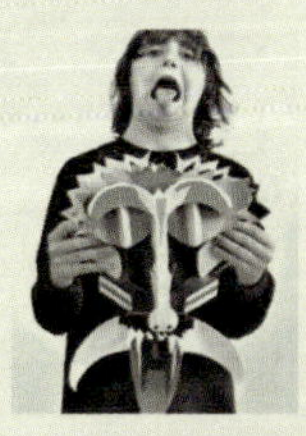
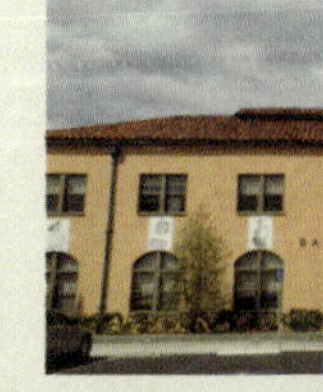
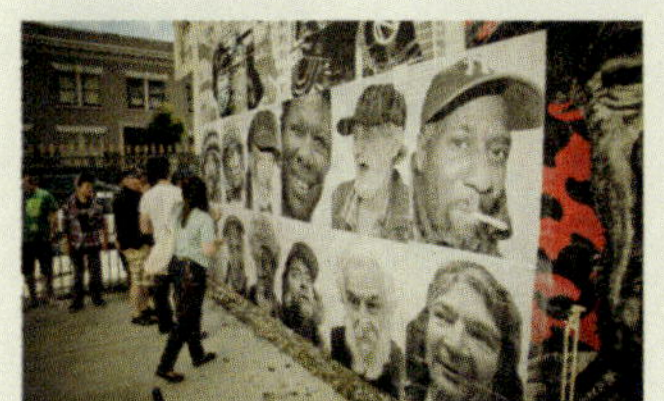
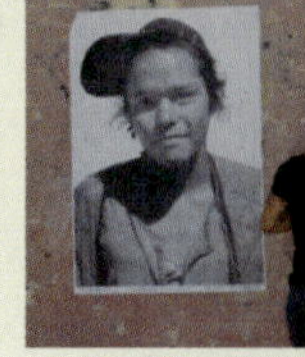

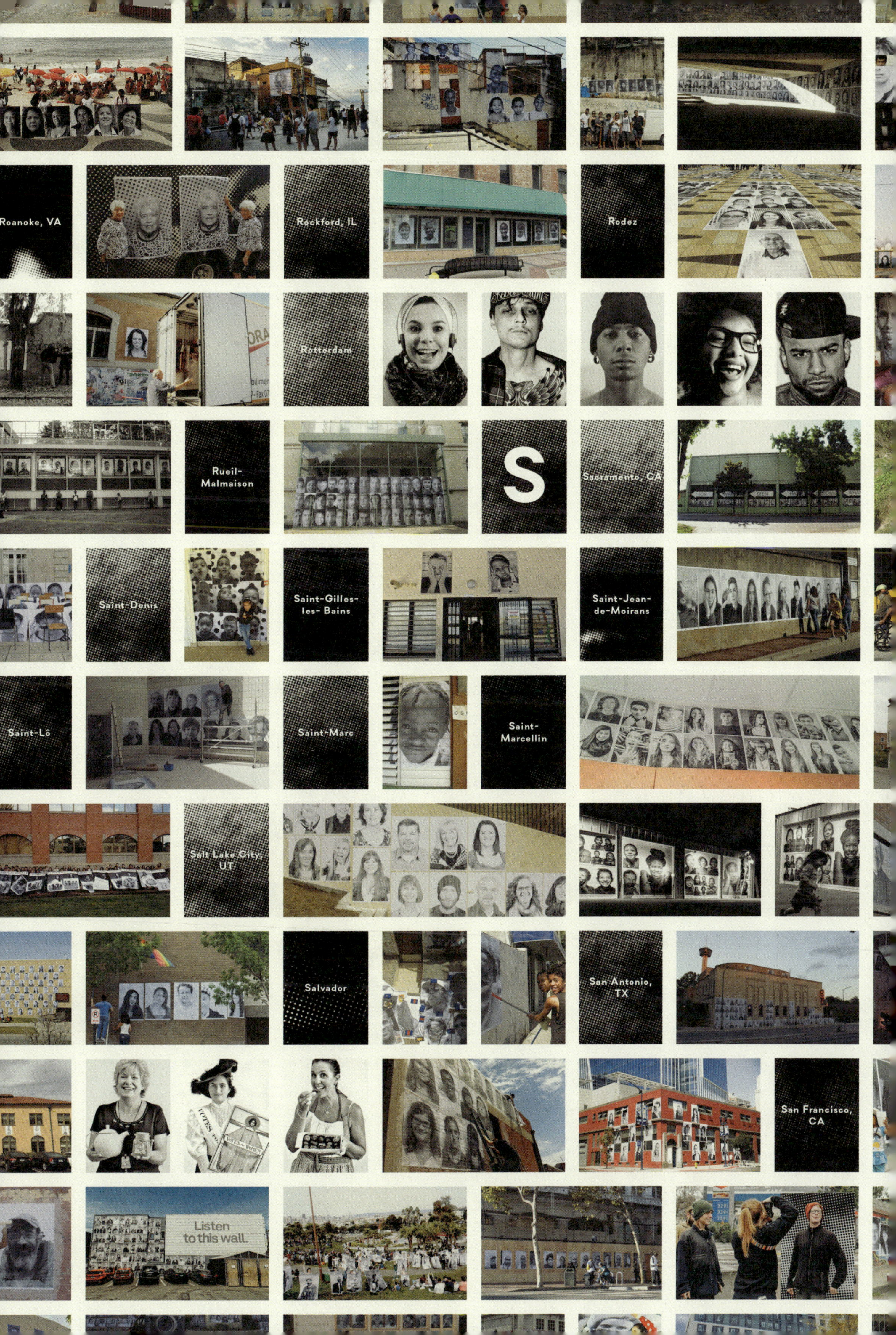

Roanoke, VA
Rockford, IL
Rodez
Rotterdam
Rueil-Malmaison
S
Sacramento, CA
Saint-Denis
Saint-Gilles-les-Bains
Saint-Jean-de-Moirans
Saint-Lô
Saint-Marc
Saint-Marcellin
Salt Lake City, UT
Salvador
San Antonio, TX
San Francisco, CA
Listen to this wall.

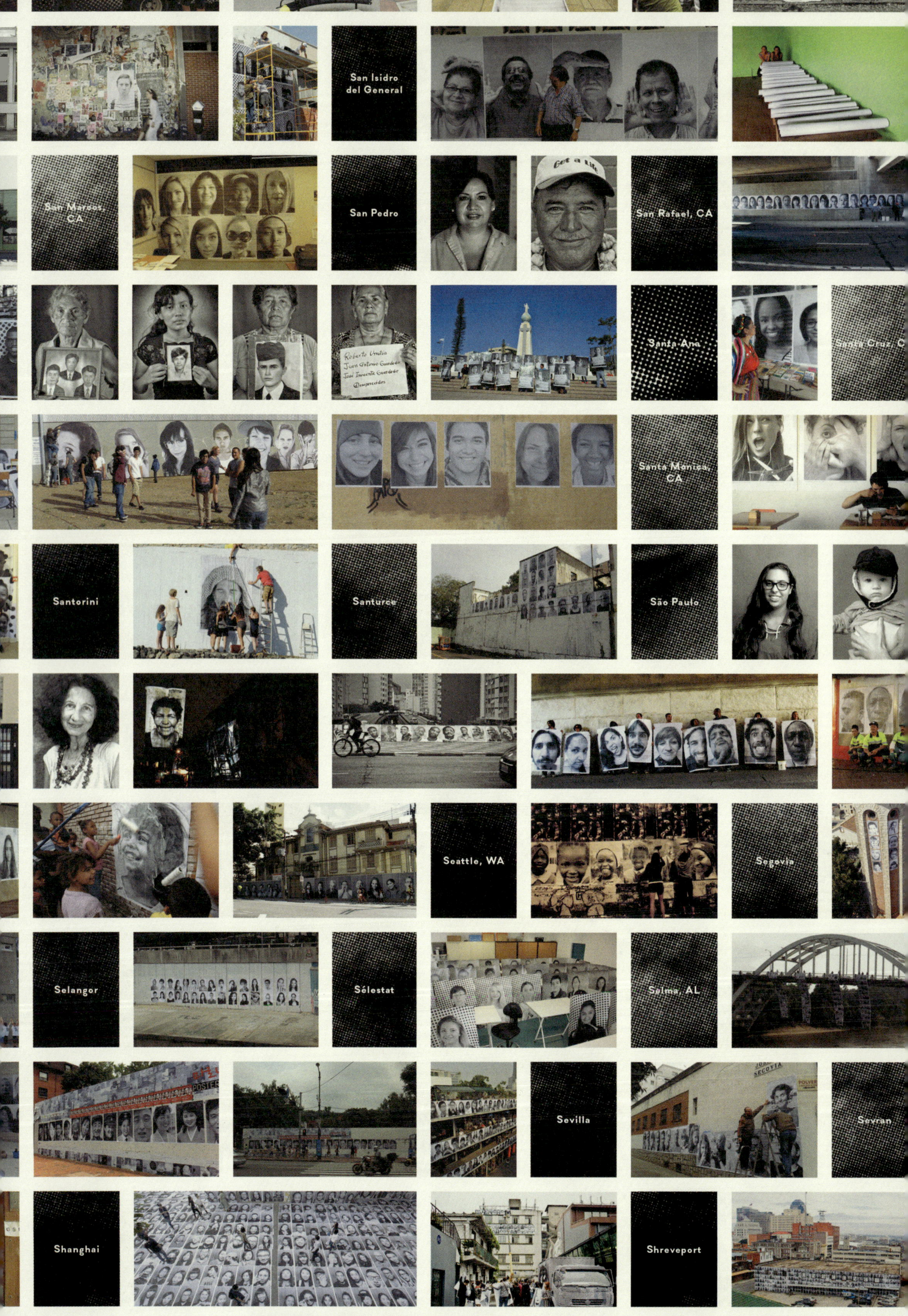
San Isidro del General
San Marcos, CA
San Pedro
San Rafael, CA
Santa Ana
Santa Cruz, C
Santa Monica, CA
Santorini
Santurce
São Paulo
Seattle, WA
Segovia
Selangor
Sélestat
Selma, AL
Sevilla
Sevran
Shanghai
Shreveport

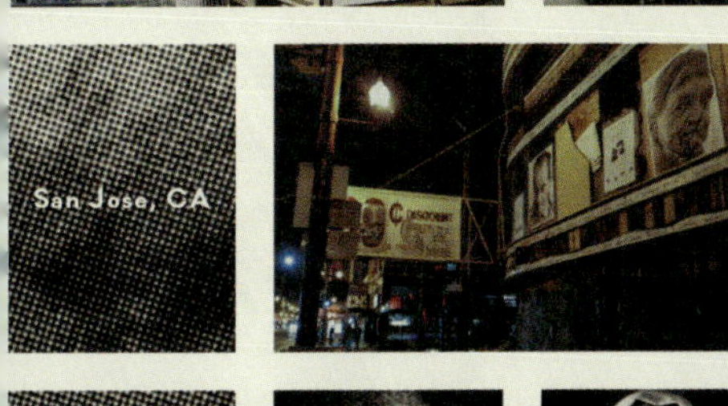

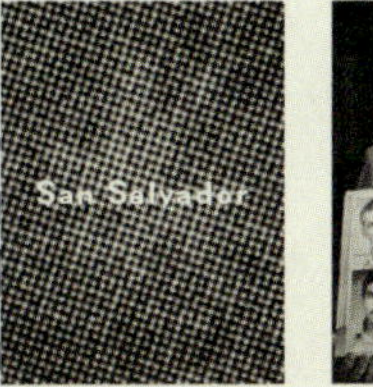

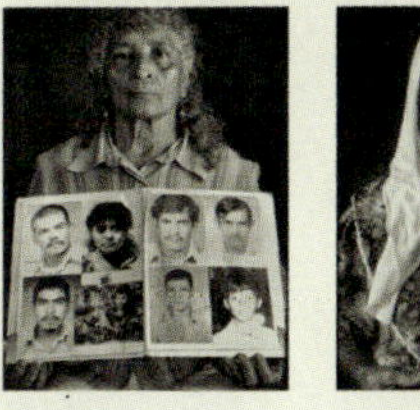
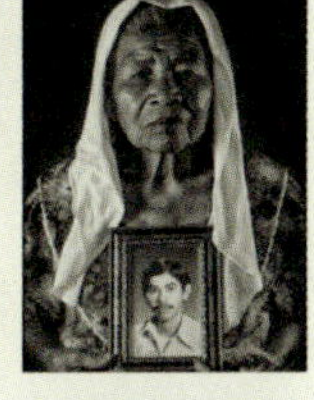
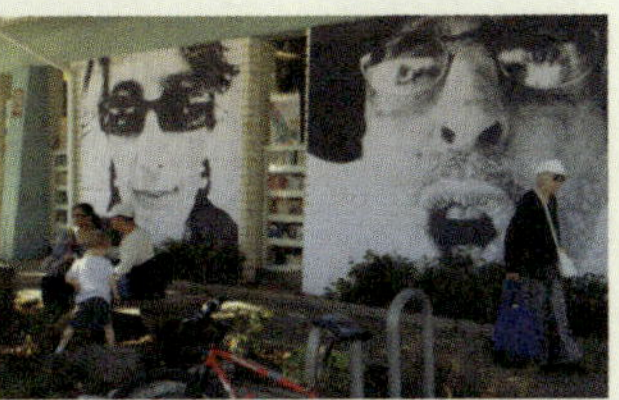
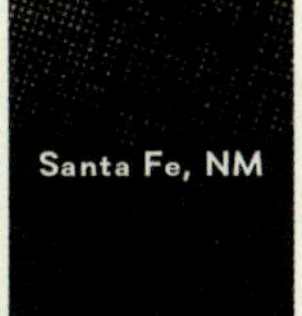

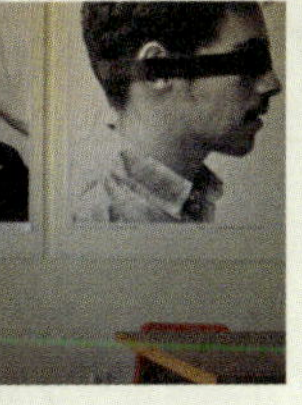
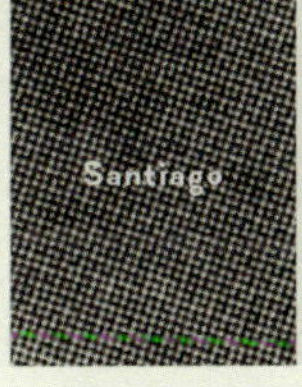

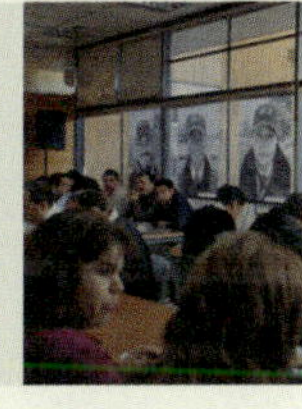
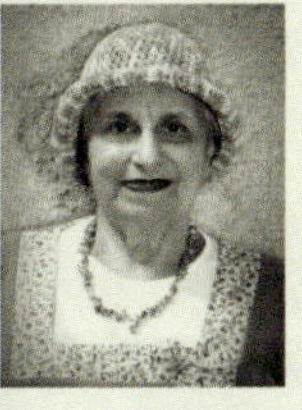
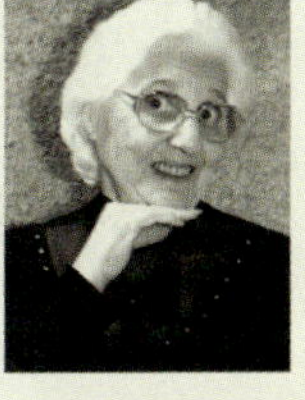
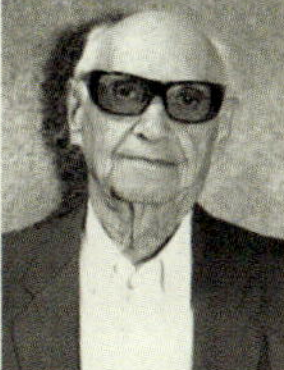
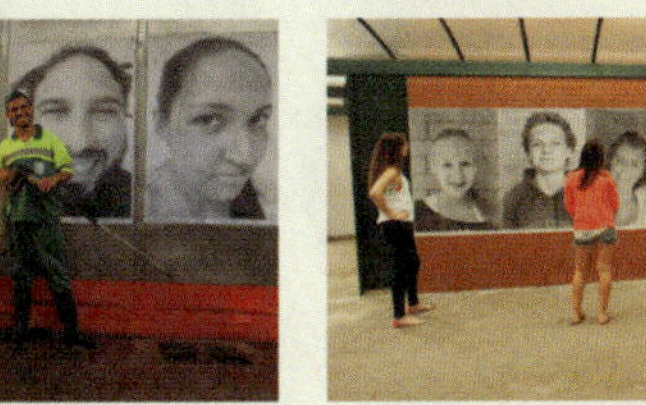
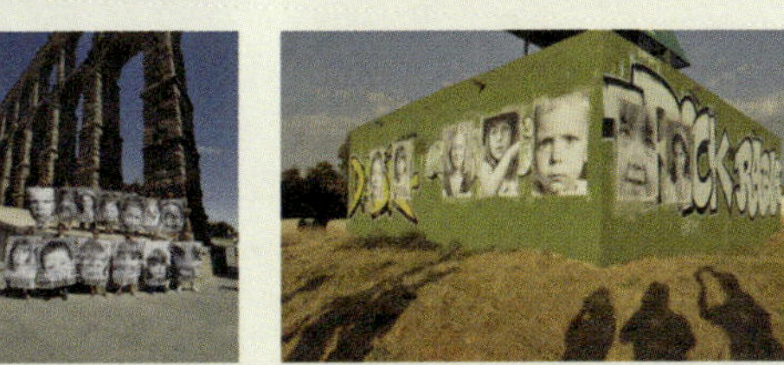
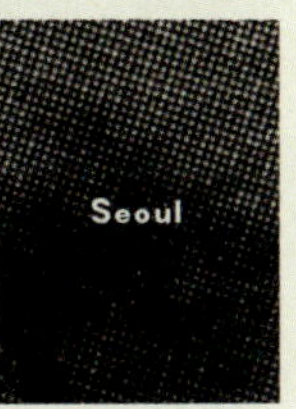

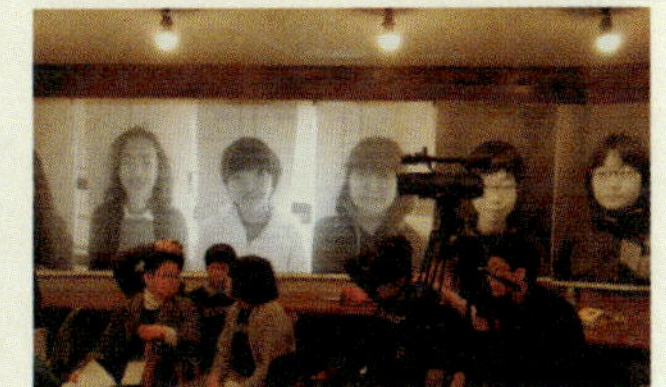
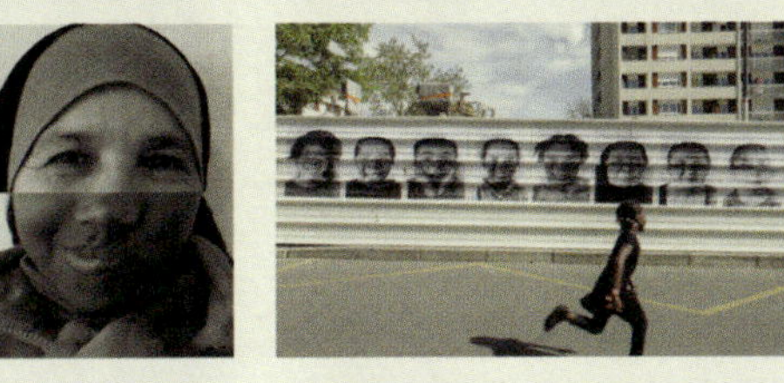
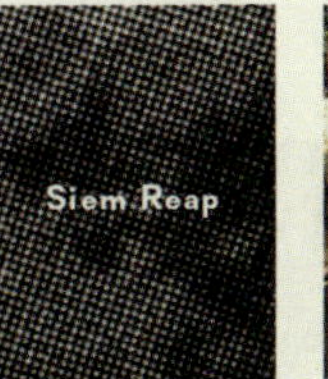

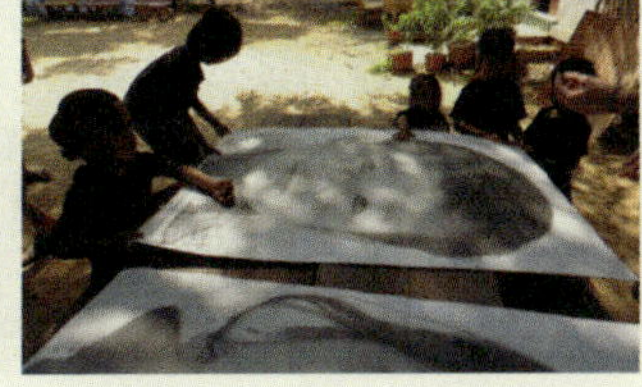

Sindos, Greece Trapped Inside, August 2016. By focusing on male refugees, this project seeks to provoke a change in people's mindsets and aims at supporting a smoother integration by improving their image. Refugee men are trapped inside in two ways: within the Greece's physical boundaries, and within themselves. They are smarting from their inability to fulfill their roles as problem solvers and providers for the family, and they are powerless in actively contributing to change in their situation. Their suffering leaves deep scars.

Singapore, Singapore Our Everyday Heroes, December 2011. "Our Everyday heroes, Inside Out:" We care about everyday women heroes of all ages, who live and inspire us, every day, in every way.

Sitges, Spain Inside Out Sitges, September 2013. The beach is an idyllic meeting point and a cultural melting pot, where we have to preserve respect and tolerance.

Soria, Spain Migrant Women's Rights, March 2013. For the awareness of migrant women's rights to the city.

Southfield, MI Education Matters, June 2011. We believe that educating students involves a strong partnership between the school, the family, and the community.

Southport, CT The Face of Southport, May 2015. Southport High School is one of the most progressive school environments within the state of Indiana. Roughly 15% of our student population are Burmese refugees, alongside South Africans, Iranians, Bulgarians, and South Americans. These are but a few of the nationalities housed within our world-cultured walls; to list them all would simply be too long. The goal of this project is to: raise awareness about our world cultures; highlight the emotion and types of people experienced in a high school environment and show the true beauty of our diversities.

Spartanburg, SC Faces of the Northside, October 2013. Tony Herbas took photos of residents on Spartanburg's Northside, where significant redevelopment efforts are just beginning. The goal of the action is to help residents see themselves as creative individuals, and empower them to be a part of the planning process to bring public art to their neighborhood.

Spokane, WA Madness, April 2014. Our intention is to bring awareness both to the stigma of the mental illness Isamu Som Jordan has and that Isamu is a light of inspiration for all of us. Mental illness can affect all people in varying ways, leaving families and communities divided. We want to demonstrate that anyone can be affected by mental illness; your neighbor, brother, mother, friend, the grocery clerk, or bus driver. We want to open a discourse to the community with this action. We want to express to the public: "It's okay to talk about this; you are not alone!" We hope that by exhibiting various people of different classes, colors, genders, and types, our action creates a new perspective and lead to a new and more hopeful method of approaching the issue.

Springfield, MA Sci-Tech Smiles, July 2014. We want to share the power of positivity. Springfield, MA, is a community laden with violence and poverty. Sci-Tech (The High School of Science in Technology) aims to be a beacon of hope starting with people sharing a smile. Our hope is to create a positive culture at Sci-Tech and to let people know that there are excellent things happening at our school!

Springville, UT Reagan Academy Middle School, May 2014. Don't Hide Your Face! Everyone should be comfortable with who they are and how they look.

St. Andrews, Scotland Glorious Survival, February 2016. Glorious Survival is the act of transcending barriers of all kinds and emerging as better human beings. As the Millennial Generation, we strive to showcase what drives, sustains, and inspires us. We have chosen to mark ourselves with these words as a reminder and celebration of how we survived, and by what ideal we forge a brighter future.

St. Gallen, Switzerland Smile the Future, November 2014. In today's world, many people don't know how to respond or react to a smile because people are too busy or too sad to smile back. People forget how to laugh and to enjoy their environment.

St. Louis, MO St. Louis Janitors, October 2012. We're protesting for our salary. Some of us have to do two or three jobs to survive. We want to become more visible so that we can negotiate.

Faces of St. Louis, September 2012. This project focused on men who are/were experiencing homelessness in order to connect them with each other, with helping staff, and to resources in the community while allowing these men to rediscover their authentic voices.

(en)Visioning Hyde Park, July 2011. North St. Louis students in fifth through eigth grade will be working to improve their Hyde Park neighborhood and document their progress using photography. Students will learn the basics of digital photography, from image capture to editing, printing, and publishing.

United in the Unexpected Fight, April 2014. The beautiful women in these portraits have been diagnosed with breast cancer at a young age. Each one is on her own journey; but together their faces convey the shared meaning of survivorship.

St. Paul, MN Inside Out Lowertown, April 2015. The goal of our project is to reveal both the scope and the diversity of the creative community that has earned Lowertown its reputation as one of the strongest arts districts in the US. Our project bears witness to the fact that an arts district is something more than a place. It is a cultural incubator where a community of culture-makers live, work, instigate, communicate, and create.

Stamford, CT Remembering September 11, September 2011. To remember the people in my community who gave their time and energy to help those in need after the September 11 attacks.

Standing Rock, ND We Still Exist, July 2011. We are the Lakota Tribe. We still exist.

Stirling, Scotland We Are Different But We Are Equal, December 2014. We are different but we are equal. We are students and we share the same ideas. We share the same kitchen but our food is different. We come from different countries but we speak one language. We study, we dream, we love, we care, we smile. "You may say I'm a dreamer, but I'm not the only one. I hope someday you'll join us. And the world will live as one."—John Lennon

Stockholm, Sweden Say It Out Loud, January 2014. Gender-based violence is the world's epidemic and up to 80% of it is linked to alcohol use. We need to stop excusing alcohol-induced violence. We have to start talking about it. Today's culture of alcohol allows violent perpetrators to hide behind the effects of alcohol. In many countries, decreased alcohol use leads to decreased violence against women.

Strasbourg, France Portrait d'une Génération Européenne, May 2014. Through this action, we would like the youth to consider the question of European identity and the power of culture.

Ils Dorment Dehors, June 2013. This is a pasting of portraits of homeless children and young adults in Strasbourg. The pasting site is an international shelter for students. Mischievous, serious, happy, or dubious: Who are they? They all live in Strasbourg, go to school, play, try to live their young lives—a young life that has seen struggle, for they were forced to flee their homes in Chechnya, Kosovo, Armenia, Georgia. These young people finally landed in France where they hope to be protected. Because they stroll around our city, they know it better than most of us do. They have all slept in the street, some of them for months. Through their faces these children tell us they are individuals, and not merely faceless figures to be dealt with. These children are just like any other children in the world: they represent our future.

Stuart, FL Treasures of the Treasure Coast, June 2014. We have chosen to celebrate the uniqueness of many great individuals in our community. We are also matching each honoree with another of similar characteristics.

Stuttgart, Germany Spatial Art Conversation, July 2014. Talking about the lived experience of the migrant worker by giving him a human face, our aim is to highlight the importance of migrant workers in a contemporary society. Western Europe's continued dependence on millions of migrant workers, especially during the worst economic crisis since the Second World War, shows that the economic system can no longer exist without their labor.

Sutton, MA Sutton Central School, May 2015. I have twelve fourth-grade students and twelve senior citizens who we would like to use in our group action to promote the idea that we are a community that is welcoming to everyone.

Suwon, South Korea Am I Ok?, October 2016. Why Don't You Shout. Through the question, we want to ask you these things: What makes you not shout? What makes you hesitate to do what you love and say who you are? And now, how about shouting something inside of you?

Sydney, Australia Diversity, Acceptance, Sharing, June 2011. Our concept statement is: Diversity, Acceptance, Sharing.

Tahiti, French Polynesia Pacific Storytellers, April 2016. A'ATA*—Smile for Peace. Joy of living and generosity are defining Polynesian values. Our action is driven by the belief that they should always be remembered and embodied by each one of us, especially, during times of increasing violence in our community. We are joy of living. We are generosity. We are Polynesian. *A'ATA means "to laugh" in Tahitian.

Tainan, Taiwan Inspiring Taiwan, December 2013. Please allow the Taiwanese to be seen. We have kept indigenous Confucius culture and manners rooted deeply in our souls. Please allow our shining personalities and characteristics inspire and bring to the world a positive outlook on life.

Taipei, Taiwan Taiwan, Keep it Up!, September 2012. We believe Taiwan can be better. We ended up creating one hundred twenty posters to form four Chinese characters on the embankments. The meaning of the characters translates as "Taiwan, keep it up!" It is a message of optimisn in the face of the troubling politics and the economy concerns we all face.

Tairawhiti, New Zealand A Shared Passion for Creativity, November 2012. We are the young and elderly, emerging and established, Maori and Pakeha, and we are all side by side to recognize and celebrate our shared passion for creativity. For each of us, our art is an expression of who we are and what we believe in.

Tamarindo, Costa Rica Camera Smiles, June 2012. Creating smiles on both sides of the camera.

Tampiquito, San Pedro Garza Garcia, Mexico Neighborhoods of Tampiquito, May 2012. Neighborhoods are the people; things can change neighbor by neighbor, street by street.

Tartu, Estonia The Great Culture Hidden Within Small Nations, July 2015. In today's world, one might not notice the great ethnic heritage that all individuals of small nations carry within themselves. An extraordinary language joined by a rich tradition-filled culture is a combination that renders each ethnicity truly unique. Sadly, it is something that is suppressed rather easily by the enemy's occupation. With this project, we wish to show the rich cultural heritage that lies within the ancient ethnicities of Estonia, Latvia, and Lithuania. Each girl represents one Baltic country and symbolizes the force of youth and the affection our community has for our nation.

Tartu as a Broad-Minded Community for Everyone, June 2015. Our idea was to draw attention to minorities and different subcultures, to the different people in Tartu. There are some emotional issues regarding minorities in Estonia, and the idea is to bring forth photos of ordinary people from different social and subcultural groups from Tartu. Intolerance is something we won't tolerate, and Tartu is a welcoming town for each individual.

Tashkent, Uzbekistan The Many Ethnicities in our Blood, January 2013. We want to show the young people of Uzbekistan: modern, open-minded, talented, ambitious, and so different. They are from Tashkent, most of them have many ethnicities in their blood, some were born in other places, many of them are trying to find their destiny in different countries now. We're for a world without borders, for living without prejudice, for different nations, cultures, and religions existing together in peace and with respect to each other.

Tbilisi, Georgia Think Globally, Buy Locally, September 2016. We want to celebrate the production of Georgia. Feel our entrepreneurial spirit and accelerate our country's development.

No to Forced Displacement of Community from Place of Origin, September 2014. Our action aimed to stand for the Khaishi community by: raising awareness of citizens of Georgia; and developing, expanding, and strengthening movement against a gigantic dam. These are portraits of inhabitants of the Khaishi community who are struggling to protect their rights to live in a place where they were born and are developing their community, and preserving their identity.

Eyes Wide Shut, March 2014. Don't shut your eyes! Six years have passed since the last Russian intervention. Thousands of IDPs had to settle in temporary places of living; people still suffer at the occupation line. By drawing attention to the cause, we encourage civil society to start thinking about the ongoing problem and to seek solutions to the occupation struggle.

Tegucigalpa, Honduras Tenemos Dignidad (We Have Dignity), August 2013. We live in what is considered one of the most dangerous cities in the world. However, we believe in positive change. We know that we can use our creativity to spread joy to others despite any difficulties we may encounter. It is possible to see the good side of things even though the majority of people do not see them.

Tehran, Iran Resistance, May 2011. For the inalienable human right to spiritual freedom.

Terwagne, Belgium Next to You, July 2016. We hope to create a bridge between refugees and citizens in Namur and share the positive spirit of these refugees so clearly visible in their portraits. Free your humanity!

The Hague, The Netherlands Escamp Inside Out, October 2014. The people of Escamp and their strength are a central focus point in this project. Platform57 strives to bring people and cultures together through presenting, maintaining, and managing visual arts in the district Escamp of the city The Hague.

Thaba Tseka, Lesotho No, I Mean It, January 2017. Lesotho has progressed to the second highest prevalence rate of HIV in the world and one out of four people knowingly or unknowingly have HIV/AIDS, however, everyone is affected by it. The ability to say no is a right we all have 1) Clear language . . . don't say no to sex when you really mean yes, MEAN IT 2) Strong body language . . . use a serious I MEAN IT face 3) Walk away!

Thessaloniki, Greece Portrait of Greece, July 2013. Crisis is not only about Greece or Greeks; it is about every country and each individual.

The Struggle is Real, 2017. We want the world to see refugees as regular people, to view them as individuals fighting for a better life, and we want to be their advocate for social change and ignite political action.

Tilburg, The Netherlands Incubate, October 2012. From joyous young mothers to grandmothers full of wisdom and experience, these women have made a significant contribution to Tilburg, and we think that all mothers deserve this level of attention; to show them in all their beauty and diversity.

Tokyo, Japan Rebuilding, October 2011. The portraits of volunteers across a wide variety of causes that help rebuild Japan—earthquake relief; food banks; domestic violence victim helpers; free ambassadors for visitors etc. Volunteers of all kinds are our local heroes.

Torcy, France Identity Belvedere, November 2014. This action is one part of a dual creative project to federate the people of Belvedere—a multicultural neighborhood in Paris's suburbs. The combination of the two projects will give an identity to the Belvedere people and convey a positive image for our community. Residents can get involved and be proud of doing so.

Toronto, Canada Sweet Salone, February 2016. I want to share with the world the beauty in black culture; it is often displayed in a negative light in the media and there is a large misconception that Africa is a strife-ridden continent when in fact Africa has so many wonderful, magical aspects to it.

Missing & Murdered, August 2015. Canadian artists draw resources to more than one thousand unsolved murders of indigenous women.

Peace of Mind, September 2015. We all have experienced some dark times in life; perhaps this dark thing—so-called Life—isn't all about choices. After all, who knows what is next, and maybe that is what makes the struggle beautiful. It's time to make peace within ourselves and stop lingering in the past. Let's make peace with the inner soul and reflect it, inside out, to our struggles. Let's face Life with a peaceful mind.

Mabin Smiles, May 2011. The fifth and sixth grades took pictures of every other smiling student and the teachers in the school. When we took these pictures, we asked the students to express peace and happiness through their picture. We want the project to have an impact on the community and everybody who passes by it. We believe that smiles can change the world.

Victoria College Students, August 2012. We are the students of Victoria College at the University of Toronto, celebrating the diversity of our stories.

Manifesto, September 2011. We are Toronto.

Toulon, France Toulon Believes in Education, June 2012. To demonstrate our belief in education, and our commitment against discrimination and for equal opportunities.

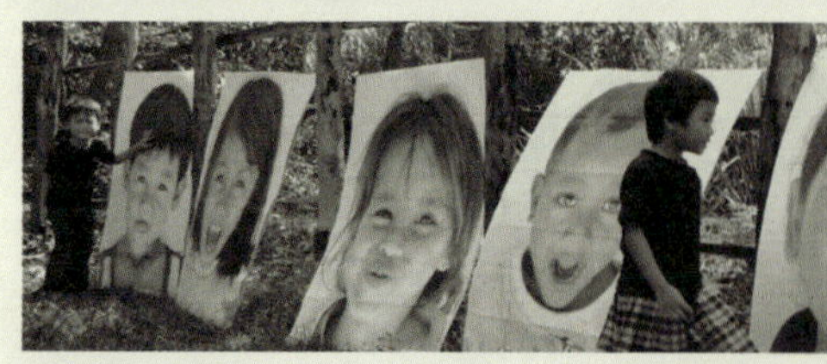

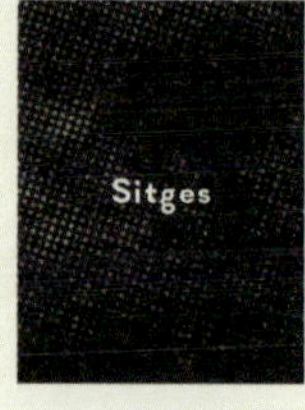

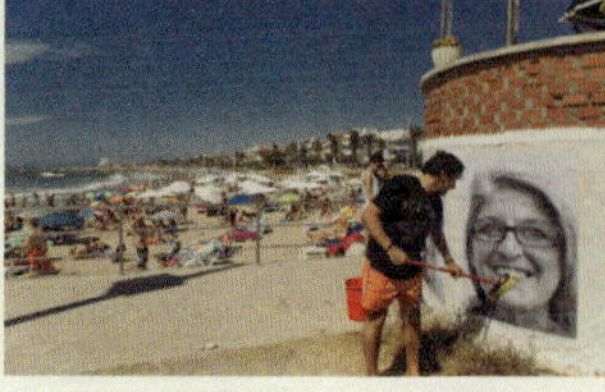

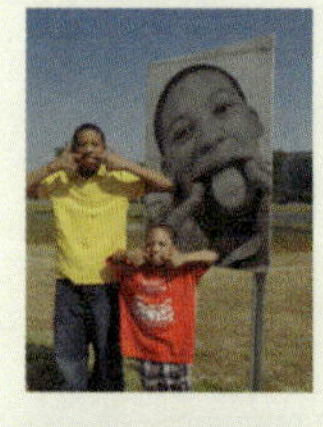

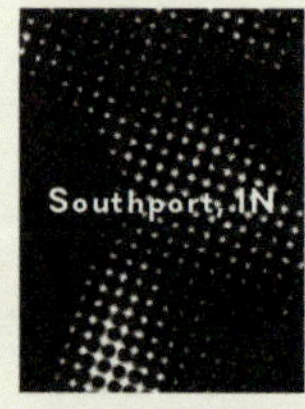

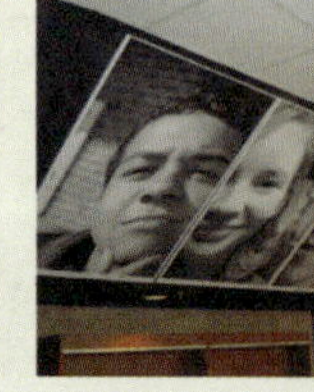

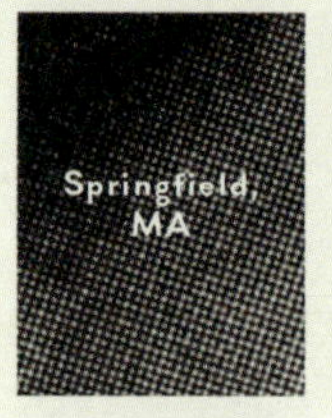

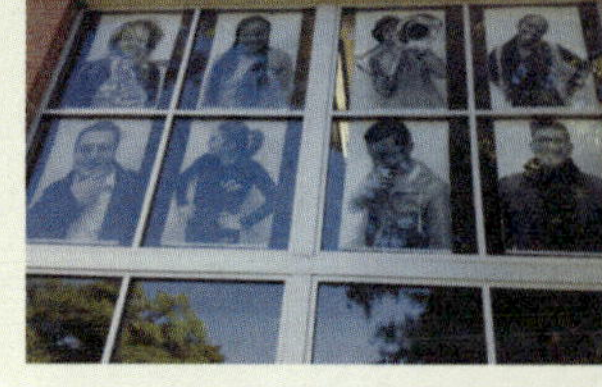

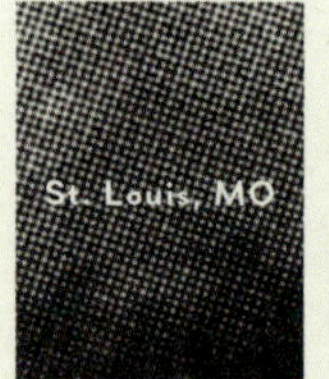

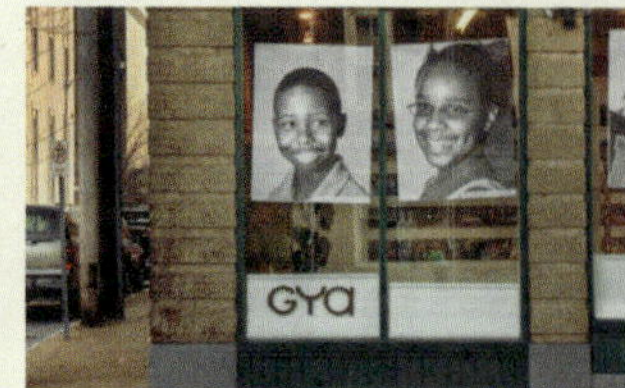

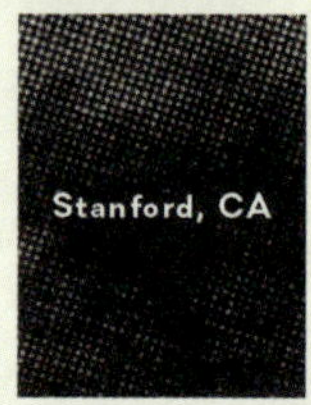

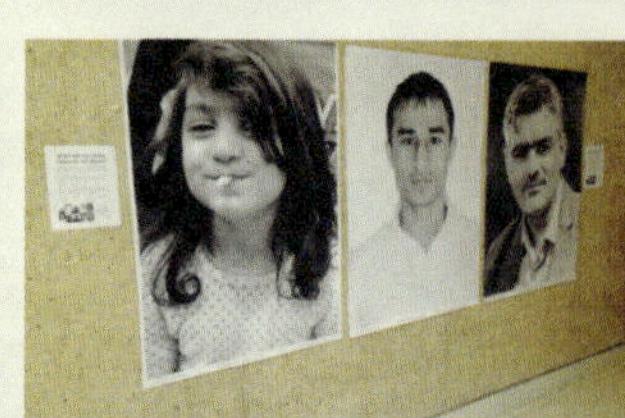

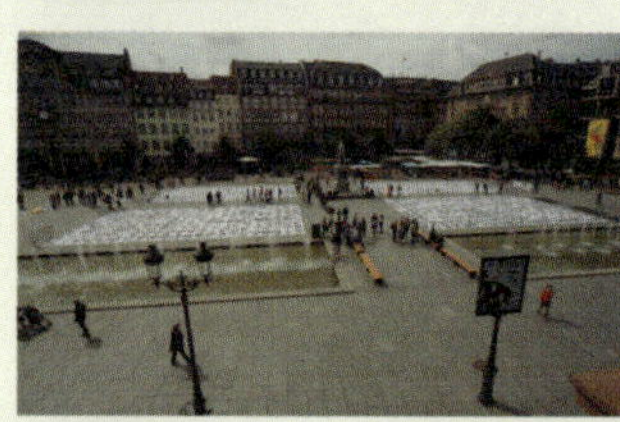

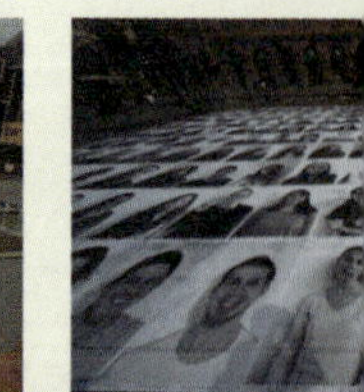

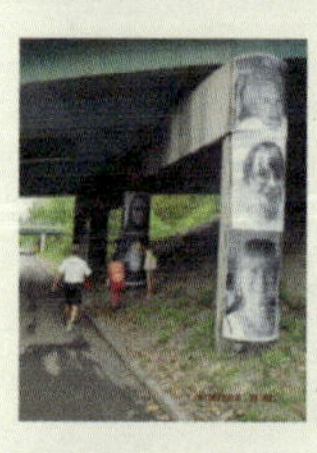

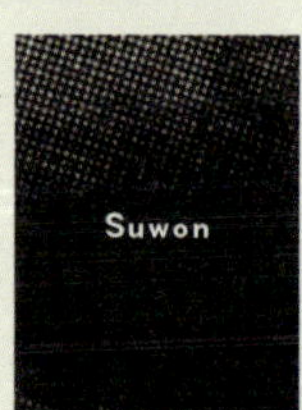

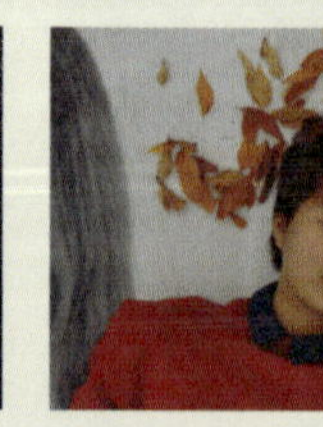

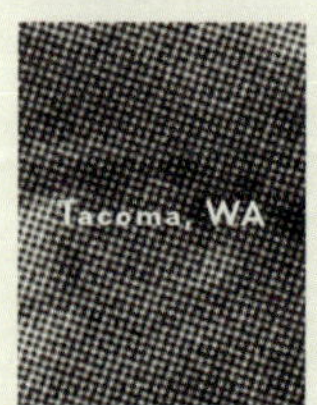

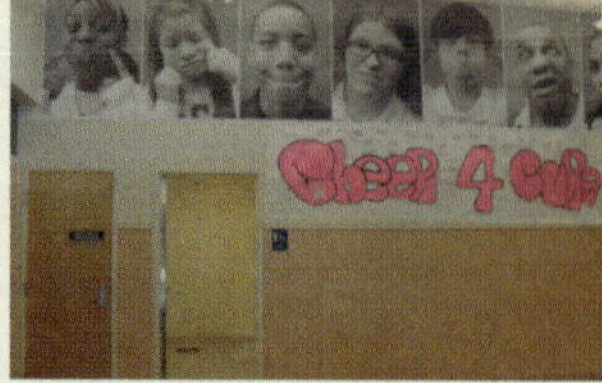

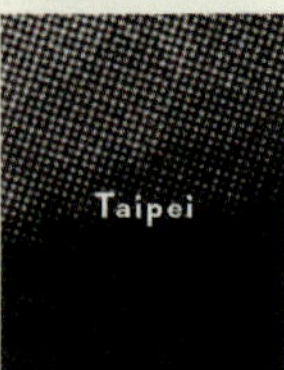

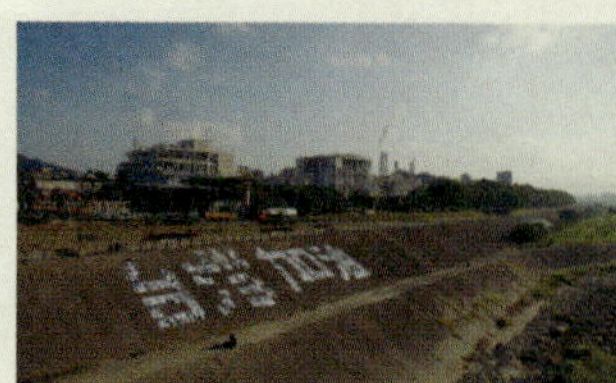

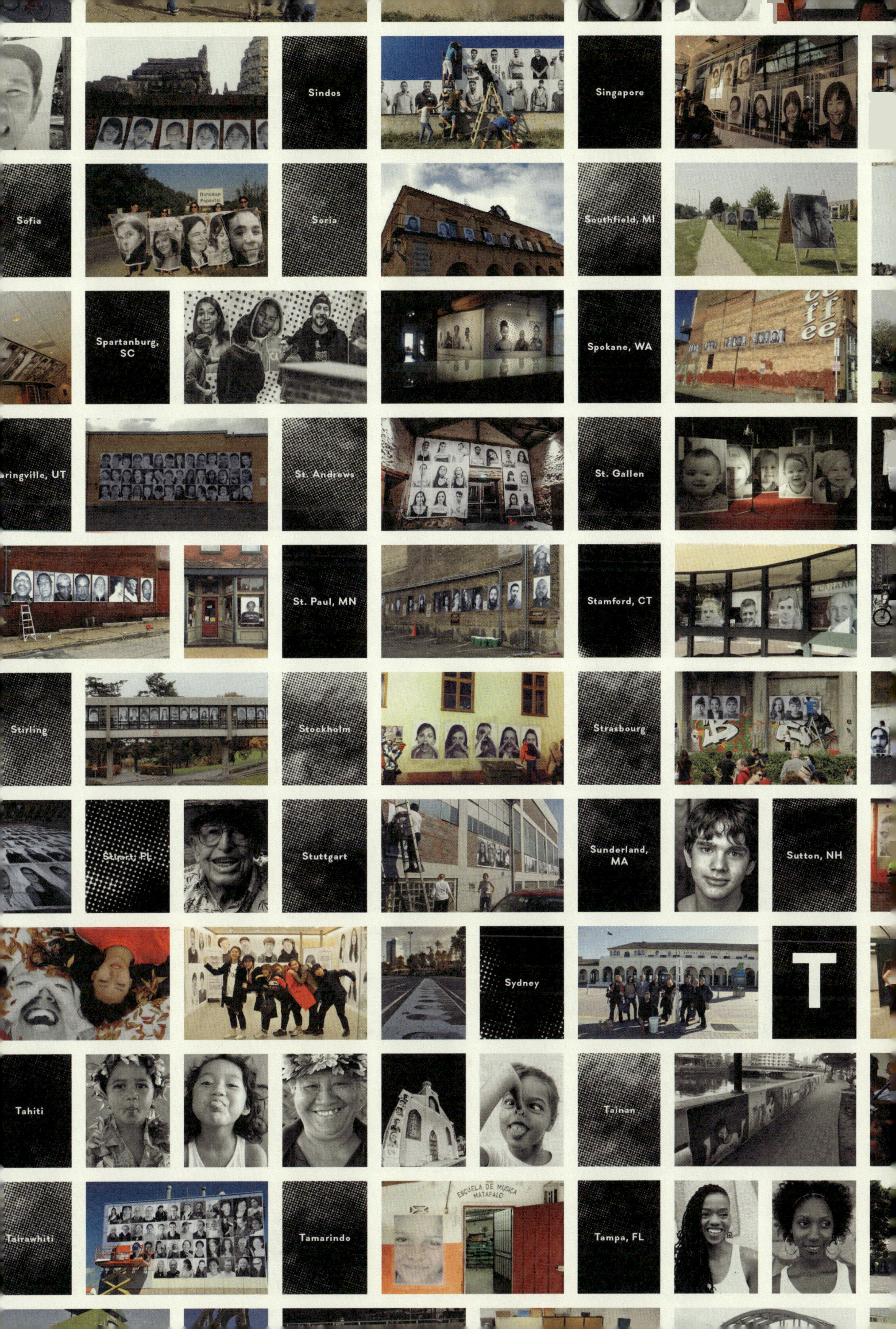
Sindos
Singapore
Sofia
Soria
Southfield, MI
Spartanburg, SC
Spokane, WA
ringville, UT
St. Andrews
St. Gallen
St. Paul, MN
Stamford, CT
Stirling
Stockholm
Strasbourg
Stuart, FL
Stuttgart
Sunderland, MA
Sutton, NH
Sydney
T
Tahiti
Tainan
Tairawhiti
Tamarindo
Tampa, FL

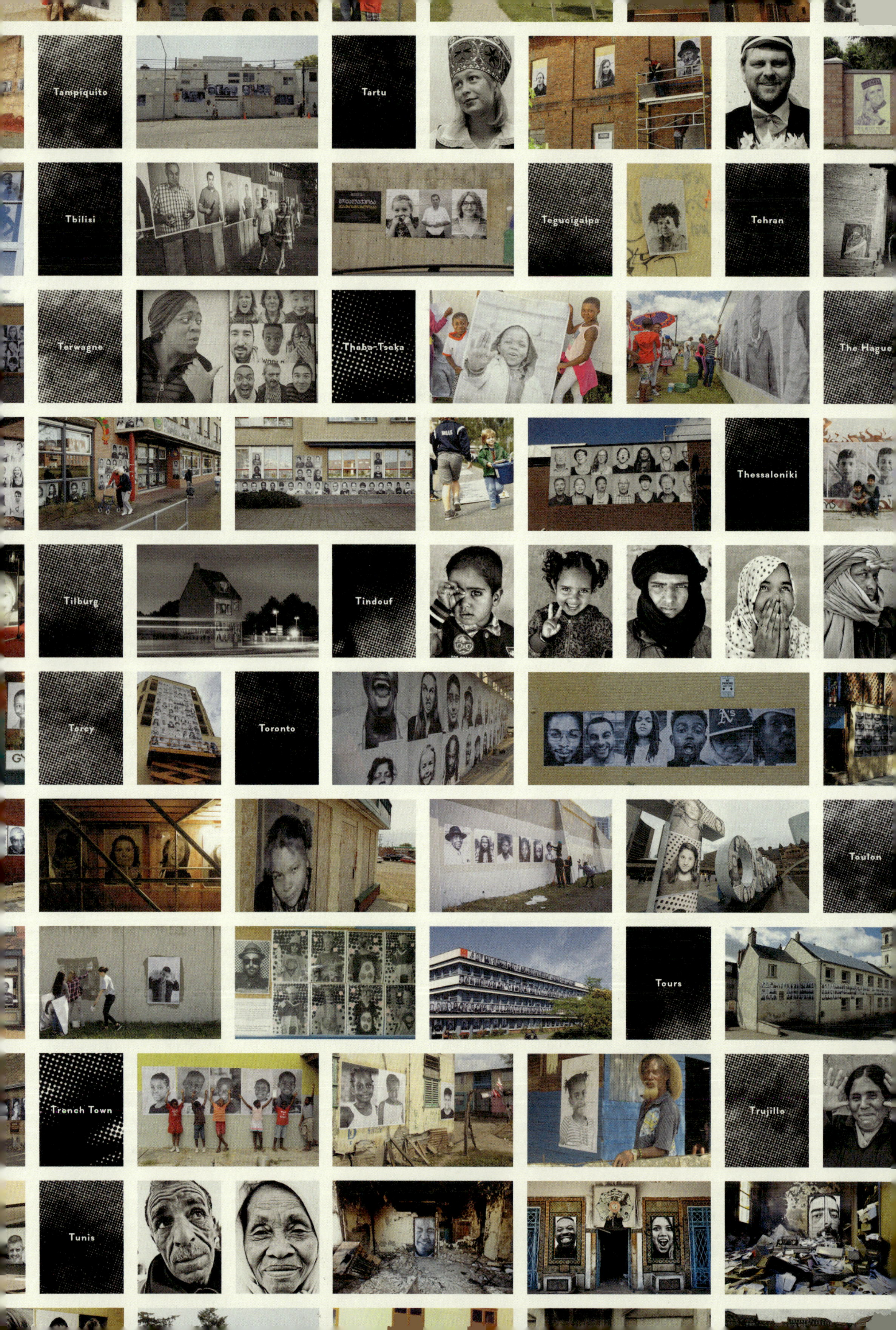
Tampiquito
Tartu
Tbilisi
Tegucigalpa
Tehran
Terwagne
Thaba-Tseka
The Hague
Thessaloniki
Tilburg
Tindouf
Torcy
Toronto
Toulon
Tours
Trench Town
Trujillo
Tunis

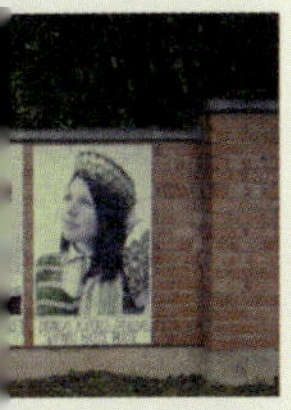
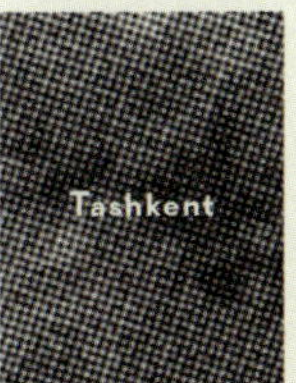

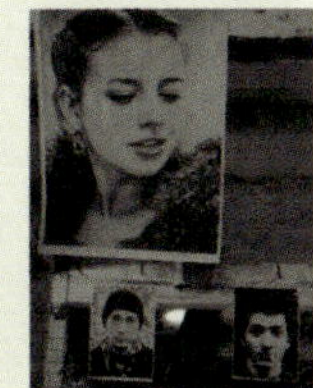
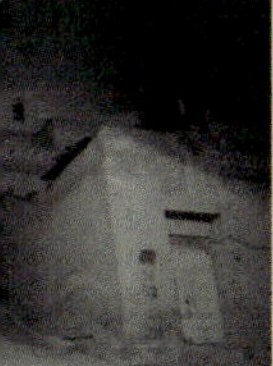
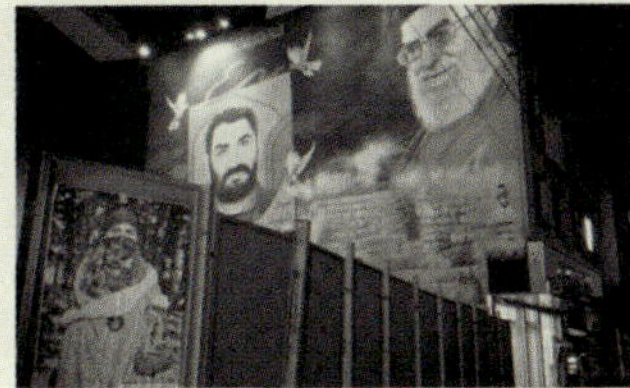
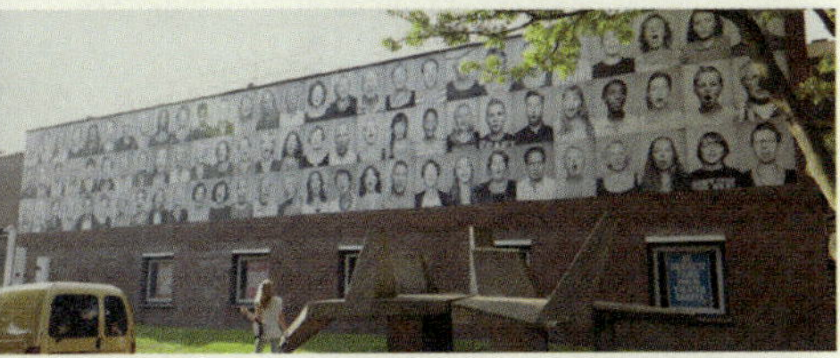
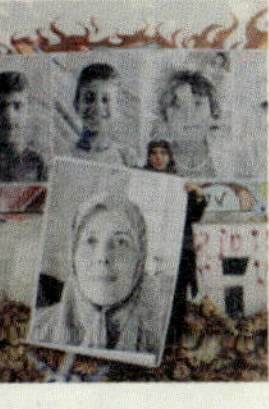
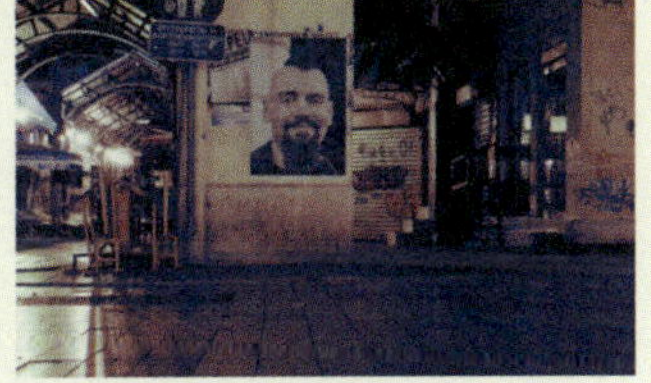
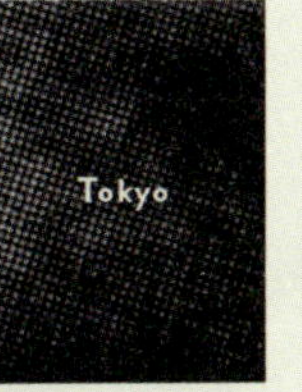
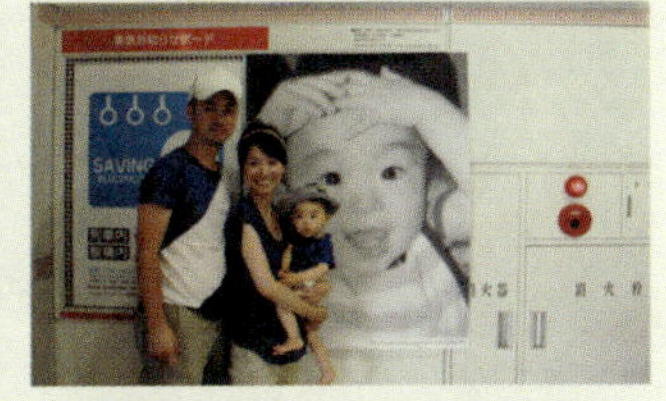
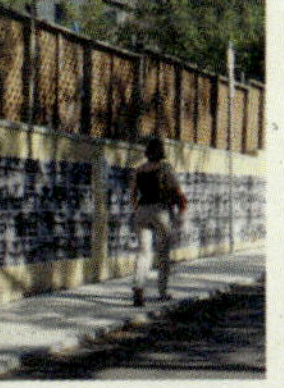

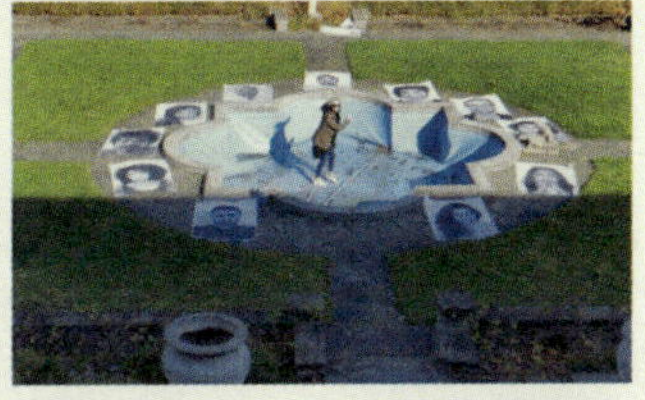
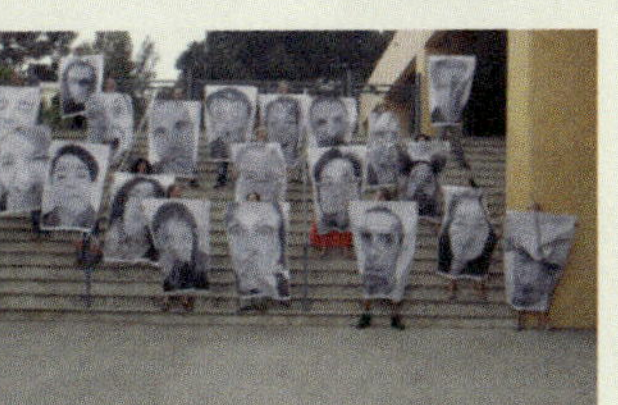
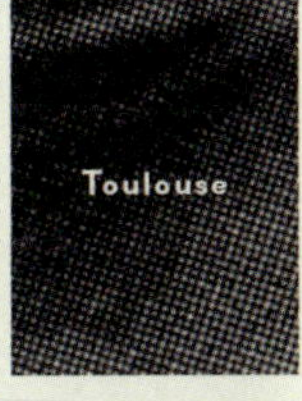

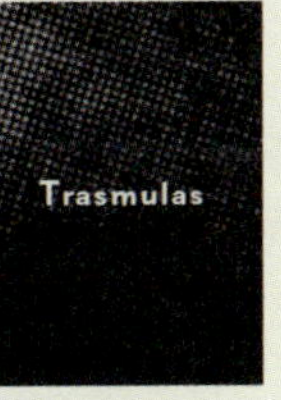

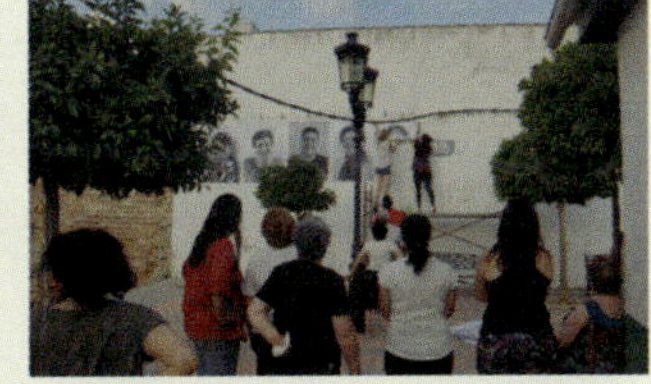
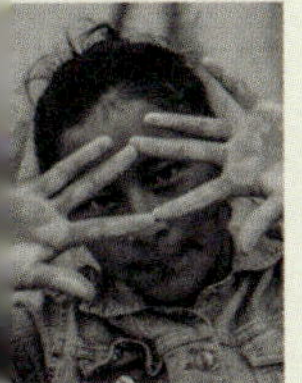
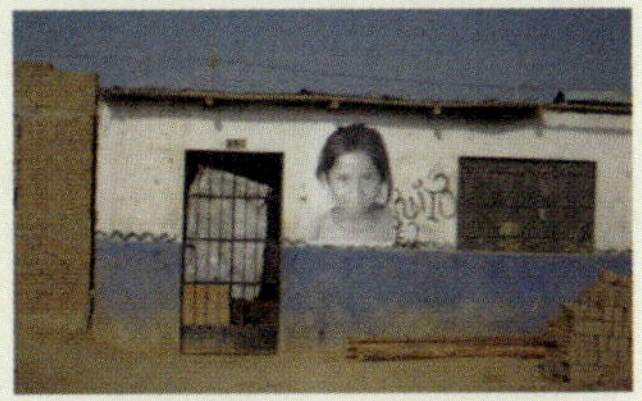
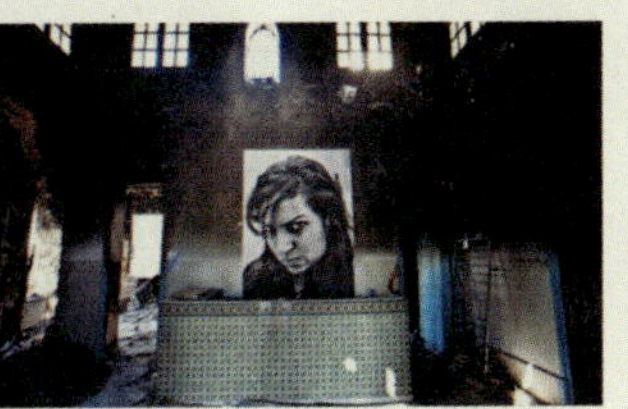
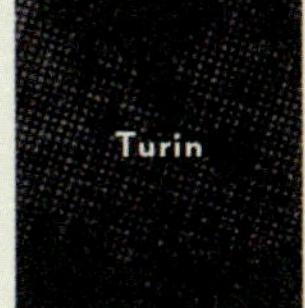

Toulouse, France La Diversité c'est Cool!!!, June 2016. To express the simple but powerful message that we are all very different but still close to one another.

Divers-Cités, May 2016. We want to show that our community is multicultural, united, and open to others and change the way our neighborhood is perceived.

Inside Out La Terrasse, June 2014. We hope that this project will help abolish the barriers between generations in our community and overcome the preconceptions attached to each of them. We hope to make people realize that they have more in common than they think. We believe that old and young can learn from each other and should consider each other as a source of wealth.

Tours, France Inside Out Sainte Ursule, March 2014. Sainte Ursule school's project signals self-acceptance and group community. Links between different portraits represent the existence of small groups inside the larger group of participants and their overarching friendship.

Trasmulas, Spain Trasmulas: Un Pueblo Pequeño, Una Gran Familia, June 2015. In an increasingly urbanized world, living in the countryside seems to be more beautiful than ever. Through this exhibition, we want to show the wealth that is hidden in the small towns that we never see.

Trujillo, Peru Mirades de el Porvenir, October 2013. Our action attempts to begin a process of opening, of breaking down stereotypes. By looking into the community of El Porvenir through our camera lens, and therefore providing a platform for community members to look back at the viewers, the people of Trujillo, we can begin to create a new reality of "the Other" and therefore challenge the negative perceptions of El Porvenir that effectively marginalize its families, its mothers, and its children.

The Skateistan Project, December 2012. We want to show the world Cerrito and its unique skate project and all the potential it has! We believe skateboarding can change situations and our big example is the Skateistan project!

Tunis, Tunisia Inside Out Tunisia, March 2011. These people represent the different faces of Tunisian society, people who agree to live with mutual respect for others.

Ulm, Germany Inside Out Project—Action Group ULM, March 2014. We want to connect art with the people, people with art, people with people. We want to build a platform for exchange, for sharing ideas, ways of expression. Art should not be an elitist religion, but a daily exercise.

Pakistan Not a Bug Splat, April 2014. Since 2004, drone strikes in Pakistan have killed an estimated 3,000+ people. While some of these were high-profile targets, a large number were civilians, including one hundred sixty children. The people who operate the drones describe their casualties as "bug splats," since viewing the body through a grainy-green video image gives the sense of an insect being crushed.

Upper Marlboro,MA Faces of Fairhaven School at Fifteen, November 2013. Fairhaven School is celebrating its fifteenth anniversary. Every summer, our students, ages four to nineteen, count the days to come back to school instead of counting the days until school lets out!

Valencia, Spain El Clot—Lives from the Hole, April 2015. I'm interested in giving visibility to the injustices I see in my surroundings, and telling their stories through images. I work with real people and their real situations, trying to understand them to develop relationships with my subjects over time.

Stop. We Are Here, May 2015. Stop. We are here.

Valparaiso, Chile Stop to Look, November 2012. Creating a community project allows us to enter the depths of people's identities, their homes. We understand that there is a need to be seen and say "this is who I am."

Vancouver, WA Kindness Matters SHS!, May 2016. The project's aim is to expose students, who, through their personal convictions and contributions to the culture of Skyview High School, is consistent with the district mission and vision in that it will foster a sense of compassion and responsibility toward the community of Skyview.

Skyview Inside Out, May 2015. This project aims to reclaim the positivity in the Skyview High School community as part of our public identity. Through this project, we intend to unify the student body, faculty, and members of the community by recognizing and celebrating students who are leaders in the academics, arts, and athletics.

Vancouver, BC Inside Out: Stories of Identity Project, March 2013. Angela has reframed the Inside Out project to include the power of storytelling as a means to bridge difference and understanding and to highlight the importance of diversity in all school communities across the district and beyond.

Varanasi, India Slums, December 2016. Children of the Varanasi slums.

Vaucresson, France À Terre le Handicap, June 2016. We chose this concept because disability stops being an obstacle when we unite in solidarity.

Vechta, Germany The Walk To Be Free, June 2014. These eight portraits represent all young women behind prison walls. With masks they protect themselves from the prejudice of society.

Vernier, Switzerland PALC—Flottaison Banque Des Serments, May 2014. Flottaison, a new action from the Bank of Oaths on the Rhône River.

Vernon, Canada Learning for Life, March 2013. We took these photos in order to give a voice to those who have the most life experience and yet are often the most silent in our society—our senior citizens. We wanted to go outside the classroom to learn from those who are inside a retirement residence.

Vero Beach, FL Help Us Read . . . It Changes Who We Become!,January 2013. By third grade, kids who aren't reading at their grade level have only a 1-in-7 chance of ever catching up.

Victoria, Australia Free from Discrimination, November 2013. "I stand up against racism." "I promote diversity." "I want to live free from discrimination." "I believe all people should be treated with respect and dignity." "People should not be bullied if they like the same sex." "I accept people's ideas even if they're different to my own." "I value all people from all walks of life." "Accept me for who I am and not for what you want me to be."

Vienna, Austria We Are (Vienna), September 2012. We Are (Vienna): How can urban interventions inspire discourse within a city?

Vila Nova de Gaia, Portugal We All Got Talent, September 2014. Everyone has a talent, something that makes us unique and adds value to society. In the cultural sector, this depends a lot on the opportunities people have to show their talent. Especially in times of economic crisis and record unemployment, musicians, singers, actors, fashion designers, and artists of all kind often struggle to be heard. We want to give a voice to local talent!

Villejuif, France Dignity in Villejuif, June 2012. Intended to restore dignity to the residents of neighborhood Hautes-Bruyeres Yvan Guibert.

Vilnius, Lithuania Is Man a Box?, June 2013. Clothing, status, address, problems—it's all temporary, it's all just a surface. We are each unique and have the potential to change!

Walled Lake, MI Water Is Good, May 2013. Water is good to US . . . WE need to be good to IT.

Warwick, NY Many Looks, One Love, May 2011. Our mission is to express our unity in diversity/see the similarities, not the differences in each other.

Washington, DC Women's March, January 2017. January 21, 2017, people from all over the country gathered in Washington, DC, to stand in solidarity in the spirit of democracy to honor the champions of human rights, dignity, and justice who have come before us, and to recognize that our vibrant and diverse communities are the strength of our country. Let's show that we stand strong and united to fight for justice and unity for all!

Washington, DC, and NYC, April 2013. I Have a Dream is a project that consist of portraits of young immigrants in the US who are fighting for the right of education for undocumented youth.

Words, Beats, & Life, September 2011. Our images show the spirit of a youth that will not be marginalized.

Critical Exposure, August 2011. Students advocating for educational reform.

Wellington, New Zealand Inside Out NZ, March 2014. The aim of this project was to show the diversity that exists in a small town like Wellington, and on a broader scale, New Zealand.

West Chester, OH Lakota West High School, November 2011. It is through the visual arts that we have found our voices and been given a platform to share our individual personalities with society.

Whanganui, New Zealand The Youth of Whanganui, June 2011. Our concept is to celebrate youth of Whanganui of all ethnicities. By displaying young individuals we wish to unite the whole community.

Wichita, KS Inside Out Fairmount Park, February 2016. This project is about overcoming the divisions between the State University and the neighborhood of Fairmount Park that has wrongly and unfairly been portrayed as a dangerous place due to crimes said to have been committed mainly by African-American men from the neighborhood, which is untrue and unjust.

Wilmington, NC Interactive Art for Community Development, March 2015. The area has a mix of low- to middle-income families, minority people who are not normally exposed to much art. We want to photograph them and then place their images on one of many abandoned or empty businesses in the area that our subjects live.

Wilmington, DE I AM, December 2011. Through art, we empower and give hope to the homeless to realize their self-worth and that they truly matter.

Windsor, CT Art Has No Borders, October 2014. Art is the great mediator. It crosses all boundaries. It is the best of humanity. More art. Less war.

Winston-Salem, NC Wake Forest Community, March 2013. The purpose of this project is to recognize the Wake Forest Community as a place of cohesion; a place where people of different niches come together to form a singular community.

Woodbridge, VA Bel Air Inside Out—Faces of Respect, May 2014. Bel Air students believe that respect can change the world and that the change could start with just one smile. We want to build understanding and respect at our school first and hope that our actions and smiles will create a chain reaction through our community and the world.

Woodlawn, MD We are Johnnycake, September 2016. Unfortunately, the United States is experiencing a period of racial tension. This is especially true in Baltimore and the outlying neighborhoods. For years, our school has had a reputation of being a "bad school" or a "school you don't want your kids to go to" and this designation stems from the fact that our school's population is generally made up of minorities. We want to show the world that our students and our school are amazing.

Woonsocket, RI Faces of Woonsocket, April 2016. The one thing all of these people have in common is that they reside in Woonsocket, RI. This is a town that has a bad reputation for drugs and crime, and this project is meant to lift up the community and to have neighbors "meet" on the city's walls.

Yerevan, Armenia Soldiers Smiling for Justice, September 2012. The Armenian society is terrified by terrible losses of soldiers we have every day. The primary concerns are suicide and non-formal relations within the army. We want to shift society's perceptions so that people here understand that soldiers are really humans, and not just expendable bodies.

Zoersel, Belgium Inside Out Zoersel, June 2013. In the psychiatric center of my hometown, Bethanië, we formed a group of people interested in making portraits. Together we photographed people we met on the street, in and outside Bethanië. The portraits were shown during the whole summer on banners in the center of Sint-Antonius Zoersel. By doing this action we wanted to reduce the gap between the village and the psychiatric center.

Zurich, Switzerland Toy—Thinking of Yves, September 2014. I think everybody who knew Yves remembers his big smile, which radiated positive energy. With my project, I want his legacy to continue to affect people who both knew and didn't know him. We shouldn't underestimate how encouraging messages and images and a smile can impact people in a positive way.

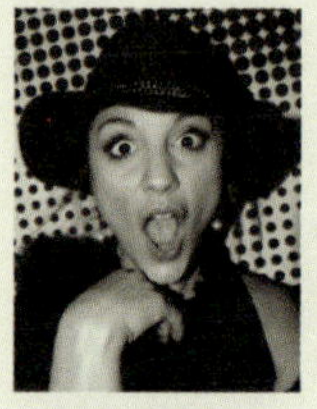
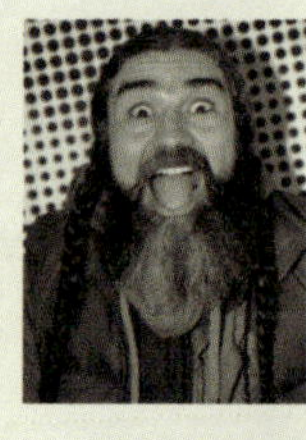
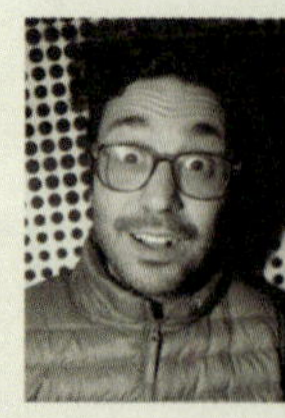
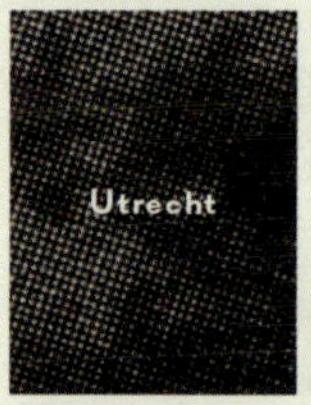

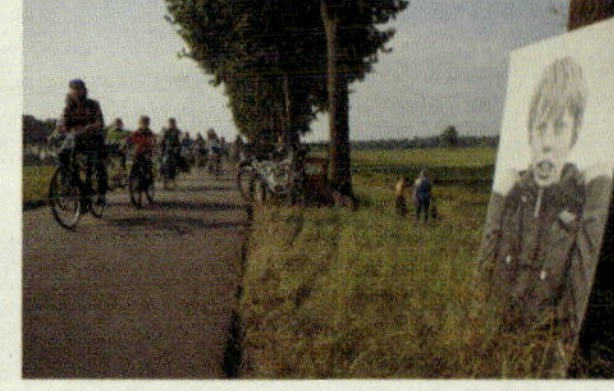
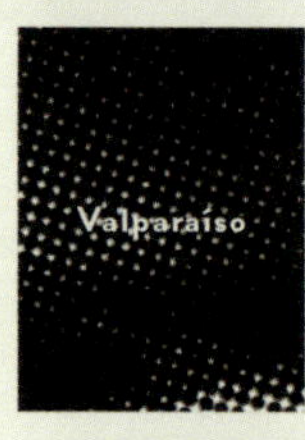

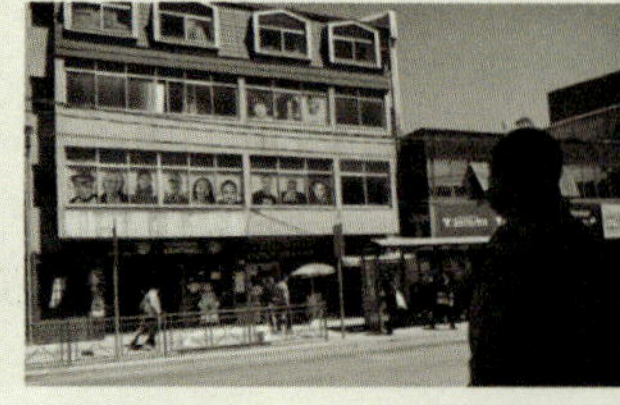
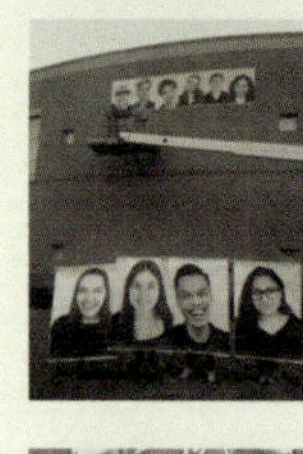
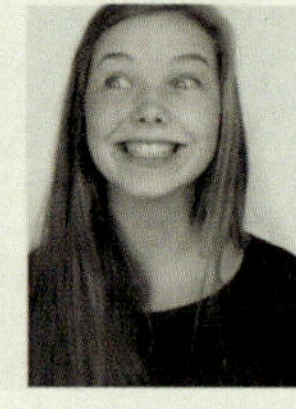
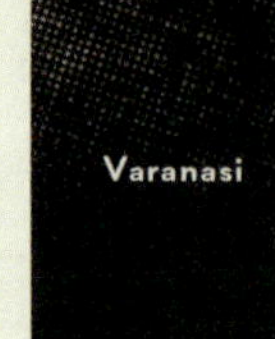

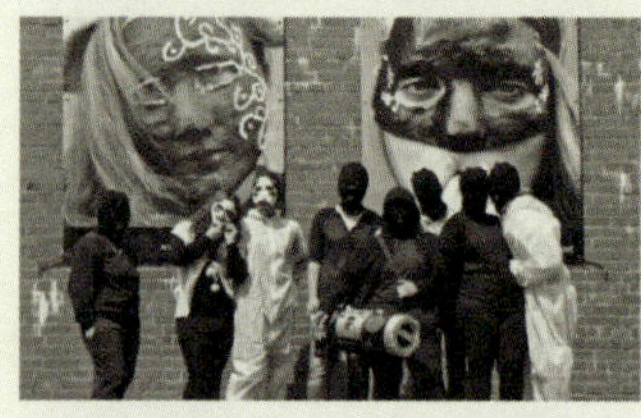
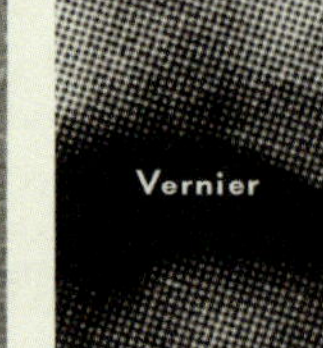

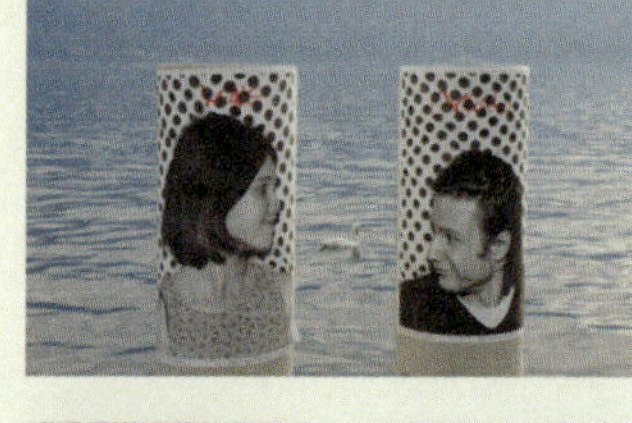
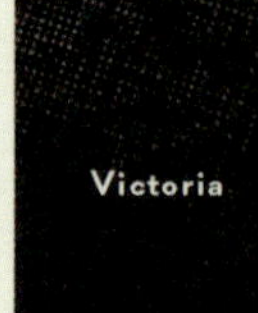

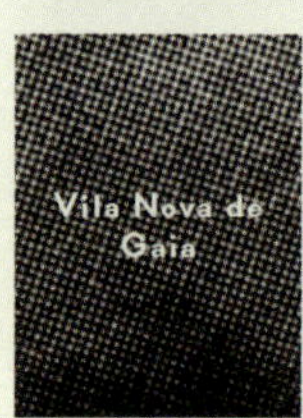

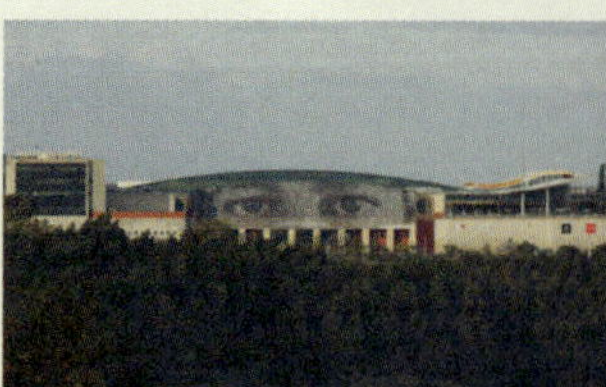
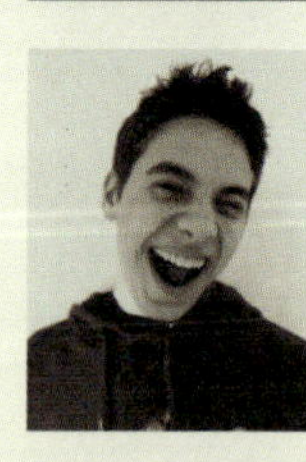
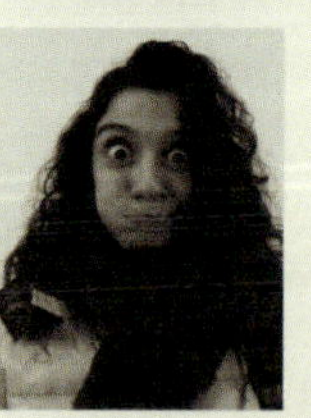
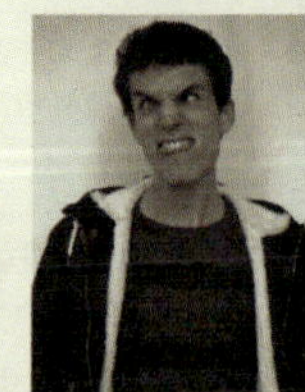
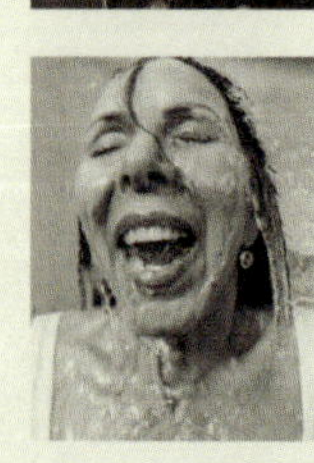
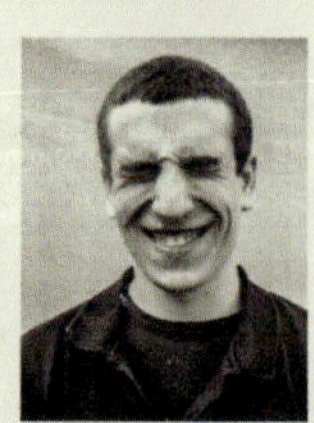
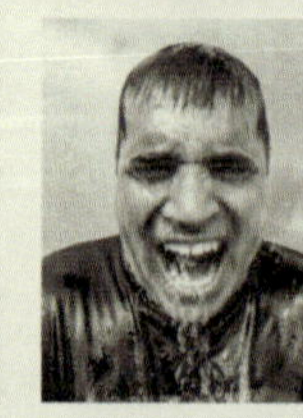
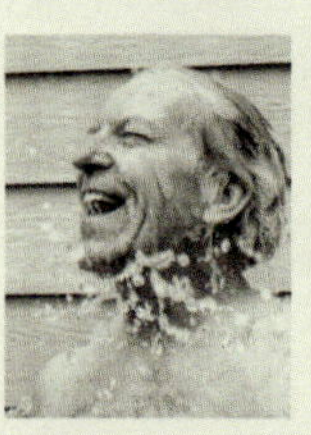
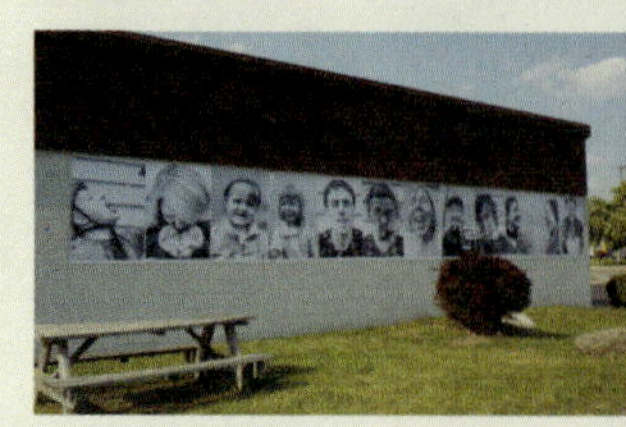

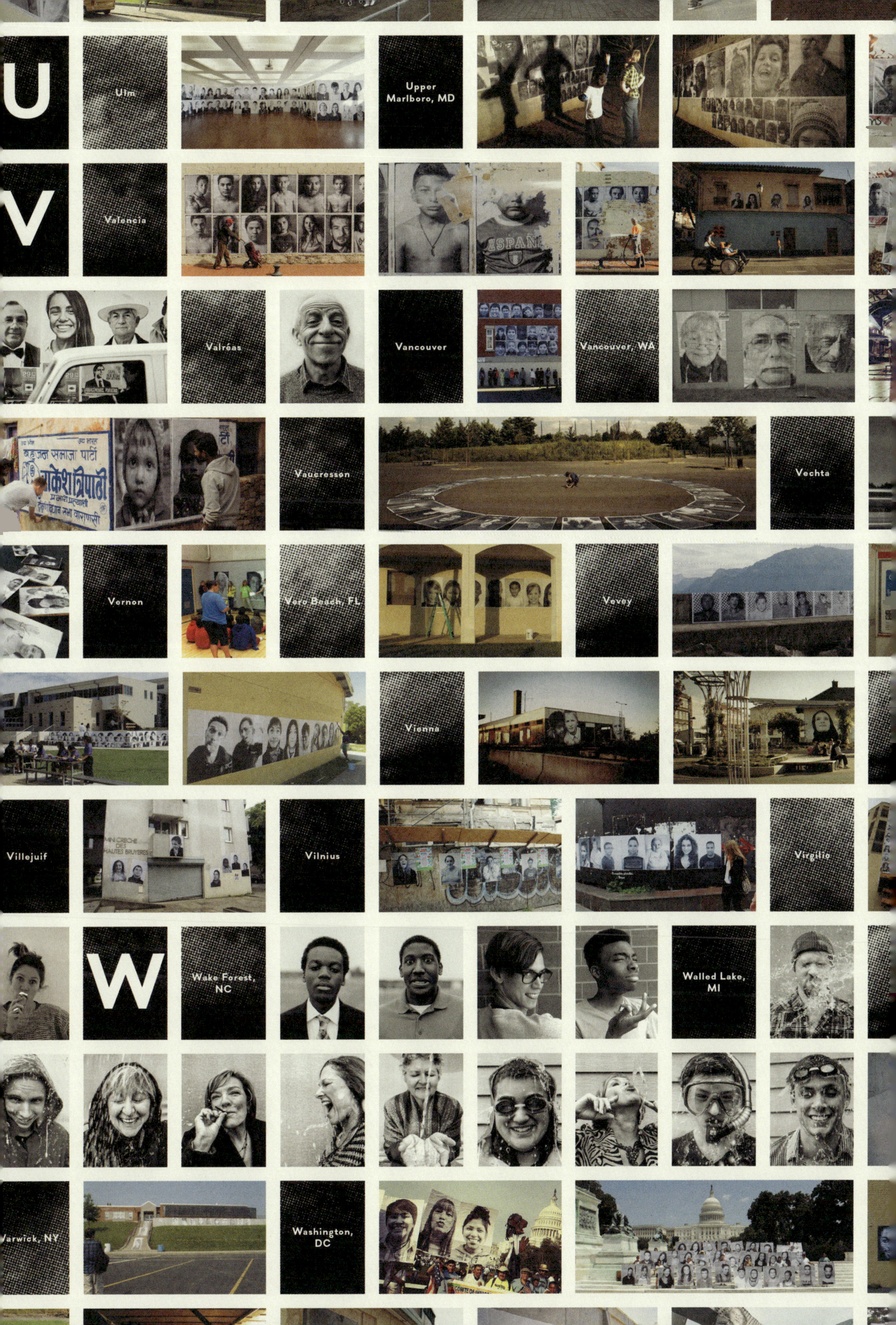

U
Ulm
Upper Marlboro, MD
V
Valencia
Valréas
Vancouver
Vancouver, WA
Vaucresson
Vechta
Vernon
Vero Beach, FL
Vevey
Vienna
Villejuif
Vilnius
Virgilio
W
Wake Forest, NC
Walled Lake, MI
Warwick, NY
Washington, DC

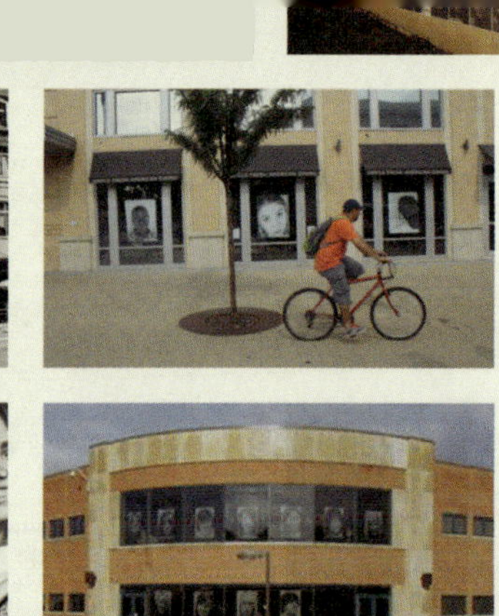

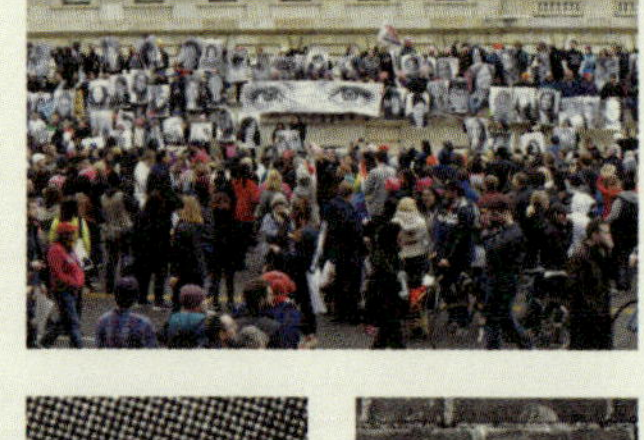

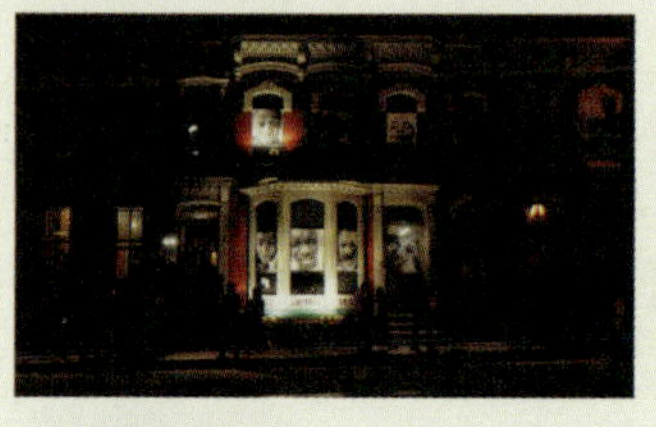

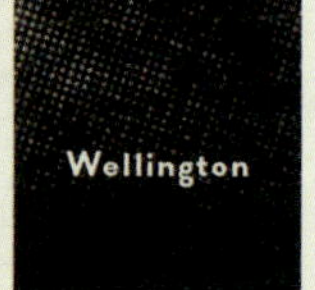

Wellington

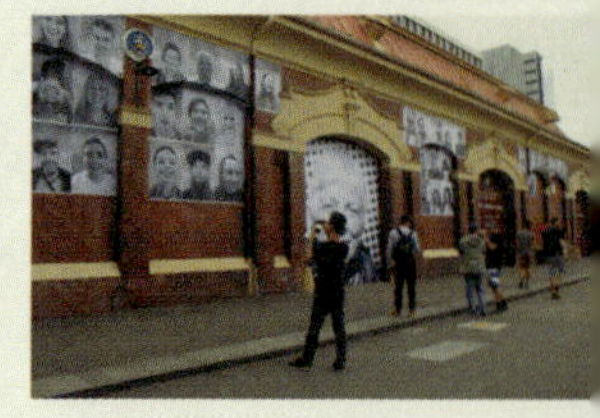

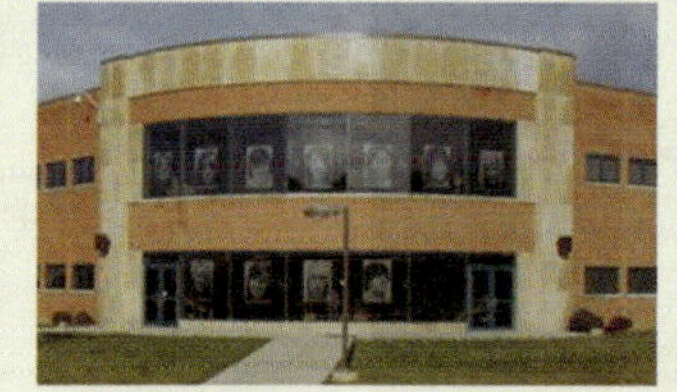

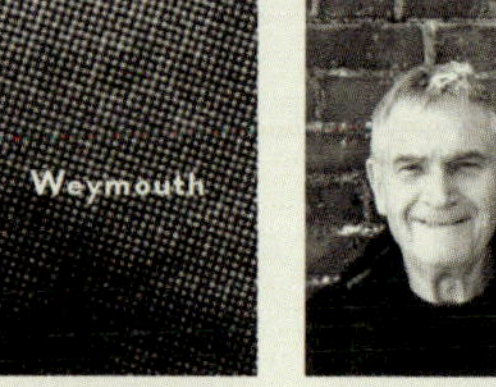

Weymouth

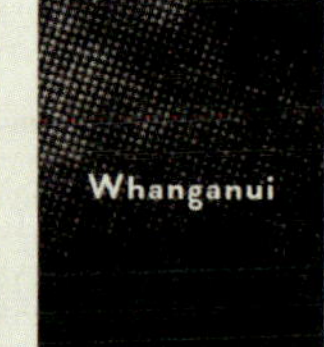

Whanganui

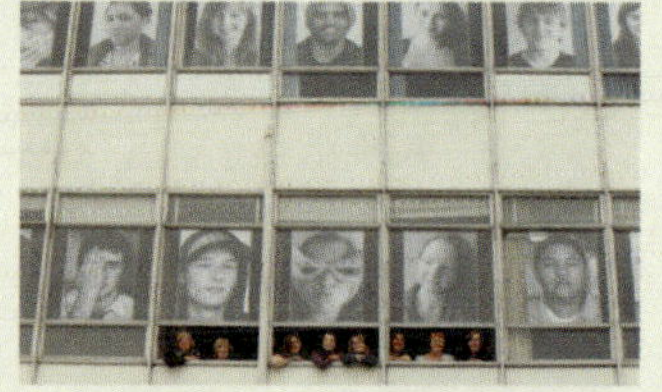

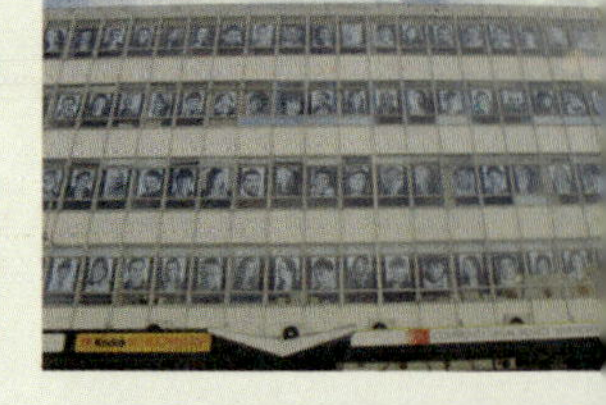

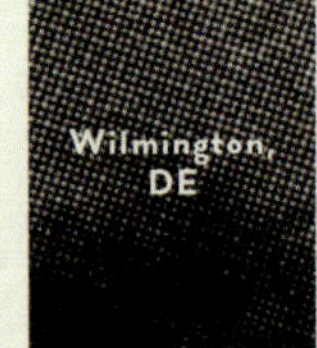

Wilmington, DE

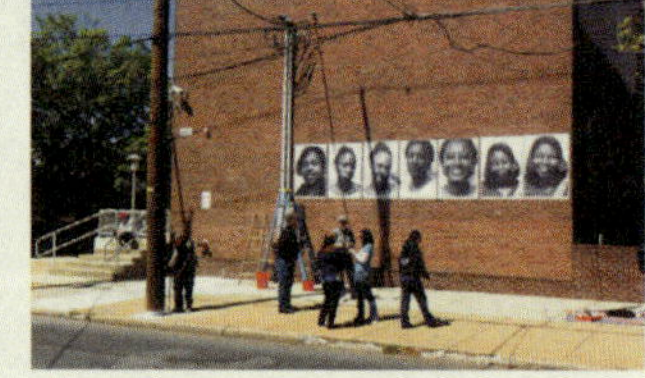

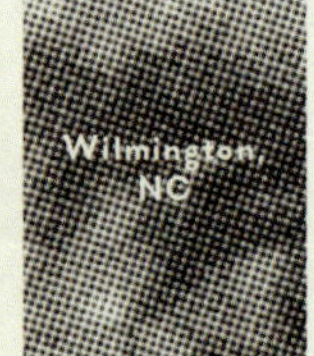

Wilmington, NC

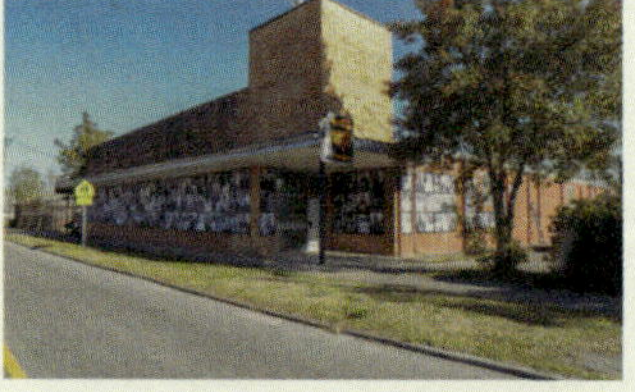

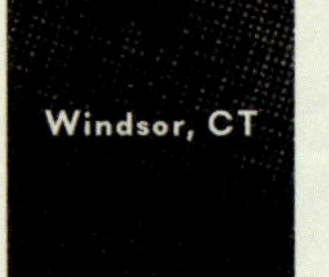

Windsor, CT

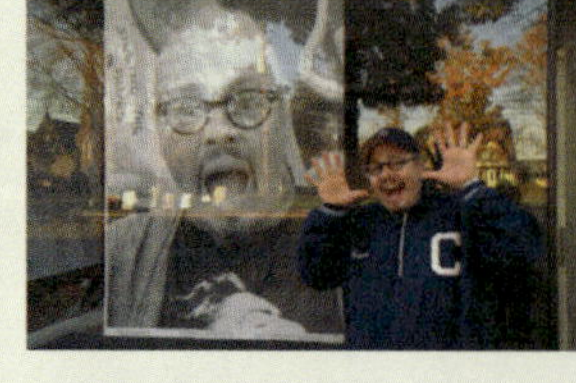

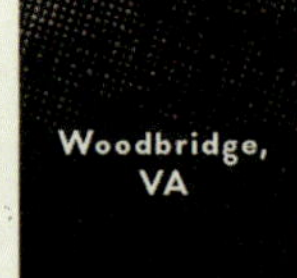

Woodbridge, VA

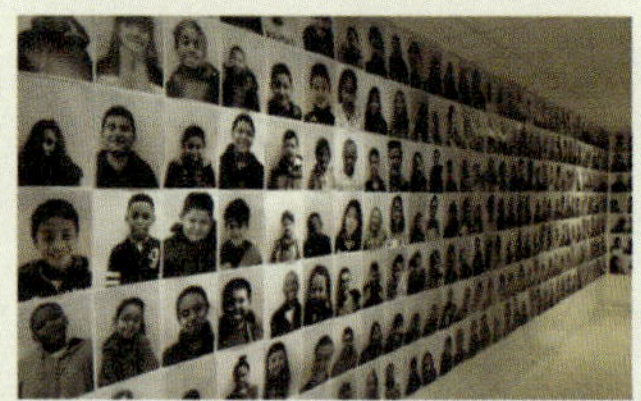

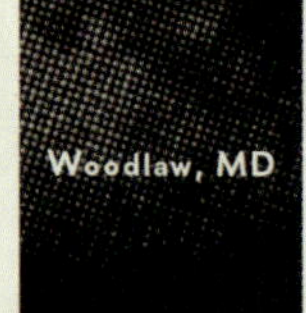

Woodlaw, MD

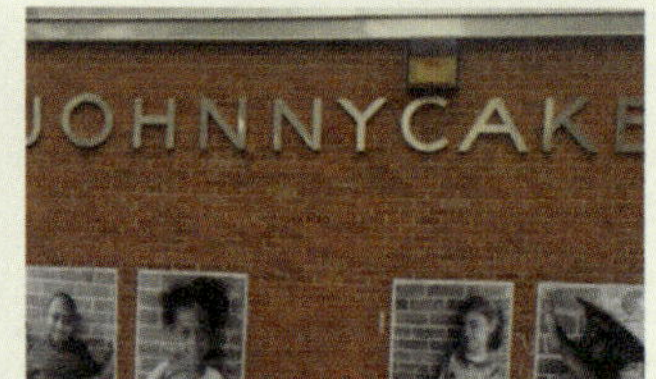

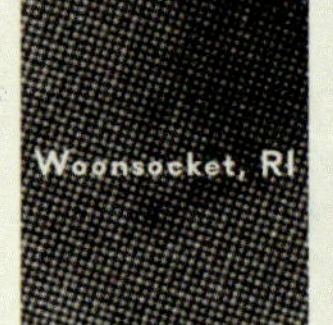

Woonsocket, RI

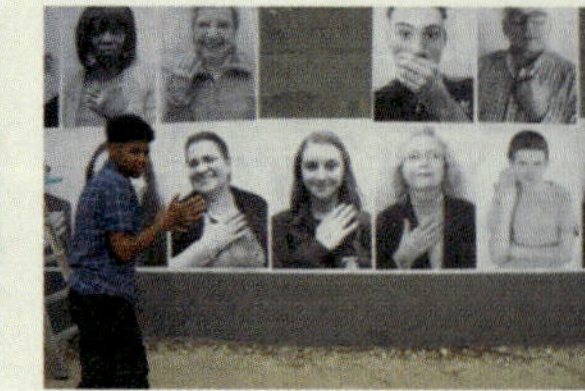

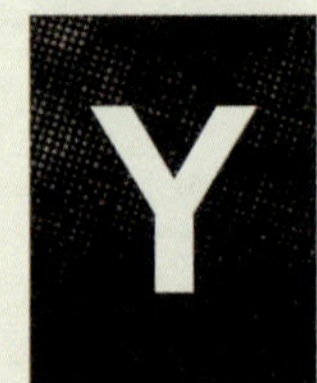

Y

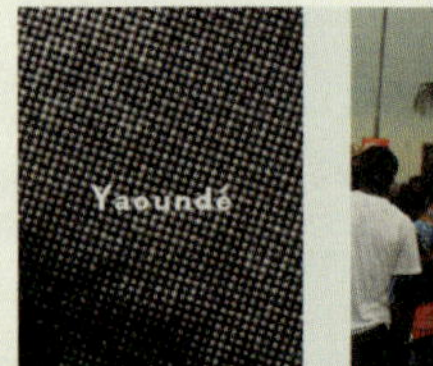

Yaoundé

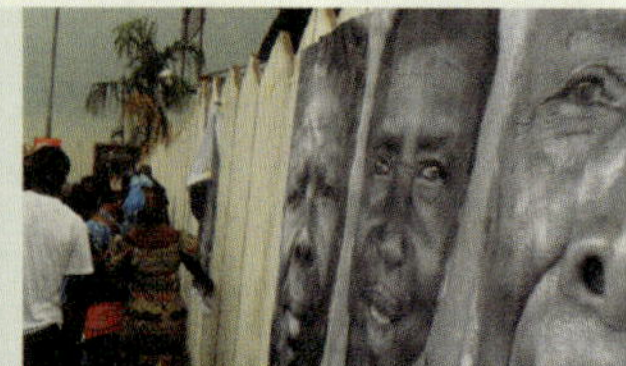

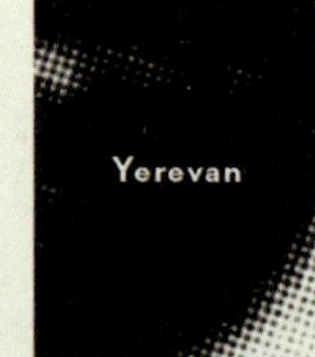

Yerevan

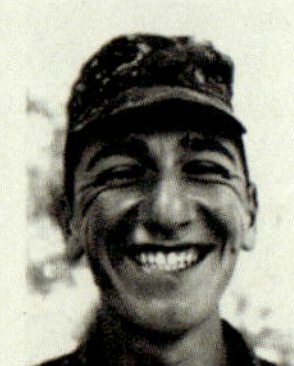

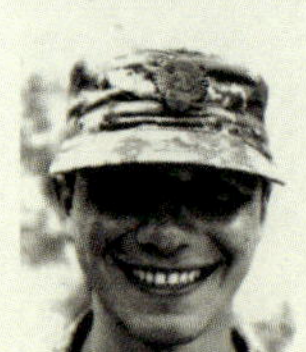

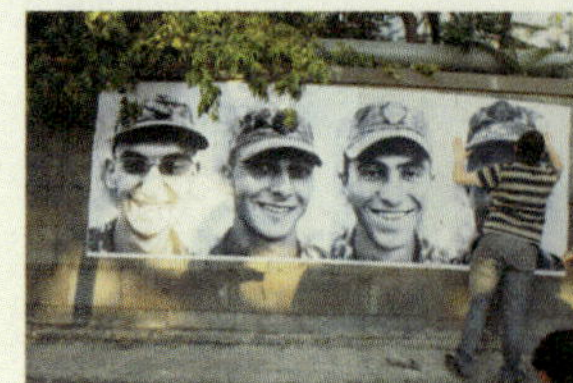

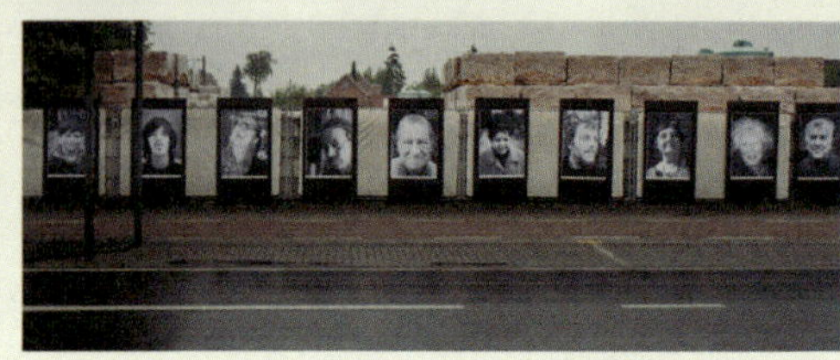

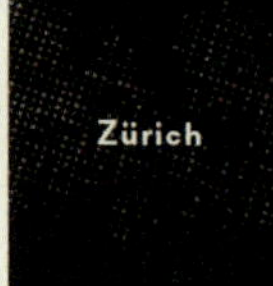

Zürich

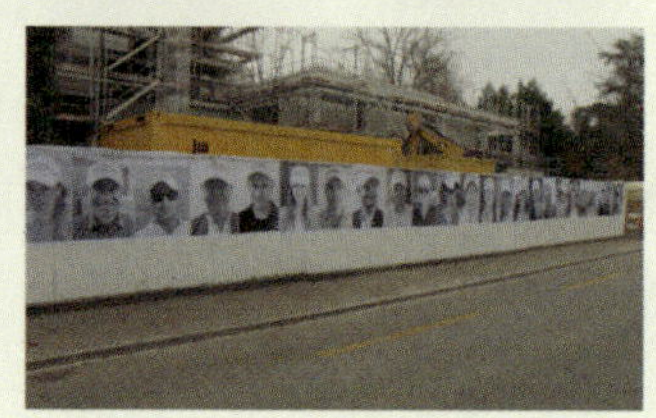

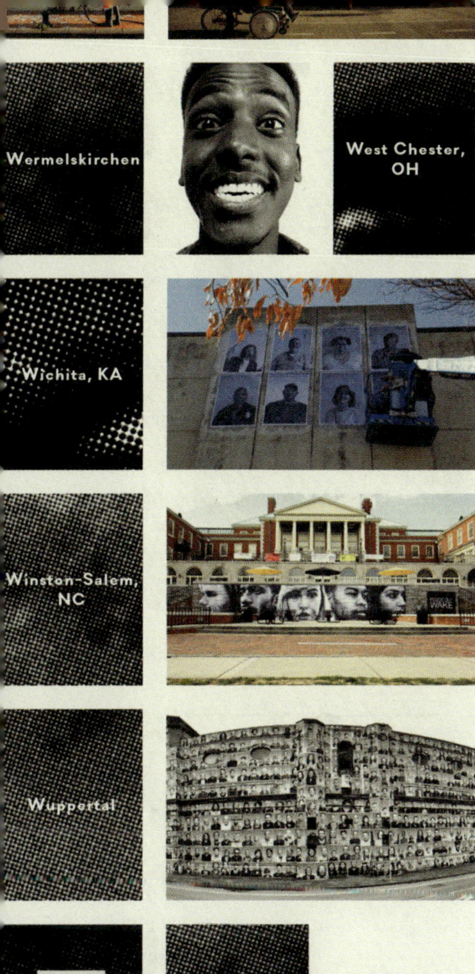
Wermelskirchen
West Chester, OH
Wichita, KA
Winston-Salem, NC
Wuppertal
Z
Zoersel

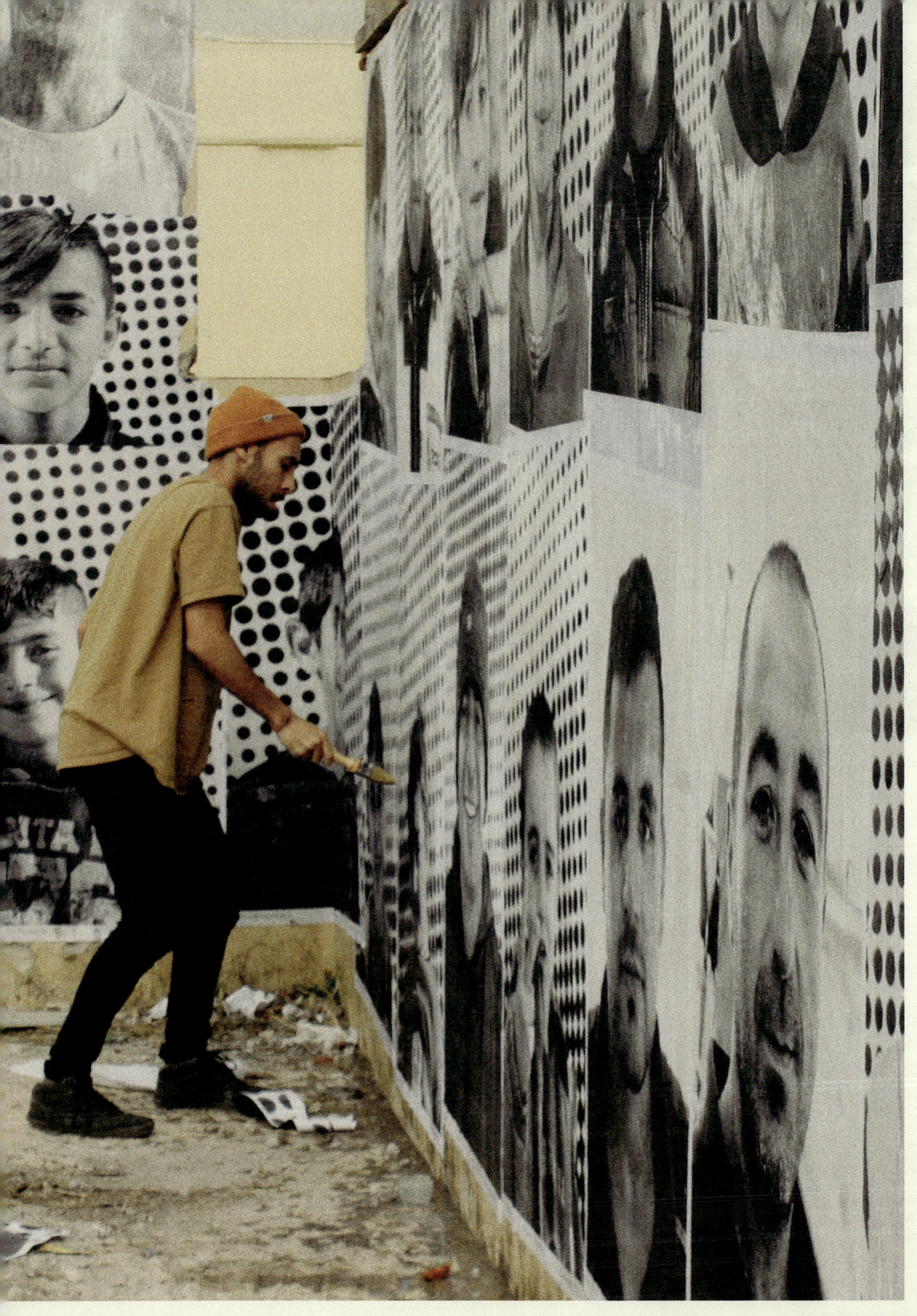

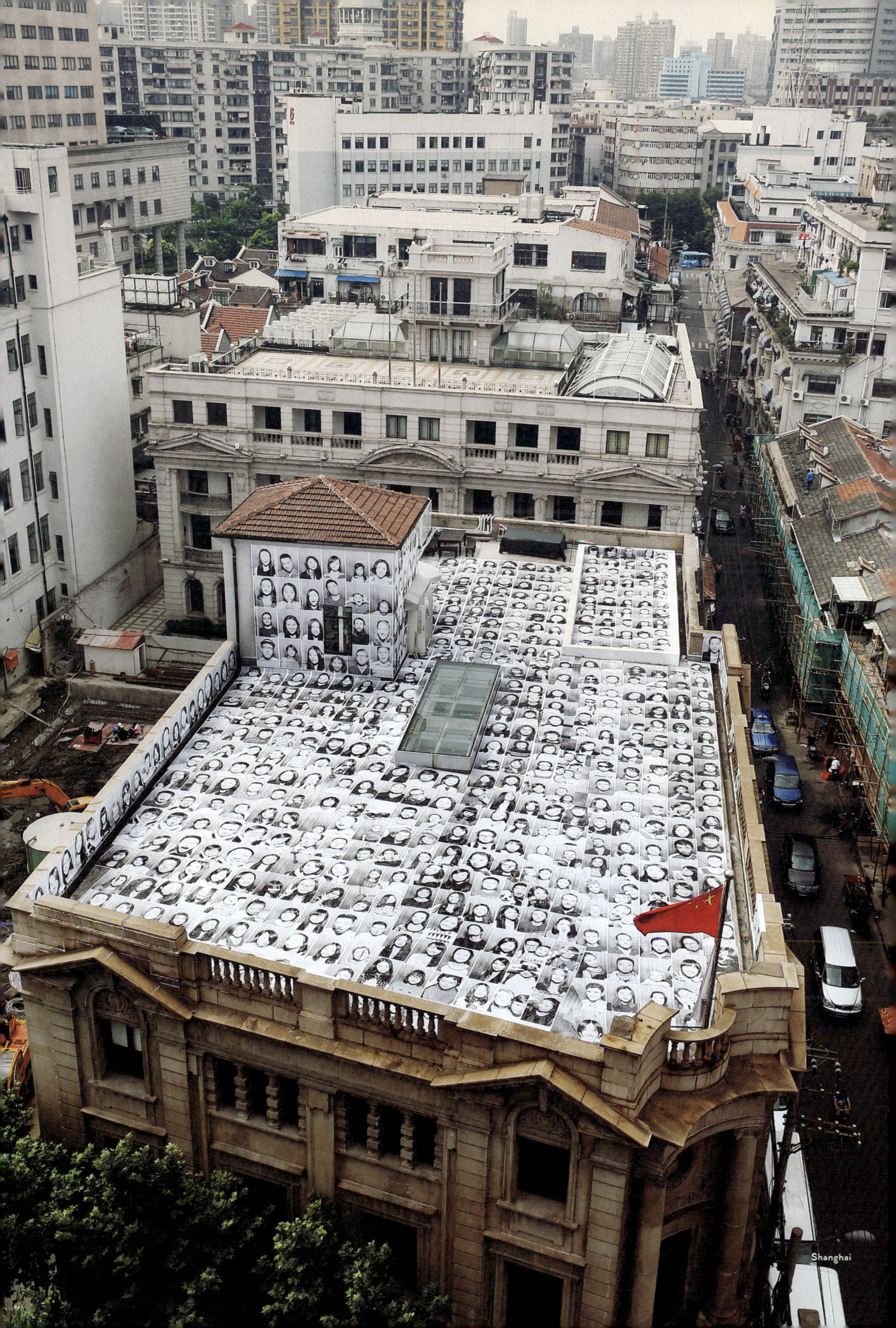

Shanghai

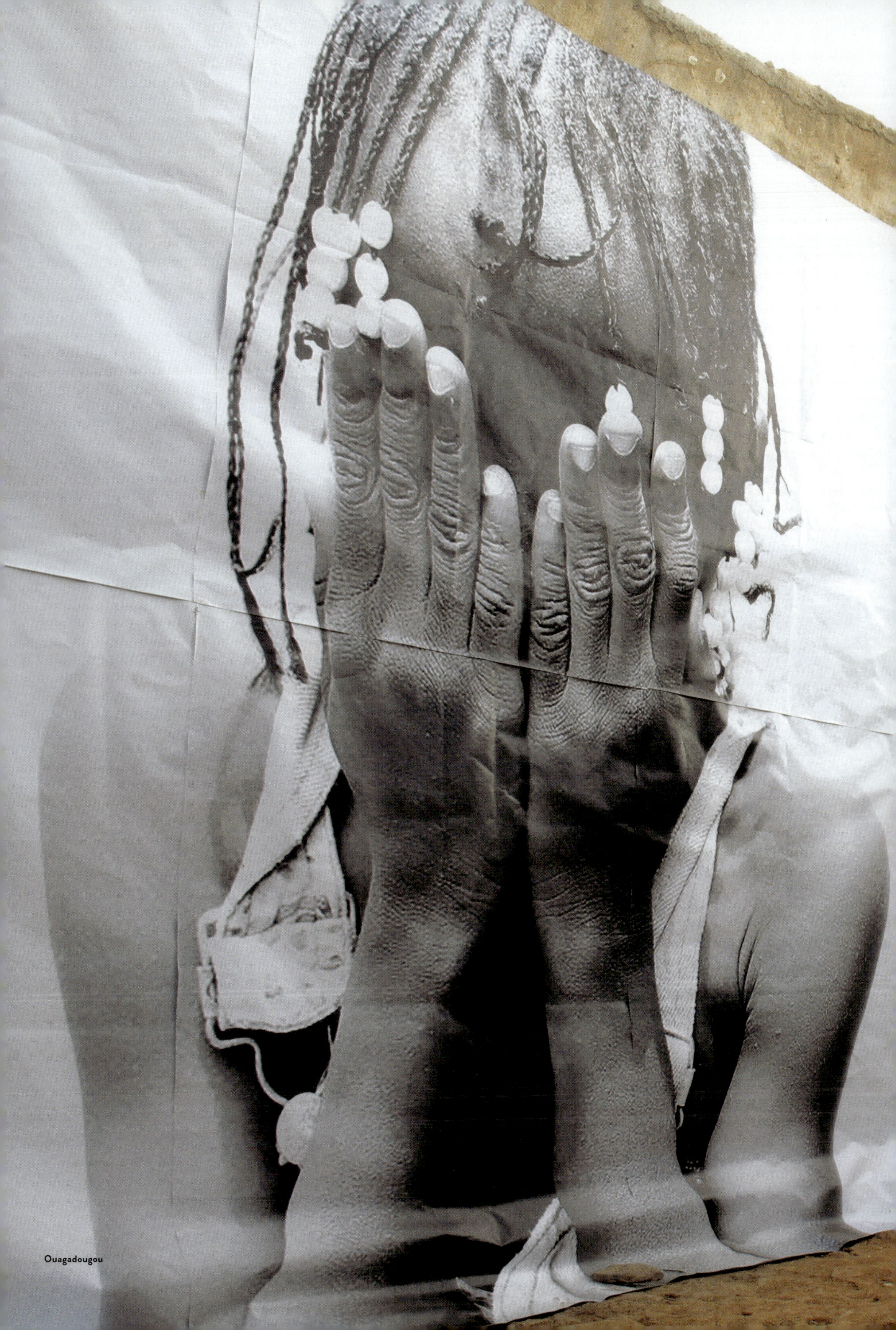

Ouagadougou

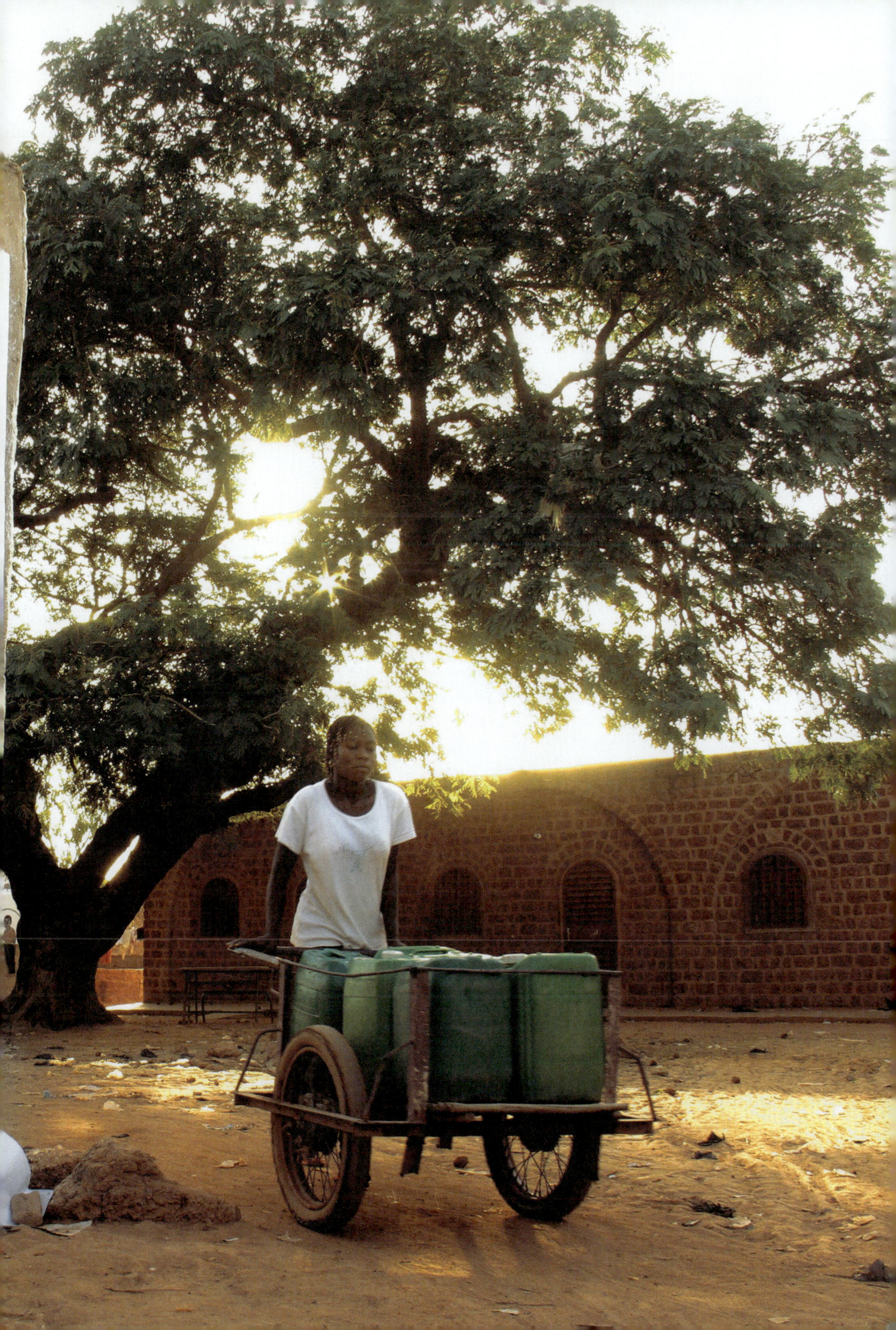

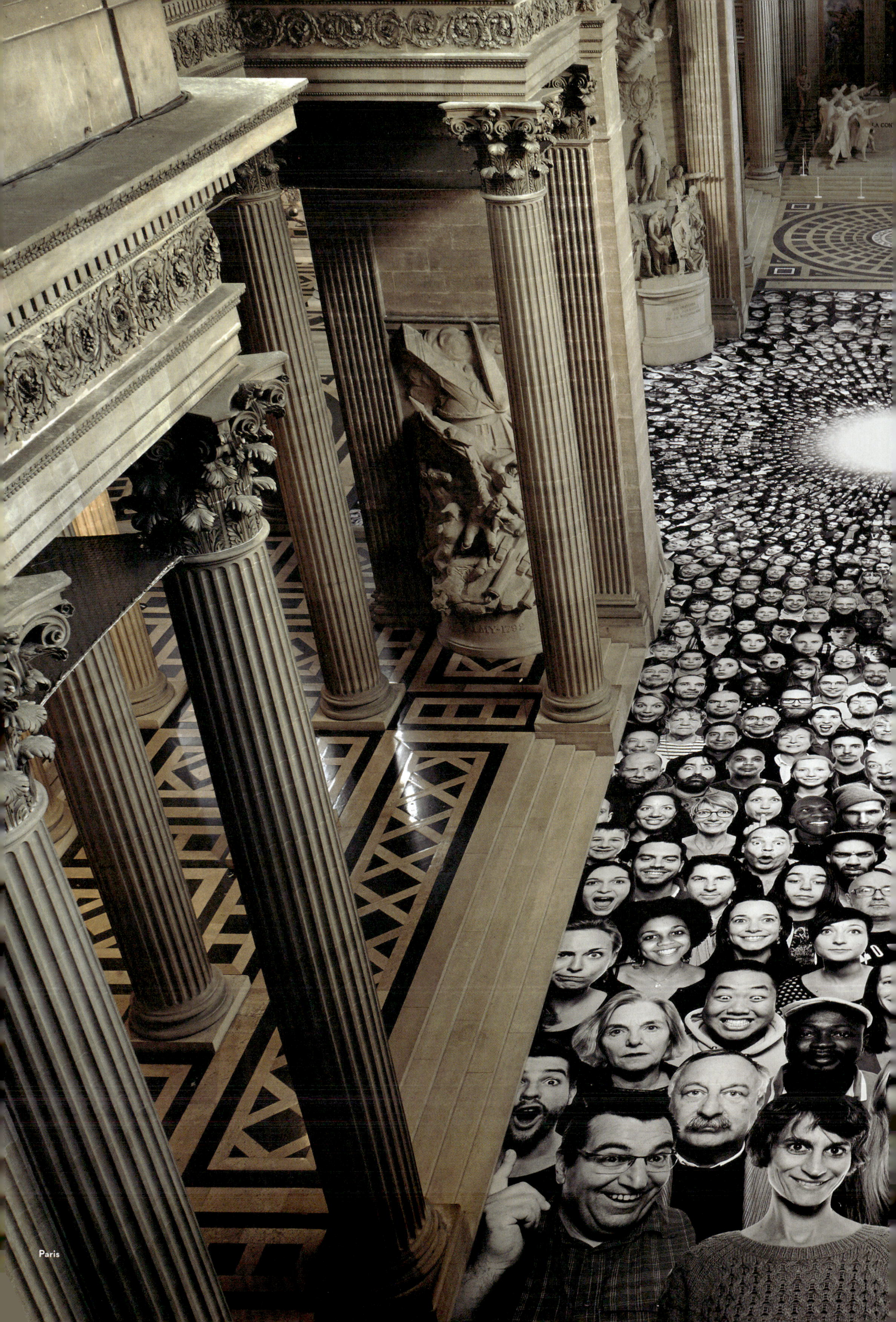

Paris

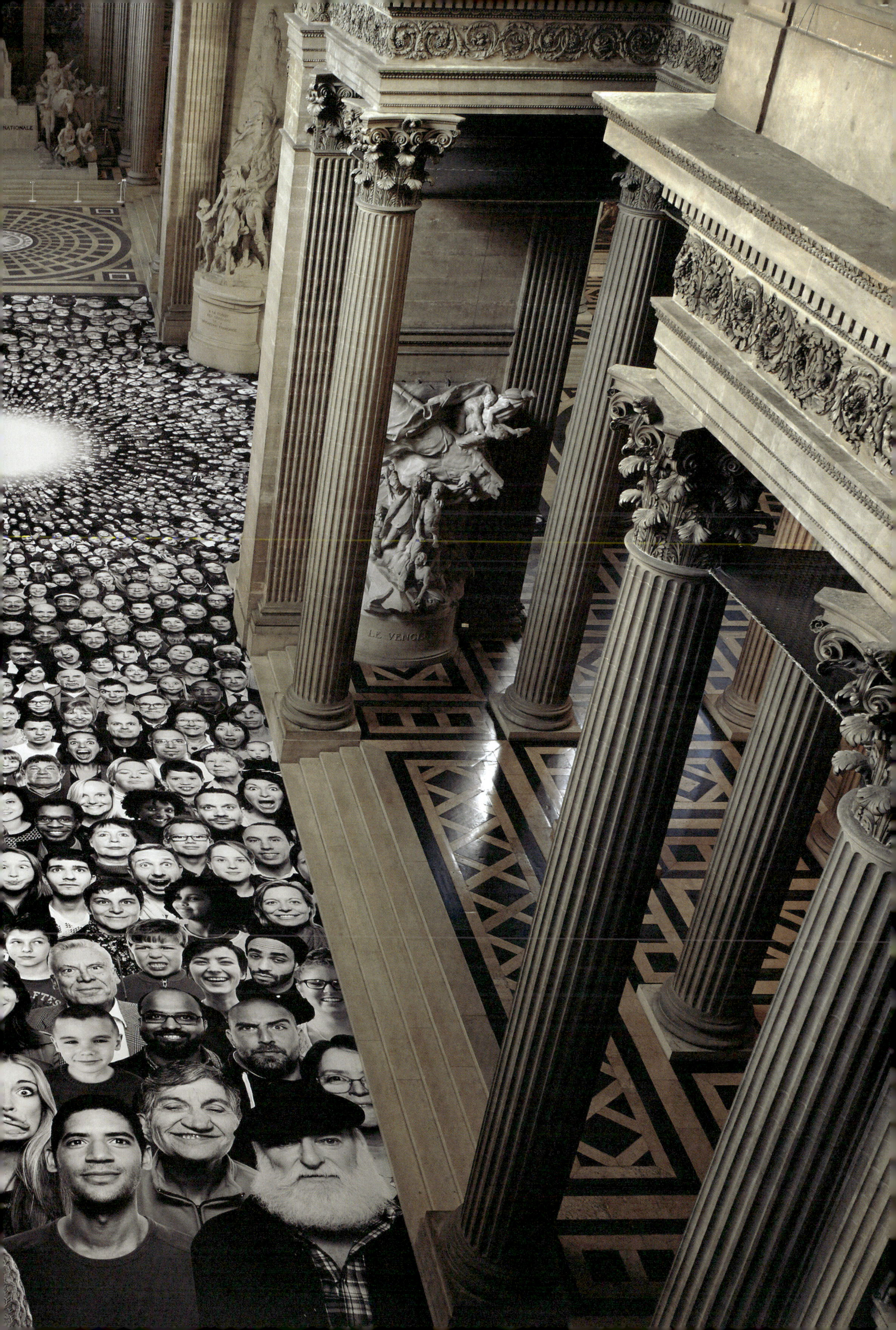

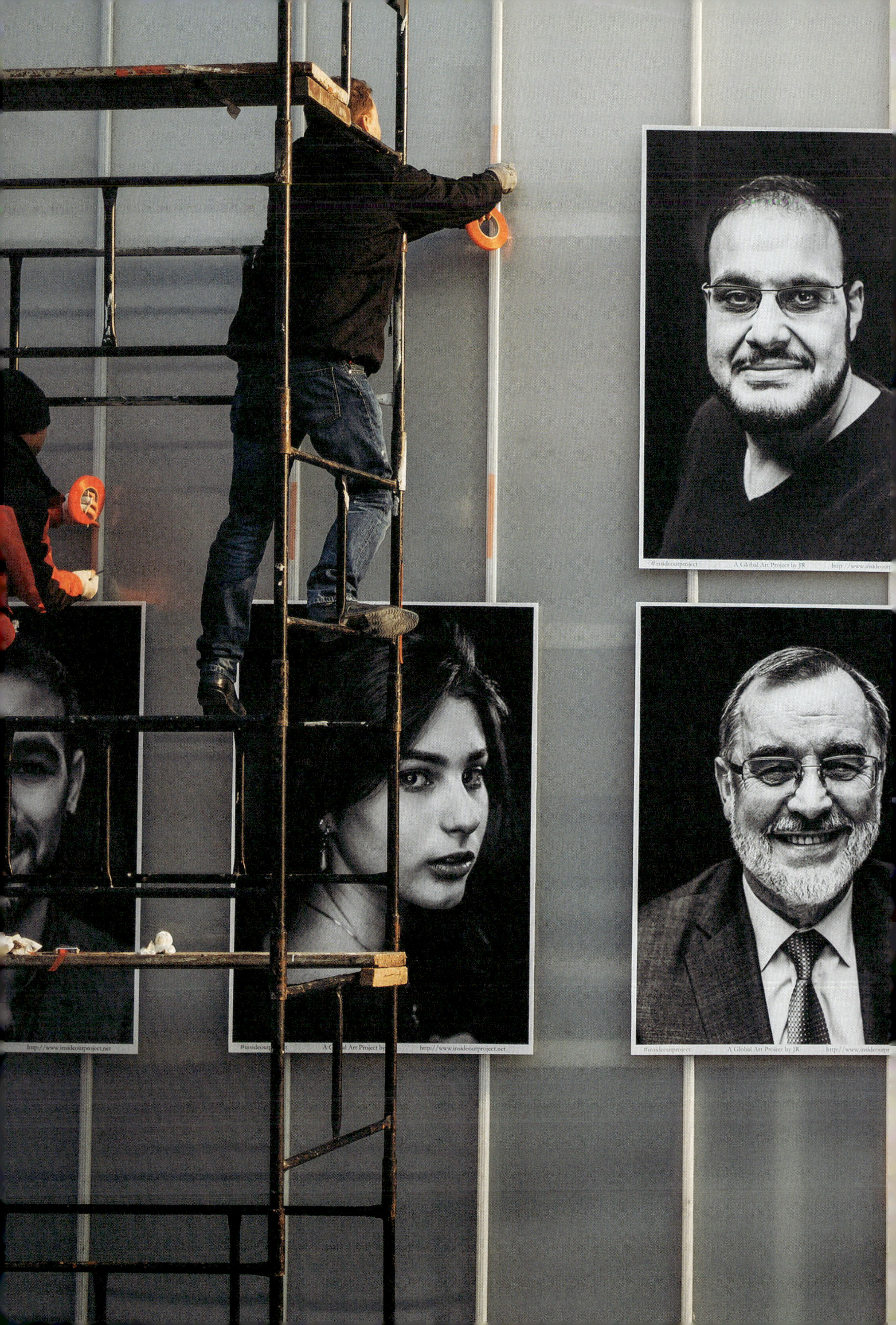
#insideoutproject
A Global Art Project by JR
http://www.insideoutproject.net

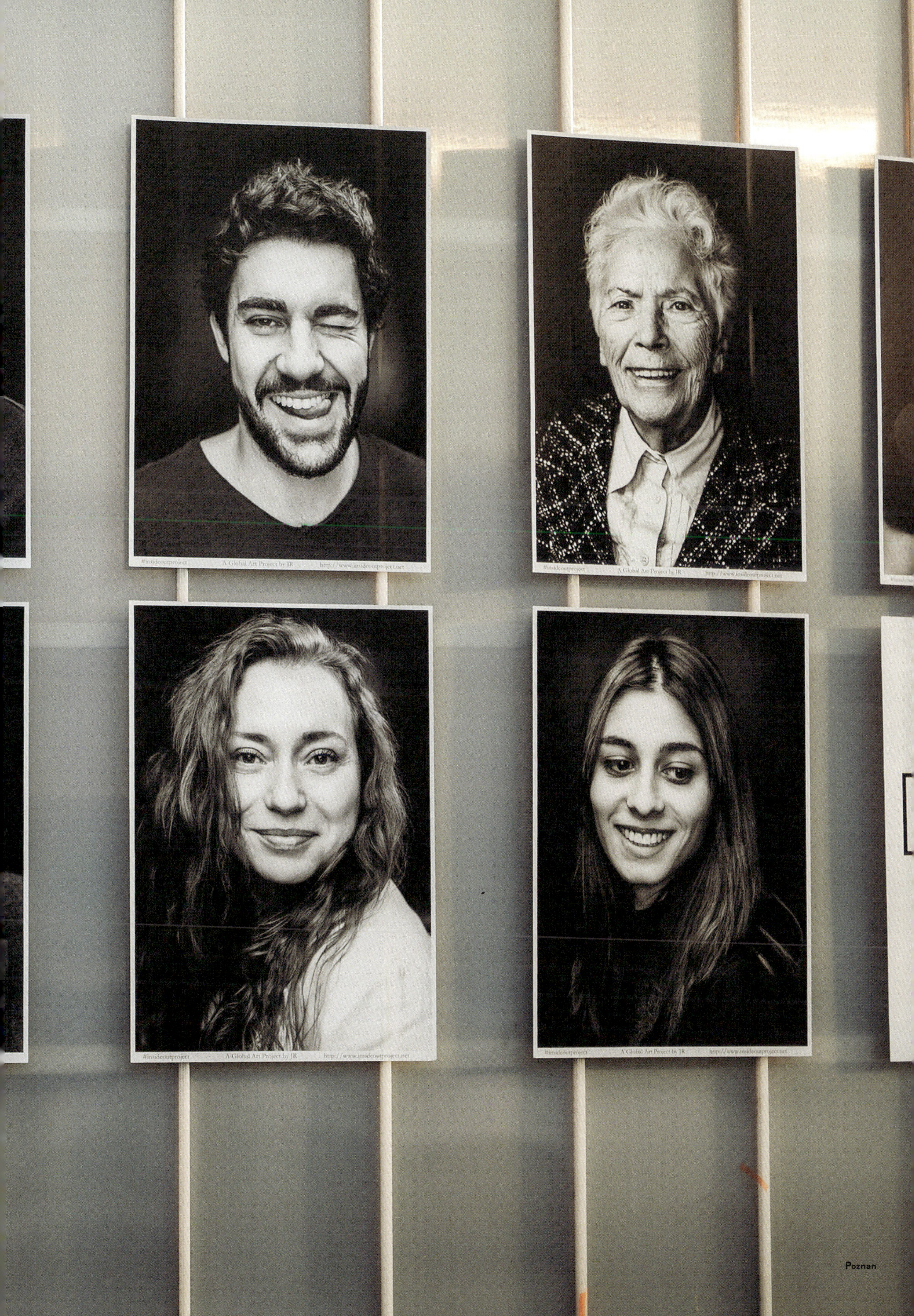
#insideoutproject
A Global Art Project by JR
http://www.insideoutproject.net

Poznan

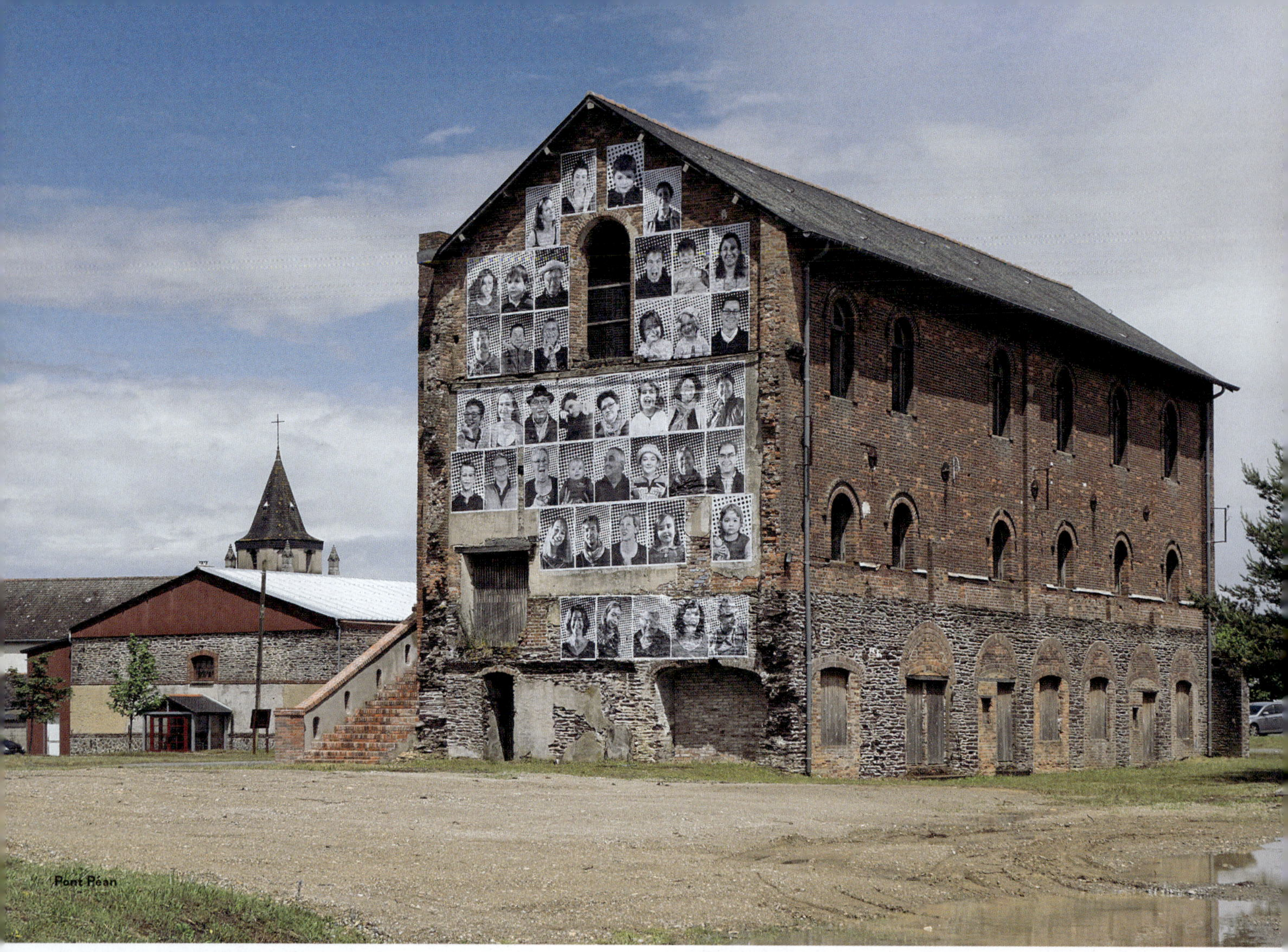

Pont Péan

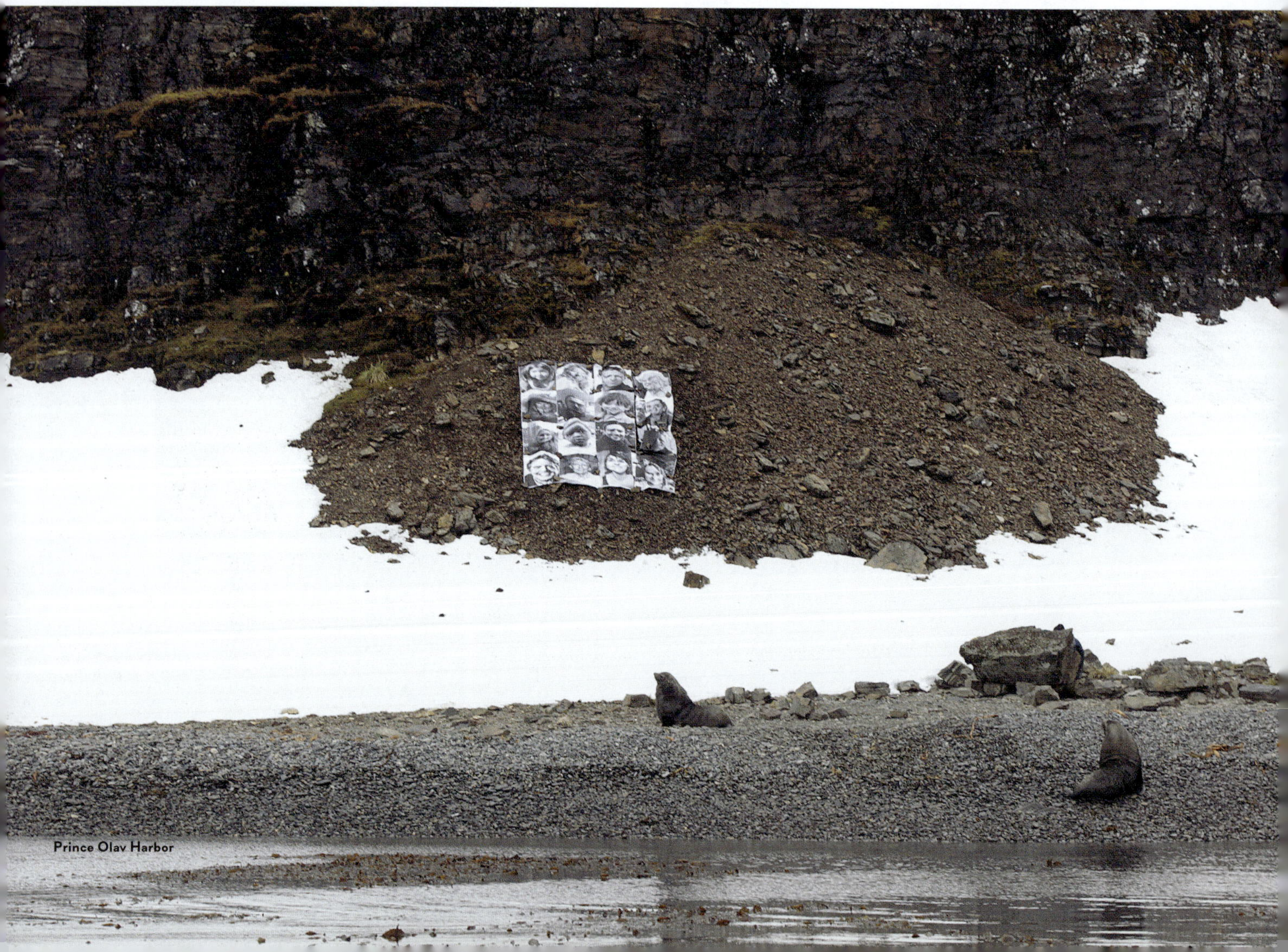

Prince Olav Harbor

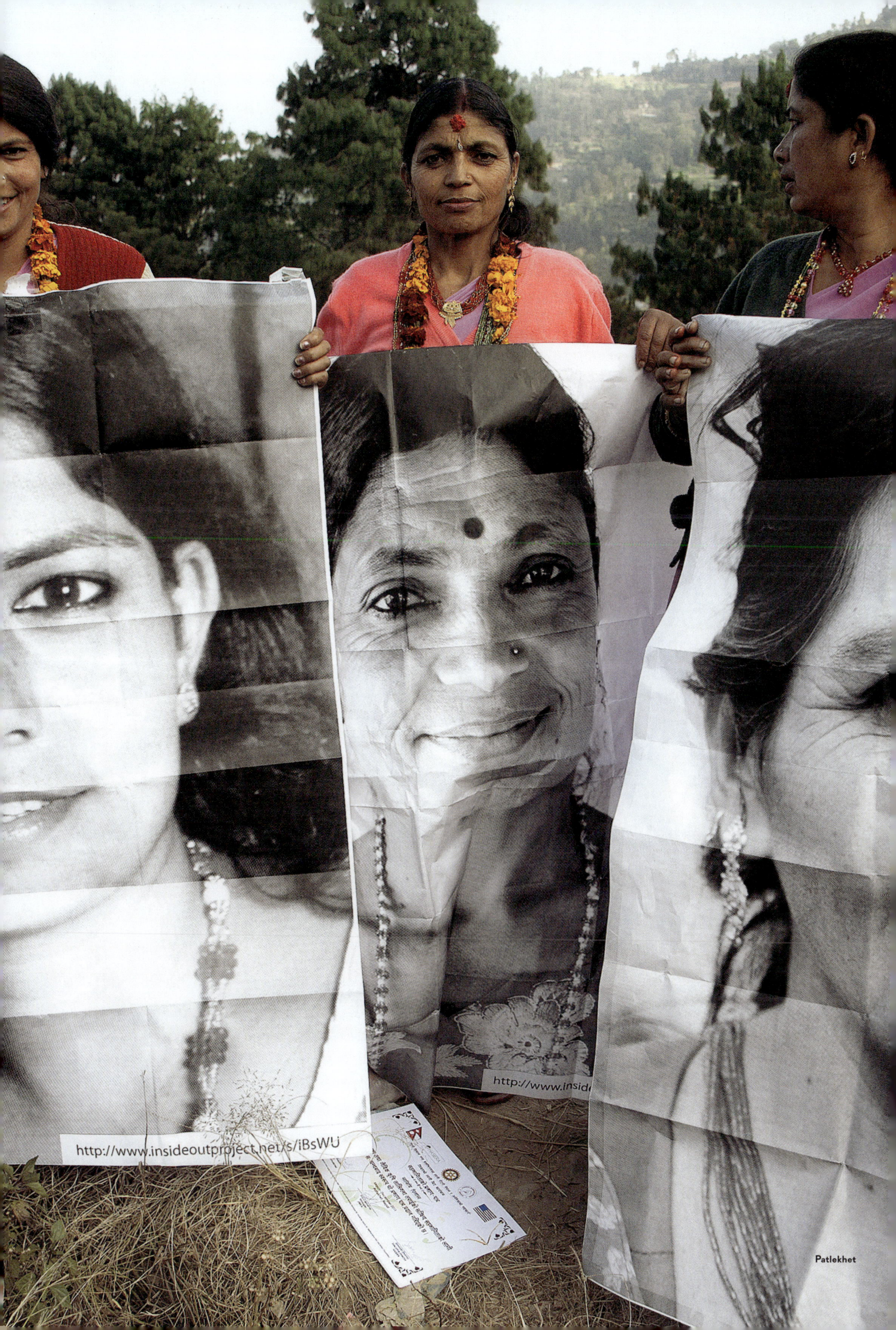

Patlekhet

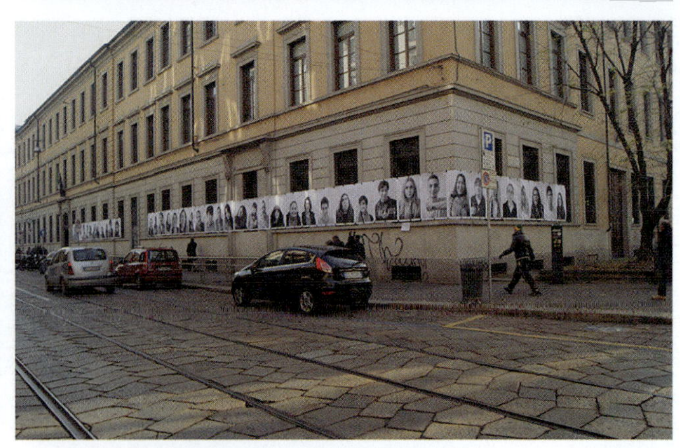

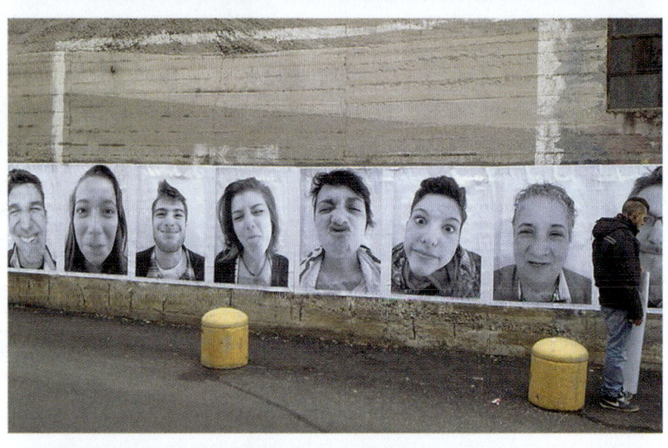

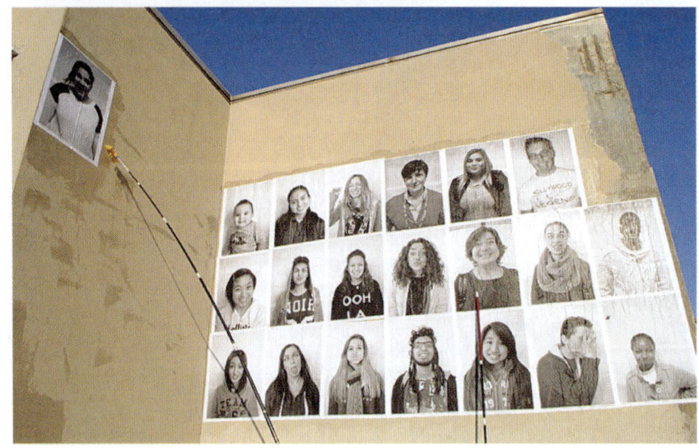

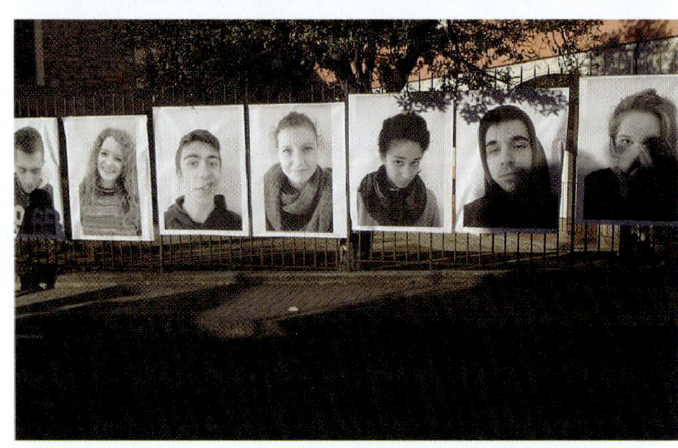

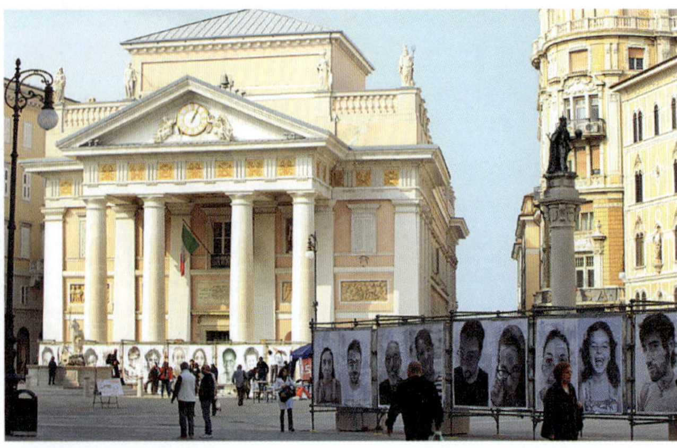

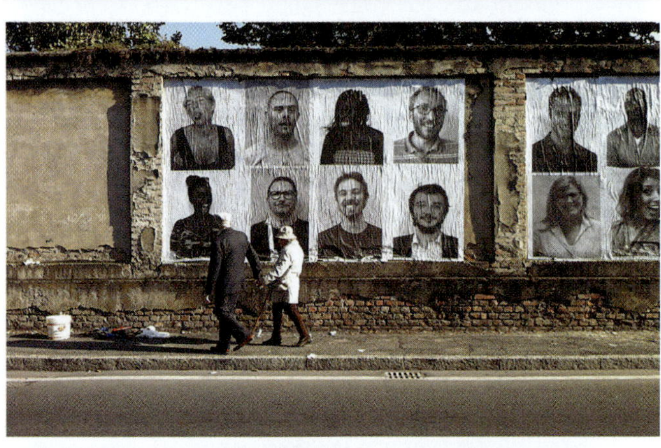

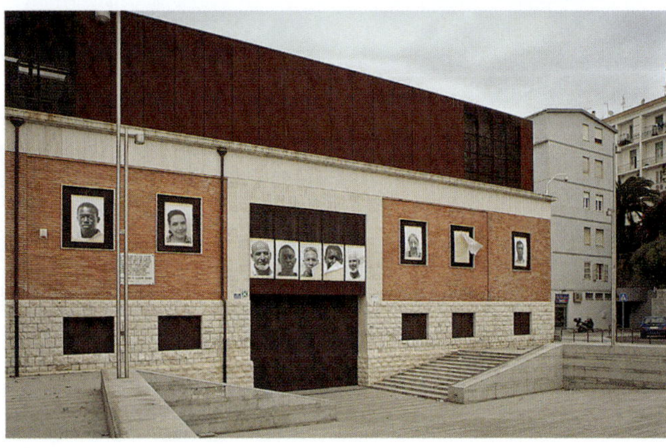

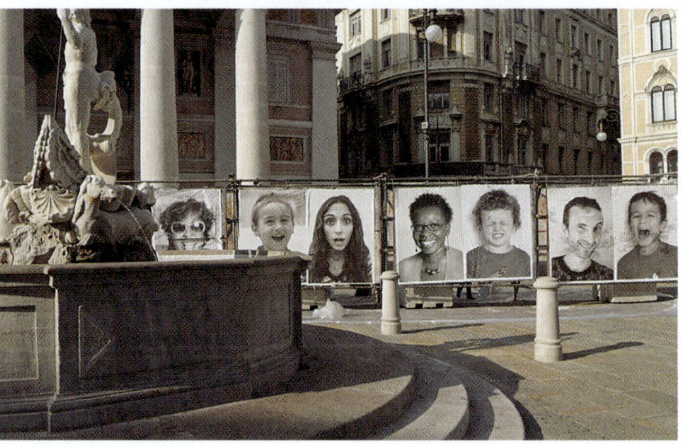

"It not only gave voice to people who couldn't say what they think, it shed light on an issue that is fundamental for every human being: human rights. Thanks to this unique and universal tool—art—we were able to have this very important discussion. It doesn't matter where we come from; if we are born and live in this country, we are all Italy."

L'Italia sono Anch'io / Inside Out Scuole

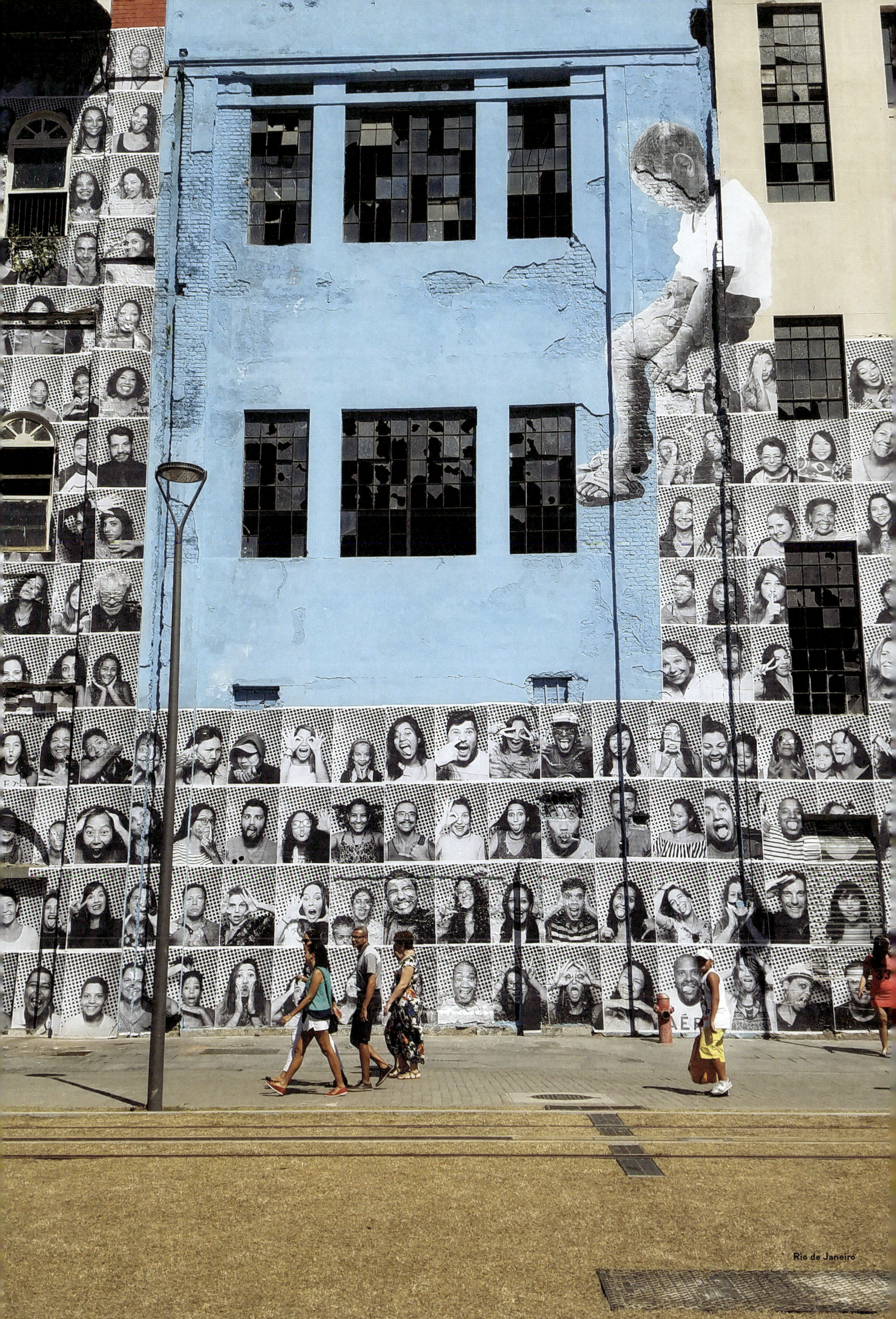

Rio de Janeiro

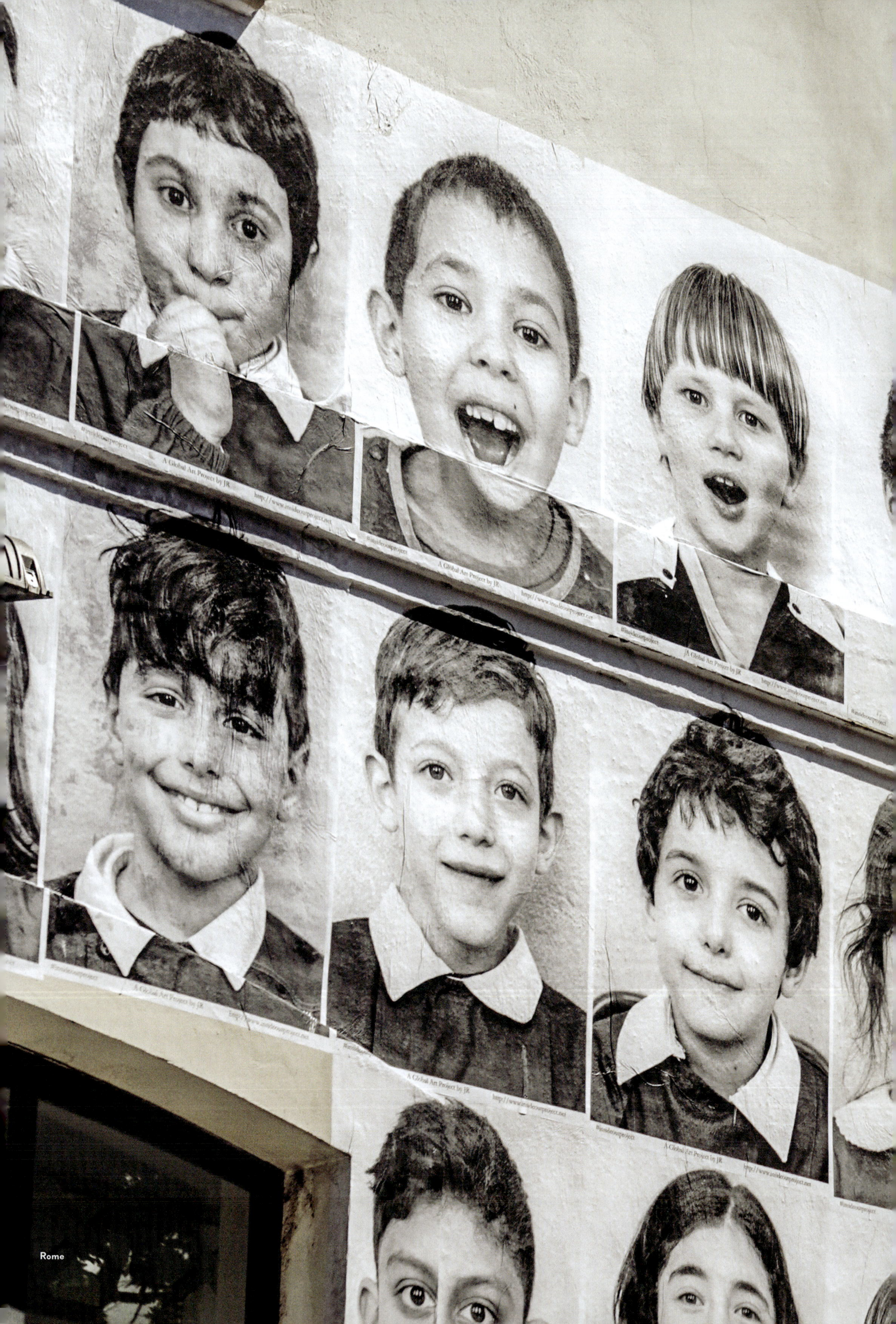

Rome

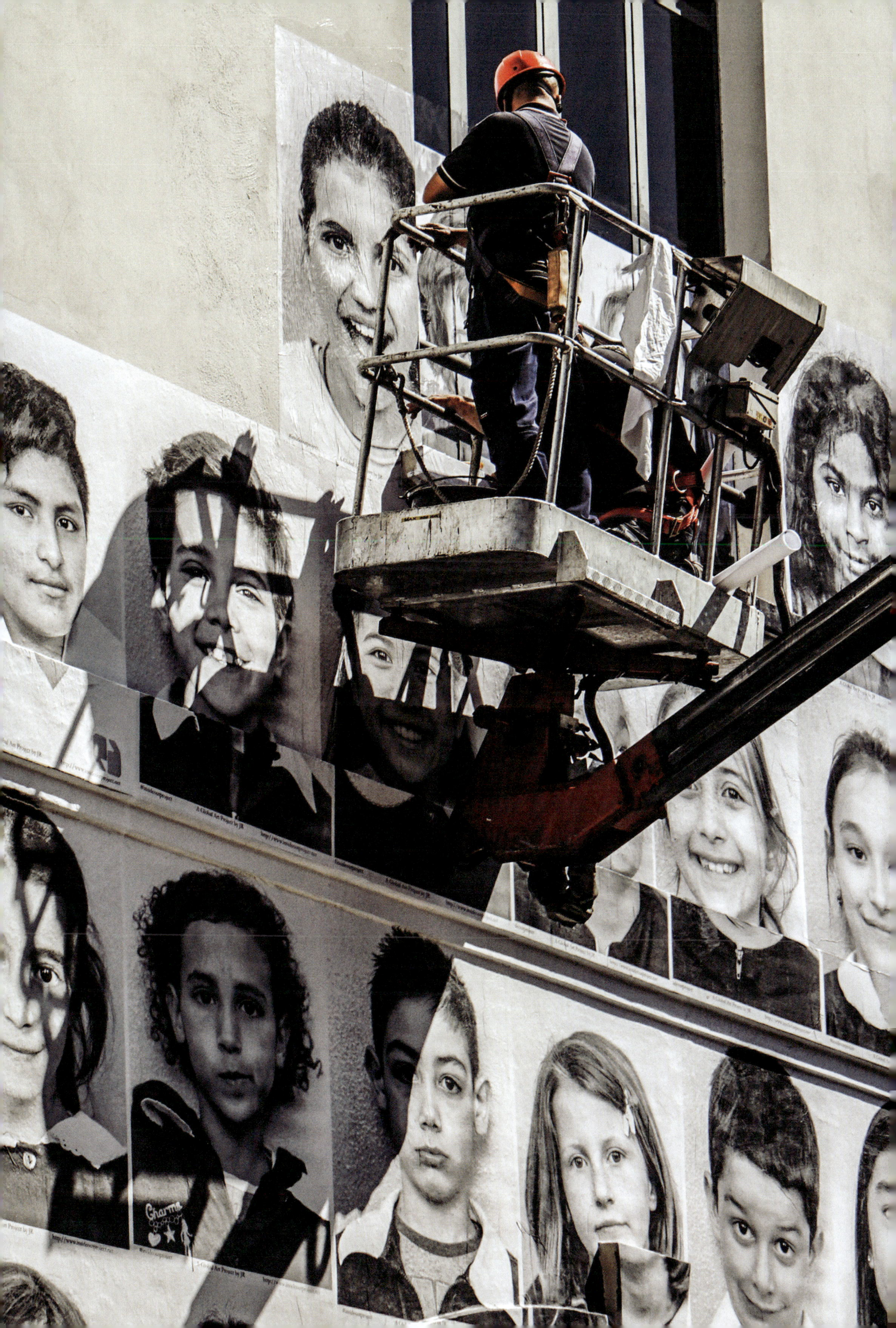
A Global Art Project by JR
Charme

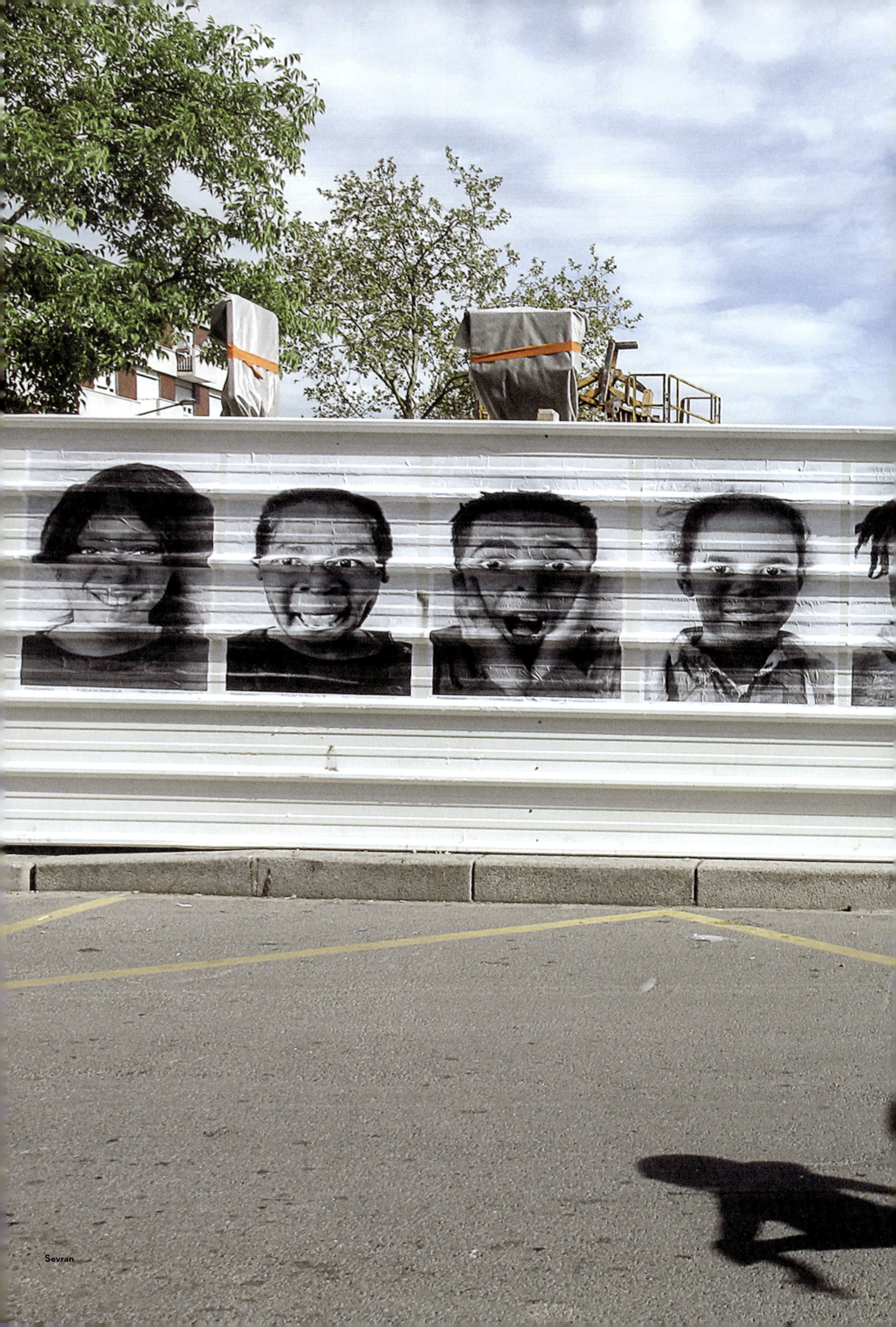

Sevran

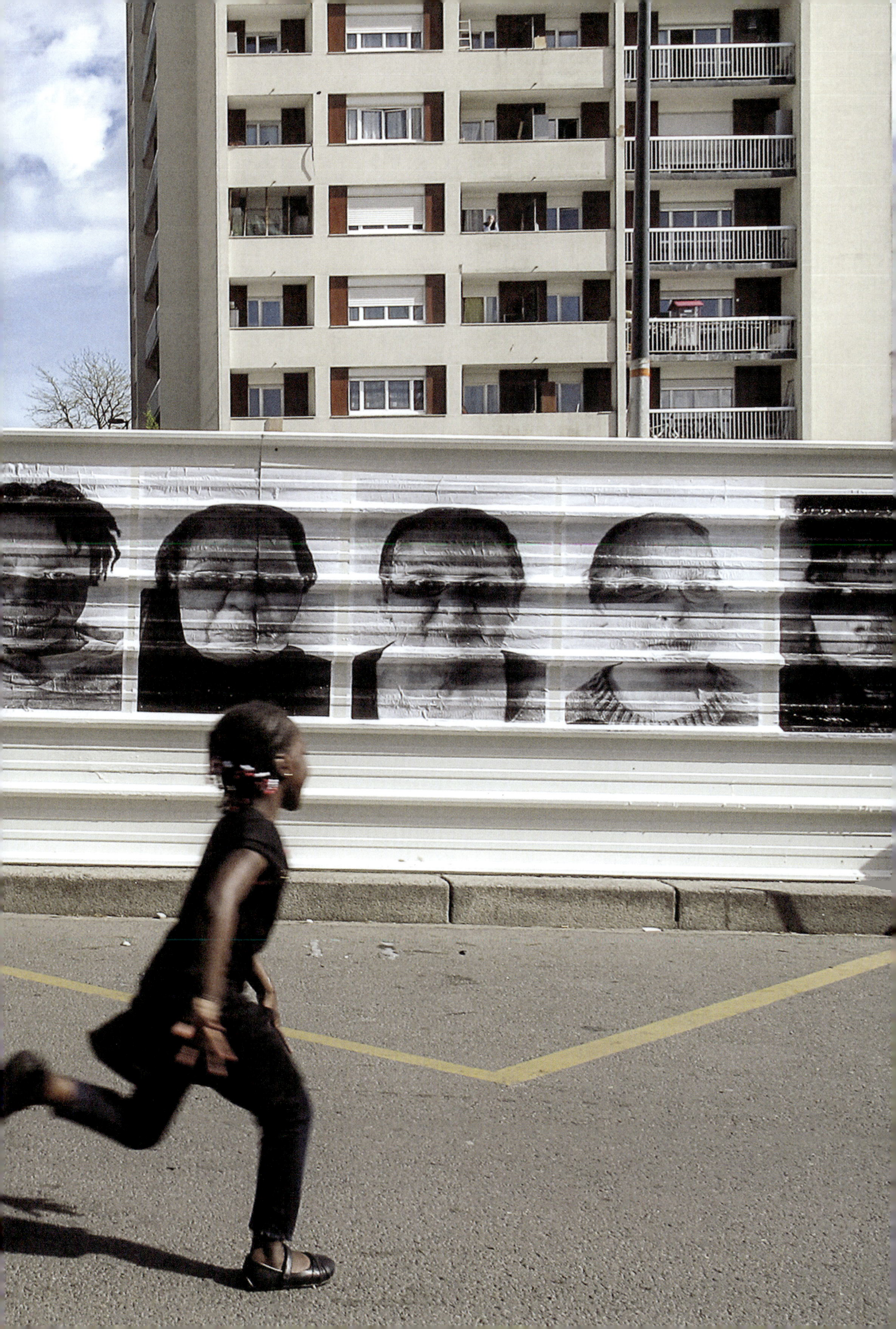

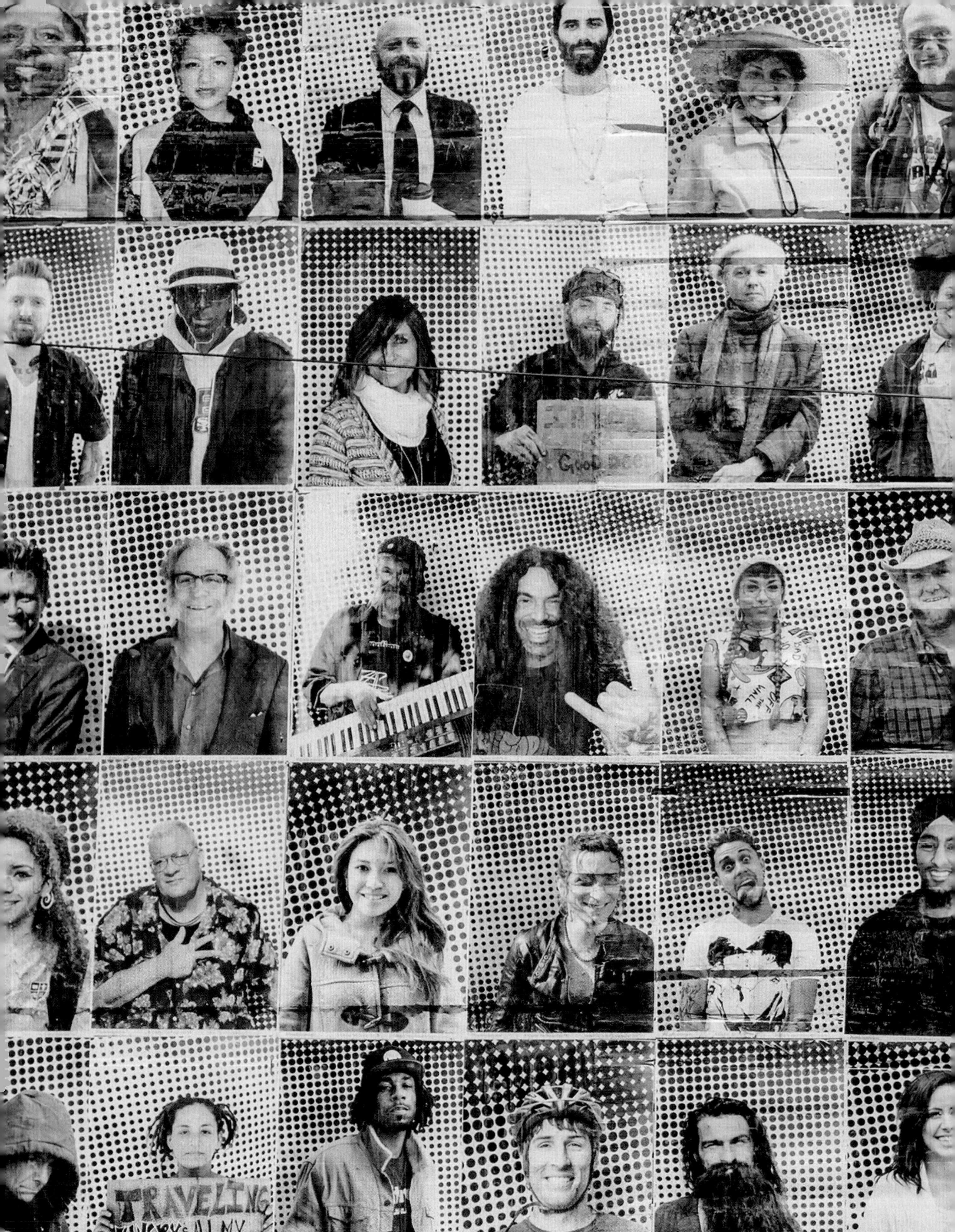

San Francisco, CA

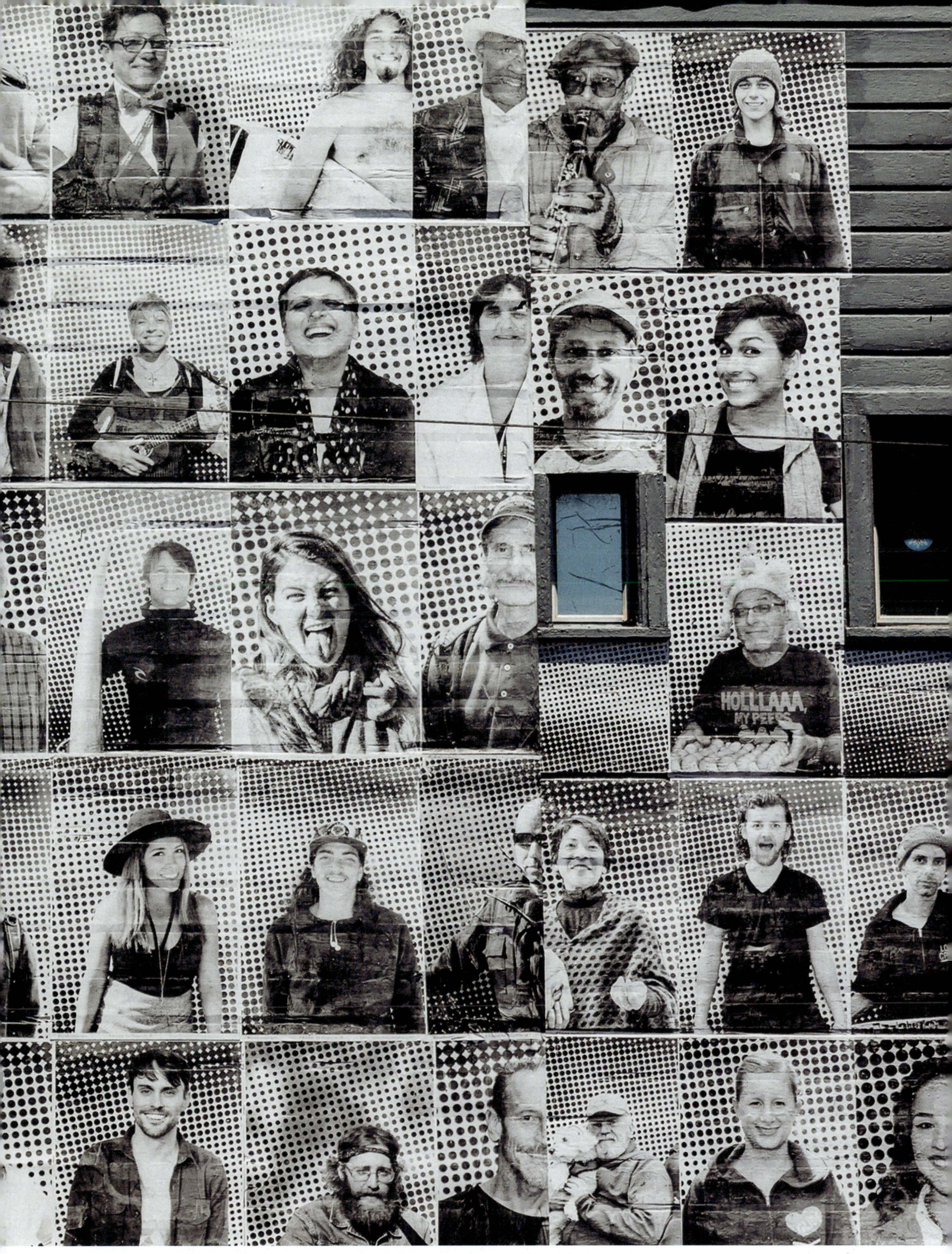
HOLLLAAA

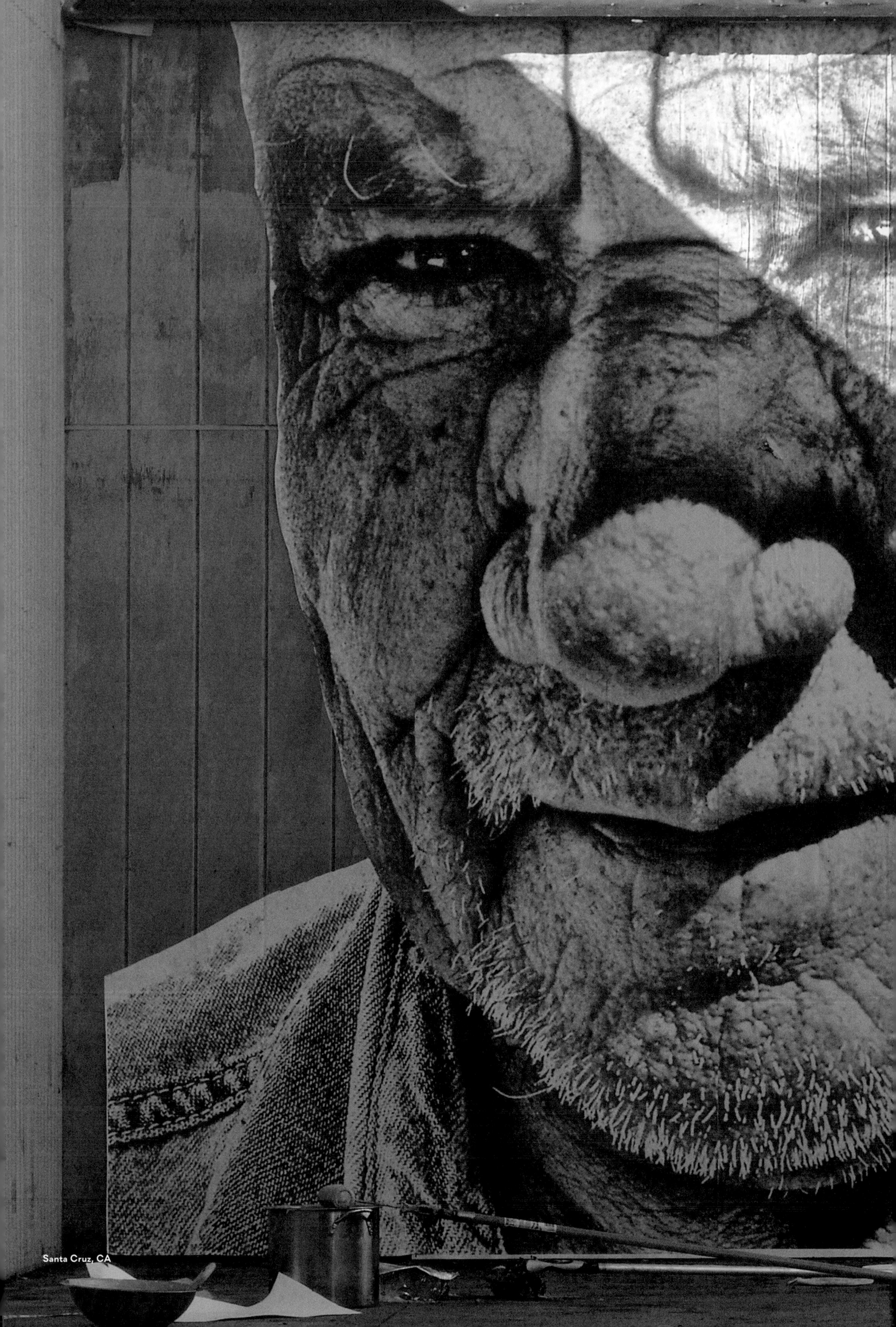

Santa Cruz, CA

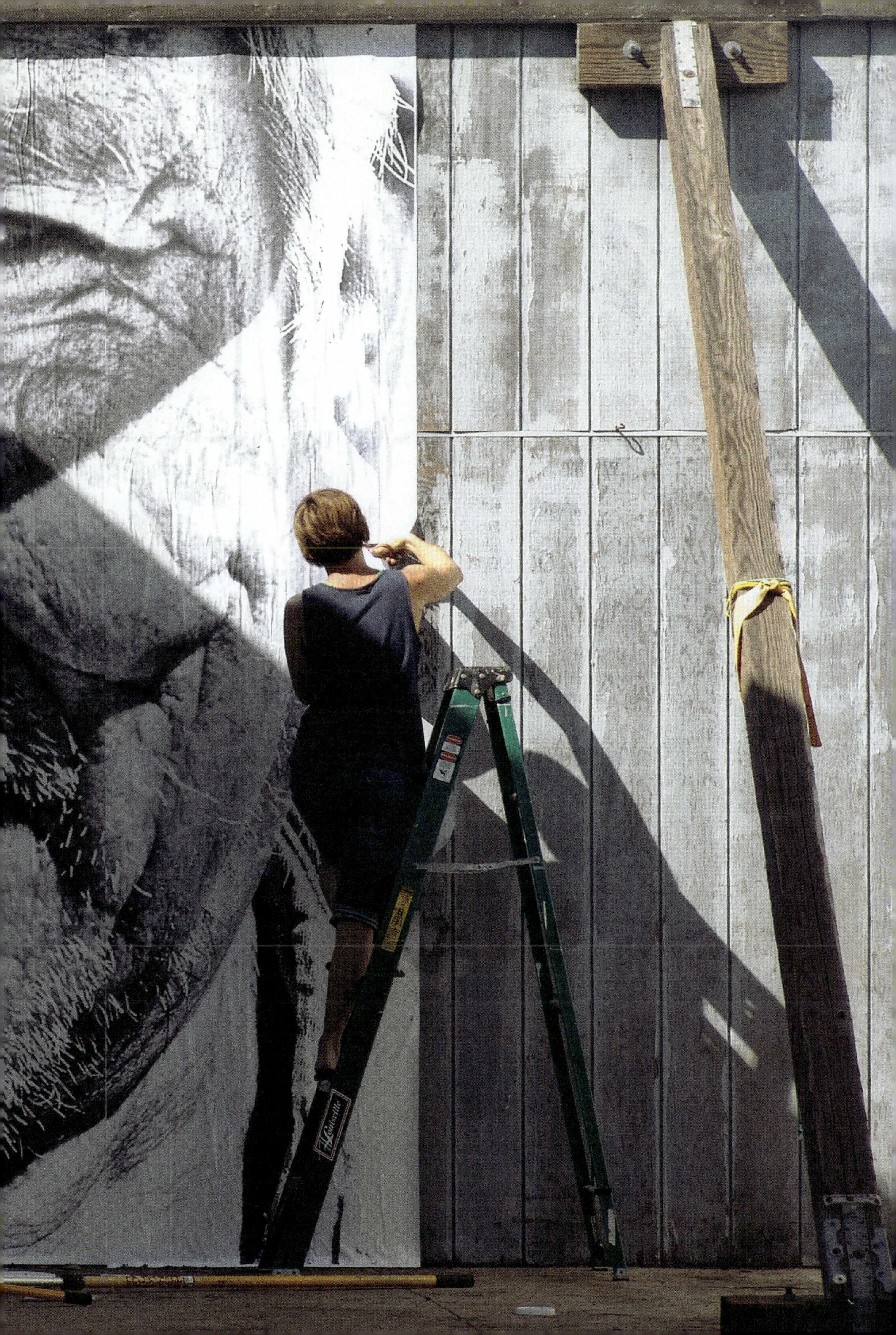

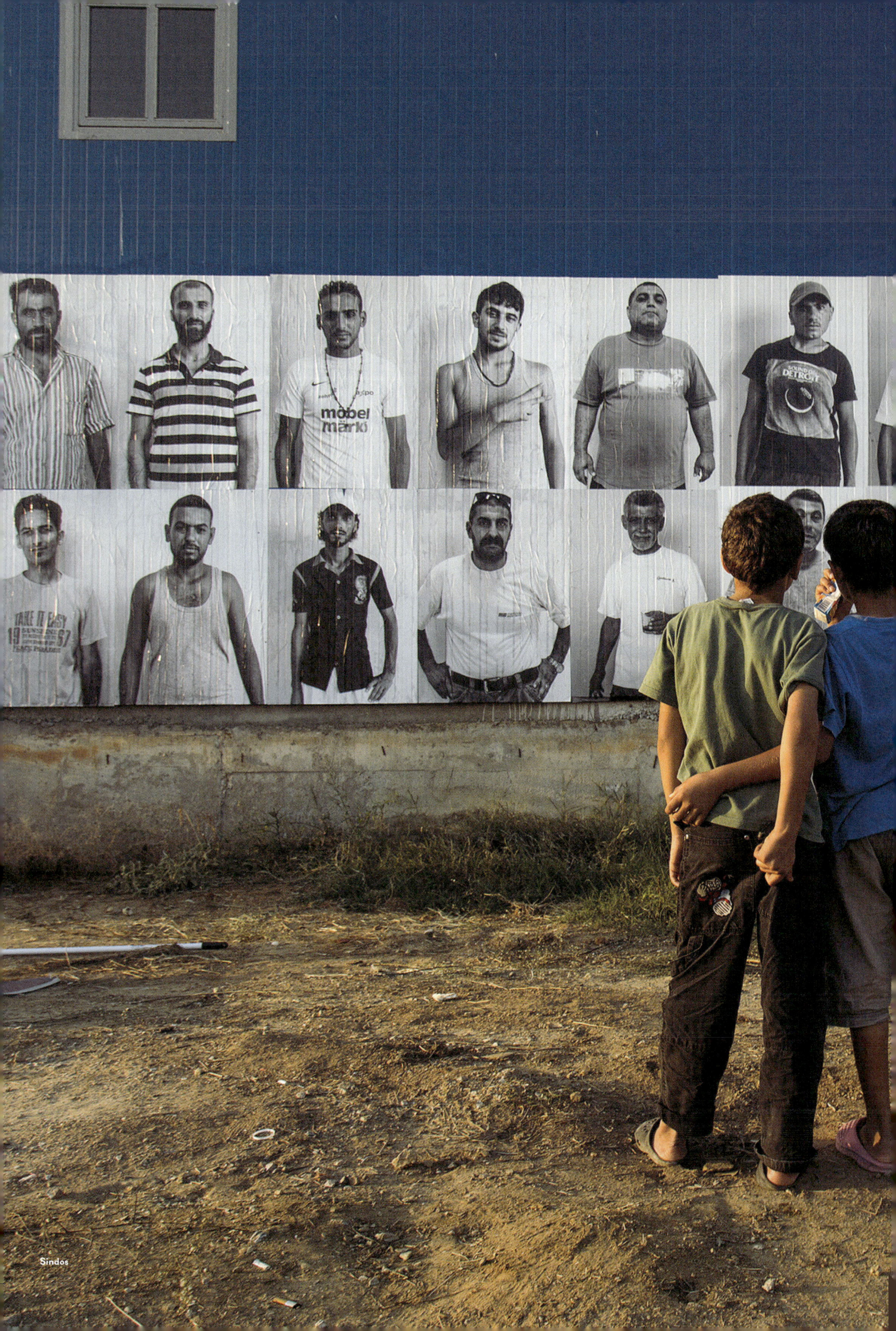

Sindos

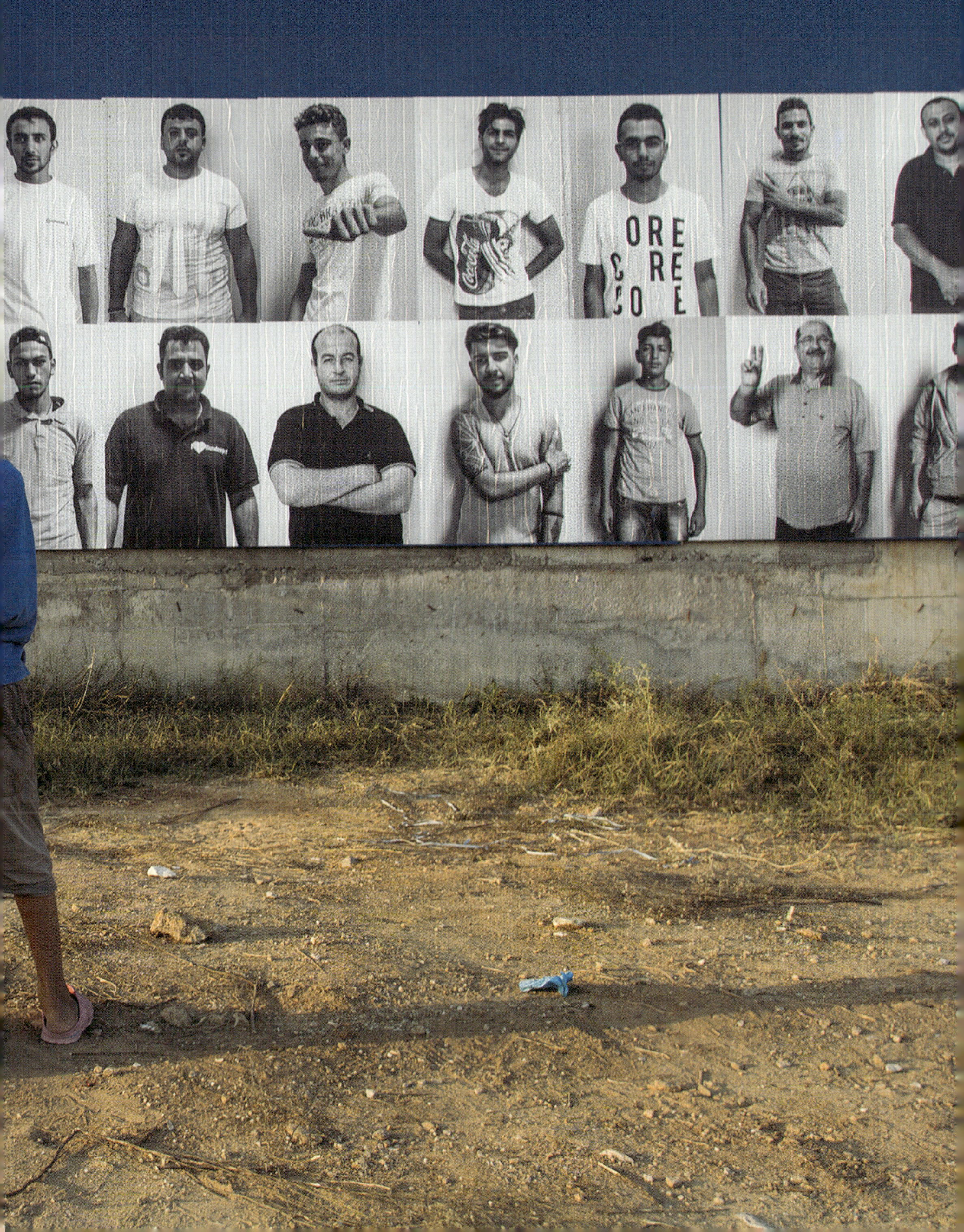

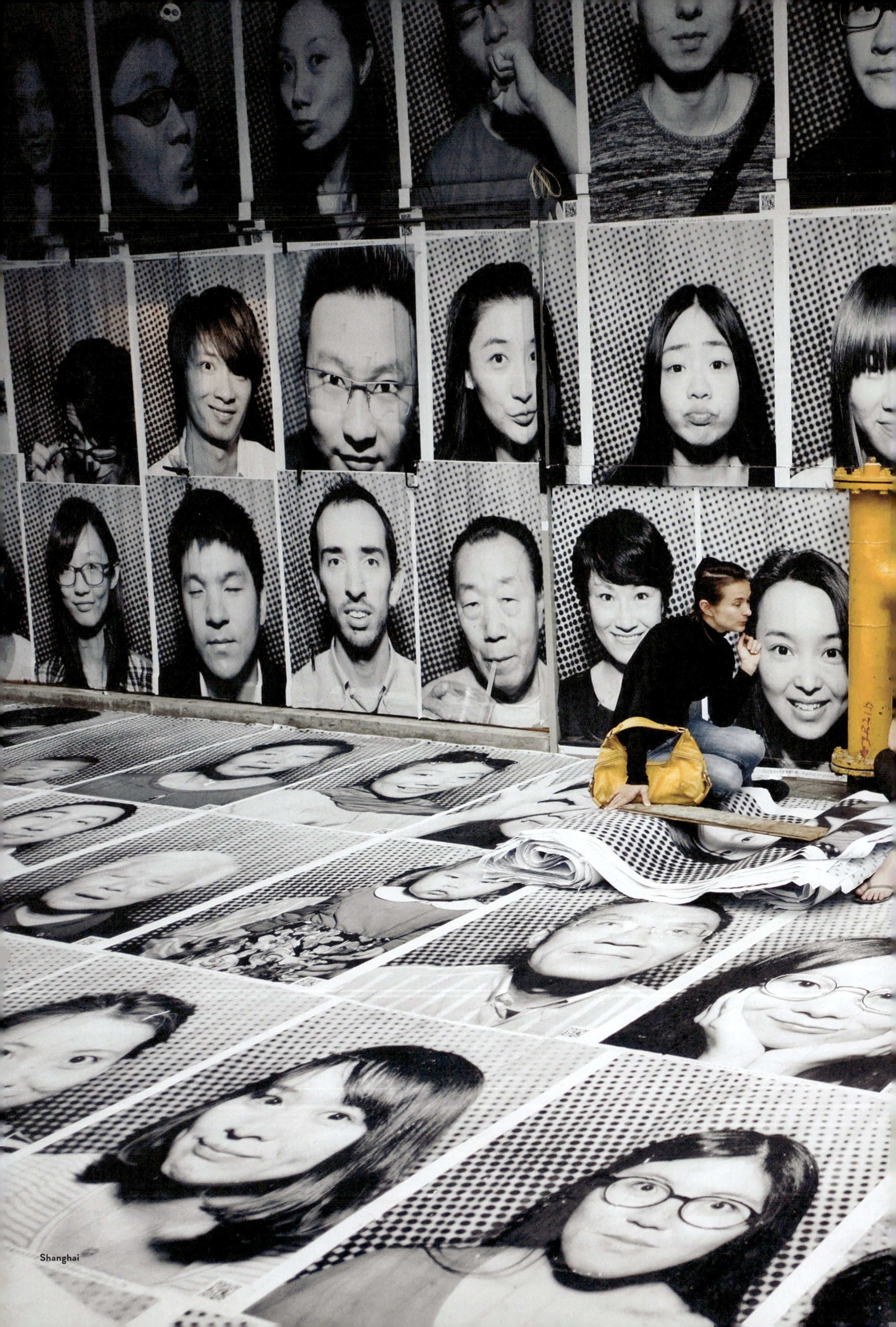

Shanghai

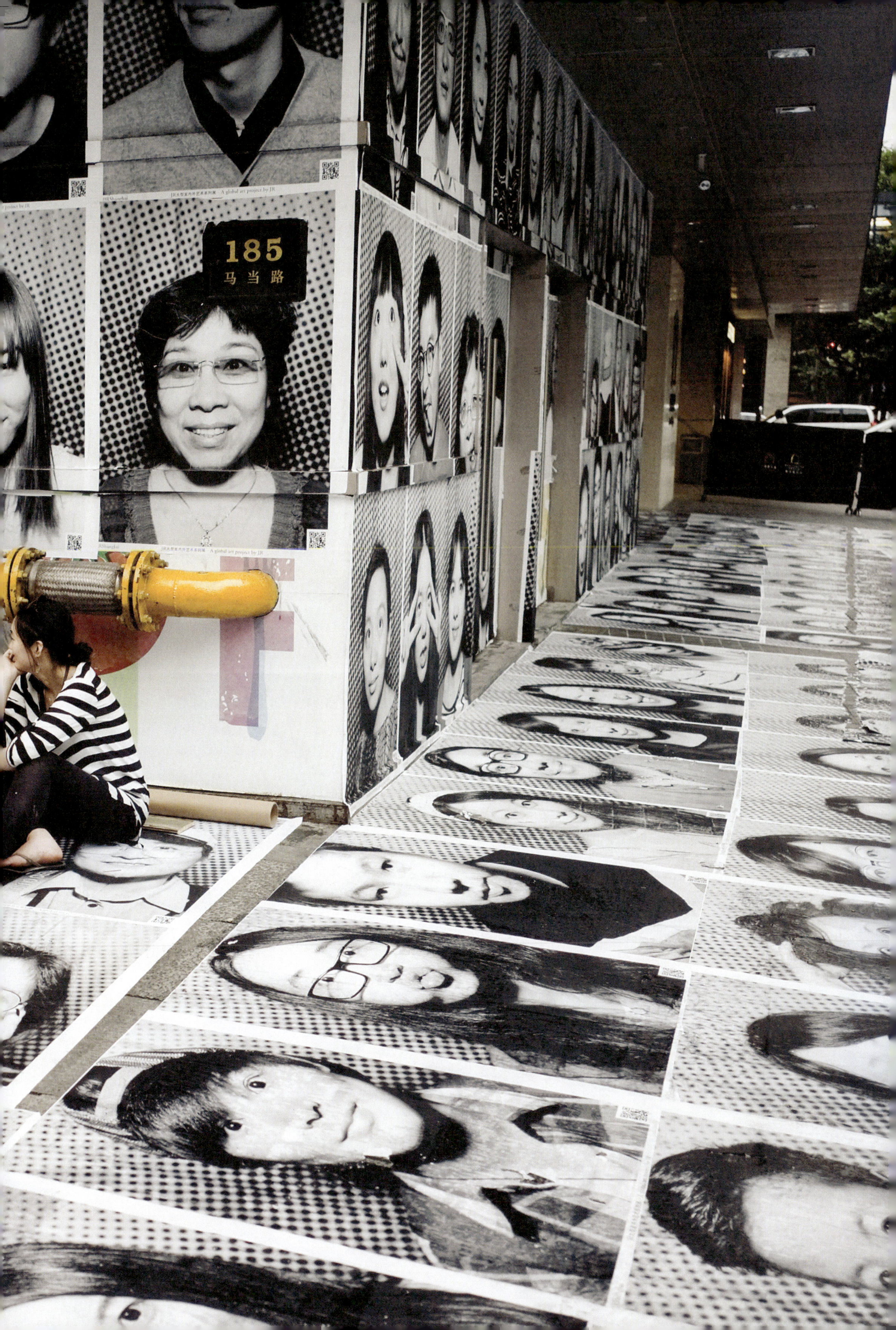
185
马当路

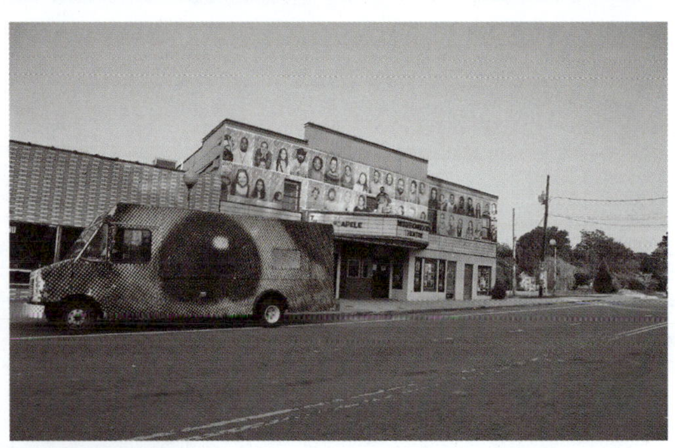

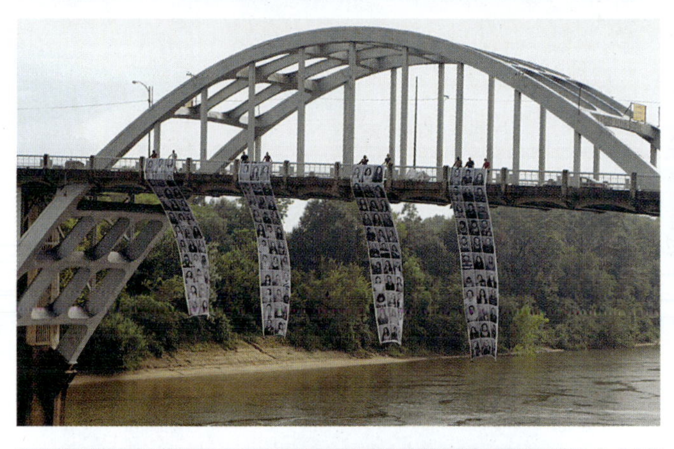

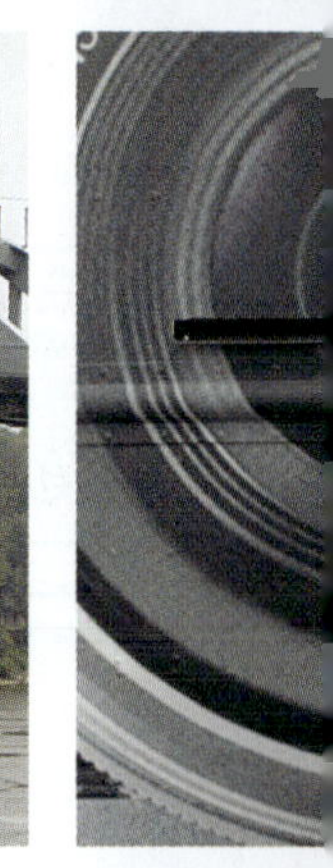

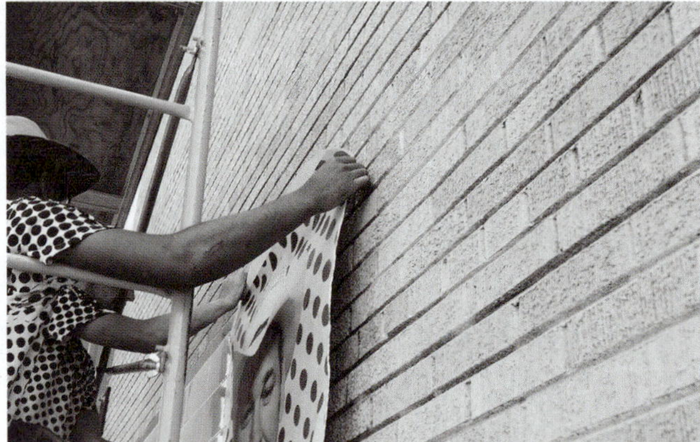

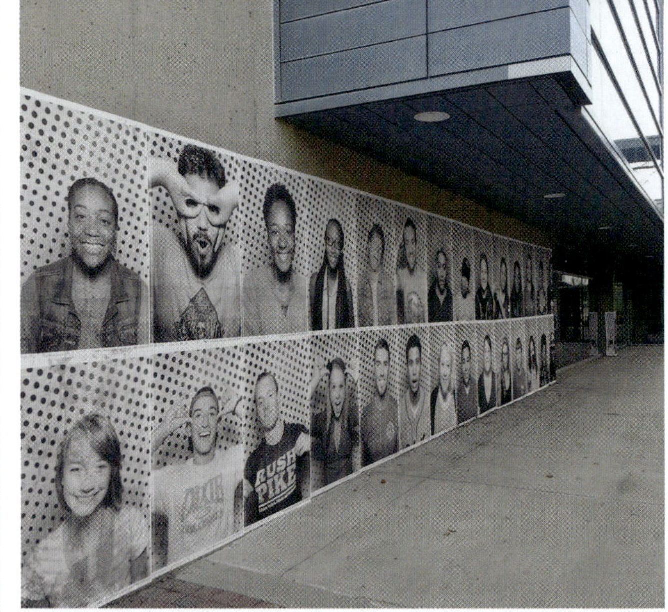

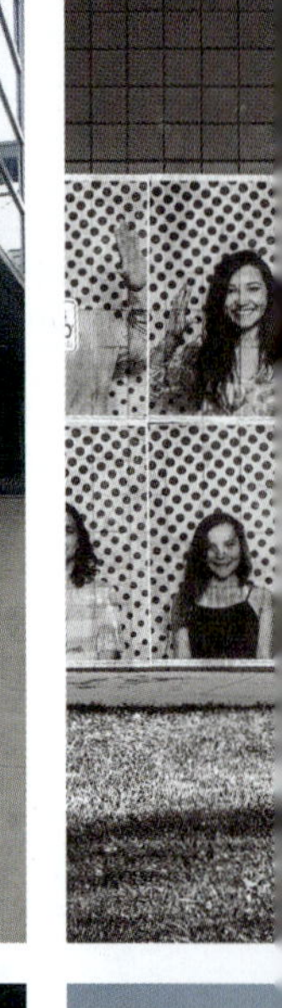

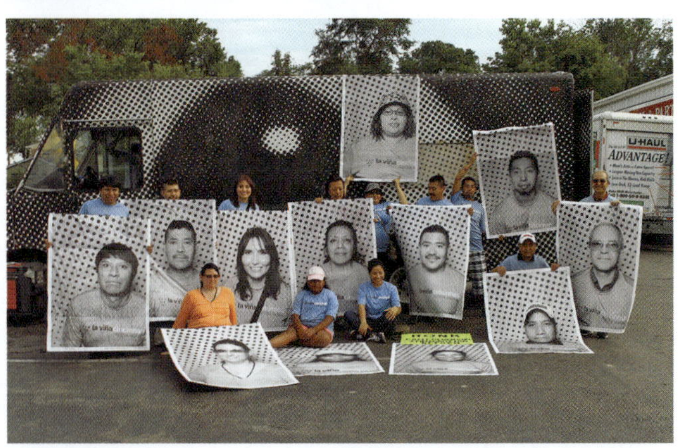

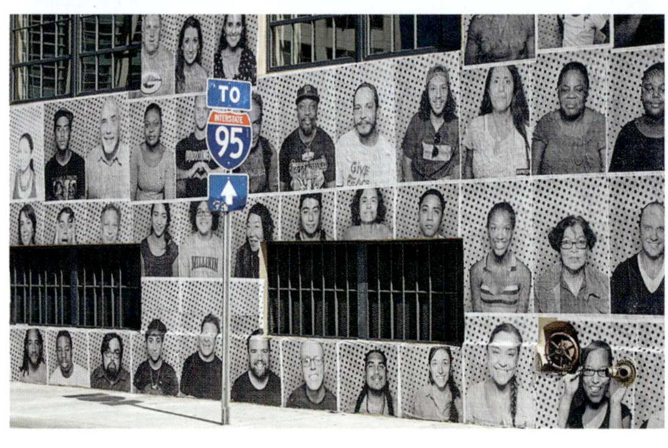

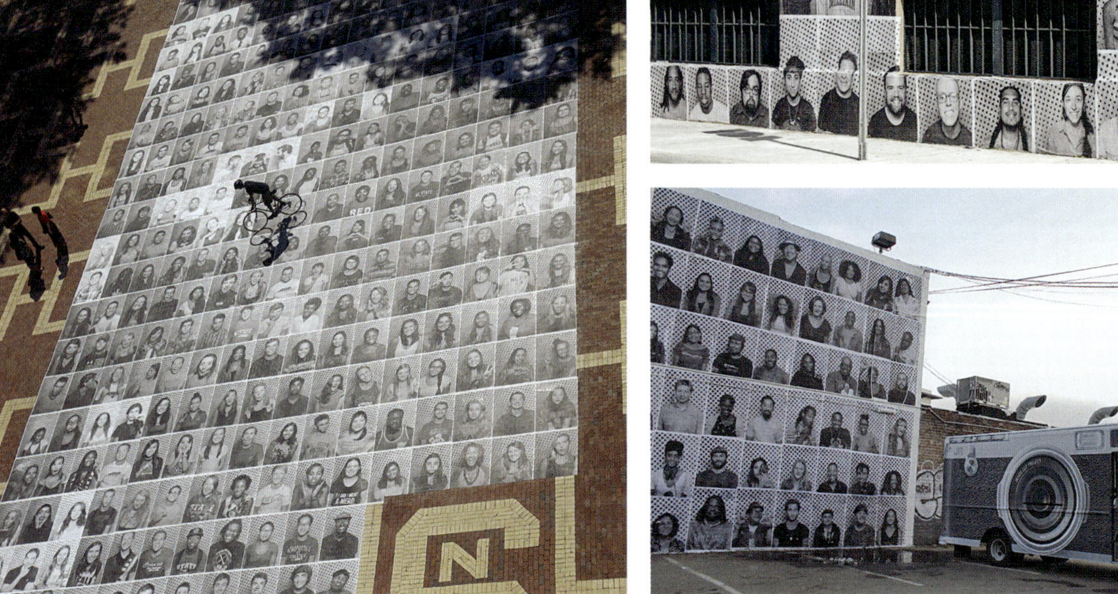

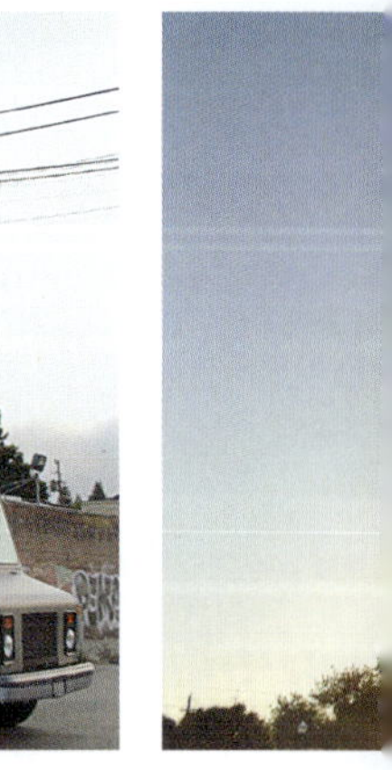

Washington, DC / Richmond, VA / Dayton, OH / Chicago, IL / Montgomery, AL / Selma, AL / Miami, FL / Raleigh, NC / Charlotte, NC / Cincinnati, OH / Sacramento, CA / Oakland, CA / San Francisco, CA / Los Angeles, CA / Las Vegas, NV / Denver, CO / San Antonio, TX / Dallas, TX / Phoenix, AZ

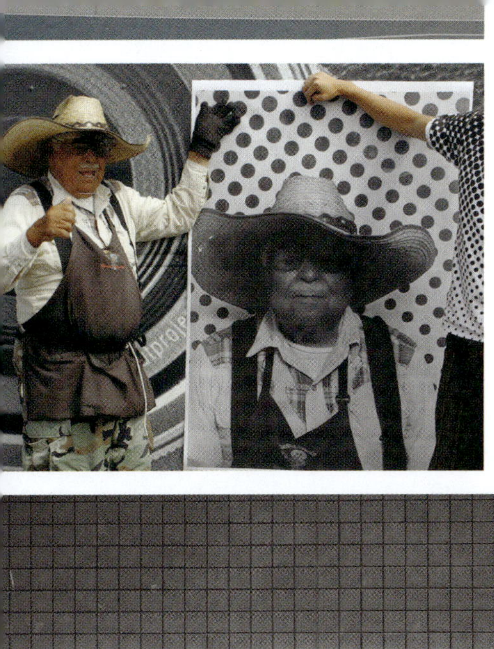
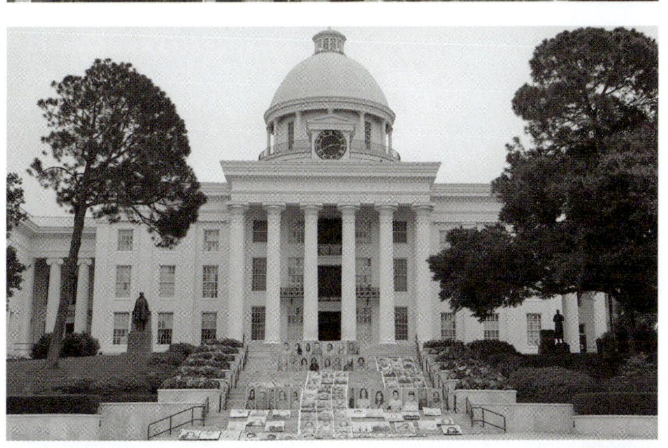
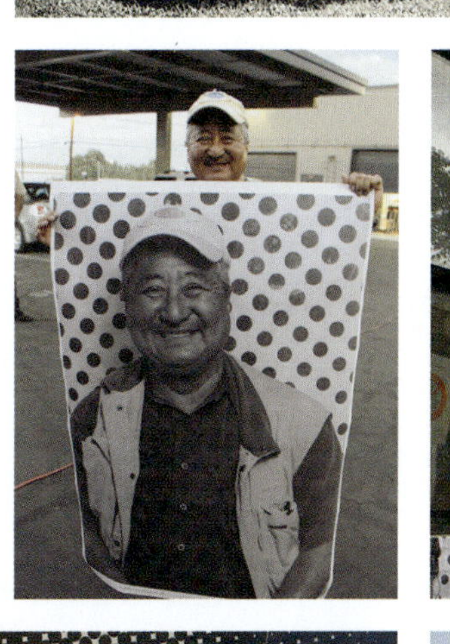
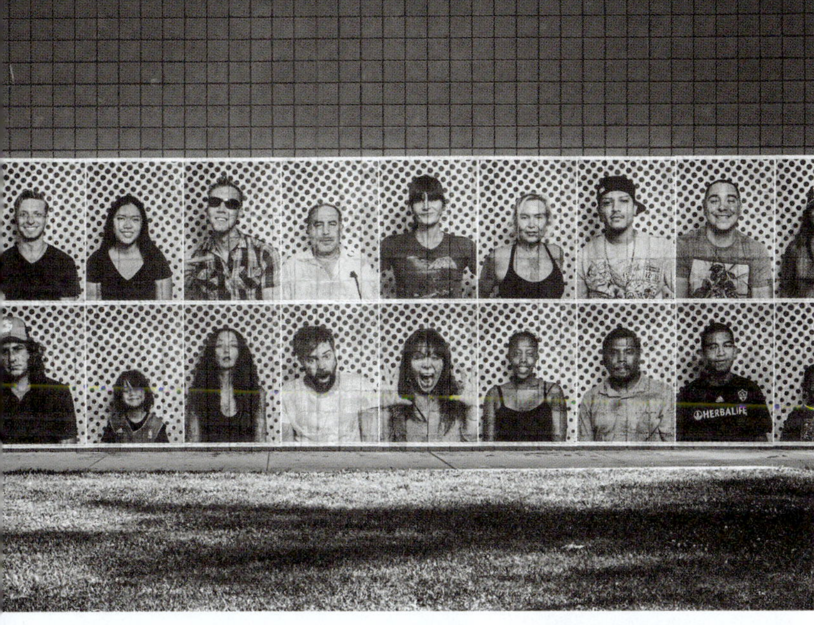

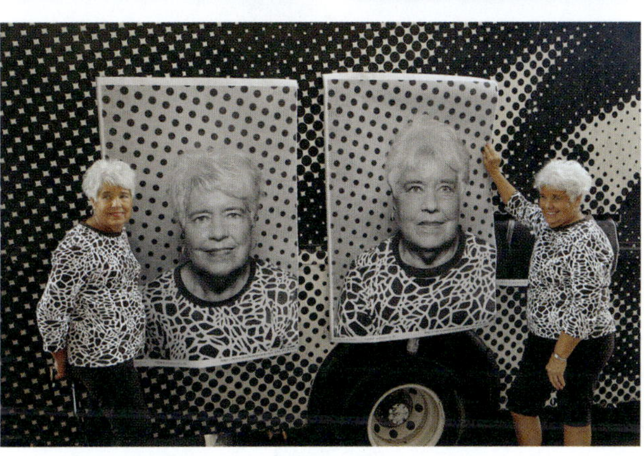
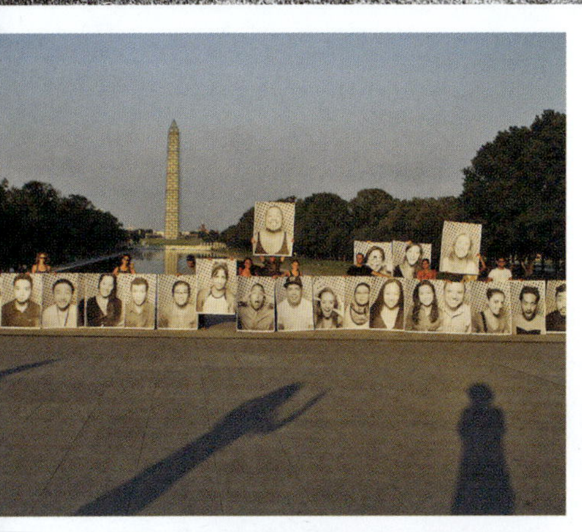
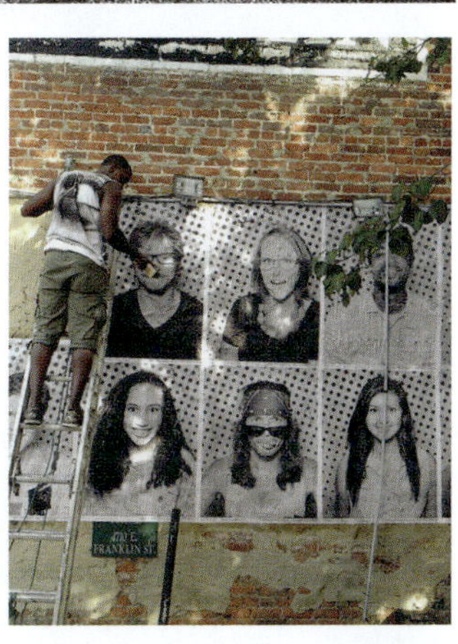
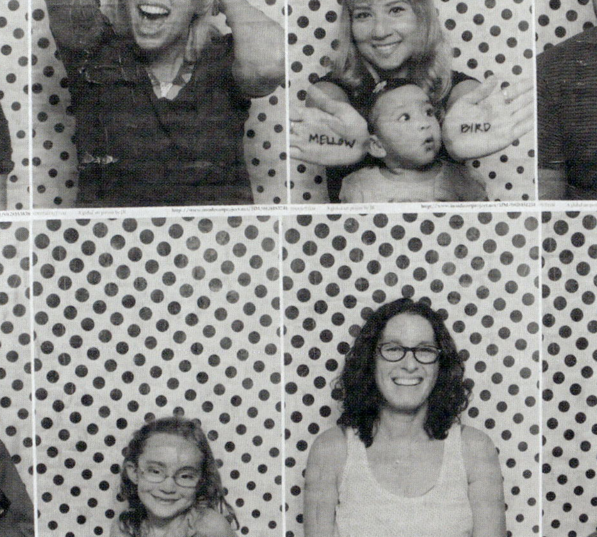

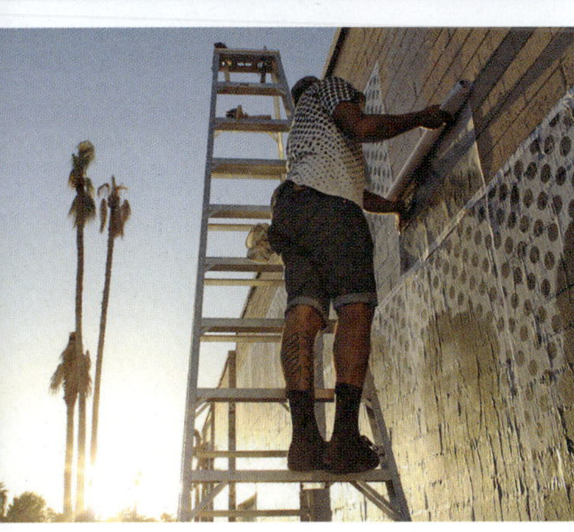
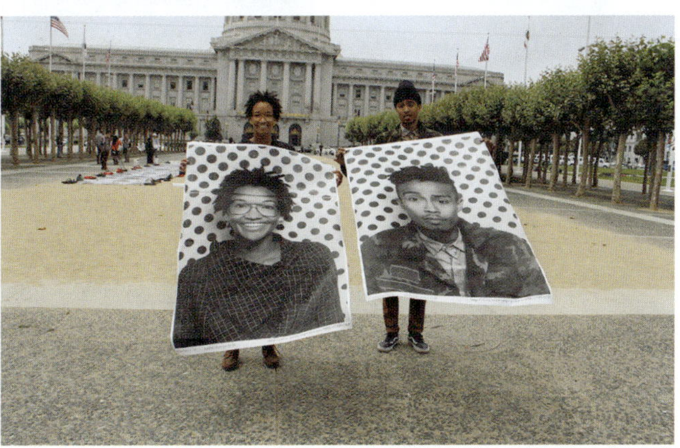
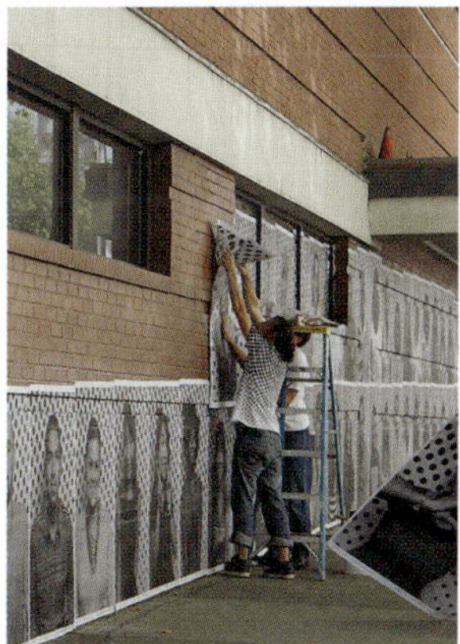

"Beyond any political debate about the eleven million undocumented immigrants living in the US, these portraits remind us that behind the numbers are real human stories. This action aimed to represent the diversity and unity of people that can call the US home. This large group action lasted four months, and utilized two photobooth trucks that traveled around the US. More than 9000 portraits were taken and pasted."

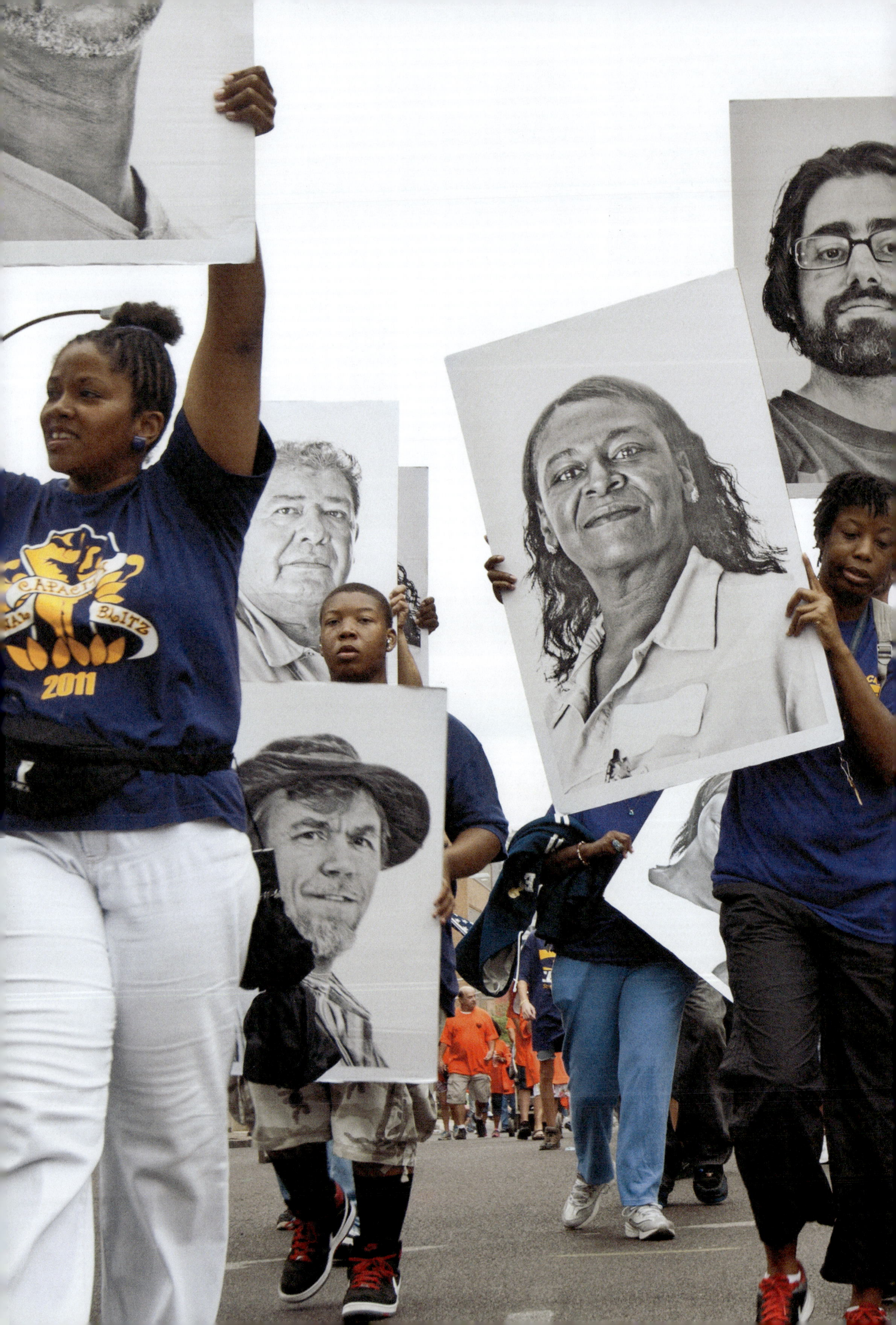
2011

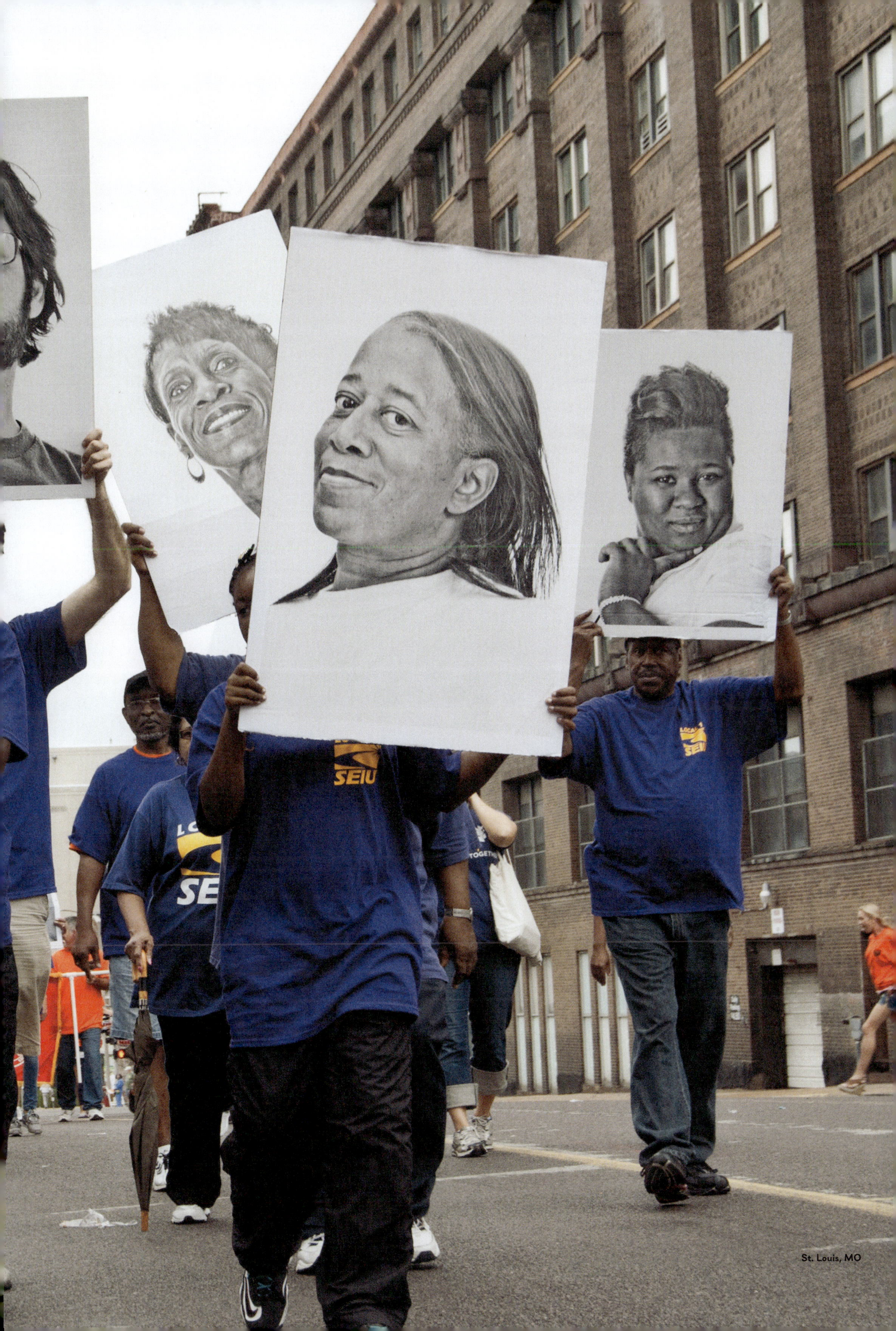

St. Louis, MO

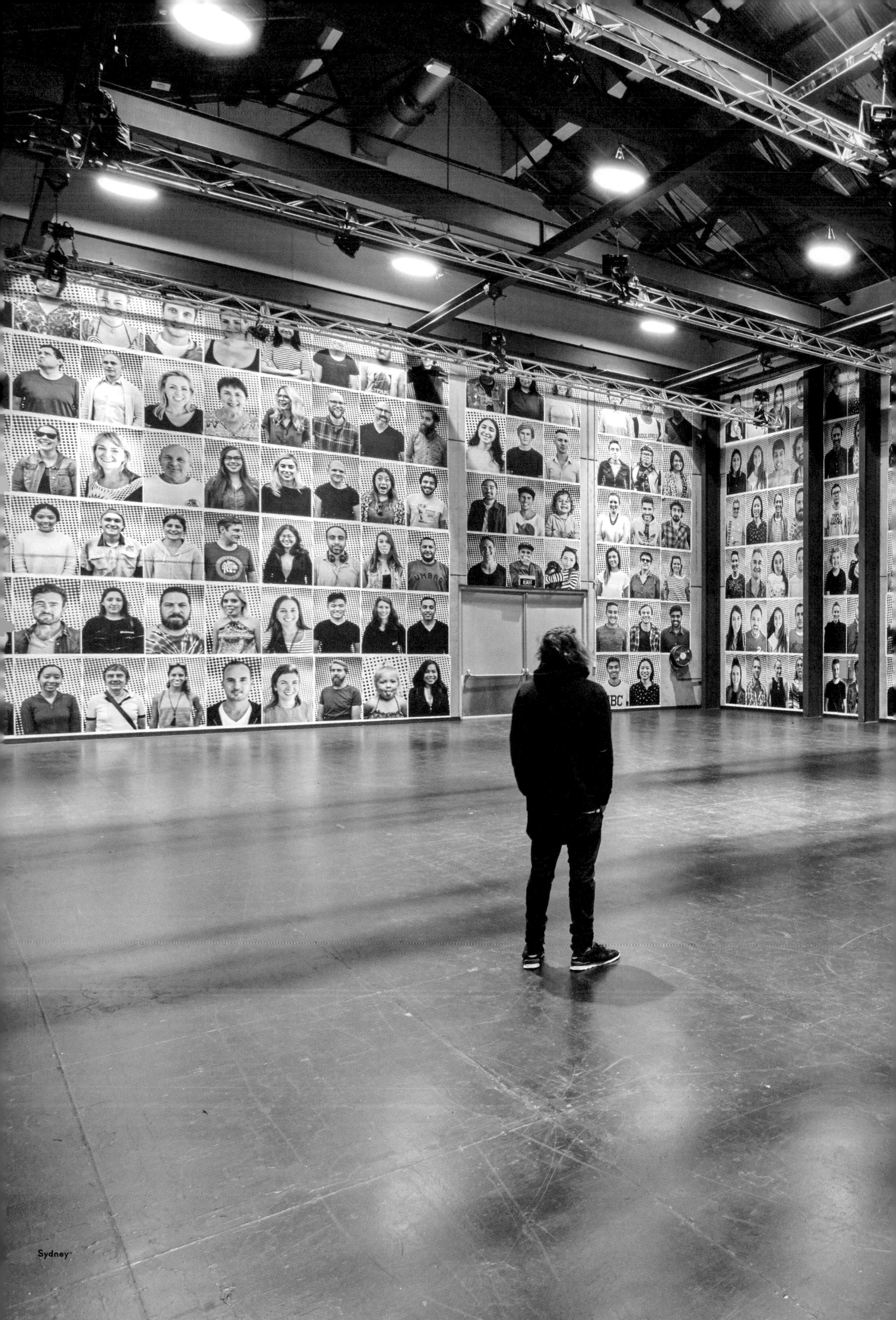

Sydney

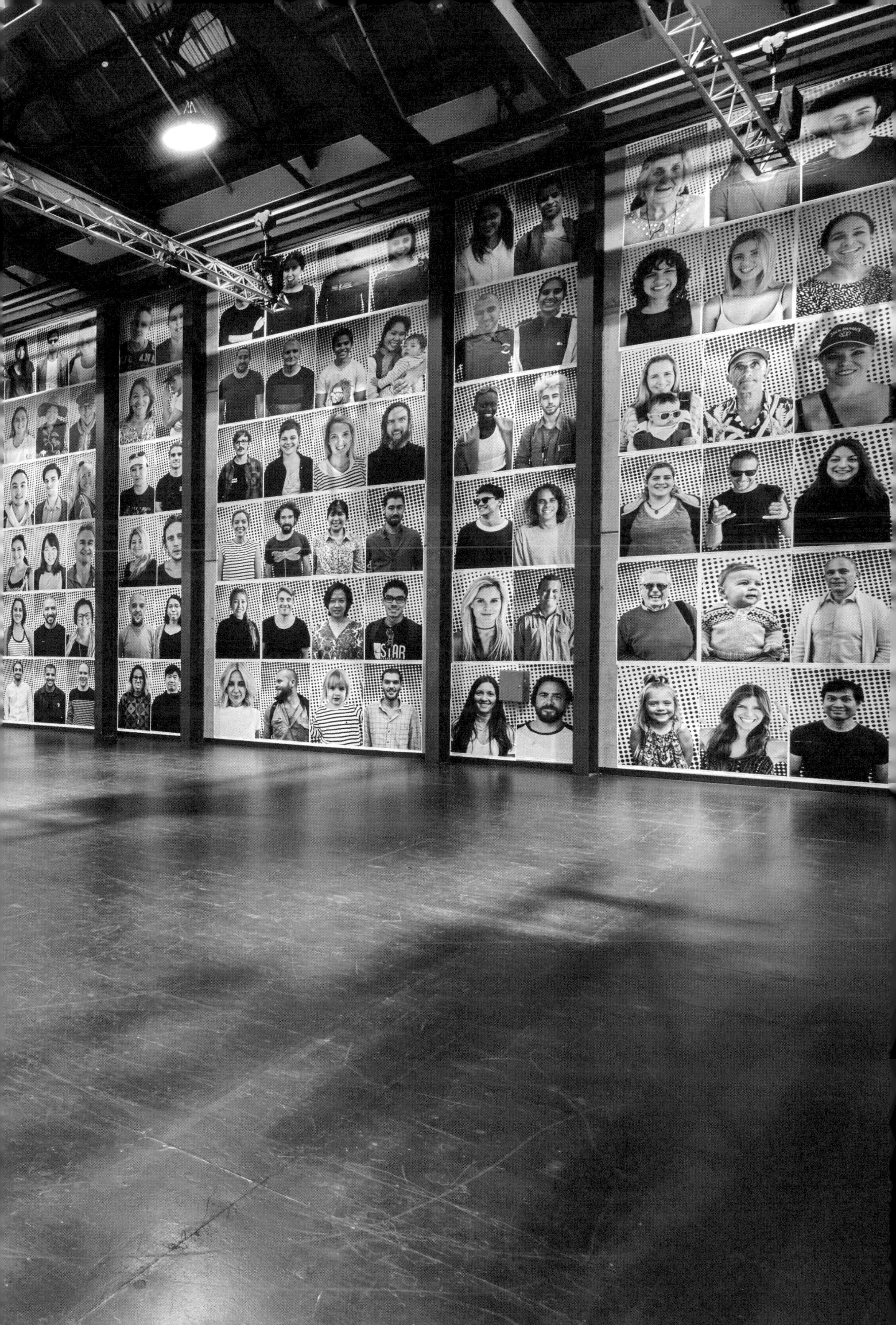
STAR

Tashkent

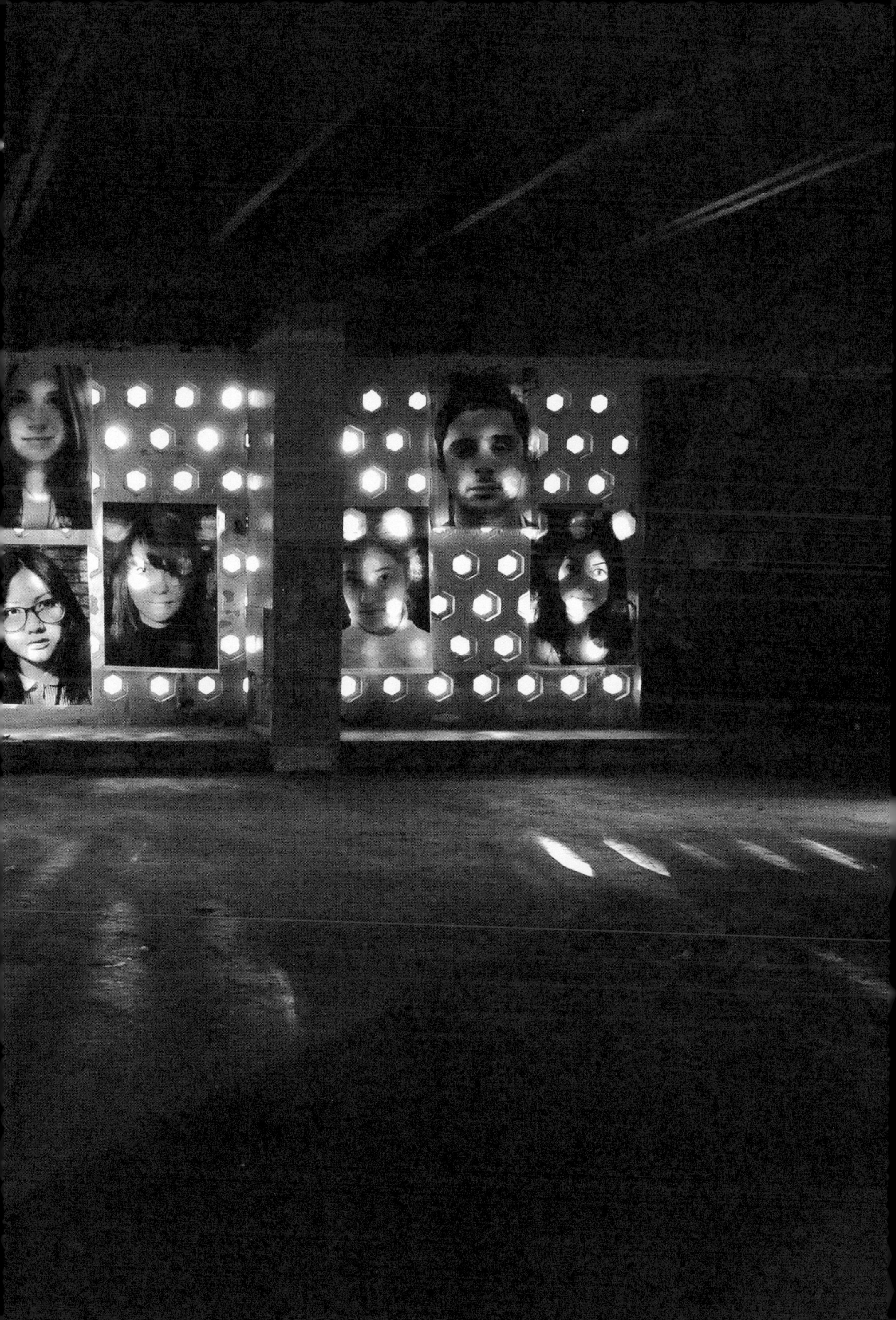

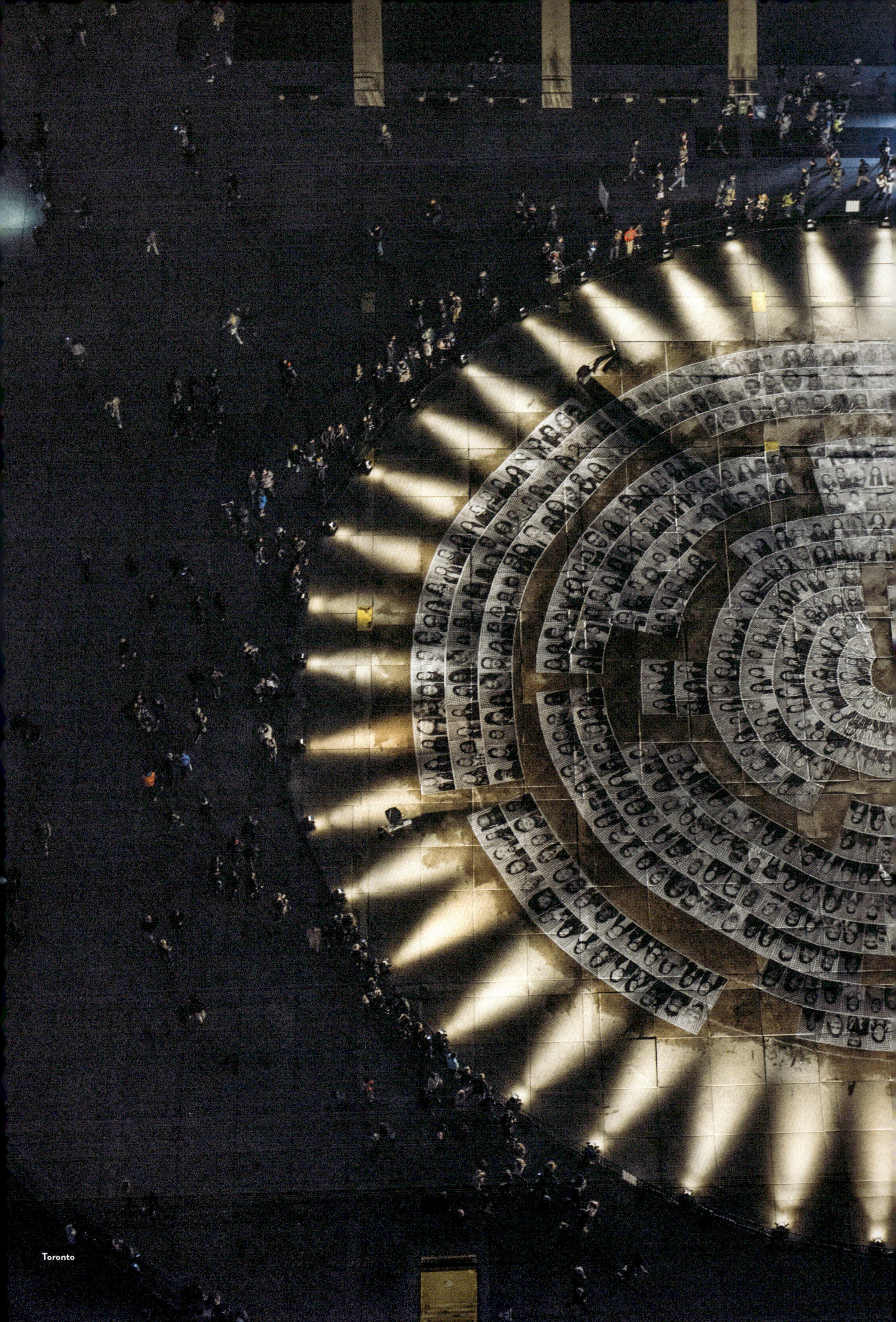

Toronto

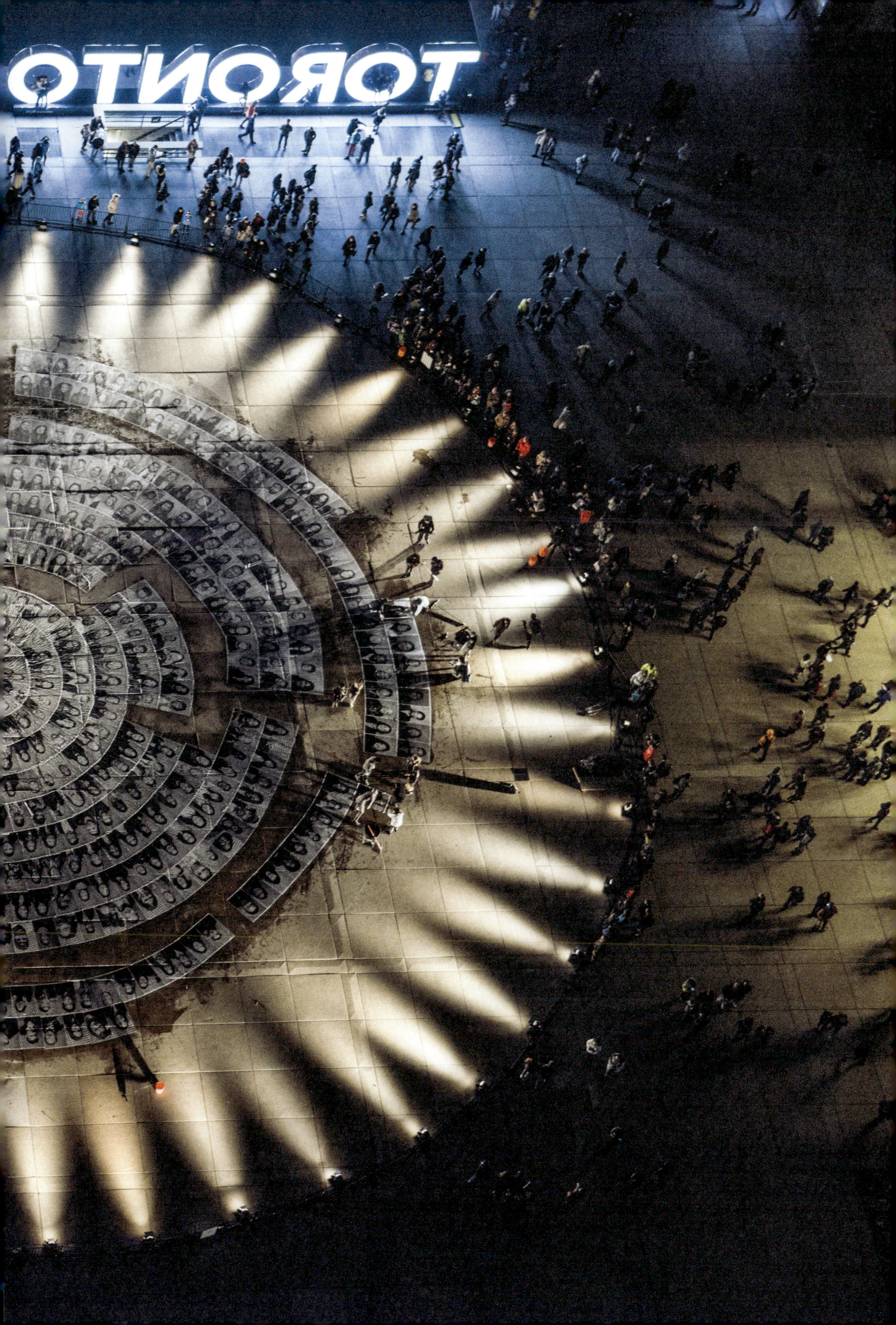
TORONTO

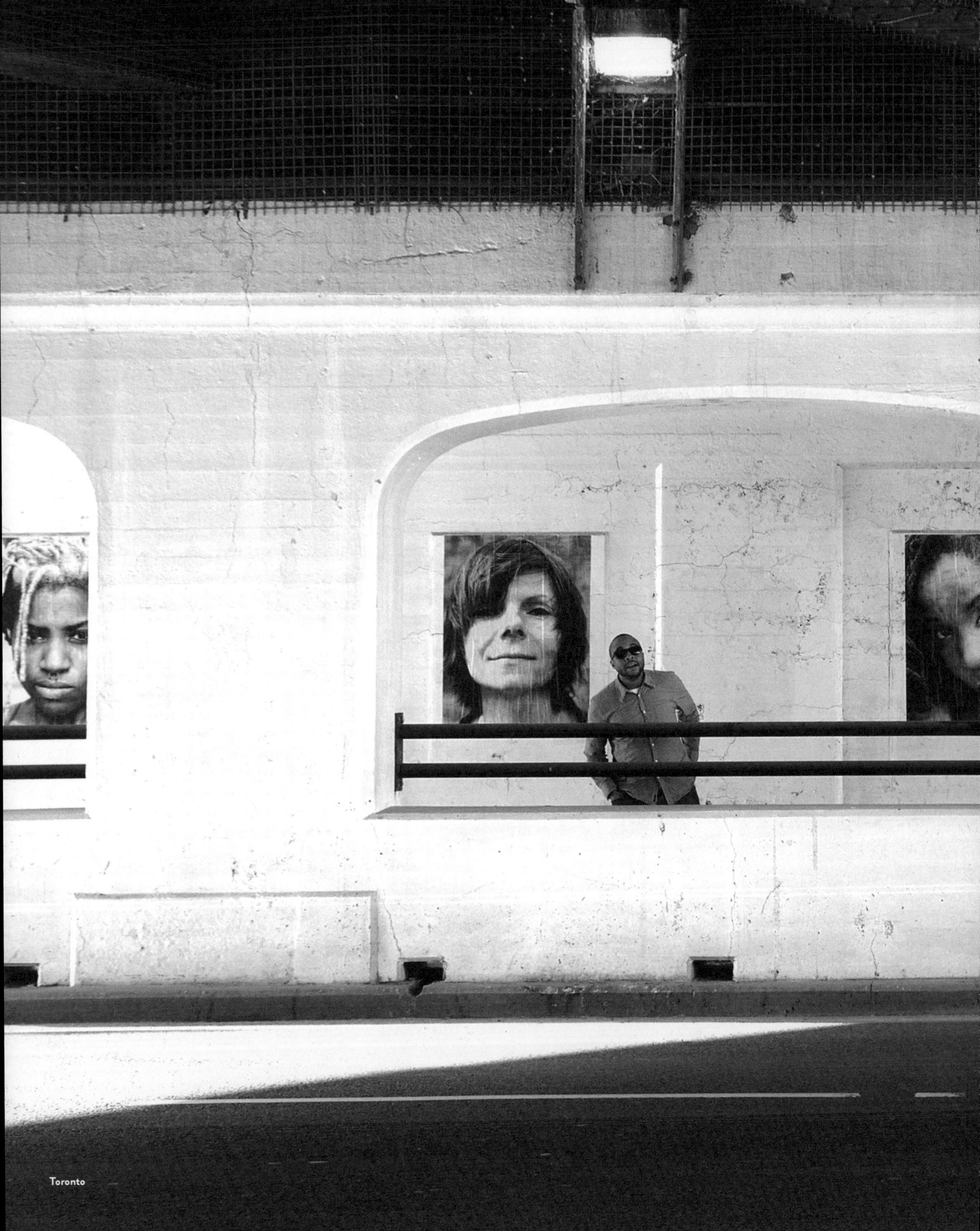

Toronto

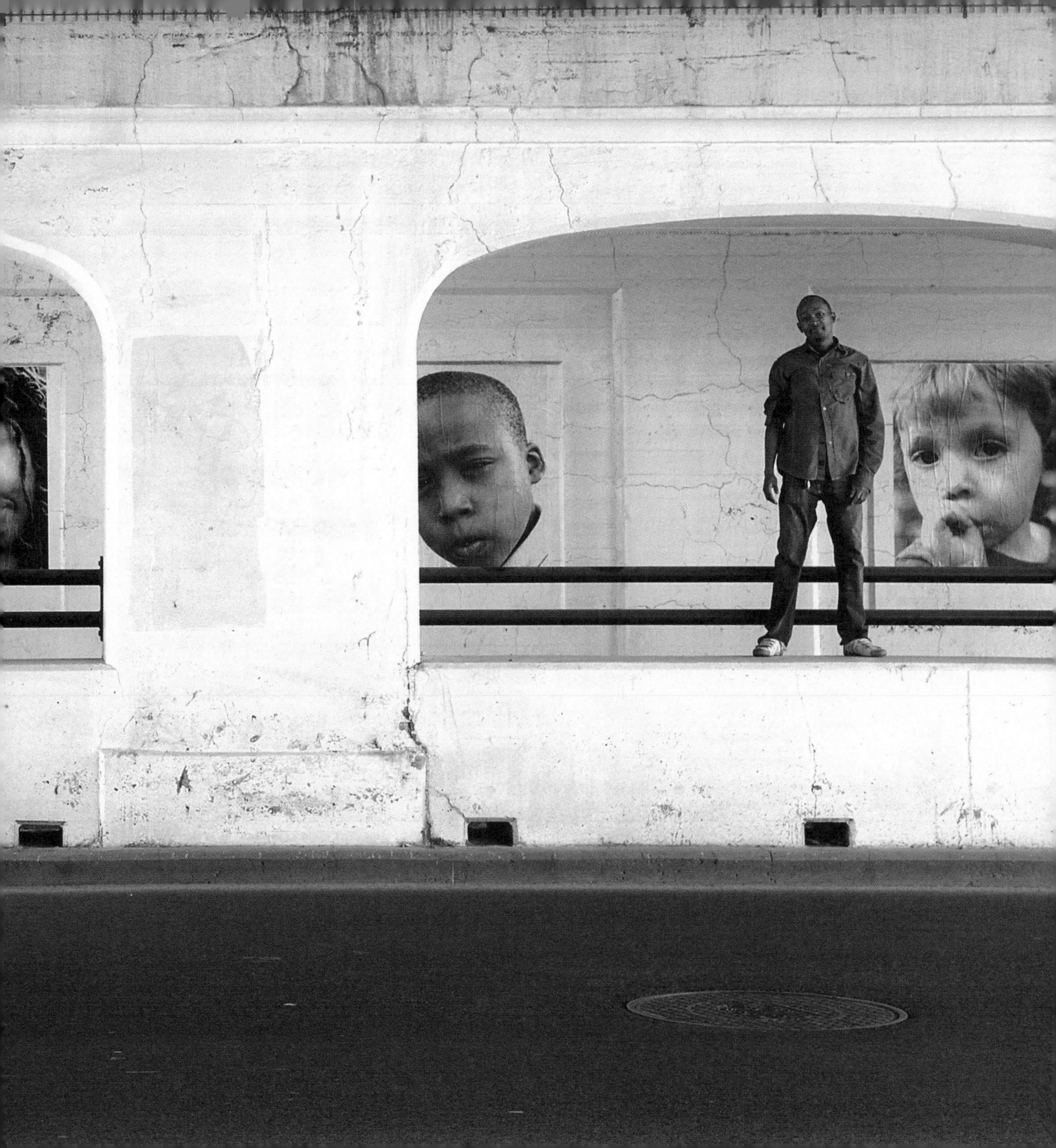

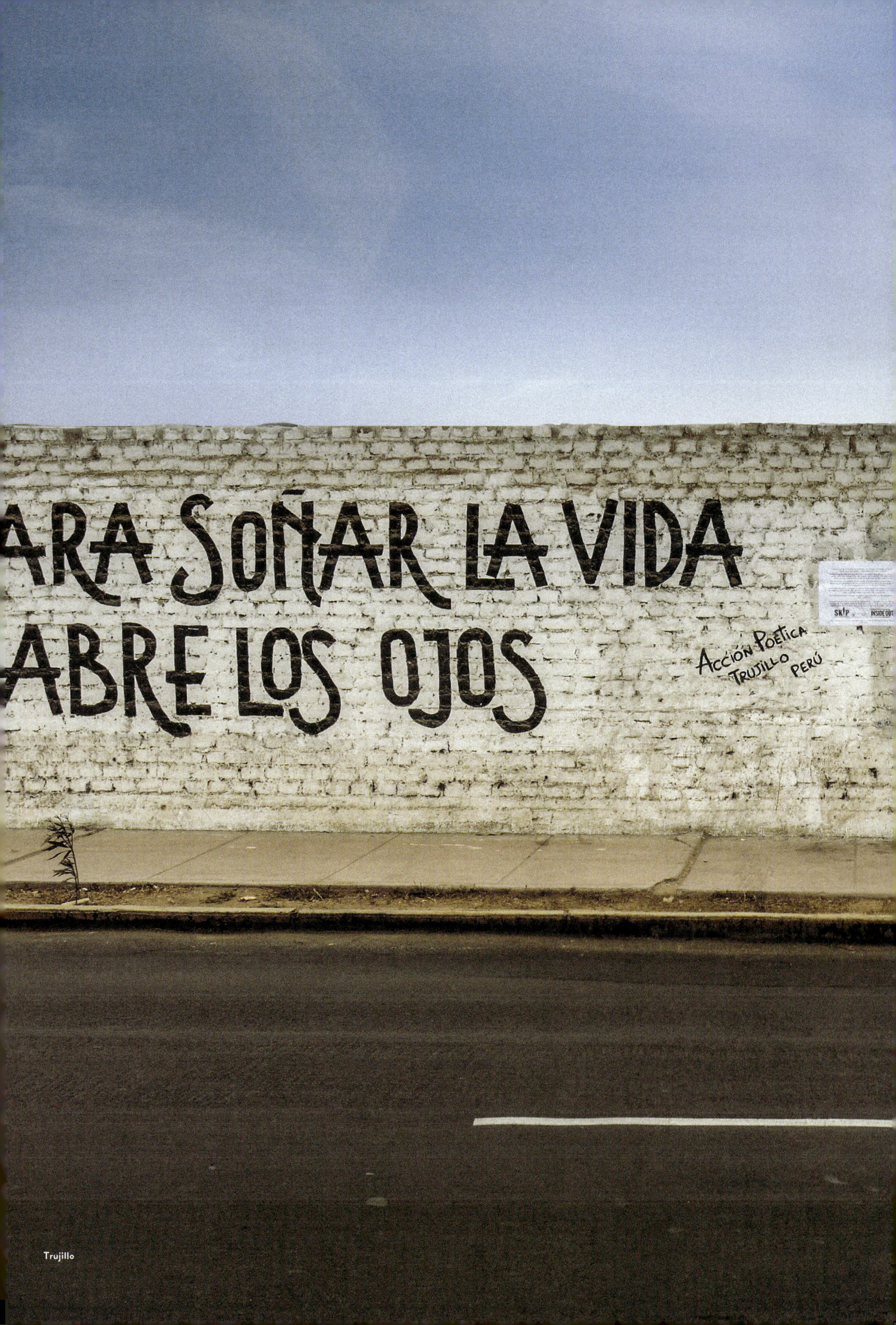

Trujillo

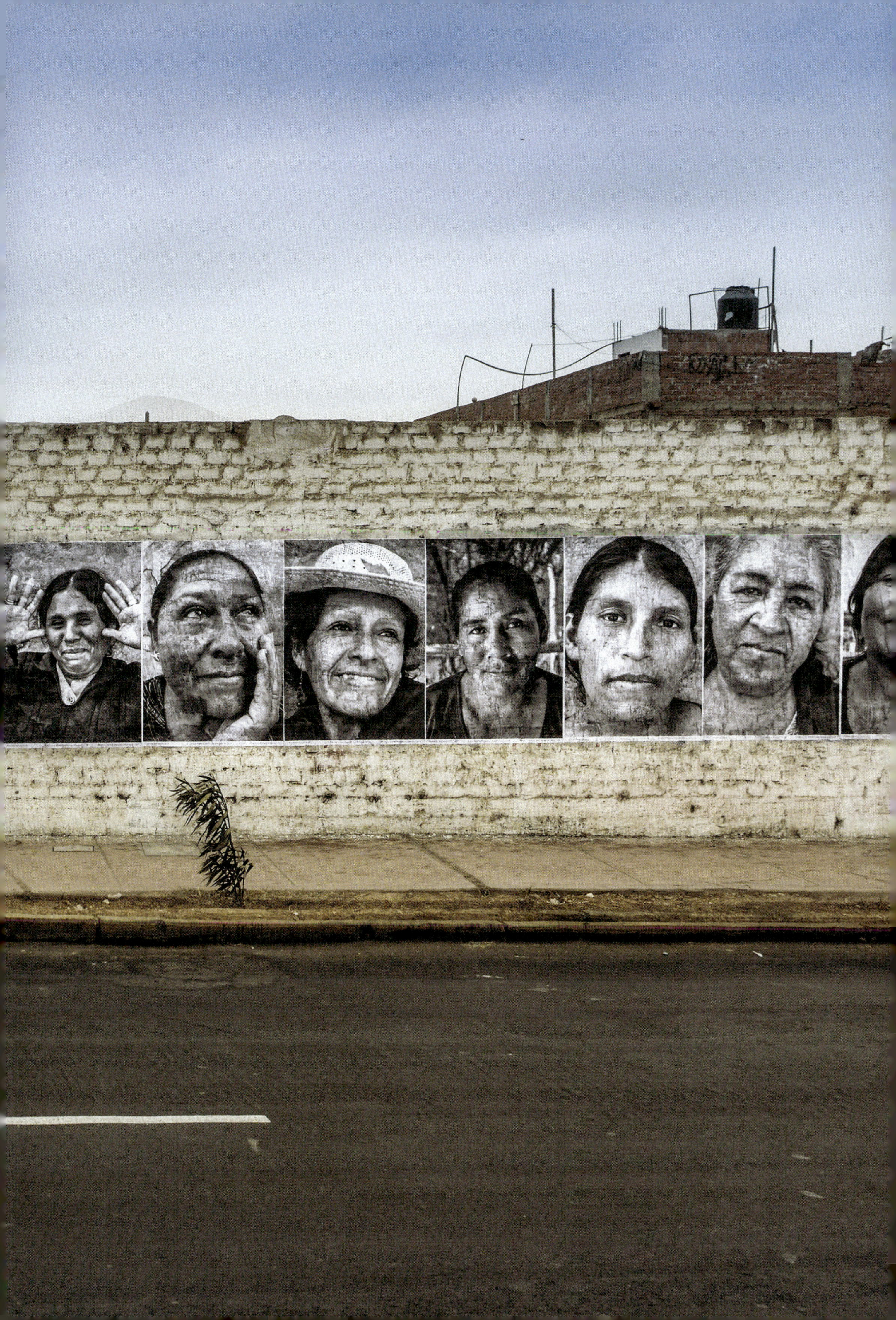

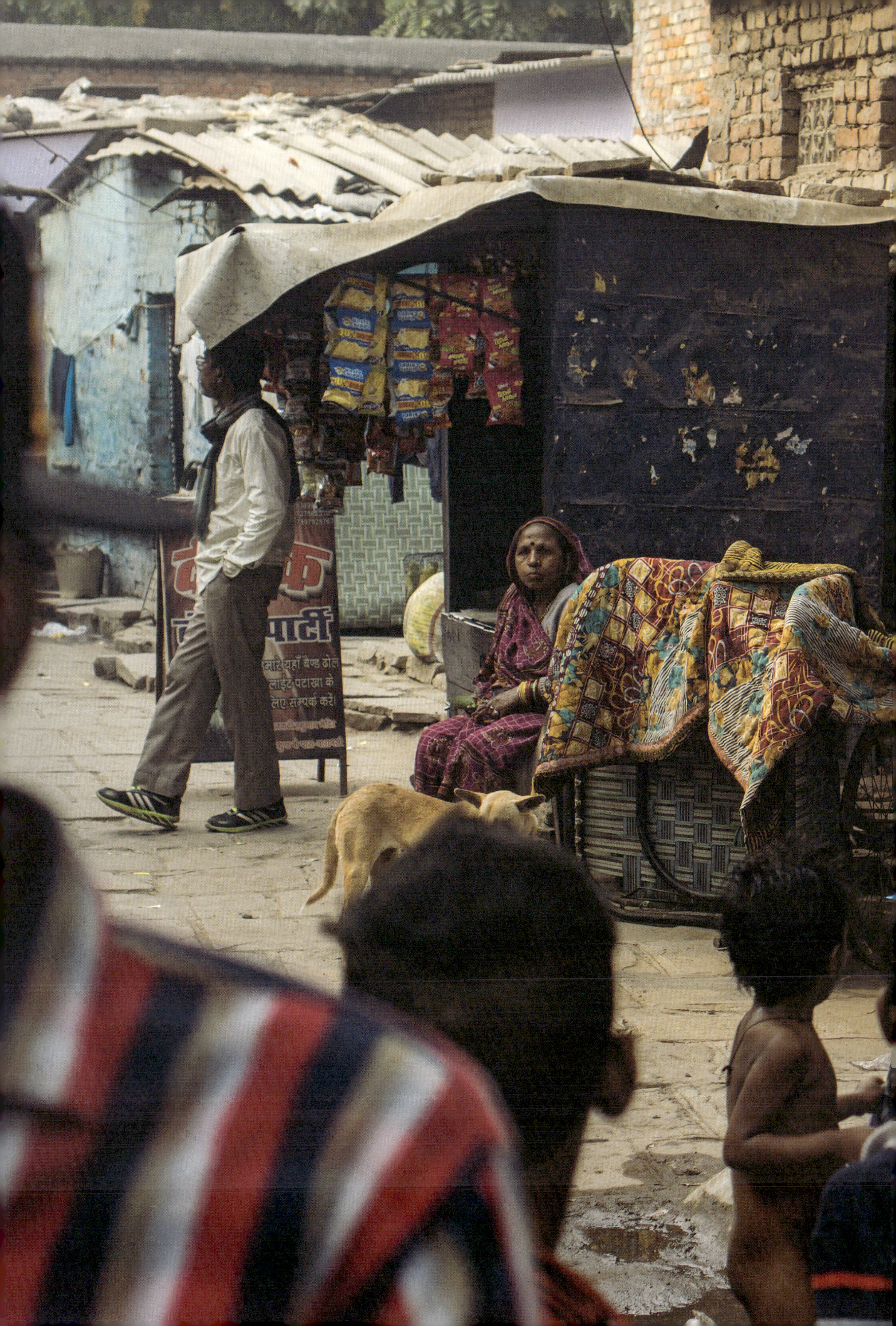
पार्टी
यहाँ बैण्ड ढोल
लाईट पटाखा के
सम्पर्क करें।

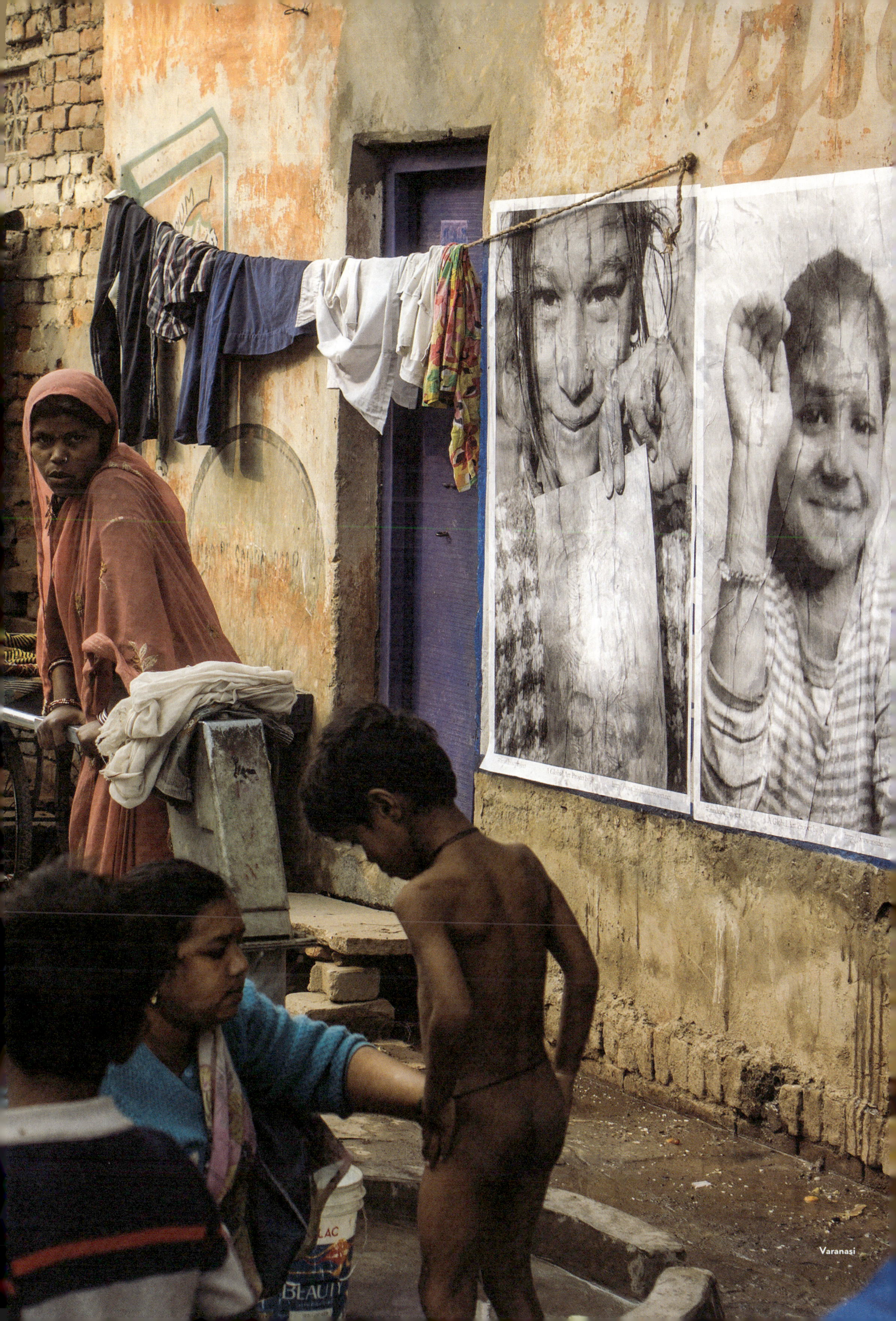

Varanasi

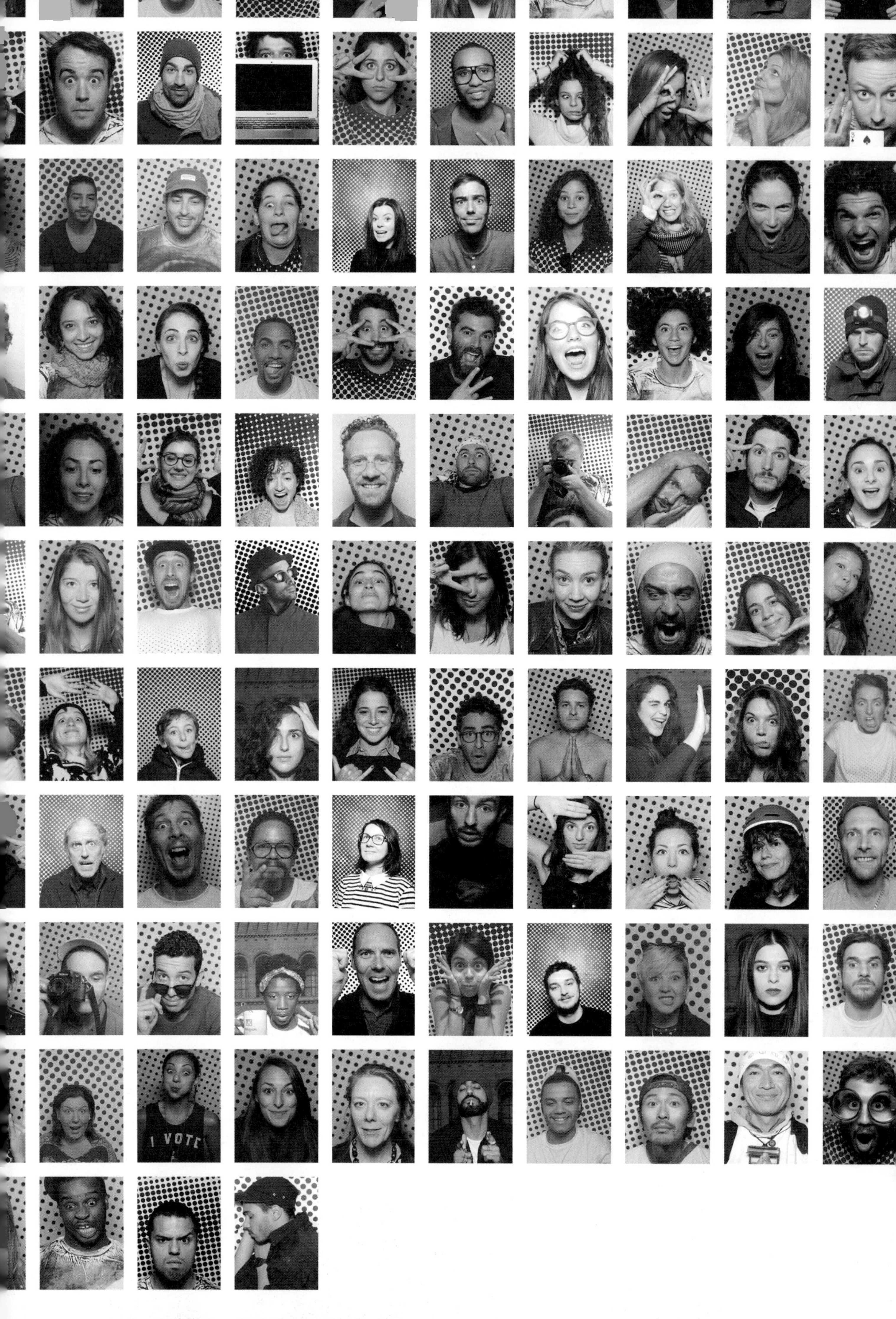

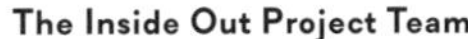

The Inside Out Project Team

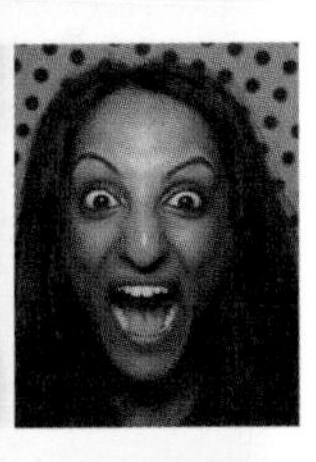

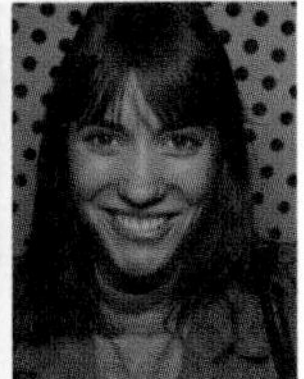

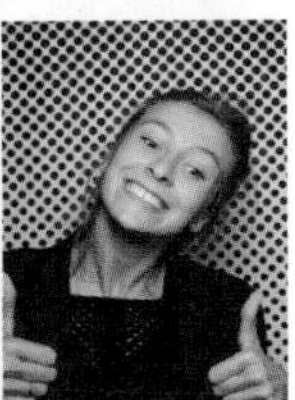

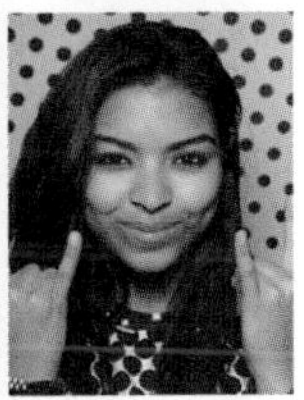

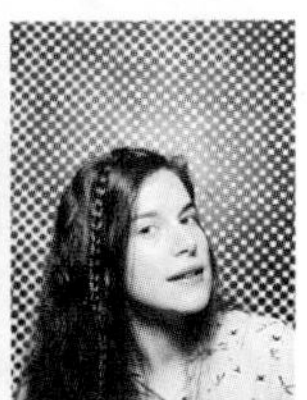

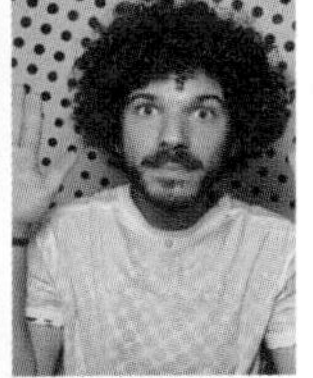

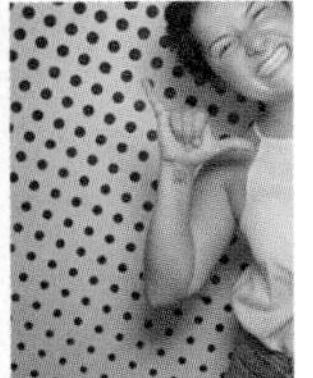

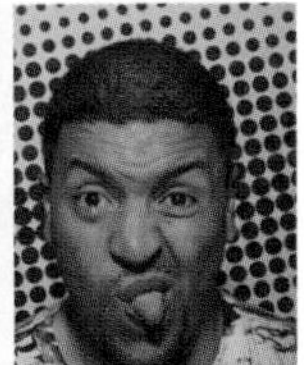

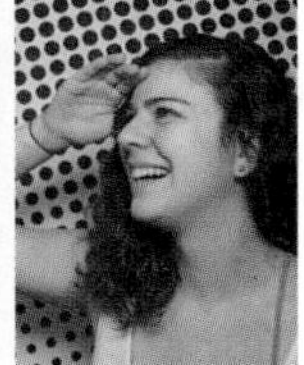

The Inside Out Project wouldn't be possible without the beautiful help and hard work of the dozens of team members, hundreds of volunteers, and thousands of group leaders all around the world who have dedicated their time and energy to allow anyone to express themselves with their portraits.

Here are some of the portraits of the Inside Out team, of past and present interns at our Paris and New York studios, and volunteers at Inside Out photobooths all over the world.

A sincere and grateful thank you to everyone who has kept Inside Out alive all these years, from the TED Prize team to the many generous donors that have helped us prove that art can change the way we see the world.

The project is free and open to everyone, at www.insideoutproject.net

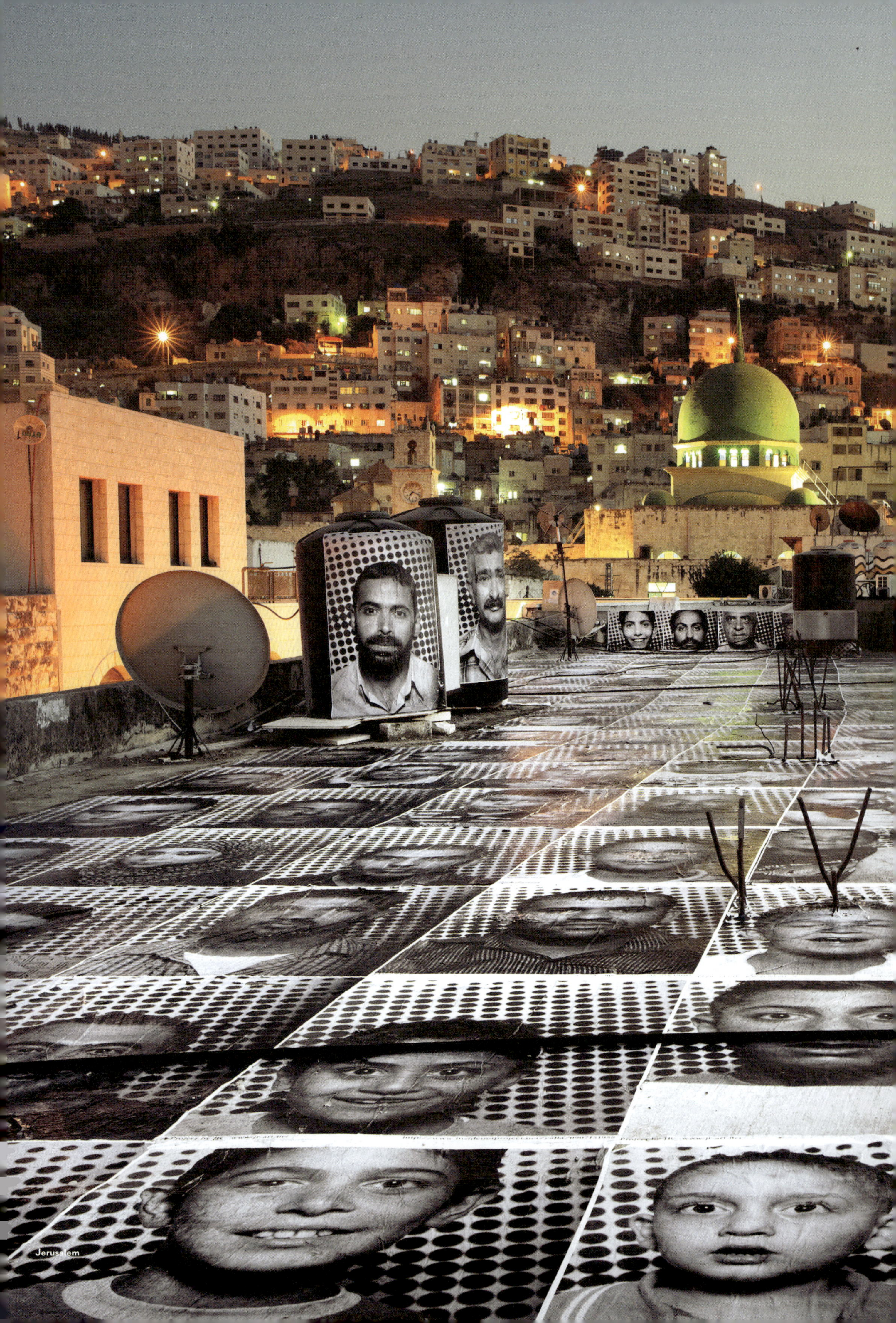

Jerusalem

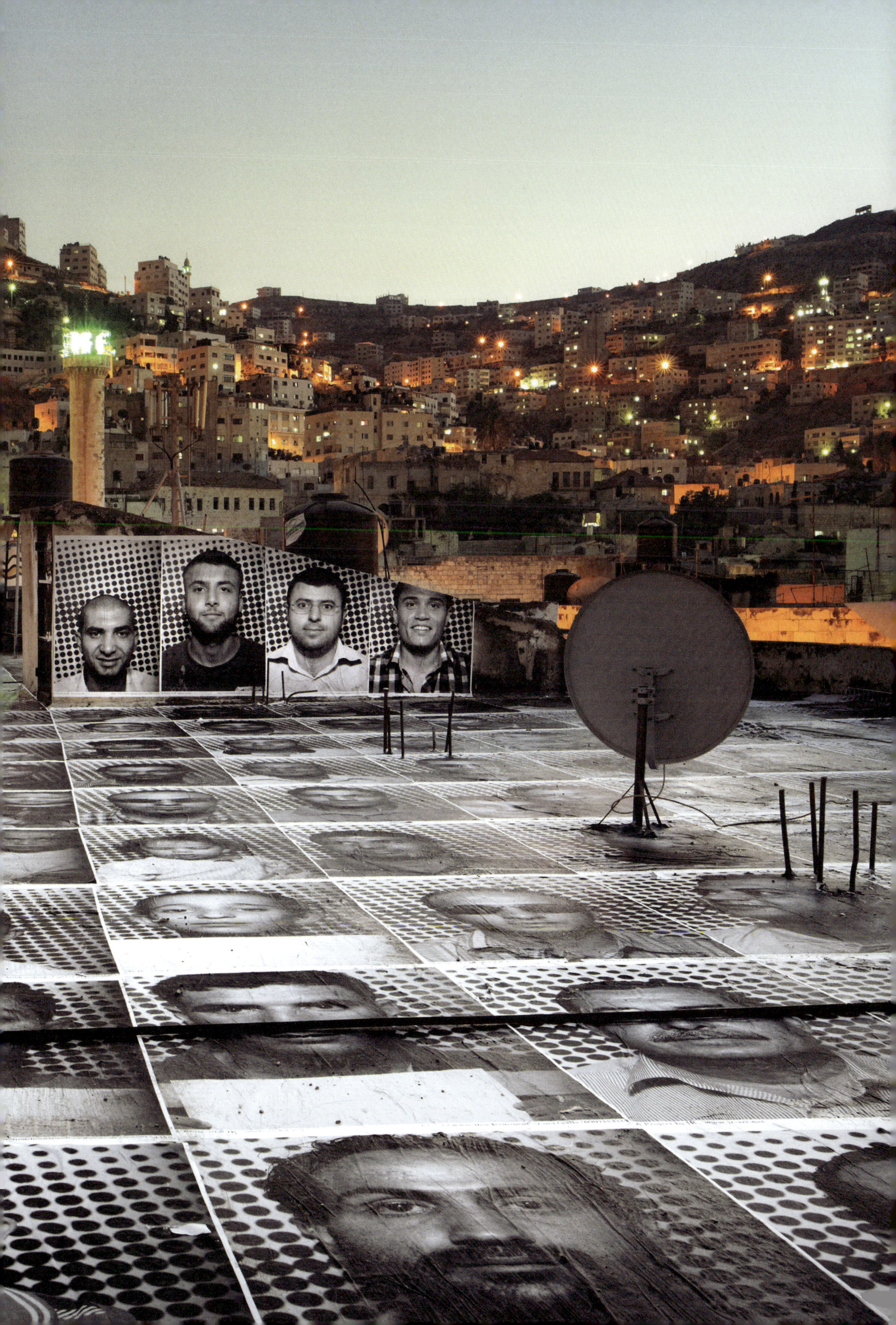

© Inside Out /L'Italia sono anch'io by ArtsFor (pp. 137, 216), ©2014 Platform57. All photos by Studio Johan Nieuwenhuize (pp. 202-203), ©Ville d'Annecy (p. 67), 1982 Creative Studios, Inc. (pp. 140–142), Eric Abdoo (pp. 138-139), Michelle Adler (p. 66), Catherine Aeschlimann (p. 138), Vincent Agnes (p. 193), Melissa Aguirre (p. 75), Maite Aizpurua (p. 143), Tania Akritidou (p. 202), Nicole Akstein (pp. 134-135), Jose Alameda Segura (p. 134), Anthony Alberti (p. 137), Francisco Alcayaga Motta (p. 129), Gilberto Alejandro (pp. 136-137), Aleksandar / Aleksic (p. 194), Suhad Alfartousi (p. 65), Kristin Alford (pp. 65, 84-85), Nida Alhamzeh (pp. 70, 129), François Allain (p. 193), Pamella Allen (pp. 140–142), Roxana Allison (p. 134), Taibah AlQatami (p. 130), Luis Alvarez (p. 201), Leopoldo Alvarez (pp. 126-127), Rahel Ambachew (p. 76), Andrew Ammons (p. 136), Camila Andrews (pp. 126-127), David Andriantsalama Rabehevitra (pp. 78-79), Ann Horak (pp. 126-127), Anonymous (p. 76), Agathe Anquez (pp. 144, 193), Allan Ansell (p. 70), Simona Antonacci (pp. 197, 218-219), Claudia Arana (pp. 70-71), Monica Araoz (p. 129), Saman Arbabi (pp. 140–142), Antonio Arcaro (p. 134), Norman Archer (p. 74), Arturo Arévalo (p. 73), Arturo Arévalo (p. 130), Polly Armstrong (p. 67), Turnpike Art Group (pp. 134-135), Omar Artalejo (pp. 126-127), Margaux Aubry (p. 66), Jared Austin (pp. 138-139), Ana Avayu (pp. 126-127), Jaime Avila Romo (pp. 136, 126-127), Lauryn Axelrod (p. 129), Lauryn Axelrod (pp. 138-139), Erika Ayala (pp. 76-77, 120-121), Tuba Aynur (p. 129), Amir Aziz (p. 202), Marc Azoulay (pp. 18-19, 132-133, 217, 182-183), Rosalieke Baak (p. 142), Bettina Bab (pp. 70, 58), Betty Baba (pp. 58, 142), Miguel Baca (pp. 126-127), Tomas Bachot (p. 207), Hayleigh Backs (pp. 138-139), Christine Baczek (pp.196-197), Patty Bafino (pp. 66-67), Nato Bagrationi (pp. 202-203, 238-239), Barry Baker (p. 77), M. Taylor Baker-Neal (pp. 194-195), Kate Balderston (pp. 140–142), Marie Bara (p. 202), Kathy Barbro (pp. 194-195), Allan Barnes (p. 199), Lisa Barnshaw (pp. 140–142), Denis Barquin (p. 73), Mallence Bart-Williams (p. 78), Simon W. Barton for Polydea (pp. 72-73), Tom Bass (pp.70, 126-127), George Beane (p. 193), Venia Beckari (pp. 126-127), Pierre-Yves Beguigneau (p. 194), Diana Bejarano (pp. 204-205), Alex Bell (p. 70), Julie Bell (pp. 202-203), Murray Bell (pp. 234-235), Antonia Belt (pp.140–142), David Beltramelli (pp. 72-73), Amina Ben Ismail (p. 71), Helene Bernard (pp.70-71), Andreu Benavent de Barbera (p. 201), Stephanie Benham (p.70), Breanna Bennett (pp. 138-139), Valérie Bentson (pp. 134-135), Michel Berger (p. 197), Ana Bernardo (p. 133), Severine Berthelot (p. 77), Marie Berthon (p. 201), Lisa Beschnett (p. 66), Jenna Biggs (p. 205), Jenna Biggs (p. 205), Aysha Bilal (p. 142), Stephane Bisseuil (pp. 209, 228-229), Enrico Bizzarro (p. 69), Eli Blizzard (pp. 138-139), Joshua Block (p. 193), Christiaan Bloem (p. 129), Ludovic Blunat (p. 202), Alexandru Bogdan (p. 201), Alana Bograd (p. 193), Joa Bohorquez (pp. 196-198, 222-223), Tamara Bokuchava (pp. 202-203), Michaela Bolotin (p. 194), Nellie Bonnefoy (pp. 140-143), Luis Borges (pp. 144, 193), Pawel Boros (pp. 76-77), Meryam Bouadjemi (pp. 132-133), Edwy Bouchez (pp. 199, 220-221), Nabil Boudarqua (pp. 126-127), Paula Bouffioux (pp. 72-73, 78, 81), Noé Bouillard (p. 194), Lila Boulbair (p. 198), Kristin Bower (p. 79), Jacob Brace (pp. 196-197), Colleen Brady (p. 137), Eraldo Brandimarte (p. 142), Vee Bravo (pp. 140–142), Katie Breckon (pp. 77, 124-125), Eliza Brennessel (pp. 138-139), Ari Briski (pp. 140–142), Angela Brown (pp. 204-205), Ellie Brown (p. 206), Sarah Bruey (p. 77), Sandy Bruyas (p. 132), James Buckley McGrath (pp. 202-203), Anne Claire Budin (p. 193), Adam Buehler (p. 77), Isaim Buenrostro (p. 129), Lara Bullock (pp. 196-197), Candido Cabana (pp. 73, 116-117), Pascal Cabaret Rueff (pp. 202-203), Cécile Cabon (pp. 76-77), Gregoire Caillaux (pp. 70-71), Jaime Cano (pp. 126-127), hugo capela (pp. 138-139), Eva Capozzola (pp. 194, 215), Kerri Carlson (p. 194), Seth Carnes (pp. 140–142, 126-127), Denise Carr (p. 73), Thibaut Carre (p. 66), Alicia Carter (pp. 202-203), Ashleigh Carter (), Tisha Carter (p. 141), Steve Carty (pp. 202-203, 242-243), Luìsa Carvalho (pp. 92, 133), John Cary (p. 133), Nany Casielles (p. 74), Natalia Castillo (pp. 126-127), David Castillo (pp. 126-127, 140–142), Celia Castro Castells (p. 198), Joana Catarina (p. 73), Christian Caujolle (p. 193), Reynaldo Cayetano Jr. (p. 196-198), Karina Cellier (p. 129), Julija Černe (p. 143), Vanja Cernivec (p.133), Héctor César (pp. 136, 126-127), Hector Cesar Garcia (pp. 126-127), Nicolas Chagnon (p. 197), Guilhem Chamboredon (p. 142), Ellen Chang (p. 69), Jeff Chang (p. 78), George Chang (pp. 70, 126-127), Fabienne Chanvillard (p. 201), Brian Charest (pp. 74-75), Zoe Charles (p. 194), Orélie Chen Fuchs (p. 138), Luke Cheng (p. 195), Fabrizio Chiesa (pp. 126-127, 140–142), Antoine Chiquet (p. 139), Christina Choe (pp. 198-199), Christina Choe (pp. 198-199), Sohee Choi (pp. 126-127), Min-Seok Choi (pp. 198-199), Con Christensen (pp. 200-201), Kate Chukhua (pp. 202-203), Ramon Ciuret (pp. 126-127), David Civitarese (p. 138), Eve Claeyman (p. 142), Ron Clewer (p. 197), Ancu Clivet (pp. 126-127, 142), Colibris (p. 58), Collège Beaucourt (p. 69), Louis Collet (pp. 144, 193), Geraldine Coltee (pp. 202-203), Zoe Condliffe (p. 130), Kim Conley (p. 130), Andreas Constantinou (pp. 126-127, 142), Scott Conti (pp. 140–142), Valerie Corcias (p. 65), Jerry Cordeiro (pp. 78-79, 148), Ricardo Cordero (p. 134), John Corker (p. 140), Benjamin Cornet (pp. 70-71), Michelle Cornwell (p. 78), Leslie Cory (p. 66), Rachel Costa (pp. 130, 160-161), Amanda Coulson (pp. 138, 178), Joelle Courvoisier (p. 70), Robi Crevatin (pp. 200, 226-227), Pamela Crimmins (pp. 140–142), Philippe Crochard (pp. 194-195), Catherine Crooke (pp. 58, 66, 69, 129, 140–142, 193, 201, 206), Yolande Cruchaudet (p. 196), Shannon Cruise (p. 77), Paulina Cuevas (pp. 126-127), Dawid Czaja (pp. 194-195, 212-213), Tineke D'Haese (p. 65), Tineke D'Haese (pp. 72-73), Louis Daboussy (p. 137), Lucca Dahan (pp. 134-135), Cody Daigle (p. 80), Annie DaMour (pp. 144, 193), Leona Dargis (pp. 132-133), Kristina DaSilva (p. 78), Everita Dave (pp. 58, 142), Giulia David (pp. 68-69), Heather Davidson (p. 134), Ryan Day (pp. 196-198), Rachel Day (p. 194), Dima Dayoub (p. 200), Petra de Bruin (p. 133), Xavier De Fougeres (pp. 126-127), Valentina de Val (pp. 126-127), Anne De Villèle (p. 74), Anne de Villèle (p. 77), Ana Dee (p. 134), Ana Dee (pp. 126-127), Mary Dee (p. 134), Margot Deerenberg (pp. 204-205), Marie Helene Deffrenne (p. 73), Mathieu Degonde (pp. 204-205), Sara DeLong (p. 69), Isabelle Delzor (p. 70), Joel Denis (pp. 200-201), Aline Deschamps (pp. 74-75, 118-119), Sean Desmond (pp. 196-198), Christiane Dette (p. 129), Marich Devise (pp. 144, 193), Laetitia Deweer (p. 200), Julien Di Giusto (pp. 126-127), Nicolás Díaz (pp. 126-127), Sarah Dibben (p. 129), Luc DIEUDONNE (p. 75), Joanna Dinning (pp. 200-201), BoB Dixon Photography (pp. 76-77), DJ Two Bears (p. 70), Ioana Dobrau (p. 193), Celsa Dockstader (pp. 142-143), KiKi Doermann (p. 129), Ellen Doherty (pp. 134-135, 168-169), Karola Dola (p. 134), Karola Dola (pp. 126-127), Teodora Dosen (p. 69), Pauline Douchamps (p. 73), James Douglas (pp. 136-137), Jerome Dubas (p. 78), Paul Duboc (pp. 198-199), Sophie Ducloux (p. 202), Dovile Dudenaite (p. 130), Sara Dudman (p. 77), Pascal Dumeste (pp. 130-131), Quentin Dumontier (p. 206), Marcus Dumoulin (p. 80), James Duncan Davidson / TED (p. 8), Shaina Dunn (pp. 140–142), Alex Duran (pp. 126-127), Vanida Duval (pp. 144, 193), Hadley Dynak (p. 193), Aurelija Dzedzeviciute (pp. 204-205), Buruk Early (pp. 202-203, 242-243), Ega MP (pp. 69, 126-127), Lilia El Goli (pp. 126-127), Assia Elhoussame (p. 72), Roslyn Ellison (pp. 202-203), Nabil Elminaoui (pp. 126-127), Jennifer Emick (pp. 196-198), Cecilia Espejo (p. 203), Florence Etienne (pp. 202-203), Tatiana Etitiene (pp. 24-25, 194-195), Niki Even Barrios (pp. 196-197), Patricia Fahy (p. 206), Fannaoui (pp. 126-127), Aurélia Faudot (p. 193), Liliane Faure (p. 194), Régine Feldgen (pp. 138-139), Eugene Femi Smart (p. 78), Dan Fenstermacher (p. 199), Magali Féret (pp. 78-79), Andrew Ferguson (pp. 60-61, 138-139, 179, 204-205), Mary-B Ferl (p. 78), Bruno Fernandez (pp. 126-127), Luza Fernandez (pp. 126-127), Agustín Fernández (pp. 136-137), Luis Fernando Garcia (pp. 126-127), Stefano Ferrando (p. 73), Mayerly Ferrucho (pp. 70-71), Alexis Figueroa (p. 198), Diego Figueroa (pp. 126-127, 136), Ron Finley (pp. 134-135), Patrick Finn (p. 73), Colleen Fitzgerald (p. 137), Melting Flash (p. 133), Guillaume Floquet (p. 137), chio flores (pp. 132-133, 165), Alice Fontaine (pp. 144, 193), Maura Fontes (p. 194), Sophie de Foucault (p. 66), Ademir Franco Hernández (pp. 136, 126-127), Romain François (pp. 142-143, 190-191), Molli François (p. 133), Christopher Franko (pp. 140–142), Marion Froment (pp. 126-127), Yuk Fung Lam (pp. 140–142), Christophe Furlong (pp. 38-39), Fabiana Futata (pp. 198-199), Adil Gadrouz (pp. 126-127), Thalia Galanopoulou (pp. 126-127), Chelsea Gallagher (p. 78), Lorena Gallardo (pp. 126-127), Belen Garcia (p. 69), Sabrina Garcia (pp. 196-197), Ernesto García (pp. 126-127, 136), Enrique Garcia Villagomez (pp. 126-127, 136), Justine Gardier (p. 74), Knox Garvin (pp. 142, 187), Julien Gaston (pp. 68-69), Charity Gates (p. 142), Eric Gauss (pp. 80, 154-155), Linda Germain (p. 129), Tiphaine Germain (p. 134), Luis German Gomez (pp. 64, 130-131, 138-139, 179), Anja Gersmann (pp. 68-69), Josh Geyer (pp. 64, 130-131, 138-139, 179), Josh Geyer (pp. 132-133), Chloé Ghozland (pp. 204-205),

Gessica Giangregorio (p. 73), Joanna Glovinsky (pp. 134-135), Lucile Gobert (p. 138), Lucila Godoy (pp. 72-73), Valentin Goëthals (p. 197), Lea Golano (pp. 138-139), Cecilia Gómez (pp. 126-127, 136), Ivan Gonzalez (pp. 202-203), Carlos Gonzalez (pp. 132-133), Mariana Gonzalez (p. 198), Silvia Ines Gonzalez (pp. 74-75), Valeria Gonzalez (pp. 140–142), Daniela González (p. 205), Stacie Gordon (p. 74), Jean-Roch Gouedard (p. 138), David Gould (pp. 122-123, 134-135), Amber Goupil (p. 193), Nathalie Goursolas (pp. 144, 193), Maria Graaf (p. 129), Peter Granadillo (pp. 72-73), Elizabeth Grandmasson (pp. 196-197), Steven Greaves (pp. 140–142, 186), Shannon Greene Robb (p. 138), LPI Mireille Grenet (p. 77), Liz Groeschen (pp. 126-127), Kim Gronneberg (p. 142), Mathieu Gruet (pp. 134-135), Nelson Guda (pp. 126-127), Amelie Guelton (pp. 144, 193), Susan Guess (p. 142), Sophie Guignard (p. 70), Celine Guillaumet (p. 143), Cristina Martínez Guillén (pp. 68-69), Benjamin Guillome (p. 133), Christelle Guisset (pp. 68-69), Karin Gunn (pp. 198-199), Victoria Gunther (pp. 70, 126-127), Sonham Gupta (pp. 73, 112), Sol Guy (pp. 52-53), Benjamín Guzmán (pp. 126-127), Nadine H. Hafez (pp. 72-73), Kat Habey (p. 129), José Luis Haces (pp. 198-199), Alex Hagiage (pp. 140–142), Gérard Hajj (p. 130), Peggy Halas (pp. 136-137), Jessica Hall (pp. 140–142), Rasha Hamid (p. 130), Annette Hansen (p. 129), Muhammad Hardiansyah (pp. 69, 126-127), Josh Haring (p. 70), Cecile harleaux (pp. 65, 86-87), Debbie Harner (p. 136), James Harrell (p. 194), Michael Harris (p. 78), Sean Hart (pp. 70, 108-109), Katya Harunzade (p. 70), Nadzirah Hashim (p. 198), Diane Hause (p. 129), Jeff Hayward (p. 80), Dave Hedges (pp. 126-127), Mark Henley (pp. 78, 52-153), Sophia Henriksson (pp. 73, 114-115), Alica Heráková (p. 70), Tony Herbas (pp. 132-133), Tony Herbas (pp. 60-61, 200-201 , 204-205), Lindsey Herkommer (p. 206), Lauren Hermele (pp. 140–142), Reuben Hernandez (p. 66), Miguel Ángel Hernández (pp. 126-127, 136), Amber Hockeborne (p. 142), Jennifer Hogan (p. 142), Lisa Holder (p. 74), Jerome Holleman (p. 205), Hojin Hong (p. 78), Matthias Hoogewys (p. 202), Philip Hoogewys (p. 142), Mauricio Hora (pp. 196-197), Joseph Huff-Hannon (pp. 196-197), Peta Huggett (p. 194), Heather Hughes (p. 143), Sarah Hughes (pp. 78-79), Matt Humphrey (pp. 134-135), August Hunt (p. 65), Shakyla Hussain (p. 131), Barry Hutzel(Bazza Design) (p. 129), Josef Ibar (p. 132), Carlos Inada (pp. 198-199), iNNoiR (pp. 126-127), Kondombo Inoussa (pp. 142-143), Wendy Insinger (p. 205), Halea Isabelle Kala (pp. 68-69), Olivia Jackson (p. 194), Megan Jacobs (p. 65), Jean Jacquemart (p. 71), Bryan James (p. 201), Sophie Jannseue (p. 74), Dominik Janovský (p. 131), Emanuel Jaramillo (pp. 70-71, 104-105), Jcs Phot'o'graphy (pp. 126-127), Jed Conklin Photography (p. 201), Staci Jennings (p. 70), Jeroen (Buffel) Meijerink (p. 205), Inge Johnsen (p. 70), Gillian Johnson (p. 193), Andri Joseph (pp. 126-127, 142), Andri Joseph (pp. 126-127, 142), JR-art.net (pp. 6, 10, 12, 14–23, 26, 28-31, 32-33, 36-37, 40-45, 56-57, 59, 65, 140–142, 193, 210-211, 240-241, 250-251), Lorena Jurado (pp. 126-127), Lucie Ella Jürgens (p. 129), Judith Kaine (p. 130), Alex Kane (pp. 142-143), Lotte Karlsen (p. 134), Alex Kat (pp. 126-127), Mahi Kaur (p. 76), Brandon Keat (p. 194), Rhea Keller (pp. 132-133), Ann Kelley (p. 134), Dominique Kelly (p. 65), Valerie Kemp (pp. 204-205), Will Kerner (p. 74), Jennifer Kessler (pp. 70-71), Jodi Kessler (pp. 206-207), Chan Kim (pp. 74-75), Joshua Kleiman (p. 193), Sophie Klerk (p. 206), Kelsey Knott (p. 142), Zeynep Kokkaya (pp. 68-69), Erica Koleff (pp. 58, 72-73), Kovi Konowiecki (p. 206), Jessica Kooiman (p. 135), Kristin Kotarski (pp. 68-69), Che Kothari (pp. 202-203, 242-243), Oscar Koto (p. 198), Georgia Koupepidou (pp. 126-127, 142), Aphrodite Koupepidou (pp. 126-127, 142), Branko Kovacevic (p. 133), Nikolas Krashias (pp. 126-127, 142), Hannah Krauth (pp. 68-69), Hannah Krauth (pp. 72-73), Connor Krezan (p. 76), Iris Krüninger (p. 205), Adam Kufeld (pp. 198-199), Yulian Kukhlevskyy (pp. 130-131), Sally Kuzma (p. 137), Karen-Sofie Kvamme (p. 206), Spiros Kyriou (pp. 126-127), François Lacroix (p. 132), Kennneth Laing Herdy (pp. 202-203), Heather Landman (pp. 136-137), Rosemary Lane (p. 207), Bob Langridge & Paul Juilliard (p. 129), Jean Lanteri (pp. 138-139, 174), Mathilde LaPierre (p. 197), Jesus Lara Flores (pp. 126-127), Simon Laraway (p. 201), Betty Lark Ross (pp. 74-75), Natalie Larrison (p. 133), Rikk Larsen (pp. 70-71), Julie Lastmann (p. 133), Robin K. Laughlin (p. 198), Myriam Laulom (p. 133), Emannuelle Laurent (pp. 136-137), Emilie Laurent (p. 70), Kim Law (p. 207), Jonathan Le Corronc Clady (pp. 68-69), Thibault Le Du (pp. 126-127), Charlotte Lebon (pp. 134-135), Guillaume Lebourg (pp. 196-197), Mimi LeBourgeois (pp. 74-75), Gabriel Lebrun (p. 205), Joey Lee (p. 201), Mina Lee (pp. 198-199), Cara Lee Wade (p. 78), Hugh Leeman (pp. 196-198), Kassandra Lefakinis (pp. 126-127), Amy Lehman (pp. 133, 165), Sophie Lelou (p. 196), Chelsey Lepage (pp. 140–142), Damien Leprêtre (pp. 166-167), Gabe Leung (p. 78), Marie Lienhard (p. 76), Light Fighter Film (pp. 196-198), Sabrina Lightbourne (pp. 138, 178), Salme Liivrand (pp. 201-202), Dave Lim (p. 201), Nelson Lima (pp. 66-67, 94-95), Elsa Liperi (p. 133), Lise-Marie (p. 76), Kristin Llamas (pp. 138-139), Samuel Llewellyn (p. 79), Athena Lobit (pp. 126-127), Christopher Lockwood (p. 74), Karen Lois Whiteread (pp. 134-135, 149), James Long (pp. 140–142), Fausto Lopez (p. 195), Jorge López Muñoz (pp. 204-205), Nathalie Lorente (p. 74), Meghan Lovett (p. 66), Monica Lozano (pp. 126-127, 130), Elle Lucas (p. 142), Elise Luce (pp. 69, 126-127), Claudia Lucero (pp. 74-75), Larissa Lucero (pp. 126-127), Iñaki Luis (p. 134), Iñaki Luis (pp. 126-127), Arnaud Lumet (pp. 130-131), Germán Luongo (pp. 136-137), Clélia Lurier (pp. 74-75), Helle Ly Tomberg (pp. 201-202), Mayli M (pp. 66-67, 93), Eileen MacAvery Kane (pp. 142-143), Jennifer Mace (p. 207), Natasha Macnichol (p. 206), Stanislav Magay (pp. 202, 236-237), Nathalie Magnee (p. 194), Swapna Maini (pp. 80, 156-157), Erica Maish (pp. 134-135), Stavros Makris (pp. 126-127), Dimitris «DeltaMi» Malachias (pp. 126-127), Massimo Malanchini (pp. 68-69), Kat Malazarte (p. 129), Lado Malazonia (pp. 202-203), Matthew Malette (p. 66), Nico Malvaldi (p. 193), Gaelle Manach (p. 131), Elias Mandouvalos (pp. 126-127), Tim Mantoani (pp. 196-197), Juan Manuel Centella (pp. 126-127, 136), Carlos Mare (p. 193), Nicolas Marie (pp. 132-133, 165), Alejandra Marín (pp. 194-195), Michael Markham (pp. 140–142), Eduardo Marques (p. 74), Barclay Martin (pp. 202, 244-245), Fabrice Martin (pp. 138, 175), Sam Martin (p. 69), Stéphanie Martin (p. 197), Hindhyra Mateta (p. 134), Steinunn Matthiasdottir (pp. 73, 111), Lasse Matthiessen (p. 129), Julia Maucurier (pp. 136-137), Christophe Maurouard (pp. 138, 175), Eraklis Mavrommatis (pp. 126–127, 142), Charalambos Mavrommatis (pp. 126–127, 142), Abigail Maycock (pp. 138-139), Silke Mayer (pp. 68-69), Gian Mazcour (pp. 18-19), Zoneziwoh Mbondgulo-Wondieh (pp. 58, 207), Kadhaffi Mbuyamba (pp. 46-47), Sandy McCartie (p. 194), Natalie McComas (p. 69), Polly McGovern (pp. 68-69), Kayla McKenna (p. 66), Teresa McLaren (p. 73), Alicia McNamara (p. 78), Molly McNeece (p. 201), Charles Meacham (pp. 68-69), Jason Meng (p. 200), Marion Méranger-Galtier (p. 77), Sienna Merope (pp. 140–142), Thierry Merré (p. 133), Kanika Metre (pp. 126-127, 69), Claire Michard (p. 75), Paul Michnewicz (pp. 194-195), Denise Mill (p. 74), Ruth Milligan (p. 76), Jean Mineo (p. 137), Kai Ming (pp. 140–142), Billie Mirk (pp. 70, 126-127), Billie Miroak (p. 73), Shaun Mitchel (p. 205), Lor Mitchell (p. 198), Roxie Mitchell (p. 77), Anastasia Mityushina (p. 65), Josh Mojica (p. 202), Cecile Monchausse (p. 193), Juan Montana (pp. 200-201, 233-234), Sarah Moon (pp. 144, 193), Elissa Moorhead (pp. 140–142), Severine Morel (pp. 144, 193), Rosi Moreno Zahinos (pp. 204-205), Marie Morillion (p. 142), Sophie Morin (pp. 140–142), Okubo Morito (p. 137), Eddie Morris (pp. 140–142), Chrystel Mounié (p. 137), Lorena Müller-Nischt (p. 134), Lorena Müller-Nischt (pp. 126-127), Ali Mumtaz (p. 130, 164), Vilma Neres (p. 197), Jason Musselman (p. 79), Nabil Myi (pp. 126-127), Franck NA PALC (p. 78), Franck NA PALC (pp. 196-197), Franck NA PALC (p. 205), Michel Nadeau (p. 194), Sierra Nallo (pp. 202-203), Dan Napolitano (p. 65), Martin Narbais (pp. 68-69), Christian Nassri (pp. 126-127), Tihomir Nedev (p. 201), Julien Nicolas (pp. 78-79), Vire Nicolas (p. 74), Liana Nigri (pp. 196-197), Elias Nikolaidis (pp. 126-127), Jaime Nimble Bear (pp. 66-67), Erik Nordtvedt (pp. 134-135), o (pp. 72-73), Marie O'Brien (p. 204), Sharmeen Obaid-Chinoy (pp. 130, 164), Gail (Mabel) Odessey (p. 132), Mabel Odessey (pp. 73-74), Foluke Ojelabi (pp. 133, 58), Katrin Olafsson (p. 194), Damiano Oldoni (pp. 46-47), Fanny Ollivier (p. 75), Christian Omar Arias Ocares (pp. 126-127), Chinenye Onukwugha (p. 74), Mauricio Tadeo Ordóñez (pp. 126-127, 136), Roshanak Ostad (pp. 58, 69), Hassna Ouali (pp. 126-127), Peter Pabon (p. 193), Gina Padilla (pp. 126-127), Stephane Pain (pp. 134-135), Jesús Palazón Jimenez (p. 138), Tori Palmer (pp. 126-127), Wartin Pantois (p. 194), Laurie Parades (pp. 68-69), Bethanie Parker (pp. 158-159), Bethanie Parker (pp. 78, 158-159), Chris Parkinson (pp. 136-137), Ben Parsons (pp. 136-137), Cheryl Paswater (pp. 140–142), Harish Patel (pp. 74-75), Coraline PAUL (p. 197), Coraline Paul (p. 202), Ander Paul Baldwin (p. 134), Morgan Pavaut (p. 77), Kimberly Pearson (p. 70), Alessandro Pelosof (pp. 198-199), Claudia Peniche Pérez

(p. 137), Hernâni Pereira (p. 205), Ernesto Perez (pp. 62-63, 135-136), Jérémy Perradin (p. 129), Rachael Perry (pp. 132-133), Hannah Peterson (p. 198), Marios Petrides (pp. 126–127, 142), Philippe Petrolese (p. 74), Ian Pettigrew (p. 80), Olivier Philippe (pp. 126-127), Evelyne Picard (p. 195), Ryma Picard (pp. 74-75), Ryan Pierce (pp. 138-139), Nirvana Pilkington (pp. 70, 126-127), Gonzalo Pino Infante (pp. 126-127), Daniela Pliego Juárez (pp. 126-127, 136), Ryan Plourde (pp. 126-127), Anamarija Podrebarac (p. 130), Burrell Poe (pp. 74-75), Damien Poeymiroo (p. 78), Albert Poghosyan (p. 206), Anik Poirier (pp. 138-139), Agata Polec (p. 133), Henry Pollack (pp. 140–142), Andrew Potoczak (p. 66-67), Steve Potoczak (p. 140), Steve Potoczak (p. 201), Pauline Poulet (p. 197), Thomas Pouplin (p. 194, P. 214), Lilian Pouységur (p. 137), Pouységur Lilian (p. 137), Laurent Poyard (p. 142), Adriana Pozos (pp. 138-139), Stephen Pratt (p. 201), Wayne Price (pp. 134-135), Adriana Prieto (pp. 126-127), Thibaut Prod'homme (p. 133), John Prosser (p. 201), Mariah Prowoznik (pp. 138-139), Anna Psaroudaki (pp. 126-127), Lau Pulic (pp. 72-73), ARTI QORMEMETI (p. 77), Douillet Quentin (pp. 72-73), Krupskaia QUEVEDO (pp. 194-195), Jorge Quintao (pp. 68-69, 100-101), Caroline Raab (p. 194), A. Radke (p. 137), Romano Raffaele (p. 77), Mizah Rahman (p. 201, 230-231), Andrew Raimist (pp. 200-201), Gianfranco Raineri (pp. 205, 246-247), Riky Ramadani (pp. 69, 126-127), Jose Ramirez (pp. 72-73), Leo Ramirez (pp. 72-73), Paul Ramirez (pp. 140–142, 184), Sofía Ramos (pp. 144, 193), Brittany Ranew (p. 66), Talía Rangil Escribano (p. 200), Chiara Ravano (pp. 72-73), Raw'n' Wild (pp. 202-203), Gypsy Ray (p. 130), Abdelmoghit Razani (pp. 126-127), Florence Raze (pp. 58, 136), Nancy Reardon (p. 200), Kristin Reed (pp. 194-195), Chris Reel (p. 66), Amy Reid (pp. 140–142), Winifred Reilly (p. 68), Cécile Reinbolt (p. 198), Frank Relle (pp. 128, 141, 180-181), Anna Renau (pp. 68-69), Olivier Rensonnet (pp. 54-55, 202), Genevieve Tran (p. 202), Maya Reyes (p. 202), Alex Rhodes (pp. 198-199), Ariadna Rico (pp. 126-127), Selim Riveill (pp. 126-127), Gilles Rivollier (pp. 132-133), Mariah Roberts (pp. 199, 224-225), Mariah Roberts (p. 199), Gail Robson (pp. 202-203), Teresa Roca Millà (pp. 68-69), Teresa Rodriguez (p. 195), Manuel Rodríguez (p. 134), Aaron Rogers (p. 70), Noela Roibas (p. 195), Jorge Rojas (pp. 196-197), Ben Rojsuontikul (pp. 78-79), Elliott Romano (pp. 140–142 /pp. 126-127), Giulio Romito (p. 142), Sofi Roncero (p. 134), Sofi Roncero (pp. 126-127), Jacob Rose (p. 201), Elyssa Rosen (pp. 140–142), Naeim Roudehchi (pp. 202-203), Etienne Rougery Herbaut (pp. 74, 113), Maeve Roughton (pp. 140–142), Jessica Ruiz Magaña (pp. 136-137), Yaël Ruta (p. 72), Michael Ryan (pp. 140–142), RymeStateofMind (pp. 126-127), Rafik Saadaoui (p. 197), Luis Felipe Sáenz (pp. 144, 193), Ozge Sahin (p. 197), Stevie Sahutske (pp. 138-139), Thomas Saint (p. 197), Theodora Sakellaridou (p. 202), Mauricio Salcedo (pp. 70-71), Javier Salcedo (pp. 198-199), Simon Saliot (p. 137), Diego San Juan (p. 134), Diego San Juan (pp. 126-127), Pep Sansó (pp. 68-69), Raquel Santamarina (pp. 126-127), Chus Sanz (p. 134), Chus Sanz (pp. 126-127), Naman Saraiya (pp. 138-141), Matteo Sarzana (pp. 137, 174), Mustafa Saudi (p. 68), Jaime Scatena (pp. 132-133), Daniel Schafer (pp. 138-139), Gretchen Schell (p. 197), Laura Scheper (p. 201), Adrien Schieber (pp. 138, 176-177), Kathleen Schmidt (p. 134), Alyssa Schukar (p. 78), Bonnie Schupp (pp. 68-69), Jean-Christophe Schwebel (pp. 126-127), Emma Scott (pp. 204-205), Kim Selig (pp. 200-201), Basil Sema (p. 65), Epiphanie Sendze Onthoi (p. 77), Rachel Shires (pp. 126-127), Stacey Shroyer Piotrowski (pp. 74-75), Margaret Silverman (pp. 58, 196-198), Teil Silverstein (p. 72), Lucie Simon (p. 144, 193), Todd Sinclair (p. 201), Nicolas Sirot (p. 66), David Skinner (p. 70), Ashley Skrabut (p. 137), Megan Smith (pp. 126-127), Shawna Snow (pp. 78-79), Sofia Zafiridou (p. 198), Sophiez Laurie (p. 65), Nathalie Soldini (p. 135), Lucia Sorce (pp. 142-143), Heo Soul (pp. 200-201), Kristina Sperkova (pp. 200-201), Kelli Stam (pp. 78-79), Jorgina Stamogianni (p. 198), Elin Stavåsen Brokvist (p. 71), Anne Staveley (p. 198), Christophe Stawarz (p. 130), Nancy Stevenson (p. 79), Thomas Stini (pp. 204-205), James Straffon (pp. 134-135), Peter Strand (p. 70), Sasha Streiff (p. 129), Fabien Strey (p. 197), Temmy Subrata (pp. 69, 126-127), Fred Suzanne (p. 66), Peter Svarzbein (pp. 126-127), Peter Svarzbein (p. 78), Michele Swanston (p. 137), Joan Sweeney (p. 142), Tara Taberner (p. 77), Alejandro Gómez Tagle (pp. 136, 126-127), Ashley Talavera (pp. 126-127), Angelique Talbot (p. 74), Katia Taschetti (p. 142), Ivo Tavares (pp. 67, 126-127), Suez Taylor (pp. 77, 146-147), Zoe Taylor (pp. 134-135), Rosina Teri Memolo (pp. 204-205), Adrien Terrier (p. 70), Denis Tessier (p. 74), The gifted school in Jerusalem (p. 129), Pictures taken by the students of the Bergen Community College Community under direction by Dr. Ellen Rosner Feig (p. 143), Tom Thiercelin (pp. 66, 90-91), Atiba Thomas (pp. 142-143), Françoise Thuriere (p. 129), Alyssa Tice (p. 207), Aziz Tnani (pp. 126-127), Terry Torok (p. 73), Saul Torres (pp. 126-127), Julien Touchard (p. 133), Pierre Touranche (p. 65), Julie Touyarot (pp. 144, 193), Alessandro Tranchini (p. 133), Jason Travis (pp. 66, 96-97), Renato Trianni (p. 201), Eva Triantafyllidou (p. 68-69), Ngoc Trieu (pp. 80, 150-151), Kate Troxell (pp. 138-139), Alta Tseng (pp. 140–142 /pp. 126-127), Maniana Tserkezou (pp. 126-127), Adrien Turpin (pp. 144, 193), Elisabeth Ulla Uksnøy (p. 71), Isabela Umbuzeiro Valente (pp. 198-199), Terri Unger (p. 129), Carlo Usuelli (p. 69), Maria Valiavko (p. 58), Rebecca Valverde (pp. 196-197), Angelina Valvi (pp. 126-127), Tim van Akkerveeken (p. 202), Julia Van Der Ryn (pp. 198-199), Philippe Van Høst (pp. 66-67), Thomas Vandekerkhove (pp. 134-135), Erwan Vappreau (pp. 194, 214), Claudia Vargas (pp. 140–142), Mireya Vasquez (p. 77), Jon Verhoeft (pp. 72-73, 110), Romain Vernede (pp. 68-69), Elena Vicente (p. 197), Vik Muniz (pp. 196-197), Camila Villa (pp. 136-137, 170-171), Olimpia Villarreal (pp. 126-127), Marie-Hélène Villierme (pp. 200-201), Kai Vorberg (p. 131), Melissa Vorselen (pp. 133, 165), Dani Wahyu Moenggoro (p. 193), Olli Waldhauer (p. 69), Olly Walker (pp. 130, 48-49), Sean Walmsley (p. 197), Brian Walsh (Thumbs Footage Photography) (pp. 70-71, 102-103), Avi Wanono (pp. 136-137), Annie Ward (pp. 194-195), Keef Ward (pp. 140–142), Manuelle Warnier (p. 134), Lola Rose Odessey (p. 71), Deva Watson (p. 193), Marie Weichman (p. 70), Raymond Weigel (pp. 126-127), Guillaume Weil (p. 70), Willie White (p. 193), Jennifer White-Johnson / Bowie State University (p.70), Joseph Will (pp. 134-135), Beth Williams (pp. 204-205), Kelli Williams (pp. 68-69, 98-99), Selena Williams (p. 206), Adam Winski (pp. 140–142), Marco Witzmann (pp. 132-133), Sascha Wolters (p. 80), Jane Woodman (p. 77), Larry Woodson (p. 79), Wei-Chen Wu (p. 201), Vassilis Xenias (pp. 126-127), Andrew Yeo (pp. 70, 126-127), Jihyun Yoo (pp. 126-127), Slim Zeghal (pp. 202-203), Ivonne Zelaya (p. 203), Zenka (p. 77), Xinyuan Zheng Lu (p. 69), Elisabetta Zucchi (pp. 134-135).

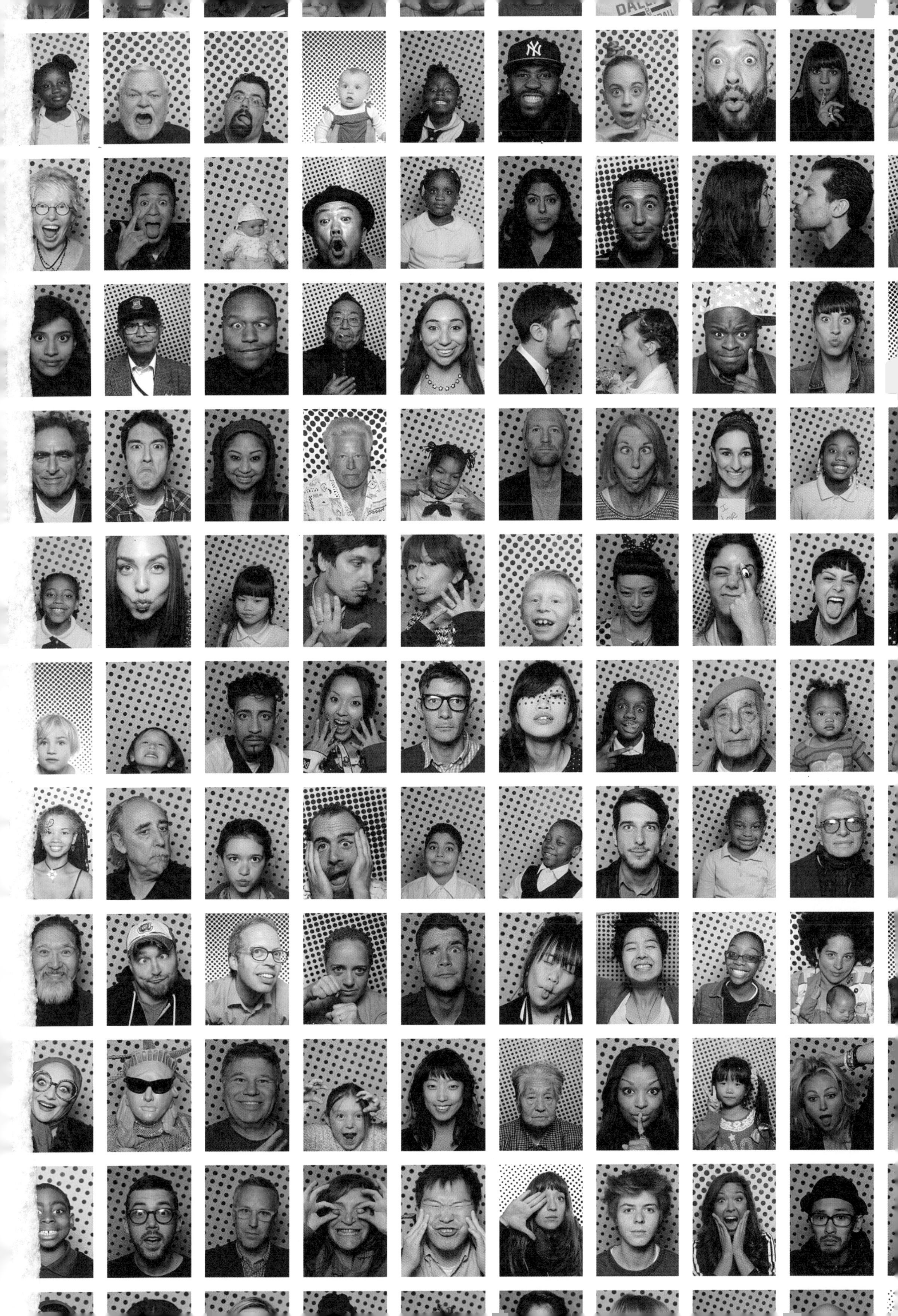

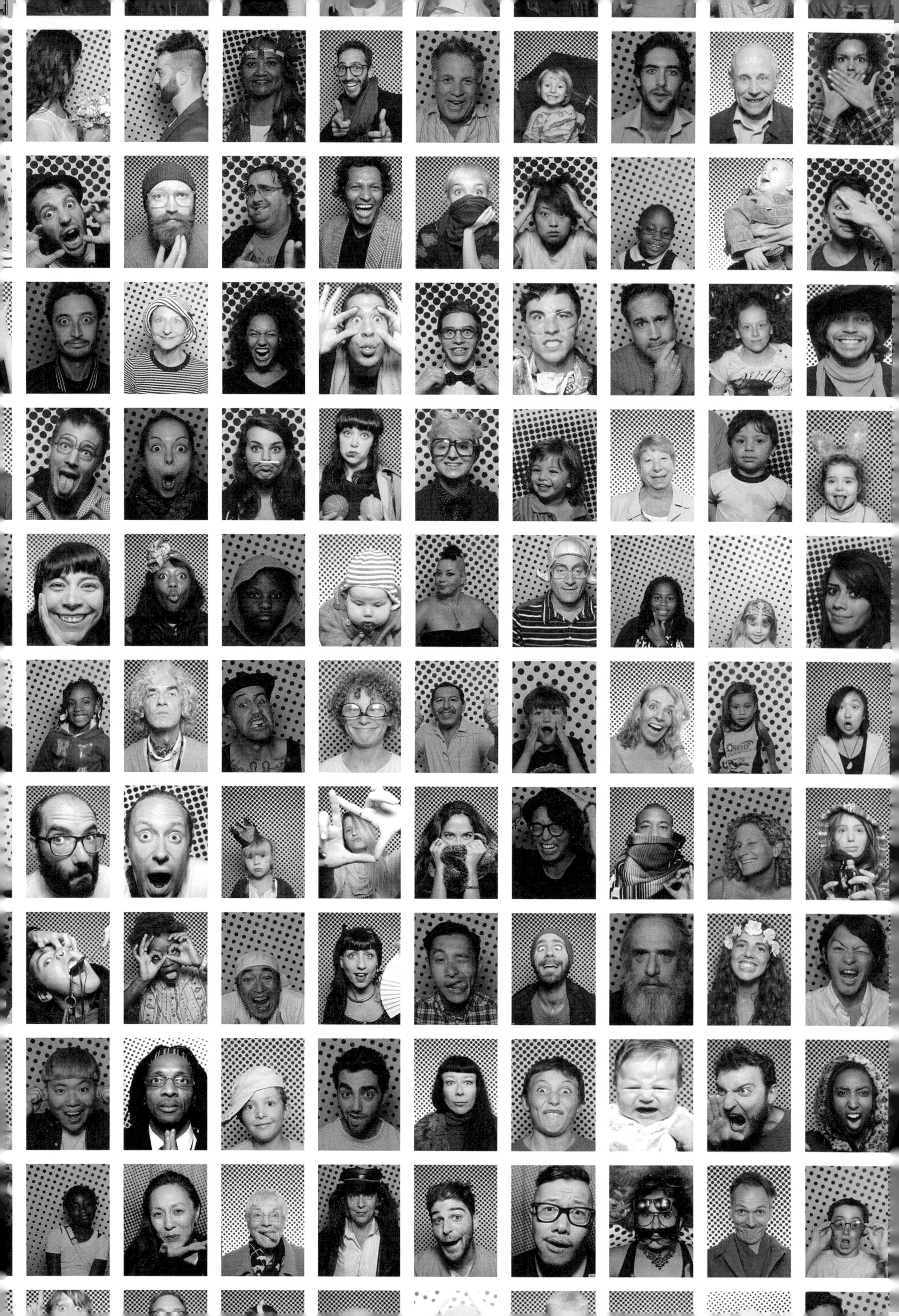